The Mystery of Romans

THE JEWISH CONTEXT OF PAUL'S LETTER

The Mystery of Romans

THE JEWISH CONTEXT OF PAUL'S LETTER

Mark D. Nanos

FORTRESS PRESS
MINNEAPOLIS

THE MYSTERY OF ROMANS
The Jewish Context of Paul's Letter

Interior design and typesetting: Dawn Allman
Cover design: Dawn Allman

Library of Congress Cataloging-in-Publication Data

Nanos, Mark D., 1954-
    The mystery of Romans : the Jewish context of Paul's letter / Mark
D. Nanos.
       p.   cm.
    Includes bibliographical references.
    ISBN 0-8006-2937-X (alk. paper)
    1. Bible. N.T. Romans—Criticism, interpretation, etc. 2. Paul,
the Apostle, Saint—Views on Jews and Judaism. 3. Judaism
(Christian theology)—Biblical teaching. I. Title.
BS2665.6.J4N36   1996
227'.106—dc20
                                              95-47643
                                              CIP

Manufactured in the U. S. A.
                                                AF1-2937
00   99   98   97   96   1   2   3   4   5   6   7   8   9   10

To Vicky, Joel and Kyle,
and Kevin

CONTENTS

ACKNOWLEDGMENTS

I want to express my sincere thanks to all who have played a role in the development of this study of Paul and his letter to the Romans, from my family and friends to the many scholars with whom I have had the privilege of discussion and with whom this work often interacts, even if critically at points.

I cannot adequately express the appreciation I have for the specialists in the field, several approached initially by this stranger, who have welcomed me and my task, taken the time to review various parts of this manuscript, provided important points to consider or reconsider, and offered encouragement and friendship, especially William S. Campbell, Warren Carter, Richard B. Hays, Donald H. Juel, Leonard V. Rutgers, Alan F. Segal, Joseph P. Schultz, Dixon Slingerland, and John H. Yoder. I want to additionally thank Leonard Rutgers for making it possible to do some research in Rome on a level that would not have been possible without his help, and William Campbell for the opportunity to present some of this material to his students at Westhill College, University of Birmingham, England, in the autumn of 1994.

This opportunity would not have been possible without the gracious consideration of Marshall Johnson and Krister Stendahl on behalf of Fortress Press. They have, along with the editorial staff, allowed this work to see the light of day; I am forever grateful. I am grateful also to the staff of Nanos & Gray who have encouraged (or is that endured?) my work on this project over the past three years; thank you. Special thanks also to my friend Dawn Allman for the design of the cover and text.

Many family members and friends have played a role as well—reading material, listening endlessly, offering encouragement—for which I am deeply grateful. I want to especially thank my wife, Vicky, and my sons Joel and Kyle, for their inspiration and considerable sacrifice. I gave them many occasions to resent the attention given to this work; they gave me nothing but support and encouragement. In this sacred circle I must also include special thanks to my friend and conversational partner, Kevin Kiser, for his keen interest and continual encouragement. And Helen Gilmore, who inspired all who knew her, and whose blessed memory lives on.

The Mystery of Romans

THE JEWISH CONTEXT OF PAUL'S LETTER

INTRODUCTION

The new level of respect among New Testament scholars for the integrity of Jewish faith and practice among members of the other Judaism(s) of the first century, from which the early Christian movement emerged and with whom it communicated, is certainly a significant contemporary development that has allowed for a long overdue reevaluation of Jewish and Christian literature.[1] More importantly, it is a welcome movement that has laid the foundation for a much more respectful understanding of contemporary Jews and their religious intentions, in addition to the much needed reinterpretation of historic Jewish faith and practice. There is a spirit of mutual respect on an

---

[1] E. P. Sanders, *Paul and Palestinian Judaism*, pp. 426-27, concludes his influential study of Palestinian Judaism thus: "On the assumption that a religion should be understood on the basis of its own self-presentations, as long as these are not manifestly bowdlerized, and not on the basis of polemical attacks, we must say that the Judaism of before 70 kept grace and works in the right perspective, did not trivialize the commandments of God and was not especially marked by hypocrisy. The frequent Christian charge against Judaism, it must be recalled, is not that some individual Jews misunderstood, misapplied and abused their religion, but that 'Judaism necessarily tends' towards petty legalism, self-serving and self-deceiving casuistry, and a mixture of arrogance and lack of confidence in God. But the surviving Jewish literature is as free of these characteristics as any I have ever read. By consistently maintaining the basic framework of 'covenantal nomism', the gift and demand of God were kept in a healthy relationship with each other, the minutiae of the law were observed on the basis of the large principles of religion and because of commitment to God, and humility before the God who chose and would ultimately redeem Israel was encouraged." Sanders gives an extensive survey of the historical and modern Christian positions in this same study.

Many other modern scholars could be quoted at this point who call for a new understanding of Jewish faith and practice in the first century and today, beginning perhaps with G. F. Moore and W. D. Davies. Excellent surveys of this new development from various perspectives are available by Calvin Porter, "A New Paradigm for Reading Romans"; J. D. G. Dunn, "A New Perspective on Paul," in *Jesus, Paul and the Law*, pp. 183-214; H. Räisänen, "Galatians 2.16 and Paul's Break with Judaism"; S. Westerholm, *Israel's Law and the Church's Faith*; K. Snodgrass, "Spheres of Influence: A Possible Solution to the Problem of Paul and the Law"; D. Hagner, "Paul and Judaism."

unprecedented level, painfully late, but perhaps the beginning of something permanent. Let us hope that the work of these scholars reaches the pulpits and Sunday school classes and permeates the cultural milieu from which Christian perceptions of "others" are born, particularly so in the case of Jews and things Jewish. Perhaps Jewish people will no longer be the victims of the hatred of those who find justification of their views and actions in the uncritical and twisted adaptation of the literature of the New Testament.

Where New Testament scholarship is concerned, the literature can now be read as Jewish correspondence, written by and for Jews and gentiles concerned with the Jewish context of their new faith in Jesus as the Jewish Messiah who had come *first* to restore the Jewish people, and *also* to bring salvation to non-Jewish people as the Savior of the world. It is now possible to approach the contingent nature of these texts without presupposing an anti-Jewish bias on the part of the writers, or the audiences they addressed. While there is considerable tension between Christian faith and practice and Jewish faith and practice where the role of Torah and halakhah (הלכה: rules of behavior) are concerned, and even with Jewish people who disagree about Jesus and the claims of gentiles to be equal coparticipants in Jewish blessings without becoming Jews, these conflicts can now be read as intra-Jewish,[2] not anti-Jewish, and certainly not anti-Semitic.[3] Simply put, we can now read the New Testament as a Jewish book.

Modern interpreters of Paul are not so quick to locate the motivations of his Jewish contemporaries who observed Torah in the traditional pejorative framework of legalistic works-righteousness. As mentioned already, many now recognize that Paul was involved in an intra-Jewish dialogue, and some even recognize that the "works of the Law" over against which Paul juxtaposed faith in Christ would have also been opposed by many of his Jewish contemporaries who stressed the universal intentions of God in electing Israel, but who did not necessarily share Paul's convictions about Jesus.[4] However, while many scholars have expressed a new level of respect for the motivations of Jewish faith and practice in first-century Judaism(s), with some recognizing the same positive intentions among later and even contempo-

[2]Dunn, "Echoes of Intra-Jewish Polemic in Paul's Letter to the Galatians."
[3]Contra R. Ruether, *Faith and Fratricide: The Theological Roots of Anti-Semitism.*
[4]Dunn, "New Perspective," pp. 190–96; R. Hays, *Echoes of Scripture in the Letters of Paul*, pp. 54–55.

rary expressions of rabbinic Judaism, few have understood Paul to share their new-found awareness.[5] Paul is regarded implicitly, often explicitly, as an apostate: Paul no longer believed the practice of Torah or Jewish halakhah were meaningful expressions of faith.[6] He is still

---

[5]M. Barth, "St. Paul—A Good Jew," p. 32, put this problem in its place: "We can be confident that Paul has thought more deeply about God's justice and about the Torah and Israel, and has shown much greater love for the law and God's people, than is possible for a modern Gentile Christian Pauline scholar and friend of Israel."

Dunn, "New Perspective," pp. 201–2, criticizes Sanders for this view and states: "The criticisms of Paul for his misunderstanding of Judaism therefore involve a double failure of perspective. What Jewish scholars rejected as 'Paul's' misunderstanding of Judaism is 'itself' a misunderstanding of Paul, based on the standard Protestant (mis)reading of Paul through Reformation spectacles. When we take these Reformation spectacles off, Paul does not appear to be so out of touch with his first-century context as even Sanders thinks. Sanders in effect freed Pauline exegesis from its sixteenth-century blinkers, but he has still left us with a Paul who could have made little sense to his fellow Jews and whose stated willingness to observe the law elsewhere (I Cor. 9.19-23) must have sounded like the most blatant self-contradiction." However, Dunn on p. 198 seems bound by the same essential perspective: "For in this verse [Gal. 2:16] we are seeing the transition from a basically Jewish self-understanding of Christ's significance to a distinctively different understanding, the transition indeed from a form of Jewish Messianism to a faith which sooner or later must break away from Judaism to exist in its own terms." See also L. Gaston, *Paul and the Torah*, pp. 4, 17–34, 65, who also criticizes this failure in handling Paul and suggests a different approach.

[6]Explicit, this view is quite common outside those responsible for the new perspective being discussed here. However, even among these scholars this position is still influential, for example, Räisänen, "Galatians 2.16," pp. 543–53; and his *Paul and the Law*, pp. 71, 77, and p. xxx contrasts with Dunn; Sanders, *Paul, the Law, and the Jewish People*, p. 144: "Finally, we have seen that, when it came to evaluating the Mosaic dispensation vis-à-vis the dispensation in Christ, Paul found the former, glorious as it had been, to be worthless"; and his *Paul and Palestinian Judaism*, pp. 550–52; F. Watson, *Paul, Judaism and the Gentiles*, builds his thesis around the assumption that Paul set out to separate his churches from the synagogues: "The law was a problem for Paul not primarily for theological reasons, but because he needed to justify the fundamental decision to abandon parts of it and break with the Jewish community, in the face of criticisms from Jews and Jewish Christians" (p. 38). See J. Gager, *The Origins of Anti-Semitism*, pp. 197ff., 213ff., 262.

Implicit, for example, Dunn, "New Perspective," p. 196: "Paul pushes what began as a qualification of covenantal nomism into an outright antithesis. . . . From being 'one' identity marker for the Jewish Christian alongside the other identity markers (circumcision, food laws, sabbath), faith in Jesus as Christ becomes the primary identity marker which renders the others superfluous." See also Dunn's essay in this same collection: "The Incident at Antioch," p. 162.

even portrayed by some as anti-Judaic.[7] At the very least, Paul is painted as arbitrary and manipulative, a chameleon lacking any integrity of conviction or consistency of application where the Jewish practice of Torah as God's elect is concerned.[8] Paul may see himself as a faithful Jew, but his contemporaries would not have, nor does the modern scholar.[9]

Put another way, Paul is essentially a "bad" Jew. He is characterized as breaking with Judaism and establishing the foundation for gentile Christianity. While some level of continuity with Judaism may be recognized, discontinuity is still most often the operating assumption for interpreting Paul's intentions and message, particularly the closer the interpreters draw to their conclusions. Their nuanced treatment of Paul eventually gives way to the ineluctable conclusion that Paul no longer subscribed to the pillars of Jewish faith and practice such as monotheism, the irrevocable election of Israel, the practice of Torah, disregarding even the place of circumcision and halakhah for Jews who believed in Jesus Christ. For example, E. P. Sanders regards Paul's ethical views as "basically Jewish," but not halakhah.[10] He considers Paul's thought "largely Jewish" and believes that his apostleship to the gentiles should "be understood within the framework of Jewish eschatological speculation." Yet Sanders concludes that Paul's "break [with Judaism] is clearly perceptible" in that Paul "denies two pillars common to all forms of Judaism: the election of Israel and faithfulness to the Mosaic law."[11] Judaism may be better understood for its truly

[7]Watson, *Paul*, albeit not in the traditional mode.

[8]See the excellent discussion by A. Segal, *Paul the Convert*, pp. 236–41, on the historical complexities of Paul's position as expressed in 1 Cor. 9:18-23. Also M. Smith, "The Reason for the Persecution of Paul and the Obscurity of Acts," in *Studies in Mysticism and Religion*, pp. 261–68, who argues that Paul's policy of "mere pretense" was a policy of "occasional conformity, which could easily be made an excuse for hypocrisy and would make it possible for legally impure and untrustworthy men to penetrate observant communities" and was therefore "the major reason for his persecution" (p. 263; cf. 267–68); P. Richardson, "Pauline Inconsistency: 1 Corinthians 9: 19-23 and Galatians 2: 11-14."

[9]Räisänen, *Paul and the Law*, pp. 71, 77, 258–65.

[10]Sanders, *Paul, the Law*, pp. 111–14, 144. For positive role of halakhah for Paul see P. Tomson, *Paul and the Jewish Law*.

[11]Sanders, *Paul, the Law*, pp. 207–8. Note this discriminating treatment of Paul in the following statement wherein Sanders is criticizing the work of Käsemann

Jewish character in faithful response to God's gracious calling and gifts; but Paul is hardly Jewish.[12]

It is no small wonder that this Paul is not well liked. Jews often perceive him as a traitor, or worse. Christians often consider him arrogant and manipulative, at the very least, and among scholars and those sensitive to the integrity of Jews and Judaism his perceived disregard for and betrayal of his Jewish heritage and the Jewish people is justifiable cause for suspicion. Some soften the edge by suggesting that Paul is uniquely modern,[13] incoherent,[14] or just inconsistent.[15] Regardless of the final position taken, it is not easy to respect the integrity of someone who is understood to be so disrespectful of the integrity of others, in this case toward his own people.

Nor is this problem with Paul a new phenomenon. It was apparently in the air during his lifetime. He was accused of apostasy and antinomianism on the one hand (Rom. 3:8; Acts 21:21), and judaizing

---

and others in their eisegetical treatment of legalism at the center of Judaism: "The prime point of accepting Christ becomes the renunciation of achievement, and those who deny Christ are necessarily guilty of self-assertion. Once this interpretation is made, it is easy enough to read Paul's 'christological objections' to Judaism as if they were directed against Jewish 'self-righteousness'. The *correct* exegetical perception that Paul *'opposed Judaism'* and that he 'argued christologically' becomes—without argument or exegetical demonstration, but on the ground of basic theological assumption—an assertion that he opposed 'the self-righteousness which is typical of Judaism'. This step has doubtless been facilitated by more than a century of reading Jewish literature as evidencing self-righteousness. But the supposed objection to Jewish self-righteousness is as absent from Paul's letters as self-righteousness is from Jewish literature" (emphasis added). This study argues that the interpretation of Paul's "supposed opposition to Judaism" is similarly absent from the text, though intra-Jewish polemic on certain points of disagreement with other Jews who believed in Jesus is evident.

[12]Räisänen, *Paul and the Law*, p. 258.

[13]For example, the two-covenant approach to Paul of K. Stendahl, *Paul Among Jews and Gentiles*, p. 4; Gaston, *Paul*, pp. 143–50; Gager, *Origins*, pp. 256–64.

[14]Räisänen, *Paul and the Law*, pp. 82–83, 255–69; cf. Sanders, *Paul, the Law*, pp. 147–48, explains the semantics of this position. Räisänen, "Paul's Call Experience and his Later View of the Law," in *Jesus, Paul and Torah*, explains that he sees old and new arguments standing side by side in Paul's writings so that Räisänen finds "the coexistence of mutually contradictory arguments within one section of a writing": "He [Paul] develops new arguments, but this does not result in discarding all the older ones" (p. 20).

[15]Sanders, *Paul, the Law*, pp. 123–32.

on the other (Gal. 1:6-10; 5:11).[16] And this characterization of Paul and
his message ostensibly continued in early Christian traditions in literature that was apparently composed by early Christian Jews,[17] although
this reading of the evidence is debatable. However, Paul defended
himself against all such accusations. Moreover, what is particularly significant but often overlooked is that Paul resisted such accusations
even to the point of suffering punishment within the synagogues
(2 Cor. 6:3-10), his early interpreters such as Luke bearing witness to
the same (Acts 21:21—26:32). According to Luke, Paul even took a
Nazirite vow, which involved sacrifice in the Temple, to demonstrate
fidelity to the practice of Torah and circumcision for himself and other
Jews who believed in Jesus (Acts 21:19-26).

In the letter to the Romans Paul built his argument around his
pathos for Israel and the obligation of Christian gentiles to adopt
proper behavior that would win the respect of their Jewish detractors
(Rom. 14:13—15:3). These gentiles must learn to live in the service of
those for whom Christ died, recognizing their obligation to those Jews
who were yet suffering vicariously on their behalf (11:11-15, 28-32). In
Romans, he also vehemently resisted the accusation that he taught
antinomianism for Christian gentiles, sparing no affection for those
accusing him of such (3:8). Further, there is no apparent debate with
Paul on the issues of monotheism, or even his definition of the nature
of faith, although the object of that faith was in dispute. Instead, Paul
argues along very Jewish lines,[18] grounding his argument in Israel's
own convictions and eschatological expectations as eloquently
expressed, for example, in his adaptation of the Shema (3:29-31)[19] and
his insistence on the certain restoration of all Israel (11:25-29). Yet
Paul's highly nuanced presentation of the gospel certainly offered the
opportunity for serious misunderstanding then (e.g., 2 Pet. 3:15-17),
even as it does today.

---

[16]Implied by his opponents' apparent claim that their preaching of circumcision
complimented Paul's; cf. Longenecker, *Galatians*, pp. 12–20; T. Donaldson,
"Preaching Circumcision: Gal. 5:11 and the Origin of Paul's Gentile Mission";
P. Borgen, "Paul Preaches Circumcision and Pleases Men," in *Paul and Paulinism*,
pp. 37–46.

[17]G. Luedemann, *Opposition to Paul in Jewish Christianity*.

[18]Sanders, *Paul, the Law*, p. 183.

[19]Throughout Romans I see the Shema as a central motif in Paul's argument:
"Hear [*shema*] O Israel, the Lord is our God, the Lord is One." See chapter 4 below
for a full discussion.

I locate in the author of Romans a very different Paul: a thoroughly Jewish Paul, functioning entirely within the context of Judaism, giving priority to Israel, even willing to give his life in the place of the Jewish people in the tradition of Moses to ensure their irrevocable stature as God's beloved for whom restoration is certain.[20] I would like to provide the reader of Paul with a new lens for viewing him and his message to Rome, an historical Jewish context that I hope will lead to the reconsideration of his intentions and message.

This study finds the Paul behind the text of Romans to be a practicing Jew—"a good Jew"[21]—albeit a Jew shaped by his conviction in Jesus as Israel's Christ, who did not break with the essential truths of the Judaism(s) of his day, who was committed to the restoration of his people as his first and foremost responsibility in the tradition of Israel's Deuteronomic prophets.[22] His dispute was not with righteous Torah-observant behavior as though Jews who pursued this course did so in order to win God's favor in the projected context of legalistic works-righteousness. He asserted that the Torah was God's gift to Israel, his covenant people. Jews observe Torah in response to God's mercy. It is a privileged obligation. At least that was the view of many Jews, including the Paul of Romans (Rom. 3:2, 31; 7:12-14; 11:28-29). Paul's problem, where his fellow Jews were concerned, was with an ethnocentric exclusivism that denied equal access to God's mercy for non-Jews, as non-Jews, the "works of the Law" by which Jewish privilege became a weapon instead of a tool, a sword instead of a plowshare (3:27-30; 9:30—10:4; 11:6).[23] The purpose of Israel's special call was in the service of universal salvation, not triumphant exclusivism. Paul argued that failure to recognize the equal status of gentiles among Jews as the people of God through their faith in Jesus Christ involved the misguided denial that the One God of Israel was the One God of the nations (3:29—4:25; 10:12-13). This was a compromise of God's

[20]Other scholars may recognize Paul as Jewish or even as a practicing Jew; however, he is (always?) interpreted as taking a compromising path at some point. I will push the implications of the observation that Paul maintained his Jewish identity and observances further as they pertain to interpreting Paul's letter to Rome and Galatians, and thus to Paul's teaching and practice as a viable expression of first-century Jewish piety.

[21]See the excellent discussion of Barth, "St. Paul—A Good Jew."

[22]Cf. Hays, *Echoes*, pp. 34–83, 168–73.

[23]Dunn, *Jesus, Paul*, pp. 194–203, 215–41.

oneness, the very heart of Jewish faith as expressed daily in the Shema. To insist that gentiles must become Jews in order to be part of the people of God is to contradict the Jewish assertion that the One God of Jews was also the One God of non-Jews, of all creation. Paul would have none of this.

But while his concerns in Romans involve Jews, they are not directed toward Jews, or Jewish exclusivism, except paradigmatically to clarify the problems inherent in the misguided views that were gaining ground among the *gentile* believers in Rome toward Jews, though perhaps springing from resentment because of the response of some Jews who may have been questioning their faith claims in Christ. Indeed, I believe that the mystery of Romans is revealed when we realize that the Paul we meet in this letter is engaged in confronting the initial development of just such a misunderstanding of God's intentions in Rome manifest in Christian-*gentile* exclusivism. In Rome, gentiles are being tempted to consider Jews excluded from God's purpose (Rom. 11): Israel has rejected the gospel; God has rejected Israel. The gentiles in Rome think Israel has now been replaced as God's people by gentiles who believe in Christ Jesus. Further, the Roman gentiles are being tempted to disregard the behavioral requirements continuous with Jewish faith and practice for gentiles (i.e., Noahide Commandments, apostolic decree) who have turned through faith in Jesus Christ to the One God of Israel as the One God of the nations (Rom. 6; 14:15-20, 21ff.; 16:17-20). Paradoxically, these gentiles are actually guilty of the same arrogant ethnocentric exclusivism that was ascribed to that part of Israel in Rome considered stumbling: judging when they ought to be serving; boasting when they ought to be grateful.

This is Paul's purpose in challenging the inherent hypocrisy of judging in 2:1-4, 5ff. and the apostrophic "Jew" in 2:17-24. This is the purpose of explaining the two kinds of predispositions in 2:1-16. On the one hand, those who "[persevere] in doing good" as they "seek for glory and honor," delighting in God's "forbearance and patience" not only toward themselves, but toward the other as well, are prepared to recognize the grace of God demonstrated in Christ Jesus that will lead themselves, and the other, to "eternal life." On the other hand, those who are "selfishly ambitious and do not obey the truth" bring upon themselves the very judgment they bear toward the other. They are the ones who boast in their privileged status, seeking "the praise of men" by standing over them and asserting the right to judge them outside God's grace. Nevertheless, there are those who seek the praise of God and the extension of his longsuffering patience toward those who are in need of the same—they focus on their own responsibility to live properly before God, the only righteous judge, who has acted power-fully on their behalf through Christ (2:1-4, 11-16, 26-29; cf. 1:16). These are the ones who conceal their privileges (circumcision and Torah observance for Jews toward gentiles [i.e., the "works of the Law"]; uncircumcision and freedom from Torah for gentiles toward Jews) and seek the best interests of the other so that they might also recognize God's grace. That is, the status of their election and special gifts are known to God, it is His praise they seek; they are not boast-fully paraded before the other in arrogance—thus, rather than provok-ing the other to resentment and blasphemy they will be attracted to respect their faith claims and worship their God. They will receive eternal life. It is in this context of bearing God's grace to the world that Israel was chosen to serve as the light to the nations. Likewise, God's grace was now given equally to gentiles believing in Jesus Christ. They are now responsible to bear that grace on behalf of those of Israel currently stumbling, rather than judging them unworthy and behaving in a judgmental manner likely to push those stumbling in a way that may make them fall (14:1—15:3).

The rhetorical debate with Judaism and the apostrophic Jew in the opening of Romans have influenced interpreters to frame Paul's argu-ment throughout Romans in opposition to Jews and "judaizers" in Rome. However, these illustrations are part of his diatribe style of teaching in Romans; they function as rhetorical devices to confront just such an error implicit in the emerging attitudes and convictions *of gentiles.*[24] The gentiles addressed are guilty of this kind of error and hypocrisy when they assume that they are now victorious, supplanting Israel as the people of God. Rather, they ought to be grateful, humbly dedicated to presenting themselves to the service of those of Israel suffering vicariously on their own behalf. In other words, early in his letter (2:1-4, 5ff.)[25] Paul laid the groundwork for confronting erroneous

[24]S. Stowers, *The Diatribe and Paul's Letter to the Romans,* pp. 93–118; W. Campbell, *Paul's Gospel in an Intercultural Context,* pp. 132–60; N. Elliott, *The Rhetoric of Romans.*

[25]For a review of the difficulty interpreters have with Rom. 2 and its ability to defy definition within most approaches to Paul's theology, see K. Snodgrass, "Justification by Grace—To the Doers: An Analysis of the Place of Romans 2 in the Theology of Paul."

gentile assumptions of this nature throughout the letter, for what the gentiles addressed cannot so easily see and correctly judge in themselves they are quick to recognize and judge in others, in this case the apostrophic Jew.[26] Such is the nature of tensions addressed in Rome.[27] The paradoxical function of this rhetorical illustration is easily recognized in chapter 11, but equally important elsewhere in Romans, as I hope to demonstrate. This is but one of the examples in Romans in which Paul turns to the eternal lessons of the Shema and exposes the error on both sides of self-serving triumphalism, calling instead for mutual acceptance of Jews and non-Jews in God's eternal plan so "that with one accord you may with one voice glorify" the One God, whom Paul maintains is "the God and Father of our Lord Jesus Christ" (15:5-12).

The interpretation of Paul's letter to Rome has been profoundly influenced by the Latin commentators of the fourth century who turned their attention to the Pauline corpus to search out the relationship of non-Jewish Christians to Mosaic Law.[28] Modern scholarship's renewed concern to understand Paul's relationship with Torah and Israel has

---

[26]The role of Rom. 2:1ff. is an address toward Christian gentile judgmentalism (the focus on Jewish judgmentalism in 2:17ff. is a rhetorical device to make the point clear by appealing to an illustration that they will readily recognize and not the focus of Paul's concern), which is further developed in the parallel language of 11:11-24 (cf. v. 18; see also 12:1-3, 4ff.; 14:1—15:3, which further indicate that the issue in Rome is the judgmentalism of the Christian gentiles). See the excellent discussion of H. Boers, "The Problem of Jews and Gentiles in the Macro-Structure of Romans," who points out on pp. 190–91: "If one takes 1:18—2:29 and 11:13–24 as brackets which set the limits within which the argument of the first eleven chapters of Romans takes place it becomes clear that what Paul is driving at in this part of the letter is that the Christian, specifically the gentile Christian, can neither boast about the sinfulness of the gentiles, because it is faith alone which separates her/him from that sinfulness, nor can she/he boast about the disobedience of the Jew, because, once more, it is only faith which brought about the reversal of their circumstances." See also W. Campbell, "The Rule of Faith in Romans 12:1—15:13," pp. 3–10; Dunn, "The Formal and Theological Coherence of Romans," in *The Romans Debate*, ed. K. Donfried, p. 250.

[27]N. T. Wright, *The Climax of the Covenant*, p. 251, succinctly captures this dynamic: "Paul could see that, in Rome, the temptation would always be for a largely gentile church to downplay or forget its Jewish roots. But if the church heeds his argument, such a possibility will never be realized."

[28]Marius Victorinus on Galatians, Ephesians, and Philippians; Ambrosiaster on all of Paul's letters; Jerome on Philemon, Galatians, Ephesians, and Titus; Augustine on Romans and Galatians; Pelagius on all of Paul's letters; and an

laid the groundwork for a thorough reappraisal.[29] Many of the answers that have dominated traditional interpretation are being reexamined and challenged by this new perspective. However, much remains to be done and the implications are sometimes staggering. Consider the following examples.

1. The contingent nature of his concern to instruct those in Rome regarding confessional and behavioral matters in a manner specific to their circumstances, even when recognized, has most often yielded to an assumption that Paul's statements are to be read as generalized ideological positions,[30] for example, on "the Jewish question."[31] But what I find in Romans is quite different: Paul, like his Jewish contemporaries, is actually concerned with "the gentile question" of proper behavior in the context of the Jewish communities of Rome. His message is prophetic and specific; he addresses proper thinking that leads to proper behavior in the circumstances facing the gentiles of Rome.

2. Paul's addressees have been assumed to function within house-churches that are separated, usually sharply, from the Jewish synagogue(s) or community(s) by the time of Paul's letter so that no deep dialogue and interaction with Jews who do not believe in Jesus Christ is really expected.[32] Although some do refer to minimal synagogue association, these references are usually limited to comments about Christian *Jews* or *former* God-fearing gentiles.[33] But the results of this

---

anonymous commentary dating to 396–405 (I am grateful to Leonard Rutgers for this information made available in a section on fourth-century Pauline commentaries in "The Jews in Late Ancient Rome").

[29]See the reviews of recent commentaries on Romans by Porter, "New Paradigm"; A. Wedderburn, "Like an Ever-Rolling Stream: Some Recent Commentaries on Romans."

[30]Note similar critique of Snodgrass, "Spheres of Influence," pp. 97–98.

[31]J. Beker, *Paul the Apostle*, pp. 59–68, critiques the problems with the traditional systematic approach, and then on pp. 69–71 Beker criticizes the ambivalent position lingering in modern scholarship as represented by W. Kümmel, *Introduction to the New Testament*, p. 312. But then Beker seems to actually offer the same kind of approach on pp. 74–93 in developing Romans as a dialogue with Jews ("the main body of the letter confronts Judaism," p. 75), even though he assumes that the church is removed from interaction with them (pp. 60–61, 89–91).

[32]This is particularly common among those influenced by the so-called edict of Claudius. See appendix 2 below.

[33]Dunn, *Romans*, pp. xlv–liv; Campbell, *Intercultural Context*, pp. 185–87 and n. 105. Both refer to Schmithals's suggestion that many of the Roman Christians were former God-fearers (cf. W. Schmithals, *Paul and James*, pp. 60–62, 115). See also Wedderburn, "Like an Ever-Rolling Stream," pp. 370–72.

investigation into the social setting of Romans suggest that the
Christian gentiles Paul addressed are still meeting in the synagogues
of Rome and that they are considered part of the Jewish community(s)
as "righteous gentiles." Within this Jewish context, however, they are
developing a subgroup identity and beginning to entertain the temptation to disregard the Jewish behavior required of them.[34]

3. Paul's opponents or audience have generally been understood to
be "judaizers" (usually Christian Jews preaching circumcision or
Torah observance for non-Jews) whom Paul sought to challenge with
the proclamation of his Law-free gospel.[35] His bias has been located
with those in Rome who no longer (if they ever did) regard Jewish
practices as essential (the "strong" versus the "weak": 14:14; 15:1) because Paul's message has been assumed to assert a Law-free gospel
and lifestyle for those who believe in Christ, whether gentile or Jew.[36]
On my proposed reading of Romans, however, the opponents appear
to be *gentilizing* Christians who by their "smooth and flattering speech"
are seeking to "deceive the hearts of the unsuspecting" Christian gentiles being addressed so that they will abandon "the teaching" of
proper "righteous gentile" behavior within the Jewish community(s)
where they worship and live (cf. 16:17-20). Paul seeks to prevent those
addressed from falling under the spell of this Law-free gospel by reminding them of their obligation to continue to obey the Jewish rules
of behavior they had already embraced when they first believed; they
will thus win the respect of the Jewish community rather than their
justifiable reproach (6:17; 12:17-18; 14:15-21 [cf. v. 18]; 15:15-16;
16:17).

4. His pathos for Israel, when granted as genuine, has been interpreted as a tacit recognition of the failure of the Jewish mission and
the reversal of salvation history. Paul may have originally understood

[34]That is, I am moving the recognition of this developmental stage in the
process, when Christianity is recognized as still functioning within and as a
Judaism, back later than the above suggest so that the implications of this association can be considered more fully as the still present backdrop for the social setting Paul addressed in Romans.

[35]Watson, *Paul*, pp. 19–22, 45–48, 109–22; Beker, *Paul the Apostle*, pp. 74–91. See
discussion above and in chapter 2 below and critiques of this reading of Paul's
rhetorical intentions by W. Campbell, *Intercultural Context*, pp. 132–60; N. Elliott,
Rhetoric.

[36]Watson, *Paul*, pp. 34–36, 94–98; Beker, *Paul the Apostle*, pp. 74–89; Dunn,
Romans, p. 798. See the discussion of "Luther's trap" in chapter 3 below.

that the gospel was "to the Jew *first* and *also* to the Greek," but he now believes that the gospel is to *the gentile first* and also to the Jew.[37] Further, the salvation of "all Israel" he now sees as possible only as the result of an eschatological miracle instead of through his preaching, that is, if he still sees the gospel going to the Jew at all.[38] I believe that Romans reveals Paul as the champion of Israel's restoration, and his prioritizing phrase "to the Jew first and also to the Greek" was descriptive of a missionary pattern to which he was committed, and for which he was willing to suffer immensely in order to ensure the salvation of the Jewish people, first and last. The failure of the gospel in this regard would have been cause for shame (1:16).

When we recognize Paul's missionary impulse and program toward Rome entirely within a Jewish worldview, albeit one shaped by his faith in Jesus as the Christ of Israel and Savior of the world, it becomes clear that he was addressing specific issues of tension in the faith and practice of those who would read/hear this letter of reminder in Rome in their current Jewish/gentile social setting. Of course, reading Paul's letter to Rome virtually independently of his other letters takes the risk of drawing conclusions about the shape of Paul's thinking and intentions that may not be coherent with evidence from his other correspondence. On the one hand, it allows Paul's thinking and intentions toward those addressed in Rome to shine through in their (original?) light. We escape the historical interpretive limitations that follow from first locating Paul's thinking, intentions, opponents, and message within Galatians or 1 Corinthians, for example, and then applying them, intentionally or not, to Romans. On the other hand, we now run the risk of exercising the same fallacious methodology in reverse.

Is the methodology of this study doomed to corrupt the larger picture of Paul and his teachings? Perhaps, but it is a risk that Paul was willing to run for his original addressees when he wrote this letter to Rome, presumably without attaching his other correspondence in order to balance the picture. Of course, that is again the strength of allowing Romans to speak alone, as it presumably did for the original audience. The message of Romans is also more pertinent today than the message of Galatians, for example, which assumes a desire among

---

[37]J. Munck, *Christ and Israel*, pp. 18–19, 120–25; Stendahl, *Paul*, pp. 28–29; Sanders, *Paul, the Law*, pp. 184, 195. See discussion in chapter 5 below.

[38]The two-covenant approach of Stendahl, *Paul*, p. 4; Gaston, *Paul*, pp. 143–50; Gager, *Origins*, pp. 256–64. Differently, Watson, *Paul*, pp. 31–32, 36.

Christians to adopt Judaic practices that can hardly be considered a contemporary problem. Romans addressed an early manifestation of the (mis)perceptions of Israel and Jews among Christian gentiles that ✓ remain influential among many in modern gentilized Christianity, a ✓ disrespect and disregard for Jewish people and their religious impulses that some may even consider inherent in Christian convictions.[39] Moreover, there is no reason to shrink back from applying what we find in Romans to Paul's other texts, particularly to those that appear most likely to challenge what is proposed herein, save for the limitations of the outline of this project. Thus, in the summary chapter I discuss an influential example that appears to pose a challenge to my conclusions; however, a full reevaluation of the larger Pauline corpus will have to wait until another time.

Chapter 1 begins with a broad outline of this study that will articulate the challenge and attempt to frame the approach of the following chapters. In particular, this chapter seeks to position Paul's purpose for writing and his intended trip, as well as the message of the letter, within the context of Paul's stated purpose. He wrote to remind those ✓ addressed in Rome of their obligation to the obedience of faith and of the irrevocable priority of Israel's restoration. The gospel is to the Jew first, and also to the Greek. Far more than rhetoric, I seek to show how this was Paul's pattern for the apostolic preaching of the gospel, even for Rome, where those addressed were still an integral part of the Roman synagogue community(s). This responsibility lies at the heart of Paul's motivations, but he fears they have lost sight of the significance of this priority in Rome. He wants to persuade those addressed to renew their commitment to this irrevocable two-step pattern, thereby doing their part to ensure the salvation of all Israel. They must ✓ seek peace with and respect from the larger Jewish community(s) and their leaders so that his planned preaching of the gospel in the synagogues of Rome will have a chance to succeed instead of being immediately and categorically rejected.

Chapter 2 briefly develops the historical situation in Rome as objectively as possible, paying special attention to the likelihood that those Paul addressed were still, in some measurable way, part of the Jewish community(s) in Rome. I discuss the general structure of the Jewish synagogue communities in Rome, explore some of the opera-

---

[39]Cf. Ruether, *Faith and Fratricide*. See the discussions of M. Simon, *Verus Israel;* Gager, *Origins.*

tive notions among Jews for the restoration of Israel, their messianic hopes, their expectations of final gentile salvation, and their program for current gentile salvation and participation among the worshiping Diaspora communities of Jews. I also discuss some of the gentile opinions of Jews and things Jewish that were prevalent in this period. Then I challenge the prevailing notions of the structure of the inter-action of early Christian gentiles with the synagogue communities of Rome, proposing that they were still functioning within the larger Jewish context. Finally, I turn attention to identifying the implied audience of Paul's "reminder" to Rome (15:15).

Chapter 3 investigates the interaction of the "weak" and the "strong" as it reflects on the historical construct I have proposed. One of the most interesting issues in this chapter lies in exploring scholar-ship's underlying presuppositions about the identity of the "weak." I then expose the hermeneutical trap that follows from the assumption that the "weak" were *Christian* Jews, an assumption that may stand in the way of understanding both the implied situation and audience in Rome, not to mention the interpretation of Paul's message throughout this letter, particularly evident in the paraenesis of chapters 12–15. This paraenesis addresses the kind of tensions that would have natu-rally arisen as this new movement within Judaism developed and at-tracted more and more gentile participants, particularly in the gentile city of Rome. Some of the Jews in Rome who did not share the same convictions, either about Jesus or about gentile inclusion by faith, would have questioned the claims of this new movement. And as this subgroup grew and began to assert some of the (mis)understandings of its essential faith, this would have led to even more skepticism and eventually to hostility within the larger Jewish community(s).

Chapter 4 develops the notions of the "righteous gentiles" and the rules of behavior for them that were operative at the time and their in-fluence on the situation in Rome, and in Paul's reminder to obey them. I also explore the relationship of these commandments with monotheistic assertions of God's oneness, and I seek to demonstrate that the crux of Paul's argument against gentiles becoming Jews was not the supersession of Christ over Law, but the implicit compromise of God's oneness that it necessarily involved. I develop the possibility that the Jerusalem Council's apostolic decree, or some form of that teaching for how gentiles ought to behave in matters of purity when associating with the Jewish community, was "the teaching" that Paul was calling for enhanced adherence to by way of his reminder to

Rome. This concept may lie behind Paul's coining of the phrase "obedience of faith" to describe the phenomenon associated with his
preaching of the gospel to gentiles.

Chapter 5 challenges the prevailing views of Paul's commitment to
and understanding of Israel's restoration, particularly in the light of his
gentile mission and the audience's triumphant assumptions of having
supplanted Israel. What has been interpreted as Paul's reconsidered,
rationalized, or revealed position on God's reversal of salvation history—no longer to the Jew first and also to the gentile, but now to the
gentile first and also to the Jew, since Israel has ostensibly rejected the
gospel—is not the message I locate in the language of Romans 11. Nor
do I find Paul expecting the non-Christian Jews to be provoked to
jealousy by gentile salvation, although this presupposition has usually
been brought to the text. Paul expected Jews to be challenged to reconsider the times in view of his ministry, that is, Paul expected them
to recognize that the promised ingathering of the nations has begun,
albeit without the sharing of some in this privileged mission. The very
Jewish Paul whom Luke portrayed in Acts can be seen also in Romans.
Luke's Paul sought the restoration of Israel, which involved the two-
step pattern of going first to the synagogues (Israel as represented in
each city), followed by turning to include gentiles in fulfillment of
Israel's universalistic expectation to bring light to all the nations. The
Paul of Romans expressed the same intention toward Rome: the mystery is clarified in the context of his missionary program, yet to be im-
plemented in the synagogues of Rome. Thus Paul was pressed to
write so that the behavior of the Christians in Rome did not preclude
the successful declaration of the gospel in the Roman synagogues
upon his planned arrival.

Chapter 6 seeks to apply the historical and interpretive construct
developed in the first five chapters to the topos of 13:1-7 addressing
the issue of subordination to authorities. This instruction has been at
the center of a lively debate about Christian responsibility to government, and has been instrumental in some very dark moments in
Christian interpretation of proper behavior. This passage has never fit
quite properly into the movement of Paul's instructions in the surrounding context of chapter 12 or 13:8ff. It appears abruptly, calls for
behavior with respect to government that has offended the sensitivity
of many (as it is usually interpreted), and makes little sense of the
likely opinion of Paul and other Jews about how to view the reign of

Nero and the many other foreign rulers of the first century. This chapter develops the proposition that the authorities are not the Romans but the leaders of the synagogues. The issue is not the payment of Roman taxes per se, but the payment of the Temple tax by "righteous gentiles" from whom it is required in their new relationship as worshipers in the Jewish community. In addition to the requirements of the apostolic decree for defining minimal purity behavior for gentiles, they are further required to obey those who interpret Torah for the synagogue community, of which they are now a part, in matters of "good" and "evil" behavior, which naturally included the payment of obligatory Jewish taxes. This is but one example of the kind of tensions this new movement within Judaism would have encountered in the fluid context of everyday life.

The Summary and Appendix 1 offers a discussion of the apparent contradiction between Paul's instructions to the "strong" in Rome and his opposition to Peter's earlier actions in Antioch when Peter had appeared to adopt behavior for the express purpose of winning the respect of his fellow Jews, that is, "the approval of men" (14:18). I examine Paul's accusation of Peter's hypocrisy in the text of Galatians 2:11-21 in the light of Paul's anxiety and victory through faith in Christ as outlined in Romans 7 and 8. This discussion helps to answer a question of extreme importance when considering first-century Christianity as a Jewish movement: How were Jews in Christ to live? Was it necessary to abandon their Jewish convictions and practices? Was it Paul's conviction that they should no longer live as Jews, or at least that they should no longer invest such a lifestyle with any real meaning beyond accommodation in order to win the respect of other Jews? In other words, the Paul of Romans is indeed coherent with the Paul who confronted Peter at Antioch as retold in Galatians. The key that unlocks this mystery has been overlooked because of the failure to apply consistently Paul's discussion of the Law and justification by faith in Galatians 2 and Romans 7, two texts that reveal a surprising conclusion to this investigation of Paul's understanding of the early churches in Rome within the context of the Jewish community(s) and place of the Law in the life of both Jews and gentiles in Christ.

Finally, Appendix 2 explains why I have not included a discussion of the so-called edict of Claudius in developing the historical situation in Rome or for interpreting Romans. I have not ignored the current of interest in this topic, which has grown in the last few years to become a foundational construct for interpreting the social setting addressed in Romans. Rather, I dismiss it as unfounded and highly unlikely. More importantly, I believe it is not helpful because it fails to make sense of the temper of Paul's letter to Rome and thus of the implied historical social situation Paul addressed. And it fails to account for later characterizations of formative Roman Christianity.

CHAPTER 1

TO THE JEW *FIRST*
AND *ALSO* TO THE GREEK

Paul sets out in Romans, strikingly and in no uncertain terms, that the very purpose of his apostleship to the gentiles is in the service of Israel's restoration (11:11-14; 25-32; 15:15-16, 31). He does not believe that Israel has rejected the good news, though some have "stumbled"; and even more important, he does not believe that God has rejected Israel, though some have been "hardened." On the contrary, in spite of how circumstances may presently appear, through Paul's apostolic ministry God is demonstrating the irrevocable priority of Israel in the faithful fulfillment of his promises to the fathers (1:1-7, 11-17; 11:11-15, 25-29; 15:7-9). For Paul, the pattern of salvation history has been and always will be, even in the midst of confronting misguided exclusivity on the part of some of the children of Jacob, "to the Jew *first* and *also* to the Greek."

In fact, Paul expects that the mystery he reveals about the certainty and process of the restoration of "all Israel" will profoundly affect the temptation toward arrogance on the part of the Christian[1] gentiles in Rome who apparently believe that Israel has both rejected the message of her restoration in Jesus Christ, and been rejected herself (11:17-32). Christian gentiles appear to believe, or at least to be

---

[1]The use of the term "Christian" is, of course, an anachronism in discussing Paul's audience, as the phrase was not yet in use, certainly not as a conceptual term to denote separation from Judaism. I will use "Christian" herein as an adjective for both Jews and gentiles to denote their belief in Jesus as the Christ; and "non-Christian" to denote those who do not believe the same. This is far more fitting than the common use of "believers" to distinguish those believing in Jesus Christ, for most Jews were certainly believers, in God if not in Jesus as the Christ. In addition, I will not use the phrase "Jewish Christian" because it assumes conversion to a new religion in a manner that Paul and the early church would not have maintained, as they saw their new faith in Jesus as the Christ of Israel first, even if also as the Savior of the nations. In fact, I contend that Paul used the terms "weak" and "strong" to provide a nuance in this distinction between faith in God but not in Christ Jesus ("weak" or "stumbling" for Jews not yet "able" or "seeing" their need to believe in Jesus as the Christ; "strong" or "able" for both Jews and gentiles believing in Jesus as the Christ, see chapter 3 below).

tempted to believe, that they have now supplanted Israel as the people of God.[2] Paul makes it quite clear that not only are they wrong, they are treading on sacred ground and jeopardizing their own inclusion in God's family. Rather than arrogance, their new position ought to result in humility and service to the stumbling children of Israel, for the fate of the children of Jacob is inextricably tied up with their own (11:11-12, 15, 22, 25-32; 12:1-3, 4ff.). Indeed, the salvation of "all Israel" is the one thing of which Paul is certain, regardless of appearances to the contrary, for:

> just as it is written,
> "The Deliverer will come *from Zion*,
> He will remove ungodliness from Jacob."
> "And this is My covenant with them,
> When I take away their sins." (11:26-27)

Moreover, Paul does not seem to be confronting an inflated view of the Torah in Rome among the Christian gentiles ("judaizing") as is often assumed.[3] Instead, he confronts the failure of the Christian gentiles in Rome to respect the role of Torah in the life of Israel as God's special gift; in fact, he emphatically elevates the status of the Torah. Note, for example, the great advantage of the Jewish people is "that they were entrusted with the oracles of God" (3:2), and elsewhere in a litany of Jewish privileges he includes "the giving of the Law" (9:4); that the "Law is spiritual" (7:14) and again, "the Law is holy, and the commandment is holy and righteous and good" (7:12); and further that "the gifts [which clearly included as central the Law; cf. 9:4] and the calling [Israel's election] of God are irrevocable" (11:29). Paul refers to the "Law of faith" (3:27) and asserts that he is not teaching that faith nullifies the Law: "On the contrary, we establish the Law" (3:31); and elsewhere that "Christ is the end [τέλος: goal] of the Law" (10:4).[4] In fact, he even regards the "love" he is calling for among his Christian gentile readers "the fulfillment of the law" (13:8-10; cf. 8:4), not a demonstration of its failure but the embodiment of its true aims. In

---

[2]D. Kaylor, *Paul's Covenant Community*, p. 159, notes succinctly their opinion (although, he incorrectly attributes this opinion to Paul, who is precisely the one opposing this view among the gentiles in Rome, see chapter 5 herein): "The gospel was working out to be not 'to the Jew first and also to the gentile' (Rom. 1:16) but to the gentile instead of to the Jew!"

[3]E.g., Watson, *Paul*, pp. 19–22, 45–48, 109–22; Beker, *Paul the Apostle*, pp. 74–91.

[4]See discussion of R. Badenas, *Christ the End of the Law*.

Romans we are confronted not with a so-called Law-free Paul, but rather with one who regards the Law as Israel's special gift from God— we meet a Paul who would be better characterized as Law-respectful.[5]

If Paul had maintained (as is generally assumed) that Christian gentiles are entirely free from embracing the Law and purity behavior, then why does he spend the greater part of this letter (chaps. 5–16) insisting on proper behavior in their service of Christ that will be both "acceptable to God and *approved by men*" (14:18)? Who are these "men" who rightfully judge the genuineness (δόκιμος) of their service in the purity matters in dispute in Rome? Is this not a clear allusion to a Law-respectful lifestyle (הלכה: halakhah):[6] walking properly

---

[5]I do not mean to suggest the doing of the Law was an "entrance requirement" for salvation, but rather the application of the Law and Jewish customs to the lifestyle of those believing in Jesus as the Christ; for the Jew believing in Christ Jesus would continue to be a Jew and thus obey the Law, and the gentile believing in Christ Jesus would continue to be a gentile and thus not under the Law, however, the gentile would now through Christ Jesus have a new relationship with Israel that made it necessary to respect the "rules of behavior" that had been developed in Judaism to define the minimal requirements of Law and custom for the "God-fearing" gentile wishing to associate with God and his people. Thus the phrase "Law-respectful gospel" is offered here to contrast with the "Law-free gospel" usually assumed to represent Paul and Pauline Christianity, incorrectly in my opinion.

[6]Literally "walking," it denotes rules of behavior in rabbinic Judaism and is a frequent idiom in the Bible as well for discussing proper behavior (e.g., Ex. 16:4; Lev. 18:3-4; Deut. 28:9; Josh. 22:5; Jer. 44:23; Ezek. 5:6-7; Dan. 9:10; Mic. 4:2); this will be discussed more fully in chaps. 2–4 below. The term "halakhah," again an anachronism as far as we know in first-century terminology, if not in practice, refers to the rules governing behavior among Jews, formulated as the practical guides for how to live out the righteousness of the Law. In Rom. 13:13 Paul calls for "proper behavior" in the same sense as Judaism speaks of halakhot or the "rules of behavior." Note also Paul's instruction to the "strong" in 14:15, "For if because of food your brother is hurt, you are no longer *walking in love*. Do not destroy with your food him for whom Christ died." These "rules of behavior" were also referred to as the "ancient traditions" (Tomson, *Paul*, pp. 34, 43–44). The Qumran community certainly had developed halakhic rulings at this time (Tomson, *Paul*, pp. 19–22, for discussion and sources), and it is possible that this was what were referred to as the "works of the Law" and the "deeds of the Torah" (e.g., 4QMMT and the discussion of Dunn, "Echoes of Intra-Jewish Polemic," p. 467), but as for Paul's application of the principles of halakhah there is some dispute. For various definitions and uses of the term "halakhah" and whether Paul applied this concept to his converts see Tomson, *Paul*, pp. 19–54, 62–68, 69ff.; Dunn, *Romans*, pp. 315–16; Dunn, "Echoes of Intra-Jewish Polemic," pp. 461-62; Sanders, *Paul, the Law*, pp. 105–7, 144; Segal, *Paul* pp. 192–94; Safrai, "Halakha," in *The Jewish People*

in matters such as food as defined by these men: 14:15—15:3) in the
context of the Jewish community?[7] They are to present the members
of their body not to their former lifestyle of "impurity" and "lawlessness" (an equally clear allusion to their former pagan behavior outside
the Jewish community), but to God as "slaves of righteousness" (6:12-
21). In fact, in view of the mercy God has extended to them, and according to the measure of their faith, as gentiles benefiting in some unfathomable way by the present suffering of some of the children of
Jacob (11:13-36), they are to present their bodies as a "living and holy
sacrifice" and turn away from viewing things as they might appear to
others (12:1-3, 4ff.). Instead they are now to commit themselves to
humbly serving those whom they had formerly regarded as "enemies"
(enemies of the gospel and thus of those being addressed) as the very
"beloved" of God "for the sake of the fathers" (12:1-3; cf. 11:25-32).
They are not to please themselves as Law-free gentiles in matters of
purity behavior. They are now to seek peace by recognizing that their
faith calls them to sacrificial Law-respectful service ("walking [halakh]
according to love": 14:15) in matters of food and drink on behalf of the
stumbling of Israel: "Do not destroy with your food him for whom
Christ died" (14:13—15:3; cf. 13:8-14; 12:9-21).

While Paul recognizes that those he addressed in Rome are believers in Jesus Christ, and though Paul is convinced they are "full of all
goodness" and "knowledge" and that they are able "to admonish one
another" (15:14), he must nevertheless come to Rome with his apostolic preaching of the gospel (his "spiritual gift") in order for their faith
to be "established" (1:11-15). And he must write this bold "reminder"
of the need to continue to obey "the teaching" they had embraced

---

in the First Century, pp. 130–32. A. Heschel, Between God and Man, pp. 175–80, explores the dialectic interdependence of halakhah and haggadah for the proper
practice of Judaism, an important note in a discussion such as ours in which this
balance is assumed.

[7]The link between δόκιμος ("approved by men") in 14:18, which means literally "tested, genuine or valuable" (Grundmann, TDNT, 2.255–56) and carries the
sense of being declared as "the real thing" and τύπον ("form of teaching") in 6:17,
which literally means "to stamp a form" or "to strike so as to leave an impression"
as in forming a coin or a wax seal (Goppelt, TDNT, 8.246–47), should not be overlooked. There is a standard/form/pattern "of teaching" by which proper behavior
(obedience: ὑπακοήν) can be judged "by men" as genuine, and it is this behavior
in the service of Christ to which the "strong" are called. Note also the use of this
language in 12:2 contrasted with 1:28. I will discuss this dynamic at work throughout Romans.

along with their faith in Christ in the face of some group's serpent-like suggestion that they could disregard such behavior in matters of food (they could "eat"), otherwise Paul's offering of the gentiles, to both God and the saints in Jerusalem, might not become "acceptable" (15:15-16, 31; cf. 6:17; 16:17-20).

If we allow these features to bear the weight in our reading that Paul apparently expected them to bear for his implied readers in Rome, we will find that a much different reading of Romans, and of Paul, emerges. The contingent nature of Romans, noted frequently in recent scholarship, can now be brought into sharper focus as it is viewed in the context of resolving the dissonance associated with Christian gentiles seeking to worship in the synagogue community(s) of Rome. Romans becomes much more than an occasional letter that is necessary in view of Paul's current collection for Jerusalem and his imminent trip to Rome, Spain, and points west in which he will include the Christian gentiles in demonstration of their indebtedness to Israel (1:9-13; 15:22-32).[8] While he is certainly concerned about matters outside Rome and seeks Roman support, requesting prayer on behalf of his trip to Jerusalem (15:30) and preparing them to serve as a base for his western trip as it extends beyond Rome to Spain (15:23-24), these are unlikely as the central reasons for addressing this "reminder" to Rome. Paul's primary purpose for writing to Rome was his concern that the situation there was deteriorating at the suggestion of those who were challenging "the teaching" that had thus far been obeyed (6:12-23 [cf. v. 17]; 14:13—15:3, 15-16; 16:17-20).

This dynamic provides a glimpse of the early Christian movement as it was developing within a Jewish environment as a viable expression of formative Judaism and suggests that the implied audience (of Christian gentiles in Rome) were meeting in the context of the syna-

---

[8]N. Dahl, *Studies in Paul*, pp. 70–74, 75ff., 88; Munck, *Christ and Israel*, with respect to the collection in noting the occasional nature of Romans. At one extreme, R. Jewett, "Paul, Phoebe, and the Spanish Mission"; and R. Aus, "Paul's Travel Plans to Spain and the "Full Number of the Gentiles" in Rom. XI 25," develop a powerful argument for the centrality of the mission to Spain, while at the other extreme Jervell, "The Letter to Jerusalem," in *The Romans Debate*, pp. 53–64, develops the profound implications of Paul's impending trip to Jerusalem. However, the opening and closing references to Paul's intentions toward Rome (and Jerusalem) and the central concerns of the argument of the letter betray the notion that Paul's primary concerns for this letter of "reminder" lay beyond Rome to the extent that these proposals suggest (cf. Stowers, *Diatribe*, p. 182; Campbell, *Intercultural Context*, pp. 14–24).

gogue community(s) and beginning to question their obligation to practice, as applicable to themselves, the halakhah heretofore developed in Diaspora Judaism for "righteous gentiles." Were they not free to "eat" all things in Christ (14:14)? This would have led the Jewish community(s) to reject the claims of the Christian gentiles as equal co-participants in the promised salvation—"blasphemy" rather than "approval" would have been the unmistakable result (14:16-18). And this would have caused the further "stumbling" of the Jewish community over the gospel—"tear[ing] down the work of God" and "destroy[ing] with your food him for whom Christ died" (14:13, 16, 20).

Paul was thereby compelled to write this bold "reminder," which he hoped would halt this process and prepare them for the procedures he would employ in the synagogues upon his arrival in Rome, when he would then implement his apostolic ministry that would "establish" them in their faith and motivate them to fulfill the responsibilities inherent in their new role in salvation history (1:11-15; 11:15—12:3; 15:14-16, 17ff.). That is, Paul wrote to Rome because it was absolutely necessary for the Christian gentiles there to understand the features he was employing through his distinctive apostolic pattern so that they (and the "stumbling" non-Christian Jews with whom they were associating) would be prepared for his arrival from Zion.[9] Upon his arrival he would execute his customary two-step pattern to ensure the restoration of the dispersed of Israel in the synagogues of Rome *first*, thereafter bringing the good news to the gentiles *also*, which was, surprisingly, a necessary part of the process of Israel's restoration, a "mystery" in which those addressed shared an extremely significant role.

Paul's concerns are those of a Jewish missionary, and his message and framework of thinking are those of one who considers himself working within the historical expectations of Israel—the Savior of Israel has come to Zion to rebuild the tabernacle of David and to bring light to all the nations—for the One God of Israel is the One God of

---

[9]G. Klein, "Paul's Purpose in Writing the Epistle to the Romans," in *The Romans Debate*, pp. 29-43, suggests that Paul's apostolic responsibility was necessary for establishing the Roman church, which is essentially correct, yet this suggestion still fails to provide a satisfactory reason for the necessity of Paul's mission to Rome. Klein's view leaves Paul looking egotistical, at the very least, for his authoritarian approach that assumes an already founded church in Rome needs his personal stamp. See Campbell, *Intercultural Context*, pp. 16–17, for criticism of Klein's position; this criticism would not, however, preclude the position suggested herein.

the whole world.[10] Paul, the apostle of gentiles, is thus the messenger of the Messiah of Israel, traveling out "from Zion" where Jesus has been named Israel's Christ, where the apostles sit on the twelve thrones of restored Israel, to the scattered children of Jacob with the good news of both Israel's restoration (to the Jew first) and the promised restoration of all creation in Christ (and also to the Greek), in this case, to Rome (1:1-16; 11:11-15, 25-27; 15:15-32).[11]

This study is committed to allowing Paul's stated purpose for his intended apostolic mission to Rome and for writing this letter, as set out in this letter, to substantially influence our understanding of the message of Romans.[12] Isn't it time we allowed Paul's explicit comments as

[10]Paul's missionary framework can be safely located in the context of contemporary Jewish eschatological notions and activity, although the exact details and extent of such activity is the topic of lively debate. See L. Feldman, *Jew and Gentile in the Ancient World*, chaps. 9 and 10, for a view that finds Jewish missionary activity prevalent in this period (but see the forthcoming review by L. Rutgers, "Attitudes to Judaism in the Greco-Roman Period: Reflections on Feldman's *Jew and Gentile in the Ancient World*"); for opposing view see S. McKnight, *A Light Among the Gentiles* (note the review of McKnight by Joseph Sievers, *Journal of the Association for Jewish Studies*, 18, no. 2 [1993]); and M. Goodman, *Mission and Conversion*. Paul's assumption that the success of his ministry to the gentiles will provoke his fellow Jews to jealousy suggests an historical situation in which a mission to the gentiles was acceptable or normative, at least within actions perceived to correspond to the fulfillment of Israel's eschatological expectations (11:13-14, 15ff.; see discussion in chapter 5 below), as does also his paradigmatic Jewish missionary in 2:17ff., that is, if the arguments in these texts are presumed to have made any sense to the original writers and audiences, or to have carried any rhetorical force. There is also the issue of Matt. 23:15 and the likely function of the *Sibylline Oracles*, which may also suggest a developed notion of Jewish missionary activity among gentiles (but now see the argument that Matthew is referring to bringing other Jews to Pharisaism, Goodman, *Mission*, pp. 70–74).

[11]Paul's use of "first" should not be limited to sequential priority as the arguments of Rom. 9–11 (esp. 11:28-29) and 3:1-2 make quite clear (cf. R. Hvalvik, "'To the Jew First and also to the Greek': The Meaning of Romans 1:16b"), but it is an important priority in the shaping of Paul's missionary strategy and plans for Rome.

[12]Every effort will be made to read Romans and make interpretive judgments with as little reference to Paul's other New Testament letters as possible, since we should assume they were unknown (or at least unavailable) to the audience in Rome based on our current information. The readers would be students of Israel's Scriptures, and Paul urged them to learn from them (15:4) and expected them to be familiar with the Torah (7:1 most likely refers to Torah). They likely attended synagogue for this exposure, which I will discuss in chapters 2 and 6 below. Obviously Paul assumed a high degree of exposure to the Scriptures if he expected

well as the many implicit ones that appear in various contexts throughout the letter to determine exactly why he felt it so important to write
to, and to personally reach, Rome? Equally important, isn't it time we
allowed Luke's understanding of these same matters, where they harmonize with Paul's stated purpose and message in Romans, to inform
our interpretation of Paul's intentions toward Rome, the probable
historical situation there, the implied audience, and of course, his
message?[13]

These observations challenge the prevailing views of Paul's purpose for writing to Rome and, necessarily, the hermeneutical assumptions that lie behind the interpretation of Romans. Was Paul opposed
to the practice of the Law and Jewish customs in the church in Rome?
Did he believe that the church needed to sever its ties with Judaic
notions of righteous behavior? Was legalism his central concern, that
is, faith versus works or grace versus law? Was the church a completely
separate institution from the synagogue that must seek to assert a

---

them to understand his message in this letter. They were also aware of some early
Christian traditions that Paul was comfortable referring to without amplification
("the teaching": 6:17; 16:17).

[13]Notwithstanding the many historical concerns associated with harmonizing
the Paul of Romans with the Paul of Luke-Acts (note the conclusion of Beker,
"Luke's Paul as the Legacy of Paul," p. 511: "The history of research has made it
abundantly clear that the attempt to harmonize the historical Paul with the Paul of
Luke-Acts has come to a radical end"), features of Luke's presentation of Paul's
view of Law-respectful behavior and his two-step missionary pattern are to be
noted in the Paul we meet in the text of Romans (see particularly chapters 4 and
5 herein). Note the challenge of Jervell, "Retrospect and Prospect in Luke-Acts
Interpretation," on p. 403: "What made the Lucan Paul possible? We have at least
three different Pauls: The Paul of the Pauline letters, the Paul of Acts, and the
Paul of the deuteropauline letters and the Pastorals. Not only by going into the
second century and later do we see the ramified tradition on the apostle to the
Gentiles. Is it possible to trace the various pictures back to the same source,
namely Paul himself, even if we know only fragments of him, namely from his letters? It should be possible to make some progress in analyzing the relation between Paul's theology and thinking on the one hand, and his acts, practice and way
of life on the other. In the tradition of Judaism behavior (according or not according to the law!) had theological significance. Halakah was normative, not haggadah.
What made the Lucan Jewish and law-observant Paul necessary? It seems that this
Paul is as necessary for the Lucan outline as the opposite is for the Pastorals. It
would be promising to study the Lucan Paul as part of the history of the Pauline
tradition." See also the comments of D. Wenham, "Acts and the Pauline Corpus
II: The Evidence of Parallels" in *The Book of Acts in Its First Century Setting*,
pp. 215–58.

Law-free interpretation of salvation and Christian behavior over against Judaism? Was his audience primarily gentiles tempted to "judaize"? Or Jews unwilling to break free from the Law as though they should? Was the purpose of Romans merely to solicit support for a stopover in Rome in route to Paul's more important destination, Spain? Or is the implied audience unimportant because Romans was merely a general or circular epistle with little concern for the particular situation in Rome? Is this letter merely his preparation for objections he anticipates in Jerusalem, addressed to the Roman congregation only in the context of working out his defense and soliciting their prayerful support for his impending trip to Jerusalem?

This reading of Romans suggests that the traditional answers to these questions are inadequate and that the historical situation addressed in Romans should be approached in a vastly different light than it has been in the past. For example, the message derived from Paul's letter to Galatia should not be allowed, as it has so often in the past, to dictate the probable interpretation of Paul's intentions toward Rome. The implied audience and the circumstances are quite different, including the important fact that Paul had an instrumental role in the development of the community he wrote to in Galatia while he had never even been to Rome. Galatians was written to confront Christian gentiles tempted to "judaize," and thus, in the opinion of Paul, to compromise the universal application of the promised salvation to all people equally through faith in Jesus Christ, whether Jew or gentile, for Paul emphatically argued that the One God of Israel was also the One God of the nations equally accessible to gentiles through faith in Jesus Christ. Thus, in Galatia, Paul urges them to "walk by the Spirit" and "through love serve one another" in the context of explaining why Christian gentiles need not become Jews (be circumcised or be under the Law) in order to behave as the "sons" of God through faith and thereby "fulfill the whole Law" (Gal. 5). This message is then, mistakenly I believe, assumed to mean that Paul opposed any notion of the continued value of keeping the Law for Christians (whether Jew or gentile), and this presupposition then becomes, intentionally or not, the hermeneutical motif assumed to lie behind Paul's message in Romans as well.

While this monograph is not the place to debate the issues and message of Galatians thoroughly, it is necessary to point out at least that Paul did not seek to disengage the gospel from any positive practice of the Law for the Christians in Rome, regardless of whether the

message of Galatians appears to indicate that Paul held such a view
(which I do not believe Galatians does indicate).[14] In Rome, clearly the
Christian gentiles were being tempted to the opposite extreme with
respect to Judaism. They were being tempted to disregard the practices of the Law and Jewish customs that Paul believed were essential
to the righteous lifestyle that should characterize their new faith in the
"God and Father of our Lord Jesus Christ" (Rom. 15:6).[15]

    Indeed, I contend that the Judaic influences evident in the devel-
opment of early Christianity in Rome are actually misunderstood
traces of Paul's success, that is, of the widespread acceptance of Paul's
Law-respectful gospel (as set forth in Romans and his subsequent
teaching in Rome) among *gentiles* who were associating with the syna-
gogue(s) of Rome because of their new faith in Jesus Christ.[16] These

[14]Perhaps the Romans had heard of the message to the Galatians, or at least a
similar message confronting some form of "judaizing" and (incorrectly) assumed
that their new faith was discontinuous with Judaism. This would have been but an
early manifestation of the views that came to dominate Christian interpretation
through the centuries. But Paul corrects just such a misunderstanding in Romans.
While Galatians corrects the error of compromising the unique monotheistic assertion of the Shema on the side of Jewish exclusivism: the Lord is *our* God and
gentiles must become Jews if they are to be his people (or at least to be equally
so); Romans corrects the corresponding error of Christian gentile exclusivism: the
Lord is *our* God and Jews who do not give up being Jewish (circumcision and
Torah/customs) are no longer the people of God (or at least not equally so). Paul
would suffer neither excluding extreme; he called rather for the inclusiveness of
asserting the Lord is One: the One Lord of Israel is equally the One Lord of the
nations—he is the One Lord of all who believe in him. I discuss this dynamic
throughout this study, particularly in chapters 3 and 4, and I will discuss Galatians
more directly in the "Summary and Appendix 1."
[15]This position will be developed in several chapters. See 16:17-18 regarding
the group opposing Paul's intentions. See Rom. 6 for issues underlying their temptation to disregard proper practice of righteousness since they are not under the
law but grace; Rom. 11 for the triumphalism in their assumed supplanting of those
Jews who do not believe in Christ Jesus; Rom. 14–15 for Paul's instructions for the
"strong" to accommodate the sensitivities of the "weak" by adopting Judaic behavior, particularly 15:1-3, for the underlying concern that if they followed Paul's
advice they were likely to be reproached for it; and chaps. 5 and 8 for Paul's
lengthy messages on how to put the persecution that would follow in perspective.
[16]See R. Brown and J. Meier, *Antioch and Rome*, for an examination of early
Christian literature that demonstrates a characteristic loyalty to Christianity's
Jewish heritage in the first two centuries in Rome. Dunn, *Romans*, p. xlviii, also
notes this characteristic and suggests rather that "the Christian groups in Rome
emerged from within the Jewish community itself, made up, at least initially, of
Jews and God-worshipping Gentiles who found themselves attracted to faith in

traces bear witness to Paul's application of synagogue rules of behavior, which had been developed in the Diaspora for "God-fearing" or "righteous gentiles"[17] seeking to associate with Jews and their worship of the One God, to the early Christian gentiles of Rome. That is, the lifestyle of these new Christian gentiles was, at the time of his letter, inextricably associated with participation in the lifestyle of the synagogue community(s). In Rome, they not only attended synagogue regularly for prayer and the reading of the Scriptures because of their new faith in Jesus as the Christ of Israel and Savior of the world, but even their house gatherings took place under the authority of the synagogue—there was, as yet, no separation of church and synagogue for Paul or for those he addressed in Romans.[18]

Messiah Jesus, and whose meetings in each others' homes would probably not, in the first instance, be thought of as opposed to the life and worship of the wider Jewish community." See discussion below.

[17]This identity is discussed fully in chapters 2–4 below.

[18]The dialogue with Jews and Judaism in Romans is often noted, yet the solutions offered generally fail to make sense of the historical situation or of how the rhetorical outline of Paul's message in chaps. 1–11 concerned with *non*-Christian Jews prepares those addressed for the paraenesis of chaps. 12–15 that is assumed to be concerned with Christian Jews. Beker, *Paul the Apostle*, p. 89, for example, asks the right questions: "If Romans is a tractate evoked by historical circumstances, why does the letter address itself to a Jewish issue and present itself as a dialogue with Jews rather than with Jewish Christians—because they, and not Jews, are members of the Roman church? . . . If Paul's concern is the unity of Jewish and Gentile Christians in the church, why does he carry on a dialogue with synagogue Jews in Romans?" Beker, however, then follows the traditional negative assumptions regarding Paul's dialogue with Judaism (that the problem is the arrogance of non-Christian and Christian *Jews* [e.g., p. 91; see N. Elliott, *Rhetoric*, for discussion of this problem in the work of Beker and others]) with his conclusion on pp. 89–91: "A dialogue with Jews, then, was necessary to determine not only the legitimate role of Jewish Christianity but especially that of the law-free Gentile mission. The key to the dialogue is the abiding faithfulness of God in the light of the faithlessness and unbelief of Israel, manifested in its rejection of Christ. And if God's act in Christ confirms his faithfulness to Israel, God becomes as well the ground of trust for the Gentiles."

But Beker's position fails to recognize that the gentiles in Rome are not questioning the grounds of God's faithfulness to themselves, and certainly not toward non-Christian Jews. They are boasting of just such a discontinuity in that they are smugly secure in their new status, assuming they have now supplanted non-Christian Jews as the people of God. They may even be grounding this notion in a misunderstanding that this was Paul's position (W. Carter, "Rome (and Jerusalem): The Contingency of Romans 3.21-26," p. 63). It is actually Paul who is concerned with the implications of their position where God's faithfulness to Israel

Thus, the historical and textual evidence that has been interpreted in the past to indicate Jewish-Christian ("judaizing") tendencies in Rome in opposition to (or at considerable distance from) Paul's gospel message demonstrates precisely the opposite.[19] This evidence actually bears witness to Paul's uncompromising application of Judaic principles for defining righteous behavior and to their dramatic impact on the development of the early church in Rome. These traces have survived in the texts of Romans and the Apostolic Fathers in spite of Roman Christianity's later disregard for these Jewish roots as it developed into a thoroughly gentile organization (the "gentilization" of the

---

is concerned. Regardless of their growing indifference, Paul must make them realize the inherent error in the position they are being tempted to take of viewing themselves as supplanting Israel.

I suggest that Beker's rhetorical question is really not so rhetorical. The historical setting involves relationships with non-Christian Jews because the early Christians were still meeting in the synagogues and functioning within the larger Jewish community(s) of Rome. This makes sense of Paul's concerns and illustrations dealing with synagogue Jews (as Beker rightly observes), and thus his confrontation of the everyday concerns and attitudes of the gentiles he is addressing in Rome as they work out their faith and practice in the context of the Jewish community(s) of Rome (which Beker's assumptions obscure).

E. Judge and G. Thomas, "The Origin of the Church at Rome," observe similarly that those addressed in Romans are still meeting "under the umbrella of the synagogues rather than forming their own church" (p. 91); however, their inferences and conclusions from this observation are quite different from those proposed herein. See also J. Ziesler, *Paul's Letter to the Romans*, p. 18: "The Romans as a church had some sort of relationship with the synagogue." See the fuller discussion of synagogues of the Diaspora and the early Christians in Rome in chapter 2 below.

[19]Brown and Meier, *Antioch and Rome*, argue throughout that "the dominant Christianity at Rome had been shaped by the Jerusalem Christianity associated with James and Peter, and hence was a Christianity appreciative of Judaism and loyal to its customs" (p. 110). However, Brown sees this tradition shaped apart from Paul's influence and in tension with his views (as does the balance of modern scholarship): "The Gentiles converted by this mission [of James and Peter from Jerusalem in the 40s] would thus have been more loyal to the Jewish heritage than were Gentiles converted in the Pauline mission. When Paul wrote to Rome in the late 50s to gain support for his collection on behalf of Jerusalem and with the ultimate hope of visiting Rome, his stance toward Judaism was more moderate than it had been at an earlier period—a change stemming partly from experience, partly from a desire to be received" (p. 212). See also R. Brown, "Further Reflections," in *Conversation Continues*, pp. 98–115.

church).[20] Indeed, consider the surviving evidence of a "conservative" attitude toward Judaism among the early Christians in Rome, which continued at least well into the second century (e.g., as seen in *1 Clement* [96 c.e.] and in *Shepherd of Hermas* [*ca.* 100-140 c.e.]),[21] as well as the observation of Ambrosiaster who reports in his commentary on Romans (*ca.* 375):

> It is established that there were Jews living in Rome in the times of the apostles, and that those Jews who had believed [in Christ] passed on to the Romans the tradition that they ought to profess Christ but keep the law. . . . One ought not to condemn the Romans, but to praise their faith; because without seeing any signs or miracles and without seeing any of the apostles, they nevertheless accepted faith in Christ, although according to a Jewish rite [*ritu licet Judaico*].[22]

I suggest that this evidence witnesses not to Paul's supposed Jewish-Christian opponents, nor to Jewish-Christian influences prior

[20]"Gentilization" as opposed to the widely recognized "judaizing" often associated with early Christian Jews. Christian gentiles prevailed over the centuries, so that by the time of Marcion he sought to rid the Christian writings of any respect for or association with Judaism or things Jewish. This tendency has obviously persisted and led to many dark moments in the history of Christianity that are easily recognized. What is less easily recognized, however, is how pervasive this "gentile" approach to Christianity really is, infecting every aspect of interpretation with a bias herein referred to pejoratively as "gentilizing." Nevertheless, I have chosen "gentilizing" over "antinomianism," for disregard for the Jewish Law and customs does not necessarily mean antinomianism, although it may. I discuss this phenomenon below in several contexts, including the development of what is referred to in this monograph as "Luther's trap" with respect to identifying the "weak" in Romans.

[21]See Brown and Meier, *Antioch and Rome*, for evidence of continued Judaic influence in Roman Christianity: pp. 159–83 on *1 Clement*; pp. 162, 203–4 on *Shepherd of Hermas*; idem, "Further Reflections," p. 102: "I argued for a Christianity in Rome, which in the period 58-96 CE was conservative toward Judaism (more so than Paul in Galatians)—a consistent attitude that I think came from Jerusalem."

[22]Citation from Wedderburn, *Reasons*, p. 51. Cf. Brown and Meier, *Antioch and Rome*, pp. 110–11. In fact, it is possible that the Christians in Rome continued to be part of the Jewish communities and synagogues for a long time as there are several references to synagogue meetings in *Shepherd of Hermas* (*ca.* 100–140 c.e.). Perhaps even Hebrews was written to the believers in Christ in Rome still meeting in synagogues; see the various comments of R. Glaze, *No Easy Salvation*, pp. 22–28; Brown and Meier, *Antioch and Rome*, pp. 139–58; Judge and Thomas, "Origin," p. 92; W. Lane, *Hebrews 1–8*, pp. xviii–lx, cxxv–cxxviii.

to Paul's letter that he sought to overcome unsuccessfully. Nor does it show that "Romans is a deliberately pacific formulation of his gospel . . . designed to win Paul a hearing and acceptance"[23] among the Christians who "are the majority at Rome and [who] have created a dominant atmosphere of loyalty to Judaism and appreciation of values in the law."[24] Rather, it points out the general misreading of Paul's position (as negative) on the place of Torah in later Christian traditions (and by modern scholarship). It demonstrates the inseparable link that existed between faith in Jesus Christ and Paul's application of Judaic halakhah for defining the righteous behavior incumbent upon the new Christian gentiles as "righteous gentiles" for both the apostle Paul and the early Christian community(s) in Rome—although the church has long since failed to recognize this profound hermeneutical key for unlocking Paul's intentions, and thus the mystery of Romans.

Romans was not written to discourage association with Judaism, or even to challenge any "judaizing" tendencies,[25] but quite the opposite. Romans was written to "remind" the early church in Rome (composed almost entirely of Christian gentiles who were associating with Jews under the authority of the synagogue)[26] of the importance of their "obedience of faith."[27] That is, Paul thought it was necessary to clarify just how important the halakhah that had been developed in the synagogues of the Diaspora to define the behavior incumbent upon 'righteous gentiles' really was now for defining the Christian gentiles' "spiritual service of worship" in their new faith as they associated with the Jews of Rome. They must "therefore," in view of "the mercies of God" shown to them as gentiles formerly outside the covenant with Israel, but now associating with Jews in their worship of the One Lord

---

[23]Brown, "Further Reflections," p. 108, cf. idem, *Antioch and Rome*, p. 212.

[24]Brown, "Further Reflections," pp. 105–6ff. Brown is correct to observe this character among the Christians in Rome, which he develops throughout *Antioch and Rome* and defends in this article. The important point here is that it need not suggest Paul had a dissimilar view which he compromised in Romans to achieve certain ends.

[25]Contrary to the creative construct of Watson, *Paul*. See the many arguments against Christian Jews or "judaizing" as the problem in Rome by Campbell, *Intercultural Context*, pp. 53–56, 164–70, including a thorough critique of Watson's construct, pp. 122–31, 132–61. See also Elliott, *Rhetoric*.

[26]See chapters 2 and 6 below.

[27]Paul's message in 15:14–32; cf. v. 18, echoing his introductory remarks in 1:5ff. of his apostolic intentions toward Rome. See chapter 4 below for a full discussion.

of both, "present" their "bodies a living and holy sacrifice acceptable to God" and "approved by men" (12:1; 14:18).[28]

Paul's adaptation of Jewish Law and customs for "righteous gentiles" attaching themselves to the synagogue(s) in Romans parallels the halakhah reported in Acts for Christian gentiles (Acts 15:19—16:4). For in Acts, the development of the "edict" that we call the apostolic decree (which is, in principle, an early version of what we now recognize in the rabbinic tradition as the Noahide Commandments)[29] appeals to the same ultimate modus operandi as Romans does for "obedience" to the halakhot governing the behavior of gentiles saved solely by "faith" in Christ Jesus. That is, the "obedience of faith" of Romans and the apostolic decree of Acts both appeal to gentiles saved by "faith" alone (without circumcision as entrance requirement) to adopt certain "righteous behavior" incumbent upon "God-fearing" gentiles associating with the synagogue in order to demonstrate their respect for the faith of the Jewish people: "For Moses from ancient generations has in every city those who preach him, since he is read in the synagogues every Sabbath" (Acts 15:21, 13-31). In fact, I believe that the "form of teaching" that Paul "reminds" the Romans to "obey from the heart" by "becoming slaves of righteousness" (Rom. 6:16-18) is an appeal to the intentions of the very same apostolic decree (though perhaps formulated differently), for exactly the same reasons as the halakhah was reportedly developed in Acts: "For if because of food your brother is hurt, you are no longer *walking* [*halakh*] according to love. Do not destroy with your food him for whom Christ died" (Rom. 14:15).

Paul's application of the intentions of the apostolic decree to the situation in Rome was probably in response to the concerns raised by Prisca and Aquila and the other small company of Christian Jews who had reached Rome, perhaps to prepare the Christians there for Paul's impending trip. There was, apparently, the beginning of a movement on the part of some Christian gentiles to disregard their inherent responsibility to the Law and to the Jewish people. They were questioning the halakhah represented by "obedience" to the apostolic

---

[28]The plain sense of 12:1ff. reaching back to the discussion of gentile salvation and obligation to non-Christian Jews in chaps. 9–11, and forward throughout chaps. 12–15.

[29]For full discussion of the Noahide Commandments and the apostolic decree see chapters 2 and 4 below.

decree in the practice of their "faith." Were they not saved by faith
apart from the Law and Jewish customs? Were they not free to
"eat"?[30] It was thus imperative for Paul to write his "bold reminder" so
they would understand the mysterious way in which their new faith
was linked with the historical faith of Israel, that is, how their new
faith was a gift of God directly linked to the vicarious suffering of
Israel on their behalf (15:14-16; 11:11—12:3, 4ff.). They would thus,
Paul hoped, be moved to enhance their adherence to the principles of
righteousness represented by the apostolic decree for the benefit of
those of Israel presently "stumbling." And they would also be prepared for his apostolic visit to preach his gospel and "impart some spiritual gift" that would "establish" them and thus bring "joy" and "encouragement" as they shared in each other's "faith" (1:11-12;
15:22-33).

The church in Rome was not yet a separate institution from the
synagogue, and at the time of Paul's letter the very suggestion that it
ever would be, in the context of Romans at least, appears to have been
unthinkable.[31] Jesus Christ was the Savior of Israel, and the nations
who were joining with the congregation of Israel were doing so as expected, "that with one accord you may with one voice glorify *the God
and Father* of our Lord Jesus Christ" (15:6ff.). The gospel represented
no break in salvation history, for it was fulfilling the promises made to
the fathers in Christ—"to the Jew first and also to the Greek" (1:16-

[30]The apparent tension in Rome was being caused by some group seeking to
persuade the Christian gentiles there to abandon "the teaching which you
learned" in the service "of their own appetites," a striking reference to the issue
of "eating" also central to the tension between the "weak" and "strong." See
Romans 6:1-23; 14:1—15:12; 16:17-18; for full discussion see chapters 3 and 4
below.

[31]Note the observation of Judge and Thomas, "Origin," that the Christians in
Rome "were not formally constituted as a church" (p. 82) as "they had preferred
to shelter under the umbrella of the synagogues rather than forming their own
church" (p. 91) until Paul arrived and set about changing things, because "it was
Paul who was responsible for organising them separately from the synagogues"
(p. 92). While their reading of Paul follows the normal assumptions I am challenging, their recognition of the prolonged relationship with the synagogues in
Rome is unusual and harmonizes more closely with the view proposed herein. See
also the remarks of H. Bartsch, "The Concept of Faith in Paul's Letter to the
Romans," pp. 41–44, 45ff., who also notes that the tensions in Rome suggest that
there was "not yet a church in Rome but only Christians who had failed to form
one church" (p. 42), although his suggestion is not explicitly that they were
meeting in synagogues.

18; 15:8-9). Thus, for Paul, the eschatological promises of the restoration of Israel and the gathering of the nations were actually unfolding before their very eyes (11:25-32; 15:4-21).[32]

These gentiles had joined the historical people of the faith. Their new participation in the congregation of the faithful of Israel made it imperative that they recognize their obligation was not to boast in misplaced triumphalism over against the practices and the faith of the Jews of Rome who were not yet persuaded that Jesus was the promised Christ or that Christian gentiles were equal coparticipants in the blessings of God through faith without the need to become Jews. Instead, their explicit obligation was to serve non-Christian Jews in love by subordinating themselves to the authority of the synagogue and to the behavior commensurate with "righteous gentiles" seeking to honor the One God of Israel as the One God of the whole world.[33] This is the very "obedience of faith" that Paul expounds throughout this compelling letter.[34]

Paul was uncompromising in his insistence on the principles of monotheism, even to the point of arguing that the current "stumbling" of the non-Christian Jews was the result of their own failure to realize the very compromise of monotheism inherent in their refusal to accept the faith of the Christian gentiles as legitimate. He saw their failure (ἀδυνάτων: "lack of strength" or "inability") to grasp this truth as the very cause of their ἀσθενήματα, their "weakness" or "stumbling" (15:1).[35] Paul challenged their ethnocentric insistence that gentiles must become Jews to be equal coparticipants in the blessings of God (3:19-31; 9:30—10:13; 14:3ff.)—for was not the One Lord the Lord of the nations as well as the Lord of Israel? Thus, for a Jew to insist that

---

[32]Is this not the plain sense of James's speech in Acts 15:13-21 as well? See chapter 5 below. Sanders, *Paul, the Law*, p. 171, observes similarly that Paul viewed his work of evangelizing and collecting money among the gentiles in the setting of "the expected pilgrimage of the Gentiles to Mount Zion in the last days": "The reign of God has come, Israel is being established, and the time has arrived for Gentiles to enter the people of God."

[33]This is the point of the paraenesis of chaps. 12–15, including 13:1-7, where the "authorities" are the synagogue leaders (λειτουργοὶ: "servants" as is Paul in 15:16, always used with religious connotations; cf. W. Bauer, *Lexicon*, pp. 470–71) rather than the state as is usually assumed. For discussion see chapter 6 below.

[34]For a full discussion of Paul's usage of the phrase "obedience of faith" and its variations see chapter 4.

[35]For full discussion of the identity of the "weak" and Paul's use of ἀσθενεῖς see chapter 3 below.

God was exclusively the possession of Israel was to deny his very oneness—to deny that all peoples, whether Jews or gentiles (non-Jews),
were unified in him as one. When Jews glorified the One God of Israel
they glorified the same God as the gentiles whom they were to en-
lighten with the knowledge that gentiles should *also* glorify the One
God of Israel—for he is truly the One God of the whole world.

Paul was equally uncompromising toward the inherent error underlying any suggestion by Christian gentiles that the One Lord was exclusively the possession of Christians, and toward any temptation to
disregard their obligation to respect the faith and practice of the non-
Christian Jews they were associating with (I propose that these non-
Christian Jews were those Paul refers to as the "weak" or "stumbling"
of Israel). For this also was to deny his very oneness and to deny that
his covenant people, whether Jew or gentile, were unified in God as
One. When the gentiles glorified the One God of the whole world they
glorified the same God as the Jews who had already been enlightened
with the knowledge that they should glorify the One God of the whole
world—for he is the faithful God of Israel (3:29-31; 11:11—12:3, 4ff.).
Paul confronted this error in his selection of the label δυνατοὶ
("strong" or "able") with its implicit critical edge, as well as explicitly
in his instructions to the "strong" Christian gentiles throughout this
letter.[36]

Romans is not a call to deny the place of Israel, nor is it a treatment
of the threat of "judaizing" among the new Christian gentiles in
Rome—for the Christian gentiles of Rome were not tempted to "judaizing" but to disrespect, and in the extreme, to "gentilizing."
Romans is rather a call to the newly believing Christian gentiles of
Rome to recognize the preeminent place of Israel, the historical
people of God (the "beloved for the sake of the fathers": 11:28), and
thus the importance of the obligation incumbent upon these gentiles
to obey the Judaic norms of righteousness and purity in their new faith
as they associate with the Jews of Rome. However, Romans includes
the unmistakable caveat that while Israel's historical place is preeminent it is not exclusive, and while the Christian gentiles must practice
the intentions of the apostolic decree they must not misunderstand
this and assume, as some were being tempted to assume in Galatia,
that they are thereby in need of placing themselves fully under the

---

[36]For full discussion of the identity of the "strong" as the essential audience
addressed in Romans see chapters 2 and 3 below.

Law (to become Jews through adapting the boundary markers of circumcision and complete Law observance) in order to be equal coparticipants in the blessings of God promised to Abraham and revealed in Christ Jesus for all who believe in Him.

Paul intended to reach Rome as soon as possible to set matters right. He would, upon his arrival, execute his customary two-step pattern of preaching the gospel in the synagogues of Rome: first, to the Jews to begin restoring the righteous of Israel present in the Diaspora city of Rome; and second, by turning to the gentiles so that they also might share equally in the fulfillment of the eschatological blessings promised to Abraham's seed.[37] However, in view of priorities he was attending to elsewhere that were continuing to delay his personal visit (15:22-25), Paul wrote his "bold reminder" (15:15-16) to the "strong" in Rome that they might fully understand the weight of their responsibility to live in love and the pursuit of peace with the "weak in faith." Paul hoped that the Christian gentiles would thus understand that their behavior was of historic importance, and must not "offend" the "weak" and thus contribute to their "stumbling" over the declaration that Jesus was the Christ of Israel, uniting Jews and gentiles in the worship of the One Lord of all humankind as promised (15:5-12).

Paul believed it was imperative that Christian gentiles embrace his epideictic[38] reminder, and thus, through their respectful "obedience to faith" represented by the observance of the apostolic decree (the halakhah governing gentile righteousness incumbent upon all gentiles who have come to believe that the God of Israel is indeed the One God of the whole world), they would respectfully become Paul's fellow workers in his mission, coparticipants in preparing the Jews of Rome for the "good news" Paul would soon declare upon his arrival. This promised salvation had begun in Jerusalem with the resurrection and preaching of Jesus as the Christ ("where Christ was already named": 15:20)[39] and continued out "from Zion" in Paul's ministry as

---

[37]This "custom" is traced by Luke and is the subject of chapter 5 below on Paul's two-step pattern for the preaching of the gospel. See Acts 28:17-31 for Luke's report of Paul's activity upon his arrival in Rome.

[38]For full discussion of the rhetorical nature of Romans as epideictic see chapter 4 below

[39]I suggest that Paul's reference was not to Diaspora cities that had received the gospel but to Jerusalem, where the Christ was "named," where the apostles sat on the twelve thrones of the restored Israel, and where Paul was not authorized to function as the apostle to Israel, for his apostleship was defined outside of Palestine to the nations. For full discussion see chapter 5 below.

he circled the Diaspora preaching the gospel and "bringing about the obedience of faith among all the Gentiles" (1:5; 15:17-25). Soon this mission would include Paul's intended trip to Rome to bring about in Rome the beginning of the "fulness of the Gentiles." This procedure would mark, paradoxically, the end of the suffering of the part of Israel presently hardened as it triggered the saving jealousy of "some of them," resulting in the eschatological restoration of "all" of Israel—for of at least one mystery Paul was certain: "all Israel will be saved" (11:11-15, 25-27; 15:22-33; 1:1-18, 19ff.).[40]

[40]For a full discussion of Paul's apostolic mission and the salvation of Israel see chapter 5 below.

CHAPTER 2

THE HISTORICAL BACKDROP
AND IMPLIED AUDIENCE

It is not the intention of this study to offer a comprehensive view of
Diaspora Jews or of the Jewish religion, in Rome or elsewhere.[1]
However, it is necessary to discuss some of the issues in Jewish faith
and practice that would have been operative in Rome at the time of
Paul's letter. We must briefly consider several general issues that
would have necessarily affected the interpretation of the language of
Romans for the original recipients; for example, (1) the role of the synagogue in the Jewish community and the parameters of its legal
authority in relation to the Jewish community, the state (Roman government), and gentiles; (2) "God-fearing" gentiles, and the halakhah
operative in defining their righteousness; (3) attitudes toward and
relations with gentiles, particularly in the matters of table-fellowship
and synagogue attendance; (4) eschatological expectations, particularly as they relate to the fate of the nations and the role of the children of Jacob dispersed among them; and finally, (5) the prevailing
attitudes of gentiles in Rome toward Jews and Judaism.

We must also discuss the probable makeup of the congregation(s)
receiving this letter, and most importantly, the probable audience Paul
was concerned to affect with this message. That is, we must seek to
understand both who was present in Rome and whom Paul targeted

---

[1] I have drawn from many excellent studies; nevertheless, there is still much
that we just do not know about the Jewish communities of the Diaspora in the first
century, and in particular, about the Jewish people and their beliefs and practices
in Rome. We can safely assume the reconstructions of the available literary, epi-
graphical, and archeological sources of the scholars included herein are accurate on
most points, especially where no available evidence suggests otherwise; however,
caution is in order because we are aware of tremendous diversity of faith and practice among Jewish people and communities in different locations, times, and circumstances. For a picture of the state of scholarship on these matter see the various discussions of G. Vermes, *Jesus and the World of Judaism;* J. Charlesworth, *The
Old Testament Pseudepigrapha and the New Testament;* L. Rutgers, "Roman Policy
Towards the Jews"; T. Rajak, "Inscription and Context: Reading the Jewish
Catacombs of Rome."

(his implied audience) as he composed this letter, matters which have a great deal to do with interpreting his intentions and his message.

DIASPORA JUDAISM IN ROME AT THE TIME OF PAUL'S LETTER[2]

The Synagogue in the Diaspora

The synagogue was the social institution ("gathering") around which Jewish community life revolved in the Diaspora, regardless of the fact that there were many different views, factions, and sects that characterized and were generally accepted within first-century Judaisms.[3] While sometimes denoting a place of assembly (e.g., Lk. 7:5; in the Diaspora often a home or a renovation of an existing structure; not the formal building structures of later times),[4] the synagogue reached

---

[2]Some archeological evidence drawn on in Rome by the following sources as first-century evidence may in fact be later. See L. Rutgers, "Archaeological Evidence," idem, "Roman Policy Toward Jews," for an argument that Jewish catacombs in Rome yield third-century c.e. and later evidence.

[3]Safrai, *Jewish People*, 2.913ff. Note that Judaism tolerated many different views as witnessed in the literature of Josephus, the Qumran Scrolls, Philo, and the other Jewish and Christian literature of the time, not to mention the differences between the views of Pharisees and Sadducees (and the diversity of opinions among those of their own sect or persuasion). This pluralism extended throughout Judaism and blended even the distinctions between Palestinian and Diaspora beliefs and practices so that it is not possible to speak of a monolithic or normative Judaism, although certain central tenets were normal in the practice of Judaism, including observance of Torah (with different views of what that meant), Sabbath observance, circumcision, and dietary halakhah (W. D. Davies, *Paul and Rabbinic Judaism*; Sanders, *Paul and Palestinian Judaism*; M. Hengel, *Judaism and Hellenism*; C. Hill, *Hellenists and Hebrews*, pp. 1–4, 5ff.; N. T. Wright, *The New Testament and the People of God*, pp. 244ff.; Dunn, *The Partings of the Ways*).

[4]There are exceptions, for example Sardis, but this was both later (third century c.e.) and still a renovation, though of a public building (A. Seager, "The Architecture of the Dura and Sardis Synagogues," pp. 79–116; cf. 80, 92; E. Meyers and A. Kraabel, "Archaeology, Iconography, and Nonliterary Written Remains," pp. 177–89; esp. 184–85). L. White, *Building God's House in the Roman World*, pp. 60–101, states on p. 64 : "In the earliest diffusion of Jewish communities into the Diaspora, local congregations probably met in the homes of individuals. The earliest synagogue buildings had little or no distinguishing architectural features"; and he notes on p. 78: "While Jewish communities are known from earlier times, the first evidence of synagogue activity in each case comes from the physical adaptation, however minimal, for religious use. Such donations came from (or at least through) the owner of the house, who first served as host to the community and

beyond the walls of any particular location in defining the organization
of the Jewish community(s).[5]

In the period we are concerned with the synagogues were institutions defining the Jewish communities as religious and legal entities in
the Roman Empire. The Roman government legally classified them as
"collegia," a term used with respect to their shared traits with "private
clubs," guilds, and other cultic associations that were legally recognized to have the same privileges: the right to assemble, to have common meals, common property, fiscal responsibilities (treasury),

---

then as its patron." On p. 92 White states further concerning synagogues: "Private
household gatherings gradually gave rise to formal establishments through a
process of architectural adaptation sponsored in large measure by private benefac-
tions." For Diaspora synagogues from archeological evidence see also E. Meyers
and J. Strange, *Archaeology, the Rabbis and Early Christianity*, pp. 140–54; S. Zeitlin,
"The Origin of the Synagogue," in *The Synagogue*, pp. 14–26.

Similarly, regarding the meeting places of the early Christians, see the significant study of early Roman Christianity by P. Lampe, *Die stadtrömischen Christen in
den ersten beiden Jahrhunderten*, in which he concludes that there is no evidence of
even rooms "reserved exclusively for liturgy" until the third century, and then in
Dura Europos, though possibly also in Rome, for example, the Roman buildings
hypothesized under S. Prisca on the Aventine, S. Anastasia on the Circus Maximus,
and S. Caecilia in Trastevere. But: "Archaeological possibilities of this kind for
liturgical assembly halls are nowhere evident for the 1st and 2nd centuries. The literary evidence that terms such as 'domus ecclesiae,' 'domus Dei' or 'sacraria' are
not yet attested for the first two centuries corresponds to this archaeological finding. The term 'basilica' used for a church is only first attested at the beginning of
the 4th century. . . . In view of the concurrence of archaeological and literary evidence, the conclusion is significant that, in the first two centuries, there were not
'house churches,' specific rooms set aside for worship in secular houses. Positively
speaking, the Christians of the 1st and 2nd centuries celebrated their liturgy in any
rooms which had been used daily in other ways by the occupants." Lampe ties
these points together: "In the pre-Constantine period, the Christians of the city of
Rome assembled in fractions on premises, scattered across the world renowned
city, which were provided by private persons. . . . The finding concerning fractionation stands against the background of *a Jewish community in the city of Rome which
had fractions*. Roman Judaism consisted of a number of independent synagogue
communities. The parallelism is amazing, whether one wishes to consider the
Jewish structure only as direct pattern or not" (cf. part 5, chapters 1 and 2, "The
Fractionation of Roman Christianity"; I am grateful to Marshall Johnson and
Fortress Press for an early transcript of the forthcoming English edition quoted
herein).

[5]G. La Piana, "Foreign Groups in Rome," pp. 347–48. Note that *proseuchē* generally referred to the building, "synagogue" to the community or its meetings. See
also H. C. Kee, "The Transformation of the Synagogue after 70 C.E.: Its import for
early Christianity," for a good discussion of the evidence.

disciplinary rights among its membership, and responsibility for the burial of members.[6] In addition to those privileges usually granted "private clubs," Julius Caesar granted the Jewish communities the privilege "to live according to their ancestral laws" because of their existence before the Roman Empire, and because of their help in the civil war in the Maccabean period.[7] These legal privileges were discussed at length by Josephus, and included the authority to interpret the Law and customs for the community,[8] exemption from emperor

---

[6]E. M. Smallwood, *Jews Under Roman Rule*, pp. 133–43, 210; H. Leon, *The Jews of Ancient Rome*, pp. 9-11; G. La Piana, "Foreign Groups," pp. 341–63; Safrai, *Jewish People*, 1.454–63; E. Ellis, *Pauline Theology*, pp. 122–45.

[7]Josephus, *Ant.* 12.3.3 (138–50); 14.10.1–11.2 (185–276); 16.1.3 (27–28); 16.6.2 (162–65); 19.5.3 (287–91); 19.6.3 (300); Philo, *Legatione Ad Gaium* 23.155–58; Claudius, *Pap. Lond.* 1912.73–105 (for a papyrus account of Claudius's own words [M. Whittaker, *Jews and Christians*, pp. 99–100]). See E. P. Sanders, *Judaism: Practice and Belief 63 BCE-66 CE*, p. 212, for a concise summary. V. Tcherikover, *Hellenistic Civilization and the Jews*, p. 83, states: "There is no doubt that the concept of "ancestral laws," where it concerns Jews, is much broader than the Law of Moses, and includes, not only the elements of the Jewish religion, but the maintenance of political institutions, the form of the regime, the methods of social organization, and the like . . . every Jewish community in the Diaspora set up synagogues for itself and sometimes even courts of justice, and these activities too were carried out in accordance with the Jewish privilege." On pp. 301–2 he states, "The permission to live according to their ancestral laws meant *the internal autonomy of the organized Jewish community in the Diaspora*. It is clear, indeed, that the same restrictions affecting a Greek city affected the Jewish community; its autonomy was not political but religious and social only. . . . The right 'to live according to its ancestral laws' meant the right to build synagogues, to maintain independent courts of justice, to educate the youth in the spirit of the Torah, to set up communal institutions and to elect officials, and the like. The Jewish community with its officials and institutions, its synagogues and courts, its economic and social life, was a miniature kingdom; and if, from the point of view of the Hellenistic state, its case was no different from that of every other 'politeuma,' from an internal point of view it was more like the autonomous Greek 'polis' than an ephemeral group of foreigners from abroad" (emphasis added). V. Scramuzza, "The Policy of the Early Roman Emperors towards Judaism," in *The Beginnings of Christianity*, pp. 277–97. But see L. Rutgers, "Roman Policy," in *Classical Antiquity*, p. 73, who points out that these privileges were developed in response to specific situations and were not a Magna Charta for the Jews: "In the earlier Roman Empire, there never was a standard Roman 'Jewish policy'"; also M. Pucci Ben Zeev, "Caesar and Jewish Law," pp. 28–37, who argues that the permission Caesar granted the Jews involved certain legal value but should not be regarded as "special."

[8]Tcherikover, *Hellenistic*, pp. 82–89, 300–302, 305ff.; Smallwood, *Jews*, pp. 133–43, 210.

worship and civic cults,[9] the right to collect and distribute the Temple tax for Jerusalem,[10] exemption from military service,[11] protection of Sabbath observance including nonappearance in court,[12] and the right to function as independent organizations without specifically seeking authorization to do so.[13]

The synagogue governed the Jewish community in religious, moral, legal, administrative, educational, and virtually every other aspect of social interaction necessary in the life of a community.[14] Essentially, the synagogue represented the independence of the community in the midst of foreign cultures in foreign lands as a place of refuge and boundary for the worship of God and practice of righteousness as defined by the Law and interpreted by the leaders of the commu-

---

[9]Josephus, *War* 2.10.4; *Against Apion*, 2.6 (77); Philo, *Legatione Ad Gaium* 23.157. See the discussion of Tcherikover, *Hellenistic*, pp. 305–7; La Piana, "Foreign Groups," pp. 376–80; Smallwood, *Jews*, p. 137.

[10]The two-drachma or one-half shekel Temple tax was paid annually by Jews outside Palestine for support of the daily whole-burnt offerings and community sacrifices (Neh. 10:32-34). Caesar allowed for its collection, treasury, and distribution. It also appears that it was customary for Jews to send supplementary gifts to the Temple along with the Temple tax as they were able. E. P. Sanders, *Jewish Law from Jesus to the Mishnah*, pp. 283–308; idem, *Judaism: Practice*, pp. 146–69, for complete discussion of Temple tax and other Diaspora payments to Jerusalem. See Josephus, *Ant.*, 14.7.2 (110) for reference to God-fearers (σεβομένων τὸν θεόν) paying this tax as well (see also 16.6.2–7 [162-173] and Tacitus, *Histories* 5.5.1, who also refers to gentiles sending their "tribute and gifts" to Jerusalem [Whittaker, *Jews and Christians*, p. 22]; discussion by S. Cohen, "Respect for Judaism by Gentiles according to Josephus," p. 428); cf. Tcherikover, *Hellenistic*, p. 308. See K. Nickle, *Collection: A Study in Paul's Strategy*, pp. 74–99, for the analogies to Paul's collection.

[11]Josephus, *Ant.* 14.10.6, 12, 13 (204, 225–30); Tcherikover, *Hellenistic*, pp. 307–8; Smallwood, *Jews*, p. 137; V. Scramuzza, "Policy," p. 289 n. 1: "The Jews could not take an oath of allegiance to the imperator since they would have to swear by pagan deities and on standards surmounted by eagles."

[12]Josephus, *Ant.* 14.10.20–25 (241-64); Tcherikover, *Hellenistic*, p. 307.

[13]Tcherikover, *Hellenistic*, pp. 81–89, 296–377; esp. 299–332; J. Jeffers, *Conflict at Rome*, pp. 38–39; W. Meeks, *The First Urban Christians*, pp. 31–36; Ellis, *Pauline Theology*, pp. 139–45; W. Wiefel, "The Jewish Community in Ancient Rome and the Origins of Roman Christianity," in *Romans Debate*, pp. 89–92; Smallwood, *Jews*, p. 135 n. 52: "The general right of assembly meant that synagogues could be formed without individual authorization."

[14]Smallwood, *Jews*, p. 210: "The Roman government recognized the Jews' moral right to practice their religion without hindrance; but its duties included the maintenance of law and order and public morality."

nity(s).[15] G. La Piana summed up the synagogue community's self-governing situation in Rome thus:

> It possessed in fact an administrative, educational, and juridical organi-zation of its own; and it exercised both directly and through the central organ of community government not only a religious and moral author-ity over its members, but also a form of civil jurisdiction in regulating contracts and settling disputes, and even a limited criminal jurisdiction with the power to inflict penalties, which were sanctioned by the pub-lic authorities. In a word the Jewish associations, taken all together, actually possessed all the essential elements of organization and gov-ernment pertaining to a city, and not merely showed the semblance of such institutions, as was the case with the collegia.[16]

Prior to 70 c.e. it appears that the synagogues usually held their meetings on the Sabbath and other holidays for worship.[17] This com-munity worship, which was understood primarily as the study of Torah and prayer when at least ten adult males gathered to do so, was the centerpiece of Jewish religious life.[18] The community would gather for the reading of the Scriptures, as well as their translation,[19] interpreta-

---

[15]Tomson, *Paul*, pp. 46–47.

[16]La Piana, "Foreign Groups in Rome," pp. 349–50. It should be noted that we do not have such evidence for Rome in particular, thus we cannot be certain this was exactly the case in Rome, although it was likely.

[17]Safrai, *Jewish People*, 2.918–19. He also mentions the possibility that there were Monday and Thursday meetings, but this is difficult to establish.

[18]Safrai, *Jewish People*, 2.915–16, 1056–60; G. F. Moore, *Judaism* 1.285; Sanders, *Jewish Law*, pp. 77–81; *Judaism: Practice*, pp. 197–208; Ellis, *Pauline Theology*, pp. 137ff.

[19]Safrai, *Jewish People*, 2.927–33, 1056–60, notes that the Scriptures were read publicly in Hebrew and translated, or there was a secondary reading of the Septuagint, because the audience spoke Greek; Meyers and Kraabel, "Archaeology, Iconography," p. 200, note that Greek was the first language of Jews in the Roman Diaspora, and cites the fact that Jewish epitaphs are 76% Greek and 23% Latin with only 1% in Semitic languages. For a full study of languages from Jewish catacombs see Leon, *Jews*, pp. 75–92; Leonard V. Rutgers, "The Onomasticon of the Jewish Community of Rome" (who has graciously provided this chapter [and others] from the revision of his 1993 dissertation, "The Jews in Late Ancient Rome," forthcoming from Brill). See Simon, *Verus Israel*, pp. 293–305, for the link between Judaism's adaptation of Greek and proselytism. For a full discussion of the Septuagint as the prevalent form of the Scriptures and the variations of Paul's quotations from the Septuagint as normative among both

tion[20] and commentary or exhortation.[21] Prayers would have included blessings such as the Shema, Kiddush, and Habdalah.[22] They also gathered regularly in the synagogue or in their homes[23] (particularly if they could not afford a separate building [note בית הכנסם: "*house* of assembly"])[24] for festivals, meals, education, and community business.

The responsibilities of synagogue leaders included both religious and practical matters of administration.[25] Although each synagogue in Rome was autonomous, they operated under the same structure and associated with the others.[26] The leadership included several positions: "synagogue ruler" (ἀρχισυνάγωγος) over religious activities; a "council" (γερουσία) for general affairs; an "archon" (ἄρχων) for non-religious affairs; a secretary (γραμματεύς); and an official for financial responsibilities (title uncertain).[27] They would have handled the many

---

[20]D. Juel, *Messianic Exegesis*, pp. 31–57.

[21]Safrai, *Jewish People*, 2.922, 927–33. This would have included comments from attendees, as is often noted in the New Testament.

[22]Safrai, *Jewish People*, 2.922–27.

[23]Meeks, *Urban*, p. 80; Meyers and Kraabel, "Archaeology, Iconography," pp. 175ff.

[24]See the discussions of S. Zeitlin, "Origin," pp. 14–26; J. Gutmann, "The Origin of the Synagogue," pp. 72–76; White, *Building God's House*, pp. 60–101; Meyers and Strange, *Archaeology, the Rabbis*, p. 141, note most evidence of synagogue buildings is from the third century c.e. and later for economic reasons; they were not yet in a position to finance public buildings in earlier periods.

[25]Safrai, *Jewish People*, 2.933–37, 942–43; Leon, *Jews*, pp. 167–94.

[26]This was not the case in Alexandria, where there was a centralized leadership; see the full discussion of Leon, *Jews*, pp. 168–70, 174–76, 193–94; Jeffers, *Conflict*, pp. 38-40; Acts 28:17ff., for example, of Paul upon his arrival in Rome.

[27]Leon, *Jews*, pp. 167–94, for a complete discussion of offices in Roman synagogues, including some additional roles such as the ὑπηρέτης as possibly the cantor, the προστάτης as the patron representing the Jewish community to the Roman government, and others, including some honorary titles. Josephus, *Ant.* 14.7.2 (116–18); 19.5.2 (280–85), relates that the ethnarch of the Jewish community of Alexandria "ruled the people, judged its cases and supervised the implementation of contracts and orders, like the ruler of an independent state." Tcherikover, *Hellenistic*, pp. 302–3, discusses the γερουσία as the council of elders, and believes that the title ἄρχων refers to the most important members of the council. He notes that the use of this title was "widespread among the Jews of the Diaspora," particularly at Rome. Leon, *Jews*, pp. 176–78, discusses the title "arcon of honor" found on four epitaphs in Rome and the suggestion of Frey that they were the

his Greco-Roman and Jewish contemporaries see Stanley, *Paul* (pp. 67–79, 340–41 on the Septuagint issue in particular).

financial and ethical issues necessary in the community affairs. For example, they were responsible to ensure correct behavior among the members, including judgment and discipline (Paul bears witness to this in his early persecution of "the Way" in the Damascus synagogues, and in the various floggings and stonings he later underwent for the same reasons at the hands of the Jewish authorities).[28] One did not simply pass in and out of membership in the synagogue community at will; if one was a member of the community one was subordinate to the synagogue leaders' authority and discipline.[29] If one

---

treasurers. See H. Sky, *Development of the Office of Hazzan through the Talmudic Period*, pp. 11–21, for an interesting discussion of later developments in this position with clear implications for the leadership roles, particularly in matters of discipline such as the administering of "judicial stripes," maintaining decorum, and signaling the beginning and ending of meetings as well as representing Jewish matters before Roman authorities. See also La Piana, "Foreign Groups in Rome," pp. 359–63; Jeffers, *Conflict*, pp. 38–40; Tcherikover, *Hellenistic*, pp. 301–6, 7ff.; J. Burtchaell, *From Synagogue to Church*, pp. 201–71.

[28]Cf. 2 Cor. 11:21-27 (Gal. 1:13-14) with Acts 14:5, 19; 16:22-23. See Acts 9:1-2 where Paul had formerly been commissioned to bind believers in Jesus Christ attending the synagogues of Damascus; 18:14-16, where Gallio expects the Jewish community to judge matters less than criminal. See Safrai, *Jewish People*, 2.942–43; A. N. Sherwin-White, *Roman Society*, pp. 100–101, notes regarding the incident at Corinth in Acts: "There is no clear evidence that the local Sanhedrins had any formally recognized right to force obedience upon their own adherents. . . . Certainly Saul's authority in the mysterious mission to Damascus derived from the high-priest and not from the local community of Jews. Only at Alexandria in Egypt is there clear evidence that the Jewish colony possessed internal self-government, in matters of the Hebraic law, under the authority of the Ethnarch" (see Josephus, *Ant.* 14.7.2 [116–18]; 19.5.2 [280–85]). He also notes on pp. 102–3, "The Jews of Corinth may not themselves have had the power of enforcement, but they might hope to invoke the proconsul's authority against a fellow Jew who interfered, as Paul certainly was interfering, with the quiet practice of their customs." But see Sky, *Hazzan*, pp. 18–20, for discussion of the disciplinary rights of the *hazzan* in local synagogues. The Mishnah discusses the discipline of flogging at length in *Makkot* 3. See also D. Hare, *Jewish Persecution of Christians*, pp. 43–46, who finds evidence that "strongly suggests that Christians were flogged in synagogues upon the authority of the local council of elders. It would seem to follow that such local councils were in the Diaspora, as in Palestine, empowered to employ various sanctions, including corporal punishment, for the maintenance of public order among the members of the synagogue" (p. 45).

[29]A. Harvey, "Forty Strokes Save One"; R. Longenecker, *Paul*, pp. 247–48; Sanders, *Paul, the Law*, p. 192.

refused to do so one was no longer regarded as a member of the community. The leaders also answered to the Roman authorities for the collection and distribution of taxes;[30] in this sense they served as representatives of the government for the Jewish community. Additional activities under their jurisdiction included schooling of children, providing lodging for travelers, and the burial of members.[31]

There were several (eleven, or perhaps many more) synagogues in Rome[32] in 55–58 c.e. when Romans was written.[33] It is likely that each operated independently, as they were characterized by the cultural makeup of the various Jewish communities that settled in Rome for different reasons, from slavery to commercial opportunity, and they had also come from a variety of locations throughout the Roman Empire.[34] The largest concentration of Jews was in the area called Transtiberinum (now known as Trastevere), where many oriental

[30]They collected the Jerusalem Temple tax and possibly Roman taxes and were responsible for their proper distribution. See Josephus, *B.J.* 2.405–7; Smallwood, *Jews*, pp. 32–33. Sky, *Hazzan*, p. 20, states that the *hazzan* represented "the Jews of Judea before the Roman authorities." See also Leon, *Jews*, pp. 191–92, on the role of the *phrontistes* as the representative from the Jewish community to the political authorities.

[31]Safrai, *Jewish People*, 2.942–43.

[32]Leon indicates at least eleven, nine of which can be located with some degree of certainty. See Leon, *Jews*, pp. 135–66, for epitaphs identifying each and additional possibilities. There is some disagreement about the exact number and some of the names. The matter of dating is also problematic, as most evidence dates from the third century c.e. and later. See the discussion of Rutgers, "Archaeological Evidence." Rutgers does note, however, that four synagogues in Rome described by Leon do include references to first-century patrons and thus reflect a situation that goes back to the first century.

In addition, consider the implications of the fact that the Jews of Rome generally lived in the densely populated and lower socioeconomic areas such as Trastevere and Porta Capena populated by the immigrants, slaves, and former slaves, and that the synagogues of the period apparently met in adapted private homes and tenement rooms that may have accommodated no more than 40 and 20 people respectively (there is no evidence of basilica structures for this period). Therefore, it is safe to assume that the number of meeting places necessary to handle the synagogue communities of some 20,000–50,000 Jews were far in excess of the eleven that Leon traces.

[33]Most date Romans at 55–58 c.e. See Dunn, *Romans*, pp. xliii–xliv, for discussion and bibliography; Sherwin-White, *Roman Society*, pp. 99–119, for interesting historical information.

[34]La Piana, "Foreign Groups in Rome," pp. 341–71; Jeffers, *Conflict*, pp. 9–12.

groups settled, but additional communities were in Subura, near the Campus Martius, and near the Porta Capena.[35]

"Righteous Gentiles," the Noahide Commandments, and the Apostolic Decree

Understanding the prevailing concept of "righteous gentiles" or "God-fearers" at the time of Paul's letter is important to understanding Judaism's views on righteousness for the non-Jew, both inside and outside the boundaries of Judaism. While rabbinic writings indicate that the salvation of gentiles without circumcision (as gentiles rather than Jews) was a topic of concern for rabbinic Judaism in the centuries following the sharp break between the church and synagogue, it was cast in more philosophical and eschatological terms.[36] There was no longer a major movement of gentiles seeking to attach themselves to the Jewish community and their worship of Israel's God. The question turned to the status of "righteous gentiles" with respect to their standing before God in the world to come, which was usually positive, at times even regarding Christians as Noahides.[37] There is, nevertheless, general agreement that the behavior and destiny of "righteous gentiles" or "God-fearers" in the context of their association with the Jewish community was of considerable concern in the period we are examining, even though the exact details of these labels are debatable.[38]

While these gentiles did not keep Jewish Law per se (the 613 com-

[35]Leon, *Jews*, pp. 135–66; La Piana, "Foreign Groups in Rome," pp. 345–47; Jeffers, *Conflict*, p. 10. See Lampe, *Die stadtrömischen Christen*; and Wiefel, "The Jewish Community," for a study of the location of early house churches in these same areas.

It is often stated that forty to fifty thousand Jews lived in Rome by the first century c.e.; however, this number is in dispute. See Leon, *Jews*, pp. 135–37, for a good discussion. Smallwood, *Jews*, p. 132, points out that the Monteverde catacomb on the Via Portuensis in Trastevere, the only one on the right bank of the Tiber, bears clear evidence of continuous use from the first century b.c.e. to the reign of Diocletian; however, this interpretation of the evidence is in dispute.

[36]D. Novak, *The Image of the Non-Jew in Judaism*, pp. 26–35; H. J. Schoeps, *Paul*, p. 251.

[37]Schoeps, *Paul*, pp. 249–58; Novak, *Dialogue*, pp. 31–34, 42–72; J. Katz, *Exclusiveness and Tolerance*.

[38]There are many terms for these gentile "sympathizers" to Judaism who were not full proselytes, but it is difficult to establish whether these terms were formal-

mandments of Torah), they kept what was later referred to in rabbinic Judaism as the "Noahide" or "Noachian Commandments."[39] These Noahide Commandments trace their roots to biblical antecedents, particularly to the Mosaic model for the laws governing the "resident alien" living in Palestine, the "stranger within your gates" (Lev. 16–26; Ex. 12:18-19; 20:10-11). In other words, the Levitical laws provided the historic halakhah for governing the minimal requirements of purity and righteousness for foreigners dwelling in the land of Israel.[40] These rules of behavior evolved during Diaspora Judaism into the seven central religious and ethical principles for the "Sons of Noah," that is, for describing the behavior of gentiles who were righteous without becoming Jews, and for those gentiles who were in the

---

ized at the time of Paul's letter (see L. Feldman, "The Omnipresence of the God-Fearers," pp. 58–63, for discussion of the various terms and settings). For the current debate on the topic of "God-fearers" in the first century see A. T. Kraabel, "The God-fearers Meet the Beloved Disciple"; and R. MacLennan and Kraabel, "The God-Fearers—A Literary and Theological Invention," pp. 46–53, who see it as operative in principle, though less formally than in Luke's usage. Feldman, "The Omnipresence of the God-Fearers" in *BAR*, pp. 58–63; Gager, "Jews, Gentiles, and Synagogues in the Book of Acts"; and McKnight, *Light*, pp. 110–15, show shortcomings of Kraabel's suggestions and develop the formal aspects of the phrase "God-fearers," including convincing historical data now available from a recently found synagogue inscription from 210 c.e. in Aphrodisias that lists Greek citizens as God-fearers (R. Tannenbaum, "Jews and God-Fearers in the Holy City of Aphrodite," pp. 54–57). See also Novak, *Dialogue*, pp. 30–32; Goodman, *Mission*, pp. 47, 113–19, 131–35, 148; and Feldman, *Jew and Gentile*, pp. 342–82, for thorough discussions.

[39]See C. Clorfene and Y. Rogalsky, *The Path of the Righteous Gentile*, for many rabbinic references and a twentieth-century orthodox spin that develops this very concept in a manner not unlike the one I am suggesting was operative in the first century.

[40]For a full treatment of the Noahide Laws see Novak, *Image*; see J. Schultz, "Two Views of the Patriarchs," pp. 43–59, for excellent treatment of the application to the fathers preceding the Sinaitic Law; Sanders, *Paul and Palestinian Judaism*, pp. 206–12; Segal, *Paul*, pp. 194–201, idem, "Conversion and Messianism," pp. 316–21, on the conversion of Izates and Josephus's use of "God-fearer" (also idem, "Universalism in Judaism and Christianity," pp. 1–29, for full discussion); K. Lake, "Note VIII. Proselytes and God-Fearers," pp. 80–88; D. Flusser, *Judaism and the Origins of Christianity*, pp. 630–32; K. Müller, "Torah für die Völker: Die Noachidischen Gebote im Beziehungsfeld zwischen Judentum und Christentum." See discussion on Noahide Commandments and the apostolic decree below and in chapter 4.

process of conversion to Judaism.[41] The "righteous gentiles" need not take upon themselves the 613 commandments of Torah that applied to Jews in their worship of the One God, but they must obey at least these seven. These "commandments" were linked to the covenant with Noah along with the rainbow (Gen. 9:1-17, 18ff.), in that they described just and proper behavior for the fathers of Israel (not only Abraham, but all his descendants until Moses received the Law at Sinai), and they became the prevailing criteria for defining the operative features of the faith and practice that would be expected to characterize all the "righteous gentiles" standing outside the covenant with Israel thereafter.[42]

The particulars of both the Mosaic model and the Noahide model for defining the behavior incumbent upon "righteous gentiles" are similar to those outlined by Luke in describing the Jerusalem council's apostolic decree in Acts 15:19-32; 16:1-5; 21:25. In general, these commandments were concerned with monotheistic issues asserted in the rejection of idolatry with its concomitant sexual and dietary characteristics. They provided the standards that gentiles without the Law of Moses would be expected to maintain if they truly honored the One God.[43] We have in the apostolic decree perhaps the best indication available of where the (fluid) process of the development and application of the notion of the Noahide Commandments were among Jews concerned with the gentile question in the middle of the first century c.e.[44]

---

[41]J. Schultz, *Judaism and the Gentile Faiths*, pp. 358–59, 360ff.; Novak, *Dialogue*, pp. 26–34, 35ff.; Schoeps, *Paul*, pp. 220–29. See McKnight, *Light*, and Goodman, *Mission*, versus Feldman, *Jew and Gentile*, for opposing views of the issue of Jewish proselytism: Was it prevalent at this time?

[42]Schultz, "Two Views," pp. 43–59; Segal, *Paul*, p. 195; Novak, *Image*, pp. 107–9, 259–69. See Gen. 9:1-7 for the text around which the rabbis developed the notion that the Noahide Commandments were binding upon all of Noah's descendants, whether Jew or gentile. It should be noted that the rabbis believed that six of these seven commandments had already been given to Adam and his descendants, with the seventh added to Noah, to refrain from eating flesh with blood in it.

[43]Sanders, *Paul and Palestinian Judaism*, pp. 269–70; Schultz, *Judaism*, pp. 361ff.; Novak, *Dialogue*, pp. 36–38, 39ff.; Tomson, *Paul*, pp. 271–74. Note that the Noahide ban on idolatry was not always necessarily understood to apply to gentiles who made no effort to associate with Israel (Novak, *Dialogue*, pp. 36–41; Flusser, *Judaism*, pp. 630–32).

[44]Segal, *Paul*, pp. 194–201; Novak, *Image*, pp. 3–35; M. Simon, "The Apostolic Decree," pp. 444–50.

The ancient Mosaic model for laws incumbent upon the "stranger within your gates," that is, for the non-Jews living in the land of Israel, included abstaining from: (1) sacrifices to idols in Leviticus 17:7-9; (2) eating blood in Leviticus 17:10-16; (3) incest in Leviticus 18:6-26; (4) work on the Sabbath in Exodus 20:10; and (5) eating leavened bread during the Passover in Exodus 12:18-20.[45]

The seven Noahide Commandments, as they were later outlined in rabbinic Judaism in the first detailed definition as found in the Tosefta of the late second or third century c.e., included matters relating to: (1) adjudication; (2) idolatry; (3) blasphemy; (4) sexual immorality; (5) bloodshed; (6) robbery; (7) a limb torn from a living animal.[46]

The four commandments of the apostolic decree drew from both these models to address the particular needs of this new Jewish movement in the middle of the first century c.e. and included: (1) things sacrificed to idols; (2) blood; (3) things strangled; (4) fornication (πορνείας).[47]

Some of the more ethical concerns did not need to be addressed because they were covered elsewhere in defining the lifestyle incumbent upon followers of Jesus Christ; however, the purity issues needed to be addressed in order for gentiles to meet the minimal requirements of holiness in the Jewish communities to which they were becoming attached through their new faith in the "king of the Jews."[48] We thus have in the apostolic decree a snapshot of a stage in the historical development from laws that had been originally addressed to gentile sojourners in the land of Israel (Mosaic model) to laws that were later developed to address the situations of the Diaspora where Jews were the ones sojourning among gentiles and living under their laws (Noahide Commandment model). The Christian model for purity laws (apos-

[45]Segal, *Paul*, p. 198.

[46]*Tosefta Abodah Zarah* 8.4 (cf. baraita in *Sanhedrin* 56a-b). See Novak, *Image*, pp. 3–4.

[47]Acts 15:20, 29. For a fuller treatment of the apostolic decree see chapter 4 below. Note also the language of the *Didache* version, which includes five of the Noahide Commandments (the same five compose the rabbinic list in *b. Yoma* 67b; *Sifra* on Lev. 18:4): "My child flee from every evil thing and what resembles it. Be not prone to anger for anger leads to *murder*. Be not lustful for lust leads to *adultery*. Be not a diviner of omens since it leads to *idolatry*. Be not a liar since lying leads to *theft*. Be not one who complains since it leads to *blasphemy*" (*Did.* 3:1-6 [emphasis added]); Flusser, *Judaism*, p. 508.

[48]Simon, "Apostolic Decree," pp. 444–50, 459; R. Longenecker, *Paul*, pp. 254–56; and the discussion in chapter 4 below.

tolic decree) thus addressed the dual tensions of a Jewish Diaspora community dwelling among gentiles and seeking to include them in their community as equals, and the requirements of holiness that would necessarily apply to those gentiles who chose to become a part of this Jewish community.

The general contours of these halakhot for the "righteous gentiles" certainly extended beyond the strict definition of these particulars to the many characteristics of behavior that would be expected to accompany worship of the One God at any given time by gentiles wishing to associate with the practice of Judaism in the worship of her God.[49] This was noted earlier in the statement of James at the Jerusalem council to explain the underlying intentions of the apostolic decree (Acts 15:21).[50]

It is important to recognize that "righteous gentiles" were welcomed by the synagogue in the first century and practiced specific Jewish customs, but without a standing as full-fledged Jews since they were not circumcised.[51] They were regarded as "potential Jews," perhaps at various stages in the conversion process.[52] The rabbis later found this semiconvert status less appealing with the rise of Christianity and modified their views of the Noahide Command-

[49]Flusser, *Judaism*, pp. 630–32.

[50]This is also the point of James's comments to Paul in Acts 21:19-26.

[51]Moore, *Judaism*, 1.325–26; Schoeps, *Paul*, pp. 249–51; M. Simon, *Verus Israel*, p. 380; Segal, *Paul*, pp. 94–101; McKnight, *Light*, pp. 12–15, 25–29; S. Cohen, "Crossing the Boundary and Becoming a Jew," pp. 26–33.

Jeffers, *Conflict*, pp. 11–12, assumes that "God-fearers" were usually not permitted access to Jewish cemeteries, for example, an important Jewish privilege (he gives no sources and this opinion is highly debatable—see the discussion of La Piana, "Foreign Groups in Rome," pp. 390-91, which notes that six to nine inscriptions from the graves of *metuentes* ["fearers of God"] have been found in Rome, at least one from the catacomb of Vigna Cimarra [n. 32]). Rutgers, "Archaeological Evidence," pp. 101–18, discusses this issue at length, including many cases of close proximity between Jewish and non-Jewish burial sites and shared materials in Rome and throughout Italy, and concludes: "To infer the 'exclusivity' of the Jewish catacombs by arguing that Jews and (full) proselytes were, and so-called 'Godfearers' were not, buried there is incorrect" (p. 112). On the general weakness of assuming materials found in the catacombs that are not clearly Jewish are not therefore Jewish see Rajak, "Inscription and Context," pp. 226–41.

[52]See Segal, *Paul*, pp. 72–114, on various views of the time; Novak, *Dialogue*, pp. 29-30; Moore, *Judaism*, 1.331–35; Schoeps, *Paul*, pp. 220–29; Lake, "Proselytes and God-Fearers," pp. 77–80.

ments; however, Judaism has always been aware of and concerned with the fate of the righteous non-Jew.[53]

Whether or not the early Christians were culled largely from these "God-fearers" as is often suggested,[54] the concept of "righteous gentiles" was operative at the time[55] and helps explain both positive and negative Jewish responses to early Christian gentiles' claims of equal coparticipation in the blessings of God.[56] Responses would have sometimes been positive because gentiles behaving righteously in worship of the One God were welcomed in the synagogue, whether to worship and learn the Scriptures or for other reasons.[57] However, it also helps explain the possible rejection of Christian gentiles who may have sought association with the synagogue; if they resisted the practice of the minimal requirements of righteousness and purity that were

[53] See Schultz, *Judaism*, pp. 362–69; Novak, *Dialogue*, pp. 31–41; Segal, *Paul*, pp. 96–105, 194–201; Sanders, *Paul and Palestinian Judaism*, pp. 207–12, for rabbinic views.

[54] Schmithals, *Paul and James*, pp. 60-62; Dunn, *Romans*, p. xlv–liv; Campbell, *Intercultural Context*, pp. 185–87 and n. 105; P. Stuhlmacher, "The Purpose of Romans," p. 238; Flusser, *Judaism*, pp. 630–32; Simon, *Verus Israel*, pp. 334–38, 408.

[55]The Qumran book of *Jubilees* dates from the first century or earlier as an independent witness to the concept of the Noahide Commandments operative in Judaism in a format similar to the apostolic decree prior to their later, formalized development in rabbinic Judaism (*Jub.* 7:20-21): "And in the twenty-eighth jubilee Noah began to command his grandsons with ordinances and commandments and all of the judgments which he knew. And he bore witness to his sons so that they might do justice and cover the shame of their flesh and bless the one who created them and honor father and mother, and each one love his neighbor and preserve themselves from fornication and pollution and from all injustice" (translation of O. S. Wintermute, in *The Old Testament Pseudepigrapha*, ed. J. Charlesworth, pp. 69–70).

[56]McKnight, *Light*, pp. 26–29, notes this same juxtaposition of Jewish kindness toward gentiles seeking association with Jews and the synagogue as pervasive: "Jewish kindness extended to gentile participation in the Jewish religion, whether it was reading Israel's holy writings, using the synagogue, or giving gifts to the temple—even if the later had some reasonable restrictions" (p. 26); while he notes resistance to gentiles is primarily due to criticism of their religious practices: "the evidence consistently bears out the view that Jews criticized Gentiles for basically one reason: pagan religion led to ethical practices that were unacceptable for those who were members of the covenant of Abraham and Moses" (p. 27). Rutgers, "Roman Policy," questions this view and suggests that the conflict was more political in nature.

[57]E. P. Sanders, "Jewish Association with Gentiles and Galatians 2:11-14," pp. 176–85; Flusser, *Judaism*, pp. 177–78.

incumbent upon gentiles wishing to count themselves among the "people of God," they would have been criticized and unwelcome.[58]

Table-Fellowship and Synagogue Attendance for Gentiles

Table-fellowship, particularly in the context of gentile participation, was a significant concern among Diaspora Jews. The many laws and customs that made it necessary generally to separate from association in gentile meals, or from the eating of many gentile foods whether in the company of gentiles or not, made table-fellowship a notable issue. Jews often avoided meat and wine, for it was necessarily tainted by idolatry in Diaspora cities, unless special provisions had been made.[59] However, Jews did eat with gentiles, given proper circumstances.[60] And in the context of "righteous gentiles" attending synagogue this matter became a regular necessity.

Gentiles attending synagogue and participating in the lifestyle of the Jewish community, or visiting Jewish homes, were expected to adopt minimal Jewish practices. This behavior demonstrated respect not only for Jewish sensitivities, but in the mind of the Jews at least, it represented respect for the righteousness of God that would be expected to accompany the faith of the "righteous gentile"—for God is holy. Thus, while considerate and polite behavior in deference to Jewish sensitivities would undoubtedly have been greatly appreciated, particularly from gentiles who were simply pagan guests, the underlying expectations toward gentiles claiming to "fear" the God of

---

[58]Note that the caution and outline of legal authority expressed by Novak, *Image*, pp. xiii–xviii, 20–35, 53–75, is respected herein; that is, I am not suggesting that Jews were seeking to govern gentiles in the larger society. I am noting that when gentiles chose to worship with and be part of the Jewish community they would have been under the authority of the synagogue and its rules for the "righteous gentile."

[59]Sanders, *Jewish Law*, pp. 281–83; idem, "Jewish Association."

[60]Sanders, "Jewish Association," pp. 170–88, for an excellent discussion of Jewish eating practices in the company of gentiles. See also Segal, *Paul*, pp. 230–33; Wright, *NT*, pp. 238–41, who largely agrees with Sanders, but believes "that most Jews most of the time felt that fidelity to Torah implied non-association as far as one could manage it" (p. 239). Hare, *Jewish Persecution*, pp. 8–10, states on p. 8: "The majority accepted the necessity of co-existence with Gentiles, and 'halakoth' were issued on the use of Gentile foods and similar matters." Tomson, *Paul*, pp. 230–36, also notes that in the majority opinion Jews ate with gentiles and were proud of their hospitality according to tannaitic literature, although the minority opinion denounced such universalism.

Israel was far greater. It was expected that their behavior would demonstrate they had turned from idolatry to worship the One God, having put off their former deeds of darkness to adopt the lifestyle of those enlightened to see the holiness of God.

It is in this context that the halakhot discussed above, represented in the various models of Mosaic Law, Noahide Commandments, and the apostolic decree, were operative in shaping the expectations of the Jewish community toward the behavioral requirements of the "God-fearing" gentile seeking association. Gentiles were welcome to attend synagogue ("a house of prayer for all peoples": Isa. 56:6-7) and participate in the Jewish community without necessarily becoming proselytes.[61] However, they were expected to adopt specific righteous behavior incumbent upon those claiming the right to worship among the congregation of Israel, certainly in deference to the Jewish people and their customs, but more importantly, to satisfy the minimal guidelines of righteousness and purity expected to accompany the behavior of gentiles claiming the right to worship the Lord of Israel as the Lord of the whole world.

Outside the synagogue the issues were not so easily resolved, for Jews simply found association with idolatry almost unavoidable when among gentiles, particularly in the context of sharing in their meals. But provisions were made: Jews simply refrained from meat and wine when questionable, ate vegetables and drank water, or brought their own food and wine.[62] Thus, while Jews saw themselves adapting a kind and accommodating posture involving some sacrifices to facilitate fellowship with gentiles, particularly table-fellowship, gentiles generally saw things differently. The underlying separatism and notable judgment of their lifestyles often offended gentiles, and, as I review below, was cause for derision and accusations of misanthropy.

Expectations of the Future

Eschatological views reflect the diversity characteristic of the entire spectrum of first-century Judaism, which included many, even

[61]McKnight, *Light*, pp. 12–15, 25–29, 74–77.
[62]We have, of course, the example of Daniel at the king's table, who refused to eat meat or drink wine, choosing vegetables and water instead in honor of God (Dan. 1:8-13, 14ff.). Other examples included Esth. 14:17 and Josephus's reference to a similar example in Rome (*Life* 14). For excellent discussions of this issue see Sanders, "Jewish Association," particularly pp. 176–85; Segal, *Paul*, pp. 230–33.

strongly conflicting, views among its members, particularly evident in their hopes for the future. Yet most if not all Jews of the mid-first century earnestly hoped for the promised restoration of Israel and the triumph of Israel's God as the One God of all the nations, which necessarily included a position on the destiny of the gentiles,[63] although it is difficult to speak of the views of the Jews of Rome specifically.[64]

This hope involved a complex web of particularism and universalism. Israel's destiny was at the fore, yet the destiny of all the world, whether through conversion, subjugation, or final destruction, was equally in view,[65] albeit through the agency of Israel and her God.[66]

[63]Concerning gentiles there was a tension that can be traced in the prophetic literature and that continues in later rabbinic literature between expectations of their destruction for ungodliness and the sufferings of Israel at their hands and expectations of their salvation, or at least voluntary subordination, as they recognize that the God of Israel is the God of the whole world. The negative expectations characterized Ezekiel's prophecies, the positive shaped Isaiah, Micah, and Zechariah. See Davies, *Paul*, pp. 58–63, 79–82.

[64]U. Fischer, *Eschatologie und Jenseitserwartung im hellenistischen Diasporajudentum*, suggests that the Jews of Rome did not have a very developed eschatology on the basis of the lack of evidence of such among the inscriptions available from the Jewish catacombs of Rome. The inscriptions we have, however, are very concise and are silent on a great many matters that were probably of great concern, although not elaborated on in this context. Furthermore, as we discussed earlier, the catacomb inscriptions in Rome arguably date later than our period.

[65]Moore, *Judaism*, 2.371; T. Donaldson, "Proselytes or 'Righteous Gentiles'? The Status of Gentiles in Eschatological Pilgrimage Patterns of Thought," pp. 3–27; P. Fredriksen, *From Jesus to Christ*, pp. 149–76; Sanders, *Judaism: Practice*, pp. 280–98, 294; idem, *Jesus and Judaism*, p. 214, lists six expectations with many references for each, including: (1) the wealth of the nations flowing into Jerusalem (Isa. 45:14; 60:5-16; 61:6; Mic. 4:13; Zeph. 2:9; Tob. 13:11; 1QM 12.13-14); (2) the gentile kings and nations bowing in service of Israel (Isa. 49:23; 45:14, 23; Mic. 7:17; 1 *Enoch* 90.30; 1QM 12.13-14); (3) Israel as the light of the nations, going out in mission and bringing them in (Isa. 2:2; 49:6; 51:4; 56:6-8; 66:18-19; Mic. 4:1; Zech. 2:11; 8:20-23; Tob. 14:6-7; 1 *Enoch* 90.30-33); (4) the destruction of gentiles and their cities and Israel's occupation of them (Isa. 54:3; Sir. 36.7, 9; 1 *Enoch* 91.9; Bar. 4.25, 31, 35; 1QM 12.10); (5) vengeance and defeat of gentiles (Mic. 5:10-15; Zeph. 2:10; T. *Mos.* 10.7; *Jub.* 23.30; *Pss. Sol.* 17.25-27); (6) surviving foreigners don't dwell with Israel (Joel 3:17; *Pss. Sol.* 17.31).

[66]Isa. 2:1-3; 11:9-10; 42:1-6; Mic. 4; Wright, *NT*, p. 268: "But that the fate of the nations was inexorably and irreversibly bound up with that of Israel there was no doubt whatsoever. This point is of the utmost importance for the understanding both of first-century Judaism and of emerging Christianity. What happens to the Gentiles is conditional upon, and conditioned by, what happens to Israel. In terms

The book of Isaiah developed powerfully the notion of the positive universal expectation of the ingathering of the nations and their certain recognition of the One Lord of Israel as the One Lord of all the world that would follow from Israel's restoration:

> And now says the LORD, who formed Me from the womb to be
>   His Servant,
> To bring Jacob back to Him, in order that Israel might be gathered
>   to Him
> (For I am honored in the sight of the LORD,
> And My God is My strength),
> He says, "It is too small a thing that You should be My Servant
> To raise up the tribes of Jacob, and to restore the preserved ones
>   of Israel;
> I will also make You a light of the nations
> So that My salvation may reach to the end of the earth." (Isa. 49:5-6)

This view informed most expectations of first-century Jews, seen clearly in the language of Paul and the writers of the New Testament,[67] but equally evident in other literature of the period:

> After this they all will return from their exile and will rebuild
> Jerusalem in splendor; and in it the temple of God will be rebuilt, just
> as the prophets of Israel have said concerning it. Then the nations in
> the whole world will all be converted and worship God in truth. They
> will all abandon their idols, which deceitfully have led them into their
> error; and in righteousness they will praise the eternal God. All the
> Israelites who are saved in those days and are truly mindful of God
> will be gathered together; they will go to Jerusalem and live in safety
> forever in the land of Abraham, and it will be given over to them.
> (Tob. 14:5-7 NRSV)

It is important to note that these hopes were not for the cessation of life in the created world and escape to some other spiritual one, and they certainly were not concerned primarily with personal salvation after death, as came to be the concern of Western individualism in

---

of the first level of covenant purpose, the call of Israel has as its fundamental objective the rescue and restoration of the entire creation."

    [67]I will investigate several examples in Acts (e.g., 13:47; 15:13-21) and Romans (e.g., 1:1-7; 10:14-18; 11:25-27; 15:7-21). See Hays, *Echoes*, esp. pp. 154-78.

later years.[68] They no doubt had personal concerns for their afterlife, but their central hope was for the restoration of this world to its intended purpose under the Lordship of the Creator.[69] Even those concerns that included the individual affirm the restoration of this world in the age to come rather than escape from this world (e.g., resurrection of the body rather than flight of the soul, renewal of the city of

[68]Wright, *NT*, pp. 278, 285, 299–301, 320–21, 322ff., 334–38; note his comments on pp. 300–301: "A word is necessary at this point about the meaning of the term 'salvation' in the context of the Jewish expectation. It ought to be clear by now that within the worldview we have described there can be little thought of the rescue of Israel consisting of the end of the space-time universe, and/or of Israel's future enjoyment of non-physical, 'spiritual' bliss. That would simply contradict creational monotheism, implying that the created order was residually evil, and to be simply destroyed. . . . Rather, the 'salvation' spoken of in the Jewish sources of this period has to do with rescue from the national enemies, restoration of the national symbols, and a state of 'shalom' in which every man will sit under his vine or fig-tree. 'Salvation' encapsulates the entire future hope. If there are Christian redefinitions of the word later on, that is another question. For first-century Jews it could only mean the inauguration of the age to come, liberation from Rome, the restoration of the Temple, and the free enjoyment of their own Land. . . . The age to come, the end of Israel's exile, was therefore seen as the inauguration of a new covenant between Israel and her god." See Moore, *Judaism*, 2.318–21; on p. 321 he states: "There is no indication that pious Jews were afflicted with an inordinate preoccupation about their individual hereafter," and on p. 319: "The ultimate salvation of the individual is inseparably connected with the salvation of the people, and inasmuch as, in accordance with the prophetic teaching, this was made dependent on the righteousness or the repentance of the nation collectively, the conduct and character of the individual concerned not himself alone but the whole Jewish people." See Sanders, *Paul and Palestinian Judaism*, pp. 125ff., 237–38.

[69]Sanders, *Judaism: Practice*, pp. 298–303, summarizes on p. 303: "When we add everything together, including the esoteric literature, we are left knowing that Jews—certainly a lot, probably most—believed in an afterlife and in individual reward and punishment. I think that this was common as a general view. . . . What is much clearer is the widespread hope of a 'new age' on this earth, one in which the God of Israel will reign supreme, being served by loyal Jews, and possibly by converted Gentiles, in purity and obedience." See Wright, *NT*, pp. 272–79, 285–86, 299–301, 320–38; on p. 278 he states: "In so far as individual Jews reflected on their own state before God, it was as members of the larger group, whether the nation or some particular sect. Sacrifice and suffering were the strange, but divinely appointed, means through which the chosen people were to maintain their status as such, and through which eventually they would arrive at redemption. In this way the wider hope would likewise come to birth: the whole world would be brought back into its divinely intended order and harmony." See H. Brichto, "Kin, Cult, Land and Afterlife—A Biblical Complex," pp. 1–54.

Jerusalem rather than pastoral bliss).[70] Israel's hope was a corporate hope of renewal, freedom, "shalom" among all the nations,[71] in fact, among all of the created order. It was rooted in the prophetic promises—in spite of the present suffering under the yoke of foreign rule with its frequently oppressive policies, Israel's Lord would ultimately rescue them from foreign dominion, which rescue was often expected to occur when their suffering for past breaches of covenant had completed its cleansing purpose (e.g., Deut. 4; 32; Isa. 40:1-2; Jer. 31:27-40; Ezek. 18; 36:24-28; Hos. 14; 2 Macc. 7:30-38; *Pss. Sol.* 7; 8.23-34; 17.26-32, 42; 18).[72] This expectation included features such as a

[70]For a review of the concept of resurrection see Brichto, "Kin, Cult," pp. 1–54; Davies, *Paul*, pp. 83–84, 285–320; G. E. Ladd, *The Pattern of New Testament Truth*, pp. 9–40, notes on pp. 39–40: "Salvation consists of fellowship with God in the midst of earthly existence and will finally mean the redemption of the whole man together with his environment. . . . In sum, the Greek view is that 'God' can be known only by the flight of the soul from the world and history; the Hebrew view is that God can be known because he invades history to meet men in historical experience." See Wright, *NT*, pp. 320–38; on p. 333: "Within the mainline Jewish writings of this period, covering a wide range of styles, genres, political persuasions and theological perspectives, *there is virtually no evidence that Jews were expecting the end of the space-time universe*. . . . What, then, did they believe was going to happen? They believed that *the present world order* would come to an end—the world order in which pagans held power, and Jews, the covenant people of the creator god, did not." On new Jerusalem see W. D. Davies, *The Territorial Dimension of Judaism*, pp. 55–61; J. Ellul, *The Meaning of the City*; rabbinic view in *Sanhedrin* 10.3.

[71]The concept of eschatological shalom is for peace in everyday relationships between all people, specifically between Israel and the nations; for a good survey of the concept in Ezek. 34:20-31; Isa. 11:1-9; 24–27; 65:17-25; Dan. 7–12; Joel 2:28—3:31 see W. Sibley Towner, "Tribulation and Peace: The Fate of Shalom in Jewish Apocalyptic," pp. 1–26.

[72]Moore, *Judaism*, 1.110–21; Sanders, *Paul and Palestinian Judaism*, pp. 170–82, 320ff.; Davies, *Territorial*, pp. 14–16, 47–48; Wright, *NT*, pp. 268–79, 299–301. Wright notes on p. 273: "Throughout both major and minor prophets there runs the twin theme: Israel's exile is the result of her own sin, idolatry and apostasy, and the problem will be solved by YHWH's dealing with the sin and thus restoring his people to their inheritance. Exile will be undone when sin is forgiven. Restoration and forgiveness were celebrated together annually at Passover and on the Day of Atonement; belief in this possibility and hope formed an essential part of Jewish belief in the faithfulness of her god. If her sin has caused her exile, her forgiveness will mean her national re-establishment. This needs to be emphasized in the strongest possible terms: the most natural meaning of the phrase 'the forgiveness of sins' to a first-century Jew is not in the first instance the remission of *individual* sins, but the putting away of the whole nation's sins. And, since the exile was the

return to the land,[73] and usually the rebuilding of the Temple—the dispersed children of Jacob[74] would return to Zion[75] where the One God would reign as king over all, and all the nations would come to worship him there also (e.g., Isa. 2:1-3; 27:12; 49:5-6; 51:4-5; 52:7-10; 56:6-8; 60–66; Dan. 7; Amos 9:11-12; Mic. 4; Zech. 8:20-23; 14:1-11; *Pss. Sol.* 11; 17.21-46):[76]

> For the LORD is our judge,
> the LORD is our lawgiver,

---

punishment for those sins, the only sure sign that the sins had been forgiven would be the clear and certain liberation from exile. This the major, national, context within which all individual dealing-with-sin must be understood."

[73]Brichto, "Kin, Cult"; Davies, *Territorial*; idem, *The Gospel and the Land.*

[74]Note that references to Jacob, the father of the twelve tribes of Israel, often have the regathering and restoration of the twelve tribes in view (Isa. 49:5); see Sanders, *Judaism: Practice*, pp. 290, 294. The regathering of the twelve tribes was a constant theme of biblical and nonbiblical literature (e.g., Isa. 49:5; 56:1-8; 60:3-14; 66:18-24; Ezek. 17; 20:42; 34; 36:9-12; 39:26; 47:13—48:35; Mic. 2:12; 4; Bar. 4.37; 5:5; Sir. 36; 48:10; 2 Macc. 1:27; 2:18; *Pss. Sol.* 11; 17.28-31, 50; 1QM 2.2, 7; 3:13; 5:1). See Sanders, *Jesus and Judaism*, pp. 95-98; Davies, *Territorial*, pp. 16–19, 20ff.

[75]Zion, of course, refers to the mountain on which Jerusalem and the temple were built (Isa. 60:14; Jer. 50:28), the very "navel/center" of the world (Ezek. 5:5; *Jub.* 8.12; Josephus, *War* 3.3.5; *b. Sanhedrin* 37a), and the place where God will dwell (Isa. 8:18; Jer. 8:19). Wright, *NT*, p. 247: "Again and again in the Pentateuch, the psalms, the prophets, and the subsequent writings which derive from them, the claim is made that the creator of the entire universe has chosen to live uniquely on a small ridge called Mount Zion, near the eastern edge of the Judaean hill-country." Also Sanders, *Jesus and Judaism*, p. 78; Davies, *Territorial*, pp. 1–35; on p. 24 Davies cites *Lev. Rabbah* 13.2 for a rabbinic view: "R. Simeon b. Yohai opened a discourse with: 'He rose and measured the earth' [Hab. 3:6]. The Holy One, blessed be He, considered all generations and he found no generation fitted to receive the Torah other than the generation of the wilderness; the Holy One, blessed be He, considered all mountains and found no mountain on which the Torah should be given other than Sinai; the Holy One, blessed be He, considered all cities, and found no city wherein the Temple might be built, other than Jerusalem; the Holy One, blessed be He, considered all lands, and found no land suitable to be given to Israel, other than the Land of Israel. This is indicated by what is written: 'He rose and measured the earth—and He released nations'."

[76]The passages are endless, both in biblical and nonbiblical literature. Wright, *NT*, pp. 208, 247, 264, 267–68, 285, 299–307; Donaldson, "Proselytes," pp. 3–27; Sanders, *Judaism: Practice*, pp. 289–90, 294–95; on pp. 289–90 he summarizes: "The chief hopes were for the re-establishment of the twelve tribes; for the subjugation or conversion of the Gentiles; for a new, purified, or renewed and glorious temple; and for purity and righteousness in both worship and morals."

the LORD is our king;
He will save us. (Isa. 33:22)

How lovely on the mountains
Are the feet of him who brings good news,
Who announces peace
Who announces salvation,
And says to Zion, "Your God reigns!" (Isa. 52:7)

And it will come about in the last days
That the mountain of the house of the LORD
Will be established as the chief of the mountains.
It will be raised above the hills,
And the peoples will stream to it.
And many nations will come and say,
"Come and let us go up to the mountain of the LORD
And to the house of the God of Jacob,
That He may teach us about His ways
And that we may walk in His paths."
For from Zion will go forth the law,
Even the word of the LORD from Jerusalem.
And He will judge between many peoples
And render decisions for mighty, distant nations.
Then they will hammer their swords into plowshares
And their spears into pruning hooks;
Nation will not lift up sword against nation,
And never again will they train for war.
And each of them will sit under his vine
And under his fig tree,
With no one to make them afraid,
For the mouth of the LORD of hosts has spoken.
Though all the peoples walk Each in the name of his god,
As for us, we will walk
In the name of the LORD our God forever and ever.
(Mic. 4:1-5; cf. Isa. 2:1-4)

That both biblical and non-biblical literature look for the kingship
of YHWH over a restored and victorious Israel is clear (e.g., Isa. 33:22;
52:7; *Pss. Sol.* 5.19; 17.1-3), as is the fact that there were expectations
of a human king or Messiah.[77] However, the exact expectations with
respect to this Messiah are not so clear.

[77]G. Vermes, *Jesus the Jew*, pp. 130–40, 159.

There were many different expectations, at different times, among each of the different Jewish groups in our period. Evidence of the basic messianic expectations surfaced from time to time, as witnessed in Josephus's concern to downplay them (*War* 6.5.4 [312–15]); Herod's and bar-Kochba's desires to fulfill them; and the understanding of the early church. The literature of the Qumran community shows a highly developed sense of a Messiah (1QS 9.11; 4Q174 1.10-13, 18), as do the *Psalms of Solomon* (17.21-32; 18), and apocalyptic literature (*4 Ezra* 11–13). Wright's summary of the various sources offers a balanced conclusion:

> Expectation was focused primarily on the nation, not on any particular individual. . . . This expectation could, under certain circumstances, become focused upon a particular individual, either expected imminently or actually present. . . . When this happened, the generalized expectation of a coming figure can be redrawn in a wide variety of ways to fit the situation or person concerned. . . . The main task of the Messiah, over and over again, is the liberation of Israel, and her reinstatement as the true people of the creator god. This will often involve military action, which can be seen in terms of judgment as in a lawcourt. It will also involve action in relation to the Jerusalem Temple, which must be cleansed and/or restored and/or rebuilt. . . . It is clear that whenever the Messiah appears, and whoever he turns out to be, he will be the agent of Israel's god. . . . Certainly there is no reason to hypothesize any widespread belief that the coming Messiah would be anything other than an ordinary human being called by Israel's god to an extraordinary task. . . . Nor is it the case that the Messiah was expected to suffer. The one or two passages which speak of the death of the Messiah (e.g. 4 Ezra 7.29) seem to envisage simply that the messianic kingdom, being a human institution, to be inaugurated within present world history, will come to an end, to be followed by a yet further "final age to come." . . . The coming of the King, where it was looked for, would thus be the focal point of the great deliverance.[78]

Roman Gentile Attitudes toward Jews and Judaism at the Time of Paul's Letter

We know much less about the views of gentiles in Rome toward Jews and Judaism in the first century. Nevertheless, we do have some

---

[78]Wright, *NT*, pp. 319–20; cf. 302–20. See also Juel, *Messianic Exegesis*; Sanders, *Judaism: Practice*, pp. 295–98; D. Aune, *Prophecy in Early Christianity*, pp. 121–26; Schultz, *Judaism*, pp. 212–14; and the many articles in Charlesworth, ed., *The Messiah*.

historical information from secular sources that allows a glimpse of some features of gentile life and religion, particularly with respect to Judaism and the Jewish people. Later, when I turn to the text of Romans, I will consider some of the characteristics of Christian gentile attitudes that appear to correspond with the prevailing views observed in this historical literature.

Many point out both the inability of pagans in antiquity to comprehend the purposeful strangeness of Jews, and the general disdain that prevailed among gentiles toward Jews and Judaism. For example, Meagher notes succinctly: "The roster of ancient writers who expressed anti-Jewish feeling reads like a roster for a second-semester course in classics: Cicero, Tacitus, Martial, Horace, Juvenal, Persius, Dio Cassius, Marcus Aurelius, Apuleius, Ovid, Petronius, Pliny the Elder, Plutarch, Quintilian, Seneca, Suetonius."[79]

It appears that Jewish insistence on separation through the observation of particular boundary markers for behavior represented a "value paradox" to the Hellenistic mind with its dream of a "universal 'politeia.'"[80] Jewish resistance to open-minded discourse, refusal to observe the community festivals and celebrations and share in the libations to the gods that commenced their meals, and their general impiety in things considered sacred were cause for accusations of atheism, barbarism, and misanthropy. Smallwood points out that the objections to Judaism were generally religious rather than racial,[81] and many point out that the issues of Sabbath, food and wine regulations, and circumcision were the most common cause for degrading remarks found in pagan literature of the time:

> The accusation of superstition was partially derived from a misunderstanding of the Jewish valuation of certain forms of ritual observance that seemed curiously primitive to the outsider—notably the dietary laws, the Sabbath regulations, and circumcision—and gained unfortunate

---

[79]J. Meagher, "As the Twig Was Bent," p. 6. For additional information see Whittaker, *Jews and Christians*, pp. 3–105; and M. Stern, *Greek and Latin Authors*, both trace many of the original documents that demonstrate Roman and other pagan authors' attitudes to Jews and things Jewish. See also Wiefel, "Jewish Community"; Sanders, *Paul, the Law*, pp. 102, 117 n. 27; idem, Sanders, *Jewish Law*, pp. 282–83; Novak, *Dialogue*, p. 30; P. Jewett, *Paul's Anthropological Terms*, pp. 45–46; Safrai, *Jewish People*, vol. 2, chap. 24; J. Gager, "Judaism as Seen by Outsiders"; Feldman, *Jew and Gentile*, chaps. 4 and 5.

[80]Meagher, "As the Twig," pp. 4–5.

[81]Smallwood, *Jews*, pp. 203–5.

support from the widely-distributed rumor, attested by writers from
Manaseas and Posidonius to Plutarch and Tacitus, that Jews worshipped
a deity with the head or form of an ass.[82]

Idolatry was woven throughout the very fabric of Roman society,
and for a Jew to live faithful to his or her God it was simply impossible
to embrace fully the prevailing practices of his or her neighbors.
Virtually all of society revolved around religious principles associated
with "the gods," from the worship of Caesar to the many household
and civic deities. This underlying idolatry extended even to the most
common forms of contact in society, particularly evident in one of the
most notable areas of Jewish concern, namely, table-fellowship:

> For most people, to have a good time with their friends involved some
> contact with a god who served as guest of honor, as master of cere-
> monies, or as host in the porticoes or flowering, shaded grounds of his
> own dwelling. For most people, meat was a thing never eaten and wine
> to surfeit never drunk save as some religious setting permitted.[83]

In addition to the religious practices that kept Jews separated there
was the issue of proselytism,[84] which was considered an "un-Roman
act" that was not usually prohibited but was discouraged and may have
led to several expulsions and to conscription,[85] a particularly offensive
punishment for first-century Jews (soldiers were enlisted in the service
of Caesar, and were necessarily trapped into the idolatrous issues associated with military duties to the "god" of Rome).[86]

[82]Meagher, "As the Twig," p. 6.
[83]R. MacMullen, *Paganism in the Roman Empire*, p. 40. See also the discussion of
P. Gooch, *Dangerous Food: I Corinthians 8–10 in Its Context*, esp. chap. 3.
[84]For a discussion of proselytism see above under eschatology and Feldman,
Jews and Gentiles; McKnight, *Light*; Goodman, *Mission*; E. Urbach, *The Sages*;
M. Simon, *Verus Israel*; Gager, *Origins*; Wright *NT*; Sherwin-White, *Roman Society*, p.
81, suggests that proselytism may not have been banned for Roman citizens at this
time.
[85]These incidents may be more the result of fears of political unrest and disor-
der than proselytism according to Rutgers, "Roman Policy," p. 68: "At best, a dislike for Judaism served to justify on a subconscious level decisions that had essentially been reached on the basis of administrative and legal considerations."
[86]Smallwood, *Jews*, pp. 205–10, 216. For more information on Jewish views of
war and violence see Safrai, *Jewish People*, 1.458–60. For a discussion of the tensions
inherent in military service under Caesar see above n. 11.

Yet there are indications of a respectful,[87] or at least sympathetic, view of Jews for their ancient traditions and their philosophy ("cult of wisdom").[88] Even their practice of Sabbath was apparently copied by some.[89] And we must account for the "God-fearers" and proselytes; they were certainly attracted to Judaism, and perhaps it was this common attraction that led to much of the disdain noted among the officials and the privileged from whose writings we draw most of our inferences.[90] Equally important is the special recognition of synagogue privileges and the right to maintain ancestral traditions throughout this period,[91] indicating a positive disposition legally and officially, at least on the part of some rulers regarding particular situations at various times.

In summary, it is fair to say that the prevailing attitudes among the gentiles of Rome to Jews and Judaism, while no doubt mixed, were often negative. Despite the general intention of kindness observed above on the part of Jews toward their gentile neighbors, the implicit, when not explicit, judgment on pagan practices made it difficult for Romans not to take offense.[92] Nor is it likely that all Romans overlooked the political and military problems associated with the Jews of

[87]See the discussion of Gager, *Origins*, pp. 55–88.

[88]Ibid., pp. 84–85, who cites Morton Smith in noting: "To those who admired Judaism it was a 'cult of wisdom' . . . to those who dislike it it was 'atheism,' which is simply the other side of the coin, the regular term of abuse applied to philosophy."

[89]Josephus, *Against Apion* 2.40 (282–85); Philo, *De Vita Mosis* 2.17–23; Gager, *Origins*, pp. 85–86.

[90]Gager, *Origins*, pp. 66, 77, 82.

[91]This was very important to Romans, who were concerned with origins, and served as the basis of Caesar's granting the Jewish community certain privileges discussed above as the right "to live according to its ancestral laws." Josephus, *Ant.* 12.3.3 (138–50); 14.10.1–11.2 (185–276); 16.1.3 (27–28); 16.6.2 (162–65); 19.5.3 (287–91); 19.6.3 (300); Tcherikover, *Hellenistic*, pp. 82–89, 300–302, 305; Smallwood, *Jews*, pp. 133–43, 210; Feldman, *Jew and Gentile*, pp. 177–200. See also Rutgers, "Roman Policy," who argues that these privileges addressed specific situations and were not an official "Jewish policy"

[92]A. N. Sherwin-White, *Racial Prejudice in Imperial Rome*, p. 87, gets the sense of this Greek dislike well in noting: "Its roots lay in the refusal of the Jewish communities to come to terms with the Hellenistic civilization, by their social aloofness from the life of the Greek cities in which they lived. . . . All this amounts to one form of modern racial bias: '*They* won't have anything to do with *us*.'" See also pp. 100–101, for summary comments on Roman attitudes, particularly toward proselytism of Roman citizens.

Palestine in the development of their opinions about Jews in Rome.[93] While no doubt some gentiles were attracted to Jewish people and the faith and practice of Judaism as well as the philosophies Jews embraced, the general views, unlike the reverence occasionally noted in some Greek cities, were for Romans apparently mixed with resentment and prejudice.[94]

Summary of Historical Issues as they Apply to Romans

Having surveyed some of the historical issues from the perspective of Judaism in Rome in the first century c.e., particularly concerning the operative principles for understanding how Jews would have responded to gentiles seeking to associate with the synagogue community within the concept of the "righteous gentile," I must ask the obvious: Would the Christian *gentiles* of Rome have sought association with the synagogue as "righteous gentiles"? And, if so, why?

Evidence indicates that in Rome Christianity and Judaism shared a common heritage, and were probably inseparable before 60 c.e., and even perhaps until the middle of the second century.[95] Secular writers and the government of Rome make no distinction prior to Nero,[96] and

[93]We should not overlook this dynamic at work. It is quite clear that the Jews of Rome were knowledgeable about and affected by events in Palestine, at times strikingly so (cf. M. Borg, "A New Context for Romans XIII," pp. 208–11). Romans would have been aware of these matters too. Romans served in Palestine in government and as soldiers. Many fought and were wounded or killed by Jewish rebels. Certainly they and their families were effected by this in ways that would have adversely shaped their views of the Jews of Rome.

[94]Some Greek examples run counter to the Roman examples, for example Sardis and Pisidian Antioch. Note the views of Gager, "Judaism," pp. 99–116.

[95]W. D. Davies, *Jewish and Pauline Studies*, pp. 20, 135, 150–52; S. T. Katz, "Issues in the Separation of Judaism and Christianity after 70 CE," pp. 43–76; Porter, "New Paradigm" pp. 266–69; Barth, "A Good Jew"; S. Bacchiocchi, *From Sabbath to Sunday*; J. Parkes, *The Conflict of the Church and the Synagogue*, p. 77: "At the death of Paul, Christianity was still a Jewish sect. In the middle of the second century it is a separate religion busily engaged in apologetics to the Greek and Roman world, and anxious to establish its antiquity, respectability and loyalty." See the introduction of Simon, *Verus Israel*. See J. D. G. Dunn, *The Partings of the Ways*, pp. 230–80, for a nice summary. See *Anti-Semitism and Early Christianity*, ed. C. A. Evans and D. A. Hagner, for a collection of excellent essays.

[96]The persecution and fire of 64 c.e. are the first indications of Roman government awareness of a separation between Christians and Jews, and even this may be simply the awareness of a new sect of Judaism known as *Christiani* (Tacitus, *Annals* 15.44.2-8; M. Grant, *Nero*, pp. 151–61; Benko as cited by Dunn, *Romans*,

there are many indications that community interaction continued to be the case well into the second century.[97] Both formalized Christianity and rabbinic Judaism found it necessary to seek to define themselves "over against" each other in the second century and thereafter, which further suggests that the umbilical cord may not have been cut earlier,[98] certainly not as early as Paul's letter to Rome between 55 and 58 c.e. Also, in Rome as well as outside Rome there are

---

p. 1). Benko, *Pagan Rome and the Early Christians*, p. 16, notes that "Tacitus saw Christianity as a 'superstition' of Jewish origin. . . . It seems that he drew no distinction between Jews and Christians." On p. 20 he summarizes: "In 64 Christians were still known as Jews."

[97]Epictetus 2.9.20-21, in the later half of the first century, "still seems to think of Christians (distinguished by baptism) as 'acting the part' of Jews" (Dunn, *Romans*, p. 1). Benko, *Pagan Rome*, p. 16, discusses the accusation in 95 when Domitian's niece Domitilla and her husband, Flavius Clemens, were "accused of atheism, for which offense a number of others also, who had been carried away into Jewish customs, were condemned, some to death, others to confiscation of property," and the possibility that "Judaism here really means Christianity" since Judaism was a recognized religion at the time and its practice was not a crime.

[98]Rabbinic views of the early Christians are difficult to trace with any certainty, noticeable in the various positions outlined in recent scholarship on the function of the Birkat-ha-Minim. The traditional view was that the Birkat-ha-Minim was probably developed between 80 and 90 c.e., perhaps to discourage Christian Jews from synagogue participation following the destruction of the Temple; cf. Parkes, *Conflict*, pp. 70-120, esp. 77; G. Alon, *The Jews in their Land*, pp. 288–94. For example, Davies, *Jewish and Pauline Studies*, pp. 136–37, suggests the defection of Christian Jews during the revolt against Rome and the struggle for survival under the sages at Jamnia with the need to protect Judaism against dissidents led to the eventual separation. Other views have been developed in recent scholarship, for example, S. T. Katz, "Issues," pp. 63–76, suggests that perhaps it refers to all regarded as heretics at this time probably including Christian Jews. For the view that the twelfth benediction was pre-Christian and thus was not against Christians see Flusser, *Judaism*, pp. 635–44; R. Kimelman, "Birkat Ha-Minim and the Lack of Evidence for an Anti-Christian Jewish Prayer in Antiquity," 2:226–44. A recent review of the various positions is now available by S. J. Joubert, "A Bone of Contention in Recent Scholarship: The 'Birkat Ha-Minim' and the Separation of Church and Synagogue in the First Century AD," pp. 351–63. Norman Cohen, "Judaism and Christianity: The Partings of the Ways," discusses second-century rabbinic views developed in opposition to Paul's theology. See C. Setzer, *Jewish Responses to Early Christians: History and Polemics, 30–150 C.E.*, for a complete treatment of the issues in the earliest period before rabbinic literature. Simon, *Verus Israel*, discusses pertinent information throughout his study; see esp. pp. 179–201, 407, on the *minim* issue.

Christianity as witnessed in the establishment of Sunday worship to distinguish

many indications of the coexistence, or even interdependence, of Jews
and Christians that characterized this period of the Christian movement, including archeological evidence,[99] shared literature such as
hymnals and prayer books,[100] the maintenance and even appropriation

---

themselves (Bacchiocchi, *Sabbath*). For a variety of thorough treatments of the sep-
aration see Dunn, *Partings*; Simon, *Verus Israel*, pp. 310–38, 369–84; L. Schiffman,
"At the Crossroads: Tannaitic Perspectives on the Jewish-Christian Schism," pp.
115–56; S. T. Katz, "Issues," pp. 43–76; C. Williamson, "The 'Adversus Judaeos'
Tradition in Christian Theology," pp. 273–96; Parkes, *Conflict*, pp. 70–120; Flusser,
Judaism, pp. 617–44; R. MacLennan, "Four Christian Writers," pp. 187–202; J. T.
Sanders, *Schismatics, Sectarians, Dissidents, Deviants: The First One Hundred Years of
Jewish-Christian Relations*.

[99]See Rutgers, "Archaeological Evidence," pp. 101–18, for many indications of
interaction in the third century in Rome and elsewhere. Note the frequency of
Christian inscriptions and artifacts in the Jewish catacombs, regarded by Leon as
an anomaly (although he notes that Christians adopted the catacomb method of
burial from the Jews, Leon, *Jews*, pp. 54–55, 66 [but did they?]), is an indication of
their interaction during this period (see Leon, *Jews*, pp. 52–53, 97 n. 6, 225, for in-
stances of Christian presence). Particularly interesting are details like the fact that
in the Monteverde catacomb, thoroughly Jewish, occasional Christian motifs sur-
vive (p. 225); and the small catacomb N. Müller found next to the Jewish catacomb
of Vigna Randanini with closures resembling those of the Jewish catacombs rather
than the Christian catacombs, with various Jewish motifs, and absent of the usual
symbols of Christianity, was but a short distance beyond the Christian catacomb of
Praetextatus and could have been either (p. 52 and notes). Also Marucchi's visit to
a catacomb he believed at first to be Christian until finding a menorah indicates the
juxtaposition of Jewish and Christian motifs that sometimes occurred (Leon, *Jews*,
p. 52; see also pp. 221, 246–47, for pertinent information). A. S. Barnes, *Christianity
at Rome in the Apostolic Age*, pp. 90–94, went so far as to suggest that the Jewish catacomb at Vigna Randanini had enough evidence of both Jewish and Christian nature that is was perhaps of Judeo-Christian origin. Also see Meyers and Kraabel,
"Archaeology, Iconography," pp. 175–210 (cf. 178–79); E. Meyers, "Early Judaism
and Christianity in the Light of Archaeology," pp. 69–79. For a thorough survey of
work from the various schools around the world concerned with this period and an
excellent bibliography see F. Manns, "A Survey of Recent Studies on Early
Christianity."

[100]D. R. Darnell and D. A. Fiensy, in J. Charlesworth, ed., *OT Pseudepigrapha*,
2.671ff., on synagogal prayers; and Charlesworth, pp. 725ff., on the *Odes of Solomon*,
which have been variously considered Jewish and Christian since their discovery
because they are so Jewish in tone yet with Christian characteristics. Charlesworth
follows those proposing they are the result of a shared community (p. 732). Also
Charlesworth, *Jews and Christians*, pp. 35–59, includes the comment of Beker in a
discussion group, noting on p. 57: "In certain ways, I would maintain, the
Matthean community is still almost part of the synagogue." The practice of meet-

of nonrabbinic and apocryphal texts in Christian literature,[101] shared language and idioms,[102] Sabbath observance and food regulations,[103] even the same forms of meeting and administrative responsibilities,[104] not to mention the context of Paul's ministry and letters as well as the accounts in Acts that take place within Israel's institutions and the synagogues of the Diaspora.[105] Indeed, there are many indications that

---

ing in synagogues for prayer is noted by Sanders, *Judaism: Practice*, pp. 202–8; see Flusser, *Judaism*, pp. 359–89 on the Tiburtine Sibyl. See Simon, *Verus Israel*, pp. 306–38, including his discussion of the adaptation of the Shema as well as Jewish rites and festivals.

[101]Christians preserved the *Psalms of Solomon*, *Testament of Moses*, *Sibylline Oracles*, *4 Ezra*, and *2 Baruch*, and appropriated passages from *4 Ezra* in 2 Esdras, used existing Jewish material in *Testaments of the Twelve Patriarchs*, combined material from the Jewish *Martyrdom of Isaiah* with two Christian works, to name several examples, not to mention the obvious influence of Jewish material on the *Didache* and other early Christian works (cf. Dunn, *Partings*, p. 235; M. A. Knibb in Charlesworth, ed., *OT Pseudepigrapha*, 2.143ff.; Darnell and Fiensy, in ibid., pp. 671ff.).

[102]Meeks, *Urban*, pp. 85–96.

[103]Apostolic decree, for example, and the discussions of Romans and Corinthians about these food issues; the *Didache* and *1 Clement* (see Wedderburn, *Romans*, pp. 50–54, for sources); see chapter 4 below on the impact of the decree on later Christian traditions; see Bacchiocchi, *Sabbath*, on Sabbath observance until the second century.

[104]Burtchaell, *From Synagogue to Church*, pp. 201–357, for important discussion; Ellis, *Pauline Theology*, pp. 129–45; Sanders *Judaism: Practice*, pp. 195–212; Meeks, *Urban*, pp. 131–39. On p. 80 Meeks notes also that they were meeting in homes, and that even the roots of the term *ekklēsia* derive from synagogue practices and language, noting also the similarities concerning judgment of internal disputes as witnessed in 1 Cor. 6:1-11 and Josephus, *Ant.* 14.10.17 (235) for Jewish practice.

[105]In Rom. 9:1-5 and 11:1ff. it is the plain sense of Paul's intention that he was still a practicing Jew completely identified with historical and prevailing definitions of what constituted "Jew" or "Israel" at the time, and deeply concerned with the division taking place over the gospel. Even his apostleship for the gentile mission is explained in the context of Israel's salvation (11:11-13, 25-32). Note too that his concern for the collection and its successful reception in Jerusalem in chap. 15 is couched in Jewish sacramental and eschatological terms fully consistent with seeing himself as a faithful Jew, and his opening comments clearly link his ministry and the work of Christ with the history and expectations of Israel's salvation (1:1-7), and with the need to bring Rome within the context of Israel's restoration through the eventual collection and declaration of the gospel that he would undertake upon his arrival in Rome (1:11-15). Acts is full of references to Paul and the early church developing completely in the context of Judaism (see esp. Acts 2:46; 5:42; 18:4, 19, 24-26; 13:5, 14, 44; 14:1; 17:1-2 [Luke describes Paul's

Christianity did develop in the context of Judaism, including synagogue attendance and the concomitant behavioral and practical rami-
fications that would have applied,[106] particularly in the case of early
Christianity in Rome, where loyalty to and appreciation of the Jewish
heritage is often noted[107] and where the location of the Jewish and
early Christian communities are the same.[108]

But the question is: Would the Christians of Rome have necessarily
sought association with the synagogues, and if so, why? The answer
we may never know entirely, but we have good reason to believe that
they would have had no concept of their faith outside the expression
of the Jewish community, initially at least, for they saw their faith in
continuity with the tradition of Israel's faith, that is, as the fulfillment
of the promised "ingathering of the nations" that was to follow the
"restoration of Israel" in Christ (Rom. 11:25-27; Acts 15:13-21). As we
shall see, this bleeds through the context of Paul's letter continually,
and there are certainly many indications that this was Paul's modus
operandi in his preaching of the gospel.[109]

"custom" to go to the synagogues first upon his arrival in any city], 10, 17). When
Paul arrived in Rome he went to the synagogue leaders first, before any other institution that may have represented those to whom he had written (Acts 28:17).
The early Christians were regarded by Jews as a "sect" within Judaism, first known
as the "Way" (Acts 24:5, 14; 28:22; note that Sadducees [5:17] and Pharisees [15:5;
26:5] are also referred to as "sects"; this label was not pejorative, but reflects the
plurality of Judaic beliefs at the time; perhaps a more refined social-scientific term
might be "factions" or "coalitions"). See also J. Jervell, *Luke and the People of God*;
Bacchiocchi, *Sabbath*, pp. 135–51; note his comment on p. 137 that Acts 1:14 appears to be a reference to those gathered in prayer in the sense that Luke understood this to be a type of synagogue meeting (προσευχή: "prayer-assembly").

[106]Paul's arrival in Jerusalem, the destination mentioned in Romans, is replete
with significance for Judaism and the continued practice of the Law for the
Jerusalem Christians and for Paul (Acts 21:15-40).

[107]Brown and Meier, *Antioch and Rome*. See discussion above in chapter 1.

[108]Lampe, *Die stadtrömischen Christen* (see n. 4 above); Wiefel, "Jewish Community."

[109]Paul's two-step pattern of preaching in the synagogues of each city he entered
first, referred to by Luke as Paul's "custom" (Acts 17:1-2), lies behind Paul's explanation of the mystery revealed in Rom. 11:25-27. His continued insistence on
the pattern of salvation history "to the Jew *first* and also to the Greek" is not
merely a literary device; it is his understanding of the way God is working in the
world, mirrored in Paul's own unmistakable preaching pattern. And according to
Luke, it was the pattern Paul even employed upon his arrival in Rome, even
though there were Christians there to whom he had written this letter (Acts
28:15-29).

The following religious questions need to be considered in this historical context as well: How would they learn the Scriptures and the way God deals with his people apart from involvement in the Jewish community, for the Scriptures were read and interpreted only in the synagogues, and primarily on the Sabbath at that?[110] How else would they learn the ways of righteousness, as there was no New Testament for them? Or how to pray "as they ought?"[111] We must come to grips with the fact that outside the synagogue environment the early Christians would have had little opportunity to learn the "Scriptures";[112] gentiles in particular would have had no previous exposure to the religious life of the people of God and the ways of righteousness associated with Judaism's monotheistic practices. When Paul appeals for the Romans to learn from the Scriptures (15:4), where else would they have had such access?[113] How could he expect his audience, primarily gentile in composition, to understand his letter replete with direct and indirect use of the Scriptures and Judaic concepts of righteousness? There would have been an almost insurmountable learning curve in bringing gentiles to an understanding of faith in Christ and the practice of righteousness without association with the synagogue and the life of the Jewish community.

But perhaps the most convincing argument is not from the educational issues but from the political and practical ones. Josephus indicated that Julius Caesar's decree forbid the assembly of foreign religious societies other than Jewish ones in the city of Rome, and according to Suetonius Caesar had "dissolved all guilds, except those

---

[110]Note that Paul urges them to learn the Scriptures in the context of explaining his hope, and practical instructions to make his hope a reality, in the midst of defining the relationship of the "weak" and "strong" as well as the "circumcised" and "uncircumcised" (15:4 in context of 14:1—15:13). On Scripture reading and interpretation see earlier comments.

[111]Does this underlie Paul's concern in 8:26-27, 28ff.? Do we see the same kind of need to learn anew in Luke 12:8-12 when Jesus tells his disciples they will learn how to say the right things when brought before the synagogue authorities for their faith in him?

[112]See Juel, *Messianic Exegesis*, for discussion of the development of early Christology as an exegetical exercise in the Scriptures of Israel to define their new faith in Jesus as the Messiah and not for the later apologetic purposes.

[113]J. Collins, *Between Athens and Jerusalem*, p. 4, notes that the Septuagint was not known in Greco-Roman literary circles. On the absence of knowledge of the Septuagint see also G. Rinaldi, *Biblia Gentium: Primo contributo per un indice delle citazioni dei riferimenti e delle allusioni alla Bibbia negli autori pagani, greci e latini, di età imperiale*. See also the discussion of Juel, *Messianic Exegesis*, p. 16.

of ancient foundation."[114] How would Christians, outside association with the synagogues, obtain the right to congregate for fellowship and worship, even in their own homes or tenement rooms,[115] unless they petitioned for designation as a "private club"?[116] Not only do we not have any evidence of such an effort, but we have good reason to believe they did not pursue such a course, as they found the authority of the synagogue sufficient (and they probably did not even consider the question!).[117] Further, even if they sought and were granted the rights of assembly of a "private club," this would not have extended to the free practice of their religion without harm or interference (e.g., they still would not have had the right to observe the Sabbath, they would

[114]See earlier discussion and *Julius Caesar* 42.3 and Josephus, *Ant.* 14.10.8 (214–16); cf. Sanders, *Judaism: Practice*, p. 212.

[115]Regarding the social status and living conditions of the early Christians and the Jews of Rome within the tenement structures of the densely populated and generally low socioeconomic conditions for the residents of the Trastevere and Porta Capena sections of Rome, see Lampe, *Die stadtrömischen Christen*; and the development of Lampe's observations by R. Jewett, "Tenement Churches and Communal Meals in the Early Church: The Implications of a Form-critical Analysis of 2 Thessalonians 3:10," pp. 23–43.

[116]Jeffers, *Conflict*, p. 41, suggests that they may have organized as informal funerary associations, which would have allowed them to meet in homes (this makes much more sense later, when Christians began to pull away from Judaism and had to accept such a compromise, perhaps after the persecutions of Nero). But he also notes that the Jewish community had many special privileges (discussed above) that would not exist outside the synagogue, including providing for the poor of their community: "until the Christians in Rome became organized, wealthy, and numerous enough to duplicate this service, they could not easily separate themselves from Judaism" (p. 40). Meeks, *Urban*, pp. 77–78, doubts that the Christians met as funeral associations.

[117]Regarding legal status see the discussions of Lampe, *Die stadtrömischen Christen*, in part 5, chap. 3, "The Fractionation of Roman Christianity," concerning the private rather than public nature of the property and possessions during the first and second centuries, hence, the lack of evidence for legal status suggested: "For lack of evidence [that the Christian groups had organized themselves as collegia tenuiorum or collegia funeraticia] the hypothesis has long been abandoned. That the groups of Christians were not *legalized* as *corpora* or *collegia* is one of the more certain statements which we can make." Wright, *NT*, p. 355, says there is no evidence they appealed to "private club" status in their defense. Dunn, *Romans*, p. lii: "The Christians were not yet clearly distinguished from the wider Jewish community. . . . Insofar as they had any legal status, they would meet presumably as a "collegium" or under the auspices of a synagogue. Here the fact that Paul never speaks of the Christians in Rome as a church ('the church of Rome') may well be significant, especially since it is so out of keeping with Paul's usual practice (1 Cor 1:2; 2 Cor 1:1; Phil 4:15; Col 4:16; 1 Thess 1:1; 2 Thess 1:1; cf. Gal 1:2)."

not have been free from serving in civic cults), nor to the right to refrain from the mandatory practice of declaring Caesar as their god
(Jews were exempt from this practice only by the institution of a special substitutionary sacrifice),[118] nor to the exclusion of military service
and other public responsibilities with their concomitant idolatry.[119]

There is good reason then, historically, to suggest that Paul's instructions in Romans may have been directed to Christian gentiles
who were in need of being "reminded" boldly of their obligation to
"subordinate" themselves to the "governing authorities" of the synagogues to which they were attached, including such matters as obedience to the operative halakhot for defining proper behavior for "righteous gentiles" (i.e., the apostolic decree, Noahide Commandments),
and the payment of taxes and other community obligations. That is,
Paul *and* the Christian Jews and gentiles of Rome both understood
their community(s) as part of the Jewish community(s) when Paul
wrote Romans, with Christian gentiles identified as "righteous gentiles" who were now worshiping in the midst of Israel in fulfillment of
the eschatological ingathering of the nations (15:5-12).[120]

THE IMPLIED AUDIENCE FOR
PAUL'S "REMINDER" TO ROME

Whom exactly did Paul have in mind when he composed this powerful letter? By this I do not mean to ask the degree to which the

[118]Delling, *TDNT*, 8.30 n. 21: "With few exceptions the Roman state did not re-
quire of Jews a proof of loyalty by emperor worship, obviously because it was seen
that their exclusive monotheism predated their attachment to the Roman empire.
In this respect Christians had no claim to exemption once they parted company
with the Synagogue as well as the state and thus declared themselves to be a newly
arisen group within the Rom. empire [Dihle]." See discussion above.

[119]All of these were special privileges granted Jews in addition to the normal
"collegia" privileges. I discussed this dynamic earlier. The later persecution of
Christians testifies to just how important this political rights issue continued to be.

[120]Many note that the earliest Christians in Rome were Jews and God-fearing
gentiles who would have naturally functioned within the synagogues during the
transition to a separate identity as Christians meeting apart from the synagogues in
house-churches (Dunn, *Romans*, pp. xlv–liv; Campbell, *Intercultural Context*, pp.
185–87; Schmithals, *Paul and James*, pp. 60–62, 115). But they do not mean to suggest that this was the case to any degree by the time of Paul's letter to Rome, particularly if they are proponents of the impact of the edict of Claudius for understanding the situation in Rome (see full discussion in appendix 2; note the
comment of P. Stuhlmacher, *Paul's Letter to the Romans*, p. 7: "They now no longer

congregation(s) Paul addressed consisted of Jewish or gentile attendees. Although we must be concerned with this question, the backdrop for understanding Paul's message really lies in uncovering the *implied* audience among the attendees. For regardless of the composition of the historical community(s), the revealing question is: Whom did Paul intend to be affected by this "bold reminder"? In what manner did he expect them to respond or change? Thus, we must be careful to distinguish between what we can know about the makeup of the congregation(s) in Rome and what we can conclude about Paul's intentions toward the implied readers/hearers of his message. In other words, our concern is not so much with who was present, but rather, with whom he was really instructing.

Failure to clarify this matter needlessly clouds the current debate concerning the reason(s) for Romans.[121] For while we may establish the composition of the audience as consisting of both Christian Jews and gentiles (there are many possibilities of the mixture, to be sure),[122] that does not necessarily inform us that Paul intended to address both parties with his message to Rome. Whom did Paul intend to inform and influence by this "reminder": Christian Jews, Christian gentiles, both

had any possibility of meeting in their congregational gatherings as a 'special synagogue' under the protection of the Jewish religious and legal privileges, but had to form their own freely constituted assemblies without leaning on the Jewish synagogues").

A few scholars push the point of the absence of reference to those Paul addressed as *ekklēsia* in his other letters, suggesting that there was not yet a unified church in Rome (cf. Dunn, *Romans*, p. lii; Bartsch, "Concept of Faith," pp. 37–45, 46ff.); or that the believers lacked an apostolic foundation and so that they were not a church (G. Klein, "Paul's Purpose in Writing the Epistle to the Romans," pp. 41–42). The closest suggestion to the one proposed herein is that of Judge and Thomas, "Origin," pp. 81–94; however, they differ completely where Paul's intentions are concerned (proposing that Paul intended to found the church in Rome "in opposition to the synagogues after Paul's arrival," which Paul was "principally responsible" for among the apostles, in contrast to Peter and James, who did not see "Christian belief" as "incompatible with Judaism, or practised under separate auspices" [pp. 81–82, 92]). They similarly propose that those Paul addressed "avoided any conflict with the synagogues" (p. 81) and "preferred to shelter under the umbrella of the synagogues rather than forming their own church" (p. 91) before Paul's arrival.

[121]Borrowed, of course, from the title of Wedderburn's *Reasons*, which has a thorough discussion of the many views that have been proposed. See also the many articles in *Romans Debate*.

[122]For example, Brown and Meier, *Antioch and Rome*, break down into four primary groupings; P. Minear, *The Obedience of Faith*, develops five different groupings.

equally, or perhaps both to varying degrees?[123] One's assumptions in this matter are telling; they necessarily and profoundly affect how one reads the text.

Paul's salutations in chapter 16 inform us that the congregation(s)[124] in Rome contained both Jews and gentiles who believed in Jesus as the Christ. He names twenty-six persons in all, from which we can develop at least some assumptions about the Jewish/gentile composition of the congregation(s).[125] Among those he apparently knew personally in Rome were Prisca and Aquila, his "fellow workers in Christ Jesus" (vv. 3-4).[126] These two Christian Jews with whom Paul had lived and worked in Corinth and Ephesus had come from Rome as a result of Claudius's expulsion of the Jews (Acts 18:1-28; 1 Cor. 16:19),[127] and they had perhaps returned to Rome to help in preparation for Paul's impending trip.[128] In addition, Paul mentions three others as his "kins(wo)men" (vv. 7, 11, 21), so we can assume that at least five of the twenty-six are Christian Jews. Lampe's analysis of the remaining names makes it unlikely that any of the other twenty-one people is Jewish.[129]

Thus some evidence suggests that the makeup of the congregation(s) was largely gentile (80% of individuals in chapter 16); however,

[123]W. Eschner, *Der Römerbrief: An die Juden der Synagogen in Rom?* suggests that Romans was written for non-Christian Jewish synagogues in addition to Christian house-churches.

[124]It is interesting to note that there appears to be perhaps as many as seven or eight congregations in Rome from the evidence in chap. 16 (P. Lampe, "The Roman Christians of Romans 16," pp. 229–30), which corresponds roughly to the number of synagogues present (see above discussion of synagogues in Rome and particularly Leon, *Jews*; Lampe, *Die stadtrömischen Christen*).

[125]See particularly Lampe, "Roman Christians," pp. 219–29, who traces many other interesting and important clues for understanding the composition of the audience, including male/female, slave/freed(wo)men, social standing, origins, etc.

[126]It is quite likely that Paul knew or had worked with a number of those mentioned in chap. 16. See the discussions of Jewett, "Paul, Phoebe," pp. 153–54; Stowers, *Diatribe*, p. 183.

[127]On the edict of Claudius see appendix 2.

[128]J. Murphy-O'Connor, "Prisca and Aquila," pp. 40–51; Lampe, "Romans Christians." Note that Claudius died in 54 c.e.

[129]Lampe, "Roman Christians," pp. 224–25, 226ff. It is difficult to be certain that names were Jewish because Jewish names from available inscriptions of the Roman catacombs suggest that many Jews followed or at least paralleled the practices of their non-Jewish neighbors in the area of naming their children. See the discussion of Leonard Rutgers, "The Onomasticon of the Jewish Community of Rome," in "The Jews in Late Ancient Rome."

the several Christian Jews among them had noticeably significant roles.[130] But the more important references for uncovering the makeup of the implied audience in Romans are those that suggest the vantage point of the implied reader. First, we must take into account the explicit references to his addressees as gentiles throughout the letter, particularly in the context of defining Paul's authority as the apostle to the gentiles:

> Paul, a bond-servant of Christ Jesus . . . through whom we have received grace and apostleship to bring about the obedience of faith *among all the Gentiles*, for His name's sake, among whom *you also* are the called of Jesus Christ; to all who are beloved of God in Rome, called as saints; (1:1-7)

> And I do not want you to be unaware, brethren, that often I have planned to come *to you* (and have been prevented thus far) in order that I might obtain some fruit *among you also*, even *as among the rest of the Gentiles*. (1:13)

> But I am speaking *to you who are Gentiles*. Inasmuch then as I am *an apostle of Gentiles*, I magnify my ministry, if somehow I might move to jealousy my fellow countrymen and save some of them. (11:13-14)

> But I have written very boldly to you on some points, so as to remind you again, because of the grace that was given me from God, to be a minister of Christ Jesus *to the Gentiles*, ministering as a priest the gospel of God, that my offering *of the Gentiles* might become acceptable, sanctified by the Holy Spirit. (15:15-16)

These explicit references are quite clear: Paul, the apostle to the gentiles,[131] was writing specifically to Christian gentiles in Rome in his

---

[130]Prisca and Aquila have an assembly in their house (v. 5); Junias was "outstanding among the apostles" (v. 7). It is important to note also that Paul refers to those who are Jews as his kins(wo)men (vv. 7, 11); if Paul had no regard for his Jewish identity as is often assumed, then it is difficult to make sense of this kind of retained identity in personal greetings among fellow Christians (equals in Christ with Christian gentiles, yet distinctively still Jewish as an active point of [positive] recognition and personal bonding), not to mention in the development of his argument throughout the letter (cf. 9:1-5; 11:1-5).

[131]While I do not agree with Gaston that Paul was concerned to address only gentiles in his apostolic ministry, his development of this theme is significant:

opening and closing comments as well as in the body of his letter, in spite of the fact that there were Christian Jews in the audience. Yet the presence of Christian Jews and Jewish themes[132] has led most if not all scholars to stop short of allowing this observation its full impact on the interpretation of Paul's message.[133] But what is perhaps most important

---

"Insofar as this reading of Paul had a starting point, it came with the conviction that one ought to take more seriously than is usually the case Paul's description of himself as the Apostle to the Gentiles. He refers to his commissioning explicitly that way, he cites his solemn promise at the Jerusalem Council to confine his missionary activity to Gentiles, and his letters are all addressed explicitly to Gentiles" (Gaston, *Paul*, pp. 7–8). See Elliott, *Rhetoric*, p. 292: "he addresses the Romans as *Gentile Christians*, and it is precisely as such that they are to respond to him as the Apostle to the Gentiles. If the letter is to be appropriated theologically in the modern situation, the exegesis presented above suggests that such appropriation might more properly read Romans along these lines: its address to *Gentile Christians as such*, rather than its mistakenly supposed systematic or dogmatic character, should give Romans whatever catholicity it may enjoy."

[132]For discussion of this shortcoming see: Campbell, *Intercultural Context*, pp. 136–41; Elliott, *Rhetoric*, pp. 105–224. See Kümmel, *Introduction*, p. 218: "The suppositions that the Roman congregation consists of a majority of Jewish Christians (W. Manson . . .), or that Paul seeks to win the Jewish Christians in Rome for the Gentile mission (Krieger), or that Paul battles against Jewish Christians who had returned to Rome, who wanted to gain ground again (Michel), can appeal only to Paul's lively discussion with Jewish arguments (cf. 2:17; 3:1; 4:1; 7:1, 4), but not to any text which characterizes the majority of Roman Christians as former Jews."

[133]Kümmel, *Introduction*, pp. 219–20, provides an excellent example: "The Epistle unambiguously designates its readers as Gentile Christians" begins his citation of the explicit passages we have just noted, including a discussion of why 4:1 and 7:1 offer no hindrance, but then he continues: "Nevertheless, the Roman congregation was certainly not pure Gentile Christian (against Munck)." His reasoning is because of the historical probability of a Jewish-Christian admixture, the call to mutual acceptance, the presence of Jewish Christians in chap. 16, etc., all of which demonstrate the presence of Jews in the congregations, but none of which negates the focus of Paul's implied audience as Christian gentiles. It is perhaps worth noting that Munck in *Christ and Israel*, p. 125, also backs away, when commenting on 11:13, from that which Kümmel accuses him of, when Munck notes that views depicting "the Roman church as consisting mainly of Gentile Christians—are not satisfactory. . . . This remark is directed to the Gentile Christians in general. In the letter to the Romans, which is a stock-taking intended for other churches than that in Rome, Paul addresses various groups to which he has had the opportunity to speak during the conflicts, and—following my modification of Manson's hypothesis—turns to the Jewish Christians in Jerusalem, and to the Jews. The letter to Rome is both a settling of accounts within the church and an appeal to the Jews." Tomson, *Paul*, pp. 58–62, would like to find the addressees

are the many implicit references in the context of these comments that demonstrate his readers' viewpoint as gentile.[134] I shall limit myself to but a few of the many contexts available, for the theme recurs constantly.[135]

In chapter 10 Paul unquestionably speaks of Israel as "them" (vv. 1-

---

to be entirely Christian gentiles, but he cannot because "there are also strong indications of a serious concern with Jews and Jewish members of the Roman church" (p. 60). Tomson's argument misses the distinction I am making here between the historical audience and those Paul was concerned to address; however, his comments on p. 61 fit my proposal nicely when he notes that "Romans in effect addresses a church in which Jews have an important place. It is also remarkable that Paul uses that self-designation, 'Apostle to the gentiles', precisely in a passage (11:13) which by exception singles out the gentiles among his readers." This observation fits perfectly with the suggestion that Paul was addressing Christian gentiles who were attending synagogue and thus very concerned with Jewish matters as they sought to understand the resistance to their claims on the part of non-Christian Jews, or at least the insistence that they adopt the halakhah of "righteous gentiles" to substantiate those claims.

[134]Kümmel, *Introduction*, p. 219, handles two passages commonly appealed to as indicating a Christian Jewish reader: "To that even 4:1 and 7:1 ff. offer no hindrance. For in 4:1 Paul imagines himself in discussion with a Jewish opponent and includes himself as a Jew with him. But the imaginary opponent is just as little to be sought among the readers of Romans as the rhetorical, apostrophic Jew of 2:17. In 7:1 he calls the readers 'those who know the law.' If Paul here actually means the Law of Moses, then he can presuppose this knowledge on the part of the Gentile Christians without more ado, for the OT was their Bible as well as that of the Jewish Christians. Gentile Christians were completely familiar with the OT through constant use in worship and instruction. Gentile Christians as well as Jewish Christians were set free from the Law through death (7:4; cf. Gal. 4:1 ff., 8 ff.; 5:1, 13: all of pre-Christian mankind stood under the Law and became free from it through Christ)." Sanders, *Paul, the Law*, p. 183, notes that Paul wrote from a Jewish perspective that conformed the gentile situation to a Jewish one: "This might have puzzled them, just as might the Jewish mode of argument, but Paul still seems to have been able to get his main points across."

[135]See Fraikin, "The Rhetorical Function of the Jews in Romans," for an excellent survey of the entire letter. He observes the same error on the part of scholars who fail to make this distinction regarding the audience and he comes to the same conclusion represented herein. Also D. W. B. Robinson, "The Priesthood of Paul," discusses at length the "we" passages throughout Romans indicate a Jewish vantage point on the issues, particularly focusing on chaps. 1–8: "This apostolic viewpoint reflects Paul's Jewishness (and therefore the representative or 'standard' character of his Christian experience) and also his defensive attitude (since he has the task of commending this experience to Gentiles)" (p. 236). Also Dunn, *Romans*, p. xlv.

3; 10:18—11:11) in the process of explaining to his audience the current state of affairs that has led to "your" salvation as gentiles in the
great plan of God (11:11-36). In chapter 11 the "you" is the "wild
olive"[136] who has been grafted in contrary to nature, who must not be
arrogant because "you" are supported by "the root" and not the other
way around, who must now understand that the mystery of God's pattern of commitment to Israel supersedes appearances to the contrary,
and who must recognize that those of Israel who appear to be "enemies for your sake" are actually suffering in the service of "your" very
salvation. This "you" is the one who must now recognize that in view
of the "mercies of God" toward "you" in this unfathomable plan of
God for the inclusion of gentiles "you" are "therefore" obligated to
"present your bodies a living and holy sacrifice" and take to heart the
humble role "you" are granted to play (12:1-3, 4ff.). This, of course,
begins the paraenesis of 12:1—15:12, which is concerned to address
Christian gentiles about their obligation to proper behavior, replete
with Judaic characteristics throughout. The former sins of those who
are now to behave properly and "lay aside the deeds of darkness" in
view of their faith in Christ are described as those sins that Jews considered characteristic of pagans: "Let us behave properly as in the day,
not in carousing and drunkenness, not in sexual promiscuity and sen-
suality, not in strife and jealousy" (13:11-14; cf. 6:19, which also assumes former pagans, certainly not Jews).

The "strong" of 14:1—15:3, 4ff. are addressed directly to forgo their
perceived freedoms from Judaic customs in matters of food[137] in view
of the priorities of the kingdom of God and instead to accommodate
the "opinions" of those "stumbling" for whom Christ died in the pursuit of peace: "For he who in this way serves Christ is acceptable to

[136]W. D. Davies, "Paul and the Gentiles: A Suggestion Concerning Romans
11:13-34," in *Jewish and Pauline Studies*, pp. 156–63, for an interesting discussion of
the underlying message of this imagery for Roman Christian gentiles in particular.

[137]"Now accept the one who is weak in faith, but not for the purpose of passing
judgment on his opinions. One man has faith that he may eat all things, but he who
is weak eats vegetables only" (14:1-2); "For if because of food your brother is hurt,
you are no longer walking according to love. Do not destroy with your food him for
whom Christ died" (14:15-16); "for the kingdom of God is not eating and drinking" (14:17); "Do not tear down the work of God for the sake of food. All things
indeed are clean, but they are evil for the man who eats and gives offense. It is not
good to eat meat or drink wine, or to do anything by which your brother stumbles"
(14:20-21).

God and approved by men" (14:18).[138] Paul wraps up this instruction
to Christian gentiles with a vision of them worshiping the One God in
one voice in the midst of the circumcised, thus fulfilling Israel's eschatological aspirations of all the nations one day recognizing Israel's
God as the God of all humankind: "Rejoice, O Gentiles, with his
people" (15:10; cf. vv. 4-12).

The explicit references coupled with the many contexts in which a
gentile audience is implied and the clear concern throughout the letter to address the need for gentiles to understand the role of historical

[138]It is worth noting that no one in Rome is addressed as thinking more lowly of
themselves than they ought, nor would the "weak" so describe themselves. The
letter is addressed throughout to those Paul is concerned to confront with thinking
too highly of themselves, to those who consider themselves to be "strong." Even
the illustration of the error of the paradigmatic Jewish missionaries in chap. 2 is a
rhetorical device to confront the same kind of error (covenantal arrogance) on the
part of the gentiles if they are judgmental toward the other when they ought to be
hoping for God's kindness toward them (2:1-4, 17-29; same message as chap. 11).
Campbell, *Intercultural Context*, pp. 136–41, discusses that the diatribe style of
Rom. 2:17-29 indicates "Paul is conducting a debate with an imaginary interlocutor who may be either a certain type corresponding to a specific vice or perhaps a
representative of a school of thought. Ch. 2:17-29 is an apostrophe to an imaginary
Jewish interlocutor in the style of the diatribe. It follows that Paul's conversation
partner in 3:1-9 may also be the same imaginary Jewish person. . . . So this is not
intended as an anti-Jewish debate. It is in fact a debate that probably often took
place among Jews at this period—even apart from the problem of Gentile
Christianity. . . . The Jew should not be seen as Paul's enemy or even necessarily
as Paul's opponent. 'He' represents a position that Paul discusses, caricatures or
even demolishes—not Judaism as such. The process depicted in such dialogical
exchanges is not *polemical*, but rather *pedagogical* and *protreptic*. . . . The Jew as the
imaginary interlocutor is purely a rhetorical fiction and the issue could equally well
be the priority of Israel in salvation history, and Gentile Christianity's attitude to
this, just as much as issues specifically relating to Jewish Christians. . . . The picture of the pretentious Jew Paul adopts here is a necessary component in his positive sketch of what it means to be a true Jew" (pp. 138–40). See Stowers, *The
Diatribe*, p. 177: "The pretentious Jew in 2:17-24 parallels characterizations of the
pretentious philosopher and is essential for the establishment of the principle in
2:25-29 that there is a true inward essence to what it means to be a Jew which can
be separated from the external trappings of being a Jew. A broader observation is
that all of the apostrophes in Romans indict pretentious and arrogant persons.
Rather than indicating a polemic against the Jew, the apostrophes in Romans cen-
sure Jews, Gentiles and Gentile Christians alike. None are excluded from the cen-
sure of the pretentious." See Elliott, *Rhetoric*, pp. 105–224, for important discussion. Hays, *Echoes*, pp. 44–46, also treats in this manner; Wedderburn, *Reasons*,
p. 126 on 2:1ff., concludes that the passage is addressed to Christian gentiles; see
also Dahl, *Studies in Paul*, pp. 70–94.

Israel, of the "stumbling" of Israel in the service of gentile salvation, of Judaic opinions of purity and proper behavior including their responsibility to accommodate those opinions, to correct their misguided and arrogant notion of having supplanted Israel,[139] and even that the "stumbling" were their "enemies,"[140] all point to the implied readers as Christian gentiles rather than Christian Jews.[141]

It may well be that Paul's letter addressed the concerns of Prisca and Aquila about the state of gentile Christian thought and practice, particularly in the face of some group suggesting that the Romans turn away from "the teaching" that they had formerly learned and obeyed

---

[139]Campbell, *Intercultural Context*, p. 171: "Paul addresses a real instance, probably the very first instance, of supersessionist theology in which Jews are displaced by Gentile believers as the new people of God, the new community of salvation."

[140]11:28: "From the standpoint of the gospel they are enemies for your sake" suggests that they are enemies of the gospel, of God's good news, thus of those addressed as His people in Rome, at least from the vantage point of the Christian gentiles being addressed.

[141]Note the similar conclusion of Fraikin, "Rhetorical Function," p. 93: "the audience is not the church of Rome in general but specifically Roman Gentile Christians. Then Romans is an epideictic discourse addressed to the Gentile Christians in Rome, intended to strengthen their awareness and assurance of God's election." See also W. Campbell, "Romans III as a Key to the Structure and Thought of Romans," pp. 257–64, who observes on p. 262 concerning the real issues in Rome evident in chaps. 9–11: This is no hypothetical situation, and the dialogue style gives no reason to believe that Paul does not address himself to a real situation in Rome where current anti-judaism was threatening the unity of the church. Paul's carefully constructed conclusion in 11:30-32 and his exhortations in 12:1f. and in 14–15 support this interpretation of ch. 11." And on p. 263 he notes: "Without appearing to be unduly specific we maintain that Paul faced two main issues in Rome (i) anti-judaism on the part of Gentile Christians, which was a cause of division among the Christian groups, and (ii) antinomianism—also on the part of Gentile Christians—some of whom were possibly former proselytes. . . . The outlook of the Roman Gentile Christians had marked similarities with that which later come to expression in Marcionism." Dunn, *Romans*, p. xlv: "Paul is clearly writing to Gentiles. . . . This is obvious from 11:13-32 and 15:7-12 and strongly implied in 1:6, 13 and 15:15-16. . . . the letter seems to be so dominated by the issue of Jew/Gentile relationships ('to Jew first and also to Greek'. . .), by questions of identity (who is a 'Jew'?—2:25-29; who are the 'elect' of God?—1:7; 8:33; 9:6-13; 11:5-7, 28-32), and by an understanding of the gospel as no longer limited to Jews as such (chaps. 2–5), but still with the Jews wholly in view (chaps. 9–11), in the hope that both Jew and Gentile can praise God together (15:8-12)." (Stowers in *A Rereading of Romans*, which appeared after this manuscript was submitted for publication, has also argued that the encoded reader is specifically the Christian gentiles.)

(16:17-18; 6:17-18),[142] a teaching that I suggest was the Jewish approach to outlining the halakhot which applied to Christian gentiles as
"righteous gentiles" when in the midst of Jews, namely, the apostolic
decree. N. T. Wright's summary of Paul's purpose for writing Romans
captures this same sense (though his interpretations of Paul's message
are not necessarily the same as those set out herein):

> The problem which Paul foresees in Rome is in fact the mirror-image
> of that which he met in Antioch. There, the church was pulled in the
> direction of maintaining the distinctiveness of Jews and Gentiles within
> the Christian church: there was an "inner circle" of Jewish Christians,
> and if gentile Christians wanted to belong to it they would have to get
> circumcised. In Rome, however, Paul foresees the danger of the (largely
> gentile) church so relishing its status as the true people of God that it
> will write off ethnic Jews entirely as being not only second-class citizens
> *within* the church, still maintaining their dietary laws when the need for
> them has past, but also now beyond the reach of the gospel *outside* the
> church, heading for automatic damnation. Paul, anxious about these
> possibilities, wishes to argue for two things: total equality of Jew and
> Gentile within the church, and a mission to Gentiles which always in-
> cludes Jews as well within its scope.[143]

With this backdrop of the historical situation in Rome and the implied audience for Paul's message as primarily, if not exclusively,
Christian gentiles who were still attending the synagogue(s) of Rome,
perhaps functioning within a subgroup identity, I now turn to the task
of seeking to understand Paul's letter.

[142]See the observation of N. T. Wright, *The Climax of the Covenant*, pp. 234–35,
247, 251, who notes on p. 247: "He suspects that the Roman church—who apparently need the warning in chs. 14–15 that the strong must bear with the weak and
not please themselves—is only too eager to declare itself a basically gentile organization, perhaps (this can only be speculation, but it may be near the mark) in
order to clear itself of local suspicion in relation to the capital's Jewish population,
recently expelled and more recently returned."

[143]Wright, *Climax*, p. 234. W. Campbell, "Rule of Faith," p. 44, notes similarly:
"Romans is an attempt to demonstrate the inherent continuity between Paul's
gospel and God's historical revelation of Himself to Israel—and thereby to deny
the legitimacy of a 'Christianity' that defines itself over against Judaism."

CHAPTER 3

WHO WERE THE "WEAK" AND THE "STRONG" IN ROME?

The identification of the "weak" and the "strong" addressed in Romans is critical for understanding the context of the original audience and how they would have read (or more likely heard the reading of) Romans themselves. The immediacy of this pursuit is heightened by the current "Romans debate," particularly by those who appeal to Paul's handling of the tensions between these two factions as the master key for unlocking the circumstances behind Paul's occasion for writing.[1] Though perhaps not as readily apparent, the identification of the "weak" and the "strong" has become equally significant for those who think the solution lies elsewhere. Even among the most extreme positions that suggest that pursuing Paul's purpose behind his comments to and about the "weak" and the "strong" is "bankrupt,"[2] decisions about what can or cannot be known about these two factions have become crucial in their conclusions. Both positions must answer at least the following questions:

1. Who were the "weak" and the "strong" in Rome?
2. What defined their *weakness* or *strength* to each other? To themselves? To Paul?
3. What was the nature of their association?
4. What did Paul intend to communicate to each of them? How did Paul hope this letter would affect their faith and behavior?

---

[1]For example, see Donfried's *Romans Debate*; see also the recent commentaries and studies in Romans listed in this bibliography. The Romans debate concerns the search to understand what factors prompted Paul to write Romans and includes major positions both for and against the situation in Rome as the impetus for Paul's letter and a variety of positions on what issues were most important in Paul's own ministry and circumstances independent of Rome that may have influenced, or even been the primary thrust of, his purpose for writing Romans. Understanding the audience addressed is central in all these positions, and many conclusions are based on decisions about who the "weak" and the "strong" were, or were not, in Rome.

[2]R. Karris, "Romans 14:1—15:13 and the Occasion of Romans," p. 66.

The answers to these questions involve significant exegetical and hermeneutical assumptions that necessarily influence any effort to unlock the purpose and message of Paul's letter to Rome for both positions. However, as we will see, some of the assumptions common to both positions need to be reexamined.

Those who believe that the purpose of Romans can be discovered by probing the text of Paul's letter for clues that reveal the historical situation in Rome, turn to the paraenesis of 14:1—15:13 as foundational.[3] In principle, they usually find it useful to work backward from the information developed in Paul's effort to unite the "weak" and the "strong" in chapters 12–15, in conjunction with Paul's introductory and closing remarks in chapters 1 and 15–16, in order to understand Paul's intended audience and message throughout the letter.[4] They essentially recognize that Paul must have laid a theological foundation in the earlier chapters that would make the ethical instructions of his conclusion both relevant and compelling.[5]

On the other side of the issue stand those who essentially maintain that little, if anything at all, can be derived from Paul's discussion of the "weak" and the "strong" that unlocks the occasion of Paul's letter. They find both the historical and exegetical evidence of "weak" and "strong" communities in Rome lacking, and thus conclude that Paul's discussion is general, perhaps but a general instruction derived from specific situations he had already faced elsewhere.[6] Some further suggest that the occasion for Romans may have even been more focused

[3]See the various articles in Donfried's *Romans Debate* for an example of the prevalence of this approach in recent studies.

[4]Minear, *Obedience*, pp. ix-x, 1ff., 6-7; etc.; also the structure/rhetoric approach that looks largely at the opening and closing, for example, L. A. Jervis, *The Purpose of Romans*.

[5]Wright, *Climax*, p. 251.

[6]Karris, "Occasion," p. 84, and others suggest Romans is but a reworking of the Corinthian correspondence where the weak and strong are concerned. G. Bornkamm, "The Letter to the Romans as Paul's Last Will and Testament," sees it as "Paul's last will and testament"; Meeks, *The Moral World of the First Christians*, p. 133: "When Paul later abstracted from this case some more general admonitions about relationships within the church (Rom. 14:1—15:13), he spoke of 'the strong' and 'the weak.'" Jewett, *Paul's Anthropological Terms*, p. 47: "For all its length, there is insufficient evidence either conclusively to identify the 'Weak' and the rationale of their abstinence or to demonstrate the source of the antinomistic self-consciousness of the 'Strong.' This would surely not be the case if the letter were composed solely to deal with concrete problems in the Roman congregation."

on issues relative to Paul's planned trips to Jerusalem or Spain than any particular, or even general, concerns in Rome.[7]

Representatives from both positions offer a wide array of explanations of who the "weak" and the "strong" were, and of what the historical situation most likely was that Paul addressed (or did not address). From these, both positions derive the purpose and message of Romans.[8] But when we look closely at the exegetical and theological inferences developed by *both* positions concerning the paraenesis of 12:1—15:13, the differences in application are surprisingly few. There is almost universal agreement (it appears to be an almost unquestioned fact) that the "weak" were *Christian Jews*[9] who still practiced the Law and Jewish customs (with most maintaining that this group would have included "God-fearing" gentiles as well), and that the "strong" were *Christian gentiles* (as well as Christian Jews like Paul who have supposedly abandoned Jewish practices).[10] A few scholars suggest, although without convincing even those who call attention to the suggestion, that the "weak" were actually Christian gentiles who had not made a complete break from Gnostic or other pagan backgrounds.[11]

[7]Jervell, "Letter to Jerusalem"; Jewett, "Paul, Phoebe"; Aus, "Paul's Travel Plans," pp. 232–62.

[8]The issue of whether to accept chap. 16, for example, as part of a letter to Rome, or an addendum to the letter to Rome attached when the letter was sent to Ephesus and other suggestions is covered well in the various articles in *Romans Debate*, particularly by Lampe and Donfried. I will assume that it was a part of the letter and refer to information that corroborates or opposes other suggestions, but refrain from making critical decisions based on the content of chap. 16. See Kümmel, *Introduction*, pp. 222ff.; Lampe, "Roman Christians," pp. 216–30; Donfried, "A Short Note on Romans 16" in *Romans Debate*, pp. 44–53; idem, "False Presuppositions in the Study of Romans," in *Romans Debate*, pp. 102–25; H. Gamble, *The Textual History of the Letter to the Romans: A Study in Textual and Literary Criticism*; M. Seifrid, *Justification by Faith*, pp. 249–54.

[9]Minear, *Obedience*, p. 9; F. Watson, " The Two Roman Congregations: Romans 14:1—15:13," pp. 203–15.

[10]Watson, "Two Roman Congregations," pp. 203, 207, for example, but this position prevails and is found in most of the literature of this bibliography.

[11]While several authors cite Rauer's suggestion that the "weak" were Christian gentiles and while they may note that it is inadvisable to allow his thesis to have been largely ignored, they all end up dismissing his thesis after a brief review because it simply fails to work. See comments on Rauer in Karris, "Occasion," pp. 68–69; Käsemann, *Romans*, p. 368; Jewett, *Paul's Anthropological Terms*, pp. 41–48, with good summary of problems. C. K. Barrett, *Romans*, p. 257, discusses view of Clement, who thought they were Pythagorean ascetes.

While ostensibly there is a great deal of disagreement concerning what this information means, and how it applies to understanding the purpose as well as the message of Romans, almost *all* appear to *agree* on at least two central points that have thus far guided their efforts:

1. The "weak" and the "strong" were *Christians*, and Paul's comments to each address tensions present in the Christian community (or communities).[12]

2. "Weak" is a pejorative term applied to *Christians deficient in their faith*, and the "weaknesses of the weak" were the result of their failure to realize the full measure of their freedom in Christ from the practices of the Law, as contrasted with the "strong," who along with Paul, have learned to "trust God completely and without qualification."[13]

These two seemingly unquestioned assumptions have had a profound impact on Christian exegesis and theology throughout the centuries, as they are central in developmental decisions about the composition of the audience and of Paul's real intentions in writing Romans. The impact is particularly telling among those engaged in the recent "Romans debate" to determine more precisely the historical setting as the necessary (or unnecessary) backdrop for understanding the original purpose of Paul's letter to Rome. As we shall see below, however, these assumptions have always been influential in the exposition of Romans.

THE PROBLEM WITH PREVAILING VIEWS OF THE "WEAK" AND THE "STRONG"

Günter Klein, a representative of those who question the prevailing conclusions that derive from the discussion of the "weak" and the "strong" for determining the historical occasion, and thus the purpose

---

[12]Minear, *Obedience*, p. 8: "not single Christian congregation" but rather the Christian congregations followed the pattern of the synagogues in that there were many different groups, just as there were many different synagogues. Thus, he concluded that the letter was addressed to different "factions" or "positions" and on p. ix says not single congregation but "on the contrary, all the evidence points to the existence of several congregations, separated from each other by sharp mutual suspicions"; Watson, "Two Roman Congregations," p. 206, says "two congregations, separated by mutual hostility and suspicion over the question of the law, which he wishes to bring together into one congregation." See also articles by Dunn, Wiefel, and Lampe in *Romans Debate*.

[13]Dunn, *Romans*, p. 798 (emphasis added). This issue will be treated more fully below.

of the message of Romans,[14] has shown that one of the inherent problems is the failure to recognize that chapters 1–11 "at no point reflect
an antagonism between Jewish Christians and Gentile Christians,"
and thus "the passage 14:1—15:13 does not deserve a key heuristic position with respect to an understanding of the epistle as a whole."[15]
Klein argues, convincingly, that the first eleven chapters do not provide the necessary "theological foundation of an intended peace set-
tlement between Gentile Christians and Jewish Christians," and that,
particularly regarding the Law, "the decisive statements" "are meant
to shed light on the situation of the non-believing Jews, in fact on non-
believers in general, and not on the situation of the Jewish Christians.
Especially Romans 9–11 cannot be regarded as a defense of Jewish
Christianity in Rome" because "unconverted Israel" is the "primary
reference."

Klein's challenge underscores the implicit weakness in the prevailing conclusions of those engaged in the Romans debate, for both positions fail to recognize, much less answer, this kind of objection.
Those who seem to recognize this kind of tension have thus far developed rather convoluted and unlikely paths. Some divide the letter
into two or more letters,[16] to two or more audiences,[17] in two or more

[14]Klein, "Paul's Purpose," pp. 29–43, seeks historical understanding, but in a
very different direction from this approach, and he ends up somewhere between
the two primary positions.

[15]Ibid., pp. 36–37. See also the question of Beker, *Paul the Apostle*, p. 89: "If
Paul's concern is the unity of Jewish and Gentile Christians in the church, why
does he carry on a dialogue with synagogue Jews in Romans?"

[16]See *Romans Debate* for many examples; Dunn, "The Formal and Theological
Coherence of Romans," pp. 247–48; idem, *Romans*, p. lxi, reviews several, including Scroggs and Schmithals.

[17]Watson, for example, offers an ingenious solution: "Paul's purpose in writing
Romans was to defend and explain his view of freedom from the law (i.e., separation from the Jewish community and its way of life), with the aim of converting
Jewish Christians to his point of view so as to create a single "Pauline" congregation in Rome. At the same time, he encourages Gentiles to be conciliatory towards
their Jewish fellow-Christians, since the union for which Paul hopes will not be
possible without a degree of tact and understanding on the part of the Gentile
Christians" (Watson, "Two Roman Congregations," p. 207; idem, *Paul*, for fuller
treatment). See Dunn, *Romans*, p. lvii; and Campbell, *Intercultural Context*,
pp. 122–60, for critiques of Watson's proposal, particularly Watson's need to dismiss
Rom. 11 in order to make his construct work and the fact that it also retains the
same hermeneutic of antithesis between Paul and Judaism, albeit in a new form,
that Watson proposes to transcend.

different locations.[18] However, it can be safely said that no one has yet provided a comprehensive solution that successfully harmonizes the audience addressed in the theological concerns of the first eleven chapters with those addressed in the behavioral instructions of the final five. I suggest that one of the reasons for this impasse, in spite of the countless efforts that have been made over the centuries to interpret Romans (usually as the most pivotal letter in any theological position) is inextricably linked with the failure to recognize who the "weak" and the "strong" (particularly the "weak") really were in Rome.

This study suggests a solution that answers the summons to harmonize the coherent and contingent features of Romans[19] while solving the very dissonance observed in the many answers to date, without compromising the features of Romans that compel one to recognize just how thoroughly "occasional" Paul's letter really was.[20] This solution respects the intentions of the text and the endeavor to find therein the clues that will unlock the historical situation in Rome and in Paul's larger ministry without necessarily separating Paul from his Jewish roots, or negating his clear concern for the salvation of Israel.[21] It respects Paul's pathos for Israel as central to his message as the representative of the Jewish people of the Diaspora and their hope of restoration, even if his apostleship is to the gentiles. The interpretation of this investigation highlights Paul's staunch defense of the principles of monotheism as the crux of his debate both with his Jewish brothers and sisters in their attitude to gentile coparticipation

----

[18]Manson, "St. Paul's Letter to the Romans—and Others," is among the many who believe Rom. 1–15 was sent to Rome and a copy was sent to Ephesus with chap. 16 added. See review of the problems with this view by Campbell, *Intercultural Context*, pp. 19–20.

[19]See J. Beker, *The Triumph of God*, pp. xx–xvi, 3–14, 15–19, for an overview of this issue (p. 15): "Paul's interpretation of the gospel consists of a complicated interplay between coherence and contingency. By 'coherence' I mean the unchanging components of Paul's gospel, which contain the fundamental convictions of his gospel. . . . The term 'contingency' denotes the changing, situational part of the gospel, that is, the diversity and particularity of sociological, economical, and psychological factors that confront Paul in his churches and in his missionary work and to which he had to respond."

[20]See Campbell, *Intercultural Context*, pp. 14–24, 31–36, for an excellent demonstration of why Romans is specifically a letter addressed to Rome and the circumstances there.

[21]This disregard for Jews and Judaism and Israel is assumed to characterize Paul by scholars of every persuasion, both Christian and Jewish.

in the blessings of God without becoming Jews, and with his new Christian gentile brethren in his uncompromising insistence on the Law-respectful behavior incumbent upon gentiles who become Christians, even though they are not under the Law—for the One God of Israel is indeed the One God of the whole world. This study thus avoids the condescending trap that characterizes almost all interpretations of the "weaknesses of the weak" as their failure to disregard the practice of the Law, as though the practice of the Law demonstrated a lack of faith. And I hope that this approach will provide another perspective in the search for the "hermeneutical key"[22] by which we can explore the mystery of the purpose and message of Romans, both for the original audience and for the synagogue and church today, as it respects the logic of Paul and his intention to build a case in the early part of his letter that will compel his audience to compliance in his summary call to service in the paraenesis of 12:1—15:13.

It is time to question these two operating assumptions in studies of Romans: (1) that the "weak" were *Christians*; (2) that their weakness was related to their alleged failure to trust God completely by breaking free from the practice of the Law. Both of these assumptions influence the process of deciding who Paul addressed in Romans, what he meant to communicate, and thus what the church should learn from this letter. They guide the interpretation of what features were operative in Paul's ministry not only toward Rome (or Ephesus or elsewhere for those who would argue such), but throughout his Diaspora ministry, and even his relationship with the Jerusalem apostles.

In fact, these assumptions create the kind of contradictions that have always riddled Christian interpreters of Romans, particularly well illustrated when they find themselves trapped, as was Luther, into dealing with the admonition not to judge the opinions of the "weak" (14:1), when by definition, their hermeneutical presuppositions necessarily engage them in the very process of judging their opinions, demonstrated clearly in the following juxtaposition of contradictions in Luther's *Commentary on the Epistle to the Romans* concerning the "weak" and the "strong." Luther clearly recognized what Paul intended to communicate: "That is, *no one should judge* the opinion or conviction of the other."[23] Luther nevertheless went on to do exactly that:

---

[22]Donfried, "Introduction," in *Romans Debate*, p. lxxi.
[23]Luther, *Romans*, p. 196 (emphasis added).

When the Apostle here speaks of the "weak," he has in mind those who
were of the opinion that they were obligated to certain laws, *to which in
reality they were not obligated*. His words, however, are directed above all
against *the Jewish error*, which some false prophets taught, distinguishing
between certain kinds of food. . . . *Against this (Christian) liberty*, for
which the Apostle contends, many false apostles raised their voice *to
mislead the people to do certain things as though these were necessary*. Against
such *errorists* the Apostle took the offensive with an amazing zeal.[24]

This, however, does not mean that we should bear *the superstitious piety*,
or rather *the show of piety* of our own time, simply because it flows from
weakness of faith. Those who do these works of piety do them *because of
their gross ignorance*. . . . Essentially, there lies at the bottom of this
error—(doing good works from necessity)—the Pelagian view.[25]

Luther recognized that Paul was clearly instructing the "strong" not
to "judge" the "opinion or conviction" of the "weak"; however,
Luther tripped into the very trap of judging them and then read this
judgment as Paul's. That is, Luther was tripped by the faulty assumption (1), that the "weak" were *Christian* Jews, into the trap of assumption (2) with its inherent, inescapable contradiction wherein he
indulges in the very same kind of *judging* Paul warned the "strong"
(which Luther considers himself) to avoid. I shall hereinafter refer to
this phenomenon as "Luther's trap," which is no respecter of persons,
for it fills every commentary on this paraenesis that I reviewed. Note
the inherent similarity in the following examples:[26]
- J. D. G. Dunn explains their faith as deficient in that they "fail to
  trust God completely and without qualification," and then states:
  "In this case the weakness is trust in God *plus* dietary and festival
  laws, trust in God *dependent* on observance of such practices, a
  trust in God which *leans on the crutches* of particular customs and *not*
  on God alone, *as though* they were an integral part of that trust."[27]
- Ernst Käsemann succinctly states, in spite of the fact that Paul is
  addressing the attitude of the "strong" as the problem: "The 'weak

[24]Ibid., pp. 194–95 (emphasis added).
[25]Ibid., pp. 196–97 (emphasis added).
[26]The list of quotes is endless to this effect.
[27]Dunn, *Romans*, p. 798 (emphasis added), is selected not because he is the most
telling example, but because he is clearly concerned to avoid these kind of misunderstandings of the text and yet falls prey without apparently even realizing it (see,
for example, his introductory comments and pp. 810–12, where he handles Paul's
Jewish concerns so well).

in faith' form the problem. These are people whose Christianity does not relieve them of doubts in the exercise of Christian liberty."[28]

- Peter Stuhlmacher is most direct: "For the strong it would be and is sin to compel the brother who is still *unsettled* in the faith to follow his or her own example, or, indeed, to demonstrate his or her (Gentile-Christian) *freedom in order to expose the narrow-minded cowardliness* of the weak (Jewish Christians)."[29]

- Paul Minear makes the same kind of statement in his often cited treatment of this paraenesis and even divides the weak into two different groups based on how much they impose their views on the strong.[30]

- Karl Barth in *Romans*, after having sensitively handled the nuances of Paul's intentions toward the "strong" and in seeking to bring the same insight to the "weak," states: "Shall not the hidden, unsubstantiated righteousness of God benefit also, and indeed precisely, the *weak in faith, the uninstructed, non-Pauline man*? Can any one with any understanding of the unparalleled mercy of God set at nought the *OTHER*, simply because he continues his busy, optimistic work on the very edge of the precipice of his unbroken morality? Does the behavior of the OTHER lie *so far outside the freedom of God* that the strong man should suppose that, though he may continue in fellowship with publicans and whores, *Pharisees* must be excluded?"[31]

- Peter Tomson takes a much more Judaic informed approach to this section than many, even criticizing those who fail to respect the "weak" in their treatment of this section: "Therefore we must take the words that follow seriously and abandon the view that Paul considers the 'weak' imperfect in faith."[32] Yet Tomson finds himself in the same trap when he refers to the "weak" as "over-sensitive Jews" with "'hyper-halakhic' anxieties regarding gentile wine and meat." Tomson makes this reference in the same context in which he observes that the issue is about "basic Jewish food laws." Why then are the "weak" characterized as "over-sensitive" or "hyper-

---

[28]Käsemann, *Romans*, p. 366, and see pp. 366–69, where he clarifies that the "weak" are the Christian Jews, concluding: "By religious descent Jewish-Christians are committed to observance of a fixed tradition which is related ultimately to the law of holiness" (p. 369).

[29]Stuhlmacher, *Paul's Letter to the Romans*, p. 229 (emphasis added).

[30]Minear, *Obedience*, pp. 8–9, 10ff.

[31]K. Barth, *Romans*, p. 510 (emphasis added).

[32]Tomson, *Paul*, pp. 242–43.

halakhic" if their concern was the observance of "basic Jewish food laws"?[33]

- Luther's trap is also not the exclusive domain of Protestantism, as the comments of *The New Jerome Biblical Commentary* clearly demonstrate when explaining this paraenesis: "The second part of the hortatory section is immediately concerned with *such minor questions* as the eating of meat and the observance of holy days. But more fundamentally it deals with the *age-old problem of the scrupulous vs. the enlightened conscience*, or the conservative vs. the progressive. . . . Paul has probably heard of *scrupulous Jewish Christians* whose judgments are based on an *insufficiently enlightened faith*. Such persons have *not really grasped* what is meant by uprightness through faith and have *sought instead to find assurance by added practices*."[34]

This brief list highlights the ubiquitous reach of Luther's trap. When these interpreters of Romans assume Paul is speaking of the "weak" as *Christians*, they inescapably stumble into the concomitant assumption that their *weakness* is evidence of lack of maturity (as measured against the strength of the "strong") to believe in God free from pre-Christian encumbrances to Torah and Jewish customs. They must then assume that Paul was "judging" the *faith* of the "weak" *deficient* because their *opinions* of proper behavior for the faithful were guided by values that Paul ostensibly believed were no longer operative for the Christian community. Thus these interpreters indulge in some version of the same unabashed judging that Luther indulged in—trapped into contradicting what they realize to be the plain sense of Paul's instruction not to judge the *opinions* of the "weak" (what the "weak" [and Paul: 14:5-6] believe to be valid acts of faith toward God) by their very act of judging such behavior (with respect to *faith*) invalid, deficient, oversensitive, or at the very least inferior.

But would Paul have considered it a sign of weakness for Jews, in this case Christian Jews, since that is who most assume to be the "weak in faith," if they continued to embrace the Law? Does keeping the Law really lie behind the "weaknesses of the weak" (15:1)? And if it does, why doesn't Paul seek to correct such a view on the part of the "weak" or urge them on to a supposedly more mature position? In fact, why does he insist that the "strong" not judge such opinions if he felt

---

[33]Ibid., pp. 244–45.

[34]J. Fitzmyer, "Romans," in *New Jerome Biblical Commentary*, p. 865 (emphasis added).

they were the cause of "weakness" (14:1)? How would he expect them ever to mature if such ostensibly flawed thinking that was keeping them from being "strong" was not confronted? Why would he instruct the "strong" to go so far as to accommodate such supposedly "weak" beliefs and practices? Wouldn't such accommodation put the "strong" at risk of going too far, that is, of "judaizing"? And why would Paul instead insist on the "weak" being "fully convinced" in their own mind that their practices of the Law are "for the Lord" (14:5ff.)? In addition, one must wonder how it is possible that the behavior of the "strong" could "destroy" the "weak" if they are Christians, whether Jews or not.[35] Just how would eating food "destroy him for whom Christ died"? Would they renounce their faith in Christ because of the eating habits of the "strong"? If so, why doesn't Paul confront such a conclusion on the part of the "weak" more directly? These observations and questions call for a thorough reevaluation of the identity of the "weak" and the "strong" and the underlying reason for their "weakness" or "strength" in Rome, as well as Paul's intentions toward each.

Must One Assume that the "Weak" and the "Strong" Are Christians?

One can hardly argue that the "strong" are not Christians. Paul, after all, includes himself in the description (15:1)! They are clearly the ones Paul is most concerned to reach with his message to accommodate, in the same spirit that Christ had, even if they are being insulted ("reproached") or otherwise judged by the "weak," whom Paul urges them to "welcome" (14:1, 3; 15:1-3). They are instructed directly as Christians to change their relative judgment of the "weak" and thus their behavior: "Do not destroy with your food him for whom Christ died" (14:15). They are, without question, a group that represents the Christian community(s) that Paul is addressing to undertake a radical "renewing of their minds" that will result in a new, humble lifestyle in their relationships (12:1-3):

> Now accept the one who is weak in faith, but not for the purpose of passing judgment on his opinions. (14:1)

---

[35] 14:15 needs to be given its proper weight in Paul's argument: "For if because of food your brother is hurt, you are no longer walking according to love. Do not destroy with your food him for whom Christ died."

Therefore let us not judge one another any more, but rather determine this—not to put an obstacle or a stumbling block in a brother's
way. (14:13)

Now we who are strong ought to bear the weaknesses of those without
strength and not just please ourselves. (15:1)

But what kind of Christians are they, or more properly, what kind of
people compose the group Paul refers to as "strong"?

The Identity and Character of the "Strong" as Christians

The opinions of the "strong" on proper practices are certainly not
Jewish, even though Paul includes himself in the appellation. Much of
what we can know of the "strong" in Rome is from how they are differentiated from the "weak" in purity behavior (14:14),[36] that is, in
their practices of matters such as food, days, and perhaps wine. They
believe they "may eat all things" (14:2); they regard "every day alike"
(14.5); and they drink wine.[37] They "regard with contempt
[ἐξουθενείτω] him who does not eat" (14.3), which suggests that they
despised or dismissed the practices of the "weak" as invalid (meaningless) before God, a disposition that Paul directly confronts as
wrong, and one that he does not share with the "strong" he addressed
in Rome.[38] Paul instructs them instead to recognize that the practices

[36]14:14 makes clear that the issue dividing the "weak" and "strong" is along
Jew/gentile lines concerning their difference of opinion in matters of purity
(κοινὸν [common] is unique to Jewish cultic language in antiquity [Dunn,
Romans, p. 800]). See chapter 4 below for fuller discussion.

[37]Implied in v. 21 as a point of distinction from the "weak."

[38]Many take Paul's comments in v. 14a to be the key to interpreting Paul's intentions in this section, perhaps inadvertently, in that they think Paul agrees with
the "strong" that these distinctions are meaningless. They assume that Paul is less
than sincere when he says in v. 14b that they are in fact "unclean" to the one who
"thinks" they are "unclean," and they thus take this as the defining issue of the
"weakness" of the "weak." But Paul is sincere and he is not saying they are meaningless in v. 14b, and if he were he would be in contradiction with not only his
statements on God's view of these actions as meaningful, but also his call to both
"weak" and "strong" to do whatever they deem to be meaningful "fully convinced" of its meaningfulness before God (v. 5). Nor would Paul spend so much
time telling the "strong" to accommodate, in fact to adopt in their own lifestyle,
the practices of the "weak." He would rather tell the "strong" to tolerate them,
and he would turn his attention to the "weak" to instruct them to grow-up, to mature in what is essential and lay aside the encumbrances, etc. No, Paul is not

of the "weak" are *just as valid before God* as those of themselves, and that they spring from the *same* faith and thanksgiving toward God as their own practices (vv. 3-13, 14ff.). And he warns the "strong" of their obligation to recognize that when their actions offend the sensitivities of the "weak" they themselves are actually the ones responsible for

---

saying that the practices of the "weak" are meaningless in v. 14, he is qualifying their importance in the prophetic tradition. Their importance, like that of sacrifice, is only meaningful when done in truth. As it was meaningless to sacrifice with an impure heart it is meaningless to assert gentile freedom as the "strong" were being tempted to do when the underlying motive is no longer right (this was perhaps a slogan of the "strong" in Rome, or of the groups seeking to influence them whom Paul opposes: 16:17-20), namely, indifference to the harm the assertion of those rights would have on "him for whom Christ died." While gentiles might be free of the Law in principle, there is a higher principle at work, and those rights must not be permitted to divide what has now been redefined in Christ, not self-pleasure but holding up the stumbling neighbor (15:1-3). They describe relations according to the flesh, that is, according to Jew and gentile, slave and free, male and female, distinctions which are real, and all meaningful, but they must not pre-empt the most meaningful thing, which is the new union possible that supersedes all relationships of fleshly distinction with a new relationship of love and honor for each other in view of the kingdom of God (14:15-18, 19ff.) This plurality is to be found in the rabbinic tradition in this same context, in fact, in a halakhah: "in the presence of a brother one is not to treat as permitted what for him is forbidden" (*b. Ned.* 15a; cf. Tomson, *Paul*, p. 252), which is exactly what Paul goes on to conclude later in 14:20: "Do not tear down the work of God for the sake of food. All things indeed are clean but they are evil for the man who eats and gives offense." It is the same intention we see so clearly in Paul's appeal of 15:1-13 to unite both in the spirit that Christ embodied (as in Phil. 2:1-11 also). No, they are not meaningless; they need not, however, in view of the knowledge of Christ, be as important for the "strong" as they may still be for the "weak," who cannot so easily transcend the differences of the flesh, the boundaries that distinguish them from gentiles. Tomson, *Paul*, pp. 247–54, follows similar lines by pointing out the issue is election rather than legalism, and on p. 250 he says: "In this ingenious way Paul is able to treat both Jewish and gentile life styles with equal respect: purity or food laws are important for Jews, not gentiles." This concept is evident in the conclusions reached in the Jerusalem Council of Acts 15, wherein it was decided that Peter's interpretation of God's intention to break down the barrier between Jew and gentile in Christ would become the operative agenda of the church (Acts 15:4-20). That is, as Cornelius, "a righteous and God-fearing man well spoken of by the entire nation of the Jews" (Acts 10:22), and his household had been "cleansed" and made "holy" by God (Acts 10:14-15, 16ff., 28ff., 34-35, 36ff.; 11:1-12, 13ff.) and had become equal coparticipants in Israel's promised salvation and inheritance of the Holy Spirit (Acts 10:44-48; 11:11-18), so too had God shown that the new community consisted not just of restored Israel, but also of "all the Gentiles that are called by My name" (Acts 11:15-18; 15:7-11, 14-17, 18ff.). See fuller discussion below and in chapter 4 below.

provoking the "blasphemy" that results (v. 16), for the (justifiable) animosity of the "weak" is a result of the failure of the "strong" to recognize the depth of their new responsibility to the "weak" in view of the sufferings of Christ (14:15—15:3).

The "strong" are the focus of Paul's instruction throughout this paraenesis. He opened with the admonition that they must now accept the "weak" for some purpose other than "passing judgment on his opinions" (v. 1). I will get to that purpose later, but here the issue to note is that Paul appears to choose the label "strong" for its negative connotations as well as its positive. They are "strong," presumably in "faith," since that is what Paul contrasts with those "weak in faith," and it is the central motif in his instruction. But their *strength* has an edge that is more properly labeled "presumption," "arrogance," and παρ᾽ ἑαυτοῖς φρόνιμοι[39]—the state of mind that Paul confronts

---

[39]To "be wise in your own estimation" (11:25) develops the warning of v. 20 when the Christian gentiles look "down" on the fate of the natural branches that have been broken off: "Do not be conceited [high-minded], but fear"; and v. 18 also: "do not be arrogant toward the branches." It also echoes Prov. 3:7: "Do not be wise in your own eyes; fear the LORD and turn away from evil." To "think more highly" of oneself than one "ought to think," that is, to be high-minded above what it behooves one to be minded, must be avoided by the "renewal" of the "mind" because one is a recipient of grace, of a "measure of faith," and thus one should now judge oneself "soberly" (to be minded so as to be sober minded: 12:1-4). Paul develops this concept of the various states of "mind" throughout the letter in the context of upward or downward direction, that is, of pride or humility, in the tradition of Scripture that the fear of the Lord is of great benefit for it recognizes the gifts of God in gratitude resulting in wisdom versus the proud of heart who rely only on themselves (11:20; 12:3; cf. v. 16: "Be of the same mind toward one another; do not be haughty in mind but associate with the lowly. Do not be wise in your own estimation" [again we see Prov. 3:7]). This concept is an echo of the temptation of Adam, who, when he was tempted to "eat" elevated himself to be "wise" like God, resulting in the wisdom that judges the other negatively instead of taking the humble direction and judging oneself in the service of the other positively (see notion of Adam's sin in 5:12-19). See also 16:19-20, where Paul contrasts being wise in evil rather than good with Satan who also elevated himself; the judging of chap. 2 on part of the audience (2:1-4, 5ff.) and the paradigmatic Jewish missionaries by way of example of their error when they do the same (2:17-24, 25ff.); the lesson of chap. 8 that the mind set on the "Spirit" no longer judges like the mind set on the "flesh" (8:5ff.), that is, it does not judge by human boundaries any longer but by God's boundaries. Note that in 15:5 Paul brings the discussion of the "weak" and "strong" to a close with the hope that they will "be of the same mind with one another according to Christ Jesus" to therefore glorify God with one voice together. Perhaps the best example of Paul's development of this theme succinctly is in Phil. 2.

as unacceptable throughout this letter.[40] And their power appears to lie in their ability to significantly affect the relationship of the "weak" toward Christ:

> For if because of food your brother is *hurt*, you are no longer walking according to love. *Do not destroy* with your food him for whom Christ died. (v. 15)

> *Do not tear down* the work of God for the sake of food. (v. 20)

These are clearly characteristics of the "strong" that Paul distances himself from and confronts as unacceptable on their part. They may be Christians, but their attitudes and actions, as perceived by Paul, embody anything but the grace of God demonstrated in Christ: they embody judgmental Christian hypocrisy of the very nature that Paul confronts throughout his letter![41]

The practices of the "strong" are those characteristic of gentiles who have come to faith in Christ without attachment to Jewish Law or customs.[42] And the attitudes that Paul confronts are those that might be expected to arise among gentiles who have come to the Christian faith without an appreciation of how their new faith is linked with the

---

[40]Barth, *Romans*, pp. 502–10, develops this same nuance in Paul's choice of the label "strong"; Jewett, *Paul's Anthropological Terms*, p. 46, observes "One thing that can be said with certainty is that they had antinomian tendencies. . . . Closely related with this antinomianism is their proud self-consciousness which expressed itself in scorn for those who were still bound by the law (Rom. 14:10) or cherished their membership in Israel (Rom. 11:17 ff.)."

[41]See 2:1-4; 11:18, 20, 23; 12:3ff., 9ff., 16-18; 14:1—15:13; 16:17-20.

[42]Wright, *Climax*, pp. 234, 247, 251; Jewett, *Paul's Anthropological Terms*, p. 45: "they are Gentile Christians with enthusiastic and libertinistic leanings. Their boasting in themselves and in their freedom from the law reveals a highly developed self-consciousness similar to that which the Gnostics in Corinth manifested"; and on p. 46: "This antinomian tendency is reflected clearly in the discussion of their rejection of the cultic law (Rom. 14:1 ff.) where Paul finds it necessary to warn against living and acting to suit oneself rather than the Lord (Rom. 14:7 ff.) and to conclude with a warning that each would have to give account for his actions at the last judgment (Rom. 14:12). Closely related with this antinomianism is their proud self-consciousness which expressed itself in scorn for those who were still bound by the law (Rom. 14:10) or cherished their membership in Israel (Rom. 11:17 ff.)." Davies, *Paul*, p. 111, comments on Rom. 6:1: "and among Gentiles, who lacked any deep acquaintance with Judaism, antinomianism was always crouching at the door ready to enter in under the cloak of grace."

history of salvation,[43] with the faith of the historical people of God embodied in the Law and Jewish customs to express righteousness and love, both toward God and humankind. Indeed, they are not unlike the kind of gentile prejudices toward Jews and the practice of their faith that were prevalent in the gentile city of Rome in the first century c.e. For in Rome, as noted earlier, the views expressed in many of the secular writings of the time were about just such issues as customs regarding food and the practice of Sabbath, not to mention circumcision,[44] that were derided as characteristic of Jews, and were cited in prejudicial remarks of strangeness, impiety, atheism, barbarism, misanthropy, and general disdain for their refusal to join in fellowship and benevolent open-minded interaction that should characterize the pax Romana. We need to recognize that this paraenesis (chaps. 12–15) follows shortly after Paul's correction of Christian gentiles' triumphant assumption of having supplanted the "stumbling" of Israel (chaps. 9–11). It appears that Paul is addressing gentiles who have grown up with just such assumptions of superiority toward Jews before they became Christians. Now, having become Christians, without a proper understanding of their roots in Jewish faith, they are allowing these

---

[43]W. D. Davies, "Paul and the Gentiles: A Suggestion Concerning Romans 11:13-24," in *Jewish and Pauline Studies*, pp. 156–63, discusses the choice of "wild olives" in this same vein and points out its lack of relative productivity as "a most forceful indictment of their lives" because they looked to Athens, the cultivated olive, the cradle of civilized life; thus Paul possibly "was deliberately turning the tables on them?" (pp. 160–61). "All this lends support to the suggestion that in that allegory, Rom 11:17-24, Paul was engaged not only with the Gentile Christians but also with the Gentile world and with its anti-Judaism. By casting Gentiles in the role of the wild olive and reserving the cultivated olive for the community rooted in Abraham, was he not in a way subtle to a modern reader but probably clear to the Christian Gentiles in Rome (whom one must assume to have achieved a degree of sophistication to be able to follow the epistle to the Romans at all) opposing anti-Judaism of the Greco-Roman world and striking a blow for his own kin after the flesh, not only within the context of the Church, but within that of the larger world?" (p. 163).

[44]J. Marcus, "The Circumcision and the Uncircumcision in Rome," pp. 67–81, discusses the possibility that the label "circumcision" was used derisively by gentiles and then later accepted by Jews as a label to be worn proudly in opposition to the label "the foreskin" used in reference to gentiles. The "Law-free Gentile Christians in Rome may have called themselves 'the strong' and their opponents 'the weak'. . . . Indeed, it is possible that there is a close relation between the two sets of terms; the 'strong' may have called their opponents 'the weak' partly because they *weakened* themselves through circumcision" (p. 80; cf. *b. Meʿila*. 17b).

prejudices to influence their present opinions and contemptuous behavior toward Jews who do not share their new faith in Jesus Christ.[45]

If we allow that chapter 16 was in the original letter we see there that some group is appealing to the Christians in Rome to indulge their "appetites" in clear opposition to "the teaching you have learned," which is causing "dissensions and hindrances" that provoke Paul to vehemently denounce them and even to liken them to Satan (16:17-20). This appears to refer to some group encouraging Law-free tendencies in specific defiance of Jewish sensitivities ("gentilizers" as opposed to "judaizers"), for the issue follows Paul's lengthy discussion to choose to "not eat" rather than to please themselves by "eating" (indulging their appetite as the serpent had encouraged in disobedience of God's command). Is this the edge to Paul's choice of the label "strong"?

We hear the echo of Paul's concern to confront Christian gentiles who boastfully presume they have supplanted Israel (11:17-32); who regard non-Christian Jews as "enemies" (11:28); whom Paul can reach most easily with the message of their own judgmental arrogance by paradigmatically illustrating this kind of behavior when it is characteristic of a Jewish missionary guilty of the same (2:17-24, 25ff.).[46] We hear the pathos of the apostle to the gentiles as he appeals to them to

[45]This is understood as the backdrop of Paul's concerns expressed throughout the letter, but particularly evident in chap. 11. See Hays, *Echoes*, for a good treatment of this issue. See Wedderburn, *Reasons*, p. 141: "Thus the Roman Christians on the one hand needed, some of them, to appreciate the Jewishness of the Christian tradition; on the other hand others of them needed to see how Paul's gospel proclaimed a God who was acting now in a way consistent with the Old Testament's record of how God had always acted in dealing with Israel." See Wright, *Climax*, p. 251: "Paul could see that, in Rome, the temptation would always be for a largely gentile church to down play or forget its Jewish roots. But if the church heeds his argument, such a possibility will never be realized." See Davies, *Jewish and Pauline Studies*, p. 138: "these chapters [9-11] reveal a Paul conscious of an emerging anti-Judaism among Gentile Christians that could draw on the endemic hostilities of the Greco-Roman pagan world to help it. He is determined to combat this."

[46]I take this passage to be a rhetorical use of diatribe. The "Jew" is developed as a paradigmatic illustration of the same error in the Christian gentile judging the non-Christian Jewish missionary so that they can recognize the hypocrisy of their own attitude being confronted in 2:1-5, 6ff. and again in chap. 11; see earlier discussions and Campbell, *Intercultural Context*, pp. 136–41; Elliott, *Rhetoric*, pp. 105–224; Stowers, *Diatribe*, p. 177; Hays, *Echoes*, pp. 44–46; Wedderburn, *Reasons*, p. 126 on 2:1ff.; N. Dahl, *Studies in Paul*, pp. 70–94.

understand that their salvation has come at great expense to Israel
(9:1-5; 11:11-33; 15:27); who seeks to give them an understanding of
how their salvation flows out from and back to the faithful concern of
God, not to mention Paul, to bring all Israel to her promised salvation
(chaps. 9–11); who hopes, in view of his "bold reminder" to "present
your bodies a living and holy sacrifice" (12:1), that he will now be able
to offer these gentiles as acceptable and sanctified (15:15-16). Is the attitude that Paul confronts in chapters 9–11 not the same kind of boast-
ful arrogance that characterizes the "strong" in Rome? Are they not
clearly the aggressor Paul confronts throughout this letter?

Indeed, the "strong" are *Christians*, for they have faith in Christ.
They are the audience Paul has continued to address throughout his
letter as gentiles (1:5-7; 11:13; 15:14-16),[47] who in view of Paul's apostleship to the gentiles need to obey his bold reminder (15:15-16) and
have their minds renewed to recognize that God's will for them is not
judgmental arrogance (2:1-4, 5ff.; 11:11—12:3, 4ff., 16; 14:1—15:3) nor
is it to continue in sin (2:5-10, 11ff.; 3:8ff.; 6:1—8:17; 12:1-3, 4ff.;
12:9—13:14; 15:14-16). His will for them is to live in righteousness
practiced in the humility that comes from setting their minds on the
things of the Spirit, recognizing that they are receivers of grace and
they must now become bearers of grace through the enabling of the
Holy Spirit—for their God is the God of all people, of Israel and of the
whole world (2:3-4, 5ff.; 3:4-26, 27ff.; 4:16; 5:1-11; 6:12-23; 8:1-30;
11:13-32; 12:1-6, 7ff., 9-21; 13:5-10; 14:1—15:3, 4-12).[48] Their
"strength" in recognizing God's grace toward themselves now com-
mends them to live, not in the position of arrogant strength that destroys the possibility of his grace being recognized by the "weak," but

---

[47]I discussed the gentile address of the letter in chapter 2 above.

[48]Paul has throughout the letter appealed to a shared value system embodied in
teaching that the audience has formerly received and honored, to which Paul calls
them to a renewed commitment in a heightened adherence. W. Wuellner, "Paul's
Rhetoric of Argumentation in Romans"; and Fraikin, "Rhetorical Function," pp.
91–93, 94ff., discuss this characteristic as evidence that Romans is of the epideictic genre (both drawing from C. Perelman and L. Olbrechts-Tyteca, *The New
Rhetoric*). This is discussed in more detail below in chapter 4. The important point
here is to call attention to the various references to a body of teaching that the
Romans are called to intensify their adherence to: 6:17, "you became obedient
from the heart to *that form of teaching to which you were committed*"; 15:15, "But I have
written very boldly to you *on some points, so as to remind you again*, because of the
grace that was given me from God"; 16:17, "contrary *to the teaching which you
learned.*"

rather in the humble position of one who lives graciously toward the "weak" in order to win them to the grace of God demonstrated in Christ (14:14—15:3, 4ff.).

The Problem with Identifying the "Weak" as Christians

When we turn to the seemingly unquestioned assumption that the "weak in faith" were Christians, whatever else they may have been, we do not find the same kind of certainty we found with respect to the "strong," either in the logic of Paul's message or in the exegesis of the text itself.

What we find is that the behavior of those called "weak" is characterized by their *opinions* of how to practice their faith as differentiated from the behavior patterns of the "strong" (14:1-3, 4ff.), however, it is not their behavior or opinions that are regarded as "weak," but their *faith*. The "weak" are understood by Paul and by the "strong" to whom he writes to be of the opinion that they should eat "vegetables" rather than "meat" (vv. 2ff., 21), regard some "days" different from others (vv. 5ff.), and, perhaps, not drink "wine" (v. 21).49 They give "thanks to God" when they eat (v. 6), though the context is concerned with that which they choose not to eat. They are, apparently, judging the behavior demonstrated by the practices of the "strong" to be unacceptable to God (v. 3),50 and further, they may be reproaching (insulting) the "strong" (15:1-3 implied as a concern of the "strong" as they consider accommodating the opinions of the "weak"). Paul's concern

[49]This reference to wine and days could be a broader statement to balance Paul's point and not actually a specific practice; Jewett says the same in *Paul's Anthropological Terms*, p. 44 (quoting from Rauer), that "formal rhythmic reasons in parallel to the expression in 14:17" may govern the mention of wine in v. 21. Also note that the issues of food may have come up because of the gathering at certain days in which meals were eaten and thus the food/drink issues would have been linked to days in the mind of the "strong." Leon, *Jews*, p. 13, notes that Roman authors believed that Jews fasted on the Sabbath, again showing a tie between food and days. See the discussion above on synagogue practices and Christian gentile associations that were likely.

[50]Dunn, *Romans*, p. 802–3, emphasizes the severity of this judgment in Paul's use of κρίνω versus ἐξουθενέω to describe the kind of contempt that the "strong" have toward the non-eating practices of the "weak," hence concluding that this issue is of far greater consequence to the "weak" than the "strong," for they see the eating of the "strong" as an indication that the "strong" are living outside the covenant and thus condemned by God; they considered them unwelcomed by God.

is to alter the behavior of the "strong" so that the "weak" are not provoked to "speak evil of" (v. 16, blaspheme: βλασφημείσθω) that
which the "strong" regard as their "good thing" (v. 16, ἀγαθόν, the
blessings of God).51

Paul regarded the "weak" as "brethren," both to himself and to the
"strong" in Rome as we see in his comments to the "strong":

> But you, why do you judge your *brother*? Or you again, why do you
> regard your *brother* with contempt? (14:10)

> Therefore let us not judge one another any more, but rather
> determine this—not to put an obstacle or a stumbling block in a
> *brother's* way. (14:13)

> For if because of food your *brother* is hurt, you are no longer walking
> according to love. Do not destroy with your food him for whom Christ
> died. (14:15)

Paul clearly regarded the practices of the "weak" to be an indication of monotheistic faith toward God, for these practices were accepted by God (vv. 2-6, 7ff.).52 Even if the "strong" did not share Paul's
opinion of the acceptability of the opinions and practices of the
"weak" toward God, for they did not apparently respect their practices
as acts of faith (vv. 1-13; cf. v. 3, where they are instructed not to
"despise"53 the "weak"), Paul did; and he intended for the "strong" to
share his opinion of the valid faith in God demonstrated by the practices of the "weak," opposing their judgmentalism along lines strikingly similar to those found in his opening comments in 2:1-3, 4ff. and
his discussion of the branches broken off in chapter 11:54

51See 10:15. Dunn, *Romans*, p. 821, notes that this is covenant language:
"*agathon* is probably best understood in a broad sense, 'the good' which sums up
all God's covenanted blessings (righteousness, salvation—cf. 8:28; 10:15) and not
merely the freedom of the 'strong'."

52Thanksgiving is practice of giving thanks at meals, an act of faith toward God.
See Tomson, *Paul*, pp. 254–58, for a good discussion.

53Minear, *Obedience*, pp. 17–18, discusses "despise" as descriptive of prejudice
and religious condescension.

54Sanders, *Judaism: Practice*, pp. 192–95, discusses how truly inseparable these
practices were for a Jew in determining their identity; they were not trivial or sub-

for God has accepted him . . . and stand he will, for the Lord is able to make him stand . . . and he who eats not, for the Lord he does not eat, and gives thanks to God. . . . But you, why do you judge your brother? Or you again, why do you regard your brother with contempt? For we shall all stand before the judgment seat of God. (14:3-12)

Perhaps most importantly, Paul describes them as "weak in *faith*" (v. 1). Paul does not describe them as "weak in *opinion*"; in fact, he instructs the "strong" not to dispute the opinions of the "weak" in Rome (an instruction that has apparently been lost in Christian theology, even among those who make this very point).[55] The "weak" practice what they practice in "faith": they have faith in "God," the One God of historical Israel, and thus they are the "Lord's" (v. 8). And they are urged to continue in the practice of their opinions "fully convinced" in their own minds (vv. 5, 22-23) that what they do is unto the "Lord"; that is, they are to continue in the monotheistic *faith* that they have, *even if that faith is characterized as "weak."*

But the question still stands: Is the faith of the "weak" described as though it was necessarily Christian? The clues we have considered thus far certainly characterize the faith expressed in the opinions and practices of those called "weak" as thoroughly Jewish. They describe the kind of separatist behavior concomitant with the boundary markers of Jewish monotheism, particularly as Jews sought to preserve their faith in the gentile world of the Diaspora.[56] Indeed, there was a long tradition of standing apart from pagan practices and their associated

---

ject to possible modification. Note also that the similarity of Paul's language of acceptance and assurance here toward the "weak" parallels the assurance he gave to Christian gentiles as the elect (the "strong"?) in the face of some threatening circumstances and uncertainty earlier in chap. 8.

[55]Luther, *Romans*, p. 206, for example; I have described this phenomena as "Luther's trap."

[56]Dunn, *Jesus Paul*, pp. 4, 137–47; idem, "The New Perspective on Paul: Paul and the Law," p. 306, says, "A sociological perspective also helps us to see how the conviction of privileged election and the practice of covenantal nomism almost inevitably come to expression in focal points of distinctiveness, particular laws and especially ritual practices which reinforced the sense of distinctive identity and marked Israel off most clearly from the other nations. In this case three of Israel's laws gained particular prominence as being especially distinctive—circumcision, food laws, and Sabbath"; Sanders, *Paul, the Law*, p. 102; Meeks, *Urban*, pp. 36–37.

idolatry, no doubt sometimes perceived as strident arrogance (and no doubt, as it is likely to surface among all deeply religious people from time to time, as exactly that),[57] but generally following from a sincere commitment not only to God's righteous commandments but also to stand as a light to the nations.[58] The insistence of the "weak" on eating vegetables when with gentiles[59] (and in many cases even when not with gentiles) rather than pagan meat is consistent with a long tradition in Diaspora cities of Jews refusing to eat meat that might have been offered to idols, or been improperly butchered so that the animal strangled or suffocated on its own blood, or simply be the meat of unacceptable animals (such as pigs, the favorite meat in Rome).[60] The ostensible refusal to drink wine when with gentiles is also consistent with Jewish practice (it is still sometimes practiced), when it is feared that the wine was associated with libations (which would have been common if not always the case), and thus with idolatry.[61] And naturally, the concern to honor certain days (i.e., Sabbath and holy days) was essential in Jewish faith, and though it was cause for derision initially in

[57]This phenomenon is Paul's concern throughout Romans and is not a Jewish problem per se, for it is the problem of his Christian audience as well. In fact, the reason it is a Jewish problem, even as it is a problem for his audience, is wrapped up in the universal plight of humankind since Adam's sin to turn their genuine acts of righteousness done in response to God's grace into an occasion for arrogance toward the other instead of grace—a persistent problem for the very ones who are noble enough to care about doing righteousness. For development of this issue see J. Ellul, *The Ethics of Freedom*; idem, *the Politics of God and the Politics of Man*.

[58]Sanders, "Jewish Association," p. 182; see the discussion of eschatology in chapter 2 above.

[59]That the "strong" only know them to eat vegetables does not necessarily mean that this was the case, for they may have eaten meat when not in company of gentiles.

[60]Sanders, "Jewish Association," pp. 176–87; Dunn, *Jesus, Paul*, pp. 4, 137–47; Sanders, *Judaism: Practice*, pp. 213–17 and nn. 11 and 13 on p. 520; idem, *Jewish Law*, pp. 272–82; Wedderburn, *Reasons*, pp. 32–34; also note that this is not the same word as "idol-meat" in 1 Corinthians. Meat was rare and usually served the dual purpose of sacrifices as well as food (Sanders, *Jewish Law*, pp. 280–81). See discussion in chapter 2 above for more information on Jewish responses to eating among gentiles.

[61]Sanders, "Jewish Association," pp. 178–79; idem, *Jewish Law*, pp. 273–75, 277. See Jewett, *Paul's Anthropological Terms*, p. 44; and discussion in chapter 2 above. Was wine a real issue in Rome or just associated with balancing the concerns of food prohibition?

Rome and other Diaspora cities, it was ultimately adopted by pagan cultures.[62]

The judgment of the actions of the "strong" by the "weak" as unacceptable to God likewise would have characterized those of first-century Jews toward the claims of Christian gentiles to be equal coparticipants in Israel's blessings without submitting even to the minimum practice of Israel's laws and customs as they were practiced by all "righteous gentiles"—if, in fact, the "strong" were resisting the practice of the halakhah for "righteous gentiles" in matters of purity as well as ethical conduct—when in the company of Jews. Buried in Paul's parallel desire that the "weak" recognize that the "eating" faith of the "strong" is "accepted by God," and that the "strong" not so offend the "weak" with their "food" that they "destroy" them (14:20: "tear down the work of God"), is Paul's inescapable Jewish knowledge that the "weak," as Jews, would simply be unable to "accept" the faith of these Christian gentiles as legitimate (as faith in the One God) without some accommodation of monotheistic righteousness.[63]

Further, the thread woven through the many themes of this letter is primarily, if not exclusively, concerned with the tensions between Jews and gentiles: covenant boundaries (Law, circumcision, food, Sabbath), and how the One God had worked faithfully throughout history to bring salvation to both equally.[64] We need look no further than the central purity statement in 14:14 or the bracketing of chapters 9–11 and 15:7-13 to see that the context of this paraenesis concerns misunderstandings in the relationship between Jews and Christian gentiles, or to the texture of Paul's discussion of the Law, faith, righteous behavior, or any of the other themes preceding the direct discussion of Israel in chapters 9–11, where the context is always defined by the universality of the One God's actions, for example, in the phrase: "to the Jew first and also to the Greek."

---

[62]Sanders, "Jewish Association," p. 180; idem, *Jewish Law*, pp. 277; idem, *Judaism: Practice*, pp. 190–212; Whittaker, *Jews and Christians*, pp. 63–73; Josephus notes envy on the part of gentiles in *Against Apion* 2.40 (282).

[63]Jews did eat with gentiles; however, they insisted on certain accommodations in order to do so; see Sanders, *Jewish Law*, pp. 282–83; Sanders, "Jewish Association," pp. 170–88; see chapter 2 above. R. Eliezer in *m. Hul.* 2:7 sums up the view of Jews less inclined toward acceptance of gentiles: "For the unstated intention of a gentile is deemed to be for the purpose of idolatry."

[64]Wright, *Climax*, pp. 231–57.

We can be certain that those Paul referred to as "weak" were practicing Jews, with perhaps the caveat that this label may have been equally applied to "God-fearing" gentiles who were among them. And we can safely disregard the suggestion that they were gentiles clinging to idolatrous practices, for it fails to account not only for the references in this paraenesis to matters of purity, but also for the tensions present throughout the letter, even more so than the inconsistencies of the major positions Klein challenged.[65]

The "Weak" Were Definitely Jews, but Were They Christians?

From the descriptions we have reviewed thus far is it necessary to conclude that the "weak" were Christians? Everything that has been said about them, or for that matter, ostensibly to them, could be said along christological lines of Jews who did not believe in Jesus as the Christ;[66] or to put it anachronistically (and without the nuanced sensitivity Paul is developing herein), to *non-Christian* Jews. Consider the following points.

1. The statements that appear directed to the "weak" not to judge the "strong" as though their practices were unacceptable to God (14.3–8) could be said to non-Christian Jews by Paul, a representative still attending, deeply concerned with, and welcome to address the

[65]Even those like Käsemann, *Romans*, p. 368, who cite Rauer decide against the probability because Paul would not have accommodated the pagan practices that would follow from this position, and he also sees the problem of the letter's context, particularly as this passage is followed by 15:8ff., where Jew/gentile is clearly at issue. Even though Jewett in *Paul's Anthropological Terms*, pp. 41–45, points to Rauer as valuable, he dismisses this position and calls for a reevaluation that accounts also for "the centrality of the circumcision and the law questions in Romans" and suggests that, in view of 15:7 and the similarity with the call to accept of 14:1ff. that "he goes on to show that Christ became the servant to the circumcised so that the promises to the Gentiles might be fulfilled. This implies that the 'Weak' and the 'Strong' may be identified with the circumcised on the one hand and the Gentiles on the other."

[66]Does this not answer Jewett's quandary perfectly? He notes that the "weak" are the circumcised and the "strong" are the gentiles (*Paul's Anthropological Terms*, p. 45) and then argues several points that lead him to conclude "that the 'Weak' in Rome were probably a small group of Jewish Christians who avoided meat out of a radicalized nomism which issued in the desire to avoid all contact with idolatry," but then realizes that this "cannot provide a completely satisfactory account for all of the evidence." But if he drops the assumption that they are Christian Jews, and concludes they are non-Christian Jews, his argument is strengthened.

synagogue.[67] And that is precisely how non-Christian Jews would have regarded the claims of the "strong"[68] if they maintained that as gentiles they were equal coparticipants with the Jews in the blessings of God without maintaining even the minimal requirements of Jewish Law and customs that gentiles had always practiced when attaching themselves to the God of Israel and, in the Diaspora, to the synagogue.[69] Non-Christian Jews would have indeed been provoked to question, and even to "blaspheme" (v. 16), the alleged "God" of these gentiles' claims.[70]

[67]Luke in Acts observes it was Paul's "custom" to attend synagogue immediately upon arrival in a city, and throughout Luke shows Paul involved with Jews, synagogues, and Jerusalem. Sanders, *Paul, the Law*, p. 192, says Paul attended synagogue and appeals to Paul's suffering at the hands of synagogue leaders as proof, 2 Cor. 11:24; McKnight, *Light*, p. 114, notes: "We can safely infer from Acts, the practice of Paul, and the evidence found in Jewish literature that the synagogue often functioned as a place for public address and for public propagation of a variety of ideas within Judaism. Paul, then, seemed to have been exploiting a normal practice in making the synagogue a platform for expounding messianic Judaism. . . . From Paul's practice we can infer that early Christians took advantage of what may have been a custom: the invitation of a Jewish visitor to address a congregation." Wiefel, "The Jewish Community," p. 92, notes that Christians were alongside non-Christian Jews in synagogues. Ellis, *Pauline Theology*, pp. 132–35, notes that Paul preached in synagogues, and only after Nero's persecutions of 65–68 c.e. do Roman authorities note distinction between Jews and Christians. Earlier they viewed churches as Jewish factions. On p. 135 Ellis notes that Paul claimed "rights of association enjoyed by the local synagogues" for his congregations. Hays, *Echoes*, p. 171, observes: "Paul stands, however presumptuous it may be for him to do so, directly in Israel's prophetic tradition." See M. Barth, "A Good Jew," pp. 8–11, 18, on Paul's use of Scripture following Diaspora Judaism, along with his style of missions and exegesis from synagogues. See fuller discussion above in chapter 2.

[68]Minear, *Obedience*, p. 20, sees this tension too: "both were assuming a pre-conversion idea of sin" (cf. p. 32).

[69]Tomson, *Paul*, pp. 46–47. Gentiles were welcome to the synagogue, provided they were willing to observe the requirements of gentile righteousness, essential decorum of respect for the God of Israel and the Law of Israel governing the boundaries of righteousness. I have discussed these requirements elsewhere as some form of what was later referred to as the Noahide Commandments (see chapters 2 and 4 herein).

[70]Wedderburn, *Reasons*, p. 116, commenting on the charge leveled against Paul, unjustly as Paul sees it in his discussion in 3:1-8, and citing Sanders in *Paul, the Law*, p. 208, says himself on p. 116: "'two pillars common to all forms of Judaism: the election of Israel and faithfulness to the Mosaic law'; it voices the criticisms that this denial would provoke amongst Jews and Jewish Christians disposed to continue to observe the Jewish Law; this twofold denial would seem to involve a

Indeed, if we assume that the early Christian gentiles in Rome associated with the synagogue, then we can immediately identify the response of the "weak" as the Jewish response to Christian gentile claims if they included resistance to the established halakhah for gentiles associating with the synagogue, that is, if they included the assertion that they need not respect the Noahide Commandments (in whatever exact format they may have taken at this time in Rome).[71] I will come back to this issue later, but here it is important to note that the "weak" need not be Christian Jews to have the kind of association Paul understands to be taking place in Rome between Christian gentiles and Jews.

The statements that appear to be directed to the "weak" may have been provided to frame Paul's weighty instructions to the "strong." They were only at the beginning (not to judge with contempt the one who eats: 14:3), and possibly at the close (to welcome gentiles who glorify God for his mercy: 15:7-9) of Paul's instructions that are otherwise clearly intended to change the opinions and practices of the "strong." I will come back to this point later when discussing Paul's instructions.

2. Paul regards non-Christian Jews as his "brethren" throughout this letter.[72] One of the most direct examples is 9:3-5, where he explains his pathos for Jews who do not yet believe in Jesus as the Christ of Israel:

> For I could wish that I myself were accursed, separated from Christ
> for the sake of my brethren, my kinsmen according to the flesh, who
> are Israelites, to whom belongs the adoption as sons and the glory and
> the covenants and the giving of the Law and the temple service and
> the promises, whose are the fathers, and from whom is the Christ
> according to the flesh, who is over all, God blessed forever. Amen.

---

twofold unrighteousness, that of an unfaithful God and that of those encouraged to flout the paths of righteousness laid down in the Mosaic Law."

[71]This association and the rules of behavior developed as halakhah to govern gentile "God-fearers" associating with the synagogue were far more influential in early Christian practice than is usually granted. The conservative nature of the faith and practices of early Roman Christianity, often assumed to be the result of the makeup of the congregation as largely Jewish (e.g., Brown and Meier, *Antioch and Rome*), fails to recognize this dynamic. Whether the early Christians in Rome were Jewish or not they would have been characterized by certain Jewish practices through their association with the synagogue. See discussion above in chapter 2.

[72]M. Barth, "A Good Jew," p. 11, recognizes the same: "He thus was more a brother than an adversary of pious Jews."

But does Paul regard non-Christian Jews as "brethren" to the "strong" in Rome who consist primarily of Christian gentiles? Certainly. Conceptually, Paul did not see faith in Jesus Christ as a break with Israel and his fellow Jews of the Diaspora. He certainly had not left the Jewish faith. Jews were the historical community of the One God, whether they believed in Jesus as the Christ or not. Thus to be a Christian, whether Jew (which would be natural to Paul) or gentile (which was a wonderful new reality that had always been part of Israel's eschatological expectation),[73] would have immediately made one a "brother" to all Jews, whether they were Christians or not.[74] We see this through the illustrations of the dough and olive tree of chapter 11, where Paul clarifies just how necessarily the faith of Christian gentiles is inextricably linked with historical Israel. And we see it dramatically in Paul's summary statements of 15:7-13, where he quotes from various Scriptures to demonstrate that the eschatological salvation of the gentiles, and thus naturally of Israel, has come—for the gentiles are now praising God in the midst of the congregation of the Jews as they praise God:

> Therefore I will give praise to thee among the Gentiles,
> And I will sing to Thy name.
>
> Rejoice, O Gentiles, with His people.
>
> Praise the Lord all you Gentiles,
> And let all the peoples praise Him.
>
> There shall come the root of Jesse,
> And He who arises to rule over the Gentiles,
> In Him shall the Gentiles hope.

The following list features some of the many examples of Paul's

---

[73]Sanders, *Judaism: Practice*, pp. 289–90, 291ff., explains hopes for reestablishment of the twelve tribes, subjugation or conversion of gentiles, new temple, purity, righteousness in worship and morals; see also pp. 291–92, 295, on gentile issues. See chapter 2 above.

[74]Meeks, *Urban*, p. 87, notes that the common use among Christians was probably taken from Jewish usage of the term, but also notes that it was used in Rome and other areas of Roman influence for members of pagan clubs and associations, although he does not suggest that it would have been used between Christian gentiles and non-Christian Jews.

parallel language in Romans when speaking of Christians, whether Jews or gentiles, and non-Christian Jews:

Christians		*Non-Christian Jews*	
brethren	1:13; 8:29[75]	brethren	9:3
adoption as sons	8:15	adoption as sons	9:4
children of God	8:16-17	children of God	9:8
the glory	8:18	the glory	9:4
Abraham as father	4:10-17	Abraham as father	4:10-17
seed of Abraham	9:7-8; 4:13-18	seed of Abraham	9:7-8; 11:1
beloved of God	1:7	beloved (of God)	11:28
called	9:24; 8:28; 1:16	called	9:7, 24; 11:29
elect	8:28, 33	elect	9:11
foreknew	8:29	foreknew	11:2

The list could go on to include other clear parallels like those given "the service" in 9:4 and those called to "service" in 12:1, just as Paul is engaged in "service" in 1:9;[76] and when speaking of election: "us, whom He also called, not from among Jews only, but also from among Gentiles" (9:24); and even the continuity of relationship to the Law[77] and covenant. In fact, one should note that many of the phrases Paul uses in chapter 8 to describe the new status in Christ of those who believe, he turns around and ascribes immediately in chapter 9 to Jews who do not believe in Christ, certainly no mere coincidence. Clearly

[75]Paul continually addressed his audience as "brethren"; see 7:1, 4; 8:12; 10:1; 11:25; 12:1; 15:14, 15, 30. What is notable in selecting 8:29 juxtaposed with 9:3 is the concept of historical lineage: Jesus is "a descendant of David according to the flesh" in 1:3; the Christian gentiles are now related to Jesus "the first-born among many brethren" in 8:29; the non-Christian Jews are "my brethren, my kinsmen according to the flesh" in 9:3. All are related to the Christ, even if they do not yet acknowledge Jesus as the Christ. Jervell, *Luke*, pp. 50–51, notes that Luke in Acts refers continually to non-Christian Jews as brethren in the same manner I am tracing here in Romans: "The consciousness of being Israel and the connection with the only Israel that Luke knows are reflected in Luke's use of the address *andres adelphoi*. . . . The designation "brothers" is more than a polite address and can, as the cited passages demonstrate, be applied only to Israelites. Thereby the solidarity and inner connection in the people of God is expressed. To be a brother means to belong to the family of Abraham, to share in the promises. *Adelphos* means Israelite (Acts 1:16; 3:12, 17; 7:23, 25 f.; 13:26)."

[76]"Service" (*latreia*) is a cultic term, and Paul uses it this way in his descriptions. See Deut. 10:12-15 for the background of this concept.

[77]This is lost in Christian theology, but Paul's recognition in 9:4 of the gift of the Law is continuous with his comments throughout Romans (3:1-2; 7:12-14) and

Paul would have called Christian gentiles "brethren" to non-Christian Jews and vice versa without any further consideration—for the One God of the nations was none other than the One God of historical Israel.

3. Paul regarded the practices of non-Christian Jews as the result of faith, and therefore unquestionably acceptable to God. He would naturally have urged the same respect from the "strong" in Rome: "Now accept the one who is weak in faith, but not for the purpose of passing judgment on his opinions" (14:1). This deep respect runs throughout the entire context of Paul's instruction, not only in chapters 14–15, but it is the very point of chapters 9–11. "For I bear them witness that *they have a zeal for God*" is often missed in the haste to get to "but not in accordance with knowledge" (10:2).

The practices in question are Jewish practices (dietary customs and calendrical observances) that predate the coming of Jesus Christ, and that Paul tells the "strong" to respect because they are done "for the Lord" and "to God," and are accepted by "the Lord" and by "God," for those who do them "are the Lord's" (vv. 3-8). Interestingly, in the first eight verses mention of Christ is completely absent; the focus is on "God," and on "the Lord"—phrases that are inclusive of non-Christian Jewish faith. Also, there is an implicit recognition that the "weak" and the "strong" regard each other as serving different "masters" (v. 4) that Paul challenges in making his point that they are wrong, for both are serving, and therefore accepted by, the same Lord.[78]

Throughout this paraenesis, particularly in the opening verses of 14:1-12, and the closing verses of 15:5-12, the theme Paul develops expounds the essence of the Shema ("Hear, O Israel! The Lord is our God, the Lord is one")[79] adapted to the conflicting judgments of the "weak" and the "strong" against each other. The One God of Israel is the One God of the nations. He is the One God: the God of the

---

should be seen in the light of the Law's continuity now represented in Christ as its true "aim" in 10:4ff., and that which formerly separated Jew and gentile is now through faith no longer a separator but a symbol of brotherhood as fulfilled in Christ (3:19-31; 4:1-25). See E. Epp, "Jewish-Gentile Continuity in Paul," pp. 87–90, for another view that also links the Law and faith in this same kind of continuity, although somewhat differently.

[78]See Rom. 10:12: "For there is no distinction between Jew and Greek; for the same Lord is Lord of all."

[79]The Shema is the central declaration of Judaism's faith in the One God. See chapter 4 below for discussion of the apostolic decree.

"weak" and the God of the "strong." The denial by one group of the
rights of the other is a denial of God's righteousness, of God's right to
judge, of God's right to make righteous ("and stand he will, for the
Lord is able to make him stand"; 14:4). This theme of radical commitment to monotheism has been woven throughout the letter as the
reason the readers must refrain from judging and focus instead on
serving—God is able to handle the judging as has been demonstrated
powerfully in his reconciling work in Christ (3:21-30; Shema seen in
theme of judging: 2:1-29; 9:10-24, 25ff., 9:30—10:4, 5ff., 8-13; 11:30—
12:3, 4ff.; 14:3-13; 15:1-12). To deny the faith of the other is to deny
the heart of the Shema:

> For not one of us lives for himself, and not one of us dies for himself;
> for if we live, we live for the Lord, or if we die, we die for the Lord;
> therefore whether we live or die, we are the Lord's. (14:7-8)

4. There are other interesting notes, some of which I will mention
later, that further demonstrate the point. For example, while Paul
refers to the "weak" as "brethren" frequently, he also refers to them
as the "neighbor" of the "strong" in Rome (15:2). This odd juxtaposition of labels used for outsiders ("neighbor") with that affectionately
reserved for insiders ("brother" and the other phrases noted earlier)
suggests a subtle tension in the definition of the "weak" that commentaries have until now failed to resolve. Further, this same tension
causes many seemingly forced outlines as commentators seek to follow the intentions of Paul's instructions throughout the entire paraenesis of 12:1—15:13.[80] These tensions are easily resolved by recognizing
that the "weak" are the same non-Christian Jews whom Paul has been
defending throughout the entire letter to the "strong" as those to
whom the gospel is given first, although not exclusively. The "strong"
are ready to dismiss these non-Christian Jews contemptuously as "enemies" of the gospel; however, Paul seeks to explain that they are not
enemies as it may appear—they are God's "beloved" (11:28), and even
their current suffering is on behalf of the "strong" (11:11, 30). Paul expects the "strong" to begin to understand their responsibility to serve
those who may appear to be antagonistic "neighbors" as their beloved
"brethren." They are to welcome the "weak" (14:1) and unite with
them in glorifying God (15:5-6), "for Christ has become a servant to

[80]For example, the strained efforts of W. Munro in *Authority in Paul and Peter*,
pp. 56–67.

the circumcision on behalf of the truth of God to confirm the promises given to the fathers" (15:7-8).

Likewise, it is often noted that Paul refrains from calling his audience the *ekklēsia*. If he was speaking exclusively to Christians, and about Christians, in chapter 14, he surely would have appealed to the illustration of the church in verses 16-17, but he did not. He instead spoke of the "kingdom of God." Was the kingdom of God a broad enough concept that Paul could easily incorporate both non-Christian Jews who believe in the God of Israel, but not in Jesus as the Christ of Israel, and Jews and gentiles who did believe in Jesus as the Christ? Is it possible that this is another indication that Paul is addressing a situation in Rome that predates the separation of the church from the synagogue as a distinct entity?

Are the "Weak" Deficient in Their Faith Because They Fail to Realize the Full Measure of Their Freedom in Christ from the Practices of the Law?

The most telling problem with assuming that the "weak" were in fact Christians is the implicit theological double standard buried in this hermeneutical presupposition, that is, the assumed superiority that surfaces in the patronizing judgmentalism of Luther's trap toward Jews and the practice of Judaism.[81]

1. To assume that the "weak" were Christian Jews who were unwilling or unable to give up the practice of the Law and Jewish customs because they were *deficient in their faith*, in that they "fail to trust God completely and without qualification,"[82] or further: "In this case the weakness is trust in God *plus* dietary and festival laws, trust in God *dependent* on observance of such practices, a trust in God which *leans on the crutches* of particular customs and *not* on God alone, *as though* they were an integral part of that trust,"[83] is indeed to fall into *Luther's trap*. Is this not the very nature of the Christian gentile presumptuousness that Paul sought to correct in this letter? Does this not totally fail to appreciate what the Law meant to Paul and any other Jew, whether they be believers in Christ or not? For it has as its underlying assumption the very arrogance that he instructed the "strong" to avoid, that is, they are to recognize that the "weak" do what they do in "faith" and

---

[81]This may be the main reason that the assumptions being questioned here have not been questioned in the past, even when they force contradictions and compromising conclusions.

[82]Dunn, *Romans*, p. 798.

[83]Ibid. (emphasis added).

"thanksgiving" to the One Lord, and because it is acceptable to God, it ought to be properly respected by the "strong." Their not eating is emphatically *not* to be regarded condescendingly as a sign of deficient faith. God "accepts" it and so should the "strong."

2. This position is guilty of an incipient contradiction in that it recognizes that gentiles become Christians (they may enter and conduct themselves as the people of God) without the need to "judaize," to become Jews (the point of the Jerusalem Council: Acts 15); however, it maintains that when Jews become Christians, they must, or at least it is maintained that it was Paul's position that they should, become like gentiles, "gentilize" as it were, in that they are expected to give up the very practices that make them Jews: circumcision, keeping the Law, observing Jewish customs—or at least they are to no longer invest these actions with any real meaning.[84] Does believing in the "King of the Jews" make it necessary, or even desirable, for one to live like a gentile? Does this not compromise the monotheistic issue, not to mention the validity of the Law, at the center of Paul's argument in

[84]There are certainly those who observe (including Dunn [e.g., *Romans*, pp. 810-12; several additional citations are noted in chapter 7 below]), though they often question whether Paul complied, that the early Christian Jews did not give up their Jewish practices, particularly in Palestine. For example, Sanders, *Judaism: Practice*, p. 195, observes: "Even ancient Christians did not criticize non-Christian Jews for engaging in temple worship, but rather for not accepting the death of Christ as the true atoning sacrifice." Gaston, *Paul*, p. 79, provides a good example: "If Paul was an apostate, did he think that other Jewish Christians should follow his example? In the light of the mutual recognition of two apostolates in Gal 2:7-9, I would assume not. Most interpreters believe that the Jerusalem church continued to keep the commandments and that Paul respected this . . . for Jewish Christians Christ probably replaced the temple as the locus of atonement but not Sinai as the locus of election. . . . The logic of Paul's theology is such as to make Jewish Christianity only a transitional period. In terms of what he does say, however, Paul speaks of apostasy only with respect to himself." On pp. 80–82 Gaston outlines some of the issues in the current context of this discussion; on pp. 135ff. he discusses further. However, I suggest that if Paul taught the generally maintained Christian position that the doing of the Law and Jewish practice were meaningless for Jews and that it would be more desirable for Christian Jews to act like gentiles, then Christianity is really only a gentile faith and might be rightly called a "gentilizing" faith, certainly an inherent compromise of monotheism. Is not the One God of the gentiles also the One God of Israel in whom those who believe in Christ Jesus now become one people, equal in status, although still both distinguished as Jews and gentiles (the central point of Gal. 3:27-29)?

Romans 3:29-31, albeit from the opposite side?[85] This assumption is pervasive in spite of the fact that the text nowhere suggests that the "weak" should act like the "strong," but rather it emphatically asserts the very opposite: the "strong" should change their *own* behavior and act like the "weak."

3. This juxtaposition can be maintained, in the current context of the discussion, only if Paul had actually abandoned, and taught other Christian Jews to abandon, the practice of Jewish customs—a questionable assumption indeed, in the light of Paul's own arguments in this very letter, not to mention in the light of Acts.[86] For when he asked rhetorically of the Jewish advantage, he answered: "they were entrusted with the oracles of God" (Rom. 3:3); and if "justification by faith apart from the works of the Law" (3:28) for both Jew and gentile nullified (made obsolete) the Law, he answered emphatically, "May it *never* be!" (3:31), for on the contrary "we establish the Law" (3:31); and if the Law, which "is holy, and the commandment is holy and righteous and good" (7:12), had become a cause of death, he answered again, "May it never be!" (7:13). Again, in 9:6, "But it is not as though the word of God has failed." And in 11:28-29, where Paul, in wrapping up his discussion of the anomaly of the situation in Rome where many Jews are not yet joining with the Christian gentiles he is addressing in believing that Jesus is the Christ, he explains their continued relationship with God thus: "from the standpoint of God's choice they are beloved for the sake of the fathers; for the gifts and calling of God are *irrevocable*."

4. To read Romans with its direction dictated by the assumption that Paul did not regard practice of the Law and Jewish custom as viable displays of faith and taught the same, based on 14:14a as the

---

[85]The reverse of Paul's argument, which would have been inscrutable to Paul, would read (I have italicized the words I have reversed to make my point): "Or is God the God of *gentiles* only? Is He not the God of *Jews* also? No, only of *Jews* who become gentiles, since indeed God who will justify the *uncircumcised* by faith and the *circumcised* through faith is one. Do we then *establish* the Law through faith? May it never be! On the contrary, we *nullify* the Law."

[86]See Acts 15; 16:1-3; 21:17-26, 27ff., and the discussion of Gal. 2 in appendix 1. Cf. Campbell, *Intercultural Context*, pp. 98–116, for an excellent discussion of the logical failure of New Testament scholars in the past on this point; see also M. Barth, "A Good Jew," pp. 21–22; Jervell, *Luke*; idem, "Retrospect"; I discuss this more fully in chapters 4 and 5 below.

guiding center of Paul's intention to compromise merely for the sake of unity in the congregation of Christians, fails to make sense of Paul's instructions in this paraenesis. Paul does identify with the "strong" in seeing that the barrier between clean and unclean has been broken down in Christ, but this is not the point he pursues as the guiding principle. If it was, the instruction to the "strong" and the "weak" would be much different. It would be about changing the opinions and behavior of the "weak," but that is precisely what he does not do, and further, it is precisely what he does not permit. He is saying that the issue of opinions pales when the context is winning the "weak" to faith in Christ. This is stated in the same context as his arguments elsewhere that in Christ there is neither Jew nor Greek, slave nor free, male nor female (Gal. 3:27-29). Certainly there still are both Jews and gentiles, slaves and free, males and females, and they are in fact different, but in Christ they are now equal and united with a higher priority toward each other than their differences dictated in the past. The "strong" are to live in view of a new age in which the pre-Christian barriers no longer dictate their response to the "weak" (they are not by their behavior to contradict the servanthood of the very one in whom they have now come to believe: 14:14bff.; 15:1-3). The "strong" are to change their *own* "opinions" and "behavior"—*not those of the "weak."*

Is the "Faith" of the "Weak" Described as Though It Were Necessarily Christian?

They have faith in God, to be sure, but do they have faith in Jesus as the Christ? The "strong" certainly do. For Paul appeals to the "strong" to follow the example of Christ by adopting behavior that accommodates the opinions of the "weak" (14:15, see also vv. 13, 20-21; 15:1-3).

Paul did not, however, ask the same of the "weak" toward the strong. The "weak" had faith in the same God, but were not Christians—they were Jews who practiced the historical faith of Israel: faith in God, the One Lord of all humankind, even if not faith in Jesus as the Christ, or in the gentile claims of coparticipation in Israel's blessings ("good things"). No, the "weak" were not Christians—*the "weak" were non-Christian Jews.*

This observation opens the door to a whole new set of hermeneutical considerations. The label "weak" is dramatically changed from a pejorative critique of the "opinions" and "behavior" of Christian Jews who continued to observe the Law because of their alleged failure to fully trust God, and all the rest of the explicit as well as implicit "judgments" of Jewish opinions that characterize Luther's trap. Instead, "weak" takes on a whole new life. It denotes *respect* for the non-Christian Jews' practice of the Law from genuine faith. The critique is not of weak or strong opinions or practices. It is not as though Jews were to become like gentiles if they were to be "strong" Christians. In other words, the issue is not Christian freedom from the Law. Rather, the implicit critique is of *faith* that fails to recognize that Jesus is the Christ, the Lord of Israel, and also the Savior of the world. For Paul, their faith is not deficient because it includes the practice of the Law and Jewish customs; it is deficient in that it is just not yet *able* to recognize that the promises have been fulfilled in Christ. But I am getting ahead of my argument. There is much exegetical work to be done before such summarizing is appropriate.

THE IDENTITY OF THE "WEAK" AND THE "STRONG" IN ROMANS

The Background for Defining Paul's Use of the Labels "Weak" and "Strong"

"The one who is weak in faith" whom Paul directed his audience in Rome to "accept[87] . . . but not for the purpose of passing judgment on his opinions" (14:1) so far into his letter must have been easily identifiable for his readers (even if they are not so easily recognized by those of us seeking to understand his message now),[88] for Paul did not find it necessary to explain who the "weak in faith" were. He introduced them suddenly, without definition, except with respect to the "measure of faith" (12:3) that they were regarded by both Paul and his audience to have: "weak" ("unable," or "not strong": ἀδυνάτων, 15:1), because they are "without strength" ("weak," or "ill": ἀσθενήματα, 15:1; ἀσθενοῦντα, 14:1; ἀσθενῶν, 14:2); in contrast to the faith Paul and his audience have: "strong" ("able": δυνατοὶ, 15:1). They must have been easily recognizable and of considerable concern to Paul, for they are central to the instructions of the entire paraenesis of chapters

---

[87]"Accept" (προσλαμβάνεσθε) implies acceptance in a home or congregation (synagogue or church, for example) or defined circle of acquaintances or friends, and it carries the sense of eating together (see, e.g., Acts 27:34).

[88]E.g., Jewett, *Paul's Anthropological Terms*, p. 3; Wedderburn *Reasons*, p. 31.

12–15, and therefore to the message of the entire letter.[89] Yet it is unlikely that either group referred to themselves or the other with these
labels in any formal way, particularly so in the case of the weak regarding themselves. Who are the "weak in faith," and how had Paul
prepared his audience to recognize them so readily without further
clarification at this point in his letter? Why are they so important to
Paul and yet, seemingly, held in such low esteem by those he addressed as "strong"? Further, what was Paul's intention toward the
"weak" and the "strong" in his instructions?

"Weak" is a very informative term, particularly when applied to
faith ("the one who is weak in faith," 14:1), and its appearance in chapter 14 was not so sudden when we look closely into its root meaning
and its application in the imagery Paul had already developed
throughout Romans. "Weakness" (ἀσθένον) is the opposite of
strength (σθένος), and carries the meaning of "powerless," "lacking
strength," and is related to "sickness" and "disease." It is the word
chosen in the Septuagint to describe Leah's eyes as "weak" (Gen.
29:17) and Samson's becoming "weak" like other men if his hair was
cut (Judg. 16:7, 11, 17).

In a manner quite different from the ordinary Greek usage for natural weakness, ἀσθενέω and ἀσθένεια developed a special character
in the prophetic literature of the Septuagint with respect to the divine
judgment that would fall upon those who rebelled against God:
ἀσθενέω was seldom used to translate the Hebrew verbs רפה (*rapa*:
"to be weak") or חלה (*ḥala*: "to be sick"), but instead was frequently
used to translate verbal forms of the root כשל (*kashal*: "to stumble,"
"to stagger"), and ἀσθένεια for the corresponding noun מכשול (*mik-
shol*: "hindrance," "stumbling block").[90] For example, in the Septuagint Jeremiah 6:21 contains both uses:

Behold, I am laying *stumbling blocks* [ἀσθένειαν] before this people.
And they will *stumble* [ἀσθενήσουσιν] against them.

Other examples include the prophetic literature of Jeremiah 18:15,
23, and especially important for Romans, Hosea 4:5; 5:5; 14:1, 9; and

[89]Wright, *Climax*, p. 251.
[90]H.-G. Link, in *New International Dictionary of the New Testament Theology*, ed.
C. Brown, 3.994; M. Barre, "Paul as 'Eschatological Person': A New Look at 2 Cor.
11:29," p. 510; Stälin, *TDNT* 1.490; D. Black, *Paul, Apostle of Weakness: Astheneia and
Its Cognates in the Pauline Literature*, pp. 13–15.

the Psalms and wisdom literature of Psalms 9:3; 27(26):2; 107(106):12; Daniel 11:14, 19, 33-35.[91]

We find the Hebrew equivalent of ἀσθενέω used in this same way in the Qumran literature, for example:

> The scorn of my enemies shall become a crown of glory,
> And my *stumbling* [kshlwn] (shall change) into everlasting *might*
> [gbwrh]. (1QH 9:25-26)[92]

> [You will bring healing to] my wound,
> And marvelous *might* (gbwrh) in place of my *stumbling* (mkshwl).
> (1QH 9:27)[93]

It should be noted that, in addition to כשל (*kshl*) meaning "stumbling," it is used in the context of the Hebrew גבר (*gbr*), which carries the same meaning as δύναμις: "might" or "strength."[94] These two phrases are juxtaposed: "weak" כשל (*kshl*) rendered "stumbling," and גבר (*gbr*) rendered "strength" in the same manner Paul contrasted them in Romans (and Corinthians).[95] In fact, Barre demonstrates that ἀσθένεια carries with it a sense of "persecution" at the hands of humans as contrasted with God's strength, his power to act in "grace" on behalf of the persecuted, a nuance that perhaps helps explain the edge to Paul's use of the two phrases in Romans.[96]

This association of *weakness* with *stumbling* parallels the imagery

---

[91]Dan. 11:33-35: "And those who have insight among the people will give understanding to the many; yet they will fall [*asthenousin*] by word and by flame, by captivity and by plunder, for many days. Now when they fall [*asthenesai*] they will be granted a little help, and many will join with them in hypocrisy. And some of those who have insight will fall [*asthenousin*], in order to refine [*pyrosai*], purge, and make them pure, until the end time; because it is still to come at the appointed time."

[92]From Barre's translation in "Qumran and the 'Weakness' of Paul," p. 218.

[93]Ibid.

[94]Ibid., pp. 218–19, cites Judg. 5:31; 8:21; 2 Kgs. 18:20; 1 Chr. 29:11 as examples.

[95]Tomson, *Paul*, pp. 194ff., 242, notes a similar sense in 1 Cor. 8 and suggests rendering "weak" as "delicate" in dietary matters.

[96]Barre, "Qumran," pp. 216–27; see also idem, "Paul," pp. 509–19. Also the link of stumbling with offense (*skandalon*) is important because *skandalo* means "trap" and is a well-established technical term in eschatological expectations of trials from God as the primary cause and humans as the secondary cause (Barre, "Paul," p. 514). Barre quotes Ps. 139 (140):4-5 and 65(66):10-11 and shows the presence of

Paul sketches throughout this paraenesis of chapters 12–15. Perhaps more importantly, it draws naturally from the overall theme of chapters 9–11, where Paul uses the same imagery to explain the anomalous current state of apparent Jewish unbelief (their "hardening" in 11:25)[97] to the audience in Rome.[98]

Paul's use of this illustration with "obstacle" and "stumbling block" parallels the usage in the prophets and is developed in the context, just as it was for the prophets, of the certainty of God's judgment upon those who are hardened (they cannot see!) God's righteousness graciously extended toward themselves until, if they do not respond to his patient kindness, they are confronted with God's righteous judgment. Note the similarity of language with Paul's earlier explanation of the phenomenon of Jewish unbelief in 9:32-33 (developed from Isa. 8:14; 28:16; see also Hos. 4:5; 5:5; 14:1, 9):

> They *stumbled* over the stumbling stone, just as it is written,
> "Behold, I lay in Zion a stone of *stumbling* and a rock of *offense*,
> and he who believes in Him will not be disappointed."

Paul has just labored to explain in chapters 9–11 how this current anomaly of Jewish unbelief has come to pass in view of the merciful, yet inscrutable, pattern of God's working through the "hardening" of part of Israel in order to bring salvation to the gentiles (11:11: "But by their transgression salvation has come to the Gentiles"; 11:12: "Now if their transgression be riches for the world and their failure be riches for

---

this language in Qumran literature as well with the same meaning (entire article, esp. pp. 511–12, 515–17), so that we can speak of a sense of Paul's awareness that the current stumbling was part of God's inscrutable plan and that the "strong" must be careful to avoid becoming instruments of wrath instead of mercy.

[97] "Hardening" (πώρωσις) is one of a group of biblical words derived from πώρος, which was a medical term for the hardened swelling of a bone after it had been broken, resulting in a callus that is dull and insensitive. See chapter 5 for discussion.

[98] What I am saying is that Paul does not break from this primary concern for how faith is defined or of his concern for the faith of Israel as he passed into the "Therefore" of 12:1 and the paraenesis that follows. Munck, *Christ and Israel*, p. 78, summarizing 9:30—10:21, says: "The Jew's disobedience and unbelief are mentioned, but without emphasis—merely as a fact. The core of the passage is God's way of salvation by faith, and His constant effort to make Israel hear and follow that way." And on chap. 11 he says: "This fundamental and central section, then, serves to explain the way of salvation opened by God in Christ—justification by faith—and to make it clear that God never tires of issuing the call to salvation, a call that includes Israel."

the Gentiles"; 11:25: "until the fulness of the Gentiles has come in"). Paul explains that somehow, mysteriously, the current "stumbling" of Israel is being used by God, not only vicariously so that God's mercy can be extended to the gentiles, but also so that it will result in Israel's salvation (11:11: "to make them jealous"; 11:12: "how much more will their fulfillment be!"; 11:26: "and thus all Israel will be saved").[99]

The "Weak" of 14:1—15:12 as the "Stumbling" of 9:30-33

The immediate context of chapter 14 contains several direct references to this same imagery and tension. The "strong" are urged, in view of God's certain eventual judgment, no longer to judge the "weak" with whom they have a difference of opinion concerning the keeping of the Law and Jewish customs: "but rather determine this— not to put an *obstacle* or a *stumbling block* in a brother's way" (14:13). We have already considered how this instruction is linked with 9:33 for Paul's use of the synonymous terms "obstacle" (προσκόμματος) and "stumbling block" (σκανδάλον) in the context of "weak" and "strong" in the same manner that they were used in the Septuagint, and in the Qumran literature, for their Hebrew equivalents.[100] But unlike 9:33, where God allows the stumbling, here the concern is that the "strong" avoid the avoidable, that is, they are to change their behavior so that their mighty actions do not cause the "stumbling" of their "brother" (the sense that we saw illustrated in 1QH 9:25-27).[101]

---

[99]Note that "hardening" refers to a process to bring about eventual salvation, not to a punishment. See Gaston, *Paul*, pp. 142–43; Wright, *Climax*, p. 247; Munck, *Christ and Israel*, p. 91.

[100]Both are connected with idolatry in the Septuagint or with their Hebrew equivalents for the Qumran texts: προσκόμματος in Ex. 23:33; 34:12; Jer. 3:3; 1QS 2.11-12, 17; σκανδάλου in Judg. 2:3; 8:27; Ps. 106(105):36; Hos. 4:17; Zeph. 1:3; Wis. 14:11 (Dunn, *Romans*, p. 817).

[101]Dunn, *Romans*, p. 817, notes that "here Paul does not seem to have the problem of idolatry as such in mind, but partly reuses the line of argument formulated in 1 Cor. 8 . . . and partly echoes the *proskomma/skandalon* link which had already become established in Christian thought through the use made of Isa 8:14. . . . The use of *skandalon* here is closer to that in Jud. 12:2—offense caused by eating gentile food. . . . The echo of 9:33 ties the offense into the Jewish failure to acknowledge Christ and anticipates the Christological plea of v. 15: Jewish-Christian offense over the foods issue is of a piece with Jewish failure to recognize the eschatological significance of Christ for Gentile as well as Jew." On p. 818 Dunn continues to develop the association with Jewish stumbling by showing the link with Mark 9:42 (Matt. 18:6, 15, 21) to show that Paul likely drew from this passage in

Instead, as a result of their determined effort (14:13: their judgment [κρίνατε] of their own responsibility), instead of their judgment (14:1: διακρίσεις διαλογισμῶν) of the opinions (responsibilities as they see them) of the "weak,"[102] they are to become the cause of something positive for their "brother." Paul is developing the echo of mutual responsibility that lies behind Isaiah 8:14 as witnessed in Leviticus 19:14: "You shall not curse a deaf man, nor place a stumbling block before the blind, but you shall revere your God; I am the Lord." This same nuance is developed in rabbinic literature: "R. Natan says: 'Whence do we know that one should not reach a cup of wine to a "nazir" nor meat cut from a living animal to a Noahide? Scripture teaches, "You shall not put a stumbling block before the blind"'" (y. Dem. 3.23).

The Imagery of "Stumbling" in Romans 14:14—15:13

This imagery follows in the context of 14:14—15:3 as Paul explains the behavior that they ought to pursue on behalf of the "weak/stumbling." Because the graphic nature of this section is often lost in the translation, I want to review the language as Paul's audience would have originally understood it. The Greek words Paul chooses offer a colorful illustration of two groups of people, with very different opinions about what constitutes appropriate worship, coming into contact with each other as they are walking to the temple to glorify God. The "weak" stumble over a stone[103] along the way, and the others face a choice.

---

his use of "brother." Probably Paul did have in mind the offense related to idolatry, for if the "strong" did not adapt monotheistic rituals they would have been regarded as idolaters and thus as a cause of "stumbling" and "offense" over their claims of coparticipation in the eschatological blessings.

[102]Paul's play on the root κρίνω and other words for judgment throughout this section juxtaposes judgment of God, of each other, and of themselves where the English renders them with different words and loses the poetic flow of this theme: 14:1: "passing judgment"; 14:3-4: "judge"; 14:5: "regards" (κρίνει) twice; 14:6: "observes" twice (φρονῶν and φρονεῖ, and see 12:3 for sense of self-judgment versus judging other from renewed mind); 14:10: "judge" and "judgment seat" (βήματι); 14:13: "judge one another"; 14:13: "determine this" (τοῦτο κρίνατε); 14:14: "thinks anything" (λογιζομένῳτο); 14:22: "condemn himself" (κρίνων ἑαυτὸν); 14:23: "he who doubts" (διακρινόμενος); 14:23: "is condemned" (κατακέκριται).

[103]Unlike Galatians, where the "stone" is immediately identified with Jesus Christ, in Romans the stone is the unwillingness to accept that the righteousness of God has been made equally available to gentiles as well as Jews in Christ—and

They may either reach out to help the "weak" gain their balance, thereby "walking according to love" (14:15) as they "bear" the "weaknesses of the weak" (15:1). Or, in view of their differences, the "strong" may just decide to "please [themselves]" (15:1) and judge the "weak" deserving of that little push likely to cause them to continue to stumble until they have fallen and been "destroy[ed]" (14:15).

In verse 15 we see language drawn from the same vein that Paul has just mined to explain how the Christian gentiles in Rome are to view humbly the grace they have received as they observe the "stumbling" of part of Israel with regard to faith in Jesus as the Christ:

> For if because of food your brother is hurt, you are no longer walking according to love. Do not destroy with your food him for whom Christ died.

Here, however, the concern has changed from explaining how they must not be conceited and think that they have supplanted Israel as though their election was the result of their own merit[104] (is this not

---

thus the stone is still Christ as he confronts the kind of self-righteous ethnocentric presumptuousness that would exclude others from the salvation of God unless their salvation promoted the status of those already in a special relationship with God, that is, unless they became Jews. The stone has the sense of the brother of the prodigal son who instead of rejoicing in the return of his brother regards him with contempt (see discussion of this dynamic in summary and appendix 1 below). See Sanders, *Paul, the Law*, pp. 37-38. Wright, *Climax*, p. 244, on 9:31-32 says: "In consequence, we have the Torah as the means whereby God becomes a stumbling-block to Israel. [His footnote says: 'Isa. 8.14, quoted here, indicates that it is God himself who is to be seen as both the sanctuary and the stumbling stone for Israel.'] 9.32b, which (oddly in Paul) has no connecting word to 32a, seems all the same to be explanatory: to pursue the Torah through works 'is' to stumble over the stumbling stone. The Torah is therefore, in a sense, the stone over which Israel has now stumbled, just as in another sense it is the crucified Messiah over which she has now stumbled. Once more, these are not two but one. And the 'one' that these two are is actually 'the covenant plan of the one God', which, expressed in Torah, was enacted in the Messiah. That is why the stumbling-stone, and the object of faith, in 9.32 f., are systematically and properly ambiguous (do they refer to God, Christ, or Torah?)."

[104]See 11:18-26, 27ff.; 12:3. This was the very message delivered to the people of Israel by Moses in Deut. 8-10 that was being delivered by Paul to Christian gentiles complete with the same kind of promise of blessing (inheritance) for living humbly in thanksgiving and grace toward both God and humanity versus the same kind of judgment (cut off) for living in pride and contempt. Wright, *Climax*, pp. 247, 251, 253, sees this very same tension in the message of chaps. 11 and 14–15.

exactly what gentile Christianity went on to claim?), to explaining
their responsibility to serve those "stumbling" so that they will in fact
recognize that the grace of God that these gentiles have received in
Christ is the very grace of God that Israel has been waiting for:

> Wherefore, accept one another, just as Christ also accepted us to the
> glory of God. (15:7)

The "strong" are now responsible for the salvation (not the condemnation!) of the "weak" in their choice of food.[105]

The word rendered "hurt" is λυπεῖται, which carries the much
deeper meaning of "offend," by causing anger or outrage, and has the
sense in the context of deliberately causing one to stumble so as to fall,
even to the point of "final eschatological ruin,"[106] a nuance that is particularly clear when this verb is coupled with "destroy" (ἀπόλλυε) as
it is in the following sentence.[107] These are used in the context of food.
Note also that the imagery is of walking, περιπατεῖς (*halakh*), which
is exactly what would be necessary for someone to stumble. Paul illustrates giving someone who is stumbling (because they are blinded
and do not see the stone in their path) as they walk next to you just
that little push (by eating offensive food) it might take to keep them
stumbling until they actually "fall" (11:11), instead of extending a
helping hand to balance them until they "stand" (14:4: "for the Lord
is able to make them stand"; 15:1: for the "strong" are "able" to "bear"
them up).

---

[105]The issue is not of the "weak" eating that which the "strong" insist is eat-
able. The issue is concerned with what the "strong" eat ("with your food") that
will offend the "weak" because it is inappropriate in the opinion of the "weak"
not so much for themselves (they were not tempted to eat like the "strong" as in
Corinth) but because it is inappropriate, in their opinion, for the "strong" to eat it.
In fact, unlike the issue addressed in Corinth, where the "weak" might be
tempted to adopt the behavior of the "strong" as desirable for themselves before
their conscience is prepared for them to do so (1 Cor. 8), in Rome the "weak" are
convinced so strongly that the "strong" must not eat the things in dispute that if
the "strong" insist on eating them the "weak," "for whom Christ died," will be
provoked to "blaspheme" the "good things" claimed by the "strong" and the
"weak" may even be "destroyed."

[106]See Jonah 4:1, 4, 9, for example.

[107]Dunn, *Romans*, p. 821; in Rom. 2:12 it is rendered "perish." Paul is talking
about being cut off from God forever.

Paul then appeals to the "strong" in verses 16-18 to live in view of the kingdom of God in their relationship with the "weak":

> Therefore do not let what is for you a good thing be spoken of as evil; for the kingdom of God is not eating and drinking, but righteousness and peace and joy in the Holy Spirit.

Again, this follows the imagery being developed, as the expected kingdom of God would be the time of shalom among all people (even the lion and lamb will be at peace with each other). Thus, they must not, as they walk together with the "weak," behave in such a manner that their claims of equal coparticipation as gentiles in the blessings of God ("good thing")[108] are "spoken of as evil" (βλασφημείσθω: are being blasphemed).[109] To avoid this reaction from those "stumbling"

---

[108]"Good" (ἀγαθόν) are the things that are done by those who "seek for glory and honor and immortality" in 2:7 (see also 2:10); it is the Law for the Jew in 7:12-13 (their privileged possession: 3:1-2; 9:4); it is that which God is working to bring about for the elect resulting ultimately in the glory of the children of God in 8:28ff. (see also 8:12-25); it is that which they must cling to rather than evil in 12:9 (see 14:20!); it is that which the "minister of God" will bring to those they praise for doing "good" rather than evil in 13:3-4; it is that which will result to their "neighbor" and thus should motivate them to "please" them in 15:2; and it is that which Paul wants them to be "wise in" while remaining innocent of evil in 16:19. The "good things" are the eschatological blessings, the promises of God that the "strong" have received in Christ Jesus.

[109]The concept of the responsibility of the "strong" to change their behavior so that their claims as Christian gentiles of sharing in the blessings of God ("good things") are not cause for blasphemy on the part of the "weak" is the heart of Paul's instruction and harkens back to his paradigmatic illustration of the Jews who would, because of their self-righteous hypocrisy, cause the same kind of reaction in reverse: the blasphemy of God by gentiles (2:17-24 so that the Roman Christian gentiles can understand why they must not behave the same way they are so quick to judge on the part of the other, for they are having a problem seeing that they are guilty of exactly the same in reverse—namely, in their claiming of special status that causes them to hold the other in contempt instead of respect. These gentiles are thereby guilty of the very same self-righteous pride and thus hypocrisy in the very claim they make to be followers of Christ even as the other fails to act in the manner of the Law—both causing the blasphemy of God instead of His praise!). Hays, *Echoes*, pp. 45–46, explores the passage in Isa. 52:5 that Paul cites and the issues relate to this point as well. Also see Smallwood, *Jews*, pp. 203–4, for the possible historical incident Paul draws from in the illustration where Josephus tells of a notorious robbery in Rome that caused the citizens of Rome to regard Jews with suspicion.

they are not to assert what they believe to be their gentile prerogatives by eating and drinking whatever pleases them without regard for the sensitivities of the "weak." Paul's argument clarifies that their freedom is not to be mistaken as their "good thing," but their new position as fellow participants in the kingdom of God.[110] They are now sharing in the fulfillment of the promises to Abraham. Interpreters err (in the same manner as the "strong") when they assume that the "good thing" is the freedom to eat and drink as gentiles, for Paul says that such freedom is *not* what constitutes the kingdom of God. Rather, because of their new position ("good thing") they are to follow Christ in seeking the best interests of the other, behavior that will be *both* "acceptable to God *and* approved by men."[111] The kingdom of God that has come in Christ Jesus demands a "renewed mind," which realizes that relationships take priority over the privilege of eating and drinking. The priority is not for the "strong" to eat or drink that to which they believe they are entitled, even if "nothing is unclean in itself." The priority is rather not to harm the "weak" who believe some things to be "unclean." Nor is the priority the seeking of vengeance and judgment, for God is the righteous judge who has reached out in patient kindness and led them to repentance instead of wrath (2:1-4; 12:16-21). Thus, by allowing God to be the judge (14:10-11), they are free to pursue the best interests of the other:

> "righteousness [14:19: "pursue the things which make for . . ."] and peace [14:19: the shalom of God's kingdom in Christ . . .] and joy [14:19: "the building up of one another"/"fellowship"] in the Holy Spirit (14:17)."

It is important to note Paul's earlier quotation of this exact accusation of himself and his vitriolic denial of the charge, taken by some to be perhaps the only thing we can know about Paul's audience in Rome[112] (however, I believe wrongly interpreted by them)[113] in 3:8:

---

[110]Dunn, *Romans*, p. 821, notes this also.

[111]Sanders, *Paul and Palestinian Judaism*, pp. 85ff., speaks of the "yoke of practical obligation."

[112]Luedemann, *Opposition to Paul*, pp. 109-11.

[113]I maintain that the audience is not anti-Pauline, nor is the struggle with Christian Jews. The opponents of Paul in Rome are urging "gentilization." Tomson, *Paul*, pp. 269ff.; and Campbell, *Intercultural Context*, pp. 31–36, also argue against the views that see the opponents as "judaizers." Note Campbell on p. 33: "Paul is addressing baptised Christians and exhorting and commanding them not

And why not say (as we are slanderously reported and as some affirm that we say), "Let us do evil that good may come"? Their condemnation is just.

This is the very same message Paul addressed in chapter 6, having explained that "faith" is the operative means for accessing the "grace" that reigns "through righteousness to eternal life" because of the "obedience" of "Jesus Christ our Lord" (3:21—5:21). He then explained that this new status is not cause to "let sin reign in your mortal body that you should obey its lusts, and do not go on presenting the members of your body to sin as instruments of unrighteousness; but present yourselves to God as those alive from the dead, and your members as instruments of righteousness to God" (6:12-13, 14ff.). Paul's message in the verse we are considering, 14:16, thus parallels the accusation quoted in 3:8 and the argument of chapter 6.

Paul in 3:8 denied the "slanderous report" (βλασφημούμεθα: blasphemous charge) that he was teaching that the righteousness of the Law should be disregarded (and instead we should do unrighteousness to provoke God's mercy) because no one was able to be righteoused by doing it completely, because no one was completely faithful to the righteousness set out in the Law (3:1-7). Paul explained that he taught instead that God was faithful to manifest in the gospel the "power of God for salvation for every one who believes, to the Jew first and also to the Greek" (1:16). God was also faithful to reveal his "wrath" "from heaven against all ungodliness and unrighteousness of men, who suppress the truth in unrighteousness" (1:18). Thus the righteousness of the Law still miraculously manifested God's faithfulness even when some were unfaithful (3:3-4). God is the judge of true righteousness; he judges the secrets in the hearts of all people, whether they have the Law to show the way of righteousness (which is a privilege for Israel) or not—by their intention to do good or to do evil, to judge the other or serve the other—in view of the grace of God shown to themselves (2:1—3:7; 3:19-21, 27-31; 12:1-3, 4ff.).[114]

Paul asserted that he is greatly misjudged if it is maintained that he abandoned the doing of righteousness by those of the faith. In fact, he

---

to live an antinomian existence. This suggests that those who slanderously reported Paul in 3:8 may be Gentile Christians who mistakenly attributed their own antinomianism to Paul's gospel of grace."

[114]Hays, *Echoes*, pp. 47–54; Wedderburn, *Reasons*, pp. 112–17; Sanders, *Paul, the Law*, p. 208.

will not tolerate the accusation because he keeps the Law and teaches
his converts to keep the righteousness of the Law as well—and he
labors to explain this fully throughout this letter—and thus we see him
laboring to explain to the "strong" that they must not behave in a
manner that will encourage this same charge against themselves for
disregarding the practices of righteousness that the "weak" deem essential for those claiming to be coparticipants in the "good things" of
God.

Verse 18 should be noted for its summarizing compression of the
entire paraenesis and its link with the imagery of slavery we have just
discussed in chapter 6 as central to Paul's message in chapter 14:

> For he who in this way serves [δουλεύων: obey as in a slave perform-
> ing responsibilities] Christ is acceptable [εὐάρεστος: brings pleasure
> to his master] to God and approved [δόκιμος: certified as the real
> thing, not as a phony to be blasphemed!] by men.

Clearly we see here that the issue revolves around the "strong"
choosing conduct that will demonstrate to the "weak," where opinion
differs, that the opinion of the "weak" regarding the approved behavior for the "strong" is recognized and observed by the "strong" as legitimate. Perhaps even a legal sense is implied—the "weak" are the
ones in position to legitimize or reject the claims of the "strong"
through their approval, or disapproval, of the behavior of the "strong."
Paul wants the "strong" to choose to serve Christ in a manner that the
"weak" will certify as acceptable to God instead of pursuing a course
that will provoke the "weak" to blaspheme the new faith claims ("the
good thing") of the "strong" in their service of God in Christ. In this
way they "let love be without hypocrisy" (12:9a). What may have appeared in 12:17b-21 to be but a general point with some sense of judicial vindication regarding their response to the hostility in question
("Take forethought for noble conduct in the sight of all. If possible, so
far as it depends on you, be at peace with all men. Never take your
own revenge,")[115] was similarly concerned with handling conflicts and
persecution now cast in the specific context of the "weak" and
"strong." The standards of purity behavior, while qualified in verse
14a, fall under the jurisdiction of the "weak" in the social setting
addressed in verses 14b-23, with verse 18 at the center of Paul's instruction for how the "strong" are to determine the behavior "accept-

[115]See the discussion of G. Zerbe, "Paul's Ethic of Nonretaliation and Peace,"
in *Love of Enemy*, pp. 177–222 (esp. pp. 188–91).

able to God" in their service of Christ: they are to walk in the manner "approved by men."

In verses 19 and 20 the image moves from the "walking according to love" to now running after someone to "pursue [διώκωμεν] the things that make for peace and the building up of one another [οἰκοδομῆς: edification]," a frequent metaphor in Pauline letters to describe the coming together of Jews and gentiles as the temple of God (Eph. 2:19-22).[116] In this passage, however, Paul is urging them to pursue "the things" that would lead to this "building up," that is, it has a future sense, contrasted with his use elsewhere when speaking of the church as a present reality (15:2: "edification" [οἰκοδομήν] of neighbor [outsider] in the view of the "strong"). This is then contrasted with the behavior that Paul seeks to halt in Rome, that is, that the "strong" would "tear down the work of God for the sake of food." The verb rendered "tear down" is κατάλυε, which actually means to "throw down," as one might throw down a stone from a building as opposed to helping put a stone in place.[117]

Note also that it is the "work of God" that Paul does not want them to throw down. This "work of God" refers back to Paul's revelation of the mysterious way that God was "building," which included the certain salvation of those whom the "strong" presently regarded as "enemies" of the gospel (11:25-36). If we assume that the "stone" of "stumbling" in 9:30-33 is the refusal to accept the equal coparticipation of gentiles in Israel's "good things," we can see that the issue being addressed in this imagery concerns an ethnocentric exclusive definition of entrance requirements that prohibits the equal coparticipation of gentiles in God's promises. The stone that the "strong" must not throw down that will further cause the "weak" to stumble is the flaunting of their new status in Christ free from the obligations of Torah and Jewish purity behavior (v. 14a)—indeed, the very stone of stumbling that would further offend the one already stumbling, thereby "tear[ing] down the work of God for the sake of food."

The imagery seems to have changed subtly. The two groups have parted company, although they are still headed in the same direction. The "strong" are challenged to catch up with the "weak" and offer

---

[116]The issue in Ephesus is different, but the use of the illustration there is telling, for the author speaks to two groups in Christ of the breaking down of the dividing wall of the fleshly differences (circumcision and uncircumcision) as one new entity. Ephesians supports the handling of 14:14 as one of priority and not meaningfulness.

[117]See Matt. 24:2; Mark 13:2; Luke 21:6; Acts 6:14 for the same usage.

them a hand as they stumble, rather than indulge the temptation to throw another stone in their path that may finally cause them to fall. And again we have the term "offense" (προσκόμματος) used to describe the sensitivities of the "weak" toward the behavior of the "strong."[118] This instruction draws from the same inspiration as Hillel's concept behind several practical principles for tolerance toward the behavior of others for the sake of social harmony:

> Be disciples of Aaron, loving peace and pursuing peace, loving people and drawing them near to the Torah.[119]

The contrast with the imagery of 9:30—10:4, 5ff. is striking: gentiles who were not *pursuing* the righteousness of God in the past must now, having become people of God, *pursue* the responsibility of "holding up" those among the historical people of God who had been in the *pursuit* of the righteousness of God but had "stumbled" over the very coparticipation of these gentiles in the good things promised to Abraham's seed. And it is this paradox that now compels these gentiles who recognize God's righteousness to *pursue* the kind of righteous behavior that will help them stop stumbling and recognize that Jesus is the Christ who has died for them (14:15: in the *pursuit* of their salvation).

We can now see the context of 12:1-3, 4ff. as it draws from the point Paul has finished developing in chapter 11 and begins the paraenesis that follows: God has graciously shown mercy to you gentiles and thus the measure of your new faith must not result in arrogant denunciation of those who do not share the same measure of faith at the present time. Instead, it should cause a sober recognition of the responsibility to pursue your gifts in the context of a lifestyle that is in the service of those suffering on your behalf, that is, "Let love be without hypocrisy. . . . Respect what is right in the sight of all men. If possible, so far as it depends on you, be at peace with all men" (12:9, 17-18).[120] This now brings together both Jew and gentile to worship the One Lord of all humankind (15:5-12; 3:26): "for the demonstration, I say, of His right-

---

[118]This follows from the intent described in v. 21, where the offender is clearly the "strong."

[119]See *m. Abot* 1:12; cf. Tomson, *Paul*, p. 252.

[120]It is important to note that the language of chap. 12 flows directly from the point made in chap. 11 to the newly grafted-in gentiles. They are the ones instructed not to be conceited in view of the grace shown to them but to serve God and others as much as they are now enabled by their measure of faith in Jesus

eousness at the present time, that He might be just and the justifier of
the one who has faith in Jesus."

The imagery of stumbling follows in verse 21 with the instruction
that:

> it is good not to eat meat or to drink wine, or to do anything by which
> your brother stumbles [προσκόπτει].

The combined thrust of the imagery of giving "offense" and causing
to "stumble" captures graphically exactly the kind of reaction that a
non-Christian Jew would have had to gentiles asserting that they are
now part of the people of God, coparticipants in Israel's salvation, yet
with no regard for the minimal requirements of Law and Jewish custom that had always been the halakhic practice of God-fearing gentiles
who turned from idolatry and attached themselves to the worship of
Israel's God. What kind of "faction" or "sect" of Judaism would teach
such a strange doctrine? The rules of conduct for "the stranger within
your gates" had long ago been adapted to issues faced by Diaspora
Jews with respect to gentile conduct.   The very essence of the
monotheistic faith that Paul was weaving throughout this letter would
be rightfully blasphemed. The complete disregard for "the faith" of
the "weak" would certainly cause great "offense" and keep them from
seriously considering the possibility that Jesus was the promised
Christ.[121] Do we not hear a clear echo of the reasoning of the Jerusalem
Council for developing the apostolic decree for Christian gentiles free
from the yoke of the Law?:

> Therefore it is my judgment that we do not trouble those who are
> turning to God from among the Gentiles, but that we write to them
> that they abstain from things contaminated by idols and from fornica-
> tion and from what is strangled and from blood. For Moses from
> ancient generations has in every city those who preach him, since he is
> read in the synagogues every Sabbath. (Acts 15:19-21)

Christ (their strength). It is also interesting to note that the gifts and responses
called for in chap. 12, like those of chaps. 13–15, are contextualized by tensions
that include interaction with those regarded as "enemies" and "persecutors" and
"authorities," among others. It is again those who see themselves as "strong" who
are being warned to recognize the source of their strength and therefore to pursue
the proper response to those not yet so strengthened in their faith.

[121]The intention of Paul's concern is that the behavior of the "strong" not so offend the "weak" that they reject the death of Christ as operative for themselves.

Paul interjects a warning to the "strong" in Romans 14:22-23 before his appeal reaches its climax in chapter 15:

> The faith which you have, have as your own conviction before God. Happy is he who does not condemn himself in what he approves [δοκιμάζει]. But he who doubts is condemned if he eats, because his eating is not from faith; and whatever is not from faith is sin.

While this is generally read as though directed to the "weak," the warning follows the flow of the text (the verses preceding and following are directed to the "strong") and takes on more character if seen as Paul's explanation of the responsibility of the "strong" (the one "eating"). The "strong" are to have their minds "renewed" rather than "conformed to this world" so that they "prove [δοκιμάζειν] what the will of God is, that which is good and acceptable and perfect" (12:2), instead of asserting their rights regardless of the impact on the "weak."[122] In other words, asserting their rights over against the "weak" is not an act of faith in practice (14:14bff.), although it could be so argued in theory (v. 14a). Moreover, in Rome, unlike Corinth, the "weak" are not attracted to or even in any way tempted to adopt the behavior of the "strong." The "weak" in Rome are convinced that the behavior of the "strong" is rightly judged as "unwelcome" by God when it fails to conform to their opinions for proper behavior among

---

[122]The very things that their renewed "minds" will "think" (φρονεῖν: 12:2-3; cf. 14:6; 15:5) will now "prove" (δοκιμάζειν: 12:2; cf. 14:18, 22) to be "God's will" and are the same things that Paul explores throughout this paraenesis. They are to prove with their renewed minds what is good (ἀγαθὸν: 12:2: cf. 12:9, 21; 13:3-4; 14:16), acceptable (εὐάρεστον: 12:1-2: cf. 14:18), and perfect (τέλειον: 12:2: which carries the sense of "without discrimination," that is, without passing judgment, which is clear throughout the paraenesis: cf. 14:1, 13). For now their renewed minds will no longer cause them to think more highly of themselves than they ought to think (12:3); rather, they will be humbly aware (judge themselves properly instead of judging the other) that the "measure" of their faith (as "strong") is the result of the grace of God (15:7), which should result in grateful service to those having less (weaker) faith instead of judgment of them (12:3—15:14). The ultimate meaning of "God's will" for them is that they no longer judge matters (or people) as they appeared according to their former mind-set governed by fleshly boundaries (discrimination). They are now to rise above discrimination and be "of the same mind with one another according to Christ Jesus; that with one accord you may with one voice glorify the God and Father of our Lord Jesus Christ" (15:5-6). Wedderburn, *Reasons*, pp. 75–77, similarly shows that 12:1-2 functions as the announcement of the paraenesis.

the people of God. The "weak" are not uncertain or wavering.[123] We must read these verses in the context of Paul's concerns in Romans, not Corinthians, where the "weak" might have actually desired to follow the practices of the "strong" as acceptable behavior for themselves, though they were unable to do so in good conscience because they were not yet mature (1 Cor. 8:10; cf. 3:1-3), a very different situation from the one being described in this paraenesis. In Rome it is the "strong" who need Paul's "bold reminder" as they are being tempted away from "the teaching" that they had heretofore observed toward one that will cause their "stumbling brethren" much harm (Rom. 6:17; 15:15-16; 16:17-20).[124]

Throughout this paraenesis Paul has been working around the edges of the double entendre implicit in his selection of δυνατοὶ ("strong"/"able") to describe their "faith." That is, the "strong" are warned in exactly the same manner as he had warned the presumptuous Christian gentiles he addressed in 11:11-26, 27ff. (for the "strong" are the very same presumptuous Christian gentiles) that they are not to be "conceited" because of their new status, "but fear," for "they were broken off for their unbelief, and you stand only by your faith . . . for if God did not spare the natural branches, neither will He spare you . . . otherwise you also will be cut off" (11:20-22). Even as the "strong" have the "ability" to destroy the one "stumbling" by throwing down a stone in their path, they also have the "ability" to destroy themselves if they choose to please themselves by the sinful act of eating in "unfaith" ("not from faith"): "but he who doubts [διακρινόμενος][125] is condemned if he eats." Again, note the

[123]Interpreters often regard the "weak," in addition to being unable to "grasp the full liberty [they have] in Christ, the consequence of which is an overscrupulous observance of formal rules," as further "plagued by an anxious uncertainty as to whether it is proper to do certain things" (Black, *Paul*, pp. 199–200). Yet these same interpreters often ascribe to the "weak" a fanaticism that can hardly be considered wavering or uncertain: "The weak do, however, show a legalistic tendency to condemn those who feel free to eat anything, and are consequently not without fault. In view of these factors, the most probable opinion is that *the weak were Jewish Christians who were more strict than the ceremonial law required and whose ascetic tendencies led to a condemnation of those who disregarded their scruples*" (Black, *Paul*, p. 205).

[124]See chapter 4 below for full discussion.

[125]"Doubting" has the sense of not judging oneself correctly as one enters a dispute with someone—again a clear reference to the instruction Paul has directed to the "strong" from 14:1 following and earlier in chaps. 11 and 12.

similarity with Paul's warning to the gentiles in the preceding argument: "you stand only by your faith . . . otherwise you also will be cut off" (11:20-22). They are instead now to see the present circumstances with the "renewed mind" called for in 12:1-3, 4ff. Believing that God is the faithful judge, they are to determine to "walk according to love" in the kingdom of God and not according to food by which their "brother" is "hurt" in a way that may "destroy" him. While this sacrifice might be expected to bring them great discomfort, Paul is concerned that they recognize that sacrificial living is the way of life, as it always had been, for the one who is "happy" (μακάριος: blessed).[126]

When Paul explains the responsibility of the "strong" (δυνατοὶ), who are "able," "powerful," or "strengthened," in 15:1 toward the "weak," he refers to the "weaknesses of those without strength" (ἀσθενήματα τῶν ἀδυνάτων), that is, he further qualifies their "weakness" (ἀσθενήματα) as their lack of "ability" or "power" as contrasted with the "strong" he is addressing:

> Now we who are strong ought to bear the weaknesses of those without strength and not just please ourselves.

His particular instruction is that the "strong" are obligated by their "strength/ability" to "bear" (βαστάζειν) the "weaknesses" (stumbling) of those who are "without strength" (lacking ability themselves). Again, interestingly, the word βαστάζειν fits the imagery Paul has developed, it means to "hold up," "carry" or "support" (cf. Gal. 6:2: "Bear [βαστάζετε] one another's burdens, and thus fulfill the law of Christ").[127] In contrast to the alternative for those with power to "please ourselves" (ἑαυτοῖς ἀρέσκειν), which echoes the selfish ambition and arrogant triumphalism that he has spoken against throughout his letter,[128] they are to use their power to "hold up" those "stumbling" so that they might "stand."

Paul instructs the "strong" in 15:2-3 to "please" their "neighbor"[129]

---

[126]Cf. Rom. 4:7.

[127]Dunn, *Romans*, p. 837.

[128]See 2:8; 11:17-29; 12:3, 16ff.; also Phil. 2 is an excellent example of Paul's meaning in this regard.

[129]This is an interesting choice of words to designate their relationship if both the "weak" and the "strong" are Christians. But this juxtaposed labeling fits well if Christian gentiles and non-Christian Jews are meeting together in the synagogue yet divided over their faith in Christ and thus each judging the other's faith "unwelcome."

for "his good, to his edification" (again οἰκοδομήν, to build; 15:2) in view of the behavior characteristic of Christ. Christ chose not to exercise his rights, serving instead the interests (the good) of the other so that they would be built up. This involved a significant choice for Christ, and it will for the "strong" as well. The "strong" are instructed to adopt accommodating behavior toward the "weak," even though it will bring upon the "strong," as it had for Christ, the reproaches of those who would consider this choice a cause for insult or shame (reproaches "fell" upon Him):

> Let each of us please his neighbor for his good, to his edification.
> For even Christ did not please Himself; but as it is written, "The reproaches of those who reproached Thee fell upon Me." (15:2-3)

Here again we sense the edge in Paul's choice of the label "strong" for his audience. They have the "ability" to believe, to see (they are not hardened!) the grace of God that has come to them in Christ, who is the very demonstration of God's saving δύναμις ("power" or "ability": 1:16; cf. 1:4 "by resurrection"), yet they fail to recognize that their "ability" carries an implicit obligation. They are no longer to be "slaves of sin" in asserting their perceived right to be "able" to eat and drink as they please free from the practice of the Law and Jewish custom in their new relationship with God. Instead, they are to become "slaves of righteousness" who are "able" to please their neighbor by refraining from offensive food and wine, thereby bearing up the "stumbling" who cannot currently see the δύναμις of God in Christ (1:16).[130] In this way the "stumbling" will *also* be "*able*" to recognize the grace of God that has come to them in Christ ("To his own master he stands or falls; and stand he will; for the Lord is able [δυνατεῖ] to make him stand": 14:4). Then those "stumbling" will "stand" in Christ rather than "fall" over him.[131] They are to help the one who is "stumbling" next to them to "stand," even if, as had been the case for Christ, the "reproaches" of the very ones they are seeking to help (or the ones who are urging them "to eat" in 16:17-18) "fall" on them in the process.

The climax of this paraenesis, in fact the final punctuation mark on

---

[130]Munck, *Christ and Israel*, p. 91. See chapter 4 below on hardening.

[131]Note also ἀσθενῶν in Rom. 5:6: "For while we were still helpless, at the right time Christ died for the ungodly"; the word translated "helpless" derives from the same root as ἀσθένεια.

the body of the entire letter, is Paul's expression of hope that these
two entities, the "weak" and the "strong" (the "stumbling" *and* those
who are "able" to cause stumbling), will come together as one as they
"accept one another, just as Christ has accepted us to the glory of
God."[132] Rather than the "weak" stumbling so as to fall, his hope and
instruction is to the end that the "strong" will accommodate the
opinions of the "weak," thereby enabling the "weak" to join together
with the "strong" in declaring the Shema:

> that with *one* accord you may with *one* voice glorify *the God* and
> Father of *our Lord* Jesus Christ. (15:6)

They would then fulfill the expectations of the prophets for the
eschatological kingdom of God, when the circumcised and uncircumcised side by side would glorify the One God:[133]

> Therefore I will give praise to Thee among the Gentiles,
> And I will sing to Thy name. (15:9)[134]

[132]Hays, *Echoes*, pp. 68–73, shows how this use of acceptance language in 14:3
and 15:7 is rooted in 1 Sam. 12:20-23, the background passage for Paul's explanation that God has not rejected Israel and of Paul's abiding commitment to Israel
in chap. 11, "For the Lord will not cast away his people, for his great name's sake,
because the Lord has gently received [*proselabeto*] you as a people for himself.
Moreover, as for me, far be it from me that I should sin against the Lord by ceasing to pray for you." Hays, p. 69, parallels this passage with Rom. 9:3 and 10:1.

[133]Hays, *Echoes*, pp. 70–74; on p. 71 he comments: "Clearly, he has saved his
clinchers for the end. After much allusive and labored argumentation, Paul finally
draws back the curtain and reveals a collection of passages that explicitly embody
his vision for a church composed of Jews and Gentiles glorifying God together.
Commentators often note that Paul has offered here one quotation from the
Pentateuch, one from the Prophets, and two from the Writings, all strung together
by the catchword 'ethnē', all pointing to the eschatological consummation in
which Gentiles join in the worship of Israel's God: truly the Law and the Prophets
are brought forward here as witnesses. . . . There is no sleight of hand here: Paul
rests his case on the claim that his churches, in which Gentiles do in fact join Jews
in praising God, must be the eschatological fulfillment of the scriptural vision."

[134]Hays, *Echoes*, p. 72: "Thus, the picture evoked by Paul's quotation of Psalm
18 is very much like the picture painted in Heb. 2:10-13: Jesus stands amidst the
congregation of his brothers, singing praise to God. Paul, of course, emphasizes for
his purposes not the solidarity of Jesus with the congregation but the fact that the
congregation is made up of Gentiles."

Rejoice, O Gentiles, with His people. (15:10)[135]

Praise the Lord all you Gentiles,
And let all the peoples praise Him. (15:11)

There shall come the root of Jesse,
And He who arises to rule over the Gentiles,
In Him shall the Gentiles hope. (15:12)[136]

My present concern has been to suggest that the label "weak" has the same sense for Paul, in its underlying usage, as it did in the Septuagint and in Qumran literature. Those so described are "stumbling." If ἀσθενείς referred, for Paul and his audience, to those who were "stumbling," then it becomes much clearer that the introduction of the phrase "weak in faith" in chapter 14 was not so abrupt, for it had already been clarified earlier in the letter, in chapters 9–11 along christological lines. There Paul had explained the anomaly of apparent Jewish unbelief in Jesus as the Christ as their "stumbling" with respect to "faith" because they were "unable" to recognize that Jesus was the Lord or the inclusion of gentiles (9:30-33; 10:8-13; 11:7-11). Before I press this point further, I want to look at some additional dimensions of the phrase "weak/stumbling in faith" that also arise earlier in the letter.

"Weak in Faith" and "Strong in Faith" Contrasted in Abraham

The phrases "strong in faith" and "weak in faith" were actually introduced early in Paul's letter to Rome, in his explanation of the kind of faith that Abraham did, and did not, have:

[135]Hays, *Echoes*, p. 72: "The quotation from Deut. 32:43, then, adds a crucial element to the portrait. . . . The Gentiles do not stand alone around Christ; they are being summoned to join 'with' Israel in rejoicing."

[136]Hays, *Echoes*, p. 73: "Similarly, the final text in Paul's catena also envisions a gathering of Gentiles and Jews around the Messiah. The full force of Paul's citation of Isa. 11:10 becomes apparent only when the reader recollects Isa. 11:11-12. . . . Paul quotes only an excerpt that prophesies Gentiles placing their hope in the 'root of Jesse,' but the quotation also works as an allusion to Isaiah's vision of God's eschatological kingdom in which the lost ones of Israel rejoin these Gentiles in being gathered at the feet of the one whom God has raised up. This allusion in turn forges an intertextual link back to the remnant theme of Romans 11."

And without becoming weak in faith [ἀσθενήσας τῇ πίστει] he contemplated his own body, now as good as dead since he was about a hundred years old, and the deadness of Sarah's womb; yet, with respect to the promise of God, he did not waver in unbelief, but grew strong in faith [ἐνεδυναμώθη τῇ πίστει], giving glory to God, and being fully assured that what He had promised, He was able [δυνατός] also to perform. (4:19-21)

God had promised Abraham that he would be "heir of the world" with his "seed" "through the righteousness of faith" (4:13), which Paul explains in the context to mean that God promised Abraham he would make him "the father" ("heir") "of many nations" ("seed"); there would be those who would "follow in the steps of the faith of our father Abraham" (4:12) from both the circumcision and the uncircumcision (4:11-12) "who believe in Him who raised Jesus our Lord from the dead" (4:24).[137] Thus the phrase "strong in faith" refers to Abraham's belief that God would fulfill his promise (the reckoning of righteousness)[138] in the promised "seed," his "faith" being "strong" enough to look beyond the present state of things that would appear to those "becoming weak in faith" as impossible (his age and Sarah's dead womb would seem to make the possibility of his having "seed" beyond hope), and thus that he would "be the father of many nations," that is, he would be the father of both those descending from his own loins (Israel) and those not from his flesh (the rest of the nations/gentiles).[139]

[137]See Wright, *Climax*, pp. 167–68, who on p. 167 says: "Thus, it may be suggested that Romans 4, like Galatians 3, argues (i) that the promises of Genesis 15, 17, and 18 always envisaged a worldwide family; (ii) that this family would be characterized by faith, not by circumcision or Torah; and (iii) that this family is to be identified with those who believe in Jesus Christ." See also Gaston, *Paul*, pp. 121–27; Hays, *Echoes*, pp. 54–57.

[138]What did Abraham expect to inherit? The focus Paul gives in Romans variously describes it as righteousness (4:22-25); forgiveness (4:3-8, 25; 3:23-26); salvation (1:16; 13:11); justification (3:24-26; 4:25); and the glory of the children of God, the redemption of our bodies that the very creation waits to share in (8:16-25); summarized nicely in 8:28-30, leading to all humankind glorifying God together in 15:5-6, 7ff.

[139]Hays, *Echoes*, pp. 54–55, says: "Paul wants to argue that Judaism itself, rightly understood, claims its relation to Abraham not by virtue of physical descent from him (*kata sarka*) but by virtue of sharing his trust in the God who made the promises. In that sense, the gospel, which invites all people, including Gentiles, into right relation with God through faith, confirms the Law; it is consistent with the real substance of the Law's teaching. This is the proposition that Paul sets out

The issue is the *measure* of Abraham's *faith*, which was prior to circumcision and the giving of the Law (the point of discussing Abraham
is to illustrate the monotheistic and Law-positive assertions of 3:29-31:
God is the One God of Jews and gentiles equally, in fulfillment of
Torah). The *measure of faith* as "weak" or "strong" *has nothing to do with
the Law* since it preceded both the Law and circumcision. It has to do
with the "ability" (strength) of Abraham's "faith" in the "ability"
(strength) of God's faithfulness to fulfill his promise through
Abraham's "seed." Those "who believe in Him who raised Jesus our
Lord from the dead" (4:24) join with Abraham in being reckoned as
righteous (4:22-25), both from Israel and the nations (4:11-12, 16: "the
father of us all"). Indeed, the Lord is One, uniting "all" who "follow
in the steps of the faith of our father Abraham" (4:12).[140]

Those "strong in faith" thus include both Jews and gentiles (circumcised and uncircumcised in vv. 9-12; those of the Law and those
without the Law in vv. 13-16) "who are of the faith of Abraham" (4:16),
for the discussion of Abraham had been introduced to demonstrate the
validity of God's justification for "the Jew first and also for the Greek"
who have received God's righteousness through faith in Jesus Christ
(3:21-30).[141] Likewise, if Abraham had been "weak in faith," it would
have had nothing to do with the Law, *for the Law had not yet been given.*
It would have meant that Abraham had faith, that he believed in God,
but that he did not believe in the promised "seed," because when he
considered the present circumstances he would have lost his

to demonstrate through his exposition of Genesis . . . the gospel confirms the
Torah. Only a narrowly ethnocentric form of Judaism, Paul insists, would claim
that God is the God of the Jews only or that Abraham is the progenitor of God's
people 'according to the flesh,' that is, by virtue of natural physical descent."

[140]J. B. Chance, "The Seed of Abraham and the People of God," pp. 391–95,
discusses the apparent contradiction of Paul's language in vv. 14 and 16 and decides that "the conclusion appears inescapable that Paul's muddled language is
rooted in his desire to argue that the seed of Abraham consists of 'both' Jews and
gentiles who have faith" (p. 391).

[141]I make the transition here to interpreting issues of Abraham's faith as operative for his audience's faith in view of Paul's movement throughout this chapter in
this same manner, especially evident in his explicit summary in 4:23-24. This was
Paul's direct instruction of how to use Scripture in 15:4. See Juel, *Messianic
Exegesis*, pp. 18, 35–57; Hays, *Echoes*, pp. 166–67, for discussions of this method
and its relationship to the exegetical and interpretive methods during this period
of Jewish history. See also Campbell, "Romans III," p. 261, who sees the illustration of Abraham "as a uniting figure in the church composed of Jewish and Gentile
Christians, and probably also as a model of 'the strong in faith.'"

confidence that God would be able to perform what he had promised—
he would not have believed God would bring salvation to the nations
through his "seed." Abraham would have been, with respect to the
promise of God, "weak in faith": believing in God but not in God's
particular promise to bring salvation to the whole world in his "seed";
that is, not believing in the restoration of the world (both Jews and gentiles in Paul's argument) through his descendants. Paul is arguing that
the line of salvation history is from Abraham to Israel to Christ to Israel
and to gentiles/nations and thus to the whole world—in Abraham's
"seed." We can thus follow what Paul had in mind when he said that
Abraham "grew strong in faith" in view of God's promise, and "therefore also 'it was reckoned to him as righteousness'" (4:22).

It should also be noted that the issue of the measure of Abraham's
faith was not in static terms. It was not a matter of faith or unfaith. He
had faith, even if it would have "grown" weak. Abraham instead "*grew*
strong in faith*." His existing faith was tested by his consideration of the
situation. When he deliberated on circumstances that appeared to
make it impossible for God to fulfill His promise to Abraham, he
trusted God in hope that God would be able to act faithfully in spite of
how things appeared (4:18, "in hope against hope he believed"). Thus
the phrase "*becoming* weak in faith" refers to a time of deliberation in
view of the appearance of present circumstances that might seem to
contradict God's promises, not to an ultimate decision not to believe (to
unfaith). It refers to faith in God, although not necessarily to faith that
God has fulfilled the specific promises in question, particularly in the
face of circumstances that are currently being questioned, in order to
make a considered decision to have faith or unfaith about them.

This graphic explanation of terms is central to Paul's message
throughout the letter: there are those who recognize God's righteousness as did Abraham ("in hope against hope he believed," 4:18), that
is, they believe in the faithfulness of God to keep his promise in spite
of appearances to the contrary ("who gives life to the dead and calls
into being that which does not exist" 4:17) in Abraham's "seed" (Jesus
the Christ) from both Jews and gentiles, and they thereby "follow in
the steps of the faith of our father Abraham" in recognizing the "righteousness of God" that has been powerfully (δύναμις) demonstrated
in Christ by his resurrection for the Jew first and also for the Greek
(1:4, 16). They are justified by faith in the risen Christ: they are "*strong
in faith*." And there are those who believe in God yet are uncertain

("waver in unbelief," 4:20; "he who doubts," 14:23)[142] that God has demonstrated his righteousness in the resurrection of Jesus as the Lord. For them, the present circumstances appear contrary to their expectations of Abraham's promised "seed." They cannot see clearly and "stumble over the stumbling stone" of whether Jesus is the promised Christ who brings the fulfillment of Abraham's promises, and thus over the inclusion of gentiles as equal co-participants in God's blessings without becoming Jews. They would be characterized as *"weak in faith"*: believing in God, but not that the Lord is One where gentile equality in the people of God through faith in Christ is concerned.

What Issues Divided the "Weak" and the "Strong" in Rome?

When we combine these historical and contextual elements we gain a much clearer picture of who the "weak" and the "strong" would have represented for Paul and his Roman audience.

The "weak/stumbling" would be those Roman Jews whom Paul has described as "the rest" of his "brethren" who have been "hardened" (calloused: 11:25) after having "stumbled over 'the stumbling stone'" (9:32) in that they do not yet consider that the present circumstances demonstrate that God's promised "blessing" in Abraham's "seed" has come in Christ Jesus (10:8—11:10); they did not yet "heed the glad tidings" (10:16) of God's righteousness demonstrated in Jesus as the Christ of Israel (10:2-4); and they did not regard as credible the gentiles claiming to be their fellow heirs in Abraham's promises without becoming Jews. They may be in the process of "stumbling," but yet not "so as to fall" (11:11). They are deliberating, but they have not yet rejected the possibility.

Simply put, the "weak/stumbling in faith" are those Jews who do not yet believe in Jesus as the Christ of Israel or Savior of the nations: they are the non-Christian Jews in Rome. They have faith in God, but not in his "seed," Christ Jesus, or in the equal coparticipation of gentiles. They are "stumbling" at the time in uncertainty, but they have not yet fallen because they have not yet actually rejected Jesus as the Christ.[143] They are "considering," as had Abraham, however, unlike

---

[142]The same basic words are used for the opposite of trust: διεκρίθη in 4:20 and διακρινόμενος in 14:23.

[143]Fraikin, "Rhetorical Function" p. 104, is close to arguing the same point when he says: "The Jew is not defined as a non-Christian but as a potential

Abraham, they are "growing weak in faith" because they are "wavering" as they are inclined not to believe that God's promises have been
fulfilled in Abraham's "seed": Jesus, the Christ of Israel and Savior of
the world in whom the "power [δύναμις] of God for salvation to every
one who believes" has been made manifest (1:16, cf. 1:4; 3:21-26).[144]
They are thus, Paul asserts, in danger of denying that the Lord of
Israel is the One Lord of all humankind, which denial will result in the
eschatological shame foretold by Isaiah (9:30-33; 10:2-4, 11–13;
3:19-31).[145]

The "strong/able" are Christians. They include Jews, like Paul and
a small group of Christian Jews in Rome; and gentiles, like the majority of the audience he is addressing in Rome, that "follow in the steps
of the faith of our father Abraham" (4:12) in that they believe (are
"able" and "strengthened" to recognize) that Jesus, by his resurrection
from the dead, has been demonstrated to be the promised "seed," the
Christ of Israel and the Savior of the world (1:4, 16; 3:21-26). They too
had been "weak" before believing in Christ: "For while we were still
helpless [ἀσθενῶν],[146] at the right time Christ died for the ungodly"
(5:6). Thus it is to the "strong" that Paul directs most (perhaps all) of
his instruction throughout chapters 12–15, for while they are "able" to
"hold up" those in the process of stumbling as they exercise their gifts
and "respect what is right in the sight of all men," they are, however,
also "able" to throw down the stone that will "destroy" them.

PAUL'S INSTRUCTIONS TO THE "WEAK"
AND THE "STRONG"

The "weak/stumbling" are characterized, as pointed out earlier, by
their differences of opinion with the "strong/able." I have made the

---

Christian. Conversely, the majority of the Jews who rejected the gospel are not
called 'the Jews.' This implies an open definition of Judaism which allows a Jew
to accept the gospel without ceasing to be a Jew. It is not the position of the non-
Christian Jews, the position of the majority of Jews, which defines what a Jew is."
This is the very nuance I have been exploring and will draw to a close below.

[144]Carter, "Rome," pp. 63–64.

[145]The juxtaposition of 9:33 and 10:11 in their respective contexts is vivid, both
concerned with the "stumbling" of Israel over the essence of God's oneness expressed in the equal access of both Jews and gentiles to salvation through faith,
and both appealing to the eschatological warning to Israel of "shame" if they do
not heed God's righteous manifestation of mercy/wrath in the promised representative of God's will.

[146]See the discussion of Black, *Paul*, pp. 182–84.

point that these differences of opinion regarding the purity practices of eating and observing days, while characterizing the "weak" as a group distinct from the "strong," are not what characterized their faith as "stumbling" or "able." The measure of their "faith" as "weak/stumbling" or "strong/able" was not determined by their observance of or freedom from the Law, even as it had not been for Abraham; it was related to their *response* to the gospel of Christ: whether they recognize that Christ Jesus demonstrates the faithfulness of God to fulfill the promises to Abraham, wherein lies "the power of God for salvation to every one who believes, to the Jew first and also to the Greek" (1:16; 3:21-26). Now we must investigate this claim further by looking into Paul's instruction to each.

Many scholars agree that most of Paul's instruction in this paraenesis is directed to the "strong."[147] However, because some instructions appear to be directed to the "weak," in concert with the unquestioned assumption that the "weak" must be Christians and that the overall thrust of Paul's instruction must therefore be equally aimed at changing their presumably "deficient" opinions, the real depth of Paul's intentions toward both groups has been missed, and often trivialized.[148]

The "weak" and "strong" are both ostensibly the focus of the instruction of 14:3-11, in what appears to be a rather balanced treatment of how each should regard the "faith" of the other. However, they are each instructed very differently. On the one hand, the kind of judging that characterizes the "weak" is much harsher than that of the "strong." They are not to "judge" the one who eats in view of God's acceptance (προσελάβετο) of him (14:3). Paul appeals to the "weak" in view of God's acceptance of the "strong" by drawing from the instruction with which he began this section when he addressed the "strong" to "accept" (προσλαμβάνεσθε) the one who is "weak" (14:1).

On the other hand, the "strong" who eat are not to "regard with contempt" (ἐξουθενείτω) the one who does not eat. Further, the following thoughts are about each recognizing that the practice of the opinions of the other are equally respected by God, for they are done in faith and thanksgiving. In fact, 14:1-12 is focused on the mutual respect incumbent upon the "weak" and the "strong" in view of the oneness of God. What we see Paul illustrating is the very essence of

---

[147]Käsemann, *Romans*, p. 374: "the tenor of the whole section is essentially an admonition to the strong."

[148]E.g., Kümmel, *Introduction*, pp. 119, 121.

the Shema adapted to resolving the tension developing in the new reality of two factions among the community(s) of God, united in that they both have faith in the One Lord, though, divided over the role of Jesus as the Christ.

One might expect, from the usual reading of this section, that Paul would instruct the "weak" to become more mature in the practice of their faith by seeing the "weakness" of their former pre-Christian opinions, and thus ceasing to put so much trust in them as important. But what he says is actually very problematic for those who suggest that the practices of the "weak" show their faith to be deficient—for Paul urges them to "be fully convinced" in their own minds. That is, Paul respects the practice of the opinions of both because God respects their practices when done in faith, and thus Paul instructs both to respect the practices of the opinions of the other.

Paul is not snared in the ineluctable trap of judging the behavior of the "weak" as the result of their faith being deficient because they continue to keep the Law and Jewish customs. The "weakness/inability" of the "weak" is not that their opinions or their practices are inferior, it is the state of their pre-Christian faith: their *wavering* in unbelief toward Jesus as the Christ of Israel and Savior of the world. Likewise, the "strength/ability" of the "strong" is not their superior opinions or practices, it is their faith, their *belief* that the faithfulness of God has been demonstrated in Christ Jesus.

All of Paul's other instructions in this section, and one could argue that this is the case throughout the entire letter, are addressed to the "strong."[149] Those that have appeared to be addressed to the "weak" have been given in the context of instructions to the "strong" for balance. The "weak" are *not* actually instructed to change their opinions or behavior, *except* as they relate to their change of attitude from nonacceptance of the "strong" to one of respect and "welcome." The appeal to the "weak" can be summarized briefly as welcoming the "strong" by not judging them to be outside God's acceptance and recognizing their own responsibility to be fully convinced in their own minds that what they practice is for the Lord. They are not directly, or indirectly, urged to change in any other manner their opinions or practices. They

---

[149]See chapter 2 above for discussion of audience. Also on the "strong" as focus of the entire letter see N. T. Wright, "Romans and the Theology of Paul," pp. 184–213.

are only to judge the "strong" as now "welcome" by God: a direct appeal to the spirit of the Shema in the context of the eschatological shalom of the kingdom of God.

We might have expected the instructions to the "weak" to be harsher than those to the "strong," but we find just the opposite is the case. The "strong" are Paul's target, and the entire paraenesis is concerned with convincing them to accept the "weak" without "judging their opinions," and further, to accommodate the sensibilities of the "weak" by modifying their behavior to mirror that of the "weak," even as Christ had. This emphasis on "acceptance" of the "weak" rather than rejection harkens back to 11:15, where Paul, in explaining to gentiles the good that has come to them through the stumbling of Israel, contrasts this present good fortune with that which shall surely result when the stumbling are "accepted":

> For if their rejection be the reconciliation of the world, what will their acceptance be but life from the dead?

Paul's use of epideictic rhetoric "to increase the intensity of adherence to certain values"[150] that they share with Christ and his apostle Paul—but that they appear to be disregarding, or perhaps are being tempted to flaunt—is clearly directed to the "strong" to explain the extreme importance Paul places on the practical dimensions of their behavior that flow from the theological arguments he has labored throughout the letter to communicate.[151] The "strong" must now

[150]From C. Perelman and L. Olbrechts-Tyteca, *New Rhetoric*, as interpreted by Wuellner, "Paul's Rhetoric," and Fraikin, "Rhetorical Function," pp. 91–105. Perelman, p. 51 notes: "The argumentation in epidictic discourse sets out to increase the intensity of adherence to certain values, which might not be contested when considered on their own but may nevertheless not prevail against other values that might come into conflict with them. The speaker tries to establish a sense of communion centered around particular values recognized by the audience, and to this end he uses the whole range of means available to the rhetorician for the purposes of amplification and enhancement." (See chapter 4 below on epideictic rhetoric.)

[151]Wuellner, "Paul's Rhetoric," p. 140, points out, again from Perelman's rhetorical observations, "the distinction between education and propaganda, with epideictic oratory serving education, not propaganda. The stalemated discussion over whether or not Romans is a missionary document can be resolved fruitfully only if we pay attention to the rhetorical genre. What is said of epideictic speeches

commit themselves to the values they share with Christ and disregard
the appeal of opposing ideas and values they may find convincing or attractive—in their relationship with the non-Christian Jews of Rome.[152]

Their triumphant assumptions of supplanting Israel as the people
of God have been dashed.[153] They are instead charged with seeing that

---

generally, is true also of Romans: in the epideictic mode the writer is 'most prone
to appeal to a universal order, to a nature, or a god that would vouch for the unquestioned, and supposedly unquestionable, values. In epideictic oratory, the
speaker turns educator.'"

[152]This sense is the heart of Paul's message in chap. 2 worked out in the instructions of the paraenesis of 12:1—15:13, particularly the attitude and service
Paul calls for in 15:1-3 contrasted with the attitude and actions Paul confronts in
2:1-16. Christian gentiles are not to be "selfishly ambitious" and seek to "please
themselves" as they hold in contempt the non-Christian Jews who are stumbling
and consider indulging in behavior that will harm them. They are rather to recognize that the patient "kindness of God" that led them to repentance must be extended not only by God to the stumbling as it had been to them as gentiles, but
they must now become bearers of that same longsuffering patience and persevere
in doing "good" as they wait for the glory of God that will be revealed in them, resulting in eternal life in the end for them and for those they bear (5:1-11; 6:12-23;
8:12-25, 28-39; 11:25-32). This is contrasted with choosing to live in contempt of
the stumbling with disregard for their justifiable sensitivities (14:13-20, 21ff.); Paul
calls this choice the pursuit of evil and the destruction of the stumbling, which will
result in their own destruction as well (2:5-6, 9, 16 [the point of the illustration of
the same kind of arrogant hypocrisy on the part of the stumbling when they act
out of contempt instead of mercy toward the gentiles]; 11:11-32; 14:20-23; 15:14-
16 [consider what will be their fate if Paul's "offering of the Gentiles" is not "sanctified by the Holy Spirit" and "acceptable"]). See Wright, *Climax*, pp. 77–98, on
Phil. 2 with this same principle. Fraikin, "Rhetorical Function," p. 92, says: "The
role Paul expects the Romans to perform is neither to deliberate nor to adjudicate
but 'to affirm the communal values which Paul and the Romans share in being
agents of the faith throughout the world.'"

[153]Interestingly, even those who see the error of the gentile assumption so dramatically, because of other operating assumptions that they just cannot shake, turn
around and say these very things. See Munck, *Christ and Israel*, for example, on
pp. 59–60: "And its adversary in Paul's day was the physical Israel, with its unbelief and hardness of heart as expressed in its persecution of the church which is
the true Israel"; contrast his statement on p. 128: "The new Israel of the church is
thus a continuation of the original Israel"; p. 136: "After the fullness of the
Gentiles has come, and as a consequence of it, all Israel—i.e., the Jews living in
the last days, which to Paul means the present—will be saved"; then again on
p. 138: "But Paul did not deny the importance of ancestry, but only man's right to
use it in making claims upon God. But now God, of his free mercy and for the sake
of the patriarchs and his earlier promises, does not forget his people Israel." My
point is simply that when one assumes that the church is synonymous with Israel

their behavior, like that of the apostle himself,[154] should be directly concerned for the eternal fate of the "weak" (14:13-15, 16ff.), because the good things they have now received are a direct result of the stumbling of Israel. They must learn to see their own history through the lens of salvation history, which means they are linked inextricably to the fate of Israel—with a history that flows through Israel and will always include Israel—"to the Jew first and also to the Greek" is an irreversible pattern.[155] They have not become part of Israel, yet they have become part of Israel's history, an extension of the historic promises made to Abraham, to the fathers—that God's blessings would extend to the whole world through Israel (Deut. 4:1-8).[156]

The task of the "strong," the "able," is thus at this particular moment in salvation history far more difficult than that of the "weak," the "stumbling."[157] They are to accommodate the practices of the "weak"

---

one loses the tension that Paul maintains, and thus one necessarily finds oneself, if one pursues historically concerned exegesis, faced with this kind of inconsistency. Paul did not see the church supplanting Israel. He did not see gentiles supplanting Jews. He saw gentiles joining with Jews in a continuation of salvation history. Gentiles share in the blessings of Israel, but they do not become Israel, for God is the Savior beyond Israel also; he is the Savior of the world. Thus gentiles need not be circumcised and take on the Law, for that would only be necessary to enter Israel, which they do not do.

[154]It is worth noting that Paul regards his ministry as the apostle to these gentiles in the service of Israel's salvation (Munck, *Christ and Israel*, p. 123, sees this in saying: "Paul is nevertheless convinced that Israel is still the chief goal of God's will to salvation" when commenting on 11:13). See chapter 5 below for a full discussion of the two-step pattern.

[155]Interpreters continue to miss the central point of Paul's instructions in chaps. 9–11, in fact, throughout the letter, when they assert that Paul saw the church replacing or becoming Israel, or gentiles as "true Jews," etc. Paul would have responded to these suggestions as he did to the suggestion that the Law was obsolete, "May it never be!" Paul insisted that Israel's distinctive role not only was maintained, but was still the priority. The church was a new entity that consisted of Jews and gentiles coming together in Christ equally, but this meant Israel and the nations had come together to give glory to the God of the whole world (8:18-21; 11:25-36; 15:5-12; 16:25-27), not that Israel alone, as now represented by the church, would give glory to God. For a full discussion see chapter 5 below.

[156]Segal, *Paul*, p. 283.

[157]That is not to say it was easy for first-century Jews to accept the practices of Christian gentiles as appropriate to God! But the contrast is recognizable when it is realized that the non-Christian Jews were being asked only to welcome these gentiles as welcome by God, and not to change their own Jewish behavior, while the gentiles are being asked to change their behavior in a major way. When these

with respect to food, wine, and days. They are to give up their gentile freedoms in Christ and follow his example of bearing reproach,[158] if necessary, in a decided effort "not to put an obstacle or a stumbling block in a brother's way" (14:13) that could "destroy" them, that is, that could come in the way of those "for whom Christ died" (14:15) so that they would not seriously consider (or reconsider) the good news. They are to follow the example of Paul's service (11:13-14; 15:1-2; 16:31), which followed from Christ's service (15:3, 7), which followed from God's service (3:21-26; 15:8), which compels them to maintain certain righteous behavior[159] to "hold up" those who are stumbling so that rather than fall they "stand" (15:1; cf. 11:11; 14:4). They are to take upon themselves the practices of the "righteous gentile" similarly

---

gentiles adopt appropriate "righteous gentile" behavior the concomitant implications of alienation in the larger gentile world and culture are enormous, not to mention the difficulty they would associate with the very practices themselves. The "strong" are thus instructed to change lifestyles in a dramatic way that will effect much more than the change in attitude that the "weak" are called to. And the reasons for this are clearly buried in the continuing and irrevocable priority of Israel in salvation history.

[158]The severity of the task is often overlooked. Imagine this kind of instruction in churches today. This kind of instruction, with its tacit reverence for Jewish Law and customs, with its inherent complications in application to gentiles, and with its confusing implications for defining the relationship of new Christian gentiles to the Jewish Law and customs, surely does not suggest that Paul was as quick to abandon the Law as is often declared. Rather, what we see is a Jew with deep roots in his Jewish faith who understands and respects the beauty of the Law and Jewish customs, but one who is now persuaded that gentiles in Christ have entered the people of God as equals, without becoming Jews. Nevertheless, Paul cannot bring himself to conclude that the Law and Jewish customs should not be operative for gentiles once they have become Christians in guiding their behavior, for they manifest the very righteousness of God embodied by Christ and the love that should now characterize this new assembly.

[159]Sanders, *Paul, the Law*, pp. 6ff., discusses the issue of requirements for those "getting in" versus those "staying in" to distinguish Paul's terminology with regard to the law. He points out that for those already in the new status, that is, Christians, "Paul often draws on the purity language of the Bible in describing behavior appropriate to being Christian, and he can also discuss that behavior as the 'fruit' of living in the Spirit. Most striking for our present purpose is the fact that he can use the language of living by the law in this context." On p. 84, when discussing the dilemma of both positive statements and negative statements about the Law, Sanders says: "I propose that the negative statements arise from the discussion of membership requirements, first of all for Gentiles and then also for

outlined in the apostolic decree[160]—"for he who in this way serves
Christ is acceptable to God and approved by men. So then let us pursue the things which make for peace and the building up of one another" (14:18-19; 15:1-3). Their goal ought to be the "acceptance" of
the "stumbling" that will result in almost incomprehensible "fulfillment" (11:12, 15; 14:1, 3; 15:7ff.), and they must be careful not to be
the cause of further "stumbling" that could instead "destroy with your
food him for whom Christ died" (14:13-15).

It is usually assumed that Paul desired that the "weak," that is,
Christian Jews, become like the "strong," that is, Christian gentiles,
by changing their opinion of the importance of keeping the Law and
Jewish customs.[161] However, when we recognize that the "weak" are
not Christian Jews, but rather non-Christian Jews, we can see that
Paul's intention toward the "weak" was to change their "faith" to faith
in Jesus as the Christ. His message actually parallels the accounts in
Acts where Paul warns those in the synagogue disputing the gospel to
be careful not to reject their promised salvation by failing to believe in

---

Jews. The positive statements arise from questions of behavior within the
Christian community . . . when he was asked, as it were, the question of what was
the necessary and sufficient condition for membership in the body of Christ, he
said 'not the law.' . . . When, however, he thought about behavior, he responded,
'fulfill the law.'" See also pp. 103–5; p. 104: "(1) Paul held the normal expectation
that membership in the 'in-group' involved correct behavior. One of the ways in
which he stated that expectation was that Christians should fulfill the 'the law' or
keep 'the commandments.' (2) In the passages in which he requires fulfillment of
the law, he offers no theoretical distinction between the law which governs
Christians and the law of Moses; put another way, he does not distinguish
between the law to which those in Christ die and the law which they fulfill."

[160]See chapter 4 below for a full discussion of the apostolic decree.

[161]Sanders, *Paul, the Law*, p. 178, concludes a discussion of Paul's practices and
teachings with respect to Jews and gentiles in Christ with just such a statement:
"If Paul's view were to be accepted, Jewish Christians could live strictly as Jews
only as long as they remained in an unmixed community. In the presence of
Gentiles, they should drop those aspects of the law which stand as social barriers.
Thus it seems that we must modify somewhat Davies's statement that 'In Christ
Jews remain Jews and Greeks remain Greeks. Ethnic peculiarities are honoured.'
That is true as long as ethnic peculiarities did not come into conflict. When they
did, the factors which separated Jews from Greeks must be given up by the Jews."
But here we see clearly that that is not necessarily the case in Paul's instructions
with respect to Rome. Notions of Jewish superiority must be given up, but not
Jewish practice. Rather, it is the gentile practices that must change in the presence
of Jews.

Christ.[162] Further, they parallel his stern warning to recognize that salvation is now open, in view of the restoration of Israel in Christ (whether they see it or not, and whether they thus realize the privilege of bearing the light as expected or not), to the gentiles as equal coparticipants in Israel's blessings: the Lord is One.[163]

Concerning the "strong," he does not want them to dispute the "opinions" of the "weak/stumbling." He rather wants them to lay aside their own rights (as gentiles free from the Law) and accommodate the opinions of the "weak/stumbling" (and of Paul!) so that they do not "destroy with your food him for whom Christ died." They ought not to let what is for them a "good thing" (their salvation as gentiles so that they worship Jesus as the Christ without the Law as entrance requirement) "be spoken of as evil" (blasphemed because of behavior characteristic of "bondage to sin" instead of that accompanying those in "bondage to righteousness": 6:12-23).[164]

---

[162]See Acts 13 and chapter 5 below on Paul's two-step pattern. What have been largely regarded as Paul's rejection of those Jews not believing his message should rather be taken in the prophetic sense of warning. He urges them not to let what has been foretold be true of them, but rather they should recognize in his turning to the gentiles that the eschatological blessings, in which they should be sharing first, have arrived as promised, and as promised, are now being brought to all the nations.

[163]Acts 13:40-41, 45-47.

[164]Wedderburn, *Reasons*, p. 141, in his concluding remarks struggles to make sense of the various audiences in Rome and makes the following interesting statement about the group "which embraced many of the practices of Judaism and remained in contact with the synagogue . . . and they by no means need have been confined to those who were Jews by birth, *Paul's gospel and ministry, like the conduct of those following such a gospel in Rome, were an object of grave suspicion.* They shared much of the misgivings, outrage even, of non-Christian Jews both at the *seeming blasphemy of Paul's account* of the story of God's dealings with Israel and the world and at the actual or threatened *immorality* of *his converts.* These two groups of Christians were divided amongst themselves over their observance or nonobservance of the Jewish Law" (emphasis added). Wedderburn follows the tradition of assuming that Paul actually proposed the kind of behavior among the Christian gentiles that we have seen Paul confront as unacceptable throughout Romans. Paul sees what the claims and behavior of Christian gentiles in Rome would appear like to non-Christian Jews. If we see that it was exclusively non-Christian Jews Paul was concerned about protecting from further stumbling, there is no need for this kind of maneuvering to find fault with Paul's gospel, as though it proposed such antinomian behavior. Paul is not the one who is causing the concern; it is precisely this kind of "immorality of" converts tempted to behave improperly when in the company of non-Christian Jews ("the deeds of darkness," 13:11-14) that Paul is confronting, but these are not *"his converts"* (1:11-15;

This is *not* mere tolerance that Paul is calling for from the "strong/able." Rather, they are challenged to live in the light of God's mercy toward the "weak/stumbling" by remembering the principles demonstrated in God's mercy toward themselves (that God has justified them and made them secure in his love and protection). The principles of God's love, embodied in the Law, must now be demonstrated in their commitment to those who now need mercy—indeed, to the "stumbling" of Israel (11:28-32).[165] They are to obey the halakhah governing the behavior of "righteous gentiles" attaching themselves to the worship of the Lord of Israel, the One righteous God of all humankind, in the service of Israel's certain salvation, albeit through an unexpected pattern of gentile involvement (11:25—12:3, 4ff.).

Paul's Hope for the Future Unification of the "Weak" and the "Strong"

When we look closely at how the "weak" and the "strong" are described and regarded, at just what differentiated them and what Paul hoped they would both do; assuming that Paul was not of the opinion that Christian Jews should abandon the keeping of the Law or Jewish customs, and that he would have opposed even the suggestion of that

---

15:14-33; 16:17-27). Paul is the one confronting this audience to halt just such behavior ("lay aside the deeds of darkness and put on the armor of light. Let us behave properly as in the day . . . and make no provision for the flesh in regard to its lusts" [13:11-14]).

The point is: How did these Christian gentiles in Rome suddenly become Paul's converts? And as we have seen throughout Romans it is precisely "Paul's account of the story of God's dealings with Israel and the world" that was intended to correct the Christian gentiles' presumptuous attitude toward Israel and the Law. It was precisely their disregard for proper behavior when in the company of non-Christian Jews that was resulting in the "blasphemy" (14:13-17, 18ff.) that Paul intends to halt with this letter. How did Paul become the protagonist of that which he stands opposed to throughout this letter?

[165]Note that the definition of their new relationship with God and the concomitant assurance of God's protection and intention to bring them to glory in chap. 8 immediately precede the discussion of the current stumbling of Israel, and Paul's concern to redefine that circumstance for the "strong" as a call not to triumphalism, but to responsibility that follows from the mercy of God as expressed in the transitional comments of 11:25—12:3 and then that define the structure of Paul's instructions in the paraenesis we have been discussing. It should be noted that the gifts described in 12:4-8 are not general. They are specific manifestations of the measure of the faith of the strong in their relationship with each other and with the stumbling (see Wedderburn, *Reasons*, pp. 78–82).

kind of behavior for himself or any other Jew (Christian or not)[166]—or
at least with an openness to the suggestion that this was his position in
Romans—a new perspective with far-reaching possibilities emerges.
This perspective respects both the integrity of the Law and the Jewish
practice of faith, and equally respects the integrity of Paul as a Jew, as
well as a Christian, who deeply loved his Jewish brothers and sisters
and who was concerned to correct behavior in Rome that he believed
jeopardized the prospect of some of them sharing his conviction in
Jesus as the Christ of Israel.

Paul was not concerned with distinguishing between Christian
Jews/gentiles who practiced ("weak") or did not practice ("strong")
the Law and Jewish customs, with the hope that all would eventually
abandon the Law and customs as they grew stronger in their faith in
Christ. His concern was rather that all the non-Christian Jews ("stumbling" in faith toward Christ) in Rome would recognize that Jesus was
the Christ of Israel, their Savior, and that they would thus believe in
Christ and become Christians ("able" to have faith toward Christ)—
Christian Jews.[167] As Christian Jews they would indeed continue to be
Jews in that they continue to practice the Law and Jewish customs in
faith, not in order to justify themselves, but because they are Jews justified by the Jewish Savior/Messiah/Christ, thus joining with gentiles
who are Christians in giving glory with "one accord" and thus "one

---

[166]W. Campbell, *Intercultural Context*, pp. 98–121, 122–53; note on p. 100:
"Because Paul cannot yield on this point [the gospel is available to gentiles on the
same terms as Jews] does not mean that he opposed all things Jewish or that he
would discourage Jewish Christians from following a Jewish lifestyle after they
had become Christians. This stipulation that Jewish Christians recognise the right
of Gentile Christians to be accepted into the people of God and continue to live
a Gentile (Christian) lifestyle, does not mean that such Jewish Christians as recog-
nised this, should not also have the freedom to continue to live in a Jewish life
style [*sic*]. New Testament scholars have in the past tended to presume that all
Jewish Christians who wished to continue to follow a Jewish life style [*sic*] must
necessarily deny the right of Gentile Christians to follow a Gentile lifestyle. But
logic does not demand this conclusion. The two positions, ie Jewish Christians
continuing to follow a Jewish pattern of life, and Gentile Christians continuing to
follow a Gentile pattern of life, are not mutually exclusive." See also Markus
Barth, "A Good Jew," pp. 7–45; Stendahl, *Paul*, pp. 11–13; Kaylor, *Paul's Covenant
Community*, pp. 171–72, 181–83; Gaston, *Paul*, pp. 7–8, 78–82, 83ff., 135ff.

[167]Fraikin puts this nicely in "Rhetorical Function," p. 98, when he observes:
"The Jew . . . is not asked to surrender being a Jew, but to become a different kind
of Jew" because "he is asked to accept also Paul's interpretation of the Christ
event on which the justification by faith is based."

voice" to the One Lord: "the God and Father of our Lord Jesus Christ" (15:6).

If my reading of Romans is correct, Paul and his audience would have understood the phrase usually translated "weak in faith" to be a highly nuanced and respectful reference to the Jews in Rome who were not Christians.[168] They had faith in God, the Lord of Israel, and were thus brothers and sisters to Paul and other Christian Jews; they were likewise brothers and sisters to the Christian gentiles because they were believers in the same God whom these gentiles had recently come to recognize. However, their faith was "weak/stumbling" (unable) with respect to: (1) their failure to yet believe that Jesus was the Christ, and (2) their failure to respect the coparticipation of gentiles in the blessings of God through faith in Jesus Christ without also becoming Jews.

This circumstance Paul ironically explains as a "mystery" that these gentiles have not been able to see (they have been hardened partially?), in light of which they have therefore grown mistakenly arrogant toward the "stumbling" as though they had supplanted them (11:16-32).[169] He explains this "mystery" so that they will now be

[168]One might ask why, if Paul means stumbling in the paraenesis of 12:1—15:13, he does not use προσκόμματος or ἔπταισαν as he had in 9:32 and 11:11. I suggest that it is because the stumbling of 12:1—15:13 is a description of their "faith" in the current situation, describing their "inability" ("weakness") to see (and its association with powerlessness as we saw earlier) and believe in Jesus as the Christ, in direct contrast to the faith of those with the "ability" to see clearly and believe. It addresses the implicit power they have over the fate of those already "stumbling," and thus it echoes the tension we saw in the Septuagint and Qumran literature where the nuance points to the secondary source of stumbling at the hands of humans instead of God. God's involvement in hardening and allowing them to stumble is, as we have seen, intended to save in the end. It is not to destroy. It is not from contempt. However, the stumbling discussed here is concerned with human acts done in contempt that will lead to destruction, whether that has been their calculated intention or not. Rashi on Zech. 1:15 ("for I was but a little displeased, and they helped forward the affliction") develops this same nuance in explaining that the nations have afflicted Israel beyond what God had intended.

[169]Interestingly, the gentiles are unable to see, as though they too, in some ironic way, were hardened/blinded to the truth that Paul is now revealing (note the play on concepts: partial hardening of Israel, meaning some of Israel cannot see versus hardening part of the gentiles, meaning they cannot see fully). Why would this be the case in Rome? This suggests again my thesis of the two-step pattern explored in chapter 5 below. And again, it reveals the nuance that Paul has mined throughout this letter to illustrate the error of presumptuous judgment of the

"able" to see what God is doing, the process he is employing to demonstrate his faithfulness and mercy, not only to Israel first, but also to the whole world.[170] He has caused a "hardening" of some of the Jews (11:25) who were "stumbling" over the "stumbling stone" that has resulted in the mercy of God to the gentiles for the purpose not only of bringing the blessings of God to the gentiles, but also to ensure that the mercies of God go to "all Israel" (11:25-32). Paul reveals in this mystery that there is a new stage in the process of salvation history in addition to the stages he had outlined in chapter 4 earlier:

> it is now Abraham to Israel to Christ to Israel and to gentiles/nations *and to* Israel *again*—and thus to the whole world.[171]

This situation thereby obligates the Christian gentiles in Rome to see their role in service to the "stumbling" and not over against them, and thus to maintain a certain accommodating behavior that is strangely familiar in Luke's description of the apostolic decree[172] (in purpose and in requirements, and Paul hopes, in their enthusiastic

---

other: since you in fact are only saved by grace you ought to be grateful and look toward the other graciously, for you are made of the same stuff (the real point of 2:1-16, 17ff. is this very message to the Christian gentiles with regard to judging the non-Christian Jews when they ought to be grateful when for the "the riches of His kindness and forbearance and patience" that has led them to "repentance" and hopeful that God is in the process of extending the same to those not yet recognizing what God has done for them in Christ Jesus). See Campbell, "Romans III," pp. 262–64; Wright, *Climax*, pp. 234–35.

[170]It is generally thought that Paul reverses his pattern in 11:25-32, in view of the realities of the situation; that is, it is assumed he has changed the pattern of the gospel's declaration from the Jew first to the gentile first because that is the way things are happening. But I do not think this is the case at all. Paul saw this reality before composing the letter and did not need to make it a central tenet if he saw it was flawed. Rather, Paul explains that the process is difficult for them to see in Rome, but that God is still faithful to the Jew first, even when it does not appear so. The anomaly is revealed when the situation in Rome is seen to depart from Paul's two-step pattern of apostolic ministry, which is the case in Rome because he has not yet been able to preach there as was his "custom." For a full discussion of this issue see chapter 5 on the two-step pattern.

[171]Again, Paul's abiding love for Israel and his resolute belief that Israel was still central in God's intentions shows through. How can commentator after commentator maintain that Paul has abandoned Israel and given up on her when we see Paul developing such complicated scenarios to affirm Israel's priority in hope, in spite of all appearances to the contrary.

[172]Acts 15:19, 20ff.; 16:1-4; 21:25; see chapter 4 below for full discussion.

response [Acts 15:31-32; 16:3-4]), so that they might not contribute to the further "stumbling" of those already in the process of doing so, but rather, they might join Paul in ensuring that the "stumbling" would soon join with themselves in declaring, together, the glories of God in Christ (Rom. 15:5-13). "Christ has become a servant to the circumcision" (15:8); so too must the "strong" (15:1-3; cf. 12:1-3, 4ff.).

The interpreters' choice of the label "weak" presumes a pejorative reference to Christians in Rome whom Paul wishes would join with those who do not practice the Law and Jewish customs (the assumptions earlier outlined as Luther's trap that follow from assuming the "weak" must have been Christians). It is not that the practice of their faith as Christians is weakened by their continuing practice of the Law and Jewish customs (would Paul have even considered such a concept?). It is rather Paul's way of describing (his euphemism, his vocabulary not yet including the term "Christian," or at least not in the same sweeping sense it has come to have) *the faith* in God of those he still considered part of the people of God who had not *yet* recognized that Jesus was the Christ of Israel: non-Christian Jews.[173] "Stumbling in faith" was Paul's phrase to describe the present anomaly of the faith of some of the non-Christian Jews in Rome. They were indeed "brethren," they were, however, in need of help to be "able" to see: (1) that the hope of Israel has come in Christ Jesus, and (2) that gentiles are now equal coparticipants in these blessings of God through their faith in Jesus Christ without becoming a part of Israel (Jews), for the One God of Israel has always intended to become known as the One God of the whole world.

Rather than cultivate the arrogance of gentile freedom from the practice of the Law and Jewish custom, Paul calls his audience to embrace the principles of love that were inherent in the intentions of the apostolic decree, so that, instead of angering the non-Christian Jews in Rome with behavior they would regard as reprehensible for gentiles claiming association with Israel and her God, they would respectfully "win" them to "faith" in Jesus as the promised Christ. Paul did not want the "strong" to misunderstand their new status in a self-righteous and triumphant way that would lead them to hold the "stumbling" in contempt, which would have made them guilty of the

---

[173]Munck, *Christ and Israel*, p. 124, makes the same kind of observation about Paul's use of "some" (*tines*) in 11:17: "It is this careful, almost covert way of speaking of Israel's unbelief and stumbling which explains the use of *tines* here, expressing an indefinite number, which the context must define further."

same misplaced arrogance they were quick to observe on the part of
the "stumbling" toward themselves.[174]

The implications for ecumenical and pastoral issues are many and
far reaching. One immediate example is that the relative faith of non-
Christian Jews in God is honored[175] (both in their faith in God and in

---

[174]This concern for humble recognition of the grace of God that has worked toward the ones who are "in" so that they do not presumptuously regard their status a result of their own doing leading to the kind of pride that hardens into disregard both for the gift they have received from God and contempt for those they
deem "outside" or less righteous than themselves, stands in the tradition of all
biblical history (it is the backdrop for Deut. and Isaiah and it is Paul's central motif
throughout Romans put succinctly in 2:1-4, 5ff.). Paul's juxtaposition of those
"able" and "unable" with the nuance that the "able" should use their "ability" for
the benefit of the "unable" as Christ had, instead of growing wise in their own estimation and holding the "unable" in contempt and acting in a manner that will
result in the "unable" being even more "unable" to recognize God's grace because of the hypocrisy they see in the "able," mirrors the message of Jesus, for example, in Luke 18:9-14. There Jesus "told this parable to certain ones who trusted
in themselves that they were righteous, and viewed others with contempt. . . . The
Pharisee stood and was praying thus to himself, 'God, I thank Thee that I am not
like other people: swindlers, unjust, adulterers, or even like this tax-gatherer'. . . .
But the tax-gatherer, standing some distance away, was even unwilling to lift up
his eyes to heaven, but was beating his breast, saying, 'God, be merciful to me, the
sinner!' I tell you, this man went down to his house justified rather than the other;
for every one who exalts himself shall be humbled, but he who humbles himself
shall be exalted." This was a frequent theme for Jesus, and he drew it back
through John the Baptist in Luke 7:29-30: "And when all the people and the tax-
gatherers heard this, they acknowledged God's justice, having been baptized with
the baptism of John. But the Pharisees and the lawyers rejected God's purpose for
themselves, not having been baptized by John." But this is not a new message
with John the Baptist or Jesus or Paul; it stands in the tradition of Israel's leaders
and prophets. It goes back through the prophets and the kings and the judges to
Moses himself in Deuteronomy, from which Paul drew much of his inspiration for
Romans. This was central all the way back to the garden—it is one of the central
concerns of the people of God that when they seek righteousness nobly they are
not caught in the seemingly ineluctable snare of self-righteous judgmentalism.
This problem is faced by everyone—it is no respecter of persons. When it is noted
in the behavior and attitudes of Pharisees or the "stumbling" it is not their special
sin. This is the same sin that the Roman Christian gentiles are guilty of as Paul addresses them. It is the sin of persons concerned with holiness, avoided only when
they recognize that their status, even as the status of the other, is a gift of God's
mercy and should result in compassion rather than contempt. See the discussion
in appendix 1 below, where this concern is traced in Rom. 7 and Gal. 2.
[175]Meeks, "Judgment and the Brother," p. 297, notes Paul's intention in this
paraenesis similarly.

their practice of the Law and Jewish custom to genuinely please God: 14:2-8), and the focus of the issue is restored to its historical context: Christianity was for Paul and the early church a Jewish faith that understood itself not as breaking from the historical faith of Israel,[176] but rather as representing Israel restored in Jesus as the Christ of Israel, with the task of bringing this "good news" to the Jews of the Diaspora (the children of Jacob) and to all the gentiles of the world who could now participate in Israel's blessing because Jesus was the promised Savior of Israel and of the world. Christians, whether Jews or gentiles, and Jews (whether Christians or not) are indeed "brothers and sisters."

THE IMPACT OF REDEFINING THE "WEAK" AND THE "STRONG" ON THE PURPOSE AND MESSAGE OF ROMANS

By demonstrating that the "weak/stumbling" in Rome were non-Christian Jews rather than Christians, this reading does much more than answer the challenge of Klein for internal consistency between the concerns expressed in the paraenesis of 14:1—15:13 and the rest of the letter. In effect, this paraenesis is raised to a new level of importance as the essential intention of the letter.[177] We see how it

---

[176]Hays, *Echoes*, p. 87: "Does he think of the church as organically continuous with Israel or as having superseded it? We saw in Romans that he argued passionately for organic continuity."

[177]Wright, *Climax*, pp. 234–35: "And it is only on the basis of the whole of Romans 1–11 that the warning of 11.13 ff.—to gentile Christians who are tempted to the arrogance of saying that Jews are now cut out of the covenant family permanently—can be understood. The theology which produces this understanding of mission in 10.14 ff. and 11.13 ff. is then, in 12–16, made the basis of the appeal for unity in the church itself: in particular, the strong must bear with the weak, and not please themselves. One of the exegetical strengths of the view I am proposing is that not only 9–11 but also 14.1—15.13 find new coherence with the argument of the letter as a whole, and the climax of the latter passage (15.7-13) can be seen in fact as the climax of the entire epistle." Wuellner, "Paul's Rhetoric," p. 144, draws together the place of the paraenesis similarly: "What happens when one sees the special parenesis in Romans . . . in the light of the Pauline intentions stated in the *exordium* and *transitus*, and reiterated in the peroration? We see that the 'logical and purposeful thought sequence' of this parenetic section functions as an *exemplum* or paradigm of Paul's basic thesis." But this investigation has shown his next statement to be in error: "Within the argumentation as a whole it functions as a digression," he then follows with: "Only by ignoring the structural rhetorical function of this whole sequence can one be surprised as Käsemann is by the complete vanishing of all references to the seemingly concrete tensions and controversies at the end when one might expect a climactic resolution. But if we

provides the immediate practical instructions for Christian gentiles who were tempted to disregard the minimum requirements expected of "righteous gentiles" when seeking association with Israel and her God, who were thus perhaps being confronted with skepticism and contempt in the presence of non-Christian Jews.[178]

We also solve the riddle of how this paraenesis flows from the instructions to give their bodies in God's service as they have their minds renewed. The various nuances of instruction toward "brethren" inside (their fellow Christians) and "brethren" outside (their neighbors, non-Christian Jews) juxtaposed in the bracketing context of 12:1—13:14 and 15:14—16:27 are not random.[179] They apply specifi-

---

place the special parenesis in its rhetorical structure, then it becomes clear that the 'exemplum' of 14:1ff. concretizes in the same way that 13:1-7 concretizes. Both concretize what is expressed in the series of *topoi* or *loci* in 12:3ff. The argumentative quality of these general and special parenetic sections is an extension of the argumentation first introduced in the *exordium*, and carried out in 1:16—11:36, and the case comes to rest not until 15:13, thus making 1:16—15:13 one 'coherent' argument." See also Meeks, "Judgment."

[178]While I cannot explore the context of 8:12-39 fully here, note that this reading opens up many statements that have not yet been freed from the heritage of systematic treatments of Romans to recognize the reality of the tensions in Rome that these new gentile converts would encounter on their trips to the synagogue for the Scripture readings, etc., when they naively in their initial visits, and defiantly later, claimed to be equal coparticipants in Israel's blessings without regard for Israel's role, for the Law, for the minimum observations of righteousness, etc.

[179]If we assume chap. 16 should be included; if not, then the balance of 15:14ff. would form the final bracket. Also note that Wedderburn, *Reasons*, recognizes the tension we have explored (he comes close to seeing the apostolic decree at work but he assumes both that the decree is not operative and that the "weak" are Christians) when he states on pp. 77–78: "The upshot of this argument is to conclude that, when Paul speaks in such seemingly general terms in 12.2 of the renewal of the Romans' minds, he already has in view *a quite concrete application of this renewal*: he wants them to view their fellow Christians in the Roman church in a new light, in the light of the new age in which they live and in the light of Christ, the representative person of that new age whom they must, as it were, put on. They must above all be *able* to *discern God's will* in the matter of *their attitude to the ritual observances which are at issue* between them, to see how they are *concretely to serve God in a manner pleasing to God*. It can also be argued that the rest of the contents of chapters 12 and 13 are far from being as general as many scholars suppose . . . we can see a whole series of seemingly general instructions which take on a new immediacy when set in the context of the situation of the Roman church when they are read in the light of what follows, particularly in chapter 14, but also in chapter 15." And he further states on p. 87: "In this way 12.2 may be said to

cally to the context of the Christian gentiles in Rome in their new association within the larger Jewish community(s), including both Christian and non-Christian Jews.

We also see how this paraenesis flows from the concerns expressed in Paul's discussion of the incomprehensible unbelief of many Jews in Christ[180] and Paul's unmistakable commitment to his "brethren." Christian gentiles must learn to understand that Israel's suffering is vicariously for their gain (11:12, 25), and ultimately will climax in Israel's success.[181] Thus the present state of the stumbling of some of Israel must be regarded not with triumphant contempt, but humbly, in recognition of the implicit responsibility that comes with their new

_____

introduce the main thrust of Paul's exhortations in Rom 12.1—15.13, a thrust that is highly relevant to, and directed towards, *a specific situation in the Roman church.*" (emphasis added). Wedderburn on pp. 79–82, gives a nice summary of the gifts in 12:6ff. as they relate to the situation between the "weak" and the "strong." Wedderburn on p. 82 interestingly notes that 12:17-21 "deals with Christians' response to ill-treatment at the hands of non-Christians." On pp. 83–84, Wedderburn reflects on 13:8-10 as it is linked with 12:9ff. by the theme of love: "Interestingly, and rather surprisingly, it is here linked to the keeping of the Jewish Law."

[180]Munck, *Christ and Israel*, p. 78, in discussing the theme of 9:30—10:21, observes: "The core of the passage is God's way of salvation by faith, and His constant effort to make Israel hear and follow that way." I merely carry that same concern into chap. 14 as Paul's operative vantage point as well. Hays, *Echoes*, p. 73, in summarizing his findings in Romans on Paul's use of the Septuagint: "In surveying the scriptural texts that sound within Paul's discourse in Romans, we have observed an extraordinary—indeed, almost monotonous—thematic consistency. In Romans, Paul cites Scripture not as a repository of miscellaneous wisdom on various topics but as an insistent witness of one great truth: God's righteousness, which has now embraced Gentiles among the people of God, includes the promise of God's unbroken faithfulness to Israel. Virtually every text that Paul cites or alludes to is made to circle around this one theme. It is as though the letter were a great parabola that picks up echoes of Scripture and reflects them all onto a single focal point."

[181]Paul saw that some Jews were stumbling because they were unable to see clearly, yet these too were destined for glory. Their suffering was somehow strangely part of God's plan so that gentiles could see and be enabled to believe, therefore receiving God's mercy (11:25-36). Some Jews were thus suffering vicariously for the sake of these gentiles' salvation. These gentiles must now learn to see that they are obligated to help those stumbling to stand; they must hold them up so they can see, for "if their transgression be riches for the world and their failure be riches for the Gentiles, how much more will their fulfillment be!" (11:12). For a full discussion see chapter 5 below on the two-step pattern.

privilege, as gentiles, of joining in the praise of Israel's One God as the One God of all the world.[182]

This paraenesis flows from Paul's discussion of how Christian gentiles, while free from the Law as both entrance requirement and empowerment for righteousness, are nevertheless slaves of righteousness in Christ, even if their new status is perhaps cause for reproach and suffering from some non-Christian Jews (when they attend synagogue or meet in their homes under synagogue authority), and from Christian gentiles who do not believe they should accommodate Jewish opinions of righteousness and purity. Thus Romans 5:1—8:39 addresses Christian gentiles who are now safely included in God's election as "righteous gentiles" without becoming Jews, with the responsibility that this implies to live *on behalf of* rather than *over against* the other—in this case the non-Christian Jew.[183] This follows from understanding how God has always reckoned righteousness toward those of faith, whether they were Jews, and as such part of the historical people of God with the privileged oracles pointing the way toward God's righteousness and mercy, or gentiles responding to what they inherently know to be right (1:11—4:25). The "able" have received a "measure of faith" not to judge the other but to serve the other, for God is surely the ultimate judge, and all stand as one in the need for his grace.[184]

This reading thus promotes a much deeper level of tension in Paul's major concerns throughout the letter: presumption—arrogance—boasting versus grace—humility—graciousness; reproaches—hope—glory versus hardening—stumbling—shame; faithfulness—righteousness—justification versus suppression of truth—unrighteous-

---

[182]Hays, *Echoes*, p. 86: "What Paul finds in Scripture, above all else, is a prefiguration of the 'church' as the people of God. . . . This way of reading is not just a contingent effect of the problems addressed in Romans. In the other letters also, Paul uses Scripture primarily to shape his understanding of the community of faith; conversely, Paul's experience of the Christian community—composed of Jews and Gentiles together—shapes his reading of Scripture. In short, Paul operates with an 'ecclesiocentric' hermeneutic." See Wedderburn, *Reasons*, pp. 88–91; on p. 88 he says: "'by God's mercies' in 12:1 Paul linked the following exhortations to the conclusion of the preceding argument: God's mercy had been a repeated theme of chapters 9–11."

[183]See Wedderburn, *Reasons*, pp. 130–38, for a discussion of Paul's development of Hab. 2:4, "shall live," in Rom. 5–8.

[184]Meeks, "Judgment," notes similarly the link between the judging of chap. 14 and that of chaps. 1–3.

ness—wrath. We see these in their historical milieu as two cultures clash, each presuming they are God's elect, yet each failing to see (each blinded in his/her own way) that this means they are recipients of God's grace not for their own selfish purposes resulting in arrogance and intolerance, but so that they might be bearers of God's grace to those who, like themselves, recognize that they need his grace, for the Lord is One.[185]

Rather than deny the valid pursuit of understanding the situation in Rome or the issues operative for Paul outside of Rome, this reading of Romans reconciles this unnecessary bifurcation with a theme that amplifies both. A clearer picture is developed: Paul is addressing the audience in Rome specifically as Christian gentiles, and even though there are Christian Jews in Rome, it is Paul's purpose to address the issues of Christian gentiles failing to understand how they fit into salvation history and how their behavior could (and should not) offend, even to the point of destroying, the non-Christian Jews with whom they were now associating in the Jewish community(s) among which they lived and practiced their faith in Christ.[186]

We see how early Christian communities were indistinguishably tied to the synagogue communities, meeting regularly in their

---

[185]The concept of election in Romans concerns this struggle. They are elected to serve the interests and needs of the other in view of God's grace toward them rather than to seek their own status or pleasure as a judgment of the other. To be chosen is a humbling responsibility, embodied in the Law of love (for "all observance is training in the art of love": Heschel, *Between God and Man*, p. 162), and in the life of Christ, the very goal of the Law, so that the elect would now take on this responsibility empowered by the Holy Spirit. Hays, *Echoes*, pp. 73–83, discusses the issue of Torah and Christ in 9:30—10:21 and says: "the word of God, now present in the Christian gospel, is the same word of God that was always present to Israel in Torah. It was so close to them that they had no need to go looking for it; yet they were unable to hear it." Meeks, "Judgment," p. 297: "Those acts of judging one another that divide the people of God run directly contrary to the universal judgment of the one God. Until the strong accept the weak and the weak the strong, the liberated and the scrupulous each other, they do not yet understand the implication of the fact that 'Christ has accepted us.'"

[186] The struggle was not within the Christian community(s) in Rome per se. It was taking place within Jewish community(s), which now included the Christian community(s) with their "righteous gentile" adherents as subgroups, though they were questioning the legitimacy of the new Christian claims of/for these gentiles. The Christian Jews were concerned that these Christian gentiles were abandoning the "form of teaching" they had learned, i.e., the apostolic decree and its broader application of deference to Israel and the Diaspora Jews. Also the matter

company (whether at synagogue for teaching and prayer/worship, or in their homes under the authority of the synagogue), and thus how important the apostolic decree was at that time in defining proper monotheistic behavior for these new worshipers of Israel's God. We gain a glimpse of churches that were not yet separate institutions when Paul wrote Romans. Nor do we find Paul involved in developing any kind of dissociating policy for the new gentile adherents of the faith, nor for those Jews who were believing in Jesus as the Christ of Israel. On the contrary, we see Paul attempting to reconcile two factions operating under the umbrella of Judaism as the one community of God, as promised, in the hope that they would ultimately welcome one another in worship of the One Lord of all the world.

This reading also sets the stage for exploring the depth of Paul's concern for the unification inherent in the collection and his trip to Jerusalem as affected by circumstances in Rome and the reports that they might generate. Further, it makes sense of Paul's intended trip to Rome (and Spain, the "ends of the earth") to preach the gospel there. He intended to begin with synagogues that he hopes will not have already been alienated and thus still receptive to his message of the "hope of Israel" (Acts 27:20ff.), followed by his characteristic turning to the gentiles with the "good news" also. This pattern had not been followed in Rome thus far, therefore, the gentiles in Rome were not yet "established" in their faith. They were not aware of how their faith was woven into the fabric of salvation history, nor were they aware of the full impact of their responsibilities as the people of God. It is in this light that we can perceive the immediate and epideictic nature of Paul's letter to the Romans.

We gain a new perspective on Paul's deep commitment to the Law, nuanced by his uncompromising concern to maintain the universal salvation that was at the heart of monotheism, for he regarded his Jewish brothers and sisters as fellow believers in the One God, though, not yet in God's Christ, the promised "seed." Rather than focusing on the assumption that "weak" is a pejorative or patronizing reference to

must be considered of Paul's sensitivity to Jews as an oppressed minority living in the kingdom of gentiles (in the case of Rome the center of the kingdom), which they see as the oppressors of the kingdom of Israel and thus of God, now confronted by gentile triumphalism—certainly one can see the inherent threat and distasteful reaction on the part of Jews, whether Christian or not, particularly if these same gentiles are tempted to flaunt their freedom from the law as a central tenet of this new coalition.

Christian Jews who practice the Law with its arrogant assumption that this is a failure to have complete faith apart from Torah, we spring Luther's trap and instead focus on Paul's continuing respect for keeping the Law as an act of faith that leads to and continues to manifest the very love of God demonstrated in Christ. And we see Paul wrestling with the tensions created by maintaining that the Law continued to be operative for Jews but was not necessary for gentiles to become coparticipants in Israel's blessings (for the blessings were actually for the whole world equally), and yet the need for gentiles to live as "slaves of righteousness," which meant in love they fulfilled the Law as they maintained the intentions of the apostolic decree— the halakhah governing the behavior of "righteous gentiles" loyal to the One Lord. Together, these observations allow us to see Paul as a faithful Jew, in fact, as a champion of Israel's historical faith, in his bold "reminder" to those in Rome whom he understood to be "righteous gentiles" through their new faith in Christ Jesus.

CHAPTER 4

THE APOSTOLIC DECREE AND THE "OBEDIENCE OF FAITH"

The Jerusalem Council, according to Luke's account in Acts 15, decided that gentiles were to be admitted as equals into the new community of Christian Jews through faith in Christ Jesus without needing to become Jews. Yet they were not to be admitted to this new faction of Judaism as pagans, for they were to respect the halakhah of the "righteous gentile" operative in Judaism at the time. These halakhot were outlined by the Council as the so-called apostolic decree (Acts 15:19-21, 28-29; 21:24-25).[1] These rules of behavior for the gentiles who believed in Jesus as the Christ demonstrated fidelity to the Judaic norms of righteousness that were operative at the time for gentiles who had turned from idolatry to the worship of the One God. In this sense one may speak of the early Christian gentiles as "righteous gentiles."[2] However, their status in this new Jewish coalition differed unmistakably from that of other "righteous gentiles" in the Jewish community(s), for even though the Christian "righteous gentiles" did not become Jews and thus were not part of Israel, they were part of the community of the Holy Spirit that represented the fulfillment of the promises of God to restore Israel (15:16) and gather in the nations (15:17)—*as equals*.[3]

This was a remarkable decision, for in the prevailing Jewish notions of the "righteous gentile" (among which there was a wide spectrum of views from complete accommodation at one extreme to total contempt

---

[1]See the discussion of the apostolic decree and table-fellowship issues in chapter 2 above, where many of the these points concerning "righteous gentiles" are developed with appropriate notation.

[2]See Simon, *Verus Israel*, pp. 334–38, 408, for development of a similar viewpoint. Also Segal, *Paul*, p. 197.

[3]Schoeps, *Paul*, pp. 250–51: "The *gere toshab* of Judaism, admitted to salvation, as it were, on an inferior level, were in consequence of the Pauline apostolic ministry equated with Jews by birth. The result which Paul fought to achieve at Antioch was just this breaking down of the wall of partition, the declaration that the Gentiles committed only to the *Derekh Eres*, or the Noachide laws, had come of age."

at the other; cf. the tensions developed in the example of Izates[4]) gentiles, who were often in various stages of the process of conversion,[5]
were to be accepted by God in the age to come, and they were accepted by the Jewish community for their fear of God, but they were
certainly not equals.[6] Nevertheless, the Council's decision was that
God had shown gentiles to be equals in view of their equal receipt of
the Holy Spirit through faith in Christ Jesus (15:8-11, 19) in fulfillment
of the eschatological promises that were expected to follow from the

[4]There is a clear line of universalism from biblical times, though not without
contrasting and exclusivistic views at the other extreme. Cf. Josephus, *Ant.* 2.3–4
(13–19). See Segal, *Paul,* pp. 96–105; idem, "Universalism in Judaism and
Christianity," pp. 1–29, for excellent discussions; J. Nolland, "Uncircumcised
Proselytes?" pp. 192–94; Sanders, *Paul and Palestinian Judaism,* pp. 207–12, for discussion of rabbinic views, both positive and negative.

[5]Moore, *Judaism,* 1.331–35, discusses the three parts of initiation for proselytes:
"circumcision, immersion in water (baptism), and the presentation of an offering
in the temple. . . . As soon as he was circumcised and baptized, he was in full
standing in the religious community, having all the legal rights and powers and
being subject to all the obligations of the Jew by birth. He had 'entered into the
covenant.'" See also Segal, *Paul,* pp. 72–114, on various conversion ideas at the
time of Paul; Novak, *Dialogue,* pp. 29–30; and Lake, "Proselytes and God-
Fearers," pp. 77–80, for conversion process.

[6]The rabbinic assertion of equality in the age to come for all who reject idolatry ("Every one who rejects idolatry is on a par with the Jew": *b. Megilla* 13a) certainly represents the view of some first-century Jews as well, particularly in the
context of the place of "righteous gentiles" in the future world. Yet the distinction
in the minority Jewish community would most naturally, in most if not all cases,
have included some disparity. "Righteous gentiles" were not Jews. We know that
Philo had to confront this issue even on the part of those who had become full
proselytes; how much more difficult was unequivocal respect for those who did
not convert. Even events like Passover naturally promote the distinction of those
who are not circumcised and their separation from the historical people of God.
Note the concerns of Peter toward Cornelius, "a righteous and God-fearing man
well spoken of by the entire nation of the Jews," yet certainly not an equal (Acts
10:22; cf. 10:9-21, 28, 34-35, 45-47; 11:1-18; 15:7-21 [Simon, *Verus Israel,* p. 278]).
Moore, *Judaism,* 1.325–26, 327ff.: "Such converts were called religious persons
('those who worship, or revere, God'), and although in a strict sense outside the
pale of Judaism, undoubtedly expected to share with Jews by birth the favor of the
God they had adopted, and were encouraged in this hope by their Jewish teachers. . . . However numerous such 'religious persons' were, and with whatever com-
plaisance the Hellenistic synagogue, especially, regarded these results of its propaganda, whatever hopes they may have held out to such as thus confided in the
uncovenanted mercies of God, they were only clinging to the skirt of the Jew
(Zech. 8, 23); they were like those Gentile converts to Christianity who are reminded in the Epistle to the Ephesians that in their former state, when they were

restoration of Israel[7] (15:13-18: James regards the gentile salvation by grace through faith a witness that Israel has been restored and thus God is now "taking from among the Gentiles a people for His name"),[8] with the unmistakable caveat that while they were to remain gentiles, they were not to behave as pagans (15:5, 19-21, 28-29). They were to obey the monotheistic tenets of the "righteous gentile" that demonstrated they had turned from idolatry to the fear of the One God, for this behavior was understood by Jews everywhere to be incumbent upon gentiles who turned to worship the One God of Israel as the One God of the whole world, as James explained in outlining the reason for developing the decree (15:21).[9]

Luke outlined these principles in the so-called apostolic decree,

---

called uncircumcised by the so-called circumcision, they were aliens to the Israelite commonwealth, foreigners without right in the covenanted promises." On the issue of gentile status see also Schoeps, *Paul*, pp. 220–29, 245–58; Simon, *Verus Israel*, p. 380; Segal, *Paul*, pp. 94–101, 265; McKnight, *Light*, pp. 12–15, 25–29; S. Cohen, "Crossing the Boundary," pp. 11–33, esp. 27.

[7]Donaldson, "Proselytes or 'Righteous Gentiles," pp. 3–27.

[8]Jervell, *Luke*, pp. 51–55, 56ff., 92–94.

[9]The real intentions of the apostolic decree are often overlooked because the context is presumed to address Christianity as a separate institution, as though fellowship was already only in the context of "Christian" Jews. The apostolic decree mirrored the purpose of the Mosaic model for the "stranger" in the land of Israel; however, the apostolic decree was concerned with gentiles seeking association with Jewish communities throughout the Diaspora, wherever Moses was read. The context was not just Christian Jews, and more importantly, not just in Christian meetings. Indeed, one could argue that the reason some Christian Jews were so concerned with this issue was because it was a matter of concern within the larger Jewish community and among its authorities, particularly in some quarters in Jerusalem that may have been putting pressure on the early Christian Jewish leaders (see R. Jewett, "The Agitators and the Galatian Congregation," pp. 198–212; R. Longenecker, *Galatians*, pp. xciii–c, 74–75). See Jervell, *Luke*, p. 144: "No matter how the complicated passage Acts 15:21 is to be interpreted in detail, the function of the verse is to validate the decree, to call upon Moses as witness. Everyone who truly hears Moses knows that the decree expresses what Moses demands from Gentiles in order that they may live among Israelites (15:15-17). The four prescriptions are what the law demands of Gentiles; perhaps Luke consciously refers to what Lev. 17–18 demands from the 'strangers' who sojourn among Israelites." Räisänen, *Paul*, p. 92 n. 257, corrects Jervell by noting that "the decree is not understood as an OT precept but as an expression of consideration for Jews or Jewish Christians who are present everywhere." Both concepts are likely. S. Wilson, *Luke and the Law*, p. 84, discusses Luke's use of κηρύσσοντας in 15:21: "That Luke chooses this term to describe Jewish preaching in the synagogues perhaps suggests that he was thinking of preaching to Gentiles who

which represents a first-century development that stands somewhere between the ancient Mosaic model for governing the behavioral requirements for the "stranger within your gates", that is, of the non-Jew living in the land of Israel (Lev. 17–18),[10] and the later rabbinic model of the Noahide Commandments that addressed the paradoxical issues that arose in Diaspora contexts, particularly after the rise of Christianity.[11] The apostolic decree needed to meet the requirements of both in the unique setting of early Christianity as an expression of Judaism. On the one hand, gentiles were attaching themselves to the Jewish community and were thus under their jurisdiction, thereby making the ethical and purity issues of the Mosaic model operative for governing the behavior of "strangers." On the other hand, this was a diaspora setting where the Jewish community was not generally in a position of authority over gentiles; they were rather the ones sojourning in gentile lands and under Roman rule. Thus, the apostolic decree offers a unique opportunity to see a developmental period in the transition from the laws of the sojourner in Israel to the laws understood to apply to the "righteous gentile" in the later discussions concerning what came to crystallization in rabbinic Judaism as the Noahide Commandments.[12]

It is likely that we have in the outline of the apostolic decree four of the most operative points in the first century c.e. of the seven Noahide Commandments outlined in the Mishnah approximately one hundred fifty years later.[13] The very concept of these laws in both early Christian and rabbinic Judaism itself bears witness to the ongoing

---

attended the synagogue (e.g., Jos. *Bell.* 2.560; 7.45) rather than the regular reading and exposition of the law for Jews, which was the main purpose of synagogue gatherings" (see also his comments on p. 95).

[10]See the discussion in chapter 2 above and Novak, *Image*, pp. 3–35; Segal, *Paul*, pp. 194–201: "Resident aliens were obliged to abstain from offering sacrifices to strange gods (Lev. 17:7-9), from eating blood in any form (Lev. 17:10ff.), from incest (Lev. 18:6-26), from work on the Sabbath (Exod. 20:10f), and from eating leavened bread during the Passover (Exod. 12:18f)" (p. 198).

[11]Segal, *Paul*, pp. 198–201; Simon, "Apostolic Decree," pp. 444–45.

[12]Other examples from this period of time include *Jub.* 7.20-21, which predates Christian origins; however, this document expresses the very different intention of showing how gentiles refused God's instruction and are thereby condemned justly (Segal, *Paul*, pp. 195–97); and *Sib. Or.* 2.93.

[13]See T. Callan, "The Background of the Apostolic Decree," pp. 284–97, for discussion of why these four were chosen and not some of the others. Also Simon, "Apostolic Decree," pp. 444–45; Segal, *Paul*, pp. 194–201, develops parallels (also Segal, "Universalism," pp. 13–27).

creative task of understanding how to apply Judaic notions of God's activity in a world where the Jewish community found itself more and more confronted by Hellenism.[14] At home and abroad, Greek philosophy and Roman authority pressed upon their historical understanding of how the world operated. Many of the historical answers were no longer adequate. How were they to understand the place of the gentile in the age to come? What was the place of the individual in the afterlife? How were they to define the community of God outside the land of Israel? And most directly for our study: How were they to accommodate gentiles who chose to fear the One God and thus sought association with the Jewish community? What aspects of Torah and ritual purity would be operative for the "righteous gentile" worshiping in their midst? These are but a few of the many questions confronting their Hebraic system of thought that had to be answered in new, creative ways.

In this context there were no doubt many prevailing opinions of the status of gentiles (e.g., the Qumran community versus the Sadducees). The Pharisees were most concerned with confronting these new challenges creatively, and as the champions of the development of table-fellowship purity at the center of everyday life it is likely that the notion of the "righteous gentile" and corresponding halakhot for their fellowship within the congregation were hallmarks of this coalition that continued to be developed in the rabbinic Judaism to which it gave birth.[15]

As noted above, the new faction of Judaism that became

---

[14]See Hengel, *Judaism and Hellenism*; and G. Theissen, "Judaism and Christianity in Paul: The Beginning of a Schism and Its Social History," in *Social Reality and the Early Christians*, for an excellent discussion of the many tensions and of acculturation in both Judaism and Christianity. Theissen, pp. 219–20, notes: "Christianity in its earliest form is to be seen as part of Jewish history. It belongs to a series of Jewish attempts at acculturation to the Gentile environment. These attempts were characteristic of the Hellenistic and Roman period. . . . The important point is that acculturation is an adaptation to the environment without a renunciation of one's own identity." Also Flusser, "A New Sensitivity in Judaism and the Christian Message," in *Judaism*, pp. 469–89.

[15]See comments of Simon, *Verus Israel*, pp. 3–64, 271–306, on the character of Pharisaism and proselytism as it developed in later rabbinic Judaism. Also Feldman, *Jew and Gentile*, and McKnight, *Light*, for differing views on proselytism. For a full study of Pharisaism and table-fellowship purity see Neusner, "The Idea of Purity in Ancient Judaism," idem, *From Politics to Piety*; Sanders, *Judaism: Practice*; idem, *Jewish Law*; Rivkin, *Hidden Revolution*.

Christianity affords the clearest view of what parts of Torah were applicable to the "righteous gentile" choosing to associate and worship with the Jewish community in the first century, particularly in matters of ritual purity. For while the Noahide Commandments occur in the later rabbinic literature, their concern was not with the same context; they were concerned not so much with gentiles choosing to attend synagogue and associate with Jews as with the place of the "righteous gentile" in the age to come.[16] The historical context had changed dramatically from the first to the second century with the emergence of both Christianity and rabbinic Judaism. In rabbinic circles the issue had become largely theoretical, concerned with recognizing gentiles outside the pale of Judaism who respected God with appropriate monotheistic behavior. Thus at the heart of the Noahide Commandments are ethical concerns, most of which are covered sufficiently in the Decalogue for the members of the Jewish community.[17]

With the birth of the Jewish faction called "the Way" (Acts 9:2), however, Jews had to delineate proper cultic as well as ethical behavior for gentiles who were to be included in the Jewish community and its daily life as equals.[18] The Decalogue and the so-called Golden Rule form the basis for the ethical guidelines (Rom. 13:8-14, for example) in the new messianic community, and the early Christian literature is replete with ethical guidance. Believing gentiles were naturally turning from slavery to sin to a lifestyle of slavery to righteousness (Rom. 6:12-23, for example: Why else would they have believed?); but the apostolic decree was developed (or adopted from the prevailing format already in place to guide the minimal cultic behavior of the "righteous

[16]See Segal, *Paul*, pp. 197–201, idem, "Universalism," pp. 2–12; and Cohen, "Crossing the Boundary," pp. 11–33, for excellent discussions of how gentiles were regarded and the various views of what was required for conversion. See Sanders, *Paul and Palestinian Judaism*, pp. 210–13, on the paucity of rabbinic literature on this topic and the fact that this issue was not as central; the concerns were for those in the covenant.

[17]That is not to say there are no ritual concerns expressed in the Noahide Commandments. Examples include the prohibition of eating "the limb torn from a living animal" at the very least.

[18]Note that Sabbath is not an issue. This may be because gentiles were observing Sabbath in order to associate with the Jewish community. The issue was how were they to behave while observing the Sabbath, and in particular, when attending synagogue. See Acts 14:1; 16:13-14; 17:1-4, 17; 18:4; Josephus *Against Apion* 2.40 (282) (Callan, "Background," p. 294).

gentile" associating with the Jewish community in the first century)[19]
as the basis for purity requirements.[20] They would learn the monotheistic ethics of love, to be sure, but they also needed to respect Jewish
sensitivities in matters of purity—for God and the community of his
people are holy. In this sense we can see that, for the Jerusalem
Council, the issue of the apostolic decree as the outline of the minimal
requirements of purity for the "righteous gentile" were not about

[19]Simon, "Apostolic Decree," pp. 444–45: "Since the regulations concerning
food, and blood in particular, are codified in chapter xvii of Leviticus, it seems
legitimate to consider that these two chapters, xvii and xviii, provide the basis of
both the Apostolic Decree and the ritual or ethico-ritual parts of the Noachian
commands in their rabbinical formulation. It is, of course, impossible to prove that
this rabbinical formulation had already been shaped and was already observed by
the God-fearers at the time when the Apostolic Decree was promulgated. I personally think it likely. It is therefore natural, or at least tempting, to consider that
the Apostolic Decree represents, basically, an extract from this Noachian legislation. It leaves aside that part of it which is strictly religious or ethical and which
the Gentile Christians were bound to observe, along with the Jewish moral law in
general, as soon as they had joined the Church; and it formulates again, in a more
precise form, those ritual or ethico-ritual commandments the observance of which
was the very condition of full religious fellowship between Gentile Christians and
Jewish Christians." Also P. Carrington, *The Early Christian Church*, pp. 102ff.; idem,
The Primitive Christian Catechism, on "Proselyte Baptism." Schultz, "Two Views,"
pp. 47–48, discusses the use of the Holiness Code of Lev. 19 by Diaspora Jewry
"as a catechism for proselytes to Judaism": "Like the first stage of diaspora Jewry's
catechism for proselytes, which according to Krauss ["Les Préceptes des Revue
des Noachides études juíves," 47 (1903), pp. 32–40] contained thirty precepts derived from the Holiness Code, the rabbinic Noahide laws were the first step taken
by a non-Jew in becoming a proselyte."

[20]Concerning the weakness of the so-called Western text of the apostolic decree
with its more ethical orientation see the excellent discussion of Simon, "Apostolic
Decree." Simon points out that the decree as an ethical guideline is quite insuffi-
cient lacking even such basics as theft. Simon clarifies the purity issues of *porneia*
as well as the more obvious food matters, demonstrating that more than just
dietary laws were at issue in this formulation of ritual rules of behavior. See also
R. Longenecker, *Paul*, pp. 254–56, who concludes on p. 256: "The fact that the
Western texts present it as an ethical pronouncement coupled with the Golden
Rule is probably due to a remodeling of the Decree to make it a rule for the whole
Church at a later time when the prohibitions of "blood" and "things strangled"
had lost their meaning. (cf. Segal, "Universalism," pp. 13–18, idem, *Paul*,
pp. 194–201, for good discussion of the two texts). I discuss the matter of purity
below, including the views of M. Newton, *Concept of Purity*, and W. Houston, *Purity
and Monotheism*. See S. Wilson, *Luke and the Law*, pp. 73–102, for the opposite
position that the decree was primarily ethical in content.

entrance requirements for salvation, but about community with God and with his people.[21]

That the apostolic decree was developed by the leaders of this new community within Judaism to address the issue of purity for gentiles believing in the God of Israel is evidence of just how thoroughly Jewish their beliefs and intentions were. They were lovers of Torah, of Israel, of the One God.[22] They were persuaded by the acts of God to welcome gentiles who recognized the King of Israel as the Savior of the nations without them becoming Jews—for God had shown them that they were equals, that the One God of Israel was the One God of all humankind. As gentiles they were welcome (without circumcision), but not as pagans (without observing the halakhah of the "righteous gentiles").[23] They were expected to maintain the minimal requirements of purity (and morality, of course) befitting those who have turned from idolatry to the worship of the One God; they were to "obey" the halakhah of the "faith" for the "righteous gentile" worshiping in the midst of restored Israel.

One of the major developments unforeseen (in magnitude) by the

---

[21]Simon, "Apostolic Decree," pp. 449–50: "We are thus led to the conclusion that the Decree represents, in all likelihood, a condensed code of levitical purity, based mainly on chapters xvi, xvii and xviii of Leviticus, but also, as regards mixed marriages, on Exodus xxxiv. 15-16. In order to be accepted into the ecclesiastical fellowship, whose spirit is still closely akin to that of the Synagogue, the Gentile Christians must be free from any form of physical defilement, and this springs from two main sources: unclean food and sexual uncleanness. This notion of levitical or ritual purity gives the Decree, considered in its dietary commandments on the one hand, its prohibition of *porneia* on the other, its fundamental unity." And on p. 459 Simon notes: "While the Noachian commands constitute a rule of life, including both moral and ritual precepts, the Decree is just a code of levitical purity, added to the ethical commandments of the Decalogue, whose observance is the very basis of ecclesiastical fellowship." See also R. Longenecker, *Paul*, p. 259; Callan, "Background," pp. 291–97; Lake, "Apostolic Council," in *The Beginnings*, pp. 208–12.

[22]See the excellent discussion of Luke's picture as thoroughly Jewish in Jervell, *Luke*, idem, "Retrospect." Note his comments in "Retrospect," p. 399: "The main point in the decree, in my view, is that keeping the law is a confession of the one and only God of Israel: God is one God (Dt 6:5). As the decree is part of the torah, the law remains valid for both the Jewish and the Gentile Christians."

[23]Jervell, *Luke*, p. 144: "Luke knows of no gentile mission that is free from the law. He knows about a gentile mission without circumcision, not without the law. The apostolic decree enjoins Gentiles to keep the law, and they keep that part of the law required for them to live together with Jews."

Jerusalem Council, but ever present in the later ministry of the apostle Paul, was the pronounced change in the makeup of the congregations.[24] It was one thing to apply the notion of the "righteous gentile" to a minority worshiping in the midst of a Jewish majority; it was quite another to confront the issues that developed when the gentiles became the majority.[25] This was the situation Paul faced, whether as the direct result of his ministry (e.g., Galatia) or not (e.g., Rome).[26] And like the Pharisee he ever continued to be, Paul sought to creatively tackle this new phenomenon by applying the essential truths of the historic faith of Israel in radically new ways that were consistent with the decisions of the Council and that reflected the dominant notions of Diaspora Judaism, but ways that dramatically reinterpreted the underlying assumptions of traditional monotheistic arguments to make sense of this new development.

These creative solutions, I believe, were based upon Paul's adaptation of the prevailing views of monotheism and the place of the "righteous gentile" in Diaspora Judaism of his time. He became the champion of a new understanding of Israel's monotheism by applying the Shema of Israel and the apostolic decree to the developmental decisions of the early congregations of believers in Jesus as they found themselves quickly populated by a growing number of gentile participants. His arguments and his rulings have been largely misunderstood, however, because they have not been considered from Paul's Pharisaic frame of reference as he creatively applied existing Judaic notions to the new historical circumstances he faced among the early community(s) of believers in Jesus Christ. Paul has thus, wrongly I believe, been seen as disregarding the Law and customs of his Jewish

[24]It was, of course, the beginning of this development that provoked the need for the Jerusalem conference that led to the announcement of the decree. But the question arose in a situation where the makeup of the congregations and the leadership was still predominantly Jewish.

[25]Jervell, "Mighty Minority," notes the issue of the changing makeup of the congregations similarly on pp. 20–21, as does Segal, *Paul*, pp. 72–93, 267–73.

[26]The observations of Hays, *Echoes*, p. 40, are quite graphic in pointing out Paul's citation of Habakkuk's protest in the opening comments in Romans echo the "military domination of the Chaldeans, 'that bitter and hasty nation,' over an impotent Israel (Hab. 1:5-11); Paul's problem arises instead from a different sort of historical phenomenon, not the occupation of Israel by a Gentile military power but the apparent usurpation of Israel's favored covenant status by congregations of uncircumcised Gentile Christians. The analogy between the situations is off-center and—precisely for that reason—metaphorical." See also Hays's comments, p. 162.

past as he developed entirely new, Christian solutions. He has, mistakenly, been made the creator of a gentile Christianity that rejected Judaism and the Law as operative,[27] rather than the champion of the restoration of Israel who fought for the inclusion of "righteous gentiles" in this new community as equals, in fulfillment of the eschatological hope of Israel and in complete harmony with salvation history as understood by James and the Council (Acts 15:13-17, 18ff.).[28]

Did Paul's understanding of equal access for Jew and gentile to God's promises through faith in Christ Jesus compromise Judaic monotheism? Paul did not believe so, for he defiantly claimed that his

[27]Examples of this position on Paul abound, some of which I review below. See, for example, Alon, *Jews*, p. 296: "The question was, would Christianity continue to view itself solely as a religious movement within Judaism, as it had been in Jesus' day; or was it to become a religion for all men and nations? An even more serious question arose out of the first: did Gentiles who came to believe in Jesus have to accept Judaism and the Jewish way of life? This question was put forward especially by Paul and his faction. Ultimately, it was their victory that transformed Christianity into a Gentile religion." Flusser, *Judaism*, p. 631, is careful regarding Paul's intentions but comes to the same conclusion: "The liberation of Gentile Christianity from the yoke of Jewish commandments was a necessary step in order for Christianity to become a Gentile religion, separate from Judaism. It is impossible to know whether Paul, and other Christians of his time, were even aware that by his 'Gospel' he helped to achieve this aim: he does not speak explicitly about the necessity of separating Christianity from its Jewish matrix and he never says that this was his intention, but it is clear that in fact such was his historical role. Paul was the most important factor in a trend which gave birth to Christianity as a distinct religion, because he deepened its Christology and stressed the inevitable necessity of accepting it for salvation, and he was the most extreme exponent of the doctrine that the Jewish way of life had no validity for Christians. The Gentile Christians in Rome, to whom Paul wrote his epistle, were surely Gentile Godfearers before becoming Christians. . . . For Christian God-fearers it was not easy to accept Paul's demand; the complete rejection of Jewish precepts was for many Gentile Christians a painful operation."

[28]See chapter 5 below on the two-step pattern for a full discussion of the concept of Israel's restoration and the ingathering of gentiles in Acts 15. See also Jervell, *Luke*, pp. 41–74; Gaston, *No Stone on Another*, pp. 200–205; Callan, "Background," p. 297: "The Apostolic Decree implies that Gentile Christians are incorporated into Israel in some way, either as converts or as a group associated with Israel without full conversion. This suggests that for Luke the core of the Christian church is that part of the Jewish people which has accepted Jesus as the Messiah sent by God. Gentile Christians are associated with this restored Israel and are dependent on its existence in order to be part of the Christian church. The Apostolic Decree seems to be Luke's oblique way of saying, in the words of Paul to the Gentile Christians of Rome, 'Remember it is not you that support the root, but the root that supports you' (Rom 11:18)."

gospel championed monotheism (e.g., Rom. 3:29-30; 10:12-13; 15:5-6, 7ff.). While it was not necessary to argue that the One God was the God of Israel, of the Jewish people, for that was unquestioned, it was necessary to ask if he was "the God of the Jews *only?* Is He not the God of Gentiles *also?*" (3:29). "*Yes*" Paul replied, "of Gentiles *also*, since indeed God who will justify the circumcised by faith and the un-circumcised through faith is *one*" (3:29-30).

Nor did Paul believe that his gospel opposed Torah. We find him following the above-mentioned monotheistic argument for the equality of gentile salvation immediately with the corresponding concern: "Do we then *nullify* the Law through faith? May it *never* be! On the contrary, we *establish* the Law" (3:31). For Paul, as for any Jew, monotheism and Torah were inseparable.

The traditional answer given for Paul's insistence that gentiles were not to become Jews is the alleged devaluation of the Law with the coming of Christ; Paul believed that the Law was obsolete and so too was being Jewish. We witness this clearly in the summary comments of Räisänen: "Paul's writings abound in statements which justify the claim that a radical critique of the Torah is the 'unmistakable charac-teristic' of his theology . . . Paul did assert that the Torah had been superseded in Christ";[29] and elsewhere, in drawing his final theological conclusions: "We find Paul struggling with the problem that a *divine* institution has been *abolished* through what God has done in Christ. Most of Paul's troubles can be reduced to this simple formula. Paul tries to hush up the abolition; he never admits that he has actually rejected large parts of the law. Instead, he has recourse to the arbitrary assertion that it is *his* teaching that really fulfils or 'upholds' the law."[30]

But this standard answer fails to account for the tensions present in this context, not to mention the balance of Paul's life and letters (he continued to be a Jew and to ground his thinking in Jewish presuppo-sitions, indeed, in the Law and in monotheism, and it was his converts that were tempted to "judaize"). What I hope to demonstrate, first, is that Paul's reason for insisting that gentiles must not become Jews was, as it was for James in his conclusions at the Jerusalem Council in appealing to the example of Peter, based not in the devaluation of Torah or Judaism but on the inherent compromise of monotheism: for gentiles to become Jews was to deny that the One God of Israel was equally the One God of all humankind (a thoroughly Jewish concern

[29]Räisänen, *Paul*, p. 50.
[30]Ibid., pp. 264–65.

that faith in Jesus Christ for all humankind was consistent with and compelled by Torah!). However, the other side of this argument for the Council, and I believe for Paul as well, was that gentiles were therefore not to disregard the faith of the Jews with whom they would now be associating in the synagogue communities. They must obey the intentions of the apostolic decree, which set out the minimal requirements of purity for the "stranger within your gates" as it was applied to "righteous gentiles" in the first century seeking association with Israel and her God. They must subordinate their freedom to worship the God of the whole world to the restrictions understood to apply to "righteous gentiles" worshiping the God of Israel in the Jewish communities with which they now sought association. The new Christian gentiles must not hurt their Jewish brothers and sisters with their food, but rather walk in love in order to win respect for their claim to be sharers in the promises of God through faith in Christ Jesus, the Savior of Israel and of the world. That is how the Council phrased the underlying intentions for the development of the apostolic decree (Acts 15:21); Paul echoed the same underlying intentions in his address (Rom. 14:14bff.) to redirect the ethical and purity behavior of the "strong" in Rome in view of the presence of those he referred to as the "weak/stumbling."

Having first examined the basis of Paul's monotheistic argument, my second concern is, then, to propose, contrary to scholarly consensus, that Paul did teach the apostolic decree, and that the tension evident in Paul's insistence on the equal status of the gentiles with Jews (the reason he would not tolerate gentile circumcision) was built around this monotheistic issue and the concomitant proper behavior of the "righteous gentile." His position was *not* built around rejection of the Law in view of the new age of Christ, but around the rejection of any ethnocentric limitation of God's salvation to those under the Law alone[31]—for the One God of Israel is the One God of the nations (3:28-31; 10:1-13). Paul argued that to insist that gentiles must become Jews to participate as equals in the promises of God is to compromise God's

---

[31]Note the similar observation of Dunn, *Partings*, p. 137: "Hence Paul's line of argument in Rom. 3.27-30: to say 'a man is justified by works of the law' is tantamount to saying 'God is the God of Jews only' (3.28-29). Thus it begins to become clear that Paul was *not* against the law as such—far less against 'good works'! What he aimed his arguments against was *the law understood and practised in such a way as to limit the grace of God, to prevent Gentiles as Gentiles enjoying it in full measure*." See also pp. 26–31, 123–27, and idem, *Jesus, Paul*, pp. 215–36; E. Martens, "Embracing the Law," pp. 1–28.

oneness, and the oneness of all humankind in him. For while the other expressions of Judaism maintained some level of respect for the "righteous gentile," it was certainly not as equals. Paul, in concert with the decision of the Council, maintained that they were in fact equals in Christ in the new community by faith alone, the "new creation" of believers in Jesus as the Christ, yet they were obliged to obey the halakhah of the "righteous gentile" as outlined in the apostolic decree to demonstrate that they had, in fact, turned from the behavior associated with idolatry to the fear of the One God (e.g., Rom. 6:12-23; 13:8-14).[32]

Christianity later, however, lost touch with the contextual tensions Paul was confronting in his insistence on the relative value of circumcision and the practice of the Law with respect to ethnocentric privilege at the point of equal access to God's blessings in Christ Jesus, because it failed to recognize that the argument was centered on the place of the "righteous gentile" in the midst of Israel as *equal co*participants in the promised salvation. Thus, what had been for Paul and the Council a highly nuanced Jewish theological battleground among themselves has come to be regarded as the position of an outsider throwing stones at his former family as though he no longer considered his ministry in the context of Israel's restoration, as though this new community replaced the historical community of Israel, making its practice of faith and Torah observance obsolete.[33] But Paul did not question whether the Law was still valid for Jews; in fact he affirmed that it was (3:21; 7:12-14; 9:2-5; 11:28-29; 15:8).[34] Paul's concern was to clarify that the Law was not for the Christian gentiles as though they were now Jews, for that would compromise that God is the God of

[32]Nickle, *Collection*, p. 55, notes similarly: "The 'Decrees' were formulated not as the fundamental requirements which a Gentile had to fulfil in order to become a Christian but as those basic regulations necessary to make full fellowship between Gentile and Jewish Christians within the same Christian community possible. As such they were not at all foreign or contradictory to Paul's conception of the relationship of the Christian to the Mosaic Law." And on p. 72 he observes about the Jerusalem Christians' need to resolve the issue of mixed communities: "Together with Paul they formulated in the 'Apostolic Decrees' a solution which did not distort or violate the gospel message."

[33]M. Barth, *The People of God*, pp. 18–19, for example, indicates a similar concern.

[34]This is clear in his entire argument throughout Romans, and lies behind his admonition to the Christian gentiles in chaps. 9–11 and the "strong" to adopt the practices of the "weak" in chaps. 14–15. See chapters 3, 5, and 8 herein for further discussion of this dynamic. Also Jervell, *The Unknown Paul*.

gentiles equally (with Christian Jews who keep Torah) in Christ Jesus (3:27-31; 4:16). The Christian gentile was to be regarded as a "righteous gentile" and obey those aspects of the Law deemed appropriate, the Torah of gentiles, one could say, with the purity issues as outlined in the apostolic decree and its broader intentions,[35] and with the ethical issues outlined variously in the Decalogue (Rom. 13:8-10), the "household tables,"[36] Judaic law and customs,[37] baptismal creeds,[38] and the "law of Christ."[39]

To challenge (what I regard as) this misunderstanding of Paul throughout most of Christian history that continues in current scholarship I herein examine the following developments in his letter to Rome: (1) monotheism, particularly as understood in the Shema and as argued by Paul in Romans; (2) the apostolic decree as the halakhah for the "righteous gentile" in the midst of the congregation of the faithful of Israel as applied by Paul to the Christian gentiles he addressed in Rome; and (3) the programmatic "obedience of faith" (ὑπακοὴν πίστεως) as Paul's unique construct in concert with the intentions of the Council's apostolic decree calling for Christian gentile "obedience" in view of their new "faith."

MONOTHEISM AND THE SHEMA
AS THE BASIS OF PAUL'S ARGUMENT

When Paul sought to explain why gentiles need not become Jews in order to become part of the people of God in view of the

[35]It must of course be recognized that views of what was appropriate behavior for a "righteous gentile" were rapidly changing in the first century, even as they were continually in debate among the many different emerging Jewish factions for defining "normative" Jewish behavior for Jews. As we have come to recognize that Judaism was not monolithic, we must naturally recognize that faith and practice among the early Judaism that became Christianity was also characterized by different emphasis in different times and places. Hence the apostolic decree was but a model; however, its broader intentions would have varied with the concerns of the various Jewish congregations that these "righteous gentiles" would join. See the discussion of P. Borgen, "Catalogues of Vices, the Apostolic Decree, and the Jerusalem Meeting."

[36]See J. Yoder, *The Politics of Jesus*, pp. 163–92, for an interesting view of these rules of subordination variously listed in Eph. 5:21—6:9; Col. 3:18—4:1; 1 Pet. 2:13—3:7. These tables may, however, be evidence from a period after Paul.

[37]Tomson, *Paul*.

[38]Carrington, *Primitive Christian Catechism*.

[39]Flusser, *Judaism*, pp. 377–85; W. D. Davies, *Torah in the Messianic Age*.

demonstration of God's righteousness through Jesus Christ, he did not give the answer that Christianity has most often given. At the very points Paul would have been expected to devalue the Torah or disregard the election of Israel in order to assert a supposed Law-free gospel or gentile Christianity, he did neither. In fact, he asserted quite the opposite. When he argued that both Jew and gentile (hence, all people) were to be judged equally (1:16—2:29), the natural question that arose was: "Then what advantage has the Jew? Or what is the benefit of circumcision?" (3:1). The issue, turned around, is: If being Jewish was an advantage then why did Paul insist that gentiles must not become Jews (through circumcision and embracing Torah) in order to become, or even after having become, believers in Jesus Christ? Why not simplify matters and just make them Israelites (through circumcision)?[40]

One might expect Paul's answer (in view of Christianity's historic position) to have been: "None! There is no advantage in being a Jew." But it was precisely the opposite: "*Great* in *every* respect" (3:2) was his emphatic reply. And his first (but not his last) reason (which ought to stop Christian interpreters in their tracks!) was that Jews possess the Torah: "First of all, that they were entrusted with the oracles of God" (3:2). While a great deal of the balance of Paul's argument beyond this first reason must wait until he has reached the appropriate moment in chapters 9–11, his first point is only concluded with a discussion of how the Law, rather than being "nullified" through faith in Jesus Christ, is actually "established" (3:31).[41] Central to this point is Paul's characteristic development of the Shema[42]—Judaism's highly charged

---

[40]The underlying question is the same one discussed in Galatians and Acts from another angle: If gentiles do not need to become Jews in order to be part of the people of God, then why did God create Israel or give the Torah? See Räisänen, *Paul*, pp. 264–69, for similar stress on this point. Sanders, *Paul, the Law*, p. 154, suggests: "Perhaps Paul saw the unfairness involved in asking Gentiles to accept the law: they would remain second-class citizens. Or perhaps he thought more radically than, for example, Peter: if Gentiles are to be brought in it means that 'all' distinctions must be obliterated."

[41]See C. Myers, "Chiastic Inversion in the argument of Romans 3–8," pp. 45–47. Actually this discussion of establishing the law continues through chap. 4.

[42]For an excellent discussion of Jewish monotheism as represented in the Shema in the first century see Wright, *NT*, pp. 248–79; Dahl, *Studies in Paul*, pp. 178–91; Sanders, *Judaism: Practice*, pp. 195–97; L. Hurtado, "What Do We Mean by 'First-Century Jewish Monotheism'?" For an extended discussion of the complete Shema see Donin, *To Pray as a Jew*, pp. 144–66; A. Millgram, *Jewish Worship*, pp. 96–100, 148–49, 192–93, 443–46, gives a good survey of the development of surreptitious methods for recitation of the Shema during the periods when the

assertion of God's oneness, of God's covenant faithfulness to Israel, his people, and their commitment to him alone, followed by the recognition that he is also the One God of all creation: "Hear [Shema] O Israel, the Lord is *our* God, the Lord is *One*" (Deut. 6:4). Paul's argument for Israel's special privilege of having Torah is grounded in his monotheistic understanding of the role of Torah, just as it is for all Jews. However, his argument turns on the *compromise* of God's universal oneness he sees in the denial of *equal* access to those outside Israel and Torah:

> Or is God the God of Jews only? Is He not the God of Gentiles also? Yes, of Gentiles also, since indeed *God* who will justify the circumcised by faith and the uncircumcised through faith *is one.* Do we then nullify the Law through faith? May it never be! On the contrary, we *establish* the Law. (Rom. 3:29-31)[43]

Paul linked his assertion of the special place of the Jew (election) with the central Jewish assertion of God as the One God, the creator, the deliverer, the faithful protector of the covenant: the God of Torah. This *particularism* ("the Lord is *our God*") and its link with the faith of Israel in the One God ("the Lord is *One*") was asserted in the face of pagan idolatry and its concomitant "deeds of darkness." But this assertion was also used by Paul to demonstrate the *universalism* embedded in the monotheistic faith of Israel—for the One God of Israel was also the One God of the nations ("the Lord is *One*"). It is at this point, where Paul demonstrates God's faithfulness to Israel as he had promised, that Paul affirms God's faithfulness to both the "Torah of

---

Shema was proscribed, including the Justinian Edict of the sixth century when the church objected to the Shema as a challenge to the doctrine of the Trinity. See Wright, *Climax*, pp. 125–36, and idem, "One God, One Lord, One People," for excellent discussion of Paul's development of the Shema in 1 Corinthians 8:1-6 and elsewhere. For evidence of the use of the Shema in a way very similar to what we find in Paul's writings in the liturgical formula of the Syrian Christians, see Simon, *Verus Israel*, pp. 307–9. For a moving presentation of the dynamics of monotheism as embodied in the Shema see Heschel, *Between God and Man*, pp. 102–7.

[43]It is worth noting that what can only be labeled gentile Christianity would have Paul saying something perhaps more like the following inversion of Paul's pointed argument: "Or is God the God of *gentiles only*? Is He not the God of *Jews also*? No, of gentiles only, since indeed God who is one will justify the uncircumcision through faith and thus will only justify the circumcision if they become uncircumcised through faith, as it were. Do we then *establish* the Law through faith? May it *never* be! On the contrary, we *nullify* the Law."

faith" (3:26-27)[44] as Israel's particular privilege (election) and to the equal inclusion of gentiles "through faith" as the descendants of Abraham also (universalism). In other words, rather than deny the special role of Israel and the Torah, he affirmed both and turned the tables, as it were, on those of Israel who would seek to deny gentiles equal access to God's promised blessings because they were not part of Israel, for the God who demonstrated his faithfulness to Israel is the one and only God. He must also be the God of the gentiles who call on the One God through faith in Christ Jesus. To assert otherwise, Paul argued, would be to compromise God's oneness.[45] They would be guilty of denying the righteousness of God as they asserted their own special place with no regard for God's worldwide intentions (the point of 10:3). It would amount to taking the position that God has not been faithful to his covenant through the Torah with Israel, or that he is not also the God of the rest of the nations, for they must become a part of Israel if he is to be their God (he is only the God of Israel; there are other gods for the nations).

We see then that the Shema of faith, with its inclusion of gentiles, by faith (the confession of the One God without becoming Jews: the point of 10:9 and context), is not a denial of Israel's election or of the "Torah of faith," but rather "establishes" Torah as a witness to the faithfulness of God to "the Jew *first* and *also* to the Greek" (1:16). For now both those of the Law (who recognize the righteousness of God demonstrated in Torah and election) and those not of the Law (who recognize "instinctively the things of the Law": 2:14-15) are able to recognize the faithfulness of God through faith in Jesus Christ, the very manifestation of the faithfulness of God as promised (3:19-26, 27ff.; 10:4-13). We see Paul's definition of how Christ "establishes" Torah and is its "goal" clearly in his summary comments in chapter 15:

> For I say that Christ has become a servant to the circumcision on behalf of the truth of God to *confirm* the promises given to the fathers, and for the Gentiles to glorify God for His *mercy*. (15:8-9)

[44]Note that Paul also says: "the Law is spiritual" (7:14). For a discussion of this view of Paul's comments on Torah in 3:26-27 see Martens, "Embracing the Law." For the opposing view see H. Räisänen, "The 'Law' of Faith and the Spirit," in *Jesus, Paul*, pp. 48–68. See also Snodgrass, "Spheres of Influence," pp. 100–103.

[45]It should be noted that this universalism was common in the interpretation of Shema at the time; however, we see that Paul was exploring an inherent contradiction between what was maintained in theory and what was maintained in practice. Note the comments of Lapide, *Paul: Rabbi*, pp. 48–50.

As Paul works through this argument we can see how unaware he was of what would become the concern of later times: Do Jews who become Christians remain Jews? Do they continue to keep Torah? These matters were so assumed by Paul in the affirmative that he does not even pause for discussion. His concern is whether the new members of the faction of Judaism that come from gentiles must become Jews and keep Torah. His question is not "Is God the God of Jews *also?*" but rather: "Or is God the God of Jews *only?*" (3:29).[46] Naturally, he would not have been concerned with developing the monotheistic and Law-positive argument we are reviewing if he believed that Israel's election and obedience to the Torah for Jews were devalued in Christ. His very argument bears witness to the fact that of course the One God is the God of the Torah-keeping Jew (3:29); the entire discussion of Jesus, the King of the Jews, would be nonsense if that were not the case. The issue is whether this same One God is also the One God of the whole non-Torah-keeping world (3:29); and Paul asserts that indeed he is the One God of all who recognize, whether through the witness of Torah (the Torah is "established": 3:31) or from the witness of their own conscience (the gentile recognition of the creator God: 1:18-24; 2:12-16) that the One God is "just and the justifier of the one who has faith in Jesus" (3:26-31; 15:8-9). Indeed, Paul is so committed to the fulfilling of Torah that he even describes the life that results from the Christian gentiles' pursuit of love in the Spirit as the fulfilling of Torah (8:4; 13:8-10).

Paul would have been surprised to hear that his teaching has been made the basis for believing a Jew lost their Jewishness (no longer kept Torah, became a gentile as it were) when they became a believer in Jesus, the One who was obedient to Torah (5:15, 17, 19) as the gift of Israel (3:2; 9:3-5; 11:28-29), so that *both* Jew *and* gentile could be saved as *Jew* and *gentile*, as children of Abraham according to promise. For Paul, as for any Jew, "the gifts" (i.e., Torah) and "the calling" (i.e., Israel) are "irrevocable" (11:29).[47] They are eternal! They do not go away with the coming of the promised one (how absurd!); they are not

---

[46]See Simon, *Verus Israel*, pp. 307-9, for an interesting discussion of the early Christian use of "but/only" from the likely first-century version of the Jewish funeral liturgy as preserved in the Samaritan version of the Shema with its "emphatic affirmation of the divine unity": "There is *but* one God; the Lord is our God; the Lord is One" (emphasis added).

[47]See the many comments sharing this same view of Paul and Torah by P. Lapide, *Paul: Rabbi*, pp. 31–56.

nullified or made obsolete; they continue to bear witness to the faithfulness of God. Certainly Jews and gentiles continue to be distinct groups clearly identifiable within the various congregations he addressed.[48] In fact, an interesting question arises in this very regard: How could Paul expect "all Israel" to be saved if he believed that his gospel was the process whereby Jews lost their Jewishness and historical Israel was nullified along with her gift of Torah? His hope and labor would more likely have been for the salvation of "all non-Israel" in that day when the disappearance of Israel as a distinct people would have testified to the completion of the promised salvation.

Gentiles are forbidden to become Jews not because becoming Jewish and keeping Torah are no longer valid acts of faith; they are forbidden because to do so would be to deny the universalistic oneness of God (he is the One God of all the nations), which would implicitly deny his election of Israel and the privilege of Torah, because if he is not the One God of all outside Israel who believe in him then he is not the One God of Israel; he is not the One God at all. His oneness has been compromised if he is *only* the God of Israel, *only* the God of the circumcised, *only* the God of Torah, and not *also* the God of the nations, not *also* the God of the uncircumcised, and not *also* the God of those outside the Torah. The Torah would not be established, and all Israel would not be saved, because the One God who called Israel and gave them the gift of Torah would not be the One God of all who believe in Him, whether the Jew first or also the Greek. And it is to prove this point that Paul turns to the illustration of Abraham, the father of all who have faith, both Jew and gentile—not to demonstrate that Israel and Torah are obsolete, for they were not even created when Abraham first believed and would thus have never even been necessary. Paul's argument is that they came later to separate those who followed the faith of Abraham until the day came to pass when the promise made to Abraham that he would be the father of many nations was fulfilled—to his own descendants *first* ("the father of circumcision to those who not *only* are of the circumcision": 4:12; "not *only* those who are of the Law": 4:16), of course, but *also* the whole world (4:13) would give "glory to God" (4:20), the One God of Abraham, and the

[48]Jervell, "Might Minority," pp. 25–26, 30, observes that even Paul's later letters like Romans indicate that the clearly distinguishable groups still live differently.

One God of all those "who follow in the steps of the faith of our father Abraham which he had while uncircumcised" (4:12).[49]

Do we not hear the unmistakable echo of the Shema of faith in the illustration of walking (halakh) in the steps of the faith of Abraham (4:12), who turned from pagan idolatry to the worship of the One God and walked in righteousness and fulfilled the very intentions of Torah before Torah was even given?[50] Indeed, the faith Paul was arguing for in the One God of the Jew first and also equally of the Greek was not a faith that made Torah, or Israel, obsolete, and it was not a faith that compromised the oneness of God by denying his universal intention toward all of his creation. The faith Paul was arguing for in the One God honored Israel as his people first, with the gift of Torah so that they might be a light to all the nations in their declaration of his oneness, the very Torah given to the people of faith, "the Torah of faith" (3:27): "Hear, O Israel, the Lord is *our* God, the Lord is *One*."[51]

Paul's linking of Torah and the Shema was not unique in Diaspora Judaism.[52] Nor was his linking of the Shema with Israel's election. Even his application of the Shema to a universalistic understanding of the One God for the inclusion of gentiles was not entirely unique, for

[49]It is notable that Abraham is referred to as "the father of circumcision" to the uncircumcised who have faith, rather than "the father of uncircumcision" to them.

[50]See the excellent discussion of Abraham's relationship with the Torah given at Sinai by Schultz, "Two Views."

[51]Lapide, *Paul: Rabbi*, p. 48, notes this same purpose in Paul powerfully: "Paul did not establish a new principle of faith or destroy the ancient principle of Torah. He neither repudiated Judaism, as numerous theologians still maintain, nor was he the founder of Christianity, as Martin Buber assumed. For him the Damascus road experience was the 'kairos' of salvation, the great turning point in God's plan of salvation, predestined since Abraham, which was to bring about the reconciliation of Jews and Gentiles. The dawning of the new age was regarded neither as a breakaway from the traditions of Israel nor as an invasion into the Gentile world, and certainly not as the abolition of Torah. Quite the opposite; it was seen as the long-awaited manifestation of the universal basic purpose of God's teaching from Sinai—a worldwide ecumenical fellowship of Jews and believing Gentiles, a "great Israel" incorporating all God-fearing peoples."

[52]Philo, *De specialibus legibus* 2.164–66; Josephus, *Against Apion*, 2.17 (165–92); Dahl, *Studies in Paul*, p. 190; L. Hurtado, "First-Century Jewish Monotheism," pp. 355, 360–65; A. Guerra, "The One God Topos in *Spec. Leg.* I. 52," pp. 148–57. Sanders, *Judaism: Practice*, pp. 195–97, points out that the Nash Papyrus of the second or first century b.c.e. was a single sheet including the Ten Commandments and the Shema that was probably used for devotional or educational purposes.

Philo similarly appealed to the One God topos and to the figure of Abraham to legitimize the inclusion of gentiles.[53] And all these concepts were united in the confession of the Shema for many Jews of the time. However, Paul's unique application of the heart of monotheistic faith becomes evident when we recognize that Philo, for example, was not concerned to include gentiles as gentiles in the people of God, but gentiles who had become Jewish proselytes. By contrast, Paul argued that to insist on gentile conversion to Judaism compromised the monotheistic faith of Israel and the core of the Shema and the Torah—for the One God of Israel is equally the One God of all the nations that turn to him, or else he is the One God of Jews only (a denial of his oneness and the oneness of all people created by him), and thus not really the One God at all.

Implicit in Paul's argument is the underlying assertion that the special role of Israel is not to indulge in an ethnocentric judgment of the gentile while gloating in the "works of the Law," that is, in their status as God's special people (which they are) to whom belong the "oracles of God,"[54] for their heritage as God's people is founded on faith that they might serve God (through the Torah of faith; he is expounding the point he begins to make in 3:27) before all the nations, bearing witness to him, not to themselves, so that the God of Israel is recognized as the God of the whole world.[55]

This paradigm ties together Paul's epideictic purpose throughout the letter. In chapters 2–4 Paul begins to develop this side of the equation for the privilege of the Jew *first* but not *only* by demonstrating that "the Torah of faith" itself bears witness to both the election of Israel (the people of faith received the gift of Torah) and God's intention to demonstrate his faithfulness to all the nations who have faith in the One God *also*, but he leaves off the balance of the argument until he has finished explaining the inclusion of gentiles in the people of God and thus their obligation to righteous behavior (chaps. 5–8). Paul then

[53]Guerra, "One God," pp. 148–57; idem, "Excursus: The 'One God' Topos in Jewish Apologetic Literature," in *Romans and the Apologetic Tradition*, pp. 84–101.

[54]On "works of the Law" as ethnocentric symbols of status see Appendix 1 below. On the "oracles" as God's word to Israel see Hays, *Echoes*, pp. 77–83.

[55]See chapter 2 above for a discussion of eschatology and chapter 5 below on the two-step pattern. Paul develops the role of Israel as the eschatological light to the nations negatively in 2:17-25, 26ff. to demonstrate what happens when it is done from self-serving ethnocentric motives; positively in chaps. 9–11 when the elect bring the light to all the nations resulting in the "obedience of faith" (15:18-21).

returns to finish up the discussion of Israel's responsibility and the current state of affairs (chaps. 9–11), which he quickly explains point to the parallel responsibility of the gentiles who have now joined the people of God toward their "stumbling" Jewish brothers and sisters "for whom Christ died" so that they might fulfill their eschatological purpose (chaps. 12–15; 14:15). All these concerns flow from his monotheistic argument for faith in Christ Jesus and the equal inclusion of gentiles in the people of God through the Shema of faith that "establishes" the "Torah of faith."

The Shema of Faith and Paul's Message Throughout Romans

I have now discussed how the confession of the One God went hand in hand with the practice of Torah for those of the Jewish faith, a juxtaposition that is outlined in the confession of the Shema (including the blessings that precede and follow in the full prayer) as understood in the first century, and as still practiced in contemporary Judaism.[56] And I have reviewed the Judaic notions of the "righteous gentile" who confessed faith in the One God and accepted the concomitant halakhot that demonstrated they had turned from pagan idolatry. In the case of the faction of Judaism that later became Christianity we saw that the apostolic decree served as an outline of some of the basic purity concerns that had been adapted from the halakhot for the "stranger" in the land of Israel to the Christian gentiles who were seeking fellowship with Christian Jews, and thus with the larger Jewish community. While general ethical matters would have been obvious, the matters of purity needed to be resolved separately. So while the early Christian gentiles were not expected to become Jews, they were expected to obey the operative first-century halakhah for the "righteous gentile" worshiping the One God in the midst of the Jewish community, for God is holy. The next question is: Can we

---

[56] It should be noted that the concept of the One God as a negative assertion over against the Trinity of Christianity was not behind the concept in Paul's time—the issue was not of numeric concern. But as Heschel, *Between God and Man*, pp. 104–5, has so eloquently phrased the issue: "Monotheism was not attained by means of numerical reduction, by bringing down the number of deities to the smallest possible number. One means 'unique.'" It is interesting to note that it was not a topic that Paul or the other Christian Jews were compelled to address; they, and the audience they addressed, understood their faith to be monotheistic. Cf. Dunn, *Partings*, pp. 205–6 and chaps. 11 and 12.

locate this concept of monotheistic obligation for Christian gentiles in Romans?

The ethical issues are certain and flow clearly from the essence of the Shema as the confession of monotheistic faith. We have already seen how Paul developed the admonition with which he drew Romans to its ethical climax around the pivotal role of the Shema in chapters 14 and 15.[57] There he clearly called for the "welcoming" of the faith of the "strong" by the "weak" and the faith of the "weak" by the "strong" because of the "welcoming" of the One God and Judge of all toward the faith of both (14:1-13). And we saw how Paul developed the obligation of the "strong" toward the "stumbling" in the context of Christian gentiles accommodating Jewish expectations of the behavior that should accompany the confession of faith in the One God for "righteous gentiles" seeking association with the Jewish community (14:13—15:13). Paul drew this admonition to a close by illustrating from the Scriptures that the eschatological expectation of gentiles worshiping in the midst of Israel had indeed begun (15:9-12), and therefore these Christian gentiles must draw from Israel's Scriptures the instruction necessary (they must learn to "hear," to *shema*) that they might "be of the *same* mind with one another according to Christ Jesus; that with *one* accord you may with *one* voice glorify *the God* and *Father* of *our Lord* Jesus Christ" (15:4-6).[58]

And we saw how Paul, in Romans 3, developed his argument for the equal inclusion of gentiles as gentiles in the people of God around the universalistic sense of the Shema of faith, at the same time affirming the election of Israel and the Torah, in fact, arguing that to deny the universalistic emphasis would be to deny the basis for the particularistic—for he would no longer be the One God.

We find this same monotheistic foundation underlying both Paul's argument for God's faithfulness and the call to proper behavior throughout Romans. Listen to the echoes of the Shema in Paul's bold "reminder" to the Romans of the roots of their faith in the "mercies of God" that necessitates dedicating their "bodies a living and holy

[57]See chapter 3 above.
[58]Note that Paul explicitly calls for worship of the God and Father, rather than of Jesus Christ, an important distinction if he is addressing the context of a mixed congregation wherein Christian gentiles are now fulfilling the prophetic Scriptures as they are meeting in the midst of non-Christian Jewish worshipers of the One God (15:9-12).

sacrifice, acceptable [welcome] to God, which is your spiritual service of worship" (12:1):

Chapter 1: It is evident in his explanation of "the power of God for salvation to *every one* who *believes*, to the Jew *first* and *also* to the Greek" (1:16), arguably the touchstone of Paul's entire message. The failure to recognize "the truth of God" turns on the failure to "acknowledge" the One God, denying the Creator the "honor" and "thanksgiving" He is due and instead indulging in pagan idolatry with its concomitant "deeds of darkness" (1:18-32), the constant theme of biblical, as well as apocryphal and pseudepigraphic literature of the period.

Chapter 2: The oneness of God as the judge of humankind without discrimination, "to the Jew *first*, and *also* to the Greek" (2:9-11), underlies Paul's admonition in chapter 2 to look to God, for he alone knows the "secrets of men," and to seek his "praise" and the good of the other rather than judging the other (Jew versus Greek, or Greek versus Jew) in an effort to win their praise, for in the very act of judging the other the knowledge of one's own responsibility to God as *the* Judge is manifested (vv. 1-4).

Chapter 3: I have already examined this explicit example of Paul's development of the implications of the Shema as the foundation of his argument that God is faithful to Israel and Torah, not to the exclusion of gentiles, but on behalf of them—for the One God of the Jews *first* is *equally* the One God of the gentiles *also*. To maintain otherwise is to compromise his oneness.

Chapter 4: Paul follows his argument in chapter 3 through chapter 4 with the illustration of Abraham, the father of faith (prior to the election of Israel or the giving of Torah, while still a gentile [and thus a representative of the worldwide purpose of God toward all his creation: 4:13, 16, 18]), to explain that through faith gentiles must be admitted as gentiles into the people of God, not because he disregards the election of Israel or the privilege of Torah, but because the purpose of election and Torah must be set in its worldwide purpose of salvation for all the descendants of Abraham: "not *only* to those who are of the Law, but *also* to those who are of the faith of Abraham, who is the father of us all" (4:16). Even as the Law is not nullified through faith (3:31), so too faith is not nullified through the Law (4:13-17); they both establish that the purpose of the other is ultimately only one thing, which is the very thing that makes Abraham "the father of us all," namely, to give "glory to God" (4:20).

Chapter 5: Chapter 5 is explosive, and I will return to it for a fuller discussion below. For the present purpose, note that Paul appeals to the concept of oneness through 5:12-21 with no less than twelve explicit citations of "one," not to mention the many implicit references characterizing his discussion of "all" and "the many." Here we find Paul's prior theological discussion in the context of explaining the equal inclusion of gentiles in God's larger purpose for choosing Israel and giving Israel the Torah of faith changes to a christological discussion as he turns to the business of admonishing the Christian gentiles in Rome on how they should live in view of their election (5:1-2, 17 begin a discussion that will carry through his next several chapters). For "the grace of God and the gift by the grace of the *one* Man, Jesus Christ" (5:15), is available to "those who receive the abundance of grace and of the gift of righteousness" (v. 17), "for through the obedience of the *One* the many will be made righteous" (v. 19). They "will reign in life through the *One*, Jesus Christ" (v. 17).

Chapters 6–8: Paul continues the discussion of the new orientation of the Christian gentiles in view of their confession of the Shema of faith "so we too might walk [*halakh*] in newness of life" (6:4), "dead to sin, but alive to God in Christ Jesus" (v. 11). We are now confronted with the full force of Paul's monotheistic argument: Gentiles are saved from slavery to sin by faith in the One God through Jesus Christ, but they are not saved in order to remain pagan idolaters; they become "slaves of righteousness" because they, like the One they have believed in, have become "slaves for obedience" (vv. 12-23). That is, they may be saved as gentiles, but not in order to remain pagan idolaters characterized by the presentation of the members of their body to sin; they are instead saved as "righteous gentiles," as those who present themselves to God, having turned from the deeds of death to those of life by the presenting of the members of their bodies as instruments of righteousness to God (6:13). I should probably note here, although I will return to this topic below, that Paul carries out this discussion of obedience to the One in the context of both ethics (law) and purity (v. 19), and further, that at the center of Paul's admonition is an appeal to "that form of teaching" to which they were "committed," a clear appeal to an existing body of teaching to which they had become "obedient" as "slaves of righteousness" when they left behind slavery to sin; a teaching that Paul now reminds them they must continue to obey (vv. 17-18). His argument includes the monotheistic insistence on the priority of Torah in chapter 7 and election in chapter 8.

Chapters 9–11: Paul returns to the additional concerns of Jewish election and Torah that he had left off after 3:2. At the center of this section is the assertion of the Shema in defining the current anomalous "stumbling" of many Jews over the confession of Christ and the gentile mission: "For there is no distinction between Jew and Greek; for the *same* Lord is *Lord of all*, abounding in riches for *all* who call upon Him; for '*Whoever* will call upon the name of the Lord will be saved'" (10:12-13). This begins a lengthy discussion of Israel's role as the bearer of "glad tidings" to all the world, and Israel's current refusal to fulfill that role but for the few, like Paul, who have accepted their responsibility as the light to the nations.[59] Paul clarifies the faithfulness of God to his one plan of salvation to the Jew first and also to the Greek, and discusses the humility appropriate for Christian gentiles in the face of the current "stumbling" of many Jews, rather than indulging any notion that they have supplanted Israel and can disregard the importance of Israel's salvation as though God was no longer committed to the people of the promises. Paul then completes this discussion with several clear assertions of the oneness of God and the oneness of humankind: "For God has shut up *all* in disobedience that *He* might show mercy to *all*. . . . For from Him and through Him and to Him are *all* things. To Him be the glory forever. Amen" (11:32, 36; see vv. 28-36).

Chapters 12–15: I have reviewed elsewhere the unifying presence of the Shema throughout this paraenesis calling for the appropriate behavioral response on the part of Christian gentiles (and non-Christian Jews) in view of the "mercies of God." We find Paul arguing the other side of the assertion that God is One: Is not the One God of the nations through faith in Christ Jesus also the One God of the "stumbling" of Israel? Is the faith that gentiles have in Christ Jesus demonstrated when they disregard the faith and sensitivities of their "stumbling" Jewish brethren? Did the One Man live in obedience, willing to accept reproach in order to serve the other in love, or did he live in disregard for the other? We also find in this section Paul affirming Torah as the way of love that will characterize the lifestyle of the Christian gentile who "behaves properly" by turning away from the "deeds of darkness" associated with idolatry and instead following the way of Christ Jesus (13:8-14):

> Owe nothing to anyone except to love one another; for he who loves
> his neighbor has *fulfilled* the law. For this, "You shall not commit

[59]Gaston, *Paul*, pp. 131–50; Lapide, *Paul: Rabbi*, pp. 48–55.

adultery, You shall not murder, You shall not steal, You shall not covet," and if there is any other commandment, it is summed up in this saying, "You shall love your neighbor as yourself." Love does no wrong to a neighbor; love therefore is the *fulfillment* of the law. (13:8-10)

Chapter 16: If we allow that the doxology of 16:25-27 is faithful in wrapping up the theme of the letter, regardless of its author, we find that the conclusion resonates with this same theme of the goal of Paul's gospel message in the One God of Israel and the nations:

Now to Him who is able to establish you according to my gospel and the preaching of Jesus Christ, according to the revelation of the mystery which has been kept secret for long ages past, but now is manifested, and by the Scriptures of the prophets, according to the commandment of the eternal God, has been made known to all the nations, leading to obedience of faith; to *the only wise God*, through Jesus Christ, be the glory forever. Amen.

Paul's monotheistic reasoning clearly lies behind his entire argument throughout Romans, both for the inclusion of gentiles in the people of God through faith in Jesus Christ, and for the behavioral responsibilities that must now characterize the lifestyle of these new Christian gentiles. They were to behave in a manner very similar to the "righteous gentile" as defined by Luke in reporting the halakhot of the apostolic decree, respecting the sensibilities of the Jewish people they were in contact with in Rome and accommodating Jewish expectations for the kind of behavior that would accompany the worship of the One God.

In the broader sense of proper behavior we see Paul's appeal to ethical behavior that results from turning to the One God and living empowered by the Spirit, thereby fulfilling the behavioral requirements of love embodied in the Decalogue (e.g., Rom. 13:8-14). The issue then becomes, Was the apostolic decree an operative concern for Paul when he addressed Rome? Do we see Paul asserting the purity issues that were embodied in the decree to the Romans?

The Purity Intentions of the Apostolic Decree Echoed in Paul's Assertion of the Shema

The apostolic decree was concerned with describing appropriate "righteous gentile" behavior for the new Christian gentiles in order to accommodate Jewish notions of purity in the community worshiping the One God. It describes the minimal purity requirements concomitant with the confession of the Shema, the behavior that follows from the monotheistic faith in the One God for gentiles seeking association with the Jewish community. The four particulars, the "necessary things" (ἐπάναγκες), outlined by Luke (Acts 15:20, 28-29) that Christian gentiles were to "keep away from," were "meat sacrificed to idols" (εἰδωλοθύτων: v. 29; "things contaminated by idols" in v. 20: τῶν ἀλισγημάτων τῶν εἰδώλων),[60] "blood" (αἵματος), "what is strangled" (πνικτοῦ), and "fornication" (πορνείας). While the apostolic decree is never appealed too or cited formally in other extant literature, the decree is recognized as operative in the thinking of the authors of Revelation (e.g., 2:14, 20, 24 for sexual immorality [πορνεῦσαι] and idol meat [εἰδωλόθυτα] and no other burden),[61] the *Didache* (6.3),[62] and elsewhere in the context of describing proper behavior in matters of food and sexual relations.[63] We find these same concerns in Paul's various paraenetic sections throughout Romans and elsewhere (1 Cor. 5:1-5; 8–10; 1 Thess. 4:3-7), and we find them in the context of Paul's concern with purity. I believe that the intentions and the particulars of the decree were operative in Paul's thinking as he addressed the Christian gentiles in Rome.

The Pharisees were the champions of bringing the purity concerns

[60]In Acts 15 we see that the decree was not still circulating as a formal document when Luke wrote, although the outline and intentions were clear, for even Luke wrote with some liberty in his description of idol meat.

[61]Simon, "Apostolic Decree," pp. 442, 451–52.

[62]C. K. Barrett, "Things Sacrificed," in *Essays on Paul*, p. 43: "there can be no doubt that the author of the *Didache* believed that to eat food sacrificed to idols was to fall into the practically unforgivable sin of idolatry."

[63]Simon, "Apostolic Decree," pp. 437–60, discusses Pseudo-Clementine *Homilies* 7.8 (pp. 447–48), and later evidence of the decree on pp. 454–59. Ehrhardt, *The Framework of the New Testament Stories*, pp. 276–90, explores early Christian observation of the decree at times "with an almost fanatic determination" (see also pp. 276, 286–89). He notes that in the second and third centuries in Rome Christians did not eat blood (pp. 282–85: cites M. Felix in *Octavius* 30.7 and others). Barrett, "Things Sacrificed," pp. 40–59, suggest that Jude and 2 Peter may also have in their background the matters addressed in the decree (pp. 41–42). Barrett also notes the issue of not eating idol food in Justin, *Trypho* 34–35, and Irenaeus, *Against Heresies* 1.6.3 (pp. 43–44); and also the substance of the decree in the *Preaching of Peter* (pp. 44–45). Tomson, *Paul*, pp. 180–86, traces post-apostolic food prohibitions.

of the Temple priests into the daily lifestyle of the Jewish community.[64] And the Qumran community's adaptation of the Temple and
priestly role for their self-definition is remarkably similar to the concepts Paul developed.[65] Paul's continual appeal to the illustration of
the community as the Temple of God,[66] to his mission and ministry as
priestly service (Rom. 1:1, 9ff., 15-16, 17ff., 25-31),[67] to his audience
as priests (1:7; 12:1-2),[68] and even as the very sacrifices of Temple
worship (1:13;[69] 6:12-13, 14ff.; 12:1-2; 15:16, 26-31)[70] mirror the notions
of his contemporaries in applying cultic purity to matters of everyday
life and community.[71] He clearly applied purity concepts and language
to matters of table-fellowship, sexual conduct, discipline, and as the

[64]Neusner, "Idea of Purity"; idem, *Judaism in the Beginning of Christianity*,
pp. 45–61; Sanders, *Judaism: Practice*, pp. 431–51; Rivkin, *Hidden Revolution*.

[65]M. Newton, *The Concept of Purity at Qumran and in the Letters of Paul*; Flusser,
Judaism, pp. 35–44; Gaston, *No Stone*, pp. 119–243; on p. 164 Gaston discusses
4QFlor 1.1-13: "This text is an exposition of the promise of Nathan 2 Sm 7, and
it interprets the 'house' which God promised to build for David as the Qumran
community. The community as the temple is the place where the holy ones, the
angels, are present, and perhaps the place above which God himself will appear.
Therefore it is holy, and the laws which applied to the priests in the Jerusalem
temple apply all the more to the members of the Qumran community."

[66]See M. Newton, *Concept of Purity*, pp. 52–78, for an excellent discussion of
Paul's view of the church as the Temple of God. Romans does not have the kind
of explicit references found, for example, in 1 Cor. 3:16-17: "Do you not know that
you are a temple of God, and the Spirit of God dwells in you? If any man destroys
the temple of God, God will destroy him, for the temple of God is holy, and that
is what you are." However, the imagery is just as clear, in Rom. 12:1-2 and 15:16ff.,
for example. See also Gaston, *No Stone*, pp. 176–205, for a discussion of this imagery of the Temple and purity in Paul. 1 Cor. 6:12-20 is clearly concerned with
food in the context of the purity of the body as God's temple, and 2 Cor. 6:14—
7:1 (note 6:16: "Or what agreement has the temple of God with idols? For we are
the temple of the living God," in the context of monotheistic ethical behavior) is
explicit and closely parallels the Qumran conceptions (Gaston, *No Stone*,
pp. 177–81).

[67]Newton, *Concept of Purity*, pp. 60ff.

[68]Ibid., pp. 70ff.

[69]Ibid., pp. 62–68, for discussion of Paul's application of fruit from priestly offerings in the light of Paul's use of fruit elsewhere in Romans and his other letters.

[70]Ibid., pp. 70ff.

[71]Ibid., for an excellent discussion of both Paul's usage of this imagery in
Romans and his other letters, as well as that of the Qumran community. See also
D. Cambell, *The Rhetoric of Righteousness*, pp. 17–18, and notes, for his comments
on the "scarlet thread of Levitical imagery running through Romans" (see also
pp. 107–30, on 3:25 as sacrificial language).

foundation of proper behavior within the community.[72] And he continually described the actions of Christ Jesus in sacrificial and priestly terms (3:25 [ἱλαστήριον as the sacrifice of Yom Kippur]; 5:2; 8:3, 34; 15:8).[73]

Paul and his contemporaries saw the issue of purity in the context of the election of Israel to the worship, as a community, of the One God in the face of idolatry, the very rejection of God and the "principal source of impurity":[74] "Purity became the guardian of monotheism."[75] Of course Paul, like his Jewish contemporaries and their forefathers in the biblical tradition, did not make the same degree of distinction we do now between ritual and ethical purity, or for that matter between ethics and purity or ritual.[76] For our present purpose we need look no further than Romans 6:19 to see Paul's indiscriminate juxtaposition of "impurity" and "lawlessness" in the context of "sanctification" and "righteousness" in describing their priestly responsibility:[77]

> For just as you presented your members as slaves to *impurity* and to *lawlessness*, resulting in further lawlessness, so now present your members as slaves to *righteousness*, resulting in *sanctification*.

We see this issue of purity in Paul's letter in the context of table-fellowship and sexual behavior that demonstrate monotheistic faith versus pagan idolatry.[78] Paul's call to practice proper behavior is based, as it was for Paul's Jewish contemporaries, on the appropriate behavior

[72]Newton, *Concept of Purity*, pp. 113–16; Gaston, *No Stone*, pp. 176–205.

[73]See the discussion of 3:25 by Cambell, *Rhetoric of Righteousness*, pp. 107–37.

[74]Neusner, "Idea of Purity," pp. 15–26.

[75]See W. Houston, *Purity and Monotheism*, pp. 123, 279. See Tomson, *Paul*, pp. 151–86, for "Laws concerning Idolatry in Early Judaism and Christianity."

[76]See Newton, *Concept of Purity*, pp. 3–4, 103; R. Longenecker, *Paul*, pp. 119–22, 123ff.; on p. 145 Longenecker notes: "While he could speak of the moral and ceremonial aspects of the Law separately, there is no suggestion that he viewed them as possessing separate validity or as being possible to separate. There is no reason to doubt that he viewed the Law, as did Judaism, as one indivisible whole."

[77]Examples abound in Romans and in Paul's other letters. See, for example, Gal. 5:19-20; 2 Cor. 12:21. Ezek. 18:5-9, 12 is an excellent prophetic example of the same juxtaposition. See the comment of Räisänen, *Paul*, pp. 25–28, 199–201.

[78]The issues of marriage and sexual conduct are treated in more detail in 1 Corinthians; for excellent discussions see Simon, "Apostolic Decree"; and Tomson, *Paul*, pp. 97–124.

for the community of people who understand themselves to be worshiping and living in the very presence of the holy God. In fact, the very dietary laws we are seeking to understand in the context of purity are equally expressive of ethics.[79] No distinction is really necessary, as Grunfeld clearly put the matter of dietary laws:

> Holiness or self-sanctification is a moral term; it is identical with what we call in modern ethics, moral freedom or moral autonomy. Its aim is the complete self-mastery of man. . . . Thus the fundamental idea of Jewish ethics, holiness, is inseparably connected with the idea of Law; and the dietary laws occupy a central position in that system of moral discipline which is the basis of all Jewish laws.[80]

Paul's argument was directed to the Christian gentiles of Rome, who had not become Jews and were thus not the people of Torah, to clarify that it was still necessary for them to practice those dietary and sexual restrictions understood to be incumbent upon "righteous gentiles" associating with the Jewish community. While it was true for gentiles believing in Christ Jesus that "nothing is unclean [κοινὸν: common][81] in itself" and that "all things indeed are clean [καθαρά]," nevertheless, things were actually impure to those who regarded them

[79]The comments of Bruce Chilton, *The Temple of Jesus*, p. 59, are interesting in this sense as he describes the "offering for sin" of Lev. 4: "Indeed, the distinctive feature of the sacrifice for sin may be derived from the sacrifice of sharings; while God consumes his portions (vv. 8-10), the priest forgoes his (vv. 11, 12; see Noth, *Leviticus*, 40). By not eating what under other circumstances he could eat, the priest reestablishes the rules of consumption. No greater support could be sought for the proposition that sanctity is more a function of what is done, by sacrificial activity, than it is a quality of space or place in an abstract sense." He discusses the actions of Jesus in terms of sacrificial purity and declares on p. 146: "In aggregate, the evidence concerning the Essenes and the Pharisees demonstrates that, during the first century, there was an ideological connection between eating, 'eschaton', and sacrifice, such that some principal sectors of early Judaism shared a typology, not only of sacrifice, but of sacrificial conceptions. Once that ideological pattern has been identified, of course, it proves to be of particular interest in understanding Jesus, as eating, 'eschaton', and sacrifice are also linked programmatically in his teaching."

[80]See I. Grunfeld, *The Jewish Dietary Laws*, p. 11.

[81]14:14 makes it clear that the issue dividing the "weak" and the "strong" is along Jew/gentile lines concerning their difference of opinion in matters of purity (κοινὸν [common] is unique to Jewish cultic language in antiquity [Dunn, *Romans*, p. 800]).

as impure (Rom. 14:14, 20).[82] A higher law applied to these "things" around which the conflict flared, namely, the responsibility for Christian gentiles to live with respect to the beliefs of the "weak," who believed that certain dietary and other restrictions applied to these gentiles when in their company: "Do not let what is for you a good thing be spoken of as evil" (14:16). Why? Because the principle of the kingdom of God superseded the principle of self-pleasure (14:15, 17). And what is the principle of the kingdom of God but the eschatological shalom that would overcome the eating sin of Adam that had led to the divisiveness of all people (Jew versus gentile in our context) as they sought their own pleasure and not the pleasure of God and of one's neighbor.[83]

Paul's view of liberty must be understood in the context of his commitment to the inherent compromise of monotheism present in any insistence on "righteous gentiles" becoming Jews. Christian gentiles are not Jews and thus are theoretically free of purity laws. Nevertheless, their assertion of freedom must be examined in the relative context of Jewish and gentile relationships and the function of Torah for each. There is a law higher than the freedom to seek one's own rights, for purity behavior applies in the context of the unification of both Jew and gentile in the eschatological restoration of God's rule on earth. That is the point of Paul's instruction to the "strong" to observe, and not to disregard any longer, the dietary opinions of the "weak" in the service of God and his shalom: "Do not tear down the work of God for the sake of food. All things indeed are clean, but they are evil for the man who eats and gives offense" (14:20). Gentiles turning to faith in the Christ of Israel need not (must not!) become Jews; however, *equally important*, they must not remain pagans, nor offend their Jewish brothers and sisters by disregarding purity behavior operative for guiding the lifestyles of "righteous gentiles" in their midst.[84] They must

[82]Grunfeld, *Jewish Dietary Laws*, pp. 11–19, among others. Even those who take this to mean that Paul no longer respected Torah purity must admit, from this digression alone, that the context of Paul's discussion of the obligation of the "strong" toward the "weak" is a matter of purity and not merely ethics.

[83]Gaston, *No Stone*, pp. 200–205, 334–65, 428–33, for the context of shalom between Jews and gentiles in Luke's writings and in Paul as founded on the restoration of Israel and the ingathering of the nations as promised. See also chapter 5 below on the two-step pattern.

[84]See also Gal. 5:13-15; 1 Cor. 8–9.

express their "faith" in "obedience" to the behavior that will be both "accepted by God" and "approved by men":

> I know and am convinced in the Lord Jesus that nothing is unclean [κοινὸν: common] in itself; but to him who thinks anything to be unclean, to him it is unclean. For if because of food your brother is hurt, you are no longer walking according to love. Do not destroy with your food him for whom Christ died. Therefore do not let what is for you a good thing be spoken of as evil; for the kingdom of God is not eating and drinking, but righteousness and peace and joy in the Holy Spirit. For he who in this way serves Christ is acceptable to God and approved by men. (14:14-18)

Paul bases this call to obey the intentions of the apostolic decree, that is, to serve Christ in a way that is both "acceptable to God *and* approved by men" in matters of "food" (14:15-18) on the principle of how Christ himself subordinated his own rights to the pleasure and best interests of the other (15:1-3). The argument is not based on compromise. It does not indicate that for Paul or any Jew there is no such thing as impurity since the coming of Christ. It rather parallels the intentions of the apostolic decree for gentiles who have come to faith in the Savior of Israel as their Savior. They do not need to become Jews; nevertheless, they do need to subordinate themselves to the operative purity rules for "righteous gentiles" in the Jewish communities of the Diaspora. Christian gentiles may be free from embracing Torah fully as Jews, but they are not free of the halakhah of the "righteous gentiles" seeking association with Israel. They must live in purity if they want respect for their claims of having turned from idolatry to the worship of the One God (13:11-14).[85]

As gentiles they are free, but not as believers. If they fail to regard the faith and practice of their new Jewish brothers and sisters they are failing to live in the service of Christ in the way "acceptable to God and approved by men" (14:18). They are rather continuing to live in sin: for "whatever is not from faith is sin" (14:23). They are called now to turn from "slavery to sin" to "slavery to righteousness" (6:12-23), or as Paul describes it in the midst of his argument with the "strong": "Do not tear down the work of God for the sake of food. All things indeed are clean, *but* they are evil for the man who eats and gives offense. . . . Happy is he who does not condemn himself in what he

---

[85]Paul argues similarly in 1 Cor. 8:4-13 from a monotheistic basis.

approves" (14:20-22). As gentiles in Christ they may be free from full observance of the purity laws; however, as people of faith in Christ they are obliged to obey a higher law, namely, subordination to the purity laws operative for "righteous gentiles" when in the company of the Jewish community (or Jewish individuals).

Paul's declaration of the purity of all things should not be taken out of its contextual argument. He is arguing, as have the prophets and leaders of Israel in biblical times,[86] and the Qumran community, and the Pharisees (from which he came), that God is the one who is to be served above self-interest, for the created order serves a higher purpose, namely, the Creator.[87] Even as Isaiah and the prophets could ostensibly speak with disregard for sacrifice and Temple in favor of worship from the heart and righteous behavior (Isa. 1:11-17; 58),[88] or recognize that idols were fashioned by humans and contained no real threat to God (Isa. 44:9-20; Jer. 10), so too Paul may seem to disregard matters of purity and belittle the relative importance of idolatrous food in favor of faith (Rom. 14:14a).[89] However, Paul is really just appealing to the inherent truth of the purity laws; they exist because the holy God has declared them so (e.g., Lev. 11:41-45; 19:2; 20:25-26). God has chosen what is pure to eat and what is impure, both for the Jew and for the gentile who worships him. Everything was created good, yet God declared to Adam, to Noah, and to Moses what was and was not to be eaten.[90] Purity is not intrinsic; it is imputed. God has spoken and it is

[86]Prophetic critique is succinctly traced by Mary C. Callaway, "A Hammer That Breaks Rock in Pieces: Prophetic Critique in the Hebrew Bible," pp. 21–38.

[87]R. Longenecker, *Paul*, pp. 65–85, on the piety of both the Pharisees and the Qumran community respecting this same sense of the importance of the intentions of love for God and others for ritual obedience to serve its true purpose. He even explores this in the context of the daily recitation of the Shema (pp. 71-73).

[88]See also Isa. 29:13; 66:1-5; Amos 5:21-24; Hos. 6:6; Mic. 6:6-8; Jer. 7:3-11. See the earlier development of this same theme in 1 Sam. 15:22; Ps. 51:17-19; Prov. 15:8; 21:3, 27. The matter is well defined by Ellul, *Politics of God*: that which originated in the service of God becomes a power unto itself and ultimately hinders the very service of God it should support. The service is not therefore essentially wrong, but it must be checked and reinterpreted from time to time to keep it on course. This is the role of the prophet.

[89]See 1 Cor. 8:4-6 for his development of the oneness of the Creator God to dismiss the reality of idolatry. See Tomson, *Paul*, pp. 189-221, for discussion of this dynamic in 1 Corinthians.

[90]Note the following Midrash: "The precepts were given only in order that man might be refined by them. For what does the Holy One, blessed be He, care whether a man kills an animal by the throat or by the nape of its neck? Hence its

so.[91] Thus, when the laws of purity are applied outside their intended purpose they are subject to prophetic criticism to set them back on course, that is, back in the service of God and of one's neighbor.

Paul's context is not disregard for the practice of purity in the matter of eating, but precisely the opposite. Paul labors to explain to Christian gentiles (not Jews, who would not need such an approach to understanding matters of purity) in a manner that he hopes they can grasp that they must not misunderstand the freedom that follows from not becoming Jews (following the same line of argument as Peter and James in Luke's account of the purpose for the apostolic decree: Acts 15). That is the point of his explanation in Romans 6 of their obligation to proper behavior even though (in fact, because) they are not under law but under grace. It does not mean they are free of either the ethical or purity requirements of their new faith as understood by Jews. They are now "slaves of righteousness."[92] That is, they are not free of the requirements of obedience that follow from their new confession of the Shema. They must obey the halakhah for the "righteous gentile" laid out in the apostolic decree as developed from the laws given first to Adam,[93] then to Noah, and then to Moses for the "stranger within your gates"—the "obedience" that follows from "faith." Paul's intentions echo those of the Jerusalem Council: Israel's faith and the purity regulations of the community must apply to gen-

---

purpose is to refine man" (*Gen. Rabbah* 44.1); and commenting on Prov. 30:5 and Deut. 14:4 concerning clean and unclean animals: "This means the precepts were given for the express purpose of purifying mankind" (*Lev. Rabbah* 13.3).

[91]Grunfeld, *Jewish Dietary Laws*, pp. 5, 12–19, 28–29. So *Sifra Aharei* 93d: "One should not say, I do not wish to dress in mixed garments, I do not wish to eat pork, I do not wish to commit illicit sexuality—but I wish to and what can I do? For my Father in heaven decreed (the prohibitions) on me thus" (from Tomson, *Paul*, p. 249).

[92]Grunfeld, *Jewish Dietary Laws*, p. 11, illuminates this essential Jewish understanding: "To the superficial observer it seems that men who do not obey the law are freer than law-abiding men, because they can follow their own inclinations. In reality, however, such men are subject to the most cruel bondage; they are slaves of their own instincts, impulses and desires. The first step towards emancipation from the tyranny of animal inclinations in man is, therefore, a voluntary submission to the moral law. The constraint of law is the beginning of human freedom, or in Rabbinic phraseology, 'None is free, except he who acts in accord with the law'."

[93]It should be noted that the Talmud (*b. Sanh.* 56b) derives the Noahide Commandments from the verse preceding the commandment to Adam not to eat of the tree of good and evil (see Grunfeld, *Jewish Dietary Laws*, pp. 42–44).

tiles who come to faith in Christ, though they need not (Paul would emphasize that they *must* not) become Jews (through circumcision and keeping the full Torah: Acts 15).

The apostolic decree provided for Jewish "approval" of Christian gentiles' claims to be equal coparticipants in God's blessings through faith. As the context of this new movement changed from the Jewish community and synagogues to a largely, and then entirely, gentile one, it is not difficult to see how the decision of the Jerusalem Council to include gentiles believing in Christ Jesus as equals ultimately led to disregard for the underlying intentions of the apostolic decree, even though the practices outlined therein apparently continued in the churches for several centuries. We see an excellent discussion of the problem already in the mid-50s in Romans 16:17-20. The position of those Paul condemns as "slaves not of our Lord Christ but of their own appetites" who "by their smooth and flattering speech . . . deceive the hearts of the unsuspecting" only too clearly adumbrates the trend that would eventually win out in the development of Christianity as a thoroughly gentile organization. Self-pleasure, which Paul confronted in the eating behavior of the "strong," triumphed over his reminder of their obligation to the "weak" with respect to certain dietary restrictions. And they, like Adam before them, were deceived into eating that which they regarded as their pleasure rather than obey the intentions and restrictions of God.[94] It is in this context that we can understand Paul's anticipation of the eschatological shalom that he hoped his addressees would participate in and that he believed God would one day bring in spite of those who were, like Satan before them, deceiving the righteous by suggesting that they should eat that which was forbidden. Paul's polemic was uncompromising: "And the God of peace will soon crush Satan under you feet" concluded his discussion of those serving their own appetites and deceiving his addressees to consider the same, causing "dissensions and hindrances contrary to the teaching which you learned" (16:17-20).

THE APOSTOLIC DECREE AND THE MESSAGE OF ROMANS

It is important to note that the major tenets of the decree were practiced by the early Christian gentiles for several centuries, although this

---

[94]For a discussion of the later Gnostic position see S. Wilson, *Luke and the Law*.

fact is not considered by most scholars to demonstrate that Paul accepted or taught it in his gentile mission.[95] Somehow it is assumed that Paul was generally unaware of the decree, or that if he was aware of it he did not accept it. Why has Christianity so overlooked this feature of Paul's missionary teaching? Consider the conclusions of several scholars who exemplify this general viewpoint:[96]

- Heikki Räisänen comments on the apostolic decree following from the decision of the Jerusalem Council thus: "It seems that Peter, Barnabas and others recognized the force of the restorative arguments . . . Paul, however, saw the situation quite differently. It is clear that over the years Paul had become internally alienated from the ritual aspects of the law. In the course of his work among Gentiles he had fully internalized the Gentile point of view and identified himself with it. While agreeing with the moral content of the Torah, Paul seldom based his ethical instruction explicitly upon it. Often complying with the ritual precepts for strategic reasons, he felt free from the law and dead to it (Gal 2.19). He had rightfully

[95]Tomson, *Paul*, p. 185, notes: "The early Christian unanimity on the prohibition of idol food makes the accepted scholarly view that Paul condoned it seem quite unlikely. If he did he would not just have been the first, but in effect the only early Christian authority to defend this position. Indeed, it would have been a miracle, resulting from pure misunderstanding, that First Corinthians was preserved at all by the early Church in its extant form." See Simon, "Apostolic Decree," pp. 454–60.

[96]I have refrained from using the comments of those who are so predisposed to seeing Paul as non-Jewish that they would naturally believe he opposed the apostolic decree, and in many cases would even question whether the decree was operative among those Paul would have supposedly opposed. It is worth noting the following comments as typical of the many scholars who categorically dismiss or radically reinterpret the historical import of the decree for Luke, or Paul: H. Conzelmann, *Acts of the Apostles*, p. 119: "For Luke, of course, the issue of table fellowship in mixed congregations was no longer a live issue. Yet he saw these stipulations as of fundamental significance. That significance, however, was not ethical, but salvation-historical, since the decree provided continuity between Israel and the church, which was free from the Law"; Schmithals, *Paul and James*, p. 100: "Those four rules make sense if they are intended to preserve the holiness of Palestine. They have a meaning, too, as a matrix of the observances recommended to a God-fearer. But as the basis for table-fellowship in particular they were inappropriate." And on p. 102, he notes that during Paul's time "the four rules were unknown to the churches."

torn down the law with its food regulations (Gal 2.18) and could say that all food was clean (Rom 14.14, cf. Phil 3.2). That is no longer a genuinely Jewish stance."[97]

- J. D. G. Dunn states regarding the apostolic decree: "Most of the gentile Christians within the diaspora congregations, particularly those founded by Paul, seem to have already moved beyond that position . . . in abandoning the hitherto characteristic hallmarks of the diaspora Jew."[98]

- Marcel Simon observes: "Paul would certainly be prepared to conform to the Decree for reasons of mere expediency, in order not to give offense to the weak brethren. But he could not, in conscience, accept it on principle."[99] Simon concludes: "While the Decree goes against the tendency represented by Paul and illustrates the triumph of what can be described as moderate or mitigated Jewish Christianity, it also amounts to a defeat of extreme, uncompromising Jewish Christianity. Paul would certainly have objected to such a document."[100]

- John Hurd notes that Paul's "previous letter" to Corinth (that is, Paul's letter preceding 1 Corinthians, mentioned in 1 Cor. 5:9) may have included the decree, which was "an uncongenial intrusion into his thought."[101] Paul had not taught the decree in his original mission to Corinth "because they had not yet been formulated";[102] the decree was part of a compromise that Paul worked out later with the Jerusalem leadership in order to gain recognition for his apostleship; however, 1 Corinthians was then written to withdraw his commitment to the decree in response to a letter from them (1 Cor. 7:1).[103]

- David Catchpole believes the decree was what was brought to Antioch by James' emissaries that Paul so opposed (Gal. 2:11-14). The decree was not a compromise and Paul was not present in Jerusalem; the decree was rather "a move back from those ideas of

[97]Räisänen, *Paul*, pp. 258ff
[98]Dunn, *Romans*, p. 811.
[99]Simon, "Apostolic Decree," p. 453.
[100]Ibid., pp. 459–60.
[101]Hurd, *The Origin of 1 Corinthians*, pp. 259–62.
[102]Ibid., p. 261.
[103]Ibid., pp. 240–70, 289–95. See Tomson, *Paul*, pp. 198ff., for criticism of Hurd.

Church and gospel which had been accepted at the conference as the basis of Gentile Christianity" that was "repugnant to Paul."[104]

- C. K. Barrett says: "In permitting the eating of εἰδωλόθυτα, Paul allows what elsewhere in the New Testament was strictly forbidden. In particular he contradicts the requirements of the Apostolic Decree."[105]

- W. D. Davies takes an interestingly nuanced position recognizing that the Noahide Commandments would have been "familiar" to Paul and even that "we can quite definitely trace the conceptions underlying those commandments in his Epistle to the Romans."[106] However, when Davies turns to the matter of the apostolic decree, which he links with the Noahide Commandments, he notes: "it is tempting and probably correct to see in the Apostolical decree an expression of these demands, a version of the Noachian commandments possibly abbreviated or in the form current in the first century. It is incredible that in any discussion on the status of Gentiles within the Church those commandments would not have been the subject of discussion, and the meaning of the decree is probably that those responsible for it, knowing themselves to be living in the Messianic Age, while they did not insist on circumcision for all Christians, did insist on their observing those fundamental demands which the Rabbis assumed to be binding on all men."[107] Davies decides finally against the decree as operative for Paul with the following comment:[108] "We cannot claim that the Noachian commandments were in any sense normative for Paul in the ethical teaching of his converts. We can claim, however, that the conceptions which gave them birth became an integral part of his theology and must have often guided his thoughts in discussions on the Gentile question."[109]

- Alan Segal concludes, on the basis of his reading of Paul's com-

---

[104]Catchpole, "Paul, James," pp. 430, 442–43.

[105]Barrett, *Essays on Paul*, p. 52; note his critique of Ehrhardt on pp. 45–46, 47ff.

[106]Davies, *Paul*, p. 115.

[107]Ibid., pp. 117–18.

[108]Davies's final position against the decree as operative for Paul is often overlooked; see, for example, the comments of Novak, *Image*, pp. 25–26.

[109]Davies, *Paul*, p. 119. Note also ibid., p. 117, where Davies comments on Burkitt, whom he quotes as saying "there was a demand for a minimum of common decency and behavior from these Gentile newcomers if they were to be received as fellow-worshippers" and then takes exception with this view: "We need not agree with Burkitt that the decree had only to deal with the problem of social

ments as indicating Paul believed the rules were inadequate and thus "totally irrelevant now,"[110] but that Paul was willing to accommodate because of his strategy for Christian unity: "The Apostolic Decree sets aside the radical ideological position of Paul, regardless of Acts' contention that Paul was a participant in the decree. . . . Throughout early church history, the dominant position is more like the *Didache* or the Apostolic Decree than Paul's ideological position."[111]

In stark contrast to this consensus,[112] however, I see the apostolic

---

intercourse and was not meant to help to ensure the salvation of Gentile Christians." This makes sense of Davies' problem in seeing the apostolic decree as operative for Paul; if Davies believes that the decree had to do with ensuring salvation for Christian gentiles then he must object. But I believe his error is in taking exception to the view of Burkitt, which allows, as does the view expressed herein, that for Paul and those who shaped the decree the decision about entrance requirements was resolved first, with the conclusion that faith alone was necessary. The tension then that the apostolic decree addressed was in the matter of proper behavior that should follow from their new status once they were in. Note also that Davies's position validates the concerns of Novak, *Image*, pp. 20–35.

[110]Segal, *Paul*, p. 235.

[111]Ibid., p. 236.

[112]The following are comments of a few scholars who believe Paul respected the apostolic decree to varying degrees, though not necessarily locating it in Romans. Ehrhardt, *Framework*, believes that Paul at first resisted the decree (when he wrote Galatians) but then changed his mind (pp. 276–77). He notes on p. 277: "The way in which St. Paul now accepted the decree, and in particular the prohibition of the eating of sacrificial meat, is highly significant for the mutual relations between the two Apostles. Not only did he not reject it any longer, but he even supported it strongly as a command of charity in favour of 'the weak.'" Tomson, *Paul*, pp. 273–74, concludes: "If 'keeping the commandments of God' for gentiles means to observe the universal or Noachian code in Paul's version, the obvious question is how this relates to the Apostolic Decree of Acts. . . . It would follow that Paul's list of the 'commandments of God' for gentiles was identical with the basic version of the Western text of the Apostolic Decree and with the three capital commandments of ancient Judaism. These considerations lead us to a hypothesis which needs further documentation but is proposed here to keep things moving. Paul's 'rule for all churches' in I Cor 7:17-20 included three 'commandments of God' for gentiles (no idolatry, unchastity and bloodshed) and may be considered as being his version of the Apostolic Decree which is basically identical to the Western text. Ignoring the tricky problem of chronology we can also infer that Paul's story in Gal 2:1-14 presupposes this version of the Decree." Also R. Grant, *A Historical Introduction*, p. 395: "Paul's letters have to do with specific problems not always, or indeed often, related to the decree. However, it would appear that his discussion of sanctification as abstention from fornication and from unclean lust (I Thess. 4. 3-7) is close to the matrimonial injunctions of the decree,

decree operating in the background of Paul's bold "reminder" to Rome. In addition to his clear agenda to explain the new status of the gentile believing in Jesus Christ as equal, though governed by the principles of behavior outlined for the "righteous gentile" in the Council's apostolic decree, several specific references suggest that his addressees share with Paul the knowledge of the decree in its original, though certainly fluid, format.[113] We have seen how central the issue of accommodating the dietary concerns of the "weak" were in order to

---

and in I Corinthians 5.1-5 he condemns a man who has violated the regulation of Leviticus 18.8. The lengthy discussion of meats sacrificed to idols in I Corinthians 8–10 is in harmony with the apostolic decree, and Paul says that the Corinthians are to give no offense to Jews (10.32). The same view is expressed in Romans 14. It looks, then, as if Paul actually continued to teach the commandments of the apostolic decree, though he did so on grounds different from those advocated at Jerusalem." R. Longenecker, *Paul*, pp. 254–63, takes a positive view of the decree, and on pp. 234–35 and 241–44, discusses why it was not directly referred to in 1 Corinthians, suggesting: "Whether or not the Decree existed or was accepted by Paul, to quote any ecclesiastical pronouncement to those ultraspiritualists who considered all such statements as sub-Christian would have immediately labeled him as beneath them in spirituality and would have closed the door to his endeavor to lead them on in true Christian liberty. It could just as well be argued that part of the criticism against Paul in the Corinthian church arose within the libertine group because he had originally delivered the Decree to them as that because he did not quote its last section in I Corinthians 6 the Decree is spurious, known to Paul only after his third journey or unacceptable to him" (p. 235). Longenecker then comments on p. 258, regarding Galatians: "We may therefore conclude that Paul's lack of reference to the Jerusalem Decree is no real evidence that he was unaware of it or refused to accept it. Nor is there any conclusive evidence that the Decree was not formulated at the Jerusalem Council, as represented in Acts 15. Accepting the early date for Galatians, Peter's vacillation was also earlier that [*sic*] the Council and does not therefore have a bearing on the question at hand. And James' statement to Paul in Acts 21:25 may be viewed just as easily as a reassurance of the elder apostles' recognition of Gentile independence within a context of brotherly forbearance as that James was telling Paul something he did not know, which was really done behind his back." And on p. 259: "Taking these two factors into consideration [Longenecker's discussion of gentile freedom yet obligation to the scruples of Jews and Paul's respect for apostolic and ecclesiastical authority in 'the guidance of Christian liberty'], I can see no reason why the Apostle would not have willingly accepted the Jerusalem Decree." See M. Bockmuehl, "The Noachide Commandments and New Testament Ethics with Special Reference to Acts 15 and Pauline Halakhah," pp. 72–101.

[113]Cf. Borgen, "Catalogues of Vices," for the variety of Jewish traditions for proselytes during this period and his argument that the two manuscript versions of the apostolic decree represent interpretations of some of the sample catalogues available.

win them to faith in Christ. Further, I find traces in the formal features of the opening and closing of the letter, in the rhetorical structure, and in several key phrases and concepts that Romans is actually Paul's exposition, by way of reminder, of the apostolic decree in view of his intended visit, and yet necessary delay.

The Purpose of Paul's Letter and His Intended Visit

The formal features of the opening and closing texts reveal Paul's intentions and expectations both in view of his current delay and with regard to his planned visit.[114] Interestingly, the language mirrors Luke's account of Paul's original declaration of the apostolic decree in Antioch, Derbe, and Lystra. In fact, the language Paul uses in Romans to describe his purpose and his anticipated reception is so remarkably similar to the language of Acts that it is surprising that this feature has apparently not been considered seriously before. I develop this issue at greater length later with respect to the two-step pattern of Paul's preaching; however, it is important to discuss here the parallels between Romans and Acts where the declaration of the decree is concerned.

Paul indicates that he regards the audience in Rome as under his apostleship, even though he has not been to Rome or apparently communicated directly with them in the past (1:5-6, 10-15; 11:13; 15:22-24).[115] Nevertheless, he is their apostle as he is the apostle of all the gentiles, responsible for the declaration of the gospel and eager to reach Rome and fulfill his calling. It is clear in his opening and closing statements (1:1-15; 15:14—16:27) that while Paul is thankful for the fact that their "faith is being proclaimed throughout the whole world" (1:8), he is, nevertheless, not satisfied with this current state of affairs where he is concerned, nor is he satisfied with their own present status.

For his part, he must "obtain some fruit" among them, "even as among the rest of the Gentiles" (1:13), a clear reference to the collection of material goods on behalf of the Jerusalem church in which he is currently engaged, and because of which he has been delayed (15:22-28).[116] This "fruit" bears witness to the Christian gentiles'

---

[114]Jervis, *Purpose of Romans*, pp. 158–64; Wuellner, "Paul's Rhetoric"; Elliott, *Rhetoric*, pp. 69–104.

[115]Jervis, *Purpose of Romans*, pp. 158–64; Klein, "Paul's Purpose."

[116]See also Paul's use of this language in 1 Corinthians and the discussion below of the collection.

obligation (they are "indebted") toward their Jewish brothers and sisters in view of Israel's current suffering on their behalf in order that
the gentiles might share in Israel's "spiritual things." The Romans
have not yet participated in this display of affection and gratitude, and
Paul asks them to "strive together with me in your prayers" for his success in this mission to Jerusalem, and for his eventual arrival in Rome
during which he intends for them to become contributors as well
(15:31-32). Paul clearly needs something from them. And this something is related to his apostolic ministry as "a minister of Christ Jesus
to the Gentiles, ministering as a priest the gospel of God, that my offering of the Gentiles might become acceptable, sanctified by the
Holy Spirit" (15:16). He is responsible for "the obedience of the
Gentiles" that results from his apostolic preaching of the gospel
(15:18-19, 20ff.), and he will not be satisfied with the situation in
Rome until he has arrived to fulfill this obligation (1:14-15), gathering
thereby the expected and necessary "fruit" (1:13; 15:27-28) that will
satisfy his ministry and permit his "service for Jerusalem" to become
"acceptable to the saints" (15:31).

For their part, Paul is concerned to "remind" them boldly of truths
of which they are aware but ostensibly questioning, particularly
under the influence of some group suggesting they serve "their own
appetites" "contrary to the teaching" that they had previously
"learned" (15:14-15; 16:17-20). Paul is concerned that their neglect of
these matters (perhaps having heard such a report from Prisca and
Aquila upon their arrival in Rome to prepare for Paul's trip) will result
in behavior that will not permit their acceptance or sanctification
(15:15-16). This certainly lies behind his admonition to offer their
bodies, in view of God's mercy toward them as gentiles, as a "living and
holy sacrifice" in their "spiritual service of worship" toward God and
toward the service of others as they are able (12:1-3, 4ff.). Moreover,
although Paul knows of their faith in Jesus Christ (even calling them
"saints": 1:7), they are evidently still lacking some essentials in their
faith, for he considers them in great need of his personal visit (he
"longs" to see them) to "impart some spiritual gift"[117] to them so that

---

[117]Wedderburn, *Reasons*, p. 97, discusses Kettunen's comments on Paul's spiritual gift: "the writing of the letter serves the same purpose as the visit that Paul
was desirous of making; the former would thus be a substitute, at least temporarily, for the latter. Then one can argue that in writing his letter Paul was discharg-
ing his apostolic task of furthering their faith. For, if he was responsible to bring
about 'the obedience of faith', i.e. the obedience of which faith is, the obedience

they may be "established" (1:11). This is no mere pleasantry; it is somehow integral to Paul's concern for their "faith." Paul wants to be "encouraged" by their "faith," and them by his, in a manner that is apparently impossible apart from his personal visit (1:12). He intends to come "in the fulness of the blessing of Christ" (15:29), perhaps another suggestion of their current inadequate standing in the mind of Paul. And as I have already noted, he intends to receive some "fruit" from among them as he has from the rest of the gentiles he has brought to the "obedience of faith" through his apostolic preaching of the gospel (in person), clearly illustrating that their current involvement fails to fulfill their complete responsibility to Israel (15:14-32; 1:13-15). Finally, he wants to receive their help in his mission to Spain (15:24), and "enjoy" and "find rest"[118] in their "company" (15:24, 32).

The imagery of Paul's expectations upon his eventual arrival in Rome to preach to those who have already believed in Christ is strikingly similar to Luke's description of Paul's earlier delivery of the apostolic decree elsewhere. Note that when Paul, Barnabas, Judas, and Silas were sent down to Antioch after the Jerusalem Council (Acts 15:22-35), they delivered the "letter" containing the apostolic decree's outline of the "necessary things" that those in Antioch who had already turned to Christ were to "observe" (φυλάσσειν: 16:4).[119] They did not find resistance to the message of the decree as might well be expected if the decree had not been an understandably significant demonstration of respect for their faith as gentiles (without becoming

---

that is inherent in faith (1.5), amongst all the gentiles, then he was responsible, Kettunen argues, not just for bringing them to faith, but also for keeping them faithful to the gospel."

[118]The "rest" is the eschatological shalom that comes from the reconciling of Jew and gentile, "weak" and "strong" in Christ. Certainly 5:1-11 and his instructions in 12:18; 13:8; 14:15-19, for example, stand behind Paul's expectation of joy and peace among those willing to subordinate their own pleasure to the interests of the other and persevere in seeking reconciliation by adopting behavior "approved by men" as well as God, the very practice of which Paul was engaged in with his trip to Jerusalem with the collection from gentile believers who recognized their indebtedness to Israel.

[119]Φυλάσσω is a deeply nuanced covenant term for keeping God's commandments, for Israel is the watchman or guardian of Torah (Ex. 19:5). Its Hebrew equivalent was a catch phrase in the Qumran community, and we see this same emphasis elsewhere by Luke in the context of the responsibility of those who truly hear God's word and for those who keep Torah (Luke 11:28; Acts 7:53; 21:24). Note also its usage in Rom. 2:25-26 for the keeping of Torah (Gal. 6:13). See Bertram, *TDNT*, 9.236–41.

Jews) in Israel's God. Instead, the multitude "rejoiced" (ἐχάρησαν) at
the "exhortation" (παρακλήσει) that was read (15:30-31).[120] As they
continued to teach in Antioch Luke tells us that the "brethren" were
"comforted" (παρεκάλεσαν) and "strengthened" (ἐπεστήριξαν:
"established") (15:32). Paul and Silas later traveled through Syria and
Cilicia "strengthening" (ἐπιστηρίζων: "establishing") the churches
(15:41). Further, when Paul and Silas continued on to Derbe and
Lystra and other cities delivering the message of necessary observance
to the commandments of the decree (φυλάσσειν τὰ δόγματα), the
churches were likewise characterized as receptive, "growing in the
faith" (ἐστερεοῦντο τῇ πίστει) and "increasing in number daily"
(ἐπερίσσευον τῷ ἀριθμῷ καθ᾽ ἡμέραν) (16:1-5).

We find then that the same kind of expectation that Paul has toward
Rome of "establishing" (στηριχθῆναι: Rom. 1:11)[121] them through his
necessary apostolic visit by imparting a "spiritual gift" that they are
yet lacking, with the result that they are "encouraged" (συμπαρακλ-
ηθῆναι: 1:12)[122] together by each other's "faith," to the end that Paul
comes to them in "joy" (χαρᾷ: 15:32) and finds "rest" (συνανα-

[120]This phenomenon suggests that during the first fifteen years or so prior to the
Council the status of gentiles in the congregations was in question. They may
have had a second-class status during this period, and they may have been
required to obey more Jewish law and customs than those represented in the
apostolic decree. There seems to be a deep gratitude suggested in their reception
of the news, and no resistance. See Jervell, "Might Minority," pp. 17–21, 22ff., and
his view that the gentiles were initially received with little restriction, and only
later, leading up to and as a result of the Council, were obligations to Jewish law
imposed.

[121]This is the passive form of the same verb (ἐπεστήριξω) that is translated
"strengthening" in Acts 15:32, 41, and both usages carry the original sense of
"supporting" as do pillars a building (Judg. 16:26, 29). See Harder, *TDNT*,
7.653–57.

[122]This is again the passive form of the same verb (παρακαλέω + συμ) that is
translated "comforted" in Acts 15:32 and that is inseparably linked with the task
of exhortation or summoning (Acts 13:15) and in Rom. 12:1 and 15:30 to introduce
Paul's "urging" of particular behavior for gentiles toward Jews in view of God's
mercy toward them in Christ (it is also a spiritual gift to be exercised in this context in Rome: 12:8; and that which they will find in the Scriptures: 15:4). See
Schmitz, *TDNT*, 5.793–99, and the summary comment on p. 799: "The meaning
'to comfort,' 'comfort,' 'consolation,' which is rare in both the Greek world and
Hellenistic Judaism, but the more common in the translation Greek of the LXX,
is influenced by the OT, and especially by Is. (and the Ps.) when the reference is
to salvation history (cf. the 'consolation of Israel' in later Judaism)."

παύσωμαι: 15:32)[123] in their company, is loaded language. It is the kind of language that was associated with Paul's apostolic preaching of the gospel to bring the "obedience of faith" among all the gentiles and with the declaration of the apostolic decree in Acts.

	Romans	Acts
Establish/strengthen	1:11	15:32, 41
Encourage/comfort/console	1:12	15:32
Joy/rejoicing	15:32	15:31

It is Paul's hope that the Romans will receive him and his message of their obligations with respect to the decree in the same positive way we find Luke describes Paul's earlier missionary reception. For the decree was not an unwelcome burden, but a powerful declaration of the inclusion of gentiles as *equals*, by faith and without becoming Jews, in the people of God. It was a sign of the fulfillment of the eschatological promise of blessings for all the world in Israel's Christ. And it was understood to be a minimal demonstration of appropriate purity behavior for association with the Jewish community (Israel, the historical people of God), on the part of gentiles who maintained they had become equal coparticipants in the promised blessings. Indeed, it bore witness to their indebtedness to Israel for her present suffering on their behalf.

I suggest that Paul had in mind a far deeper intention than pleasant fellowship and congeniality in his opening and closing address. The language chosen to communicate his expectations upon his planned arrival in Rome, and the immediacy of this letter in view of his unavoidable delay, should be considered in the context of Paul's personal apostolic preaching of the gospel (his "spiritual gift") and his continued commitment, as recorded by Luke, to proclaiming "obedience" to the apostolic decree for gentiles who come to "faith" in Israel's Christ as the Savior of the world (the "obedience of faith"). Paul was "reminding" the "saints" in Rome of their responsibility to behave in keeping with the intentions of the apostolic decree, even though their current status (as gentiles turning to faith in Christ Jesus) represented an anomaly, for it fell outside the circle of the authorized apostolic mission from Jerusalem out to the nations by Paul (since he, the "apostle

---

[123]Rest was a significant eschatological concept linked with persevering obedience for the early Christian communities (Heb. 3:12—4:16).

to the gentiles," had not yet reached Rome: 15:17-23). His letter to
Rome began the process of preparing them for his intended personal
visit to "preach the gospel to you also who are in Rome" (1:15: though
they have already heard the gospel!) and thereby bring them back
within the pattern of the apostolic preaching of the gospel (to the Jew
first and also to the Greek, the pattern traced by Luke as Paul's "custom" [Acts 17:2] of preaching in the synagogues to restore Israel first,
followed by turning to the gentiles), thereby "establishing" their
"faith" and bringing about in Rome (as the beginning of his western
apostolic mission) the appropriate "obedience of faith" characteristic
of the eastern spiral of his mission to date (Rom. 15:19-23).[124]

Paul's Epideictic Reminder to "Obey from the Heart" That "Form of Teaching" to Which They Were Already "Committed"

Paul appeals throughout Romans to a specific body of teaching, the
nature of which has generally confounded scholarship. But as we
approach the context of each of these references anew, recognizing the
rhetorical structure of the letter as an epideictic discourse that "sets
out to increase the intensity of adherence to certain values, which
might not be contested when considered on their own but may nevertheless not prevail against other values that might come into conflict
with them,"[125] we can begin to recognize just how clearly this body of
teaching lies behind Paul's, and his audience's, understanding of the
purpose and message of this "bold reminder" to Rome (Rom. 6:17;
15:15; 16:17).

    Perelman points out that the speaker who appeals to epideictic dis-
course "tries to establish a sense of communion centered around par-

[124]Note that the pattern of his eventual visit to Rome in Acts 28:15-31 was to
proclaim the gospel to the Jews first as though no church already existed, and then
later to turn to the gentiles. I discuss this pattern and its application to Rome fully
in chapter 5 below.
    [125]From Perelman, and Olbrechts-Tyteca, *New Rhetoric*, p. 51, as applied to
Romans by Wuellner, "Paul's Rhetoric," p. 140. (See also this same application to
Romans by Fraikin in "Rhetorical Function," pp. 91–105.) See also D. Aune,
"Romans as a 'Logos Protreptikos,'" p. 280ff., who discusses how the epideictic
nature of Romans can be understood in the context of Romans as a *logos protreptikos*: "That is, Romans is a speech of exhortation in written form which Paul
addressed to Roman Christians to convince them (or remind them) of the truth of
'his' version of the gospel (Rom. 2:16; cf. 16:25; Gal. 1:6-9; 2:1) and to encourage
a commitment to the kind of lifestyle which Paul considered consistent with his
gospel" (pp. 278–79).

ticular values recognized by the audience, and to this end he uses the whole range of means available to the rhetorician for the purposes of amplification and enhancement. In epideictic oratory every device of literary art is appropriate, for it is a matter of combining all the factors that can promote this communion of the audience."[126] Further, it must be noted that in the epideictic genre the speaker is educator, not propagandist, and the appeal is to values that are beyond question.[127] "The role Paul expects the Romans to perform is neither to deliberate nor to adjudicate but 'to affirm the communal values which Paul and the Romans share in being agents of the faith throughout the world.'"[128]

The values to which Paul appealed for enhanced adherence were clearly not general. He carefully explains as he begins to close his letter that the message therein has served as a bold reminder concerning matters of which they were already aware, yet of which he, as the apostle to the gentiles and thus their apostle, is concerned that they may fail to give their proper due:

> But I have written *very boldly* to you on *some points*, so as to *remind* you again, because of the grace that was given me from God, to be a minister of Christ Jesus to the Gentiles, ministering as a priest the gospel of God, that my *offering* of the Gentiles might become *acceptable, sanctified* by the Holy Spirit. (15:15-16)

We see that the failure would not only be on the part of the Romans addressed, but also on the part of Paul's "offering," which is tied to his trip to Jerusalem with a collection for Israel that he is concerned may not be found "acceptable."[129] This offering will become acceptable only when it has been properly "sanctified by the Holy Spirit," the very imagery I have reviewed in the context of purity language as applied to the intentions of the apostolic decree for demonstrating the valid faith of gentiles who have turned from idolatry, with its

[126]Perelman, p. 51, from Wuellner, "Paul's Rhetoric," p. 140.
[127]Ibid.
[128]Fraikin, "Rhetorical Function," p. 92, quoting Wuellner.
[129]In this context the suggestion of Jervell, "Letter to Jerusalem," that Paul has his trip to Jerusalem in the forefront of his mind as he writes to Rome makes sense of the tension evident in Paul's closing concerns. While Jervell's notion helps to understand the centrality of the collection and Paul's imminent trip to Jerusalem, it fails to deal with the need to address the reality of the situation in Rome underlying Paul's intentions, the clues for which are many. See chapter 5 below.

concomitant deeds of darkness, and who are now seeking association with the Jewish community as they join in worshiping the One God (6:1-23; 8:1-17; 12:1-2; 13:11-14; 15:16).

There are two additional direct references to a specific body of teaching to which Paul is appealing, and in both cases the context is likewise concerned with appropriate conduct for gentiles who now have faith in Christ in matters of their outward expression of obedience. I examine these contexts in more detail below; it is important, however, at this juncture to review them as they throw light on the nature of the shared values that Paul is addressing in this epideictic reminder.

First, in Romans 6:17, in the midst of explaining why they must not sin with their "mortal body" (6:12) or continue to present the "members of your body to sin as instruments of unrighteousness," but rather present themselves to God "as those alive from the dead, and your members as instruments of righteousness to God" (6:13), even though they "are not under law but under grace" (6:15), Paul identifies a specific body of teaching to which they were already committed in the past:

> But thanks be to God that though you were slaves of sin, you became *obedient from the heart to that form of teaching* [τύπον διδαχῆς] to which you *were committed*, and having been *freed from sin*, you became *slaves of righteousness*. I am speaking in human terms because of the weakness of your flesh. For just as you presented your members as slaves to *impurity* and to *lawlessness*, resulting in further lawlessness, so now present your members as slaves to *righteousness*, resulting in *sanctification*. (6:17-19)

Here again we see Paul's concern with outward expressions of obedience to the faith they have in their heart. The imagery is of an offering of the members of their body in cultic terms paralleling the imagery of 12:1-2. This commitment to specific righteous behavior results in sanctification, his concern for his audience with regard to the acceptability of his offering of the gentiles (15:15-16, 31). And the focus of the entire discussion follows from the need to explain "in human terms" the behavior that is appropriate for gentiles who have come to have faith without being under the Law (the issue he is addressing throughout chap. 6):[130] the very "obedience of faith" that ought to characterize their "slavery to righteousness" in Christ.

What is important to note at this point is that Paul is not appealing

---

[130]The "weakness of your flesh" speaks of their position outside the Law, of gentile versus Jew, a relationship that should no longer dictate their view of Jews

to vague notions of proper behavior. He says they are aware of, and in the past have been committed to, "obedience" (ὑπηκούσατε) to a specific catechism: a "form of teaching" (τύπον διδαχῆς) that accompanied their freedom from sin and new life as slaves of righteousness. Here, in Paul's first discussion of the concept of Christian freedom in this letter, we find a clear reference to a body of teaching to which they are obliged to continue to adhere. For those predisposed to believing that Paul maintained no obligation outside faith, the question is well framed by Schlatter: "With the teaching does not the law come back into the community?"[131]

Dunn comments that "most understand the phrase to refer to a fixed catechetical formulation or creed, already so well established and so well known that Paul could refer to it without further detail," and adds that "since the emphasis is on practical outworking of Christian commitment, there is a good deal to be said for this view."[132] However, Dunn is uncomfortable with this approach and decides: "Although use of common parenetical themes is evident later in the letter (see 12:9-21; 13:1-7 and 13:11-14), Romans is too early for us to be confident that a particular pattern had become already sufficiently well established to be recognized simply by the phrase τύπος διδαχῆς."[133]

If the apostolic decree is allowed to have been operative from the time of the Jerusalem Council, however, then we readily solve both the issues of law keeping and of understanding how Paul could appeal to a pattern of teaching that had already been concretized well before Romans. In fact, if the apostolic decree was the "form of teaching" to which Paul appealed, the message of presenting the members of their body to pure and lawful behavior that results in sanctification makes sense and avoids the trap of the usual bifurcation of faith versus works or grace versus law. This view makes sense of Paul's concern to remind them of the necessary "obedience" that should characterize their new "faith" as gentiles who have turned from idolatry and the associated

---

or of "proper behavior" now that they are a part of the people of God through faith in Israel's Christ. This same issue is at the heart of Paul's message in chaps. 9–11 to confront Christian gentile arrogance that flows from mistaken notions of supplanting Israel—they have come to have faith without a proper understanding of their relationship to Israel and the flow of salvation history. These are problems in the forefront of Paul's mind as he writes; however, they will only be fully rectified by his apostolic visit (see chapter 5 below).

[131]Schlatter, as cited by Dunn, *Romans*, p. 343.
[132]Dunn, *Romans*, p. 343.
[133]Ibid., p. 344.

"deeds of darkness" to the One God and thus must learn to "behave properly as in the day" (13:11-14), thereby demonstrating their love and obligation for their neighbor and actually fulfilling the law (13:8-10; and the point of 14:1—15:3):

> For he who in this way serves Christ is acceptable to God and approved by men. (14:18)

Second, in Romans 16:17-18, Paul harshly criticizes some group disturbing those he is addressing in Rome:

> Now I urge you, brethren, keep your eye on those who cause dissentions and hindrances *contrary to the teaching which you learned*, and turn away from them. For such men are *slaves* not of our Lord Christ but *of their own appetites*; and by their smooth and flattering speech they deceive the hearts of the unsuspecting.

Here again Paul appeals to "the teaching" (τὴν διδαχὴν) that they have already learned in the past as the basis for his admonition to enhanced adherence. Dunn observes:

> διδαχὴ is not a regular Pauline word (but see 6:17 and 12:7), but, as the full phrase indicates, it must refer to the traditions the Roman Christians received when they were converted and baptized. . . . It is to be noted that Paul can take it for granted that such basic teaching, no doubt including a fair amount of Jesus tradition, had been given to (a) church(es) which others than he had founded—so much must it have been typical throughout the Christian mission.[134]

Indeed, Paul alludes to "the teaching" in appealing for enhanced adherence as readily as one might refer to the wedding vows, without considering any need to recite them formally in order to remind someone of the obligations incumbent upon them now because of their former confession of "the vows" when the privileges so clearly outweighed the burden of the responsibilities. The context of "the teaching" as beyond dispute and Paul's vitriolic characterization of those now causing "dissensions and hindrances contrary" to "the teaching" as "slaves not of our Lord Christ but of their own appetites" again parallels the language that would be expected if Paul was appealing for obedience to the intentions of the apostolic decree.

It is interesting to note that it is their "hearts" that are threatened

[134]Ibid., p. 902.

by deception, paralleling his language in 6:17 that they were "obedient from the heart to that form of teaching to which you were committed." The threat is from those who are slaves of their own "appetites" rather than Christ. The issue follows Paul's summary
discussion of dietary accommodation in chapters 14–15 and concludes
with an appeal to his audience from the imagery of the garden and of
the eschatological kingdom of peace from which he had argued in
14:16-17: "but I want you to be wise in what is good, and innocent in
what is evil. And the God of peace will soon crush Satan under your
feet" (16:19-20).

The imagery of Adam's sin in the context of eating that which was
forbidden through the deception of the serpent by his "smooth and
flattering speech" clearly sets the context for the "dissensions and hindrances" that Paul is so concerned to address. I believe this group is
suggesting that the "strong" need not accommodate the faith of the
"weak" in matters of dietary law.[135] This group is seeking to convince
them to disregard the intentions of the apostolic decree, "the teaching" that they had "learned" leading to slavery to "our Lord Christ"
rather than "their own appetites." They are likely those from whom
the "strong" feared reproach if they "held up" the "stumbling" by accommodating their sensitivities in matters of food rather than seeking
to please themselves in the indulgence of their perceived freedoms in
Christ (15:1-3). In fact, it is entirely possible that "nothing is unclean
in itself" (14:14) was the slogan of this group, who "by their smooth
and flattering speech" were twisting the truth to "deceive the hearts
of the unsuspecting" into asserting their freedom and judging the
opinions of the "weak" (14:1) by disregarding the obligations of the
apostolic decree toward those "for whom Christ died" (14:15). Thus
Paul would have found it necessary to contextualize the truth of
Christian gentile freedom from the Law with the reasoning of the
apostolic decree:

> For if because of food your brother is hurt, you are no longer walking
> according to love. Do not destroy with your food him for whom Christ
> died. Therefore do not let what is for you a good thing be spoken of as
> evil; for the kingdom of God is not eating and drinking, but righteous-
> ness and peace and joy in the Holy Spirit. For he who in this way
> serves Christ is acceptable to God and approved by men. (14:15-18)

In each of these appeals to a specific body of teaching that the

[135]Contra ibid., p. 904.

audience had formerly embraced, and that Paul is now calling in this epideictic letter for a renewed commitment to by way of reminder, the central theme of the context is the outward expression of "obedience" from the "heart" by gentiles who have turned to Christ by "faith."[136] And the particular contexts are all concerned with matters of purity, of sanctification for those formerly enslaved to sin but now enslaved to righteousness. Each context allows for Paul's concerned reminder to be an appeal to the intentions of the apostolic decree as it was outlined by the Jerusalem Council, namely, that their faith claim to be coparticipants in the blessings promised to Abraham will be respected by the Jewish community as valid (14:16, 18).[137] Paul hopes, in harmony with James, that when the "stumbling" of Israel witness "obedient" gentiles calling on the name of the Lord they will realize that the ingathering of the nations (gentile salvation) is taking place before their very eyes, which means that the eschatological restoration of Israel has in fact already begun, as promised, and they will be provoked to reconsider the gospel of Jesus Christ (Acts 15:15-18; Rom. 11:11-15, 25-27).[138]

THE "OBEDIENCE OF FAITH" AND THE APOSTOLIC DECREE

Throughout this study I have noted that Paul's epideictic intentions in his bold "reminder" to Rome echo the very intentions of the apostolic

---

[136]Fraikin, "Rhetorical Function," p. 93: "In order to complete the description of the rhetorical situation in Romans, we may anticipate the discussion of the *exordium* and put forward the conclusion that the audience is not the church of Rome in general but specifically Roman Gentile Christians. Then Romans is an epideictic discourse addressed to the Gentile Christians in Rome, intended to strengthen their awareness and assurance of God's election. It is in this discourse that the Jews and Israel play a significant role."

[137]The link between τύπον ("*form* of teaching") in 6:17, which means literally "to stamp a form" or "to strike so as to leave an impression" as in forming a coin or a wax seal (Kittel, *TDNT*, 8.246–47) and δόκιμος ("*approved* by men") in 14:18, which means literally "tested, genuine or valuable" (Grundmann, *TDNT* 2.255–56) and carries the sense of being declared genuine (the real thing!) should not be overlooked. There is a standard/form/pattern "of teaching" by which proper behavior (obedience: ὑπακοήν) can be judged "by men" as genuine, and it is this behavior in the service of Christ to which the "strong" are called. Note also the use of this language in 12:2 and 1:28.

[138]Fraikin, "Rhetorical Function," p. 98, observes similarly: "We are faced, then, with the interesting fact that Paul, in a discourse whose goal is to strengthen

decree as recorded by Luke. The common theme underlying both is the call to "obey" the halakhah of the "faith" for the "righteous gentile" worshiping in the midst of restored Israel, demonstrating their "sanctification" as they present their bodies as "slaves to righteousness" with a lifestyle that will promote the eschatological shalom among Jews and gentiles. They are to seek peace above all else: "Respect what is right in the sight of all men. If possible, so far as it depends on you, be at peace with all men" (12:17-18). They are to "walk according to love" by accommodating, in matters of dietary purity, the "opinions" of their "brothers" who may otherwise "stumble" and "blaspheme" their "good thing." These Christian gentiles thereby demonstrate the presence of the promised shalom of the eschatological "kingdom of God" in a convincing manner that is both "acceptable to God and approved by men" (14:13-18, 19ff.).[139]

Paul wove this dynamic theme of Christian gentiles presenting their "bodies" to "obedience" through proper ethical and purity behavior (6:19; 12:1) in view of their "introduction by faith into this grace in which we stand" (5:2; 12:1: "by the mercies of God") throughout the fabric of Romans. I suggest that Paul's fascinating programmatic phrase "obedience of faith" (ὑπακοὴν πίστεως: 1:5; 16:26), which appears in the midst of these contexts throughout this letter (ὑπακοή from ὑπακούω [ὑπό and ἀκούω]: 1:5; 5:19; 6:16; 15:18; 16:19, 26;

---

the Gentiles in the gospel, provides them with the arguments by which he would make his understanding of the gospel and its consequences credible to Jews. It is not simply that the theological categories used by Paul are Jewish (what other theological framework could we expect Paul to use?), but that it is important for the Gentiles that their position be credible in the eyes of Jews. Their experience of salvation is certainly not dependent on these arguments, but at this point it seems necessary for them to have a theology of their experience that relates them to Israel. The fact that the argument is meant to bring a Jew to understand their position reveals the weight of Judaism. Why would they care whether a Jew will accept them and their salvation if it is not because they are (through Paul) claiming entry into a story which belongs to the Jews from old?" I discuss this more fully below in chapter 5.

[139]The issue of eating for Adam, and now for the "strong" in Rome, is a symbol of a deeper issue: the asserting of one's right to control one's own destiny in the face of God and other humans. In contrast with Adam and the "strong," Jesus obeyed God's voice and sought peace, willing even to be wrongly reproached in the service of the "weak" rather than to seek his own pleasure (15:1-3). This is the character of the kingdom of God to which they are called by faith in the obedient One.

[ὑπακούω and ἀκοή: 10:16-18)[140] actually knits together and succinctly defines the various strands of this message to Rome expounding the distinctively Judaic nature of the "obedience" that ought to
characterize the lifestyles of Christian gentiles professing "faith" in
the One God.

Countless pages have been and will be written about this thematic
construct. It has, of course, been disconcerting to many that Paul, the
supposed champion of "faith alone" and founder of gentile
Christianity, would be so concerned with articulating a theme inherently concerned with "works." Naturally, I will explore the distinctive
Jewish texture applied to the particular contexts of Paul's argument for
this "obedience of faith." However, I need not review here the extensive background work of Don Garlington, tracing the biblical and
nonbiblical Judaic notions that stand behind this phrase.[141] I will rather
draw from his research and continue to concern myself with Paul's application of these notions in his letter to Rome. It is important to note
that I agree with Garlington that Paul's prime objective in the development of this thematic phrase is tied up with the explanation of *his*
gospel with a particular focus on its application to gentile believers in
Christ.[142] However, my approach, unlike Garlington's, is not grounded
in the assumption that Paul coined this phrase to articulate "a reversal
of his heritage as a Jew,"[143] nor that "Israel's distinctiveness has now
passed away in Christ,"[144] nor to "epitomize his position as over against
that of his rivals," who are understood to be "his Jewish kinsmen and

---

[140]Note the comment of Dunn, *Romans*, p. 856, on 15:18: "the thematic
ὑπακοή (v 18) provides a thread which unites missionary impulse, theological rationale, and parenesis (1:5; 5:19; 6:16); and the citation of Isa 52:15 (v 21) links directly back into the argument of chaps. 9–11, where it could easily have been used
(cf. 9:30; 10:16, 20)."

[141]I became acquainted with the work of Don Garlington while in the course of
writing and I am indebted to his thorough development of the background of the
phrase in Judaism. While I strongly disagree with his conclusions regarding Paul's
polemical intentions in the choice of this phrase, I just as strongly agree with many
of his conclusions concerning the development of this language with regard to
both the terms "faith" and "obedience" and will draw from his work many useful
insights. The works considered are D. Garlington, *"The Obedience of Faith":
A Pauline Phrase in Historical Context*; and three articles that appeared in *Westminster
Theological Journal*, "The Obedience of Faith in the Letter to the Romans," part I
in 1990, vol. 52, part II in 1991, vol. 53, and part III in 1993, vol. 55.

[142]Garlington, *Obedience*, p. 3.

[143]Ibid., p. 247.

[144]Ibid., p. 259.

the Jewish Christian missionaries who countered his gospel with their insistence on circumcision, the food laws and the special days of Israel, etc., as prerequisites to salvation."[145]

I have already discussed the failure of these traditional assumptions to account for the tensions in Rome where the opponents are tempting the "strong" Christian gentiles to disregard for the Judaic roots of their faith and away from accommodating the behavior acceptable to their "stumbling" Jewish brothers and sisters ("gentilizing" as it were), rather than toward any kind of "judaizing."[146] In Rome the implied audience was tempted to see their faith displacing that of the "natural branches" so that they need not be concerned with seeking the respect of the Jewish community toward themselves in matters Jews considered unquestionably important for the demonstration of authentic faith on the part of gentiles claiming to have become part of the community of God's people, namely, obedience to the halakhah of the "righteous gentile" on the part of the Christian gentiles in matters of purity, not to mention moral behavior. Thus, while I believe it is helpful to see the "antithetical and polemical" application of the phrase "as regards those with whom Paul disagrees,"[147] I do not agree with Garlington's traditional assumptions about who it was Paul opposed, or why he opposed them. Moreover, I believe the texture of the phrase demonstrates "a comprehensive ethical principle in Paul"[148] in the context of his argument for how his gospel affects gentiles who join the community of faith that is actually *Law-respectful*, that is in agreement with the notions of many of his Jewish predecessors and

---

[145]Ibid., pp. 3, 253. Garlington's leap from the background of the language in Judaism to Paul's supposed polemic against the law and Judaism is grounded in traditional assumptions about Paul's negative view of the law and Judaism. Hence, his movement to explain Paul's intentions in adopting the phrase in contrast to the prevailing views of his contemporaries in Judaism is quite different from the approach developed herein.

[146]See also Wright, *Climax*, pp. 234–35, 251.

[147]Garlington, *Obedience*, pp. 3, 5–6, 265–68. I do agree, where Garlington draws from Dunn, that the issue involved the sociological dimension of ethnocentric exclusion. Paul did oppose limiting the One God to Jews *only*; however, this does not mean he took the position that God was not for Jews *at all*, which position is inherent in reading Paul as rejecting his Jewish heritage as though the One God were for gentiles *only* since the coming of Christ, including those Jews who become gentiles in that they are understood to necessarily reject the Law in order to take up faith in Christ.

[148]Garlington, *Obedience*, p. 3.

contemporaries,[149] and that, in fact, parallels the intentions of James
and those Christian Jews who met in Jerusalem and framed the necessary laws for Christian gentiles contained in the halakhot of the
apostolic decree.[150]

The Background for Paul's Adaptation of
the Phrase "Obedience of Faith"

The concept of the "obedience of faith" has a rich Jewish heritage, although it is important to note that the phrase is not found in this exact
form before Paul, and that it was his development of the terminology
that probably stands behind its later establishment in Christian teaching.[151] The word rendered obedience is ὑπακοή, which is derived
from ἀκούω ("hear" with ὑπό: "by hearing") and includes in its range
of meaning "give ear to, answer, heed."[152] Significantly, there is no
word "obey" in Hebrew,[153] and the Septuagint renders the Hebrew
shema (שמע: "hear"), with its heritage of responding obediently to
what one hears, and as the central expression of Jewish monotheistic
faith in the Shema, with the term ὑπακούω.[154] Thus obedience has
the clear sense of how one "responds"[155] to the word of God in faith:
the hearing response of faith or the Shema of faith, one could say. To
respond with other than obedience demonstrates a failure to have
heard, and is "tantamount to unbelief."[156] This concept of hearing obediently is intimately connected with keeping the covenant: Israel has

---

[149]Contra ibid., p. v.

[150]Garlington, "Obedience of Faith," part II, pp. 67–72, makes a similar point,
although cast in a different way when discussing the Jewish character of the idea
of perseverance as "precisely loyalty to the Mosaic standard in the face of widespread apostasy" (p. 69). He notes: "The bottom line then is that *the obedience of
faith which finally justifies is perseverance, motivated by love.* Indeed, it is when Paul's
doctrine of the obedience of faith is allowed to speak for itself that any superficial
tension between him and James dissipates immediately" (p. 68). If he were to
allow for the purpose of the apostolic decree as I have argued, then his comments
would support my position on Paul's use of the phrase "obedience of faith."

[151]Dunn, *Romans*, p. 17.

[152]Ibid., p. 17; Garlington, *Obedience*, pp. 11–14.

[153]Garlington, *Obedience*, p. 11.

[154]Dunn, *Romans*, pp. 17–18. Note also that the rabbinic tradition uses this as
the terminology of exegesis, including for the halakhic tradition (*shemua* [שמועה]:
"what is received"). See Kittel, *TDNT*, 1.218.

[155]Dunn, *Romans*, p. 17.

[156]Garlington, *Obedience*, p. 11, from F. W. Young.

heard God's voice and accepted the responsibility to obey his commandments, which obedience will result in God's blessing (Deut. 4:1-14, 33, 36; 5:1-5, 22-27; 6:3-25; 7:12ff.; 8:1ff.; 11:13-27); but failure to believe and listen to his voice will lead to the curse of destruction (Deut. 8:20; 9:23; 11:26-28).[157]

Equally rich in meaning is πίστεως ("faith"), which renders the Hebrew אמונה (*emuna*) in a seamless blending of both trust and commitment as it defines the obedient character of the one who trusts God.[158] When one trusts in God one obeys God; faith and works are inextricably woven together in the response of trusting faith.[159] Garlington puts it succinctly: "In a real sense, then, to speak of faith *is* to speak of obedience. 'Faith and obedience are one action. Faith has to be proven by obedience.'"[160] Paul develops his use of faith from this Biblical background and on common ground with his Jewish contemporaries: "faith is right hearing."[161] There appears to have been no argument with Paul's understanding of faith among his audience or even among his opponents, although the object of that faith was debated. Faith and obedience are as inseparably linked in Paul's understanding as they are in Judaism, and he might just as well have penned the argument of James that "faith without works is dead" (Jas. 2:14-26; 1:22-27).[162]

Paul's construct, ὑπακοὴν πίστεως, with two largely parallel terms: "obedience" and "faith" (in its genitive form), has been the

---

[157]Garlington, *Obedience*, pp. 11–13.

[158]Garlington, "Obedience," part I, pp. 209–10.

[159]Ibid.; idem, *Obedience*, pp. 9–14, 233–35.

[160]Garlington, "Obedience," part I, p. 210. So too G. Davies, *Faith and Obedience in Romans*, p. 28: "Obedience for Paul, is more comprehensive than faith as mere believing; it involves *doing* also."

[161]Käsemann as quoted by Garlington, "Obedience," part I, p. 210. He further quotes F. W. Young: "To really hear God's word inevitably involves one in an obedient response in action prompted by faithfulness to and faith in the God who is revealing himself in and through particular historical events. Not to respond in obedient action is tantamount to unbelief—and so the prophet chastises his people for their blind eyes and deaf ears (Isa 6:9-10), which betray their faithlessness. This inevitable consequence of failing to hear is rebellion or disobedience. But rebellion is not just the willful disobedience of one who has heard. Rebellion is the sign that one has not really heard, since *to hear implies a faith-obedience response.*"

[162]Paul's point in Rom. 14:23 that "whatever is not from faith is sin" defines the activity appropriate toward God and one's neighbor. One's "works" toward his or her neighbor demonstrate one's "faith" toward God. See also Garlington, *Obedience*, p. 233 n. 1.

subject of lively grammatical and theological debate. The major positions for the proper translation of this phrase include:[163]

- *objective genitive:*
  "obedience to the faith" (to a body of doctrine)
  "obedience to faith" (to the authority of faith)
  "obedience to God's faithfulness attested in the gospel"
- *subjective genitive or genitive of source:*
  "the obedience that faith works"
  "the obedience required by faith"
  "obedience that springs from faith"
- *adjectival genitive:*
  "believing obedience"
  "faith's obedience"
- *genitive of apposition:*
  "the obedience that consists in faith" (faith as an act of obedience).

There is good support for each of these positions, although the genitive of apposition appears to be weak.[164] The subjective genitive and adjectival genitive are clearly favored in recent works.[165] However, in the end one's grammatical conclusions seem to be shaped more by one's theological understanding of the contexts than the other way around. In our case, the crucial concern is the larger context of Paul's argument throughout Romans for "obedience of faith *among all the Gentiles*, for His name's sake, among whom you also are the called of Jesus Christ" (Rom. 1:5-6; 15:18: "resulting in the obedience *of the Gentiles*"). That is, Paul's phrase is not applied to *all*, inclusive of Jews who believe in Jesus, but is rather aimed at articulating his apostolic responsibility toward bringing *gentiles* to the "obedience of faith" that follows from the powerful work of God in Christ toward those outside the covenant promises of Israel, although inside the intentions of God's promises in Abraham to *all*.[166] That is not to say that Jews believing in Jesus as the Christ of Israel are not equally obedient or

---

[163]See C. Cranfield, *Romans* 1.66; Garlington, "Obedience," part I, pp. 205–7, 224; Dunn, *Romans*, pp. 17–18.

[164]While faith and obedience are parallel terms they do maintain some distinction that this conclusion fails to uphold. Why bother with the phrase if Paul's point is the faith of the faith? See also the comments of G. Davies, *Faith and Obedience*, pp. 28–30; Garlington, "Obedience," part I.

[165]See the discussions of Garlington, "Obedience," part I, pp. 205ff.; and Davies, *Faith and Obedience*, pp. 25–30.

[166]Contra G. Davies, *Faith and Obedience*, p. 29, where he misses this distinction between Jews and gentiles.

believing, but to note that the contextual concern of Paul's adaptation of the phrase is specifically in reference to the situation of *gentiles* who come to faith in Jesus Christ and highlights appropriate monotheistic behavior that accompanies such a confession.[167] There is a clear call to proper behavior at the heart of Paul's "obedience of faith" that has gentile responsibility to become "slaves of righteousness" instead of continuing as "slaves to sin" at the center of his concern.[168]

Paul's bold "reminder" to the Romans of God's faithfulness and of the behavior that is appropriate for gentiles who recognize God's mercies toward themselves in Christ has been developed in the context of his apostolic mission everywhere he has preached the gospel (15:18-19). He has been bringing gentiles to the "obedience of faith" so that his "offering of the gentiles might become acceptable" both to God and to the Jerusalem saints he will soon visit with the collection of gentile "fruit" (15:15-16, 25-32; 1:13). While the Roman Christian gentiles have certainly heard the gospel and believed outside Paul's apostolic preaching of the gospel (15:22-23), and while both their "faith" (1:8) and "obedience" (16:19) are known to Paul and others, he is nevertheless intent upon reaching Rome and preaching the gospel to them (1:15). He must impart "some spiritual gift" to them that will cause them to be "established" in some way they are yet lacking (1:11-12), receiving "fruit" from them as from among the rest of the gentiles he has reached (1:13) so that he might "offer" them also up to God and the Jerusalem saints (15:15-32). He is compelled to write to these gentile believers of the nature of their faith and the appropriate obedient behavior of love toward the "weak" non-Christian Jews in their company until he can finally arrive to bring about this "obedience of faith"

---

[167]Dunn, *Romans*, p. 18: "In linking the thought of 'obedience' to 'the nations' Paul's train of thought may still show the influence of Ps 2 (v 8—God's son given the nations as his inheritance and the ends of the earth as his possession; cf. 1:3-4) and Isa 49 (vv. 6-7—God's slave/servant given as a light to the nations . . . princes prostrating themselves; cf. 1:1). More probable still is the likelihood that Paul had in mind the importance of obedience within Jewish self-understanding—obedience as Israel's proper response to God's covenant grace (as particularly in Deut 26:17; 30:2; the Shema of course begins שמע ישראל, "Hear, O Israel" [Deut 6:4], though the LXX translates שמע here as ἄκουε). The point would then be that Paul intends his readers to understand the faith response of the Gentiles to the gospel as the fulfillment of God's covenant purpose through Israel, the eschatological equivalent of Israel's obligation under the covenant."

[168]Garlington, "Obedience," part I, pp. 211–12, for similar observation of the "transfer of lordship" inherent in Paul's development of the phrase; however, he fails to note that the distinction is with respect to gentiles.

personally.[169] And the time is imminent. Paul is wrapping up his eastern missionary spiral out from Jerusalem and returning with the
"fruits" of this mission even as he writes to Rome. His next spiral will
be from Jerusalem, "where Christ is already named," westward; it will
begin with Rome and reach toward Spain, the biblical ends of the
earth[170] (15:18-25, 26ff.).

We must thus recognize the paradigmatic phrase "obedience of
faith" as inclusive of much more than the initial act of gentiles believing in Jesus Christ; rather, it speaks of the comprehensive *lifestyle* of
those who come to believe in the righteousness of God revealed in
Christ Jesus—a lifestyle that Paul is concerned to "boldly remind"
them of the importance of in his absence, and which he is anxious to
soon "proclaim" to the Romans himself.[171] For if their lifestyle is characterized by the "obedience of faith" rather than the "deeds of darkness" it will bring honor to their claim to share in the "good things" of
God rather than "blasphemy" (14:16); indeed, it will bring honor to
the "name" (reputation) of Christ in the Jewish community: "Jesus
Christ our Lord, through whom we have received grace and apostleship to bring about the obedience of faith among all the gentiles, *for
his name's sake*, among whom you also are the called of Jesus Christ"
(1:4-6).[172]

Paul's Use of "Obedience" Theme Throughout Romans

Paul develops the theme of the obedience that must characterize the
faith of those he is addressing in Rome, not in opposition to the faith
of Israel, but rather in direct continuity with and even in the service of
Israel. Their faith is like that of the "righteous gentiles" who recognize the truth of the Creator God and seek eternal life (1:18—2:16;
3:19-31). It is like Abraham's faith (4:10-25), Isaac's faith (9:7-29), and
Moses' faith (10:5-13). Indeed, Paul's point is that their new faith is
continuous with Israel's faith and connects them with God's faithful-

---

[169]G. Davies, *Faith and Obedience*, p. 27, notes similarly: "It is an ethical dimension, therefore, that undergirds Paul's desire to visit (and no doubt also to write to)
the saints at Rome."

[170]Cf. Aus, "Paul's Travel Plans," pp. 232–62.

[171]See the similar comments of Garlington, "Obedience," part I, pp. 211–13,
214ff.

[172]Dunn, *Romans*, p. 18, sees the context of this concern, although he treats it
quite differently.

ness to Israel and to all of humankind in Christ (1:16-17; 3:21-31; 4:12, 16; 9:1-29; 10:5-21; 11:20-32; 15:4-12).

Interestingly, while Paul is addressing Christian gentiles, he does not address the many contexts of Christian gentile interaction with other gentiles in a gentile city like Rome. It is the context of Christian gentile faith and the practice of that faith in the light of Israel's role in salvation history and in the midst of the behavioral concerns of the Jewish community(s) with which they now have contact that Paul addresses. While Paul's concern throughout Romans involves faith and obedience (the "hearers" and "doers" of chap. 2 and the character of Abraham's faith in chap. 4, for example), I will confine myself to tracing Paul's development of this theme in those contexts where the explicit usage of "obedience" (ὑπακοή) occurs, noting the Mosaic texture of the behavioral issues addressed in the context of "faith" for those responsible for serving Christ in a manner "acceptable to God and approved by men" (14:18).

Paul opens Romans with a powerful retelling of salvation history that casts the resurrection of Jesus Christ and Paul's bondage to the apostolic proclamation of this "good news" that brings "all the Gentiles" to the "obedience of faith . . . for His name's sake" in the context of the fulfillment of the historic promises to Israel through David's seed (1:1-7).[173] Paul makes quite clear from the beginning that the order of God's salvation for humankind is now, as it has certainly been in the past, "to the Jew first and also to the Greek" (1:16; 2:9-10; 9:24; 15:8-9).[174] The risen Christ is the Savior of Israel first, and also of the whole world. He is the promised Son foreseen by David (Pss. 2:7-11; 110), who will rule over Israel and who "will surely give the Gentiles as Thine inheritance, and the ends of the earth as Thy possession" (Ps. 2:8). In fact, the role of historical continuity is so clear in Paul's introduction to those in Rome that Garlington makes the following comment before developing his polemical viewpoint of Paul's position as discontinuous with Judaism:

---

[173]Garlington, *Obedience*, p. 236, notes: "In Rom 1.3-4, then, Paul underscores to his readers that the subject of his gospel is a *thoroughly Jewish* Messiah the Son of David prophesied, as it is commonly agreed, by Ps 2.7 (Ps 110), and, therefore, the fulfilment of Israel's eschatological expectations; he has now been 'installed' (ὁρίζειν) on none other than the throne of his father David (cf. Lk 1.32)."

[174]Paul clearly has this same order in mind throughout Romans; see, for example, 3:19-21; 4:16; 9–11.

This reflection on Rom. 1.3-4, especially as supported by the OT passages briefly surveyed, would lead one to believe that if an informed
reader of Romans went no further than v.4 of the letter, he would have
no cause to suspect that Paul was championing any other than an un-
modified Jewish conception of the Messiah in his relation to Israel and
the Gentiles.[175]

Paul's language here echoes Luke's development of Amos 9:11-12
in Acts 15:16-18 to explain that the restoration of Israel has taken place
first, followed by the gathering in of the gentiles "for His name's sake"
(Rom. 1:5) in fulfillment of the eschatological promises:[176]

> After these things I will return, and I will rebuild the tabernacle of
> David which has fallen, and I will rebuild its ruins, and I will restore
> it, *in order that* the rest of mankind may seek the Lord and *all the
> Gentiles who are called by My name*, says the Lord, who makes these
> things known from of old. (Acts 15:16-18)[177]

Paul's conception of gentiles glorifying the name of Israel's God
mirrors the views of many of his contemporaries outside the Christian
Jewish coalition.[178] On the one hand, the Lord's name is inextricably

[175]Garlington, *Obedience*, p. 237.

[176]Ibid., p. 245: "it is a short step from Amos' 'all the nations who are called by
my name' to Paul's 'the obedience of faith among all the nations for the sake of
his name'." See N. Dahl, "A People for His Name."

[177]Note the Qumran use of this same complex of passages (4Q174 1.10-13:
Amos 9:11; 2 Sam. 7:11-14; Ps. 2:1) to discuss the restoration of Israel.

[178]Garlington, *Obedience*, pp. 242–47, recognizes that Paul's development of the
theme is consistent with Jewish views of the time, yet he concludes that because
Paul has in mind the name of Christ he has necessarily broken with "his heritage
as a Jew" (pp. 245–47): "Consequently, if in 'the obedience of faith among all the
nations' we see Paul's continuity with Jewish precedents, in 'for his name's sake'
we see the discontinuity" (p. 246). This conclusion fails to recognize that the
gospel is still to "the Jew first and also to the Greek," a distinction Paul maintains
throughout Romans (11:25-29; 15:5-12, for example) in harmony with the conclusions of the Jerusalem Council (Acts 15:16-18) for explaining the inclusion of gentiles in the people of God in the name of Christ Jesus. The addition of gentiles by
faith was seen as the fulfillment of Israel's promised salvation, not the negation of
it. Jewish identity is not threatened by gentiles recognizing the One God of
Israel—it is fulfilled. The issue Paul wants to address is the appropriate "obedience" that must accompany this confession of the One God among gentiles saved
by faith alone (as gentiles, that is, without becoming Jews) so that their faith
claims will be respected, rather than blasphemed in the Jewish community (the

linked in biblical and apocryphal literature with his covenant people Israel:[179]

> But now, thus says the LORD, your creator, O Jacob, and He who formed you, O Israel, "Do not fear, for I have redeemed you; *I have called you by name; you are mine!*" (Isa. 43:1, also vv. 6-7; 44:5)

> Have mercy, O Lord, upon the people *called by thy name, upon Israel*, whom thou hast likened to a first-born son. (Sir. 36:12)

On the other hand, the hope of Israel was *also* that *the name* of the One God would one day be recognized by all the nations:

> And all the Gentiles who are *called by My name*. (Amos 9:11)

> And I will say to those who were not My people, "You are My people!" And they will say, "Thou art my God!" (Hos. 2:23)

We see in Paul's opening comments the unmistakable blending of the "obedience of faith among all the gentiles for His name's sake" with Israel's historical faith in God's promises. Gentiles calling on the name of the One God through faith demonstrated in obedience to the operative halakhot for "righteous gentiles" represents no break with Israel's faith or the practice of Torah. Their faith is in Israel's Christ, their gospel was declared to Israel first, their salvation is at Israel's present expense, their obligation is to help the "stumbling" of Israel stand—yet, just as importantly, they are now equals through faith in Christ without becoming Israelites. Paul builds on this foundation throughout Romans until the audience in Rome can comprehend his universal vision of the eschatological promises being fulfilled by Roman Christian gentiles "glorifying" the name of the One God, "the God and Father of our Lord Jesus Christ," in the midst of Israel ("Rejoice, O Gentiles, with His people": Rom. 15:10) with "one voice" in "one accord" through their "obedience" to "that form of teaching to which you were committed," so that the faithfulness of God to Israel followed by the mercy of God toward gentiles might be

---

point of Paul's argument in 14:13—15:12 that I discussed in chapter 3 above that explains the need Paul saw for this "bold reminder" to Rome).

[179]Garlington, *Obedience*, pp. 242–45.

made manifest to those of Israel yet "stumbling" (15:5-12; 6:17; 11:11-14; 14:13—15:3).

In 5:12-19 the theme of "obedience" (ὑπακοῆς) as contrasted with the sin of Adam's disobedience defines Jesus Christ and those who believe in him. Adam "heard" and was "obedient" to another voice that he had more faith in than the voice of God. Adam ate that which God had told him not to eat; he is the type of "disobedience" (παρακοῆς) for all people (5:18-19),[180] even for Israel, those who have not eaten that which is forbidden ("even over those who had not sinned in the likeness of Adam's offense": 5:12-14, 15ff.). Unlike Adam, Jesus Christ was the obedient One restoring humankind to life: "through one act of righteousness there resulted justification of life to all men" (5:18). He fulfilled the intentions of Torah, and unlike Adam he did not embrace the voice of the tempter, he did not "eat," as it were. He heard the word of God, believed, and obeyed. They have thus come, through faith in the "one Man, Jesus Christ" (5:15), into a relationship with the One God and Father of "the many"; that is, of both the circumcised to whom the promises are fulfilled in Christ and the uncircumcised to whom God has shown his mercy (15:6-9), for "through the obedience [ὑπακοῆς] of the One the many will be made righteous" (5:19).[181]

Chapter 6 flows from the position Paul has argued in chapter 5 and clarifies the behavioral responsibilities of gentiles who now have faith in the obedient One yet are not under the Law: they are to present their bodies as "slaves for obedience [ὑπακοὴν]" (6:16; see vv. 12-19). The questions Paul addressed were framed for gentiles accepted by faith into the people of God without becoming Jews. Are those gentiles who now believe in God, yet without becoming part of Israel through circumcision and Torah, to continue to live in sin "in the likeness of Adam's offense" (5:14)? Are they "to continue in sin that grace might increase" (6:1)? Shall they sin because they "are not under law but under grace" (6:15)? Simply put, are they to live in disobedience, having believed in the obedient One? "May it never be!" (6:15) was Paul's emphatic reply.

As gentiles they had formerly followed Adam and been "obedient"

[180]For a full discussion of Adam's role in contemporary Judaism and the various uses of Adam typology see Wright, *Climax*, pp. 18–40, 56–98.

[181]The context of the "all" and the "many" is concerned with the distinction between Jews and gentiles being broken down in their common humanity in Adam, and now in Christ. Garlington, "Obedience," part III, pp. 111–12, notes similarly that the πάντε of 5:12 is "ethnically qualitative, not quantitative."

to a voice other than God's (which defines the sin of idolatry),[182] for "you are slaves of the one whom you obey, either of sin resulting in death, or of obedience resulting in righteousness" (6:16). They had formerly been "slaves of sin" who "presented your members as slaves to impurity and to lawlessness, resulting in further lawlessness" (6:16-19). But now that they have believed in the grace of God through the obedient One they have been "freed from sin" and have become obedient themselves:

> But thanks be to God that though you were slaves of sin, you became obedient [ὑπηκούσατε] from the heart to that form of teaching [τύπον διδαχῆς] to which you were committed, and having been freed from sin, you became slaves of righteousness. (6:17-18)

They are now to "present your members as slaves of righteousness, resulting in sanctification" (6:18) rather than to the "impurity" and "lawlessness" of their former "slavery to sin." This righteousness to which Paul is calling for enhanced adherence is no mere generality; it is outlined in a specific body of teaching they have learned and obeyed in the past. And, as noted earlier, it is framed in contrast to the "impurity" and "lawlessness" that characterized their former pagan lifestyles before believing in the obedient One.

Paul's language here of presenting their bodies to righteous behavior in view of the grace of God toward them in the obedient One mirrors that of the cultic language of 12:1ff. (and 15:15-16, 18): "I urge you therefore, brethren, by the mercies of God, to present your bodies a living and holy sacrifice, acceptable to God, which is your spiritual service of worship." And similarly, Paul's instruction to adopt this "obedient" behavior is framed in the context of recognizing God's mercies to them as gentiles saved by faith. This necessarily involves them in the responsibility to "prove what the will of God is, that which is good and acceptable and perfect" (12:2), an unmistakable call to flee their former pagan lifestyles ("do not be conformed to this world, but be transformed by the renewing of your mind": 12:2) and to adopt the standards of Mosaic behavior that apply.[183]

In 10:14-21 we meet the theme of "hearing" in defining the current

---

[182]Garlington, "Obedience," part III, pp. 108–9, discusses the language of the Wisdom of Solomon (14:29-31; 15:2-3) where sin and obedience to lifeless idols are drawn together, among other examples.

[183]This language must be understood following Paul's discussion of the Christian gentiles' present state in the context of Israel's stumbling and the warn-

status of those of Israel "stumbling" over the confession of Jesus as Israel's Christ and over the equal inclusion of gentiles. Here the Romans are informed that "faith comes from hearing and hearing by the word of Christ" (10:17), which Paul is engaged in declaring. Paul describes his apostolic preaching of the gospel to Israel and the nations in eschatological fulfillment of restored Israel's responsibility to bring salvation to the ends of the world.[184] The issue of obedience to Torah is not present in this context—Paul is concerned to clarify that even those of the Law must obey the message of the gospel through faith in Christ Jesus (10:8-12), regardless of their faithfulness to Torah. We thus see that when the thematic ὑπακοή is applied to Israel's response it does not carry the same sense of responsibility to proper behavior, for the "stumbling" Jews in question already obey Torah, even if they do not yet obey the good news of Christ.[185]

When Paul explains his missionary accomplishments and the reasons for his delay in reaching Rome in 15:18-24, 25ff. he once again

---

ing to flee from arrogance. Paul then spells out the behavior appropriate for gentiles who recognize the mercies of God toward them in Christ. Note the comments of Wedderburn, *Reasons*, pp. 77–87, on Rom. 12:1—15:13 as addressing "*a specific situation in the Roman church*" (p. 87), so that rather than being "as general as many scholars suppose" (p. 78), "the upshot of this argument is to conclude that, *when Paul speaks in such seemingly general terms in 12.2 of the renewal of the Romans' minds, he already has in view a quite concrete application of this renewal: he wants them to view their fellow Christians in the Roman church in a new light, in the light of the new age in which they live and in the light of Christ, the representative person of that new age whom they must, as it were, put on. They must above all be able to discern God's will in the matter of their attitude to the ritual observances which are at issue between them, to see how they are concretely to serve God in a manner pleasing to God*" (pp. 77–78).

[184]Gaston, "Israel's Misstep in the Eyes of Paul," pp. 312–17, 322–24, discusses the context of chaps. 9–11 in terms of the Jewish missionary issue, in which he sees Paul accusing some Jewish missionaries of their failure to be a light to the gentiles as they ought. On p. 316 he clarifies: "The righteousness of God for Gentiles, which is the goal of the Torah, has now been manifested, and it is the failure of Israel to acknowledge this, which is what Paul holds against them."

[185]Paul cannot mean here that all Jews have heard the gospel as witnessed in his continuing ministry to inform Jews in each city of the work of Christ on their behalf (his pattern of preaching where Christ has not been named and his plans for Rome and Spain, for example: 15:17-24), and by his explanation in chap. 11 of his intention to provoke his fellow Jews to jealousy by his ministry to the gentiles (of course, Luke takes this view in that Paul continued to enter synagogues first with the gospel, including upon his arrival in Rome; note also that in Athens Paul speaks as though all the world is present at his speech and therefore informed, clearly not meaning any beyond those present to hear the message: Acts 17:30-31).

speaks of the "obedience of the Gentiles" (ὑπακοὴν ἐθνῶν) as the outcome of his apostolic proclamation of the gospel (15:18-19), echoing his language in 1:5. This discussion is framed by the preceding explanation of why he has written this bold reminder in view of his unavoidable delay in reaching Rome personally so that his "offering of the Gentiles might become *acceptable*, sanctified by the Holy Spirit" (15:15-16), followed by the concern to complete his collection of gentile "fruit" which he hopes will be "*acceptable*" to the Jerusalem saints, and for which he seeks their prayers (15:22-32). Again, as in 1:5, it is specifically *gentile* "obedience" that Paul's missionary activity elsewhere has been bringing about, "by word and deed, in the power of signs and wonders, in the power of the Spirit" (15:18-19).[186]

The underlying motive for Paul in calling attention to this particular result of his apostolic ministry is drawn out of the distinction between those to whom Paul has personally proclaimed the gospel and the Roman Christian gentiles whom Paul has not yet been able to reach with his gospel, who have not yet been "established" by his "spiritual gift" (1:11) as they will be when he comes to them "in the fulness of the blessing of Christ" (15:29) "in order that I may obtain some fruit among you also, even as among the rest of the Gentiles" (1:13). Certainly much more than the initial confession of faith in Christ is in view, because they have already made such a confession. As Garlington notes: "Paul envisages not only the believing reception of his gospel by the nations but also their constancy of Christian conduct."[187] Outside this distinction it is difficult to make sense of Paul's intentions toward Rome and their current state of affairs in contrast to his ministry elsewhere "resulting in the obedience of the Gentiles by word and deed," of which he is willing even to boast (15:17-18).

Chapter 16 has two references to ὑπακοή, verses 19 and 26, although the authenticity of the doxology containing the second is a matter of some dispute. Paul refers in 16:19 to "news" of the "obedience" (ὑπακοή) of the Roman Christians having reached to "all men," which likely means, as it has throughout Romans, that their reputation is a matter of note among both Jews and gentiles. This reference is contained in the midst of 16:17-20, wherein we find Paul's vitriolic condemnation of some group that has been causing "dissensions and

---

[186]Note that ἐθνῶν, if taken as a subjective genitive, further enhances this point that it is specifically the obedience of the gentiles being emphasized here (Garlington, "Obedience," part I, pp. 217–19).

[187]Garlington, "Obedience," part I, p. 222.

hindrances [σκάνδαλα: stumbling blocks, offenses]" as they seek to "deceive the hearts of the unsuspecting" through "their smooth and flattering speech" into disregarding or disobeying "the teaching which you learned [τὴν διδαχὴν ἣν ὑμεῖς ἐμάθετε ποιοῦντας]." This group is characterized as "slaves not of our Lord Christ but of their own appetites [κοιλία: stomachs]" in opposition to the "teaching" they had "learned" and of which Paul has reminded them in this letter.

Unlike the "slavery to Christ" Paul had urged in 14:18, which is "acceptable to God and approved by men" in that it seeks peace through accommodating the faith of the other ("and not just please ourselves": 15:2) in matters of diet ("stomachs": 16:18; "eating and drinking": 14:17), this group is apparently proposing that they ought to "please themselves."[188] Their serpentlike speech as "smooth and flattering" in the service of their "stomachs" rather than in the service of Christ, coupled with Paul's desire for the Romans addressed to "be wise in what is good, and innocent in what is evil" until "the God of peace will soon crush Satan under your feet," all point to the temptation of Adam. Clearly Paul has the garden of Eden in mind, and he sets the disobedience intended by this beguiling group urging them to serve their own appetites against the "obedience" of his audience to "the teaching" that they had learned in the past. This context parallels the concerns of 6:15-20, wherein Paul reminded them they had become "obedient from the heart to that form of teaching to which you were committed, and having been freed from sin, you became slaves of righteousness."

Interestingly, it is the unsuspecting "hearts" of Paul's audience that this group is seeking to deceive in matters of diet that depart from "the teaching," even as it was their former "obedience from the heart" to which Paul had earlier referred in calling for enhanced adherence to "the form of teaching." And what was Adam's sin but hearing and obeying a voice other than God's, a voice he did not suspect of the deception intended. That voice led to the Fall, humankind's stumbling into a state characterized by the "deeds of darkness," where self-satisfaction leads to "strife" (13:11-14). For the voice of the serpent,

[188]Ibid., part I, pp. 214–15, is aware of the ethical dimension in this context and finds it thus necessary to seek to balance the evidence that it was a body of doctrine in question, a bifurcation that my approach obviates any need for because I assert that the body of teaching was actually concerned with both ethical and purity matters.

banished thereafter to his "belly," promised that they would be "like God, knowing good and evil" if they would but "eat" (Gen. 3:5).

Paul's call for his audience to be "wise in what is good, and innocent in what is evil" suggests that they must not eat that which is forbidden, namely, that which departs from "the teaching," even as Adam was not to eat from the tree "of the knowledge of good and evil" (Gen. 2:17). For even though God had created "every tree which has fruit yielding seed" as "food" for Adam (Gen. 1:29), and one might legitimately maintain that "all things are clean" and thus that Christian gentiles are free to eat as they choose (Rom. 14:14a), the picture changes when God separates by divine command what is allowed and what is not. Hence, they must not be deceived into rethinking "the teaching which you learned" from the perspective of this group who present their freedom to eat as it had appeared in the garden: "For when the woman saw that the tree was good for food, and that it was a delight to the eyes, and that the tree was desirable to make one wise, she took from its fruit and ate; and she gave also to her husband with her, and he ate" (Gen. 3:6).

"The teaching," like the Torah, calls for hearing obedience to God's voice, believing his word in matters of purity and proper behavior. Thus Paul calls for continued obedience to "the teaching" rather than considering the temptations of this group that lead to "dissensions and hindrances [σκάνδαλα: stumbling blocks or offenses]." Their continued "obedience" in the service of Christ and those "stumbling" is more important than their appetites, and will promote the eschatological shalom of the kingdom of God through behavior that is "acceptable to God and approved by men" (14:15-18) until "the God of peace" comes to "crush Satan under your feet."[189]

The final doxology (16:25-27), while perhaps a latter addition,

---

[189]Seifrid, *Justification by Faith*, p. 201, notes along similar lines: "This final warning against agitators from outside the church has a dual function. First, it is meant to ensure the continued 'obedience' of a basically Gentile church. The term ὑπακοή implies the exclusive allegiance to the God of Israel effected by the Gospel, which Paul has repeatedly described in Jewish terms at crucial points in the letter. His earlier warnings against Gentile pride find practical expression in this exhortation, which connotes the avoidance of idolatrous practices. Secondly, the faithfulness of the Gentiles to the teaching they had received would prevent further division. Paul closes with a promise of victory over Satan from the 'God of peace,' alluding to an end to the conflict between Jews and Gentiles in the church."

nevertheless pulls together the major themes of Romans faithfully.[190]
Here the theme of the declaration of the gospel "to all the nations,
leading to obedience of faith," is in fulfillment of "the Scriptures of
the prophets, according to the commandment of the eternal God,"
once again emphasizing the continuity of Paul's proclamation with the
historic expectations of Israel for the salvation of the nations. But most
importantly, Paul's doxology is built around the preaching of *his*
gospel, around "the revelation of the mystery" that *he* has revealed, in
order that God may "establish" them.[191] Their faith is yet incomplete.
This bold reminder calling for enhanced adherence to values that they
had formerly embraced, but that they question now (as their faith is
not yet "established" by Paul's visit), sets out the apostolic gospel in
view of Paul's delay so that they will continue to obey "the teaching"
as they begin to understand the mystery of how their "faith" obligates
them to observe the intentions of the apostolic decree as "slaves of
righteousness" in the service of Israel's respect and salvation: "for he
who in this way serves Christ is acceptable to God and approved by
men" (14:18).

We can see a clear outline to Paul's argument once he has explained
the continuity of the "obedience of faith" for gentiles with the historic
faith of the descendants of David (the flow of his opening address in
1:1-7). The "obedience of faith among all the Gentiles" is no polemic
against the Torah practice of historical Israel. It rather bears witness to
the continuity of the gentiles' faith with the faith of Israel, with the
Torah of faith that is "established" through faith in Christ, for the
"goal of the Torah" is faith in Israel's Christ as the Savior of the entire

---

[190]Dunn, *Romans*, pp. 912–14, believes it to be a later addition; nevertheless he
notes that "the doxology succeeds quite well in summing up the central themes
of the letter." Garlington, "Obedience," part I, pp. 201–3, believes that the verses
are authentic but states (p. 201 n. 1) that even if they are not "these words are a
fitting climax to the burden of Romans 14–16."

[191]Garlington, "Obedience," part I, pp. 204–5: "Of course, it is precisely the historical realization of the μυστήριον which Paul envisages in his preaching of
Christ. Analogous to 1:5, faith's obedience on the part of the Gentiles is the goal
to which the revelation of the mystery looked. Consequently faith and the obedience of faith assume a distinctively eschatological character. Seen in this light, 'the
obedience of faith' is to be regarded as a phrase of some significance for the understanding of Paul. It is, in other words, *his own articulation of the design and purpose
of his missionary labors*: God is *now* bringing his purposes to pass in salvation history through Paul's gospel, i.e., the preaching of Jesus Christ (v. 25). Paul's commission then is to be viewed as nothing less than the eschatological actualization
of the eternal plan to create faith's obedience among the nations."

world (3:27-31; 4:11-12, 16; 9–11; 10:1-13; 15:5-12). The "obedience of faith" is the obligation incumbent upon gentiles who have come to faith in the One God through Christ Jesus, who as gentiles are now equally part of the historical people of faith, although they are no longer pagans but "righteous gentiles" who must obey the halakhot incumbent upon gentiles who turn to God and associate with his people. They must learn to live the life of the sanctified (6:22; 15:14-16), which will be "acceptable to God and approved by men" (14:18). They must declare in "one voice" in the midst of Israel the Shema of faith (15:6)—for God is One.

The "Obedience of Faith" and the Apostolic Decree

The programmatic "obedience of faith" echoes the spirit of the Jerusalem Council's intentions in setting forth the need for the Christian gentiles of Rome to obey the particulars outlined in the apostolic decree. Paul was concerned to remind them boldly of proper monotheistic behavior for "righteous gentiles" in their association with non-Christian Jews, and specifically in halakhic matters of dietary and sexual conduct (12:1—15:3). He told the Romans that he was "confident" they were "full of goodness, filled with all knowledge, and able also to admonish one another" (15:14); however, he was concerned that they might give ear to those in Rome suggesting they need no longer obey "the teaching" which they had learned and obeyed since their introduction to the faith, and thus that their behavior might not be "acceptable" to the "stumbling" in the Jewish community among whom they worshiped, nor to the saints in Jerusalem (6:17; 14:14-18, 19ff.; 15:15-16; 16:17-18). Thus he wrote this epideictic reminder of the "obedience of faith" so that they would have a better understanding of how their faith was inextricably linked with the fate of Israel, regardless of appearances to the contrary, hoping thereby to forestall any departure from "the teaching" until he could arrive in person to "establish" them with his apostolic proclamation of the gospel that brought gentiles everywhere to the "obedience of faith for His name's sake."

This powerful letter, in addition to shaping their practice of the faith until Paul's arrival, was probably also intended to demonstrate that the Christian gentiles in Rome were, in spirit if not yet in practice, sharers in the collection of "fruit" that bore witness to their understanding of indebtedness to Israel for the "good things" in which they were now participants at Israel's current expense, furthering the chances for the "acceptance" of this gift and thus of Paul's ministry to the gentiles by the Jerusalem saints (15:17-32; 1:11-15).[192]

Whatever grammatical construct one might prefer, the "obedience of faith" articulated Paul's uncompromising commitment to the deeper intentions of the Shema, embracing both the election of Israel and the inclusion of gentiles *equally*—for God is *One*! The contours of Paul's argument have been overlooked because interpreters have misunderstood his focus on gentile inclusion through faith alone, ostensibly dismissing Torah obedience as obsolete. However, if we recognize that Paul was addressing Christian gentiles tempted to consider themselves as having supplanted Israel and thus no longer obligated to obey "the teaching" of the apostolic decree (for why would they need to be concerned with the "acceptance" of the "stumbling" of Israel and their "opinions" of proper purity behavior for "righteous gentiles"; if Israel has been cut off they are free to eat all things!), then we can readily follow Paul's nuanced discussion of circumcision and Torah.

Paul had to balance carefully his reminder of *obedience* to Law-respectful behavior for "righteous gentiles" with the clarification of their *equal* standing, through faith alone, that is, without becoming Jews—for if they became Jews it would compromise God's oneness. It would mean that the One God of Israel was not also the One God of all the nations through Jesus Christ. Faith and Torah are not in conflict, although they are certainly in tension. Indeed, faith establishes Torah, which will be clear to the "stumbling" of Israel when the Christian gentiles among the non-Christian Jews of Rome demonstrate by word and deed the "obedience" of their "faith," glorifying "the God and Father of our Lord Jesus Christ," who has demonstrated his faithfulness to the circumcised by fulfilling the promises to the fathers, and to the gentiles by his mercy—declaring with "*one* accord" in "*one* voice" the very Shema of faith in the *One* God (15:5-12):

Hear O Israel, the Lord is *our* God, the Lord is *One*.

[192]Nickle, *Collection*, pp. 119–22, 127–29.

CHAPTER 5

PAUL'S TWO-STEP PATTERN AND THE RESTORATION OF "ALL ISRAEL"

Throughout this study we have considered the context of Paul's apostolic ministry in the light of his two-step missionary pattern: "to the Jew first and also to the Greek" (Rom. 1:16; 2:10).[1] His opening and closing addresses indicate that Paul must reach Rome to bring them within the two-step pattern God had appointed for the restoration of Israel and salvation of the world, regardless of the fact that some gentiles in Rome had already believed in the good news before many of the Jews in Rome had even heard it (Rom. 1:5-17; 15:14-33; Acts 28:14-23, 24ff.). They were struggling because their faith lacked a proper foundation (it was not "established": Rom. 1:11)—and they were ignorantly supposing that their new position in salvation history involved supplanting Israel (11:1, 11-32).

While Paul must reach them in person to set matters right, he cannot risk waiting to address them in some fashion, for he has heard of a group beguiling them into outright disregard for "the teaching" they had learned to obey in the past (16:17-20; 6:17). They are being tempted by this group to abandon respectful righteous and purity behavior that they had been observing and that Paul maintains is still necessary on behalf of their witness to the "stumbling" Jews in Rome, and perhaps equally necessary with respect to the acceptability of Paul's offering in Jerusalem. Thus he writes in the hope that they will take the instruction in this bold epideictic reminder to heart and continue to obey the operative halakhah for "righteous gentiles" who have turned to the One God of Israel as the One God of the whole

[1] Paul's "custom" of going to the synagogue first upon his arrival in a city he has not preached in previously, before he would turn to preach to the gentiles in that location, is captured succinctly in this phrase, which operates throughout Paul's argument in Romans along the same lines traced by Luke in Acts 17:1-2. See the similar observations of P. Richardson, *Israel in the Apostolic Church*, p. 136; Munck, *Christ and Israel*, pp. 18-19. Although the historical reliability of Luke's construct is in dispute, we are interested in Luke's picture of Paul in Acts as it parallels and sheds light on a new way to read the message and mission of the Paul we meet through Romans. The question of accuracy in Luke's account is left to the work of others.

world. He hopes they will thereby win respect among the "stumbling" in the Jewish community toward their claim to be coparticipants in the "good things" promised to Israel. In fact, Paul fears that if he does not write in view of his continued delay the Christian gentiles in Rome may grow conceited toward the "stumbling" of Israel and disregard "the teaching" of the apostolic decree "to serve Christ" in a manner "acceptable to God and approved by men" (14:18). They might, in effect, if they abandoned this principle, be throwing down another stumbling stone in the path of those "stumbling" that could eventually result in their fall—a prospect so unthinkable that Paul must risk writing boldly, to those who may not see themselves responsible to his authority, of their obligation toward Israel represented in "obedience of faith."

I have thus painted Paul's intentions toward Rome on the same canvas as Luke, and somewhat at odds with the pattern as it is usually traced in Romans. I have found Paul to be a champion of the restoration of Israel first (not its rejection) before the gentile mission had commenced, even as did Luke.[2] Even when the gentile mission had begun it was still thoroughly colored by the necessity of Israel's restoration (11:11-15, 16ff.). In fact, Israel continued to be Paul's unmistakable priority even through his apostleship to the gentiles.

What then are we to do with Romans 11:11-32, wherein Paul appears to have accepted that the original pattern has been reversed with gentile salvation becoming the step that will then lead to Israel's restoration? How do we reconcile Paul's pattern in Acts 28:14-17, 18ff., where upon his arrival in Rome he went to the Jewish leaders first before turning to the gentiles, with the Paul of Romans 11 who appears to have abandoned such a notion?

---

[2]Of course, many do not trace the pattern in Luke-Acts in the manner I am proposing. They see the Jewish rejection of the gospel, not its restoration, as the reason for turning to the gentiles with the gospel message, and thus they would not sense the tension I am proposing to resolve between the account in Acts and Paul's message in Romans. For they would find it natural that Paul based his mission to the gentiles as described in Romans upon this same principle of the rejection of Israel. I am indebted to the work of Jervell, *Luke*, pp. 41–74; idem, "Mighty Minority," for reading this pattern in Acts (see his work for opposing views as well). See J. T. Sanders, *The Jews in Luke-Acts*, chaps. 3 and 4, pp. 263, 283, for recent and thorough critique of Jervell's construct. But see the critique of Sanders's views in C. A. Evans, "Is Luke's View of the Jewish Rejection of Jesus Anti-Semitic?" pp. 29–56, 174–83; and C. Evans and James A. Sanders, *Luke and Scripture: The Function of Sacred Tradition in Luke-Acts.*

In other words, while Romans 11:11-32 and its setting in chapters 9–11 is widely recognized as the clearest evidence of Paul's continued commitment to empirical Israel, it has nevertheless served as the basis for concluding that the "mystery" Paul revealed was the reversal of the pattern of salvation history because he believed Israel had rejected the gospel and would only be restored after the gentile mission had been completed (the "No" of Israel led to the "Yes" of gentiles).[3] It is generally maintained that by the time Paul composed these chapters he had begun to accept the failure of the mission to Israel as originally intended, and was pushing his expectations for Israel's salvation into the distant future. So while Paul affirms the priority of Israel's restoration, he moves it back in the pattern of salvation history: it is only after "the fulness of the Gentiles has come in" that "all Israel will be saved" (11:25-26).[4]

Or does he? I will reexamine this passage at length and its relationship to the two-step pattern affirmed elsewhere in Romans and

[3]Munck, *Christ and Israel*, pp. 18–19, 120–25; on p. 123, he summarizes the view of most: "He has changed the sequence of events that prevailed in the minds of the earliest disciples—first the preaching of the gospel to Israel, and then to the Gentiles—to the sequence we have learned to know in the preceding pages: the gospel was first to be preached to Israel, but because of Israel's unbelief the Gentiles are now to hear it, and when they have received it Israel will also be saved; but in spite of this, Paul is nevertheless convinced that Israel is still the chief goal of God's will to salvation." Munck's chart, p. 123:

Survey of the Idea of Mission Within Earliest Christianity

	Jews	Gentiles	Jews
Jewish Christianity	YES	YES	
Paul	NO	YES	YES
The Post-apostolic Church	NO	YES	

See also Stendahl, *Paul*, who draws from Munck's work and states succinctly on pp. 28–29: "Whenever Paul went to a new city, Acts depicts him as going first to the synagogue where he preaches, albeit with little success. . . . But I rather think that Acts intentionally records this pattern: Paul had to register the 'No' of the Jews before he was allowed to bring the gospel to the Gentiles. This is what is theologically expounded in Romans 9–11." Sanders, *Paul, the Law*, p. 195: "The main thrust of Paul's argument should now be summarized: the eschatological scheme has been reversed; Israel will be saved not first, but as a result of the Gentile mission, through faith in Christ. Some of Israel has been broken off, and this allows time for the completion of the Gentile mission; but if Gentiles are grafted into the olive tree, 'all the more' will the natural branches be regrafted (11:24)."

[4]Even Jervell, "Mighty Minority," p. 29, reads Paul this way: "It does not make sense to Luke to talk about the future of Israel in the way Paul does in Romans 9–11." See Sanders, *Paul, the Law*, p. 184: "It is not until Romans, probably the last

throughout Luke's account in Acts. For I believe that this passage has been heretofore separated from its most natural meaning for Paul and for those he addressed in Rome, hiding his graphic commitment to an approach that he believed was thoroughly dedicated to restoring Israel first, and last, in the context of bringing God's promised blessings to all the world through Christ.

PAUL'S TWO-STEP PATTERN IN ROMANS AND REFLECTED IN ACTS

Luke reports that Paul, upon reaching Rome, was greeted by a small group of brothers and sisters, presumably the same ones to whom he had written his earlier letter (Acts 28:15). However, the rest of Luke's narrative essentially disregards these brothers and sisters, and Paul turns his attention immediately to the task of addressing the leaders of the Jewish community (28:17, 18ff., 23ff.). It is almost as if the gospel had never before been proclaimed in Rome, for Paul's priority and pattern was, as it had been in cities of his eastern spiral that had not yet heard the gospel, to proclaim the good news in the synagogues first (17:1-2). He set about the task of restoring Israel represented in the Diaspora city of Rome. Once the Jewish community had heard, indicated by the division of his listeners into those "being persuaded by the things spoken, but others would not believe" (28:24), Paul gave his characteristic warning (from Isa. 6:9-10) to those departing that "this salvation of God has been sent to the Gentiles; they will *also* listen" (28:24-28; cf. 13:40-41, 46-48).[5]

Paul knew that there were already Christian gentiles in Rome, and he was intimately aware of their faith and obedience, having written his bold reminder to these very ones. Why then does Paul speak of his intention to preach the gospel in Rome to those who already believe the gospel? Luke also knew about these "brethren." How then could Luke understand Paul to speak of a decisive turning to gentiles with the good news as though the gentiles in Rome had not heard the gospel before? And how could he consider the Jewish community(s) to be so uninformed of the Christian message prior to Paul's arrival?[6]

---

of Paul's surviving letters, that he reflects on the failure of the mission to Israel. . . . The traditional scheme has gone awry. The restoration of Israel has not taken place, and so he revises the scheme, as is well known: God will save the Jews after the Gentiles enter, not before (Rom. 11:13-16)."

[5]See discussion below in the excursus on "the fulness of the Gentiles."

[6]See appendix 2 below for discussion of this paradox.

The answer to these questions lies in recognizing the deeply nuanced language of Paul's address to the Romans. Paul's unrelenting intention was to reach Rome as the springboard for his western apostolic ministry to preach the gospel to the ends of the earth (even though they have already heard the gospel in Rome: Rom. 1:8, 14-15) and gather "fruit" from them as he has from "among the rest of the Gentiles" (1:11-13) whom he has brought to the "obedience of faith" during the eastern spiral of his apostolic ministry (which is the reason for his delay, so that he might put his "seal on this fruit of theirs" by "offering" it in Jerusalem, where he hopes it will be "accepted" by the "saints": 15:14-32). Paul must bring to Rome a "spiritual gift" that is necessary for their faith to be "established" in the "fulness of the blessing of Christ" (1:11ff.; 15:29).

Thus the language of Luke becomes clear when read in the light of Paul's own missionary intentions for the proclamation of the gospel "to the Jew first and also to the Greek" upon reaching Rome.[7] Although there are Christians in Rome, the foundation of their faith is incomplete because they have not yet been brought within the divine two-step pattern that begins with the restoration of Israel in each new location first, before the gospel proclamation can fully incorporate gentiles into the people of God.[8] Since Paul *has not yet been to Rome* to exercise his apostolic responsibility by preaching in the synagogues of Rome before turning to the gentiles, that is, before exercising his "spiritual gift" that will "establish" them in the faith in the "fulness of the blessing of Christ," their faith may be real, but it represents an anomaly in salvation history.[9] And it is just such an anomaly that ex-

---

[7]This reading makes more sense of Paul's pattern in Rome according to Luke's account as but another example of the customary two-step pattern that would be repeated in yet future cities if the story of Acts was to continue beyond Rome, rather than as an indication that Luke regarded the mission to Israel complete with Paul's arrival in Rome (contra Jervell, *Luke*, pp. 64, 174). It also respects the caution of Knox and Sanders regarding Acts; this study is based on a reading of this pattern in Romans that parallels Acts and thus suggests the reliability of Acts regarding Paul's missionary pattern (Sanders, *Paul, the Law*, p. 181; J. Knox, *Chapters in a Life of Paul*).

[8]I thus answer the tension seen so clearly by Klein, "Paul's Purpose," p. 40, that the usual views fail to account for the fact that Paul "regards the Romans both as Christian brothers and as missionary objects."

[9]Klein, "Paul's Purpose," p. 40, notes similarly: "These riddles can be solved quite easily, however, if we assume that Paul was in a unique situation, and that he was dealing with addressees whose faith was beyond question but who still were lacking the authentic apostolic stamp." Klein also notes, pp. 41–42, that this

plains why they are being tempted to see their new status in Christ as supplanting the role of Israel, and as the reason why they are beginning to listen to some group that is proposing that they need not respect the "opinions" of the "stumbling" of Israel in matters of ritual purity (the apostolic decree) for "righteous gentiles."

Paul must reach Rome to bring them back within the divine two-step pattern, beginning with the restoration of Israel and then by fully turning to the gentiles. They will then understand the continuity of salvation history.[10] They will really know how their "Yes" of faith is rooted in the "Yes" of Israel's faith, and they will understand how they are deeply indebted to the "stumbling" (who have thus far said "No"), who may appear to be their "enemies," but who are actually servants of their very salvation (11:11-14, 15ff., 28-29, 30ff.). They will then begin to share Paul's deep commitment to the "Yes" of "all Israel" by seeking peace and adopting behavior in their service of Christ that is "acceptable to God and approved by men" (14:18; cf. 11:11-15, 16ff., 25-32; 12:1ff., 14-21; 13:8 ff., 11-14; 14:13—15:3).

This reading makes sense of the importance of the collection as the demonstration of gentile indebtedness to Israel and as the center of his apostolic ministry that is causing his necessary delay.[11] Paul incorporates them in this "fruit" vicariously by way of prayer until they are actually established (15:26-32).[12] And he prepares them to share in this

---

may account for the notable absence of the concept of *ekklēsia* in Romans: "Paul's refusal to use this term is commensurate with a Pauline ecclesiology which holds that the temple of God exists only where the apostle has laid its foundation (1 Cor. 3:10-17)."

[10]Campbell, "Romans III," p. 260: "The question of continuity between Judaism and Christianity was a real issue among the Roman Christians."

[11]Nickle, *Collection*, pp. 129–43; Richardson, *Israel in the Apostolic Church*, pp. 145–46; Aus, "Paul's Travel Plans," pp. 232–62; Munck, *Christ and Israel*, pp. 9–13, 50, 73, 109, 120–22, finds this theme helpful in explaining chaps. 9–11 because the collection is that which will provoke Israel to jealousy; Wedderburn, *Reasons*, pp. 66–91, weaves the theme of collection throughout the letter. See M. Green, *Evangelism in the Early Church*, pp. 272–73: "The collection, and the varied delegation of delegates who brought it, were representatives of the gospel's fruit among the Gentiles, bringing their offerings and themselves to Mount Zion in fulfillment of the ancient prophecies." See J. Beker, "The Faithfulness of God and the Priority of Israel in Paul's Letter to the Romans," p. 331: "In other words, the Roman church is asked to acknowledge the priority of the Jew in the gospel by the apostle to the Gentiles, Paul."

[12]Bjerkelund takes this even further, stating that Paul's safety and the acceptability of the collection are the real purposes for writing Romans (Wedderburn, *Reasons*, p. 71). Also Jervell, "Letter to Jerusalem," who reads Romans entirely in

offering as a demonstration of their commitment to those suffering on their behalf upon his arrival (1:13; 15:14-15, 29-31).[13] Paul will then be able to put his "seal" on the "fruit" of the Romans' future offering as a demonstration of their indebtedness to Israel too.[14]

This reading also makes sense of the fact that Paul did not regard his powerful and comprehensive letter (considered everything from Paul's "compendium of Christian doctrine"[15] to his "last will and testament"[16]) adequate for the proclamation of the gospel or the establishing of their faith.[17] The gospel for Paul could not be separated from

the light of Paul's Jerusalem trip. See Wedderburn, "Purpose and Occasion of Romans Again," pp. 200–202.

[13]Wedderburn, *Reasons*, pp. 71–72, suggests that Paul may not ask for a contribution at this point because (1) Paul may be treading carefully in the matter of his authority over them; and (2) it was too late to receive a collection from them before his departure for Jerusalem. But I suggest that they are not yet established and thus are not entitled to make this contribution until they have been brought within the apostolic pattern and had their faith properly founded upon the restoration of Israel. This view also answers Wedderburn's discussion on pp. 72–75.

[14]Is it possible that Paul regards his offering in Jerusalem as the "seal" of the faith righteousness of the uncircumcised in the same manner that circumcision served as the "seal" of Abraham's faith (4:11)? This would make sense of the universalism present in this gesture in the same way as the universalism is present in Abraham's fatherhood of both circumcised and uncircumcised who have faith in the One God. Note Paul's use of the sense of a "seal" in 14:18 for the appropriate behavior he is calling the "strong" to embrace that will be "'approved' by men" which carries the sense of "authenticated as the real thing" (see chapter 3 above for discussion of this verse).

[15]The famous statement of Philip Melanchthon, *Loci communes*, in 1521.

[16]Bornkamm, "Letter to the Romans."

[17]Contra Jervis, *Purpose*, pp. 158–64, who recognizes the strong apostolic context of the letter but concludes on p. 164: "The function of Romans is to preach the gospel by letter to the Christian converts in Rome. . . . Paul created this letter to be capable of standing on its own; to function so as to accomplish his present goals for the believing community at Rome." The issue of the noninterference clause (see Klein, "Paul's Purpose"; Wedderburn, *Reasons*, pp. 27–29, for the issues), wherein Paul is assumed to have not come to Rome yet because he will not build on another's foundation or preach where Christ was "named" (Rom. 15:20), seems to misread Paul's language in 15:17-25, in addition to obviously contradicting the purpose behind this letter, not to mention his intended trip. Klein's suggestion, which is one of the few to deal with this matter head on (pp. 38ff.), is that the reason Paul can go to Rome is that he does not regard them as having an apostolic foundation. This agrees with the tension I am seeking to explore herein; however, his reading of the text fails to explain why Paul has been prohibited from going in the past but is free to go now; what has changed? I suggest that Paul is saying he is delayed by the eastern spiral of his mission, which will not be

his personal apostolic mission "from Zion" to restore the dispersed of
Israel and bring light to the nations.[18] Until then the Jews of Rome
have not yet heard and thus Israel has not been restored, nor have the
gentiles been properly included or established. Yet this "reminder"
was urgently necessary in order to check those trends that might in-
hibit success upon his trip to Rome. For if the gentiles grow "conceited" and judgmental toward the "stumbling" of Israel (believing
that they have supplanted Israel as God's people)[19] and disregard
proper behavior (the "obedience of faith" as represented, for example,
in the apostolic decree), further offending the Jewish community before his arrival from Jerusalem, they in fact jeopardize the salvation of
those "for whom Christ died" (14:15; cf. 11:11ff.; 14:1ff.). They must
not let their claim to share in Israel's "good things" be "blasphemed"
because of "food" (14:14-18). Paul must write, and he must arrive, to
bring about the restoration of Israel and the commencement of the

completed until he goes to Jerusalem, "where Christ is named" (where the
apostles sit on the twelve thrones as the judges of restored Israel in Jesus the
Christ: Luke 22:30; 24:44-49; Acts 1:1—8:2 clearly show the progression from
Jerusalem where Christ is named first [2:14ff.; 3:16-26; 4:8-20] before the mission
turns out to Samaria and then to the nations [1:8]) to put his "seal" on the collection. Only then will he be free to travel "from Zion to Rome" and begin the
western spiral of his apostolic mission, thereby providing the proper foundation
they have not yet benefited from in Rome. See Gal. 2:1-10 and Rom. 15:15-32 for
Jerusalem's place in Paul's thought and missionary strategies.

[18]Note the similar observation of Klein, "Paul's Purpose." See Campbell,
Intercultural Context, p. 81: "Romans has traditionally and, in our opinion, wrongly
been regarded as a summary of Paul's theology. This designation would have more
substance were the letter regarded as a summary of Paul's theology of mission
which in fact can be seen to occupy a substantial part of the letter when chapters
9–11 are included in the discussion."

[19]It is often assumed that in chaps. 9–11 Paul is engaged in explaining that God
is faithful to Israel as though the Christian gentiles were concerned with this matter: If he was not faithful to Israel how could they be assured he would be faithful to themselves? (cf. Beker, *Paul the Apostle*, pp. 77–78; Campbell, *Intercultural
Context*, pp. 170–75). While this matter is certainly a significant concern of Paul, it
does not make sense as the present concern of the gentiles addressed. They appear rather to be growing comfortable with the developing notion that Israel has
fallen and they have stepped into Israel's place. As long as God is faithful to themselves all is well, and they do not seem to be concerned otherwise. Paul (and the
Christian Jews who have alerted him of this attitude in Rome) is concerned that
they should (must!) understand the unquestioned faithfulness of God to Israel, albeit in sometimes unfathomable ways, so that they will not draw just such false
conclusions about God's intentions toward Israel, and hence such superior conclusions about themselves.

gentile mission, the two-step pattern for the apostolic proclamation of the good news that Israel's Messiah is also the Savior of the world.[20]

In spite of the fact that we can locate features of Paul's two-step pattern in Romans that reflect and clarify Luke's formalized understanding of Paul's "custom" of going to the Jews first before turning to the gentiles,[21] if I am to maintain that this pattern was operative for Paul in Romans I must confront the seemingly insurmountable obstacle of Paul's revelation of an ostensible reversal (to the gentile first and then to the Jew) in 11:25-26 and its surrounding context:

> For I do not want you, brethren, to be uninformed of this mystery, lest you be wise in your own estimation, that a partial hardening has happened to Israel until the fulness of the Gentiles has come in; and thus all Israel will be saved; just as it is written . . .

How are we to understand the Paul of Romans who continues to announce a message of equality delivered in a clearly discriminating program "to the Jew first and also to the Greek," with the Paul who communicated 11:25-26, which appears to invert this pattern in concluding the order must now be to the gentile first and then also to the Jew?

The Context of Paul's Concern

This language comes in the context of Paul's lengthy explanation that the current phenomenon of Israel's "stumbling" and failure to fulfill her role of bringing the good news to the nations is inextricably linked with the beginning of the gentile mission that he and the remnant are carrying out on Israel's behalf:

> I say then, they did not stumble so as to fall, did they? May it never be! But by their transgression salvation has come to the Gentiles, to

[20]D. W. B. Robinson, "Priesthood of Paul," p. 232, captures this sense when he observes: "We may state that the aim of Romans is to show the Gentiles how their hope rests on Israel's Messiah: how that through the prior fulfillment of the promises to Israel a stepping stone is made for the Gentiles."

[21]Note Dunn, "Formal and Theological Coherence of Romans," p. 249, observes: "It is precisely the tension between 'Jew first but also Greek' (1:16), which Paul experienced in his own person and faith and mission, which also provides an integrating motif for the whole letter."

make them jealous. (11:11)

> Inasmuch then as I am an apostle of Gentiles, I magnify *my ministry*,
> if somehow I might move to jealousy my fellow countrymen and save
> some of them. (11:13-14)

Paul, in the context of 11:11-29, 30ff., clarifies that while part of
Israel may have "stumbled" it is not "so as to fall" but in order that
they will be provoked to jealousy as the gospel brings salvation to the
gentiles in fulfillment of the prophecies. It is for this very reason that
Paul magnifies "his ministry" as the "apostle of Gentiles" (v. 13). He
hopes it will "move to jealousy my fellow countrymen and save some
of them" (v. 14). Paul frames the purpose of his apostolic ministry with
the vivid contrast between the present "riches" that have come to
gentiles through the "stumbling" of some of his brothers and sisters
(who have not believed in Christ or in the salvation of these gentiles)
and the unfathomable success that will be realized by both the
Christian gentiles and Israel when his apostolic ministry has at last fulfilled its destiny:

> Now if their transgression be riches for the world and their failure be
> riches for the Gentiles, how much more will their fulfillment be. . . .
> For if their rejection be the reconciliation of the world, what will their
> acceptance be but life from the dead? (11:12, 15)

Even though Paul is bringing the gospel to gentiles it is in the service of Israel's eventual restoration, which will be incomparably superior to the present circumstances that have been benefiting the gentiles, even as life is incomparably superior to death. He expects his
"stumbling brethren" to recognize *in his ministry to the gentiles* that the
eschatological promises are being fulfilled;[22] but they are missing out
on their prophesied privilege of serving as restored Israel's light to all
the nations.[23]

It is important to note that it is not the salvation of the gentiles per
se, but "his ministry" that he magnifies and expects to provoke some
of his "fellow countrymen" to jealousy—the bringing of gentiles to

---

[22]Paul's intentions are often read here as though his ministry demonstrated that
Israel's promises have been nullified, as though Israel has been rejected and will
not fulfill her promised destiny as a light to the nations.

[23]See B. Longenecker, *Eschatology and the Covenant*, p. 264: "For Paul, gentile
faith in the Jewish Messiah is the actualization of the Jewish hope for the eschatological ingathering of the nations."

"obedience of faith" as they recognize Israel's Christ as the Savior of the world. Strangely, interpreters assume that Paul expects Jews to be jealous of the *salvation* of gentiles. This would imply that gentile salvation (becoming part of the people of God) is undesirable to Jews or that it necessarily suggests to Jews that they are no longer the people of God unless they convert to a new (gentile) religion as early as Paul's letter to Rome. Is that really Paul's view? Would it be the view of his fellow Jews about what it would mean to claim that the Jewish eschatological promises were being fulfilled? More importantly: Does this not presuppose that Jews wanted to exclude gentiles from salvation even though Jewish eschatological expectations were generally full of this very hope? What sense does this make of the Jewish missionary impulse, arguably a normative feature of the time? Would not the turning of pagans to the worship of the God of Israel have been cause for celebration? There is also another logical problem with the usual handling of this text: Even if a visible salvation of gentiles was something to be jealous of, then the Christian gentiles' claims would have provoked anger perhaps, and separation, but it is unlikely that they would have produced the kind of jealousy that Paul seems to be looking for that will lead to a *positive reevaluation* of the gospel.[24]

In spite of this common assumption, Paul does not say that Jews will be jealous of gentiles being saved, which would be but the other side of the exclusivistic triumphalism he is confronting among Christian gentiles. He explicitly says it is *his ministry* that will be the cause of jealousy for some of them, which is a very different point. It suggests exactly the opposite of the usual view, namely, that Paul assumes his fellow Jews will see in his success among the gentiles that their own Jewish universalistic hopes are being fulfilled, albeit somehow without their coparticipation in this fantastic privilege as they have expected. Hence they would be jealous of Paul's ministry and reconsider his declaration that the hope of Israel has come in Christ Jesus.

Paul expects them to be jealous of his ministry, which reveals a failure on their part and suggests that a measurable missionary program toward gentiles was present in Jewish communities of Paul's time, or at least that one would be intelligible and enviable within the scope of

[24]See R. Bell, *Provoked to Jealousy*, for a full discussion of the range of meanings possible for "jealousy." In this passage Paul speaks of a positive jealousy, i.e., emulation (pp. 39–43). See also D. W. B. Robinson, "The Salvation of Israel in Romans 9–11," pp. 92–95.

their eschatological expectations. Note also Paul's language to describe Jewish missionaries concerned with the gentile mission earlier
in this very letter (2:17-24); it is for him a present concern on the part
of his "stumbling brethren" to bring gentiles to faith in the One God.
A kind of positive competitive jealousy seems to be in view. That is,
the "stumbling" are not expected to be provoked to jealousy by gentiles sharing in salvation as they bless the One God (as is usually assumed in interpreting this passage); the salvation of the gentiles
should provoke unmitigated rejoicing! This is a sign of the promises
fulfilled, the eschatological shalom that will bring all the nations to the
worship of Israel's God as the One God of all. Yet the fact that gentiles
are becoming coparticipants in the eschatological blessings through
Paul's ministry as Israel's representative and *not their own* quenches the
rejoicing, for it bears witness against them. It signifies that *they* are
those suffering the eschatological curse ("hardened": vv. 7-10 from
Deut. 29:4; Isa. 29:10; Ps. 69:22-23), that *they* are standing outside the
promised blessings, while *Paul* is fulfilling Israel's eschatological privilege of bringing light to the gentiles.[25] They are among those whom
the prophets warned of hardness of heart. Their privileges are being
enjoyed by Paul and a remnant of Christian Jews who are bringing the
good news to the ends of the earth. Thus Paul hopes their jealousy
toward his ministry will awaken them to the reality of the times so that
they will "not continue in unbelief" (Rom. 11:23), so that he might
"save some of them" (v. 14),[26] indeed, so that the fullness of the blessings (the resurrection? 11:12, 15, 26) may come.[27]

Finally, it should be noted that this expectation of jealousy presup-

[25]Even as Luke portrayed Paul warning them in his account of Paul's later ministry to the Jewish leaders in Rome (Acts 28:24-28).

[26]It is difficult to understand the position of those who maintain that Paul has
abandoned a mission to Jews when even his ministry to gentiles is on behalf of his
Jewish brothers' and sisters' salvation. It is also important to note that Paul sees
the way to salvation for his brethren is through faith in Christ, and that his expectation is for "some" of them to turn from their present "unbelief." Paul does not
appear at this point to expect "all" Jews to share his "faith."

[27]W. Campbell, *Intercultural Context*, pp. 92–93, makes an important point where
the jealousy motif is concerned vis-à-vis the view that the "final restoration of
Israel would be the work of God himself ": "One question still remains unan-
swered—what is the relationship between the jealousy resulting from the fullness
of the nations and the final conversion of Israel? As we noted, this outcome is generally taken to be by the direct action of God Himself—but the jealousy motif
suggests that it is in fact the winning of the representatives from the nations which
causes Israel's restoration."

poses close contact with Paul and his mission and firsthand knowledge of the response of these gentiles; Paul expects them to regard himself and his ministry within the context of Judaism and the concerns of the Jewish community. If Paul's ministry is not taking place within the confines of the Jewish community, then they would neither know about it nor really care, at least not enough to provoke the kind of extensive and positive reaction Paul intends. There is no reason or precedent for this kind of emulative jealousy on the part of the Jewish communities toward what would have been regarded, if identified outside Judaism, as a pagan movement. If Paul's ministry was successful in appealing to Jews and considered a non-Jewish or apostate movement, it may indeed provoke fear, even anger, but what is there to be jealous of?

Paul develops the imagery of an olive tree[28] to clarify further why the Christian gentiles in Rome should not consider that the "stumbling" of Israel are supplanted by themselves and thus no longer God's "beloved."[29] They have received the same grace that the "stumbling" stand in need of and they must "not be arrogant" toward the

---

[28]This motif may have had a more literal sense for Paul's audience as there was possibly in Rome a Synagogue of Olives or Olive Tree, although Leon questions this interpretation (Leon, *Jews*, pp. 145–46). For a possible explanation see W. D. Davies, "Paul and the Gentiles: A Suggestion Concerning Romans 11:13-24," in *Jewish and Pauline Studies*, pp. 158–59. See also the discussion of A. Baxter and J. Ziesler, "Paul and Arboriculture: Romans 11.17-24," pp. 25–32, who show the likelihood that Paul's illustration followed plausible botanical processes and that the main point is to argue for the rejuvenation of the tree that no longer produces proper olives: "a tree that was exhausted, unproductive, or diseased, in order to re-invigorate it" (p. 27).

[29]See Davies, "Paul and the Gentiles," in *Jewish and Pauline Studies*, for a full discussion of the olive tree allegory. On pp. 159–63 Davies suggests that Paul may have chosen the olive tree over the vine, which would be more natural for Jews, because the olive was a powerful symbol of Athens and Greek culture, in order to emphasize the sharp contrast between wild and cultivated olive trees. Wild olive trees were unproductive and bore no useful fruit; thus this was "a most forceful indictment of their lives," turning the tables on those who generally looked down on Jews and their culture by "implying the superiority of the Jewish tradition and the inferiority of the Hellenistic." "By casting Gentiles in the role of the wild olive and reserving the cultivated olive for a community rooted in Abraham, was he not in a way subtle to a modern reader but probably clear to the Christian Gentiles in Rome (whom one must assume to have achieved a degree of sophistication to be able to follow the epistle to the Romans at all) opposing the anti-Judaism of the Greco-Roman world and striking a blow for his own kin after the flesh, not only within the context of the Church, but within that of the larger world?"

natural branches that have been temporarily "broken off" so that they themselves "might be grafted in." Indeed, Paul continues to illustrate the fact that even the branches that have been "broken off" are separated unto the Lord in the service of gentile salvation: for "if the root be holy, the branches are too" (vv. 16-17).[30] The "rich root of the olive tree," which appears to signify the remnant of restored Israel that Paul in his ministry to the gentiles represents (cf. vv. 1-10),[31] "supports" all the branches, both the gentiles who are grafted in from a "wild olive tree" and the natural branches of the "cultivated olive tree."

Paul thus explains that the grafting in of the gentiles does not support the root, "but the root supports you" (v. 18), a significant metaphor that Paul expects will deepen the impact of this challenge to their temptation toward arrogance in their new status.[32] Here,

---

[30]The illustration of the "root" may very well be drawn from "the root of Jesse" as applied in Isaiah, whom he has just quoted often in this argument, most recently in v. 8. See his application of this exact language in 15:12 for the "root of Jesse" as the ruler and hope of the gentiles in the congregation of Israel among whom the gentiles worship (15:5-12).

[31] Jervell, "Mighty Minority," p. 23, sees this same meaning, and comments on 11:18 that "the root that sustains you" means: "The Jewish Christians carry the church." Munck, *Christ and Israel*, pp. 110–11, comments similarly on 11:5: "But here, in chapter 11, the remnant concept is put forward in preparation for the message that the whole of Israel will eventually be saved; the stress lies on the fact that there is at least a remnant which stands as testimony that God's grace toward the chosen people has not ceased." So also D. Johnson, "The Structure and Meaning of Romans 11," pp. 93–100; he notes on p. 99: "In Rom 16.5 and I Cor 16:15 Paul refers to the first converts of his ministry in an area as the ἀπαρχή. They are the foreshadowing of the greater, eventual redemptive work of God. Likewise, the remnant within Israel is the ἀπαρχή among the Jews. It adumbrates God's final redemptive work among his people. . . . What is true of the first fruit will of necessity become true for the whole lump; the essential character of the root inevitably becomes the essential character of the branches. It belongs to the nature of things. Just so, it is inevitable that the remnant will some day find its fulfillment in the full inclusion of the Jews, when "all Israel will be saved." See also Richardson, *Israel in the Apostolic Church*, p. 130; Callan, "Background," p. 297. Davies, *Jewish and Pauline Studies*, pp. 154–57, sees the root as Abraham, which Jews are attached to by nature while gentiles are not, and he uses the root motif as the Jewish advantage (pp. 134, 144–46, for relationship of Abraham as father of Jews, and p. 147, for his use of this language in the same manner pursued herein). On first fruits as the remnant see also Dahl, *Studies in Paul*, p. 151; Beker, *Paul the Apostle*, p. 90.

[32]This point makes the suggestion of many that the root here is a reference to Abraham unlikely. Why would they be tempted to disregard Abraham? They believe they have priority not over Abraham, but over Israel. If they are disregarding

buried in language that ostensibly reverses the order of salvation his-tory with the "Yes" of gentiles preceding the "Yes" of Jews is a strik-ing reminder that the gentile inclusion *follows from Israel's restoration*, not the other way around. Even those cut off are "holy," separated to suffer vicariously for the sake of bringing God's mercy to the gentiles, preserved by the remnant "root."[33] The fate of Israel precedes and supports the fate of the nations. The "Yes" of the believing "root" as well as the "No" of those "cut off" precedes and supports the "Yes" of the wild olives grafted in, but there is still more—both the believing root and the wild olives are not the end of God's plan but now must

---

Israel then they are disregarding the remnant of restored Israel that Paul counts himself among (as well as the part hardened whom the remnant preserve in God's unfathomable plan), who represent the maintenance of all Israel's priority and cer-tain salvation before a merciful God. Again, we must focus on the desired result of Paul's language here to dissuade Christian gentiles from the notion that they have supplanted Israel as God's people. Note the comment of H. Räisänen, "Paul, God, and Israel," p. 188: "Most interpreters identify the ῥίζα with Israel. Logically, it should perhaps refer to something else, since Israel seems to consist rather of branches. Paul, however, is not famous for keeping his comparisons always strictly in order, and in any case there is no great difference between the alternatives. Gentiles are proselytes, Israel is the people. Gentiles are not to boast, for they do not support the root, they are supported by it."

[33]Hays, *Echoes*, pp. 60–63, illustrates this imagery powerfully, explaining Paul's application of Ps. 44: "If exilic Israel's suffering is interpreted by the psalmist not as punishment but as suffering for the sake of God's name, then perhaps even the temporary unbelief of Israel can be understood as part of God's design to encom-pass Jews and Gentiles alike with his mercy" (p. 61). Hays continues: "it is clear that the breaking of the branches is God's act, aimed at salvation of the Gentiles. . . . By describing the fate of unbelieving Israel in the same language that he had used to describe Jesus' death, Paul hints at a daring trope whose full implications subsequent Christian theology has usually declined to pursue. What Paul has done, in a word, is to interpret the fate of Israel christologically . . . Israel under-goes rejection for the sake of the world, bearing suffering vicariously" (p. 61). By combining 11:21 and 8:32 and linking these with Abraham's near sacrifice of Isaac, Hays suggests: "The parallels between these three beloved ones 'not spared' are too rich to be fortuitous. Abraham did not spare his son Isaac but bound him to the alter, only to receive him back through God's intervention. God did not spare his son Jesus but offered him up to death for the world, then vindicated him through the resurrection. God did not spare his people Israel but broke them off like branches for the sake of the Gentiles; surely that is not the end of the story, 'for if their rejection means the reconciliation of the world, what will their acceptance mean but life from the dead?' (Rom. 11:15). In each case, the rejection/acceptance pattern plays itself out to the vicarious benefit of others" (p. 62). See also N. Dahl, "The Atonement: An Adequate Reward for the Akedah?" in *Jesus the Christ*.

recognize their responsibility to those of Israel who initially said
"No"—"For if their rejection be the reconciliation of the world, what
will their acceptance be but life from the dead?"

So the final results are not yet in. Not all of Israel has been restored,
hence, rather than responding with "conceit" to those now cut off, the
Christian gentiles instead should "fear" the same fate and seek to continue in God's "kindness," that is, they should continue in humble
"faith" by presenting their bodies to God and his purposes, and to the
service of the "stumbling" according to the "measure of faith" they
have been "allotted" (11:20-23, 30-32; cf. 12:1-3, 4ff.).[34] Israel has not
fallen; she has been divided. Rather than arrogantly assuming they
have replaced a fallen Israel, the gentiles are to recognize they must
be servants of Israel's salvation even as Paul is, *for it is Israel's success
and not her failure* that will bring the "revealing of the sons of God" for
which the "creation" is anxiously longing (8:19).[35] It is only natural that
those now "broken off" will be "grafted into their own olive tree" "if
they do not continue in their unbelief" (11:23-24). What is unnatural
is the current state of affairs wherein it has been necessary in the design of God for some branches to be temporarily broken off in order
that wild olive branches can be grafted in. This division of Israel, with
the present suffering on the part of some of the natural branches,
should cultivate a sense of gratitude for God's mercy and a sense of responsibility to suffer now on behalf of those temporarily broken off so
that they may be grafted back in. This will result in "riches" beyond
measure, the groundwork for Paul's message in chapters 12–15.[36]

---

[34]The message of persevering in suffering is woven throughout Romans; significantly, it is clearly in the context of relations between Christian gentiles and
non-Christian Jews in 15:1-5, 6ff. (5:1-5, 6ff.; 8:31-39; 12:14-21; 16:17-20).

[35]Baxter and Ziesler, "Paul and Arboriculture," p. 29, do a nice job of pointing
out that the purpose of ingrafting in this illustration is "the rejuvenation of the
tree. This is why the process would be undertaken at all. It would enable the in-
grafted branches to become fruitful, but the rejuvenation of the whole tree would
be the primary aim. If, as we suggest, it is likely that Paul knew this, then the figure is used primarily to stress God's intention to save Israel (v. 26)."

[36]Hays, *Echoes*, p. 62: "Paul's grasp of the logic of this 'pattern of exchange' is so
firm that he can write, 'I used to pray to be myself accursed and cut off from Christ
for the sake of my brethren, my kinsmen by race' (Rom. 9:3). The prayer sounds
peculiar or even heretical by subsequent Christian standards, but it embodies
Paul's fundamental conviction that the people of God do and should manifest in
their own lives a conformity to the sacrificial example of Jesus Christ, a pattern
which is rooted in the story of Abraham and Isaac and—paradoxically—reenacted
in Paul's own time by the 'breaking off' of Israel. Thus, when Paul in Romans 8

Paul's illustration has prepared the Christian gentiles in Rome for a revelation that he believes will finally level the temptation to regard the "stumbling" of Israel arrogantly. He presents a "mystery" that they apparently have not realized before, a mystery that he believes will keep them from being "wise in your own estimation." It is to this revelation we now turn.

EXEGESIS OF ROMANS 11:25-29

> For I do not want you, brethren, to be uninformed of this mystery, lest you be wise in your own estimation, that a partial hardening has happened to Israel until the fulness of the Gentiles has come in; and thus all Israel will be saved; just as it is written,
>
>> "The Deliverer will come from Zion,
>> He will remove ungodliness from Jacob."
>> "And this is My covenant with them,
>> When I take away their sins."
>> From the standpoint of the gospel they are enemies for your sake, but from the standpoint of God's choice they are beloved for the sake of the fathers; for the gifts and the calling of God are irrevocable.

The Purpose of Paul's Revelation

Paul is determined to correct the misguided views that would lead to triumphal conceit toward the "stumbling" of Israel. He does not want them to be "uninformed" or "wise in your own estimation," and so he reveals a "mystery."[37] Thus, we must interpret Paul's revelation in the

---

quotes the words of Psalm 44, 'For your sake we are being killed all the day long; We are reckoned as sheep to be slaughtered' he is sounding a theme that reverberates in complex patterns with and against his letter's other images of election, faithfulness, and sacrifice. This quotation prepares the way for his direct exhortation in Rom. 12:1: 'I beseech you then, brothers, through the mercies of God to present your bodies as a living sacrifice.' That is what is required of the eschatological people of God; God's elect must suffer and groan along with—and even on behalf of—the unredeemed creation (cf. Rom. 8:18-25)."

[37] "Mystery" (μυστήριον) draws from Jewish apocalyptic language the sense of "divine secrets now revealed by divine agency" through visions, heavenly journeys, or the interpretation of Scripture (Qumran exegesis: *1 Enoch* 104.12), often, as here, to explain "the puzzle of Israel's defeat or failure or chastisement" (Dunn, *Romans*, pp. 678–79, 690–91). On p. 679 Dunn captures the sense of Paul's use of the term: "As the apocalyptist's revelation was a response to the anguished cry

context of the following question: How does the "mystery" Paul reveals deliver new information certain to confront the temptation toward Christian gentile arrogance? The difficulty of this task becomes apparent when we look closely at the usual interpretations of what Paul means in asserting that "all Israel will be saved."

1. Many consider "all Israel" to be the church composed of believing Jews and gentiles, although the language chosen to explain this phenomenon differs.[38] But this is simply another way to say that Paul has substituted the church for Israel or that the church is the true or spiritual Israel.[39] What point would this make? They already believe that Christian Jews and Christian gentiles compose the church, don't they? How would revealing that after the "fulness of the Gentiles has come in" all *Christians* would be saved be significant, or even sensible? Nowhere does Romans refer to the church as Israel. Moreover, this fails to maintain the tension between gentiles and Jews that underscores this entire argument, not to mention the balance of the letter.[40] Is this not an example of the very supplanting of empirical Israel that Paul is arguing against in this text?

2. Some suggest that Paul is referring to the believing "remnant" of Christian Jews.[41] This too is redundant and hardly motivates gentiles to humility. They already recognize that Jews who believe in Jesus as the Christ are saved, don't they? What does this position tell us about the "stumbling" of Israel? Are they cut off and supplanted as the Christian gentiles already suppose?

3. Others believe that "all Israel" refers to the whole of Israel to be

---

'How long?' (Dan 8:13; 9:20-27; 12:6-8; *4 Ezra* 6.59; *2 Apoc. Bar.* 26; and cf. particularly the sequence in *4 Ezra* 10.38-39 and *2 Apoc. Bar.* 81.3-4), so the mystery revealed by Paul provides an answer to the anguish he expressed in 9:1-3 and 10:1. That Paul was moving in the same circle of thought is sufficiently indicated by such parallels as Isa 6:10-13; Zech 1:12-17; Rev 6:10-11; *4 Ezra* 4.33-37 and *Apoc. Abr.* 28.3–29.2."

[38]Wright, *Climax*, pp. 249–51; M. Getty, "Paul and the Salvation of Israel," p. 459.

[39]Richardson, *Israel in the Apostolic Church*, discusses the historical shortcomings of this view. See the discussion below.

[40]So too Jervell, "Mighty Minority," p. 25, states: "The concept of the Jewish Christians constituting the centre of the church, that is the idea in Rom. 11, demands that it is actually possible to distinguish between Jewish and Gentile Christians."

[41]For proponents of this view see the discussion of Dunn, *Romans*, p. 681. See also J. Lambrecht, "Israel's Future According to Romans 9–11 An Exegetical and Hermeneutical Approach," in *Pauline Studies*, pp. 46–54.

saved after the gentile mission is complete.[42] While the people as a whole is the most likely meaning of "all Israel," which I will explore below, how does this interpretation affect Christian gentile arrogance? Does the inverted order of salvation history (gentile first, then Jew), which these interpreters suggest Paul is revealing and which might indeed lead Jews to humility,[43] lead to the salvation of Jews in a manner that provides a humbling and motivational message for Christian *gentiles*?

4. Some develop the idea that "all Israel" will be saved by an eschatological miracle such as the return of Christ.[44] It is particularly difficult to see the motivational message in this solution. If God will miraculously save all Israel at the end of some period of time (i.e., the parousia),[45] what impact does that have on gentile presumption toward the "stumbling"? How does it make sense of Paul's desire to provoke jealousy through his ministry as the motivational stimulus?[46] Besides, isn't this just another form of triumphalism: "We will win in the end!"? How does that combat the arrogance of the gentile assumptions? As wonderful as this reading is (in its usual intentions), it simply fails to account for the purpose of this revelation. Further, it suggests that the gospel is not effective in the end, which would have been cause for Paul to abandon his continuing concern with a Jewish mission, or to be ashamed of the power of the gospel, positions he certainly denied (1:16).

5. Still others suggest that all Israel's salvation is independent of

[42]Dunn, *Romans*, p. 681. Sanders, *Paul, the Law*, p. 195; Davies, *Paul and Rabbinic Judaism*, pp. 75–76.

[43]Dunn, *Romans*, pp. 679, 693.

[44]Munck, *Christ and Israel*, pp. 136–38. Differently developed by O. Hofius, "'All Israel Will Be Saved': Divine Salvation and Israel's Deliverance in Romans 9–11," pp. 19–39, who on pp. 36–37 states: "The apostle certainly does *not* have in mind a further, end-time evangelistic proclamation of the gospel to Israel by the church, followed by Israel's believing in the gospel which it has heard *preached*. 'All Israel' is *not* saved by the *preaching* of the gospel. By no means, however, does that imply a 'Sonderweg,' a way of salvation which bypasses the gospel and faith in Christ! Rather, Israel will hear the gospel from the mouth of Christ himself at his return—the saving word of his self-revelation which effects the faith that takes hold of divine salvation. When 'all Israel' encounters the *Kyrios* at the parousia, it encounters the *gospel!*"

[45]Dunn, *Romans*, p. 692; Sanders, *Paul, the Law*, pp. 193–96; Käsemann, *Romans*, pp. 312–14.

[46]Similarly noted by Wright, *Climax*, pp. 249–51; differently, Goodman, *Mission*, p. 166.

Christ or the gospel.[47] But again, the question of how this revelation
provokes much more than indifference from the gentiles addressed
must be asked. In fact, while the proponents of this view explicitly
seek to propose a modern view that is respectful of Jews and Judaism
in Paul's theology, paradoxically, their position excludes Jews from
Christ and makes little sense of the situation of Paul and other
Christian Jews, their mission, or their suffering for their confession
that Jesus was Israel's Messiah. Nor does it make sense of Paul's sor-
row or his intention to provoke jealousy in this same text.
Furthermore, the "disobedience" of some of Israel is in the present
tense; it is "now," just as the mercy shown to them through the inclusion of gentiles is in the "now": "so these [Jews] also now have been
disobedient, in order that because of the mercy shown to you [gen-
tiles] they also may now be shown mercy" (11:31).[48] While this view is
attractive and allows for excellent dialogue,[49] it does not make for very
good history, it fails to account for many of Paul's statements in
Romans and elsewhere,[50] and most importantly, it does not deliver the
motivational impact this context demands.

The restoration of "all Israel" was already clearly promised in
Scripture and developed in contemporary apocalyptic traditions—it
represented no mystery.[51] How would the revealing of the salvation of
all Israel, especially as suggested above, affect Christian gentile attitudes in a new and powerful way? Is complacence Paul's aim? For all
of these will take place with or without gentile humility; God is surely
committed to Israel's salvation regardless of the failure of gentiles,
even as he is committed to the salvation of the gentiles regardless of
the failure of some of Israel (e.g., 3:3ff.). Moreover, how does revealing an inverted order of gentile first before Jew differ from what the

[47]Stendahl, *Paul*, p. 4; Gaston, *Paul*, pp. 143–50; Gager, *Origins*, pp. 256–64.

[48]Robinson, "Salvation," pp. 95–96.

[49]Note the comments of Sanders, *Paul, the Law*, pp. 192–99; Segal, *Paul*, pp. 279–82.

[50]See the critical discussions of this position by Campbell, *Intercultural Context*, p. 78; idem, "Salvation for Jews and Gentiles"; Räisänen, "Paul, God"; R. Hvalvik, "A 'Sonderweg' for Israel"; Wright, *Climax*, pp. 252–57.

[51]Dahl, *Studies in Paul*, pp. 152–53. On apocalyptic views see D. Allison, "The Background of Romans 11:11-15 in Apocalyptic and Rabbinic Literature," pp. 229–34; E. E. Johnson, *The Function of Apocalyptic and Wisdom Traditions in Romans 9–11*, pp. 124–31, 162–63, esp. p. 126 n. 55; Aune, *Prophecy*, pp. 252–53; Sanders, *Paul and Palestinian Judaism*, pp. 147–82. See also the discussion in chapter 2 above.

gentiles already believe? From what Paul has been assumed to have argued in the preceding verses? And how would the knowledge of that motivate a change of heart? Learning that their salvation now precedes Israel's stands a better chance of feeding conceit than it does of checking it. Moreover, how do these solutions explain the reasons behind Paul's continuing intense concern for a Jewish mission, albeit, at least in this passage, through his mission to the gentiles?[52]

I suggest that the "mystery" is not so much *that* "all Israel" will be saved, although it is likely that the Christian gentiles need to be reminded of this irrevocable promise as it applies to the non-Christian Jews in Rome: the "mystery" reveals *how* "*all*" Israel" is being saved. Nor is it so much that gentiles are saved first, that appears to have been their opinion already. It is *why* they are being saved before the part of Israel that has been "hardened."

"Mysteries" are revealed to change present as well as future expectations, and thus behavior. The "mystery" will surprise them. Things are not as they appear to be; that is, God is working differently than they currently realize in Rome with regard to the non-Christian Jews whom they consider "enemies" of the gospel. The tension that is at the center of Paul's concern, namely, to inform so as to change Christian gentile perceptions that are leading to disregard for those presently broken off, is wrapped around the surprising *process* God is employing in the restoration of Israel, in addition to asserting the *fact* of that restoration.

The "mystery" Paul reveals is that Israel has been divided and thus the two-step pattern is operative in spite of appearances to the contrary: God is still committed to the program of "to the Jew first and also to the Greek." His audience in Rome will then see that:

• Israel has not fallen and they have not supplanted Israel in spite of how things might presently appear; rather, they have become co-participants in the process of Israel's restoration.

• The salvation of the gentiles has not preceded the restoration of "all Israel," even if it has preceded the restoration of "some," that part which has been "hardened."

• Those branches presently "broken off" (the "part hardened") are

---

[52]Note the explicit concern for investigating the reasons for the mission of Paul and the early Christians and not just the nature and course of that mission in the concluding discussion of Goodman, "The Consequences and Origins of Proselytizing," in *Mission*, esp. pp. 160ff.

serving in the initiation of the gentile mission through their present suffering (as a sign that Israel's restoration/pruning has begun and thus that the gentiles must now be reached) until those who "do not continue in their unbelief" are again "grafted into their own olive tree."

- Even Paul's ministry to the gentiles is, in part at least, to provoke those presently "hardened" to reconsider the message as they see the eschatological promises to restored Israel carried out by Paul as Israel's representative bringing light to the nations, thus saving "some" who are now "broken off" who might not have otherwise stopped to reconsider the message.

- The branches are not supporting the root as they may suppose, but the remnant of restored Israel (the "root") is supporting both the branches that believe ("wild" [gentile] as well as "natural" [Jew]) and their current ministry to the gentiles is engaged in restoring those of Israel presently "hardened."

So the "mystery" is not so much *that* Israel is "stumbling" or will be saved, although it may be in part the reminder of these truths, but rather it is *why* Israel is stumbling and *how* Israel will be saved. And it is not that the gentile "Yes" precedes Israel's "Yes." The "mystery" is that the process God is employing to ensure Israel's "Yes" includes the temporary division of Israel, that is, it includes both the "Yes" of the remnant of presently restored Israel *and* the "No" of that part of Israel presently hardened (Yes/No) in order to initiate the gentile "Yes," and only "then, in this way" will the "Yes" of "all Israel" be completed.

God is involved in restoring Israel *through* the apostolic ministry, pruning those who are hardened so that the representatives of restored Israel may turn to the gentiles with the good news as promised. Israel is in the process of being divided so that she may be finally restored, and this process involves the suffering of those hardened, but certainly not their destruction. They may be grafted in again, joining with the remnant in constituting the restoration of "all Israel." To this end Paul has dedicated his life, and now he reveals this "mystery" so that his audience in Rome will likewise dedicate theirs.

This kind of revelation of how God is working differently than they currently assume would lead the Christian gentiles to reconsider their present status and role with regard to those "broken off" in the manner that makes sense of the balance of chapter 11 and the paraenesis of chapters 12–15. The Christian gentiles in Rome must realize that somehow the very hostility of those they regard as "enemies" is inextricably bound up with the "good news" to them: the "stumbling" are presently suffering on their very behalf (11:11, 30-31). They may appear to be "enemies," but they are actually "beloved" (11:28). This will open their eyes to how God is working toward them so that they can recognize that their obligation toward the "stumbling" is not to "grow wise in your own estimation" but to "think so as to have sound judgment, as God has allotted to each a measure of faith" (12:1-3, 4ff.). Rather than judging the "opinions" of the "stumbling" and disregarding the halakhot that applied to themselves as "righteous gentiles" when in their presence, they will see the depth of their responsibility to "bear the weaknesses of those without strength and not just please ourselves" as they refrain from destroying "with your food him for whom Christ died": "For he who in this way serves Christ is acceptable to God and approved by men" (14:13—15:1, 2ff.). And, of course, this would lead to Paul's vision of Christian gentiles confessing the Shema of faith in the midst of Israel "with one accord" in "one voice" glorifying "the God and Father of our Lord Jesus Christ" (15:5-12). His "offering" of the gentiles might then be found "acceptable" both in the sight of God and in the sight of Israel, where he is bringing the "fruit" of the gentile believers who in the "obedience of faith" recognize that they are "indebted" to Israel, for "the Gentiles have shared in their spiritual things" at great expense (15:14-32).

This reading makes sense of the power of the "mystery" to motivate Paul's mission to the gentiles on behalf of the "stumbling" of Israel and to effect a change in thinking and behavior on the part of the Christian gentiles in Rome, but does it make sense of the text of 11:25-28? To this question I now turn.

"A partial hardening has happened to Israel. . ."

Paul reaches back to the metaphor of hardening to illustrate the mystery of how God is dealing with a divided Israel. He has employed "stumbling" over the "stumbling stone" and the breaking off of branches as well as "hardening" to communicate the status of "the rest" as distinguished from "the remnant" of empirical Israel (11:7). "Hardening" (πώρωσις) is one of a group of biblical words derived from πῶρος, which was a medical term for the hardened swelling of a bone after it had been broken, resulting in a callus that is dull and insensitive.[53] Πώρωσις was used interchangeably with πήρωσις, "maiming" or "blinding," so often that there was eventually little or

[53]K. L. and M. A. Shmidt, *TDNT*, 5.1022–28.

no awareness of their difference in meaning, as their biblical contexts often overlapped.[54] These terms were frequently used to express the process of "strengthening" people in their resolve so that they persisted in the course which they had chosen, particularly when they might otherwise lose heart.[55] This process served the people of God, although often (but not always: e.g., Josh. 11:20) it was their adversary's hardening, such as Pharaoh's, that was necessary to bring about the eventual good.

Paul described the "hardening" of part of Israel ("the rest": οἱ λοιποὶ) in 11:7-10 from Deuteronomy 29:4, Isaiah 29:10 (cf. 6:10) and Psalm 69:22-23 in language similar to Luke's recording of Paul's language in Rome (Acts 28:25-27). This same kind of language with regard to Israel was developed in other literature of the time, as Wright observes:

> The explanation for the apparent inactivity of the covenant god at the present moment is that he is delaying in order to give time for more people to repent; if he were to act now, not only would the sons of darkness but a good number of the sons of light would be destroyed in the process. As a result of this process of delay, those who do not repent will be "hardened" so that, when the time comes, their punishment will be seen to be just.[56] (See, e.g., 2 Macc. 16:12ff.; Wisd. 12:19ff.; Sir. 5:4; *4 Ezra* 7:17-25; 9:11; 14:32.)

Paul is not describing rejection, but temporary discipline, a "strengthening" in the course they have chosen for themselves that demonstrates it is time to turn to the gentiles with the gospel *also*. Munck develops this implicit logic in Paul's use of hardening:

> The apostolate is a testimony to God's gracious will toward Israel, while at the same time Israel's unbelief expresses God's hardening of their hearts. In a way, chapter 10 makes the problem logically insoluble. The logical contradiction, however, includes the very factors that point the way to a solution. God's hardening implies a redemption purpose toward the Gentiles. The apostolate—and, as we shall see, the remnant—testifies to God's will to save, which is to achieve its purpose after the hardening has fulfilled its function. God hardens in order to save, and he will therefore save the obdurate as well.[57]

[54]Shmidt, *TDNT*, 5.1027–28.
[55]R. Forster and V. Marston, *God's Strategy in Human History*, pp. 155–70.
[56]Wright, *NT*, p. 271.
[57]Munck, *Christ and Israel*, p. 91.

There is an important distinction to note in Paul's choice of "hardening" to describe God's part in this process being revealed ("to Israel has happened": τῷ Ἰσραὴλ γέγονεν). "Hardening" has happened to "part of Israel"; he does not say "disobedience" or "unbelief" "has happened" to them. This nuance is maintained in the Biblical accounts, particularly noticeable in the case of Pharaoh, to recognize that while God may "strengthen" them in their chosen course to accomplish his purpose for his people, he does not choose their course for them. They have chosen not to believe; God has "strengthened" them in this course so that "salvation [comes] to the Gentiles, to make them jealous" (Rom. 11:11).[58] Or, as he will go on to phrase it in 11:28: "From the standpoint of the gospel they are enemies for your sake." They have been "hardened" in their chosen path in order both to bring the gospel to the gentiles, and to "save some of them" who are presently denying the gospel by provoking them to jealousy as they recognize that the promised ingathering of the gentiles has begun without them: the commencement of step two is thus revealed through the part "hardened." The present "stumbling" of "the rest" of Israel is somehow, in the "depths of the riches both of the wisdom and knowledge of God" (11:33), a blessing and not a curse, bringing salvation to the gentiles and provoking those of Israel who may not have reconsidered faith in Christ Jesus to do so. Moreover, once "the fulness of the Gentiles comes in," those hardened will no longer be so affected. Although they may not all choose faith in Christ Jesus at that time, they will no longer be "strengthened" in their "stumbling" in order to bring the gospel to gentiles, or in order to manifest their own need for grace. The temporary role of hardening will be over, and Paul hopes, so too will be their "stumbling."

"Partial hardening" (ἀπὸ μέρους) can be taken to mean "part" of the people were hardened, or that those who were hardened were only hardened "partially."[59] However, the discussion of chapters 9–11 has been concerned with that "part" of Israel that has been "stumbling,"

---

[58]This same distinction can be maintained in many of the accounts in Acts wherein the initial "wavering" with respect to Paul's gospel was not the signal to turn to the gentiles, but the signal to warn them not to bring upon themselves the cursed hardening the prophets had foretold. It was only when some of them became opposed to the gospel, sometimes violently, that Paul then turned to the gentiles fully (Acts 13:40-46, 47ff.; 18:4-6; 19:8-10; 28:23-28).

[59]For "part" of the people see Wright, *Climax*, p. 247; Dahl, *Studies in Paul*, pp. 152–53; Munck, *Christ and Israel*, p. 132. For all of Israel "partially" hardened see Gaston, *Paul*, p. 143; Dunn, *Romans*, p. 679.

not with all of Israel stumbling "partially." Certainly all Israel is not "hardened," even "partially"—after all, Paul and the remnant are the "holy root" that make the "branches" holy.[60] The viewpoint that would take this as all of Israel is partially hardened, even if for only a specific period of time, is based on a view of Israel rejecting the gospel, which was not Paul's view; it was precisely the view he was confronting as wrong.[61]

The context of Paul's explanation is how the present status of "the rest" of 11:7, the "some" of 11:14, 17, the "these" of 11:24, 31, and the "enemies" who are "beloved" of 11:28—while "stumbling," and "broken off," and "hardened"—have not "fallen" (11:11), although the Christian gentiles he is addressing are tempted to think so. The issue is one of quantification: the *hardened* part in contrast to the *remnant* part, who see and believe along with the newly grafted-in Christian gentiles.[62]

Paul has revealed the final phase of step one ("to the Jew *first*"): the "hardening" of "part" of Israel in their unbelief is not the conclusion of Israel's history, it is not a final punishment; it is part of the division of Israel that sets up the benefits of step two. For even the unbelief of "some" is being used in God's grand design; as we shall see, it was a sign to initiate the gentile mission as well as to restore "all Israel."

"until the fulness of the Gentiles has come in. . ."

This is the critical point around which turns the interpretation of Paul's revelation, and its expected impact. What would his audience understand him to mean?

"Until" (ἄχρι), functioning here as a conjunction, followed by the usually untranslated (genitive) relative pronoun οὗ, draws from the prepositional meanings "until" or "during," and gives this point a sense of future time and temporal sequence after which the hardening

---

[60]I find the suggestion that Paul or any other Christian Jew could have considered themselves "hardened" in the sense Paul is describing here simply incredible, though that would be the logical result of the qualitative view.

[61]Fraikin's otherwise wonderful treatment of Paul's handling of Israel breaks down when Fraikin concludes that Israel has rejected God, something Paul does not do ("Rhetorical Function," pp. 101–2).

[62]One could argue that God has "strengthened" Paul and the "remnant" in their resolve to fulfill their ministry on behalf of the salvation of "all Israel" even as he has "strengthened" the "stumbling" in theirs so that the gentile mission could be undertaken, but the context is here concerned with the process God is employing for the "part" of Israel "hardened" in their unbelief.

will have fulfilled its purpose: "until the time when."[63] After or during this time of hardening "the fulness of the Gentiles" takes place and the "strengthening" of part of Israel will have fulfilled its function.

Just what did Paul mean by "the fulness of the Gentiles"? Suggestions range from his forthcoming journey to Jerusalem with the collection[64] to his return to Jerusalem after his planned trip to Spain (the "ends of the earth": Tarshish) which would complete the period of preaching preceding the parousia,[65] to the entrance into the kingdom of God of "the full number that God has decreed from the beginning,"[66] to an apocalyptic time when "there will be a mass conversion and pilgrimage of the Gentiles to Zion (e.g., Isa. 2:2-3; Tob. 13:11),"[67] and even to seeking the answer in Luke 21:24: "and Jerusalem will be trampled underfoot by the Gentiles until the times of the gentiles be fulfilled."[68] Most take "fulness" to have a numeric quality: "the full number intended by God."[69] Munck is among those who take issue with this numerical approach, demonstrating several reasons for its weakness, and concluding instead that it means "the gospel will be first preached to all the Gentiles":[70] "'The fulness of the Gentiles' must signify the goal that the totality of the Gentile world— admittedly in a representative form—should hear the gospel, that is, both that the gospel should be preached to them, and that they should hear and believe."[71]

There is certainly no linguistic reason why "fulness" (πλήρωμα) should take on a numeric quality, as it has to do with "that which is

[63]Dunn, *Romans*, pp. 679–80.

[64]Munck, *Christ and Israel*, pp. 120–21.

[65]On Spain as the Tarshish of Isaiah and NT times and thus of Paul's ministry to the ends of the earth (Isa. 60:9; 66:18-24) see Aus, "Paul's Travel Plans," pp. 232–62, esp. pp. 237–46, 249–52; for his view of the significance of Paul's return to Jerusalem see pp. 256–62, stating on p. 260: "He has already won representatives there [eastern Mediterranean] from the major Gentile cities and nations to present them and their gifts to the Messiah in Jerusalem. He wishes to complete his eschatological task by also evangelizing in the area so often mentioned in the eschatological visions of the OT as the extremity of the world, Spain (Tarshish)."

[66]Dahl, *Studies in Paul*, p. 153, although not his final interpretation.

[67]Dunn, *Romans*, p. 691. See Wright, *Climax*, pp. 231–57, for the many problems with this and other eschatological approaches.

[68]Munck, *Christ and Israel*, pp. 135–36, discusses this view.

[69]Dunn, *Romans*, pp. 691, 680. So too Delling, *TDNT*, 6.302; Bauer, *Lexicon*, p. 672.

[70]Munck, *Christ and Israel*, p. 135.

[71]Ibid., pp. 133–35.

brought to fulness or completion."[72] It is best understood playing off
Paul's usage of πλήρωμα in Romans 11:12 to describe how much more
the "fulfillment" of Israel will transcend the current "riches" now
being realized as a result of Israel's stumbling, even as life is greater
than death (v. 14).[73] If Paul meant to communicate "the full number"
of gentiles in a numeric sense his point would have been better made
by using the same adjective he uses for Israel's destiny: "all" as in "all
gentiles saved first and then all Israel," certainly the sense the text is
most often given.

I suggest that the answer lies elsewhere. Paul employs the term
πεπληρωκέναι (perfect infinitive active of πληρόω) in Romans 15:19
to describe the "completion"[74] of his preaching of the gospel that has
brought the "obedience of faith" throughout the eastern spiral of his
ministry and heretofore kept him from reaching Rome and his western destinations.[75] Further, he intends to come eventually from Jeru-

---

[72]Bauer, *Lexicon*, p. 672.

[73]Munck, *Christ and Israel*, pp. 120–21: "If we assume, as do some commentators, both that the ἥττημα of the Jews alludes to the fact that in every city they
have refused to receive the gospel, and that the remark is thus current and practical as regards Israel's fall at the present day, then it is natural to take what follows
as also current and practical. The ζῆλος, then, which Paul is to stir up, and that
fullness of the Gentiles which is to lead Israel to salvation, are also to be interpreted as something current and practical. In this passage we get a glimpse of
Paul's thoughts as he collects the gift to Jerusalem and gradually realizes that this
journey with the collection may turn into a manifestation, a promulgation of the
fullness of the Gentiles, something that will impress not only Christians but the
Jews in Jerusalem as well. Both in Romans and in Acts we see that the journey to
Jerusalem concerns not merely the Jerusalem church but the non-believing Jews
of that place as well. Romans 15:31 speaks of the unbelievers in Judea as well as
of the saints in Jerusalem, and in Acts 21:11 it is said of Paul that the Jews shall
deliver him into the hands of the Gentiles (cf. Matthew 20:19, of Jesus; cf. Acts
21:20 [omit: τῶν πεπιστευκότων]). Paul goes up to Jerusalem fully expecting to
effect the great turning point in the life of his people by bringing with him a rep-
resentation of the fullness of the Gentiles."

[74]Bauer, *Lexicon*, p. 671. Dahl, *Studies in Paul*, p. 154, touches on this association
between 11:25 and 15:19-23 for understanding Paul's intentions, although he does
not pursue it.

[75]Used also in Col. 1:25 and 2 Tim. 4:17 in this same manner for the preaching
of the gospel to gentiles. Both contexts are very similar as well, Colossians even
mentioning the mystery of gentile salvation (1:25-27). Munck, *Christ and Israel*,
makes much of this similarity and concludes: "'The fulness of the Gentiles' then
signifies the achievement of the goal toward which Paul is striving during his
preaching of the gospel to the Gentiles: the completion of that preaching"
(p. 134).

salem to Rome "in the fulness [πλήρωματι: dative of πλήρωμα] of the blessing of Christ" (15:29). I propose that this associated use of πλήρωμα/πληρόω in these various contexts is no mere coincidence.

This process will be completed when "the fulness of the Gentiles *has come in*" (εἰσέλθη is the aorist subjunctive of εἰσέρχομαι: "come [in, into], go [in, into], enter"), which again carries the sense of time, "going, entering, beginning"; and figuratively it means to "come into something or share in something."[76] Since the context deals with a period of future time, εἰσέλθη carries the sense here of events that are coming or beginning. Munck concluded that it might be best rendered "begins": "until the fulness of the gentiles begins."[77] Particularly interesting is the observation of Dunn that Paul, who seldom uses this verb, may draw this usage of εἰσέρχομαι "on a pre-Pauline tradition which stems from Jesus" where it is frequently employed "in talk of entering into the 'kingdom' or into 'life.'"[78] This suggests that Paul has in mind with his choice of this particular verb the "*incoming* of Gentiles to Zion."[79]

This verb is generally seen as describing what will occur after the completion of Paul's ministry, or after all gentiles have been reached with the gospel, or after all gentiles have believed either down through history or at some far-off eschatological moment. But I suggest that it is describing the (eschatological) process taking place in Paul's ministry (yet in the future for Rome since he has not yet been there), not some distant eschatological event (i.e., the parousia).[80] It is what will occur after the hardening of part of Israel has completed its function, signaling that it is time for the fullness of the gentiles to *begin*.

A close look at Luke's account of Paul's missionary program clarifies Paul's language in Romans. Luke traces Paul's two-step pattern of

---

[76]Schneider, *TDNT*, 2.676–78; Bauer, *Lexicon*, pp. 232–33; Munck, *Christ and Israel*, p. 132.

[77]Munck, *Christ and Israel*, p. 132.

[78]Dunn, *Romans*, pp. 680–81.

[79]Ibid. (emphasis added).

[80]Segal, *Paul*, pp. 281–84, notes similarly that Paul was meditating on events he was experiencing and not the final fate and destiny of history. For other examples noting the present aspect of Paul's meaning, in various ways and not necessarily similar to the pattern described herein, but in tension with an apocalyptic expectation, see Dahl, *Studies in Paul*, pp. 152-54; Munck, *Christ and Israel*, pp. 112–13, 120–21, 136; C. Stanley, "The Redeemer will come," pp. 140–41; Richardson, *Israel in the Apostolic Church*, p. 146; Wright, *Climax*, pp. 249–51; F. F. Bruce, *Paul*, p. 335; D. W. B. Robinson, "Salvation," pp. 92–96.

going to the Jews in each location first before turning fully to the gentiles with the gospel, precisely what Paul is indicating in revealing this
mystery to the audience in Rome.

Excursus: The "Fulness of the Gentiles" in Luke's Portrayal of Paul's Two-Step Missionary Pattern

Luke sketched the outline of Acts around the striking success (not the
rejection) of the apostolic mission to Israel which represented the
restoration of Israel as promised (Acts 15:13-18)—appealing constantly
to the multitudes of believing Jews to highlight this point (Acts 2:41, 47;
4:4; 5:14; 6:1, 7; 9:31, 42; 12:24; 13:43; 14:1; 17:10-12; 19:20; 21:20).[81]
This pattern progresses from the initial "three thousand souls" of 2:41
and "five thousand men" of 4:4 through the "multitudes" of 5:14, including even "a great many of the priests" (6:7), to the eventual observation of James to Paul upon his arrival in Jerusalem: "You see, brother,
how many *thousands* there are among the Jews of those who have
believed, and they are all zealous for the Law" (21:20).

Just as important as the focus on the thousands of believing Jews is
Luke's ineluctable concern to communicate the fact that they represent
faithful Jews, orthodox Jews, Jews who are respected by their peers for
fidelity to the Law and to Israel (2:41; cf. 2:5 "devout"; 6:7 "priests";
17:11 "noble"; 18:8 "leader of the synagogue"; 21:20 "all zealous for the
Law"; 21:24 "walk orderly, keeping the Law"; 22:3; 24:16-17; 25:8).[82]
Further, these are Jews for whom the restoration of Israel is of utmost
importance (1:6; 2:46; 3:1, 21; 5:12; 10:9ff.; 11:2; 15:1-18; 21:20—22:3ff.;
23:6; 24:14-21; 26:4-7; 28:20). Moreover, the Jews who do not accept the
gospel or even oppose it are not pictured as rejecting some new faith or
institution; rather, they are rejecting Abraham and Moses and the
prophets, they are rejecting the hope of resurrection and the Messiah—
thereby cutting themselves off from the promises to Israel (3:19-26;
13:46; 14:1-4; 17:3; 23:6-10; 24:14-21; 26:22-23).[83]

---

[81]Jervell, *Luke*, pp. 44–46.

[82]Ibid., pp. 46, 51.

[83]See Richardson, *Israel in the Apostolic Church*, appendix C, for a discussion of
the common exclusivist tendency for Jewish sects or factions, particularly the
Qumran community, to define themselves as the purified remnant representing
Israel and the others as outcasts. P. Esler, *Community and Gospel in Luke-Acts*, pp.
65–70, discusses the sociological dimension of this development from reform
movement to sect and concludes on pp. 69–70 "that central to Luke's composition
of a unique history, which encompassed the Jesus story and its sequel in Acts, was
an ardent desire to present Christianity as the legitimate development of Judaism.
. . . He presented their new faith as if it were old and established, as the divinely

What Luke reveals is an Israel sharply divided over Jewish concerns: many Jews in each synagogue community believe that this is the good news promised to Israel, and many do not (4:1-4; 5:12-20; 6:7-14, 15ff.; 9:28-29; 13:16-41, 42-51; 14:1-4;[84] 17:1-5, 10-13; 18:4-11, 19-20; 19:8-10; 28:17-27). Those who believe continue within the Jewish institutions; they are not converts. They are believers in Israel's promises, worshiping in Israel's institutions, and keepers of Israel's faith and Torah.[85] They function within Judaism, in the manner in which Luke would label a "sect" of Judaism (28:22).[86] Those who do not are warned that they risk being purged from the people of God. Jervell summarizes this dynamic with striking simplicity: "The picture is clear: Israel has not rejected the gospel, but has become divided over the issue . . . 'empirical' Israel is composed of two groups, the repentant (i.e., Christian) and the obdurate. It is important for Luke to show that the Jewish Christian church is a part of Israel."[87]

We are thus prepared to recognize that for Luke the commencement of the gentile mission was based not on Israel's rejection but on the belief that her promised restoration had begun, with the inherent obligation to proclaim this message to all the nations (Acts 15:13-18). For Luke "Israel" always refers to the Jewish people.[88] "Israel" does not refer to the church, and Luke does not know of a "new Israel." The mission to include the gentiles in the people of God is conceived in Jewish terms: they are admitted as "righteous gentiles" and taught to obey the appropriate halakhah as outlined in the apostolic decree (15:19-29). The continuity of salvation history is maintained through the restoration of historical Israel to which gentiles are now attached through faith in Israel's God, although without becoming Israelites

---

sanctioned outgrowth of Judaism. . . . In other words, Judaism was a faith which carried within itself the seeds of its own transformation. So Luke could console his fellow-Christians with the message that it was not they but Jews still attending the synagogue who had abandoned the God of Abraham, Isaac and Jacob, of Moses and of David."

[84] This is an interesting passage in which even the "multitude of the city was divided; and some sided with the Jews, and some with the apostles," who are still clearly Jews divided over a synagogue matter (v. 1).

[85] Jervell, *Luke*, p. 142: "The mark of distinction between Christian Jews and other Jews is not law or circumcision. The mark of distinction is that the Christian Jews believe *all things* in the law and the prophets, which includes the acceptance of the circumcised Messiah promised the people and now come."

[86] Esler, *Community and Gospel*, pp. 68–69, discusses that αἱρέσεως would be better understood as "parties or movements within Judaism and not sects whose members could no longer be said to belong to the wider Israel."

[87] Jervell, *Luke*, p. 49.

[88] Ibid., pp. 43, 49, 53ff.

themselves. Again Jervell sums up this important basis for the gentile mission poignantly:

> Luke's explanation is very simple, perhaps too simple: The church is Israel, and it is Israel because it is "filled" with penitent and pious Jesus-believing Jews, circumcised Jews. The church is not the other or new Israel in relation to the old. The church is merely Israel, the old Israel living in the Messiah epoch of the history of the people of God. We should notice, however, that it is not the church as a whole which is called Israel, but the law-obedient Jewish Christians within the church.[89]

In Acts, the apostolic mission to the gentiles was thus sketched as restored Israel's eschatological mission "to proclaim light both to the Jewish people and to the Gentiles" (Acts 26:23; cf. Luke 24:44-47; Acts 1:6-8; 3:18-26;[90] 9:14-15 [cf. 22:12-21; 25:14-20, 23]; 13:46-48). Likewise, the Jerusalem Council appealed to the manifestation of Israel's restoration (not rejection) by the eschatological ingathering of the nations in fulfillment of prophecy in concluding that gentiles were to be admitted to the people of God without becoming Jews (Acts 15:13-18).[91] Even Paul's warnings to those questioning his message are a sign of prophetic fulfillment, not rejection (13:40-41).

Paul's declaration of "turning to the Gentiles" in Acts 13:46, often regarded as demonstrating that the gentile mission is predicated upon the rejection of Israel, indicates quite the opposite for Paul. Paul explained that he was doing so, that he *must* do so, to *fulfill* the prophetic "commandment" of God to be a light for the gentiles in bringing salvation to the whole world:

> It was necessary that the word of God should be spoken to you first; since you repudiate it, and judge yourselves unworthy of eternal life, behold, we are turning to the Gentiles. For thus the Lord has commanded us, "I have placed you as a light for the Gentiles, that you should bring salvation to the end of the earth." (13:46-47)

The mission to the gentiles was not understood by Jews to indicate their own condemnation; it would one day be their privilege to declare

---

[89]Jervell, "Mighty Minority," p. 28.

[90]Jervell, *Luke*, pp. 58–60, for an excellent discussion of Abraham's seed as Israel and "the families of the earth" as gentiles so that Peter's meaning is that this news is for Israel "first."

[91]The example of Cornelius is not concerned with whether gentiles should hear the message or be saved; the issue is whether they are to remain gentiles or become Jews (Acts 10), just as it was at the Council. See Jervell, *Luke*, pp. 64–67.

the One God of Israel to the nations. Paul's declaration follows the
warning of 13:40-41 to be careful lest they become the recipients of the
prophetic curses which witness that they have failed to share in the
blessings:

> Take heed [βλέπετε: "watch" or "be careful"] therefore, so that
> the thing spoken of in the Prophets may not come upon you:
> "Behold, you scoffers, and marvel, and perish; for I am accom-
> plishing a work in your days, a work which you will never
> believe, though someone should describe it to you."

Paul's warning cannot mean that Jews should "be careful" lest the
gospel goes to the gentiles.[92] He is warning them, in keeping with the
conclusions of the council, not to fail to recognize that the restoration of
Israel is taking place before their very eyes, made manifest not so much
by the gospel going to Israel, but by the gospel going to the gentiles as
a sign of Israel's eschatological mission, and thus as a sign that Israel's
restoration had indeed begun. Paul was warning them not to miss the
significance of what was taking place in his apostolic ministry; beginning with the proclamation of the good news to Israel *first* to restore and
cleanse Israel as promised, and then bringing this good news to the nations *also*. Paul was pleading with them: "Watch out! Do not let yourselves be among those purged!"

It is not because of the rejection of some of his fellow Jews that Paul
turned to the gentiles, but in spite of their rejection.[93] Their failure will
not stand in the way of the purposes of God.[94] Their rejection functioned rather as a *sign* that Paul's first step was completed—Israel (as
represented in that location) was restored (at least in part), having heard
the good news. Now it was time to begin step two, to fulfill God's commandment to be a light to the gentiles, so that God's promises to all humankind could be completed. The pattern of salvation history as traced
in Paul's apostolic ministry by Luke is based on the "Yes" of Israel first,
with the "No" on the part of some of Israel signaling that the restoration was now well underway so that the eschatological function of restored Israel as the messenger of the good news to the nations could
now *begin*, bringing about the full "Yes" of believing gentiles who proclaim the One God of Israel as the One God of all the world.

Of course, one must recognize that although Paul had decidedly
turned to the gentiles in Pisidian Antioch, his ministry to Israel was far

---

[92]Ibid., pp. 60–64, 165. Note that the issue among Jews, even in their accusations against Paul, are not about gentile converts but about their relationship to
the Law and circumcision.

[93]Ibid., p. 63.

[94]Precisely Paul's point in Rom. 3:3ff.

from complete. Throughout the rest of Acts he continued to go first to the synagogues of each city he entered, and only after the audience was divided over his message did he turn to the gentiles of that city (14:1-4; 17:1-5, 10-13; 18:4-11, 19-20; 19:8-10; 28:17-27). This two-step pattern ("custom") throughout his ministry reveals that Paul was taking the good news of Israel's blessings throughout the Diaspora to the children of Jacob first, restoring and purging, until all of Israel had heard. Only then, as the representative of restored (albeit divided) Israel in each new location, did he turn fully to step two and the matter of including gentiles among the people of God. Paul's apostolic ministry maintained the continuity of salvation history: the gospel brings Israel's restoration first, only then as a representative of restored Israel did Paul turn fully to bring light to the gentiles so that they might also share in the promised blessings, or in Paul's turn of phrase: "until the fulness of the Gentiles begins."[95]

Paul's intention in Romans is to communicate his forthcoming preaching of the gospel in Rome. He is not speaking of when the gentile mission is finished, but when it is begun, signaling the *commencement* of the gentile mission that will complete the purpose of "strengthening" part of Israel in their unbelief. Paul thus revealed information about a period of time in the future that would not be obvious to the Christian gentiles without knowledge of this mystery, a period that would not come "*until [the time when]* the fulness of the Gentiles *begins*" its purpose with regard to the part of Israel presently hardened. This period of time would be recognized by his audience as "the fulness of the Gentiles," a phrase he apparently thought they would be able to understand in the context he was developing. After all, he expected this concept to impact them significantly, resulting in their humble recognition of the plight of the "stumbling" of Israel and their self-offering on Israel's behalf (Rom. 12:1-3). However, just what Paul intended by this phrase has not been so obvious to interpreters since, and most suggestions fail to come close to anything that would have motivated a change of heart for his readers.

This "mystery" is set in the future, "until the time when," because while Paul has worked this way in the east he has not yet been to Rome and the west. The gospel has not yet turned "*fully* to the in-

---

[95]Jervell, *Luke*, pp. 57–60, observes that even the speeches to gentiles speak of the commission to Israel and are directed to Jews, while the speeches to Jews speak of the gentile mission.

gathering of gentiles" in Rome (even though some gentiles there have heard and believed it) *until* the gospel has gone first to the representatives of Israel there (the synagogues), dividing Israel as it restores the remnant and prunes the part hardened, and *only then* turning *fully* to *the gentiles* ("until [the time when] the fulness of the Gentiles begins"), not to condemn the part hardened, nor to make them angry, but to provoke them to jealousy so that he might "save some of them." The "fulness of the Gentiles" is thus the full *commencement* of the gentile mission in a given location when Paul, having *first* proclaimed the good news to Israel and having reached a decisive point in which the division is clear (Jews believing in Jesus as Israel's Christ are the remnant of restored Israel, and Jews not believing this are those presently hardened), warned those rejecting his message and turned *fully* to proclaim the gospel to the nations *also*.

The mystery of 11:25-28 in its surrounding context resonates with Paul's uncompromising intention to save his "stumbling brethren," even in, or as he seems to indicate, especially through his apostolic ministry to the gentiles. He hopes that his ministry provokes them to jealousy leading to faith, for it demonstrates to his brothers and sisters that the eschatological promises of the "ingathering of the gentiles" are now being fulfilled before their very eyes: Israel has been restored and her representatives are turning fully to bring the light to believing gentiles as foretold—"beware, lest you suffer the curse and not the blessing," is his warning cry. "Beware, lest gentiles embrace fully what you deny yourself." Part of Israel has been hardened to her salvation "until the time when the fulness of the gentiles begins"—step two, when God "opened a door of faith to the Gentiles" (Acts 14:27), the time when Paul turns to "fully preach the gospel of Christ" (Rom. 15:19; cf. Acts 13:46) to gentiles (as he has throughout the eastern spiral of his apostolic mission resulting in "obedience of faith" among gentiles), thus initiating the "fulness of the blessing of Christ" (Rom. 15:29; Acts 13:47-49) for those formerly outside the promises of God so that "as many as had been appointed to eternal life believed" (Acts 13:48).[96]

This reading answers the call to recognize the motivational stimulation intended in the revealing of this mystery to the Christian gentiles in Rome who believe Israel has fallen and they have supplanted

---

[96]Rom. 15:18-19, 20ff., 29; Acts 13:46-49.

her: "May it never be! But by their transgression salvation (comes) to the Gentiles, to make them jealous" (Rom. 11:11).[97]

Now they can see that even Paul's very apostleship to the gentiles is intended for the salvation of Israel (11:13-14). They are somehow, in God's unsearchable judgments and unfathomable ways, benefiting from the "stumbling" of the part of Israel, whom they are so quick to condemn for not believing what they now believe (11:30-36). Certainly, this is cause for humility where arrogance had once been tempting, laying the groundwork for the commitment Paul urges from 12:1 onward toward God, brothers and sisters, enemies, neighbors, and the "stumbling" of Israel—the very bearing of the "weaknesses of those without strength" (those "unable" to yet believe as they do themselves) in the tradition of the suffering of Christ Jesus (15:1-3).

"and thus all Israel will be saved. . ."

We come now to the real goal of Paul's ministry, regardless of how things may appear at the present time to those unaware of the mystery: the restoration of "all Israel" as God had promised.

"And thus" (καὶ οὕτως) is descriptive of a process and is perhaps best translated "and thus, in this manner or way,"[98] which allows the phrase to carry both the sense of the process and of time, playing off the earlier "until the time when . . . begins." This balance allows one to avoid the bifurcation most interpreters find necessary to support their larger reading of Paul's message here.[99] Paul is telling his reader both *how* and *when* God is saving "all Israel," though it need not have the commonly assumed sense of cataclysmic finality.[100]

Most importantly, it is "all Israel" (πᾶς Ἰσραὴλ) who "will be

[97]D. W. B. Robinson, "Salvation" p. 93, notes: "The final and summary statement of 'the mystery' in 11:25f., then, looks back, not to the olive tree illustration, but to the earlier intimations of the chapter (11:11-14) about 'provoking to emulation.'"

[98]Wright, *Climax*, pp. 249–50; Bauer, *Lexicon*, pp. 597–98; Munck, *Christ and Israel*, p. 152; Beker, *Paul the Apostle*, p. 314; D. W. B. Robinson, "Salvation," pp. 93–94; Dunn, *Romans*, p. 681: "the basic sense of οὕτως is 'thus, in this manner,' referring to Paul's conviction that conversion of the Gentiles will be the means of provoking Israel to jealousy and converting them." Compare also the usage in Gal. 6:2. So too Sanders, *Paul, the Law*, pp. 193–94.

[99]Wright, *Climax*, p. 249, for example.

[100]Ibid., p. 249ff., argues against this common reading too.

saved" (σωθήσεται).[101] While Paul's reference to Israel's restoration generates little debate,[102] being a common theme of Jewish eschatology (e.g., Deut. 30:1-5; Neh. 1:9; Jer. 23:3; 29:14; Ezek. 11:17; 36:24; Amos 9:11-15; Mic. 2:12; 4:6-7; Zeph. 3:19-20; Zech. 10:8-10; Sir. 36:11; Bar. 4:37; 2 Macc. 2:18; *Jub.* 1.15, 22-25; 50.5; *Pss. Sol.* 17.26-28; 1QSa 1.1-6; 4Q174 1.10-13),[103] the introduction of "all" has created a great many interpretations.[104] Whom does Paul mean for his audience to understand by "all Israel"?

It is difficult to imagine in a letter that maintains throughout the distinction between Jews and gentiles (whether they be Christians or not), particularly in this context of explaining the destiny of empirical Israel to Christian gentiles so that they will realize the current state of the "stumbling" of Israel is not as it appears, that Paul would suddenly

[101]Stanley, "Redeemer Will Come," p. 139: "In the tradition, as in Scripture, the verb σώζειν and its cognates (σωτήρ, σωτηρία, and so on) are used often to describe what Yahweh will do when he comes to restore his people." Sanders, *Paul and Palestinian Judaism*, pp. 125–46, 212–38, for rabbinic literature on topics concerning salvation.

[102]See the discussion of eschatological expectations of salvation primarily conceived in corporate terms of Israel's restoration rather than individual salvation in chapter 2 above. See especially Wright, *NT*, pp. 273, 300–301, 334–38; note his comments on pp. 300–301: "A word is necessary at this point about the meaning of the term 'salvation' in the context of the Jewish expectation. It ought to be clear by now that within the worldview we have described there can be little thought of the rescue of Israel consisting of the end of the space-time universe, and/or of Israel's future enjoyment of non-physical, 'spiritual' bliss. That would simply contradict creational monotheism, implying that the created order was residually evil, and to be simply destroyed. . . . Rather, the 'salvation' spoken of in the Jewish sources of this period has to do with rescue from the national enemies, restoration of the national symbols, and a state of 'shalom' in which every man will sit under his vine or fig-tree. 'Salvation' encapsulates the entire future hope. If there are Christian redefinitions of the word later on, that is another question. For first-century Jews it could only mean the inauguration of the age to come, liberation from Rome, the restoration of the Temple, and the free enjoyment of their own Land. . . . The age to come, the end of Israel's exile, was therefore seen as the inauguration of a new covenant between Israel and her god."

[103]Allison, "Background," pp. 229–34; Dahl, *Studies in Paul*, pp. 152–53; Dunn, *Romans*, p. 681; E. Johnson, *Function*, pp. 124–31, 162–63; Aune, *Prophecy*, pp. 252–53.

[104]See Sanders, *Paul and Palestinian Judaism*, pp. 147–82, for a thorough discussion of R. Joshua's statement that "All Israel—there is for them a share in the world to come" (literal translation of Sanders [p. 182] for *m. Sanh.* 10.1) and related statements in rabbinic literature (also pp. 367–83 for this theme in *Jubilees*).

shift his meaning of "Israel" to that of "true" or "spiritual" Israel (by which most really mean to say that the "church" has supplanted Israel, the very point Paul is arguing against).[105] This interpretation owes more to the presupposition that Israel has been rejected than to what Paul is affirming here, notably, to counter just such an assumption on the part of his audience.[106] No, indeed the church has not supplanted Israel as the people of God; rather, the foundation of the church is built on the shoulders of the restoration of "all Israel."

While Paul does make a distinction among Jews between the "remnant" and the "part hardened" so that he can say "they are not all Israel who are descended from Israel" (Rom. 9:6), it makes little sense of Paul's revelation to read this as "all the remnant of Israel will be saved" or "all the remnant of Israel and believing gentiles will be saved." First, it misses the point of Paul's explanation for the role of the remnant, evident most clearly in his own ministry to the gentiles as the representative of the whole of Israel in order to save "some" of them. Second, it reveals no mystery, certainly not one that would affect Christian gentile attitudes as Paul proposes this information will do; they already accept that there are Christian Jews, albeit a very small minority of the congregation in Rome.

"All Israel" was a common idiom for corporate Israel,[107] for Israel as "a whole," that is, as a people, even if every individual was not necessarily present (e.g., 1 Sam. 25:1; 1 Kgs. 12:1; 2 Chr. 12:1; Dan. 9:11; *Jub.* 50.9; *T. Levi* 17.5; *T. Jos.* 20.5; *T. Ben.* 10.11; Ps.-Philo 22.1; 23.1). Paul has maintained a distinction throughout between the "remnant" and

---

[105]For discussion of the historical development of this substitution see Richardson, *Israel in the Apostolic Church*, pp. 131–32, 146–47, 200–206. Richardson (pp. 205–6) points out that Justin Martyr was the first to call the church "true Israel" (ca. 160). Wright, *Climax*, pp. 249–51, discusses problems with usual substitution and suggests a "Pauline polemical redefinition" wherein gentiles join with the remnant of Christian Jews to make a "whole people." Notwithstanding Wright's keen awareness of the process Paul is describing, his view seems to be but another way of saying that Israel is the church. Paul, however, continues to maintain a distinction between Israelites and gentile believers in Christ, between Israel and the community of believers in Christ inclusive of gentiles, between natural and wild branches, etc. See also the comments of Campbell, *Intercultural Context*, in his essay on "Paul's Strategy in Writing Romans," pp. 132–60.

[106]Dahl, *Studies in Paul*, pp. 157–58: "Gentile Christians soon came to believe that God had rejected Israel, that, much to the advantage of the Gentiles, he had gathered for himself a new people from among them; Jewish Christians they treat as a special case."

[107]Dunn, *Romans*, p. 681.

the "rest" (Rom. 11:5-7, 8ff.), and his goal in provoking his brothers and sisters to jealousy was to "save *some* of them" (v. 14). So here it is some of his brothers and sisters from the "part hardened" that he sees coming back to join the "remnant" of Christian Jews in restored Israel: "and thus, in this way, all Israel shall be saved."[108]

The two-step pattern can be clearly seen operating in this language. While Dunn does not have my reading of this two-step pattern in mind (and while he may well object to my conclusions), he reads the tension similarly:

> The way in which the pendulum had swung *from* Israel *to* the Gentiles and would swing *back again* to Israel had already been clearly enough articulated (10:19; 11:11-14): Israel would be saved by being made jealous at the sight of Gentiles enjoying what had been their privileges (9:4-5), and so provoked into abandoning their unbelief in Jesus their Messiah and into acceptance of the gospel (1:16).[109]

There are two steps here: one, the division of Israel evident when some (the part hardened) deny Paul's message, which indicates that the remnant have been restored, and thus that it is time for step two, the initiation of the gentile mission (the fullness of the gentiles), when

---

[108]Dahl, *Studies in Paul*, p. 153: "The context makes clear that 'all Israel' refers both to the remnant and to 'the others.' Paul does not affirm that every individual Israelite will attain salvation, but that God will grant salvation to both parts of his people, to those who have rejected Christ as well as to those who have believed in him." So too Dunn, *Romans*, p. 681; Munck, *Christ and Israel*, p. 136; Johnson, "Romans 11," pp. 100–103.

It is likely that Paul hoped this would include all of his brothers and sisters, as in every individual one of them. But the text here is concerned with revealing the process that God is employing for bringing about the restoration of Israel in a surprising way more than it is concerned with explaining how every Jew will be saved. Even the term "salvation" tends to color the focus for the later reader of Romans in a way that it would not for a first-century audience, for whom the restoration of a people would have been a more present concern than the individualism of our Western culture since then.

[109]Dunn, *Romans*, p. 691 (emphasis added). Dunn seems to see the swing from Israel due to the rejection of the gospel, as do most (e.g., Munck, *Christ and Israel*, pp. 18–19, 120–25; Stendahl, *Paul*, pp. 28–29), and he believes also, as do most, that it is gentiles' appropriating Israel's blessings in their salvation that will provoke Jews to jealousy rather than Paul's ministry fulfilling the privileges of Israel as the cause for jealousy; however, he sees that the process is the point of Paul's message in a manner that suggests the accuracy of the reading I am suggesting herein.

the positive response of gentiles bears witness to the truth of Paul's message of Israel's present restoration, which triggers a jealous reconsidering of the good news he proclaimed, "and thus, in this way, all Israel will be saved."

The future sense in Paul's language is significant, and necessarily eschatological; however, it need not describe the parousia or any cataclysmic apocalyptic event in the distant future initiated by God: in Rome, the process of "fulness of the gentiles" (turning to the gentiles with the gospel) has not yet "begun."[110] Paul has not yet been to Rome to carry out this pattern in the "fulness of the blessing of Christ" and

---

[110]Paul has argued that the power of God for salvation has already been demonstrated, and for the Jew first (1:16). Paul is not arguing here for a new act of God (parousia) in order to save Israel, as though the first act had failed (perhaps the context for understanding Paul's concern with not being ashamed of the gospel; indeed, perhaps it helps explain the larger complex of shame/hope woven throughout Romans). Paul is involved in a process that may appear to some to be failing (or rather to have failed), but he is arguing that it has not failed even if it does appear to be failing from their limited vantage point in Rome before the mystery of what is really happening is revealed (a position later Christian interpreters find difficult to recognize as they look back on the evidence which suggests that it did ultimately fail in Paul's time, a view adumbrated in the opinion of the Christian gentiles in Rome). He is explaining the results of his apostolic ministry that follow from the process he is describing, including provoking his "stumbling" Jewish brothers and sisters to jealousy and reconsideration of the gospel. Note how the observation of Gager, *Origins*, pp. 259–60, harmonizes with this point: "A final modification involves the eschatological framework that determines all of Paul's activity. We need only mention here that Paul certainly expected the final events (Rom. 8:18-25; I Cor. 14; I Thess. 4:13-18) in his own lifetime. When he speaks of the *pleroma* of the Gentiles who are to come in and of Israel's return, he is thinking in terms of years—not even decades, let alone centuries or millennia. The preconditions for the final events were well underway. On Paul's shrunken globe, the *pleroma* of the Gentiles seems to have been equivalent to what lay between 'Arabia' (Gal. 1:17) and Spain (Rom. 15:24). In short, all of these momentous events were well underway and pressing forward to their end as Paul wrote his letters. Thus when we read of Israel's trespass, failure, and rejection, we must remember that for Paul their duration was to continue for 20 years, not 2,000." Also Dunn, *Romans*, p. 18: "Paul seriously contemplated this outreach being achieved within his lifetime, as the last act before the end and the necessary preliminary to the salvation of Israel (1 Cor 4:9; Rom 11:13-27)." Räisänen, "Paul, God," p. 191, also notes this tension: "If 11:25-26 is interpreted in the light of v. 12 (τὸ πλήρωμα αὐτῶν corresponds with τὸ πλήρωμα τῶν ἐθνῶν) and vv. 14-15, it seems quite possible that Paul expected the final conversion of Israel to take place in the course of his—and others'—proclamation of the gospel. While a miracle is necessary, it is perhaps not worked through a deus ex machina but is worked through the agency of God's apostles."

thus has not yet "fully preached the gospel of Christ" as he has in the eastern spiral of his ministry. He will soon, and when he does come from Zion to Rome to exercise his "spiritual gift" they will be "established" in the faith and recognize how God has been working with and through the restoration and division of Israel, as well as through the gentile mission, in order to bring about the eschatological restoration of "all Israel" as promised. They will then understand the critical importance of continuing to "obey the teaching they have learned," the halakhot of "righteous gentiles" worshiping in the midst of the Jewish community as outlined in the apostolic decree for Christian gentiles. They will respectfully commit themselves to demonstrating love for those "for whom Christ died" by confessing the Shema of faith in "one accord" with "one voice" in the One God, "the Father of our Lord Jesus Christ," in a way that is "acceptable to God and approved by men." "And thus, in this way, all Israel will be saved."

"Just as it is written, . . ."

"The Deliverer will come from Zion,
He will remove ungodliness from Jacob."
"And this is My covenant with them,
when I take away their sins." (11:26-27)

This process, while set out anew in Paul's revelation, was foretold by the prophets; it is not a new idea even if it is a new way to understand an old one.[111] Paul supports his revelation, or derives it, from a combination of Isaiah 27:9 and 59:20 (also possibly Isa. 2:3; Mic. 4:2; Jer. 31:34), passages that "portray Yahweh as a military hero who comes to rescue his people from a state of 'darkness' and 'captivity'."[112]

---

[111]See Hays, *Echoes*, pp. 34–83, 154–92, for a brilliant description of Paul's development of the prophetic literature and themes in Romans, particularly Deuteronomy, Isaiah, and the Psalms. Note Hays on p. 171: "Paul stands, however presumptuous it may be for him to do so, directly in Israel's prophetic biblical tradition. He does experience present time as a time of God-dominated events; he does see his own ministry as part of the consequential flow of time from Abraham to the present. He does believe that God is speaking through him. Hence, the freedom of his intertextual tropes. The circumspect sense of temporal estrangement from Bible time is completely lacking from his readings of the text. Also lacking, therefore, is the dutiful desire to preserve and repeat the precise words of a holy 'once upon a time' when God was present and spoke to his people; God speaks now."

Paul's choice of these particular passages is portrayed eloquently by
Christopher Stanley:

> Though the story is not identical, the obvious parallels between this
> passage [Isa. 27:9] and Isa. 59.20—63.7 make it easy to see why an an-
> cient reader (who worked from the premise of a unified Scripture)
> might have felt compelled to interpret the one passage in the light of
> the other. Even today, reading the two passages with a view to harmo-
> nization produces a stereophonic effect that could hardly be missed by
> a reader attuned to the cadences of both passages. In one ear sound the
> woeful confession of sinful Israel; in the other, the impassioned plea of
> the "righteous" for vindication. Yahweh's "coming" answers to both of
> these needs, not only removing the ungodliness of his people but also
> rescuing them from their oppressors. The picture of the divine warrior
> marching forth from his sanctuary to destroy his foes becomes a cipher
> for the armies of Israel advancing in the power of Yahweh against their
> ungodly neighbors. In both scenes the victory is complete: the nations
> and their rulers submit not only to the armies of Israel but also to Israel's
> God. Both passages reach their climax in the return of the dispersed
> children of Israel to their land, in the one case by the supernatural ac-
> tivity of Yahweh himself, in the other by the hand of the defeated na-
> tions. The final scene shows the fulfillment of all the dreams and aspi-
> rations cherished by Yahweh's people over the years: eternal peace and
> security in their own land, immeasurable wealth and prosperity, the rule
> of justice and righteousness in every sphere of life, honor and tribute
> from the surrounding nations, and above all the presence of Yahweh
> among his holy people. What Jew could fail to find hope and reassur-
> ance in such a glorious future?[113]

Much is made of Paul's substitution of ἐκ Σιὼν ("out of [*from*]
Zion") for ἕνεκεν Σιὼν ("*for the sake of* Zion").[114] A host of explanations have been offered, ranging from a memory lapse to an intentional
corruption of the text to the adaptation of an earlier Christian tradition.
Stanley's explanation seems the most probable, namely, that this is not
a Pauline adaptation but rather Paul was quoting from a contemporary
Jewish tradition: "the expectation that Yahweh would come 'out of
Zion' to 'redeem' his people (especially those in the Diaspora) from
their pagan overlords was common in early Judaism."[115] While Jews in

[112]Stanley, "Redeemer Will Come," p. 120.
[113]Ibid., pp. 130–31.
[114]For an excellent discussion of the variations in this citation see Stanley, *Paul
and the Language*, pp. 166–71; idem, "Redeemer Will Come."

Palestine would be awaiting the Deliverer who comes *to* or *for* Zion, those of the dispersion would be awaiting the Deliverer who comes *from* Zion, after having first delivered the land he would then come to bring them back from their exile (examples of the Lord's reign reaching out ἐκ Σιὼν are many, e.g., Pss. 14:7; 110:2; Joel 4:16; Amos 1:2; Mic. 4:2).[116]

How will "the Deliverer" accomplish this task of restoring "Jacob" (regathering the dispersed of Israel)?[117] The Deliverer, which need not be taken christologically to make sense of Paul's application here,[118] will "come out from Zion." This is set in the future, as is the revelation of the mystery ("he will come": ἥξει). *What* will the Deliverer do? He will "remove ungodliness from Jacob." *When* will he do this? "When I take away their sins" as God has promised in his "covenant."[119] Paul thus cites this Scripture to parallel the mystery he has just contextualized for his audience: the process that God is employing (*how*: "and thus, in this way") to ensure the salvation of "all Israel" (*what*), which will come after the function of hardening has accomplished its task of signaling the initiation of the gentile mission in each diaspora city and is thereafter removed (*when*: "until the time when *the fulness of the Gentiles* begins").

Pinchas Lapide noted similarly that the tension was not so much in *what* Paul was teaching, but in Paul's view of where Israel was in relation to *when* these things were to take place:

> The dawning of the new age was regarded neither as a breakaway from the traditions of Israel nor as an invasion into the Gentile world, and certainly not as the abolition of Torah. Quite the opposite; it was seen as the long-awaited manifestation of the universal basic purpose of God's teaching from Sinai—a worldwide ecumenical fellowship of Jews

[115]Stanley, "Redeemer Will Come," pp. 126ff.

[116]Ibid., pp. 132–35. Note that ἕνεκεν Σιὼν occurs only here in the Septuagint.

[117]Sanders, *Judaism: Practice*, pp. 290, 294; M. Barth, *People of God*, p. 43. See the discussion in chapter 2 above.

[118]While this may be taken to refer to Christ, it may just as well be taken to refer to God (e.g., 2 Cor. 1:9-10), or even to Paul as apostle/messenger. Isaiah uses the phrase for the Lord (5:29; 44:6; 47:4; 48:17; 49:7, 26; 54:5, 8; 59:20). See Stanley, "Redeemer Will Come," p. 137. See also the discussion both for and against a christological interpretation by Hvalvik, "Sonderweg," pp. 92–95, 101, and his discussion of why the citation of this Scripture need not be taken as a reference to the parousia of Christ.

[119]See the discussion in chapter 2 and above on sin and salvation for first-century Judaism. Note here Zeph. 3:14-20; Jer. 31:27-40.

and believing Gentiles, a "great Israel" incorporating all God-fearing peoples . . . The bedrock of the entire Hebrew Bible is impregnated with this vision of universal salvation. It is not by chance that the Great Book begins with the portrayal of a single universe and closes with the vision of a reunited humanity. Its *leitmotif* is and remains *one* God, *one* world, and *one* single human family, whom all Israel has been chosen to serve. . . . This is the pledge which was given three times to our fathers, Abraham, Isaac, and Jacob. Since then this world-embracing tradition has not ceased to raise its voice among the people of Israel. The message of the prophets reverberates time and time again in the Talmud, in Midrash, and in the other rabbinic writings: no bearer of God's image is without salvation, and the Jewish people, small, weak, and plain as they are, are held divinely responsible for calling all of their human brothers and sisters to the single lordship of one God—a united states of all humanity, that *basileia* [kingdom] of God which will finally encompass all nations in an undivided worldwide rule of peace and justice. That this gospel of biblical reconciliation, as Stuhlmacher calls it, is the *kerygma* [proclamation] and task of Israel as well as the final goal of world history was as familiar to Paul as it was to his rabbinic colleagues. What made them opponents of this solitary student of the Pharisees was neither the question of what was to happen to the Gentiles, nor who would finally bring about reconciliation, but solely when all of this was to occur.[120]

This reading throws light on Paul's description of his apostolic missionary pattern that has brought gentiles to the "obedience of faith":

> *from* Jerusalem[121] and round about as far as Illyricum I have *fully* preached the gospel of Christ. And thus I aspired to preach the gospel, not where Christ was already named [Zion],[122] that I might not build upon another man's foundation [the twelve on Israel's thrones];[123] but as it is written,

---

[120]Lapide, *Paul: Rabbi*, pp. 48–49.

[121]Note the observation of Hengel, *Pre-Christian Paul*, p. 25: "So we must assume that 'from Jerusalem' is to be related strictly to his person: his missionary career began from the Holy City. He left Jerusalem and was called to become a messenger of the gospel by his vision of Christ on the road, shortly before he reached Damascus."

[122]Note Paul's comments elsewhere that he had not preached originally in Jerusalem (Gal. 1:11—2:10). See Sanders, *Paul, the Law*, p. 186, for similar note that Paul did not preach in Jerusalem.

[123]See Luke 22:28-30; Acts 1; Gal. 1–2. Note the comment of Sanders, *Paul and Palestinian Judaism*, p. 104: "The fact is that the number twelve itself, 'apart from the details of any individual saying', points to 'all Israel.'"

"They who had no news of Him shall see,
and they who have not heard shall understand." (15:19-20; cf.
10:14-21; Isa. 52:6-15)[124]

He is the apostle to the gentiles (nations), the messenger of the
Deliverer who has begun to restore Israel ("Hear, O Israel, the Lord is
our God") and the God of all the nations ("the Lord is One"). The
messengers have brought the good news to Zion of her salvation:

> How lovely on the mountains are the feet of him who brings good
> news, who announces peace and brings good news of happiness, who
> announces salvation, and says to Zion, "Your God reigns!" (Isa. 52:7)

Paul is thus charged with bringing the good "news" of Israel out to
those of the Diaspora dwelling among the gentiles *first*, and light to all
the gentiles *also* (Isa. 52:10: "The Lord has bared His holy arm in the
sight of all the nations; that all the ends of the earth may see the salvation of our God"), which surprisingly is *also* part of the process of
Israel's restoration, for it was necessary to demonstrate to "some" of
the children of Israel that they had departed from God's mercy in
order to provoke them to jealousy, so that they might reconsider and
now "obey" the good news that they will have "heard" (Rom. 10:14-
21; 11:30-32).

F. F. Bruce, who in no way intended to communicate the two-step
pattern I am proposing here, observed Paul's intentions similarly,
although certainly differing on the particulars:

> His own apostolic ministry was the means in the divine purpose for the
> accomplishment of this "mystery." Isaiah in his day had been cleansed
> and sent by God to people whose hearts were "hardened" against his
> message by their very hearing of the message (Isaiah 6:9f.); so Paul had
> been cleansed and sent by God, not directly to the people whose hearts
> were hardened against the message, but to convey that message and its
> saving benefits to others so that the people with hardened hearts might
> begin to covet those benefits for themselves and at last embrace the
> message with which the benefits were bound up. Thus the history of
> salvation would be consummated, and Paul had a distinctive part to play
> as God's chosen instrument in bringing about the consummation. In the
> light of the initiatory revelation and its progressive unfolding in his

---

[124]Bracketed interpretation added.

ministry he knew himself to be, under God, a figure . . . of eschatological significance.[125]

Paul cited these Scriptures to demonstrate that the foundations of
the "mystery" he was articulating were present in the message of the
prophets that foretold his apostolic ministry on behalf of the scattered
of Israel and the nations. Paul's role was in the service of Israel's
promised restoration: the Deliverer has come to Zion in that Jesus has
been named the Christ of Israel, and now Paul is responsible for bringing this good news out "from Zion" to the dispersed among the nations to complete the restoration of "all Israel," in this case to Rome.[126]
The pattern that Paul is employing to this end necessarily involves the
inclusion of the gentiles (they will also hear the good news), and it
even necessarily includes a proper understanding of these matters on
the part of the Romans addressed, for their "proper behavior" is crucial for success. They are also involved in this process as their "obedience of faith" wins respect among the children of Jacob who are not so
quickly persuaded of the message, rather than blasphemy of their
"good things." Even the pattern for provoking jealousy involves them
so that Paul's ministry in fulfillment of Israel's eschatological privilege
of bearing God's light to the gentiles may be magnified, thus causing
"some of them" to seriously reconsider the message Paul
proclaimed.[127]

---

[125]Bruce, *Paul*, p. 335. Note also Käsemann, *Romans*, p. 313: "The end of v. 25
states the precondition of the parousia and the related conversion of all Israel to
which the apostle is contributing by fulfilling his own commission and which he
probably hopes to see in his own lifetime."

[126]Räisänen, "Paul, God," p. 191, also notes this tension.

[127]Note that this reading accounts for the observation of Sanders, *Paul, the Law*,
p. 194: "Despite the surprising character of the mystery, the explanation of the salvation of Israel in 11:26a is still 'historical'; that is, it is connected with the missions of the apostles" without the paradoxical problem he sees in Paul's proof-
texting (pp. 194–95): "But the proof-text which Paul quotes to establish the fact
that all Israel will be saved has nothing to do with the gentile mission. . . .
Although Paul three times in Romans 11 connects the salvation of Israel with his
own mission to the Gentiles, the quotation in 11:26b-27 assigns that salvation to
the Redeemer; that is, it puts it outside the bounds of the apostolic missions alto-
gether. Paul treats the quotation in 11:26b-27 as if it proves the point that the Jews
will be saved as a result of the Gentile mission, but it does not do so."

"From the standpoint of the gospel they are enemies for your sake, but from the standpoint of God's choice they are beloved for the sake of the fathers; for the gifts and the calling of God are irrevocable."

Paul rounds off his discussion of this mystery with another effort to develop and then resolve the tension between the way his audience views their circumstances with regard to the "stumbling" of Israel— enemies of the gospel—and the way Paul regards them—beloved of the fathers. They appear to be enemies of the gospel to the audience in Rome, which informs us that they are crossing paths regularly or else this enmity would not be so developed. This further suggests that the community(s) of Christian gentiles are not separated from the synagogue community(s) and are seeking acceptance therein, but are perhaps being met with some skepticism and rejection, even blasphemy of their good things (14:16). This would make sense of Paul's focus on hope and his continual concern to address their security in God's love and elective purposes in spite of opposition to their faith claims (5:1-5; 8:12-39; 12:9-21; 15:4-5, 6ff.). And it would make sense of his bold reminder to obey the intentions of the apostolic decree (6:15-23; 12:1-3; 13:11-14; 14:13—15:3; 15:15-16; 16:17-20).

Paul's point here is that things are not as they appear. While some Jews may appear to be enemies of the gospel, the Christian gentiles must realize that in the purpose of God it is "for your sake." These Jews are suffering this "hardening" in their "stumbling" vicariously, in order for "salvation to come to the Gentiles." Further, they are suffering in this current state "until the time when the fulness of the Gentiles begins," which will provoke them to jealousy and "save some of them." This present state must thus be viewed from God's vantage point (Christian gentiles must be "transformed by the renewing of your mind" so as to have "sound judgment": 12:1-3), for their current enmity is but temporal and does not bring harm as it appears; rather, it brings good, for "we know that God causes all things to work together for good to those who love God, to those who are called according to His purpose" (8:28).

Paul's message is clear: Israel has not been rejected by God, although it may appear so now. The "stumbling" of Israel are suffering, but not thereby condemned. The Christian gentiles must learn to see them through the eyes of God. For they are "beloved for the sake of the fathers, for the gifts and the calling of God are irrevocable" (11:28-

29; cf. 9:1-5; 3:2; 11:1-2). They are the seed of Abraham, those for whom Abraham's belief in God's righteousness is rooted. God has made promises to them through Abraham, Isaac, and Jacob, through Moses and David, through the prophets, and through Jesus Christ, the very one the gentiles have now come to believe in. God has not "strengthened" some in their unbelief in order to destroy them. He has done so in order to save gentiles too, and in order to demonstrate their common need for God's grace, as some of them have lost sight of the foundation of their election in God's grace and need this process to bring them back around to reconsidering the "good news" (11:30-32). Without this process they would not have turned back from the course they were choosing that was leading them away from the faith of their fathers, a change of course that they would have been unable to recognize because without the "ingathering of the gentiles" they would not have realized the time of fulfillment had come.

Maintaining the distinction between Jews and gentiles represented no problem for Paul. In fact, he promoted the distinction in order to emphasize that gentiles were not Jews and thus must not be circumcised and keep the Law, Israel's special "gift." His particular concern, however, was to promote as well that this distinction, even if it demonstrated Jewish *advantage* in the order of God's plan, did not result in, and must not be developed to suggest, *inequality*. Those advantages were on behalf of the whole world, not for self-congratulation. They are the elect, the light of all the nations. The purpose of election is to communicate in a special way God's truth to those who would otherwise be unable to understand, to those who do not speak the language, one might say. Israel's priority (to the Jew *first*) is real, but it is in the service of God's universal plan, which is for the gentile *also*, and *equally*. So now the Christian gentiles' election is not to result in conceit, but in the service of those suffering on their behalf, the "part hardened," as they join with Paul in the service of the salvation of "all Israel" by presenting their "bodies a holy and living sacrifice" and by learning to recognize that their responsibility is commensurate with the "measure of faith" they have been graciously given so that they might serve "him for whom Christ died."

They are different, *Jews* and *gentiles*—yet *equal* in Christ. The distinction remained, but discrimination did not. When the balance swung toward Jewish failure to recognize gentile equality, Paul's message was necessarily weighted to emphasize the gentile prerogative of faith alone (e.g., Galatians); however, when gentile priority was cause for arrogance, as in Rome, he swung around to make it equally clear that Israel was first, that faith demonstrated the truth of the Law, and that even the mission to gentiles was underscored by the priority of the Jew in salvation history.

THE "FULNESS OF THE GENTILES" AND THE RESTORATION OF "ALL ISRAEL"

Things are not as they appear in Rome. The mystery Paul reveals is that the root still supports the branches, that is, Israel's restoration and even her pruning precede and support the gentile mission. Furthermore, even the initiation of the gentile mission, which commences with a warning to the "stumbling," is in the service of the restoration of Israel, that they might be provoked to jealousy as they see the fulfillment of the promises in Paul's apostolic ministry to the gentiles taking place before their very eyes without their participation as expected ([un]realized eschatology!). Indeed, with the initiation of the gentile mission the "fulness of the Gentiles *begins*," step two, "and thus, in this way, all Israel will be saved," even as the prophets foretold: The Deliverer will come from Zion to regather the dispersed children of Israel, Jacob will be restored, and the gentiles will be drawn to the light and worship the One God of Israel as their own, as the One God of all the nations. Paul is concerned that they do not misunderstand the role of those who appear to be enemies in Rome: they are "beloved" and suffering "on your behalf" that God might show his mercy to all, to Israel and to the nations. "Therefore, on behalf of God's mercy to you in this grand design, *present yourselves. . . .*"

Of course, we cannot be certain this is what Paul meant to reveal in this "mystery." Even less can we be certain this is what his audience in Rome heard. However, some clues suggest the possibility, even though they are not normally taken to do so. The attachment to Judaic practices, recognized as a kind of conservatism in matters of Jewish practice, has been often noted in the development of the church in Rome through the early centuries. While this has been taken to mean there were many influential Jews, or that the audience was former gentile God-fearers who clung to Judaism in spite of the supposed intention of Paul to dissuade them from this course, it just as well might indicate that my reading of Paul's message promoting respect for Judaic practices was actually taken to heart by those gentiles he addressed, at least for a while.

At the very least, this reading of Paul develops the tensions likely
to have surfaced in the gentile capital of the world as some gentiles
embraced a Jewish Savior, while seeking perhaps to strip him of his
Jewish context and meaning in the face of opposition to their equality
from the Jewish community wherein they had sought respect and assurance but had not found it, at least not unequivocably.[128] This would
account for the constant theme of perseverance in the face of suffering in Romans. And it would account for Paul's passionate and unrelenting intention to reach Rome (and Spain and points west, the biblical ends of the earth),[129] preceded by this bold *reminder* to *obey* "the
teaching" they had learned in the past with regard to righteous behavior ("slaves of righteousness") for those believing in the One God
of Israel as the One God of all the world. He must write, and he must
come to Rome, in order to bring them within his apostolic charge
"from Zion" out through the Diaspora, bringing the children of Jacob
their promised restoration *first* and light to all the nations *also*, in order
that he might provoke "the rest" to jealousy and "save some of them."
For *then* the hardening will have completed its function in the vicarious service of both Israel and the nations, bringing Paul's apostolic
calling with its deeply painful conflicts to its eschatological climax:[130]

and thus, in this way, all Israel will be saved.

---

[128]Not to mention the many tensions involved with their identity in the gentile
community as semi-Jews, particularly among their families, friends, employers,
masters, etc.

[129]Aus, "Paul's Travel Plans," pp. 232–62.

[130]Räisänen, "Paul, God," p. 196, notes this tension, though interpreting it quite
differently: "The issue in Romans 9–11, then, is not merely the 'justification of
God.' Paul is in effect concerned to justify his own activity as a preacher of the
gospel. He is not constructing abstract theology. He is struggling to find peace and
consolation in view of the nagging problem of Israel's rejection of his message.
The answers found by him diverge on the theoretical level. Each of them, however, serves to give him consolation and reassurance—and, he must have hoped,
his audience confidence in him and his task. Things are not the way they are by
chance. God is in control."

CHAPTER 6

ROMANS 13:1-7: CHRISTIAN OBEDIENCE TO SYNAGOGUE AUTHORITY

This chapter seeks to take up the challenge laid down in my approach to Romans thus far, namely, to recognize that Paul and the Christians addressed in Rome understood themselves to be working within the boundaries of Judaism and the Jewish community(s) of Rome. I now apply the implications of this paradigm to the interpretation of Romans 13:1-7.[1] I will assume that Paul addressed the Christians gentiles in Rome within the context of their association with the synagogue(s) for the *obedience of* their new *faith* by instructing them to subordinate themselves to the *institutional* requirements of the synagogue(s) in addition to the ethical and purity halakhot that had been developed for "righteous gentiles" worshiping in the midst of the congregation of Israel.

We must examine this passage in the light of the historical milieu, and then see if my proposal harmonizes Paul's purpose and message in the paraenesis and in the larger context of the letter. In other words, I first must make sense of the assumption that, historically, the early Christians in Rome (*gentile* as well as *Jew*) associated with the synagogue(s) in a manner in which this reading of 13:1-7 makes sense. This begs several questions we have been examining throughout this study: What was the synagogue like? Would the Jews of Rome have welcomed gentiles? If so, what halakhot would have been operative? How would Christian gentiles have been governed? Were there Jewish expectations that could have accounted for the phenomenon of the claims of the Christian gentiles and their desire to seek association with the synagogue? How would gentiles have regarded the Jews and their practices, opinions, and authority? I have examined many of these earlier; here I need to apply them to a new way to read this text and see if my thesis makes sense exegetically, in the topos of Romans 13:1-7, and in the context in which it is embedded.

Romans 13:1-7 has traditionally played a pivotal role in determining

---

[1] J. I. H. McDonald, "Romans 13.1-7: A Test Case for New Testament Interpretation," pp. 540–49, sets out just such a task.

the various issues of Christian relations to power, the state, and the complexities of civic responsibility.[2] But was Paul, when he addressed the political matter of "subordination" to the "authorities" in Rome, actually concerned with the context of Christian responsibility to the empire or state? I suggest that the hermeneutical presuppositions brought to the text of Romans heretofore have so dictated the direction of the prevailing interpretations that the natural sense of the text, the likely historical tensions in Rome, and Paul's intentions in this address have been largely overlooked with the result that Paul's instructions have been sadly misapplied in the history of the Christian faith.[3]

[2]R. Stein, "The Argument of Romans 13:1-7," p. 325, for example, begins his study thus: "The clearest passage in the New Testament dealing with the relationship of the Christian to the State is found in Rom 13:1-7. Although other important passages discuss this issue, nowhere else is the argument as clearly and as carefully constructed." E. Bammel, "Romans 13," p. 365, pushes the implications of this passage even further in his opening comments: "Chapter 13:1-7 of Paul's letter to the Romans became perhaps the most influential part of the New Testament on the level of world history," followed by the caveat: "This happened in spite of the fact the interpretation of the passage has never been found easy and is nowadays more disputed than ever before." Bammel draws his argument to a close with the following provocative proposal (p. 381): "The development of Pauline theology has not been sufficiently investigated. . . . We are bound to admit that the passage appears just as much a foreign body when seen from the general viewpoint of Pauline theology as it is evidence for an exceptional case when viewed historically. Therefore, whatever its biblical theological significance may be and however great the momentum it gathered in church history has been, in an account of the Pauline view of the state Romans 13 must be given its place rather in a side aisle than in the nave."

[3]The tragic results of the traditional interpretation of this text are too many to number here. Many sensitive readers of this text have struggled to free it from the implications that have been applied all too often to destructive ends, in this century in the supportive, or at least permissive, position of many churches in their dealings with Hitler and the Nazi regime. Moreover, the traditional interpretations have not successfully accounted for the fact that this letter was addressed to Rome during the reign of Nero by a Jewish man whose worldview was thoroughly informed by the prophetic writings and who had, along with his whole generation, seen the continual destruction of their people and interests under the tyrannical reigns of Herod and the Roman rulers (how could one involved in declaring the Jesus crucified by Romans as King of the Jews be assumed to be so naive as to ascribe Roman authority, ostensibly without caveat, to the ordering of God?). It is in this context that the wealth of apocalyptic literature of this period was born with many veiled references to Rome as "Babylon." These are simply not times in which the posture toward Roman authority was unequivocally positive, to say the least. Moreover, Paul's categorical critique in 1 Cor. 6:1 of the unrighteous authorities administrating civic courts must be considered, as well as his hope for the

This approach thus offers an interpretation of Paul's intended message that may appear radical at first, yet it successfully harmonizes the many tensions juxtaposed in Paul's larger paraenesis of 12:1—15:13 with his particular instructions in the topos of 13:1-7 in a way that, historically, allows the coherence of Paul's message to prevail. Specifically, this reading develops the tensions that likely underscored the need for his audience to be "reminded" of the importance of "subordinating" themselves to the "governing authorities" by paying special attention to the historical situation in Rome at the time of Paul's letter, with the assumption that 13:1-7 should harmonize with the context of the surrounding textual issues, as well as the larger themes Paul addressed throughout the letter.

It is my contention that Paul's instructions in 13:1-7 are not concerned with the state, empire, or any other such organization of secular government. His concern was rather to address the obligation of Christians, particularly Christian *gentiles* associating with the synagogues of Rome for the practice of their new "faith," to subordinate themselves to the leaders of the synagogues and to the customary "rules of behavior" that had been developed in Diaspora synagogues for defining the appropriate behavior of "righteous gentiles" seeking association with Jews and their God.[4]

Paul intended for the Christian gentiles of Rome to regard the "stumbling" of non-Christian Jews (9:30-33) in a new light (11:25ff.) so that they would realize how God was at work, even in the current anomalous state of affairs. He revealed the mystery that the "stumbling" of some of the children of Israel was actually in the vicarious service of bringing the gospel to gentiles (11:11-15, 25-32);[5] thus they are now indebted to love those "stumbling" as both "brethren" and

---

resurrection in 1 Cor. 15:24ff.: "when He has abolished all rule and all authority and power." Borg, "New Context," pp. 208–11, discusses the relationship of tensions in Rome and Palestine for Jews in Rome regarding their attitudes toward Roman rule. See also J. D. G. Dunn, "Romans 13.1-7—A Charter for Political Quietism," pp. 55–68; and the critique in J. Ellul, *Anarchy and Christianity*.

[4]The Christian gentiles, indeed all Christians in Rome (it is not uncommon to find mention of Christian Jews continuing to attend synagogues in other studies, hence the emphasis placed herein on Christian gentiles), would have associated with the synagogues for a variety of reasons as discussed in chapter 2 above. See Jeffers, *Conflict*, pp. 40–41, for similar observation, although he does not arrive at the same conclusions.

[5]On the vicarious nature of the present "stumbling" state of Israel in Rom. 11 see particularly Hays, *Echoes*, pp. 60–63; Dahl, *Jesus the Christ*, pp. 137–51; and the discussion in chapter 5 above.

"neighbors" and to live with those "stumbling" in harmony (peace: 12:17-18) as they obey the halakhot defining proper behavior for the people of God (6:12-23; 12:17; 13:8-14; 14:18-19; 15:15-16). Because of the suspicion of the non-Christian Jews toward the new claims of these gentiles (perhaps for their failure, in the eyes of the synagogues, thus far fully to adopt righteous [Law-abiding] behavior commensurate with their claim to share in Israel's "good things": 14:16), those Paul referred to as "stumbling" may have appeared to be "enemies" (11:28) and could certainly be regarded as "neighbors" (outsiders) more than "brethren" (insiders: see 15:1 vs. 14:10, 13, 15). However, their leaders are to be obeyed, for their authority is from God and is recognized even by the Roman emperor for the execution of their responsibility to oversee the behavior of the Jewish communities, to which these Christian gentiles were now attached through synagogue attendance and when meeting in their homes under the authority granted the synagogues.[6]

Paul instructed the Christian gentiles composing the group labeled "strong"[7] to adopt proper behavior so that they would not cause the further "stumbling" of the "weak," who were the non-Christian Jews of the Roman synagogues (14:13—15:3). In 13:1-7 Paul clarifies that, in addition to his instructions throughout the letter calling for the willing "obedience" (ὑπακοήν) to the rules of "righteous behavior" that should accompany their new "faith" as they associate with the synagogue community (ethical and purity issues),[8] they must also "subor-

[6]Synagogue responsibilities and privileges included the oversight of the Jewish community's behavior with respect to Jewish and Roman law including proper discipline as warranted, the collection of both Jewish (and perhaps some Roman taxes?) and their proper distribution, general administration and orderly assembly including such matters as festivals, common meals, property, education and schooling, and burial of members. These same features would have applied to "righteous gentiles" associating with the synagogue community, and thus would have applied to the early Christian gentiles making a claim to be a part of the people of God when they attended synagogue. Note the comment of Segal, *Paul*, p. 252: "Living in faith apparently causes suffering for the believers, perhaps directly from Jewish persecutors or indirectly by the Romans for not observing Judaism, thus not deserving the protection of Judaism's legitimacy." For more information see chapter 2 above on historical issues.

[7]The "strong" would include all Christians, as we discussed in chapter 3 above, but the thrust of Paul's usage in Romans is determined by the gentile composition of the audience.

[8]Paul's central concern throughout the letter is the "obedience [ὑπακοήν] of faith" (1:5; 15:18; 16:17-20, 25-27; and see Dunn, *Romans*, p. 856; e.g., presenting

dinate" (ὑποτασσέσθω)[9] themselves to the rules of community behavior and to the "governing authorities" charged with ensuring compliance therein (institutional issues), including the payment of the
two-drachma Temple tax (13:6-7).

In recent years it has been more common than the past for scholars
to note that the beginnings of Christianity were thoroughly Jewish,
and that the early Christians (generally scholars are describing
Christian *Jews* or *former* God-fearing gentiles in the context of these
statements, not Christian *gentiles*) attended synagogue and respected
the practices of Judaism.[10] The following study pushes this observation a bit further, asserting that the Christian *gentiles*, as well as the
Christian *Jews* in Rome originally understood the practice of their faith
in the context of the Jewish community(s), although some group was
planting the seeds that later gave birth to the concept of a separate and
superior institution that need not respect its Judaic "roots,"[11] and this
new development precipitated the crisis Paul hoped to correct with
Romans, his "bold reminder" of the "obedience of faith."[12] That is, I
propose that the Christians in Rome, primarily gentiles at the time,
shared Paul's Judaic views and did not yet recognize their new faith
outside the definitions of righteousness that were operative in the synagogue community for guiding the faith and behavior of the "righteous gentile" seeking association with Israel, her people, and her God;

---

their members as "instruments of righteousness" in chap. 6 [cf. 6:17], and their
bodies as "living sacrifices" in chap. 12 so that Paul can "offer" them to God "as
acceptable, sanctified in the Holy Spirit" in chap. 15 [cf. 15:15-16, 18; 1:5]). See
chapter 4 above for full discussion.

[9]Käsemann, *Romans*, p. 351, "Whereas ὑπακούειν usually designates free obedience ὑποτάσσφαι emphasizes more strongly the fact that a divine order rules
in the divinely established world and that this entails super- and sub-ordination."
Also Yoder, *Politics*, pp. 174–75.

[10]See discussion in the introduction above.

[11]If we allow that chap. 16 was part of the original letter we can see this issue
explicitly in 16:17-20, when viewed in the light of Paul's comments in chaps.
11–15 to correct the temptation of the Christian gentile audience (the "strong") to
question their obligation to respect the faith of the "stumbling" of Israel, or to accommodate the righteous behavior that the "weak" saw as incumbent upon the
"strong" for the practice of their faith to be respected. Note the similarity of Paul's
language about those serving their appetites and the belly in seeking to deceive
the "strong" with the same choice of language for Philo in *Virtues* 34.182 and the
author of 3 Macc. 7:11 to describe apostasy for Jews as characterized by abandoning the dietary customs. I have discussed this dynamic in chapter 3 above.

[12]15:15-18, 19ff., 31; see chapter 4 above.

they were, however, being tempted by some group to begin questioning this view in the manner that ultimately prevailed in the Christian
tradition in spite of Paul's warnings.

EXEGETICAL FEASIBILITY

"Let every person be in subjection to the governing authorities" begins what has traditionally been regarded as an abrupt transition, lacking either conjunction or joining particle, and with a change to third
person.[13] This topos has been regarded as a major change of topic,
often beyond the grasp of many to reconcile with the surrounding context.[14] Nevertheless, Paul wrote this paraenetic topos as though there
was no major transition in topic from the issues he was in the midst of
addressing in chapter 12, and which he then picked up again without
the usual marks of transition in 13:8.[15] Namely, Paul led up to 13:1-7
by addressing several issues that are generally treated as independent
concerns in the larger paraenesis: how to live properly with regard to
"one another" (12:5, 10, 16); "saints" (12:13); those who "persecute
you" (12:14); those who "rejoice" or "weep" (12:15); the "lowly"
(12:3, 16); and those who do "evil toward you" in such a way that it

---

[13]Dunn, *Romans*, p. 759.

[14]This topos has been regarded as everything from "an independent block"
that "in view of its singular scope it can be pointedly called an alien body in Paul's
exhortation" (Käsemann, *Romans*, p. 352) to "a self-contained envelope completely independent of its context" that "actually interrupts the context" as an
"alteration" that ought to be recognized as a later "interpolation" (J. Kallas,
"Romans XIII. 1-7: An Interpolation," pp. 365–74). For additional arguments for
a later interpolation see Munro, *Authority*, pp. 16–19; J. C. O'Neill, *Paul's Letter to
the Romans*, pp. 207–9. Minear, *Obedience*, p. 88, having shown how "every command becomes applicable to the kind of behaviour-change which Paul wanted to
produce among the strong in faith" throughout chaps. 12 and 13, then comments
on the "pericope concerning obedience to the governing authorities" in 13:1-7:
"Here I must admit that I am unable to find particular reasons in the Roman situation for Paul's inclusion of this teaching."

[15]Kallas, "Romans XIII. 1-7," p. 366: "A careful examination of the closing parts
of chapter xii on the one hand and xiii. 8f. on the other reveals that the two chapters would read more smoothly if this strangely intrusive section were omitted."
Kallas continues to demonstrate the similarities with the synoptic material in
chap. 12 and 13:8ff., which are "homogeneous material" into the midst of which
"the envelope of xiii. 1-7 is thrust." (See F. F. Bruce, "Paul and 'The Powers That
Be,'" pp. 78–96, for a critique of Kallas's position). Stein, "Argument," p. 326, is
guarded yet observes: "Even if there are ties with the immediately surrounding
materials, it must nevertheless be admitted that the ties are at best loose."

could provoke a desire for "revenge" (12:17-21); and then beginning in 13:8 Paul continued his instructions with the concern for living properly in love toward "your neighbors" (13:8-10), followed in chapters 14 and 15 by the admonition to the "strong" to "welcome" the "weak in faith," who are variously referred to as both "brothers" and "neighbors." Paul appears to move around with little internal coherence. Were his instructions really as disjointed as most commentators suggest?

I suggest that there is no conjunction to announce a break in Paul's larger paraenetical concerns of 12:1—15:13 because there is no conceptual change of focus in 13:1-7.[16] The entire section, including *"every* person" of 13:1-7, is concerned with addressing the new lifestyle of the Christian *gentiles* in response to the gospel's revelation of the "mercies of God" toward themselves,[17] so that they would be committed to "proper behavior" in the congregation of the people of God to which they now belong as new members of the synagogues of Rome through their "introduction" by "faith" in Christ Jesus. These same Christians who saw the "stumbling" non-Christian Jews as "enemies of the gospel" in 11:28 (and who were most easily reached with Paul's call to resist "judging" by paradigmatic appeal to the same kind of "judgmental" behavior when witnessed in the life of the apostrophic Jew in 2:17ff.) are now being instructed on how to live in view of the "mystery" of God's unwavering commitment to those "stumbling" as God's very "beloved" (11:25-29, 30ff.). The Christian gentiles may see those "stumbling" ostensibly as enemies in that they

---

[16]My approach obviates the need to argue that this section develops a line of thinking regarding the state that is alien to Paul's views and practices in other texts, or even to consider that fact that outside of this topos we cannot be certain of Paul's views of the state as discussed by Kallas, "Romans XIII. 1-7," pp. 365–74. See also Bammel, "Romans 13," p. 367 ff., for a similar observation that "the stamp of the pericope is thus a Jewish and not a genuine Pauline one," although he follows a different line than Kallas. Bammel also discusses the issues that result from the need to reconcile the traditional interpretation of Rom. 13 with 2 Thess. 2:6ff. (pp. 375–81).

[17]Ridderbos, *Paul*, p. 321: "It may not be forgotten that Romans 13:1-7 forms a subdivision of the paraenetic part of the epistle that begins with 12:1, and is therefore characterized by the qualification given there of the Christian life as 'liturgy,' the service of God in everyday life. Viewed in this context Paul's intention becomes more transparent: obedience to earthly authorities is also involved in what Romans 12:1 ff. calls the spiritual sacrificial service, the placing of oneself at the service of God in virtue of the mercy of God shown to the church. This obedience is a submitting of oneself to the order appointed by God."

question these gentiles' claim of entry into the historical people of
God by faith in Christ without becoming Jews (by "the gospel"). By
their new association with the synagogues through faith in Christ,
however, they are to recognize that those "stumbling" are not only
their "neighbors" whom they must "love" even in the face of "evil"
(12:17-21), but they are also their "brethren" for whom "Christ died"
(14:15). They are instructed to "respect what is right in the sight of all
men" (12:17), and further, "so far as it depends on you, be at peace
with all men" (12:18). They are now responsible to have their "minds
renewed" (12:1-3) so that they will "behave properly" (13:13) in their
service of Christ in a way that will be "approved by men" (12:17;
14:18) as they "bear" the "weaknesses of the weak" "for his good, to
his edification" (15:1-3).

And just who are these "enemies," "neighbors," and "brethren"
whom they must learn to see anew and from whom they seek "approval"? They are the "stumbling" non-Christian Jews with whom
they now associate under the "authority" of the synagogue, the "weak
in faith" who do not yet recognize that Jesus is their Christ nor the
legitimacy of these gentiles' claims to be equal coparticipants in the
promised blessings without becoming Jews; and most importantly for
this study, they include the "governing authorities" (ἐξουσίαις
ὑπερεχούσαις) of the synagogues.

Paul utilizes several phrases to describe those in authority to whom
the Christian gentiles are to "subordinate" (ὑποτασσέσθω) themselves:

1. "governing authorities" (ἐξουσίαις ὑπερεχούσαις), who derive
their "authority" (ἐξουσίαις) "from God" (v. 1);

2. "rulers" (ἄρχοντες: v. 3) who are not a "terror" (φόβος) to "good
behavior" (ἀγαθῷ ἔργῳ) but to "evil" (κακῷ);

3. a "minister of God" (θεοῦ γὰρ διάκονός: v. 4) "to you for good"
(σοὶ εἰς τὸ ἀγαθόν); however, he is also an "avenger" (ἔκδικος)
"who brings wrath upon the one who practices evil" (εἰς ὀργὴν τῷ τὸ
κακὸν πράσσοντι) because "it [authority] does not bear the sword
for nothing" (οὐ γὰρ εἰκῆ τὴν μάχαιραν φορεῖ);

4. "servants of God" (λειτουργοὶ γὰρ θεοῦ: v. 6) "devoted"
(προσκαρτεροῦντες) to the collecting of "taxes" (φόρους).

1. "Governing authorities" (ἐξουσίαις ὑπερεχούσαις). The
Greek phrase means literally "superior authorities" or those in
"higher" or "stronger" positions of "authority."[18] It has been tradition-

---

[18]Delling, *TDNT*, 8.524.

ally assumed to refer to the institution of the state, and contextually to the Roman Empire. Some point out that this phrase, especially when viewed in concert with the other references to those in authority, is a reference not to the state or empire but to local and regional authorities involved in the administration of Hellenistic cities, "ranging from the tax collector to the police, magistrates, and Roman officials. . . . bearers of power with whom the common man may come in contact and behind which he sees the regional or central administration."[19] In addition, Jan Botha points out that the terms describing those in power do not indicate "abstract 'institutions' or 'systems.' Rather, their lexical sense is specifically related to personal relationships."[20] In other words, "it is not the *right, domain* or *means* of control that is in focus, but the persons who exercise that control":[21] "It is a relationship between *people*, with the subordinates vying for honor or praise from the authorities."[22]

Since these phrases were used in the administration of the Hellenistic style of government to describe those who interfaced with the people on their behalf, it is possible that these are the "authorities" Paul has in view. However, this approach, like the traditional one, fails to make sense of Paul's willingness to invest these authorities with God's "ordering" ($\delta\iota\alpha\tau\alpha\gamma\hat{\eta}$) or "appointment" ($\tau\epsilon\tau\alpha\gamma\mu\acute{\epsilon}\nu\alpha\iota$). After all, Paul was not blind to the evils of the empire and its idolatrous foundations, nor was any first-century Jew who was waiting for the "kingdom of God" to bring justice to the earth, particularly in the period of Nero's reign, a period of prolific apocalyptic literature filled with symbolic language to cloak bitter political critiques of Rome as "Babylon."[23] Furthermore, while it is plausible that non-Romans of other cities throughout the Roman empire nurtured some independent political notions within the scope of their new faith in Jesus, it is difficult to imagine, within the limitations of Paul's personal relation-

---

[19]Käsemann, *Romans*, pp. 353–54; Wilckens, *TDNT*, 8.565ff. I am not discussing the proposal of those who suggest that this is a reference to the angelic order. For a discussion of this view and why it is not tenable see Käsemann, *Romans*, pp. 352–53; Dunn, *Romans*, p. 760; Stein, "Argument," p. 328.

[20]J. Botha, *Subject to Whose Authority?* p. 213.

[21]Ibid., p. 41.

[22]Ibid., p. 214.

[23]Wright, *NT*, pp. 268–72, 279–80, 281ff., 299–307, 333ff.; L. Schottroff, "'Give to Caesar What Belongs to Caesar and to God What Belongs to God': A Theological Response of the Early Christian Church to Its Social and Political Environment," pp. 238–40.

ship to those addressed and the overall concerns of this letter, that the Christian gentiles in Rome (Romans!) needed to be made aware or even reminded by Paul of their obligations toward the Roman government, particularly with respect to the particular Roman officials with whom they personally interacted.

Paul need not invest the "authorities" with such a commission from God in order to explain the need to be "subordinate" ("to place or order under": ὑποτασσέσθω)[24] to the rules of the secular government to curb any "enthusiastic" or "spiritualistic" tendencies that may have been operative among the new Christians in Rome,[25] nor to recommend the level of compliance necessary to avoid stirring the government to issue another edict against the Jewish community, "with whom the Christian groups were still largely identified."[26] However, even if one of these were the case, it seems that Paul would have given such instructions without identifying the empire's government with the "ordering" (διαταγῇ) of God (cf. 1 Cor. 2:8; 6:1).[27]

Paul winds his theme of "subordination" (ὑποτασσέσθω) around the concept of the legitimacy of the "authorities" (ἐξουσίαις) he is calling his audience to willingly "place themselves under" rather than "resist" (ἀνθέστηκεν), for God is behind the "ordering" (διαταγῇ) of their authority, and those who resist are thus resisting the very

[24]Yoder, *Politics*, pp. 170–92. Yoder reads "the powers are under God" as a reference not to the divine instituting or mandating of the authorities but rather to providential permission.

[25]Contra Käsemann, *Romans*, pp. 354, 359; contra Ridderbos, *Paul*, p. 323. This was also the position of Calvin; see D. Steinmetz, "Calvin and Melanchthon on Romans 13:1-7," pp. 74–81. In Romans there is no evidence of such tendencies; further, this makes little sense of the fact that Paul is addressing primarily Roman gentiles in Rome and not those suffering occupation as might be the case elsewhere. How would the Christian faith at this time lead to such alleged political tendencies that this appeal to the ordering of God would be necessary?

[26]Contra Dunn, *Romans*, pp. 768–69. If the usual Pauline assumptions are maintained, why would Paul be so concerned with protecting the synagogues, with whom he and his communities were presumed to compete? Interestingly, Dunn ties the Christians to the Jewish community much as this reading does; however, his meaning was that they were mistakenly being identified with the Jewish community (p. 769). See also Dunn, "Political Quietism?" pp. 55–68. Differently argued by Borg, "New Context," pp. 205–18. See appendix 2 below.

[27]Note the comment of Wright, *NT*, p. 333, in answering the question of what first-century Jews believed was going to happen: "They believed that *the present world order* would come to an end—the world order in which pagans held power, and Jews, the covenant people of the creator god, did not."

"authorities" with whom God has been working ("ordering").[28] Those who resist bring upon themselves the "judgment" (κρίμα) they will receive, for those in authority are in the business of "praising" (ἔπαινον) those who do "good" (ἀγαθὸν) and "avenging" (ἔκδικος) those who "practice evil" (κακὸν πράσσοντι).

It is often assumed that Paul was simply restating a well-known and widely followed Jewish platitude to "pray for the welfare of rulers": Jews must be subordinate to the government authorities under whom they find themselves until the day of the Lord.[29] However, what is missing in Romans 13:1-7 is the characteristic criticism of those foreign powers in the present evil age. For the call to subordination in Judaism carried an implicit, if not always explicit, judgment of such foreign governments, even if God was somehow using their evil intentions to accomplish his ultimate goals.[30]

---

[28]Yoder, *Politics*, p. 175, succinctly captures the essence of the language: "The term *hypotassesthai* is not best rendered by *subjection*, which carries a connotation of being thrown down and run over, nor by *submission*, with its connotation of passivity. Subordination means the acceptance of an *order*, as it exists, but with the new meaning given to it by the fact that one's acceptance of it is willing and meaningfully motivated."

[29]While Daniel speaks of God giving power to the king (1:2; 2:37ff.; 5:18) and the *Letter of Aristeas* of God standing behind the king (15), the sweeping sense of Paul's comment appears far greater, encompassing the whole system of government. Further, Paul's expressions διάκονός θεοῦ and λειτουργοὶ are uncommon with reference to secular powers. Bammel, "Romans 13," p. 374, thus concludes: "Taken together this amounts to a fairly extended theology of order which goes far beyond the acclamation or prayer for the king" before discussing the "obvious" "difference" (p. 380) with Paul's comments regarding the state here with his apocalyptic message of 1 Thess. 5:3; 2 Thess. 2:6ff.: "The Thessalonians passages and Romans 13 represent two different types of understanding of the state, which have little in common" (p. 381). Note also the observation of J. Friedrich, W. Pöhlmann, and P. Stuhlmacher, "Zür historischen Situation und Intention von Röm 13, 1-7," p. 158, that this positive reference to taxation in Rom. 13:6-7 is unparalleled in Jewish literature of this period.

[30]This critique included Israel's own kings (1 Sam. 8); it was even uttered by Israel's kings (Eccl. 3:16: "In the seat of justice there rules wickedness"), and it was understood to lie behind the necessary cooperation during this period of chastisement at the hands of foreign domination (Isa. 48:5-7, 8ff.; 10; Jer. 29 [cf. v. 7]; 34; Wis. 6:1-11). As long as the laws of the king did not interfere with the practice of the laws of God they were to be obeyed, but martyrdom was better than forced idolatry as well as other sins against the Law (Dan. 3; 2 Macc. 7 [cf. vv. 1-2, 15, 30-38]). While rebellion against the king was punishable even to the extent of death, the Maccabean revolt and Zealot uprisings found their justification in the monarch's disregard for God's Law. See the discussion of Biblical periods and

Paul's unmitigated description of the governing authorities as the servants of God and of his "ordering" makes little sense in the context of the Roman empire or of Hellenistic government, and we know only too well from history since these words were penned that it is simply not true of many administrations of power. Yoder's caveat helps:

> God is not said to *create* or *institute* or *ordain* the powers that be, but only to *order* them, to put them in their place. It is not as if there was a time when there was no government and then God made government through a new creative intervention; there has been hierarchy and authority and power since human society existed. Its exercise has involved domination, disrespect for human dignity, and real or potential violence ever since sin has existed. Nor is it that in his ordering of it he specifically, morally approves of what government does. The sergeant does not produce the soldiers he drills, the librarian does not create nor approve of the book he catalogs and shelves. Likewise God does not take the responsibility for the existence of the rebellious "powers that be" or for their shape or identity; they already are. What the text says is that he orders them, brings them into line, that by his permissive government he lines them up with his purpose.[31]

Yoder's penetrating observation helps bring the issues into focus; however, he still must blink, as it were, at the notion of the government's authority when describing it as representing God's "permissive government." This is precisely the point that Paul would be expected to make but did not.[32] He was unrestrained in granting that the

---

rabbinic legislation in Schultz, *Judaism*, pp. 169–72; note also his discussion of the rabbinic position that discriminated between rulers who came to power and "who reigned by force of arms" rather than by "the order of a prophet or through the consensus of all Israel": such rulers "could be disobeyed or even forcibly removed from office without fear of legal sanction or reprisal" (p. 170). See J. Katz, *Exclusiveness and Tolerance*, pp. 48–55, 106–13, for discussion of how the tension of messianic hope and desire for the welfare of gentile rulers was resolved in later situations. This same critique is evident in Jesus' reaction to the tax question (Matt. 22:15-22) and in the attitude of the early church toward the Roman Empire as empowered by Satan (cf. Luke 4:6-7; Rev. 12–13; 18; see the discussion of Ellul, *Anarchy and Christianity*, pp. 45–88). See also Wright, *NT*, pp. 286–320; Moore, *Judaism*, 2.112–18.

[31]Yoder, *Politics*, p. 203.

[32]Christian theologians have often found it necessary to develop the nuance that Paul appears to inscrutably ignore, for example, to deal with tyrants or threatening opponents: "A strange casuistry was adopted to explain that power comes

"authorities" were under "appointment" (τεταγμέναι: "established") "by God" and that they would reward good and punish evil. But this was certainly often not the case for Roman government and its rulers, and the early Christians, particularly Jews, were only too clear on this. How can we account for this dissonance? Was Paul simply naive? That just does not make sense of the situation, or of Paul.[33]

The New Testament and the sources noted earlier when reviewing the government of the Diaspora synagogues have another usage for the "authorities" (ἐξουσίαις). As we shall see, it was a clear reference to those in charge of the government of the synagogue, an institution that in fact has been "ordered" by God to interpret righteousness for his people, for the praise of those who do good and the discipline of

---

from God only when it is gained in a legal, legitimate, and peaceful way and exercised in a moral and regular way" (Ellul, *Anarchy and Christianity*, p. 79). Steinmetz, "Calvin and Melanchthon," p. 80, notes that "Calvin and Melanchthon are both uneasy about the absolute endorsement of state power that Paul seems to offer. Each tries in characteristically different ways, to soften that endorsement. . . . On the other hand, if Calvin and Melanchthon offer little in the way of restraint on the powerful, Paul offers even less. His statement is absolute; theirs at least is qualified. Both commentators have softened the seemingly harsh character of Paul's dictum by introducing qualifications not found in the text." See also the discussion of Schottroff, "Give to Caesar," pp. 238–40. For a survey of the various interpretive methods of handling the political thought arising from this issue see W. Parsons, "The Influence of Romans XIII on Pre-Augustinian Christian Political Thought," pp. 337–64; idem, "The Influence of Romans XIII on Christian Political Thought II: Augustine to Hincmar," pp. 325–46.

[33]Note Paul's attitude in 1 Cor. 2:8 and 6:1 toward government. Ridderbos, *Paul*, p. 322, observes the same when commenting on suggestions that Paul had a favorable experience of Roman government or that he would not have written so if he had foreseen the persecution that was to come under Nero: "But in the first place such a conception attributes to Paul a naively optimistic evaluation of the existing political order that bears no relationship to what he himself had already experienced and to what since the death of Jesus had repeatedly been the experience of the Christian church." Dunn, "Political Quietism?" p. 67, notes: "For one thing Paul does not idealize the situation he is addressing. He does not pretend the authorities of whom he speaks are models of the good ruler. His advice does not particularly arise out of his own experience of Roman protection and the 'pax Romana'. He and his Jewish readers in Rome knew well enough the arbitrary power of Rome." If Paul knew they were meeting outside the special privileges of the synagogue, would he have been comfortable with such a statement? After all, they would have had to face a great number of matters of conscience, not the least of which was emperor worship itself. Some caveat from Paul seems warranted in the traditional approach.

those who do evil.[34] This institution derives its life from God's "gift" to Israel: the "ordering" (διαταγῇ) of the covenant with Israel, the Torah, the very word of God.[35] This institution, Paul had just emphatically asserted in response to Christian gentile presumptuousness in the face of Israel's current "stumbling," represents the faithfulness of God to his promises, for "the gifts and calling of God are irrevocable" (11:29). And since association with the synagogue would have involved the recognition of a new authority for the Christian gentiles in Rome (whereas they were unmistakably familiar with the authority of the empire from birth) it makes much better sense of the need for the kind of instruction Paul gives here, calling for (willing) subordination in view of the synagogues' responsibility to interpret God's word on matters of proper behavior (good and evil). This is particularly the case if the synagogues' interpretation involved them in some commitments to behavior they found cumbersome and unnecessary, because they had been saved as gentiles and not Jews, by faith and not by the Law. But does this make sense of Paul's use of "authorities" (ἐξουσίαις)?

Luke used "authority" (ἐξουσίαν) to describe the synagogue "authority" which he understood that Paul represented in his mission against the first Christians (who were, one should note, found not in an institution separate from the synagogues but in the synagogues).

[34]The institution of the synagogue makes more sense of the need for willing subordination for those who are just now beginning to attend. The Roman government is clearly in authority, but attending synagogue and associating with the community is a choice of subordination. Also, if the synagogue is guilty of tyranny, it is for being overly zealous in its interpretation of righteousness and thus less tolerant of improper behavior, not of the kind of tyranny that would accompany the empire or state.

[35]It is important to note that διαταγῇ (literally "instruction" [Delling, *TDNT*, 8.36) only occurs in one other case in the New Testament, and that is in relation to the Law as "ordained (διαταγὰς) by angels" in Stephen's speech (Acts 7:53). Note also that Justin in *Dial.* 67.7 used it to denote the "decreeing" of the Torah by Moses (Delling, *TDNT*, 8.36). Might this make more sense of the underlying issue of "angels" some suggest are the "authorities"? (See the dismissal of this suggestions by Ridderbos, *Paul*, 325–26; and Käsemann, *Romans*, 352–53.) See Gal. 3:19 for similar usage relating angels to the giving of the Law. We meet the same sense of the ordaining of the Law and its interpretation in Josephus, *Against Apion*, 2.18 (173–78): "For ignorance he left no pretext. He appointed the Law to be the most excellent and necessary form of instruction, ordaining, not that it should be heard once for all or twice or on several occasions, but that every week men should desert their other occupations and assemble to listen to the Law and to obtain a thorough and accurate knowledge of it, a practice which all other legislators seem to have neglected."

Unaware of Paul's experience on the road to Damascus, when told of his need to seek out Paul (Saul at that time) in Damascus after the appearance of the Lord to him, Ananias expressed his concern with the following notation in Acts 9:14:

> And here he has authority [ἐξουσίαν] from the chief priests [ἀρχιερέων] to bind all the ones calling upon Thy name.

Paul ascribes the same "authority" to his mission when he explains to Agrippa in Acts 26:10-12:

> not only did I lock up many of the saints in prisons, having received authority [ἐξουσίαν] from the chief priests [ἀρχιερέων], but also when they were being put to death I cast my vote against them. And as I punished them often in all the synagogues, I tried to force them to blaspheme; and being furiously enraged at them, I kept pursuing them even to foreign cities. While thus engaged as I was journeying to Damascus with the authority [ἐξουσίαν] and commission [ἐπιτροπῆς] of the chief priests [ἀρχιερέων] . . .

Note that Jesus also refers in Luke's Gospel to those in synagogue government as "authorities" (ἐξουσίας) in the same context we are concerned with in Romans 13 (Luke 12:11):

> And when they bring you before the synagogues and the rulers [ἀρχὰς][36] and the authorities [ἐξουσίας], do not become anxious about how or what you should speak in your defense, or what you should say.

The context of Jesus' instruction is concerned with the future appearance of those who believe in him before those governing the synagogues who may oppose the notion of Jesus as the Christ of Israel. Jesus tells his followers that in that day they must not deny him before humans, for to do so is to deny him before God, but to be assured that the Holy Spirit will assist them in the right confession when necessary. Is this not an adumbration of the position Paul took as the representative of the synagogue's authority when he sought to cause those of "the Way" to "blaspheme"? And is this not the same sense we have

---

[36]I have not yet taken up the issue of "rulers" (ἀρχὰς); nevertheless, note that Luke also refers to "rulers" (ἀρχὰς) alongside the "authorities" of the synagogue, as does Paul in our passage in Romans.

before us in Paul's instructions to the Roman believers if their "faith" in Jesus as the Christ is being challenged when they attend synagogue?

We have then a parallel use of "authorities" in Luke and in Acts applied similarly in Romans 13:1-7.[37] The references in Luke and Acts take place clearly in the context of synagogue government and in the context of the role of their "authority" vis-à-vis enforcement of the confessional and behavioral requirements of the Jewish community;[38] and in the case of Acts, in the context of Paul's own experience with synagogue "authority" in its disciplinary role. It would be natural for Paul to apply this same language in Romans if he was addressing Christians, particularly Christian *gentiles*, meeting in the context of the synagogue, perhaps under some duress, and beginning to question the extent of their obligation to the "authorities" therein.

2. "Rulers" (ἄρχοντες). This term is used of both religious and political leaders, and in the context of the Greek-speaking "private clubs" it referred to the chief officer or magistrate.[39] For my purpose it is worth noting that a papyrus from the mid-first century b.c.e. states that all the members of a particular pagan association are to "render obedience to the leader of the association and to his assistant."[40] In the case of the synagogues the "ruler" entrusted with the conduct of worship was called an *archisynagogus* (ἀρχισυνάγωγος)[41] while the one concerned with nonreligious affairs was elected annually and referred to as an *archon* (ἄρχων).[42]

Again Luke sheds considerable light on the usage of the term in the Jewish community, quoting from a Septuagint passage on Moses when

[37]It is interesting to note the suggestion of Pelagius in his fifth-century commentary on Romans: "Alternatively: 'Higher authorities' can mean ecclesiastical authorities," by which he is no doubt referring to church authorities (T. De Bruyn, trans., *Pelagius's Commentary on St. Paul's Epistle to the Romans*, p. 136).

[38]Note also the discussion in Matt. 23:2-3, 4ff., of the synagogue authorities sitting on the "seat of Moses," and Jesus' admonition, "therefore all that they tell you, do and observe," has this same sense. See Rivkin, *Hidden Revolution*, pp. 252ff., for a full discussion. For the historical accuracy of Luke's understanding of synagogues and their practices see R. Oster, "Supposed Anachronism."

[39]Jeffers, *Conflict*, pp. 36–37; Delling, *TDNT*, 1.488–99; Käsemann, *Romans*, pp. 356–57; Tcherikover, *Hellenistic*, pp. 301-5 and n. 22, 29, 36; Sherwin-White, *Roman Society*, pp. 133, 143. See the discussion in chapter 2 above.

[40]G. Horsley, *New Documents Illustrating Early Christianity*, 1.28–29.

[41]Beyer, *TDNT*, 2.91; Tcherikover, *Hellenistic*, p. 303.

[42]Leon, *Jews*, pp. 167–80, 193–94.

his legitimacy was questioned by an Israelite injuring his neighbor (Acts 7:27, 35): "Who made you a ruler [ἄρχοντα] and judge [δικαστὴν] over us?" In addition to the earlier noted incident where Luke used "rulers" in the context of the synagogue "authorities" (Luke 12:11), Luke writes of the "ruler of the synagogue" (ἄρχων τῆς συναγωγῆς) in Luke 8:41, and "the Jews and their rulers" (Ἰουδαίων σὺν τοῖς ἄρχουσιν) when speaking of the Diaspora synagogue of Iconium in Acts 14:5.[43] It is important to observe that Luke frequently refers to the "rulers" of the Jewish people, and he especially uses the term in the context of the Sanhedrin as those responsible for delivering Jesus to the Romans (Luke 14:1; 18:18; 23:13, 35; 24:20).

The comments of Käsemann, struggling to dissociate the term from its traditional application, are interesting for my proposal: "They are disciplinarians in relation to individual and group emancipation, which presupposes human autonomy or religiously based equality. For this reason the function of those who have power to punish moves to the foreground, and the community is assured that it has nothing to fear if it behaves properly."[44] This observation fits neatly my proposal that the "rulers" in Romans 13:3 were synagogue "authorities" who would have represented a "terror" (φόβος: "fear") to those practicing "evil," and "praise" (ἔπαινον) to those doing "good,"[45] whether in the sphere of religious or nonreligious, perhaps financial, obedience to the rules of the community.[46]

3. "Ministers" (διάκονός). "Ministers of God" or "servants of God" (θεοῦ διάκονός) became, in the Christian tradition, the title of the office of "deacon." Literally, διάκονός had to do with serving, "waiting at tables," thus, often with the service of food, although not necessarily.[47] In Romans 11:13 Paul speaks of his apostleship to the gentiles

[43]Also in Matt. 9:18, 23.

[44]Käsemann, *Romans*, pp. 356–57.

[45]Compare with 14:16 the concern that they behave in such a way that their good not be blasphemed. Perhaps this praise had a formal sense of recognition, for example, as embodied in being called a God-fearer.

[46]For the role of the "hazzan" in rabbinic literature, though traceable in the second temple period, see Sky, *Hazzan*, pp. 1–21.

[47]Beyer, *TDNT*, 2.81–93. Leon, *Jews*, p. 190, discusses the fact that we have one inscription from a Jewish catacomb that refers to a ὑπηρέτης, a term used by Luke in Luke 4:20 for a synagogue servant who apparently brought out the Torah scroll to be read at the service, like the modern cantor. He notes that the fact that we have only one inscription in Rome suggests it was not generally the term used

as his "ministry" (διακονίαν); in 12:7 he encourages the fulfillment of the gift of "serving" or "ministry" (διακονίαν); and twice he uses it as a verb in connection with his collection for the Jerusalem saints (15:25: διακονῶν; 15:31: διακονία). He also speaks of Christ's having become a "servant" (διάκονον) of the circumcision in his faithfulness to confirm the promises of the fathers (15:8).

It may be possible to stretch the context of food across all these references by exploring the issue of table-fellowship, particularly in light of the discussion in 14:1—15:4, which explicitly demonstrates this concern as central in Rome, though it is not necessary to do so.[48] The term describes "service" usually in practical matters and grows out of the sense of humbly loving one's neighbor, often related to serving food and thus to matters of table-fellowship (Luke 10:40; 12:37; 17:8; 22:26ff.), perhaps including the issues that would have arisen in relation to gentiles eating in the context of the Jewish community.

It is difficult to see why Paul should be assumed to have referred here to "servants" of the empire as "servants" or "ministers of God," regardless of their capacity.[49] However, it is not difficult to see how Paul could speak of them as "ministers" or "servants of God" (θεοῦ διάκονός) who have been "appointed" in the "ordering" of God for the discipline of the synagogue congregation, and as the "avengers for wrath" (ἔκδικος[50] εἰς ὀργὴν) to those "practicing evil" in the "service" of the "good" of the congregation of Israel: the protectors of holiness among those assembling before God. But what are we to do with Paul's reference to the "sword" (μάχαιραν)? Did the synagogue "authorities" have swords? I will return to this point after we look at

---

to designate this service or it was used to refer to an office that was not regarded special enough to be mentioned on one's epitaph. Leon notes also that Krauss, to the objection of Frey, believes that "the Jewish hyperetes was the prototype of the deacons of the early Christians" (p. 190 n. 2). See Sky, *Hazzan*, 31 n. 44, on Epiphanius's translation of "*hazzanites*" as "*Diokones*"; Leon's ὑπηρέτης suggestion on 35 n. 67.

[48]See the interesting example of this in Galatians by H. Beyer, *TDNT*, 2.88–89.

[49]Ogle, "What Is Left," pp. 260–62, suggests that the term should be rendered "servant-leaders" with reference to the leadership of the church. See also J. Robinson, *Wrestling with Romans*, p. 137, who notes the parallels between Paul's function as servant and that of the "state."

[50]ἔκδικος refers to a legal action, literally "he who by an offense places himself outside the limits of the law" and thus has the sense of "contrary to the law." Hellenistic usage took on the meaning of a legal officer "defending, avenging the right" (Schrenk, *TDNT*, 2.442–45).

Paul's next description of the "authorities" as "servants [λειτουργοὶ] of God."

4. "Servants" (λειτουργοὶ). Paul speaks of the "servants of God" (λειτουργοὶ θεοῦ) in the context of the collection of taxes, and says that they are "attending continually" (προσκαρτεροῦντες) to this service. This is a most interesting reference, and it has been the topic of several interpretations challenging the traditional views by emphasizing the function of the church in this paraenesis.

The concept of λειτουργέω derives from service to the community or society versus service for an individual, and its application extended to many religious functions for the priest or cult in Greek society, in the Septuagint, and in rabbinic Judaism.[51] In the New Testament its usage draws from the priestly functions,[52] and we see it used in this context by Paul to explain why he has written his bold reminder to the Romans (15:15-16):

> But I have written very boldly to you on some points, so as to remind
> you again, because of the grace that was given me from God,
> to be a minister [λειτουργὸν] of Christ Jesus to the Gentiles, ministering as a priest the gospel of God, that my offering of the Gentiles
> might become acceptable, sanctified by the Holy Spirit.

The term λειτουργοί was used of "public servants" and government officials who would have been concerned with taxes, but would Paul call them *"servants of God"* and would he speak of their devotion to this task with such reverence? Käsemann finds this inscrutable: "The idea that the authorities constantly seek to be God's servants is obviously exaggerated if not wholly incredible."[53] Yoder develops this concern further and suggests that προσκαρτεροῦντες in the context of λειτουργοί should be rendered "they are ministers of God *to the extent* to which they busy themselves" or "*in that* they devote themselves" or "they are ministers of God *only to the extent to which* they carry out their function" or "they are ministers of God *by virtue of* their devoting themselves" to their functions.[54] Yoder finally suggests that "there is nothing in the text to make sure that Paul does not intend

[51]R. Meyer, *TDNT*, 4.215–25.
[52]Strathmann, *TDNT*, 4.226–31; page 230: "The context thus shows us that λειτουργὸς had for Paul a sacral ring."
[53]Käsemann, *Romans*, p. 359.
[54]Yoder, *Politics*, pp. 207–10.

"ministers of God" to refer to Christians. This would also fit quite
smoothly in the context: The Christian is subject for the sake of conscience; it is for this reason that Christians pay taxes because
Christians also, as ministers of God, devote themselves to the end that
the good be approved and evil reprimanded."[55] Indeed, Yoder's suggestions make much more sense of the fact that Paul speaks of the
"continual devotion" of the ministry of these people "unto God" in
the matter of "taxes" than the traditional understanding of this passage, which sees the "authorities" of the empire or state as continually
devoted to God's service.

There is, however, another possibility to explore. Drawing from
Paul's application of λειτουργὸς to his function as a "minister of
Christ Jesus to the Gentiles, ministering as a priest [λειτουργὸν] the
gospel of God, that my offering of the Gentiles might become acceptable" (15:16), which he inextricably linked with his own "continual
devotion" to the collection for the Jerusalem saints as an example of
the Christian gentile's indebtedness to the suffering of Israel (1:10-15;
15:15-33), we may perceive a clue to the historical usage of
λειτουργὸς in the context of the Temple tax.[56] This would make
sense of their "continual devotion" to the collection of taxes as "servants of God." That is, the function of the "servants of God" within
the Jewish community was to devote themselves to the collection and
safe delivery of the Temple tax to Jerusalem. This "privilege" for the
synagogues of the Diaspora was very dear to the life of the Jewish
community and the source of tension in the larger gentile communities in which they dwelt.[57] In fact, it was a constant source of resentment in the Diaspora, and it had apparently been a matter of debate
among Jews in Palestine during this period as well.[58]

[55]Ibid., p. 210; also see the comments of Ogle, "What Is Left," pp. 260-62;
Robinson, *Wrestling*, p. 137.

[56]Nickle, *Collection*, pp. 74–99, develops this connection.

[57]Tcherikover, *Hellenistic*, pp. 308, 330, 371–77; see the discussion of synagogue
privileges in chapter 2 above.

[58]See the discussion of W. Horbury, "The Temple Tax," pp. 265–86. The payment of this tax may have become common practice only during the Hasmonean
period (pp. 277–78). The Pharisees interpreted Ex. 30:13 to mean that this tax
should be paid by everyone annually; however, the Qumran community appears
to have taught that it should be paid only once in a lifetime (4Q159; Horbury,
pp. 279ff.), and according to a mishnaic discussion the payment of the tax did not
apply in Galilee, which arguably "reflects a first-century Galilaean reluctance to
pay the half-shekel annually" (pp. 280-81).

There are historical references indicating that "righteous gentiles" paid the Temple tax during this period. In particular, Josephus mentions that the vast wealth of the Temple was directly related to the extensive contributions of Jews and σεβομένων τὸν θεόν ("God-fearers") from around the world, and Tacitus refers derisively to those gentiles ("people of the worst sort") who, "renouncing their ancestral religions, would send their tribute and gifts there [to Jerusalem] in heaps."[59] If the newly Christian gentiles in Rome were expected to pay this Temple tax as "righteous gentiles" when attending synagogue, and if they were hesitant to see this as an obligation incumbent upon them in the practice of their new faith since they were not actually Jews and did not enjoy the full privileges of Jews (and were even suffering the rejection of the legitimacy of their claims), *then* we can make sense of the need for Paul's instruction. They were obligated to pay (τελεῖτε: "pay what one owes")[60] the Temple tax to those collecting it as the "servants of God."

Interestingly, in Matthew 17:24 we have the term τελεῖτε linked directly to the payment of obligatory taxes (whether Roman poll taxes or Jewish Temple taxes),[61] and Jesus, though not without some criticism of the obligation (apparently in concert with contemporary Qumran and Galilean positions that questioned the Pharisaic interpretation of the responsibility to pay the Temple tax annually),[62] subordinated himself to those having the authority to collect the tax so that he would "not give them offense" (μὴ σκανδαλίσωμεν αὐτούς). This is certainly the same sense that we have traced in Paul's concerns throughout Romans 12–15.

This suggests that the λειτουργοὶ θεοῦ are none other than those responsible for the collection, safekeeping, and annual distribution of the Temple tax within the Jewish community in Rome, and that Paul's concern is that the Christian gentiles in Rome would understand they are not only obligated to pay this tax by the interpretation of the Law as understood by those in authority (13:4-5: ὀργὴν: "wrath"); they are

[59]See Josephus, *Ant.*, 14.7.2 (110) for reference to God-fearers (σεβομένων τὸν θεόν) paying this tax (see also 16.6.2–7, [162-173]). See Tacitus, *Histories* 5.5.1 (Whittaker, *Jews and Christians*, p. 22), cf. S. Cohen, "Respect," p. 428.

[60]Delling, *TDNT*, 8.60.

[61]Sherwin-White, *Roman Society*, pp. 126–27, suggests that this is most likely the "censum" (κῆνσον) poll tax begun in Judea in 6 c.e., not the Temple tax as is commonly assumed. However, Horbury, "Temple Tax," makes a convincing argument for the Temple tax.

[62]Horbury, "Temple Tax," and n. 58 above.

further obligated by their responsibility (13:5: συνείδησιν: "conscience") to demonstrate graphically that their claim of sharing in the
"good things" promised to Israel is legitimate through their willing
payment of the Temple tax, so that they might not cause offense but
win their respect as "righteous gentiles," thereby "holding up" (15:1:
βαστάζειν: "bear") those "stumbling" until they are "strong" enough
to see and believe in Jesus as the Christ (15:1-3; 14:9-18, 19ff.).[63]

The Problem of the "Sword" (μάχαιραν).

I now turn to the issue of the "sword." Did the synagogue "authorities" have "swords"? Paul's mention of the "sword" in this paraenesis
has certainly been one of the central reasons for the traditional and
seldom challenged presuppositions that Paul was dealing with the
"authorities" of the state or empire. But when we approach this paraenesis from the vantage point of synagogue "authorities," the matter of
the "sword" is contextualized in several important ways.

First, the "sword" (μάχαιραν) is a "knife" used in circumcision
(Josh. 5:2) and in the offering of Isaac (Gen. 22:6, 10), and a "dagger"
or "small sword" (Judg. 3:16) as opposed to a sword proper
(ῥομφαία).[64] It could also be used symbolically or metaphorically
(Prov. 5:4 for the effect of a harlot; 12:18 for words; 24:22 for ruin; 25:18
for false witness; 30:14 for the teeth of the wicked; Isa. 49:2 for the
Lord's mouth; Eph. 6:17 for the word of God [Heb. 4:12]). In Roman
law it was used in the defining of *ius gladii*, "the right of the sword."[65]
The μάχαιραν was the "symbol of judicial authority . . . like the pis-
tol worn by a traffic policeman or the sword worn by a Swiss citizen-
officer, it was more a symbol of authority than a weapon."[66]

Paul's use of μάχαιραν here could fittingly describe the discipli-

[63]Schmithals, *Paul and James*, p. 109 n. 18, notes that Matt. 17:24-27 "provides
evidence for the fact that in Jewish-Christian circles the Temple tax was indeed
paid, but it declares at the same time that in principle Christians are exempt from
this payment. It should be made only from tactical considerations, so as not to give
any offence . . . the reason given for the payment means in practice: for the sake
of peace with the Jews, to avoid persecution, 'the disciples of Jesus pay the
Temple tax as free sons, merely in order not to give offence.'"

[64]Michaelis, *TDNT*, 4.524–27.

[65]Sherwin-White, *Roman Society*, pp. 8–11, 74ff.

[66]Yoder, *Politics*, p. 206. Yoder further qualifies the use of μάχαιραν: "In the police function, the violence or threat thereof is applied only to the offending party.
The use of violence by the agent of the police is subject to review by higher authorities. He applies his power within the limits of a state whose legislation even
the criminal knows to be applicable to him."

nary function of the synagogue "authorities."[67] Paul had certainly been engaged in such disciplinary functions under the "authority" of the synagogue in his former manner of life against "the Way." And he had likewise been the victim of such "authority" applied to himself by those rejecting his contention that Jesus was the Christ and that gentiles could now, by faith and without becoming Jews, become equal coparticipants in the blessings of the One God promised to Abraham's seed. The synagogue "authorities" would have had every right to remove gentiles making such claims if they were unwilling to adopt the "proper behavior" of "righteous gentiles," including the payment ("rendering") of the two-drachma Temple tax (for the support of the community sacrifices in Jerusalem) to demonstrate their fidelity to the holiness of God, the Law, and his people. And if they persisted in attending without "subordinating" themselves to the "authorities" they would have been subject to discipline, though capital punishment is questionable.[68]

This fits Paul's description of the purpose of the "bearing" (φορεῖ: "wearing," "carrying") of the "sword" as the "avenger of wrath." "Wrath" (ὀργήν) is a deeply nuanced phrase in Judaism and thus for Paul. God's wrath is linked with his covenant with humanity, with the recognition of the One God and his elect people who were no longer to worship other gods.[69] It is a central theme of the monotheistic faith of Israel. For the early Christian gentiles to make the monotheistic claims they would be making without "necessarily" (ἀνάγκη: 13:5)[70] adopting the "proper behavior"[71] of "righteous gentiles," including payment of the Temple tax, would have been the source of the synagogue "authorities'" justifiable "wrath" as the legitimate representatives of God's "order" in the congregation of the people of God

[67]The office of *hazzan* described in the Mishnah included the responsibility for order and discipline in the synagogue, including the administration of "judicial stripes" in the courts of the local synagogues (Sky, *Hazzan*, pp. 13–21; esp. 18–19). Note that Sky traces evidence of this office in this period and earlier (pp. 1–12). See *m. Makkot* 3 for discussion of disciplinary flogging, including the *makkot mardut* of the local courts; also the comments of Hare, *Jewish Persecution*, pp. 43–46.

[68]Alon, *Jews*, pp. 206–12.

[69]Fitchner, *TDNT*, 5.396.

[70]Paul says that subordination is "necessary" as in compulsory responsibility (1 Cor. 9:16; 2 Cor. 12:10). See Grundmann, *TDNT*, 1.344–45.

[71]The theme of gentiles repenting and adopting righteous behavior flows throughout Paul's letters and Acts. In this context see, for example, Rom. 1, 2 and 6 as well as the intentions throughout chaps. 12–15; also Acts 26:20 for concise use in this same way.

(13:2-5; note this contextual concern on the part of the authorities in 13:11-13; 14:15-16).

But there is another possibility for Paul's use of μάχαιραν here; he could have had a symbolic or metaphoric intention. If Paul used "sword" figuratively here for the "word of God" it would neatly fit my proposed understanding of the context of Paul's remarks in this paraenesis. The "authorities" of the synagogues were the interpreters of the Torah (God's word to Israel, the Law), and they would unquestionably have been responsible for the application of the Law to the synagogue community, including Christian gentiles seeking association with the synagogue as "righteous gentiles." The "authorities" would judge behavior (and faith claims) based on their interpretation of Torah even as the writer of Hebrews spoke of the "word of God" as "living and active and sharper than any two-edged sword [μάχαιραν], and piercing as far as the division of soul and spirit, of both joints and marrow, and able to judge the thoughts and intentions of the heart" (Heb. 4:12). The synagogue "authorities" would naturally praise good behavior according to their understanding of the word of God; and they would administer God's wrath on those who compromised the monotheistic tenets of the faith as set forth in the Law. Indeed, they would have been "servants of God" on the "seat of Moses" (Matt. 23:2ff.)[72] interpreting Torah and halakhot for the community, and continually dedicated to the collection, safekeeping, and distribution of the Temple tax for Jerusalem, the dwelling place of God and of his word.

Does a figurative application of the "sword" appear forced? Consider Paul's use of the image of the "armor [ὅπλα] of the light" in the context of Romans 13:12, a mere eight verses after his use of the imagery of the "sword." Is Paul's use of "armor" there not figurative?[73] Consider also that "wear" (φορεῖ) has the sense of being a customary and continuous action, comes from the same root as "tax" (φόρος: literally "carrying"),[74] and although seldom used in the Septuagint, among its several appearances two are figuratively linked with the "carrying" of wisdom, the Law, or mercy on the tongue.[75]

Certainly no one would argue that Paul intended for his audience

[72]Rivkin, *Hidden Revolution*, pp. 252ff.

[73]Consider also the use of the image of the "sword" in the letter to Ephesus (6:17): "the sword [μάχαιραν] of the Spirit, which is the word of God," in the context of discussing the "whole armor [πανοπλίαν] of God" (v. 11).

[74]Weiss, *TDNT*, 9.78–83.

[75]Ibid., 9.83–84.

literally to "put on armor," or even metaphorically in that they should adopt the moral behavior of a soldier. That would defy the plain sense of the text and of Paul's contextual intentions to urge a new lifestyle characterized by "proper behavior." In fact, Paul's exact phrase in 13:13 that is translated "proper behavior" is εὐσχημόνως περιπατήσωμεν, which is literally "let us walk [*halakh*] decently." And his concerns are the Judaic norms of "proper behavior" that I have described earlier for the "righteous gentile" leaving behind the behavior associated with idolatry and pagan culture ("the deeds of darkness" as characterized by idolatrous parties and festivals and cultic prostitution, and by the strife resulting from resistance to the "authorities" described between the "strong" and "weak" of chap. 14):

> Let us therefore lay aside the deeds of darkness and put on the armor of light. Let us behave properly as in the day, not in carousing and drunkenness, not in sexual promiscuity and sensuality, not in strife and jealousy. (Rom. 13:12-13)

In summary, Paul could have intended the usage of "sword" figuratively for the disciplinary authority inherent in the responsibilities of the synagogue leaders, the same sense normally applied to the image of the sword in the traditional interpretations of this topos, that is, "the sword is the symbol of the executive and criminal jurisdiction of a magistrate, and is therefore used of the power of punishing inherent in the government"[76] (enemy nations may be literally ruled by the Roman sword, but Romans and Rome were ruled by Roman law!).[77] In other words, synagogue officials may be said to have the authority of the sword even though they did not literally use it to discipline their members, that is, they have the right to govern their membership— just as the local Roman or Hellenistic officials may be said to have the

[76]Sanday and Headlam, *Romans*, pp. 367–68.

[77]While the sword might possibly be enlisted in capital punishment in some extreme cases during this period (decapitation, preceded by whippings), most often punishment involved fines and beatings (even strangulation was more common than the sword). In Rome any such official punishments were the jurisdiction of judicial magistrates; they involved Roman laws and courts. Rome was not under a police force in the manner of a rebellious colony or province where the Roman governor enforced order through the troops under his command. The "right of the sword" (*ius gladii*) had to do with the power over soldiers under one's command, not ordinary citizens. For full discussion of Roman law and punishment see Sherwin-White, *Roman Society* (*ius gladii* on pp. 8–11); J. Stambaugh and D. Balch, *The New Testament in Its Social Environment*, pp. 30–36.

authority of the sword, though they would not have literally used a
sword in the exercise of their duties, for example, in the case of those
responsible for the collection of taxes. Or Paul could have intended a
metaphorical interpretation: the synagogue leaders were the legitimate interpreters of the word of God ("carrying" the Torah "ordained
by angels") for the behavioral requirements for the congregation of
God's people, including the "righteous gentile" in their midst.[78] In
both scenarios the context of the synagogue and the role of the "authorities" to praise good and protect the congregation from evil in the
administration of their responsibilities as servants of God, including
the behavioral requirements of the "righteous gentile" and their obligation to pay the Temple tax, respect the plain sense of Paul's intentions in 13:1-7 and in his larger paraenesis of 12:1—15:13. Paul was
concerned with outlining the kind of behavior that should characterize the "renewed [nonconforming!] minds" of gentiles who "present"
their "bodies a living and holy sacrifice, acceptable to God, which is
your spiritual service of worship," in view of their having received the
"mercies of God" in the present, temporary situation characterized by
the vicarious suffering of the "stumbling" of Israel and their rulers, to
whom they must now be "subordinate."

"Render to All What Is Due Them."

Paul wraps up this small paraenesis on subordination to the authorities
with the admonition in 13:7 to:

> Render to all what is due them: tax [φόρον] to whom tax is due; cus-
> tom [τέλος] to whom custom; fear [φόβον] to whom fear; honor
> [τιμὴν] to whom honor.

[78]Steinmetz, "Calvin and Melanchthon," p. 76, notes that in medieval exegesis
the authorities were both secular and spiritual, and the sword referred to both the
"physical sword of temporal magistrates and the spiritual sword of ecclesiastical
prelates." Interestingly, Luther "argues that Paul had in mind both secular and
spiritual authorities. Having made this point, Luther shows very little curiosity
about secular rulers, who seem to him to be doing a capable enough job—certainly
better than the spiritual authorities whose stewardship of the Church has left it in
rags and tatters. [Cardinal] Sadoleto, on the other hand, agrees with Luther's reading of Paul's intention, but not with Luther's criticism of the Church. For Sadoleto
the papacy is unarguably the highest of the higher powers. He therefore heaps
scorn on the Protestants who grovel before petty German princes (whose title to
power is often, to say the least, ambiguous) while rebelling against the spiritual
sword held by the Church, given directly to Peter by Christ."

This instruction is certainly linked with Paul's continued point in the following verses (v. 8):

Owe nothing to anyone except to love one another; for he who loves his neighbor has fulfilled the law.

I explore this link below; however, it is important to note here that Paul is not really through with his instruction concerning payment of what is "due" the "authorities" in verse 7, for "love" is the real motivational issue that ties together his concerns in 13:1-7 with his larger concerns throughout this paraenesis.

Each of the four elements bears closer examination and can be directly linked to the four categories or functions of synagogue leadership just reviewed, albeit in the pattern of reverse order, or chiastic inversion.[79] They are extremely flexible and lend themselves to interpretation by their context; in fact, the traditional translations of these terms are generally based on alternate or secondary meanings in keeping with the hermeneutical presuppositions brought to the text.

Paul instructs his audience to "render" (ἀπόδοτε: "to give back, repay") to all what is "due them" (ὀφειλάς). This phrase carries the sense of fulfilling an obligation or expectation, in this case, what is "due," which is a popular concept for Paul, expressing the sense of obligation to Judaic norms of righteousness as the halakhah that should not be disregarded in the Christian community (1 Cor. 11:7, 10), and in the context of the "weak" and the "strong" it is used to urge the obligation of the "strong" to accommodate the opinions of proper behavior as understood by the "faith" of the "weak" (Rom. 15:1).[80] But most relevant is Paul's use of ὀφειλέται/ὀφείλουσιν to describe the "obligation" (ὀφείλουσιν) of Christian gentiles to participate in the collection for the Jerusalem saints, for they are "indebted" (ὀφειλέται) to share with them in the "service" (λειτουργῆσαι) of their "material things" by reason of having shared in Israel's "spiritual things" (15:15-32; 1:11-13).

Paul's language is charged with deep allusions to the "reasonable

[79]Myers, "Chiastic Inversion," notes that "chiastic inversion has a more significant impact on the organization of Paul's argument in Romans than has been recognized previously" (p. 34). Stein, "Argument," pp. 325–43, explores the chiastic character of this passage.

[80]Hauck, *TDNT*, 5.562–64. The point of contention between the "weak" and "strong" is the application of halakhah for "righteous gentiles" to the Christians in Rome.

service of worship" incumbent upon the Christian gentiles of Rome; they must pay that which the "authorities" in their service of God as the legitimate interpreters of his Law (of good and evil) are seeking from them, both in the areas of "taxes" and "proper behavior" and out of the sense of duty as well as service.

1. Paul first says to render "tax" (φόρον) to the one collecting the tax, clearly drawing from the instructions he has just given to recognize they must pay the "servants [λειτουργοὶ] of God" continually devoted to the collection of taxes. Paul's use of φόρον for taxes with his choice of φορεῖ for the "wearing" of the sword are no accident. Both draw from the same root meaning of "carrying" or "bringing" a "gift" or "tribute," usually a tax. It differs from τέλη, which often refers to tolls and taxes paid to a foreign power such as the emperor.[81] Thus, we have another indication that those "carrying" the "sword" as the legitimate "servants of God" do so in the particular function of "carrying" the taxes. I propose that these taxes were not those of the empire but those of Diaspora Jewry, the two-drachma Temple tax collected annually for the support of the community sacrifices in Jerusalem.

2. Paul then instructs the payment of "custom" (τέλος) to whom custom is due. The translation of τέλος here as "custom" derives from the presuppositions brought to the context, and as Delling points out it is not possible to arrange all statements using τέλος with lexical certainty, as more than one meaning are likely when this word is used.[82] The noun τέλος derives from a verb meaning to "carry out" or "fulfill," and it carries the sense of "final destiny," "results," and the "end."[83] In this particular case "custom" or "tribute" may be the proper translation of the word; however, it should be noted that only in Matthew 17:25 of all the many appearances of τέλος in the New Testament is it rendered so (see, for example, Rom. 6:21-22 as the "result"; 10:4 as the "goal," "aim," or "end").

The word τέλος has a variety of other primary meanings that are suitable for translating Paul's usage here. It is worth considering the context of Paul's use here in the light of his usage of "perfect" (τέλειον) in 12:2 at the beginning of this paraenesis to describe the "will of God" that is "proved" by those who have their "minds renewed" because they "present your bodies a living and holy sacrifice,

[81]Weiss, *TDNT*, 9.81.
[82]Delling, *TDNT*, 8.54.
[83]Ibid., 8.49–61.

acceptable to God, which is your spiritual service of worship" (12:1-2). Paul may have in mind the indebtedness of the Christian gentiles to being "perfect" as defined by the synagogue servants (διάκονός) for halakhah applicable to their behavior as "righteous gentiles." This would make sense of Paul's use in Romans 6:21-22, translated "results" or "outcome" in the context of "eternal life" when explaining their obligation to "present yourselves to God as those alive from the dead, and your members as instruments of righteousness to God" (6:13ff., 21-22).

The translation of "custom to whom custom," fully consistent with the use of τέλος in the Greek world with "obligations" and the "fulfillment" of responsibilities,[84] would then be: "the fulfilling of good results to those concerned with the results of your righteous behavior," in the context of fulfilling the halakhot applicable to the "righteous gentile" associating with the synagogue. This would infer payment of taxes as well as ethical behavior. This is consistent with rendering "customs" in the sense of Judaic customs of behavior, rather than the somewhat redundant rendering of τέλος as another statement of "tribute" or "taxes."

3. The rendering of "fear" (φόβον) to those due φόβον has provided an opportunity for those uncomfortable with Paul's seemingly indiscriminate legitimizing of the "authorities" to explore what would be, if the traditional understanding of the "authorities" as states and empires is assumed, a necessary caveat.[85] Yoder is most eloquent in demonstrating that Paul could not have meant to "render everything to government."[86] Yoder explains:

> Often this text is read as a sort of list of all the four kinds of things that are due to government; taxes, revenue, respect, and honor. Such an interpretation is quite common. It makes nonsense, however, of the prior invitation to be discriminating and to render to each just what is his due.

[84]Ibid., 8.49–51.

[85]The concern to soften Paul's radical language, ostensibly concerning the ordination of the state in the traditional interpretation, is an ancient phenomenon. See the discussion of Schottroff, "Give to Caesar," pp. 238–40: "The radicality and singularity of Rom. 13:1-7 becomes clear if one compares this text with a philosophical explanation from antiquity of the power of the state, about different constitutional forms and their quality. A philosopher who is a loyal supporter of the government will naturally differentiate between good and bad constitutions" (p. 238).

[86]Yoder, *Politics*, p. 211.

It is therefore a much more serious reading of the entire passage to hear in this text, as do Cullmann and Cranfield, an implicit allusion to the words of Jesus. "Render to each what is due to him" means to render to Caesar what belongs to him and to God what belongs to him. Taxes and revenue, perhaps honor, are due to Caesar, but fear is due to God.[87]

The problems with this rendering of Paul's intention in his application of "fear" here are several. The very structure of the verse and its relationship to the prior instructions belies this kind of discrimination; Paul would have structured his language to make this kind of emphatic point (e.g., 1 Pet. 2:17).[88] But perhaps more telling is that Paul and his heirs, like the Jewish community (and Peter),[89] did use φόβον to describe "respectful" behavior toward those in "authority" in various interpersonal relationships (household tables) when addressing those in "subordinate" positions (e.g., wives in Eph. 5:33; slaves in Eph. 6:5).[90] This understanding of the community dynamic is rooted in the historic understanding of the responsibility of those in authority to nurture obedience to God's Law in the family, in the community, and in the land. Indeed, fear of God is tied up with fear of the Law and those responsible for its interpretation in the community of God.[91] Finally, "fear" is a central concept in the designation of "righteous gentiles." They are "God-fearers" who have willingly adopted certain tenets of Judaic halakhah to govern their proper behavior while dwelling among the people of God.

"Fear of God" is understood to lie behind "fear of men" in the very sense that Paul would naturally speak of rendering "fear" to those of

[87]Ibid.

[88]Stein, "Argument," pp. 342–43, notes that all four of these "are addressed to πασιν ('all of them') whose immediate antecedent is the authorities or ministers of God in 13:6."

[89]1 Pet. 2:17-18; 3:2; even in the context of pointing out to "fear God" Peter instructs slaves to fear humans in positions of authority, i.e., their masters.

[90]Balz, *TDNT*, 9.215–18. Note that "fear" or "respect" was used in this same manner in *1 Clement* and the *Didache* in defining proper interpersonal relationships. See Carrington, *Primitive Christian Catechism*, for more on early Christian catechisms and subordination. See Yoder, *Politics*, pp. 163–92 on household tables and subordination.

[91]See Josephus, *Against Apion* 2.39–42 (276–78, 288–96), stating in 2.39 (276–77): "for though we be deprived of our wealth, of our cities, or of other advantages we have, our law continues immortal; nor can any Jew go so far from his own country, nor be so affrighted at the severest lord, as not to be more affrighted at the law than at him."

the synagogue in positions of "authority" to interpret proper behavior and to collect the Temple tax as well as to administer other community obligations. In this case Paul may particularly have in mind "respect" for the rulers (ἄρχοντες). This approach again allows the plain sense of the text to come through without the need to be concerned with providing a caveat that Paul, dealing with the "authorities" of the synagogue rather than the assumed empire or state, did not sense the need for.

4. The rendering of "honor" (τιμήν) is generally downplayed as though it were a mere redundancy. However, τιμήν was a very rich word that was originally tied to recognition of one's control of one's property and possessions ("respect"), and even when it acquired its more ethical qualities it was still, for example, used to render "payment" and "price" in the Septuagint (Job 31:39; Gen. 20:16; 44:2; Ex. 34:20; Lev. 5:15, 18; Num. 20:19); and in Leviticus 27:2-27 it is used for the estimation of vows and dues.[92] "Honor" has the sense of proper moral behavior in accord with the Law as well (e.g., Gen. 38:23; 1 Sam. 15:30; 2 Sam. 6:20).

It is perhaps noteworthy that we are aware of at least four epitaphs from Jewish catacombs in Rome that refer to individuals who were, in addition to the more common duty of *archon*, also called *archon* "of all honor" (πασής τιμής). This appears to be a higher office, a combination of offices, or at least an *archon* who was more highly "honored" than an ordinary *archon*, and may have something to do with their responsibilities as they relate to treasury.[93]

The combination fits my proposal nicely: Paul calls the Christian gentiles of Rome to "honor" the higher authorities (ἐξουσίαις ὑπερεχούσαις) as the interpreters of "good" and "evil" in the execution of their official responsibilities, including the payment of the

[92]Schneider, *TDNT*, 8.169–80. See 1 Tim. 5:17 for an interesting use with payment to presbyters. Other New Testament uses with the sense of material goods include Rev. 21:26; Acts 4:34; 5:2-3; 7:16; 19:19; 1 Cor. 6:20; 7:23. Note also that in Matt. 15:5, 6 and Mark 7:11, 12 honoring parents includes financial support, and see Matt. 27:8 for the value of the thirty pieces of silver for Judas.

[93]Leon, *Jews*, pp. 176–78, discusses the various possibilities. Particularly interesting here is the suggestion of Frey that "the secondary meanings of τιμη as value, price, evaluation, census, regards this officer as most probably the financial executive of the congregation charged with collecting the dues, taxes, and other revenues and with making disbursements; in other words, a sort of treasurer." Leon notes that Frey's conclusion is not clear since the preceding definite article that would be conclusive is missing.

taxes and any other financial and administrative obligations incumbent upon them in their new association with the Jewish community.

We can now see the richness of Paul's call to "obligatory" behavior in 13:1-7 in the context of the synagogue and the concomitant behavioral and administrative requirements incumbent upon the Christian gentiles attending as "righteous gentiles." Indeed, we see what may have been four very specific instructions that may follow, in chiastic order, their obligations to four specific roles of synagogue leadership. That is, each of the activities they are indebted to render may be linked to the particular concerns of each of the four different roles examined for synagogue leadership, though I am hesitant to insist on such a relationship:[94]

Synagogue leadership role	to be paid
1. ἐξουσίαις ὑπερεχούσαις (higher authorities)	4. τιμήν (honor)
2. ἄρχοντες (rulers)	3. φόβον (fear)
3. διάκονός (ministers)	2. τέλος (custom)
4. λειτουργοὶ (servants)	1. φόρον (tax)

The chiastic pattern of Paul's admonition was thus:

[A] Authority #1: ἐξουσίαις ὑπερεχούσαις (higher authorities)
  [B] Authority #2: ἄρχοντες (rulers)
    [C] Authority #3: διάκονός (ministers)
      [D] Authority #4: λειτουργοὶ (servants)
      [D'] Payment due to authority #4 (λειτουργοὶ): φόρον (tax)
    [C'] Payment due to authority #3 (διάκονός): τέλος (custom)
  [B'] Payment due to authority #2 (ἄρχοντες): φόβον (fear)
[A'] Payment due to authority #1 (ἐξουσίαις ὑπερεχούσαις): τιμήν (honor)

Moreover, we are prepared for the play on words and concepts that underlie the next verse in Paul's letter, when those who have just been told to pay what they "owe" (v. 7: ὀφειλάς) are alternately instructed not to "owe" (ὀφείλετε) anyone anything, "except to love one another" (v. 8). For we can now see that this follows the same pattern he had developed with respect to the "authorities," namely, beyond the obligatory "subordination" to those in "authority" for "wrath's sake"

[94]See the chiastic structure of this passage proposed by Stein, "Argument," pp. 339–43, who suggests that these references to authority figures overlap in a manner that actually strengthens my proposal.

there lies the more important motivation of "conscience." Paul develops this juxtaposition of relations according to fleshly distinctions (gentiles vs. Jews), which are to be abandoned along with the "deeds of darkness" that had characterized their "slavery to sin" in the past (certainly directed to Christian *gentiles*, not Christian Jews), as they learn instead to live in "love," which naturally fulfills the very intentions of the Law that may have been in dispute (the teaching of loving behavior in holiness before God toward one's neighbor).[95]

CONTEXTUAL FEASIBILITY

Paul's Instructions in 13:1-7 in the Context of
the Paraenesis of 12:1—15:13

Many commentators note the need, but few manage to follow through on the importance, of reconciling Paul's concerns in the topos of 13:1-7 with his contextual concerns throughout the balance of the paraenesis of 12:1—15:13,[96] much less those of the entire letter, wherein Paul deals with the tensions of redefining faith in Christ for his audience (particularly for *gentiles* newly introduced to "faith" in the One God of historical Israel) in relationship to Israel, the Law, and the anomalous "stumbling" of non-Christian Jews whom the audience ostensibly considered "enemies" of the gospel.[97]

[95]Heschel, *Between God and Man*, p. 162, is eloquent: "Above all, the Torah asks for *love: thou shalt love thy God; thou shalt love thy neighbor*. All observance is training in the art of love. To forget that love is the purpose of all *mitzvot* is to vitiate their meaning."

[96]See my earlier discussion of those who cannot reconcile this passage with the surrounding context or their views of Pauline ideas and thus come to various conclusions, some arguing that this topos must be a later interpolation. Dunn, *Romans*, p. 768, is a notable exception. While Dunn calls for this consideration and makes some effort to provide suggestions, his suggestions fail to provide an acceptable answer. It is historically unlikely that Roman gentiles would have represented a threat to the Jewish community, upon becoming Christians, because they were more resistant to Roman law and taxation than the Jewish community. However, Dunn's suggestions do respect the need to address the historical tensions and coordinate with the suggestions I will offer below, particularly his notice of the possible missionary sense of the admonition (though differently than he was suggesting).

[97]The concerns of chaps. 9–11 immediately precede the "Therefore" of 12:1 that begins this paraenesis. In chaps. 9–11 we see that the tensions underlying Paul's concerns throughout the letter are concerning the interaction of Christian gentiles with non-Christian Jews. Paul confronts the temptation to arrogance over

This study seeks to bring the instructions in the smaller paraenesis of 13:1-7 into harmony with the several parallel tensions that exist between:

- Christian *gentiles* and non-Christian *Jews* as the focus of chapters 9–11 (the "stumbling" of 9:30-33)
- Christians and their "brethren" as the focus of much of chapters 12 and 14 (12:9, 13; 14:10, 13, 15, 21)
- Christians and their "neighbors" as the focus of many instructions in chapters 12–15 (13:8-10; 15:1-2)
- Christians and their "enemies" (12:14-21 as those who persecute, curse, and intend evil; 15:3 as those who would reproach)
- The "strong" (Christians) and the "weak" (non-Christian Jews) of 14:1—15:3.

If Paul was addressing tensions resulting from the new association of Christian gentiles within the synagogue communities in Rome, as seems to be the case often throughout the letter, then the following scenario is likely:

First, the Christian gentiles found some of the halakhot governing their behavior as "righteous gentiles" difficult to accept (e.g., dietary restrictions), particularly in the light of the attractive argument that some group was making that they need not be concerned with Judaic practices of righteousness (the plain sense of 16:17-18 for the group Paul opposes), for they were saved by faith alone (the misuse of Paul's teaching that he confronts in 3:8; 6:1-23; and turns around on the "strong" in 14:14b-17).

Paul's admonitions in chapter 12 and the balance of chapters 13–15 appear to address the need to observe these behavioral requirements and the concomitant obligation to seek peace with any non-Christian Jewish "brethren" who may have been reluctant to accept Christian

---

against those "stumbling" as unacceptable and dangerous, and calls instead for the recognition of responsibility to serve the "stumbling" and understand the vicarious nature of their plight. Further, he explains that those appearing to be "enemies for your sake" "from the standpoint of the gospel" (11:28) are in fact "beloved for the sake of the fathers" "from the standpoint of God's choice" because the "gifts and calling of God are irrevocable" (11:28-29). He explains this in the context of revealing the mystery of the Christian gentiles' role in the designs that God was employing to bring about the salvation of all Israel (11:25-27, 28ff.). See also 9:1-5, where it is clear also that Paul does not regard the non-Christian Jew as the enemy but as his "brethren" who he would willingly suffer vicariously to bring to faith in the gospel (11:13 in defining his ministry to gentiles as really in the service of those "stumbling"!).

gentiles, or may have been even hostile toward the association of these
Christian gentiles (15:3: the "strong" fear "reproach" from the
"weak"), or may have been disputing their claims to be equal coparticipants in the blessings of God (14:16: blaspheming their "good
things").

Paul's admonitions in 12:9-21 are clearly concerned with how to in-
teract in love with both "brothers"[98] (insiders) and "neighbors" (outsiders) who may have even done them "evil." The juxtaposition of relationships fits the proposed understanding of the historical tensions.
The "measure" of their new "faith" is worked out in the context of
the synagogues; in the context of multiple definitions of which "faith"
is appropriate (the tension of 14:1-12, 13ff. between the "weak" and
the "strong"). The practice of their new faith is thus tested by the historic definitions of faith operative in Judaism, including the apostolic
decree (Noahide Commandments) for defining the proper practice of
faith for the "righteous gentile." If they were disputing or resisting
these definitions in their synagogue attendance, which appears to be
the case in the context of payment of the Temple tax and the dietary
regulations that are at issue between the "weak" and the "strong,"
then they would meet with disapproval from their Jewish
"brethren"—"neighbors"—"authorities," whom they may consider
their "enemies."[99] The legitimacy of their faith would be disputed. We
would then understand why Paul does not want them to take "revenge" but rather wants them to be humbly[100] concerned with "overcoming evil with good" as they "respect what is right in the sight of all

[98]Paul used the term "brethren" to refer to Christian gentiles now related to
Jesus, "the first-born among many brethren" in 8:29 and of non-Christian Jews as
his "brethren, my kinsmen according to the flesh" in 9:3. All Jews are related to
Jesus, the "descendent of David according to the flesh" (1:3). Paul continually
used the term "brethren" in this letter for both Christians and non-Christian Jews
in the sense I have developed, for they were now worshiping God together, even
if not Jesus as the Christ. For additional uses of "brethren" that refer variously to
Christians and non-Christian (as well as Christian) Jews as insiders see also 7:1, 4;
8:12; 10:1; 11:25; 12:1; 15:14, 15, 30, and the fuller discussion in chapter 3 above.

[99]Barth, *Romans*, p. 484, notes the relationship between the enemies mentioned
at the end of chap. 12 and the rulers of chap. 13 in defining the revolutionary nature of Paul's epistle. A. Webster, "St. Paul's Political Advice to the Haughty
Gentile Christians in Rome: An Exegesis of Romans 13:1-7," pp. 277–82, also explores Paul's language in the context of the tensions within the community and
with the Jews of Rome, though he reaches different conclusions.

[100]12:16 repeats the central concern of 12:3 not to think more of one's new
status than is prudent.

men. If possible, so far as it depends on you, be at peace with all men"
(12:17-18; 14:13—15:6).[101]

Further, the concerns of 13:8-14 deal with fulfilling the loving intentions of the Law by turning from pagan practices ("lay aside the
deeds of darkness": are the behaviors outlined still a temptation for
the Christians Paul was addressing?) to the practices that characterize
Judaic norms for righteous behavior ("put on the armor of light" and
"behave properly"[102]) in view of the need to "make no provision for
the flesh in regard to its lusts" (a clear concern to overcome Jew-
gentile barriers and see their relations anew in Christ).[103]

In this context Paul's concern with the commandments of the Law
(even quoting them to illustrate his point: 13:9) have depth, for they
would have been unquestionable measures of the validity of the
Christian gentiles' claims in the synagogues. "Owe nothing to anyone
except to love one another. . . . Love does no wrong to a neighbor; love
therefore is the fulfillment of the law" (13:8-10) is a call to the Judaic
norms of righteous behavior, not to earn salvation but because of it.
They were saved by faith, but not in order that "sin reign in your mortal body that you should obey its lusts, and do not go on presenting the
members of your body to sin as instruments of unrighteousness; but

---

[101]Zerbe, "Paul's Ethic," p. 187, ties together these passages similarly, though
he is working within the traditional definition of the state in 13:1-7: "The exhortation to nonretaliation and good deeds in relation to hostile outsiders (Rom.
12:14, 17-21) complements the exhortation to submission in relation to ruling authorities (Rom. 13:1-7). The two passages are linked thematically; both passages
address the question of responding to and minimizing conflict with the surrounding world." So too Schottroff, "Give to Caesar," p. 224: "Romans 12:14-21 presupposes that Christians will come into dangerous conflicts with persons who are
not Christians: enmity (12:20), persecution (12:14), and evil directed at Christians
(12:17, 19) are mentioned; these are situations that call for divine retribution. If
the sequel, then, discusses the behavior vis-à-vis powers of the state, it is clear that
this discussion about obedience toward the state occurs against the background of
already present as well as anticipated conflicts of Christians with the society and
the power of the state. The assumptions of 12:14-21 and 13:1-7 are identical. The
content of 13:1, therefore, also connects to the content of 12:21: the good, which
overcomes evil, is here equivalent to subordination to the power of the state."
(One need but substitute "synagogue" for "state" to see my point reinforced in
these parallel observations).

[102]Literally "walk" properly in 13:13, certainly a reference to "halakhah" for the
"righteous gentile."

[103]Paul uses the term "flesh" to distinguish between Jews and non-Jews, circumcision being a very real distinction in the flesh.

present yourselves to God as those alive from the dead, and your members as instruments of righteousness to God" (6:12-13, 14ff.). Do we not hear an echo of Paul's concern that wherever he has preached the gospel it results in "the obedience of the Gentiles by word and deed" (15:17-19); was this not the very "obedience of faith" of which he wrote "boldly" to "remind" the Roman Christians?

The admonition in 14:1 to the "strong" to "welcome" the "weak" without disputing their opinions may be the practical outworking of the admonition in 12:9-21 for the "strong" to seek peace by overcoming evil with good, that is, by extending the very "welcoming" to the "weak" that they themselves (the "strong") were presently being denied (by the "weak"). The "strong" need to respect the "measure" of the "faith" of the "weak" without disputing the particulars of their practice; for their faith is legitimate before God (14:1-12: is this not the classic issue between Christianity and Judaism?). Moreover, the "strong" need to accommodate the "opinions" of the proper practice of the faith as defined by the "weak" so that they do not cause the "weak" to "stumble" further and "blaspheme" the claims of the "strong" (the issue in 14:16—15:3), thereby missing the most important message that the "strong" should be devoted to demonstrating in their lifestyle: that Jesus is the Christ who has come for the "weak" to "confirm the promises given to the fathers" even as he has come for the "gentiles" Paul is addressing to "glorify God for his mercy" (14:13-18; 15:1-9).

Paul's instructions to the "strong" in chapters 14–15 echo his instructions in chapter 12 to serve humbly and in love with "respect for what is right in the sight of all men" in the pursuit of "peace," as far as they are "able" (δυνατὸν: "strong" [12:17-18]); and they tie back equally into his instructions in chapter 13: "Do you want to have no fear of authority? Do what is good, and you will have praise from the same. . . . Render to all what is due them. . . . Owe nothing to anyone except to love one another; for he who loves his neighbor has fulfilled the law. . . . Let us behave properly as in the day . . . put on the Lord Jesus Christ, and make no provision for the flesh in regard to its lusts" (13: 3, 7, 8, 13, 14). The "strong" are to accommodate "proper behavior" as defined by the "weak": "For he who in this way serves Christ is acceptable to God and approved by men. So then let us pursue the things which make for peace and the building up of one another. Do not tear down the work of God for the sake of food" (14:18-20).

As Paul brings this paraenesis to its crescendo he envisions gentiles

praising God in the midst of Israel as they recognize that the One God
of Israel is indeed the One God of the whole world (15:9-12):

> "Therefore I will give praise to Thee among the Gentiles,
> And I will sing to Thy name."
> And again he says,
> "Rejoice, O Gentiles, with His people."
> And again,
> "Praise the Lord all you Gentiles,
> And let all the peoples praise Him."
> And again Isaiah says,
> "There shall come the root of Jesse,
> And He who arises to rule over the Gentiles,
> In Him shall the Gentiles hope."[104]

Christian gentiles worshiping the One God in the midst of the congregation of Israel—my point exactly!

Thus, Paul has covered a lot of ground in this paraenesis to convince the Christian gentiles that they should adopt the behavior incumbent upon "righteous gentiles" seeking association with Israel.
First, in service of Christ as the "acceptable" behavior before God
(14:18); second, in service of peace as the "approved" behavior before

---

[104]Hays, *Echoes*, pp. 68–74; on p. 71 he notes, "Clearly, he has saved his clinchers for the end. After much allusive and labored argumentation, Paul finally draws
back the curtain and reveals a collection of passages that explicitly embody his vision for a church composed of Jews and Gentiles glorifying God together.
Commentators often note that Paul has offered here one quotation from the
Pentateuch, one from the Prophets, and two from the Writings, all strung together
by the catchword *ethne*, all pointing to the eschatological consummation in which
Gentiles join in the worship of Israel's God: truly the law and the Prophets are
brought forward here as witnesses. . . . There is no sleight of hand here: Paul rests
his case on the claim that his churches, in which Gentiles do in fact join Jews in
praising God, must be the eschatological fulfillment of the scriptural vision."
Again on p. 72 he notes, "The quotation from Deut. 32:43, then, adds a crucial element to the portrait. . . . The Gentiles do not stand alone around Christ; they are
being summoned to join 'with' Israel in rejoicing." And finally, on p. 73: "Similarly,
the final text in Paul's catena also envisions a gathering of Gentiles and Jews
around the Messiah. The full force of Paul's citation of Isa. 11:10 becomes apparent only when the reader recollects Isa. 11:11-12 . . . Paul quotes only an excerpt
that prophesies Gentiles placing their hope in the 'root of Jesse,' but the quotation also works as an allusion to Isaiah's vision of God's eschatological kingdom in
which the lost ones of Israel rejoin these Gentiles in being gathered at the feet of
the one whom God has raised up. This allusion in turn forges an intertextual link
back to the remnant theme of Romans 11."

non-Christian Jews (14:18—15:2), to the end that both Christian gentiles and non-Christian Jews might with "one voice glorify the God and Father of our Lord Jesus Christ" (15:6, 5-12).

In addition to clarifying the above reasons for the Christian gentiles to adopt the halakhot of the "righteous gentile" in their moral and religious behavior, he also found it necessary to address some of the additional community (institutional) requirements incumbent upon them in their new association with the synagogues. Strictly speaking, these Christian gentiles could have adopted "righteous behavior" and still disputed the Jewish community's administrative authority, particularly with regard to their payment of the Temple tax; hence the need for the admonition of 13:1-7.

The synagogue leaders had the "authority," and the power that necessarily accompanies such responsibility, to govern the behavior of the Jewish community. This jurisdiction extended to many administrative areas such as the responsibility, both to the Jewish community and to the Roman authorities who granted them their rights,[105] to collect taxes (Roman taxes[?] and the Jerusalem Temple tax)[106] as well as to discipline improper behavior, whether religious, moral, or social, including the right to physical punishment.

The need for Paul's address in 13:1-7 becomes clear in this context. It was necessary to "remind" the Christian gentiles of Rome of their need to "subordinate" themselves to the synagogue authorities, for

---

[105]It is obvious that the Jewish community would have to report to some governor under whose jurisdiction they would fall, and there is much evidence of communication on the part of both Jewish communities with Roman government and of government decisions regarding Jewish communities. In addition, Leon, *Jews*, pp. 191–92, states that the prostates is the equivalent of the common Latin term *patronus*, and that most scholars interpret the prostates as "the official who defended the interests of the congregation in the community at large, especially in its relations with the political authorities. He would have been a sort of legal representative of his congregation."

[106]It is not hard to imagine resistance on the part of gentiles to paying a tax to the Jerusalem Temple, particularly if they were tempted to regard the Temple as obsolete (as gentile Christianity later claimed and characteristic of the kind of thinking Paul challenges in chaps. 9–11 and 15). Taxes were already considerable, and there was a general discontent in Rome with respect to any new taxes; it is not difficult to imagine a negative response to the Temple tax (see Dunn, *Romans*, pp. 772–73). In fact, the special privileges that made the payment of the Temple tax possible were the occasion for animosity in the larger gentile communities in which the Jewish community dwelt (Tcherikover, *Hellenistic*, pp. 308, 330, 371–77). Paul, however, appears to consider the issue beyond dispute.

they were serving God's people in the execution of their responsibilities to maintain order, collect taxes, and generally attend to the administrative matters of the community. These Christian gentiles, because of their new association with the synagogue, are obligated to subordinate themselves to the synagogue authorities and their demands ("wrath" or "praise") whether they like it or not; in addition, they are obligated to "behave properly" for "conscience sake" in the pursuit of peace and respect for their claims in Jesus Christ. Paul considers the issue of Christian gentile obligation clear; they associate with the community and they are to subordinate themselves to the concomitant requirements, willingly and with the clear understanding that if they fail to comply they will be justly disciplined; however, his preeminent concern is not with their institutional responsibility but with their conscientious commitment to the salvation of the house of Israel, for certainly "all Israel shall be saved" (11:26).

THE FEASIBILITY OF THIS PROPOSAL AS DEMONSTRATED IN PAUL'S EXAMPLE OF "SUBORDINATION" (A FINAL CONCERN)

Am I standing on solid ground in suggesting that Paul instructed the Christian gentiles to be "subordinate" to the synagogue "authorities" and "behave properly" as defined by the Judaic norms of righteousness? Did Paul "subordinate" himself and those he was with to the synagogue "authorities"? Did he adopt and insist that those with him adopt "proper behavior"? To these questions I now turn.

Paul, in his own life, as recorded in Acts and gleaned from comments in his letters, is perhaps the best example of just how extensive the "authority" of the synagogue was in the first century, functioning as the center of the Jewish community's activities, as the protector of its welfare, and as its powerful disciplinarian. Prior to his belief that Jesus was the Christ, Paul carried out one of the most extreme examples of the disciplinary authority of the synagogues that we have record of:[107]

> Now Saul, still breathing threats and murder against the disciples of
> the Lord, went to the high priest, and asked for letters from him to
> the synagogues at Damascus, so that if he found any belonging to the

[107]A. Hultgren, "Paul's Pre-Christian Persecutions of the Church: Their Purpose, Locale, and Nature," pp. 107–10, discusses the nature of Paul's persecutions as intensely zealous, though not violent, as is often assumed.

Way, both men and women, he might bring them bound to Jerusalem. (Acts 9:1-2)

And I persecuted this Way to the death, binding and putting both men and women into prisons, as also the high priest and all the Council of the elders can testify. From them I also received letters to the brethren, and started off for Damascus in order to bring even those who were there to Jerusalem as prisoners to be punished. (Acts 22:4-5; cf. 26:9-12)

For you have heard of my former manner of life in Judaism, how I used to persecute the church of God beyond measure, and tried to destroy it. (Gal. 1:13)

It is important to note that the authority of the Jewish leaders was restricted to an official format. Paul could not indiscriminately enter any synagogue and execute justice; he had to obtain "letters" authorizing his activities that he then presented to the synagogue upon his arrival. Nor was he concerned with anyone outside the jurisdiction of the synagogue; "the Way" was a "sect" within Judaism that he intensely opposed,[108] apparently because of his concern to preserve the "ancestral traditions" he understood to be threatened by this new faction (a likely allusion to the perceived threat [by Paul] that this group was compromising Jewish practices through gentile coparticipation in the congregation of Israel).[109] The comments of Dunn are particularly interesting in the context of this reading as he develops the association of the "sword" with "zeal":

The reason Paul persecuted the church was out of "zeal" . . . an important word in the history of Jewish self-identification, particularly in the

---

[108]Ibid., p. 101: "Whatever his views as a Christian apostle were concerning the relationship between Judaism and Christianity, it is clear that originally as a persecutor he looked upon the church as close enough to Judaism, if not under it (as a sub-community), to cause concern for the latter. In some way the Christian movement was considered the business of the Jews in an official way." See Richardson, *Israel in the Apostolic Church*, p. 46.

[109]Gal. 1:13-14; Phil. 3:5-6. See Dunn, *Partings*, pp. 120–22. Räisänen, *Paul*, p. 253, "It would seem natural to infer that the status of the Gentiles, and thus the status of circumcision, was an important bone of contention between Paul the Pharisee and the Christians persecuted by him." Different approaches include M. Smith, "The Reason for the Persecution of Paul," pp. 261-68; Hultgren, "Paul's Pre-Christian Persecutions," pp. 103–4; M. Hengel, *The Pre-Christian Paul*, pp. 63–86.

senses echoed here—zeal for God, zeal for the law. In Jewish circles the
classic examples of this zeal were well known and highly regarded . . .
Simeon and Levi . . . Phinehas . . . Elijah . . . the Maccabean revolt. . . .
In every case the *zeal* referred to was a dedicated defence of Israel's distinctiveness. . . . And in every case the zeal was expressed by taking up
the sword and by resort to open force. . . . This is clearly the zeal which
Paul has in mind in recalling his own career as a violent persecutor (Gal.
1.13-14; Phil. 3.5-6)—*zeal for the law expressed* in defence of Israel's
covenant distinctiveness *by the sword*.[110]

Just as revealing, perhaps even more so, was Paul's continued subordination to the synagogue after his "conversion" to faith in this very
same "sect" of Judaism through his own faith in Jesus as the Christ. In
fact, his first public action was to "proclaim Jesus in the synagogues"
at Damascus, to the very same people he had set out to bind for punishment (Acts 9:19-22; 26:9-21). While it is clear that most Jews were
not so violently opposed to this new faction (Paul refers to himself as
more "zealous": Gal. 1:13-14), some sought to turn the tables on him.
Paul escaped the immediate threats in Damascus, and from time to
time elsewhere as well. He does not appear to have subordinated himself to the threat of the mob.[111] However, he continued to live and
work under the "authority" of the synagogues, and he suffered both
the frequent rejection of his ideas and even serious punishment at the
hands of its leaders. Even his final appeal to Roman citizenship was
likely tied up with his insistence on reaching the synagogues of Rome,
even if in chains (cf. Acts 22:22-29 with his immediate actions upon
reaching Rome in 28:16-17, 18ff.; Rom. 1:15-18; 15:22-32).

Luke portrays several incidents of synagogue discipline, and Paul
speaks directly of his various sufferings, including physical punishment in the very sense that might be associated with the authority of
the sword, at the hands of the Jewish authorities (Acts 14:5, 19; 16:22-
23; 2 Cor. 11:23-26).[112] Indeed, Paul bears witness in his own life to the

[110]Dunn, *Partings*, pp. 120–22 (emphasis added).

[111]Sherwin-White, *Roman Society*, p. 97, makes similar mention of the mob issue
at Iconium and Lystra.

[112]See also 2 Cor. 6:1-10 for Paul's rationalizing of this phenomenon. Though he
has done "good" and sought to give no "offense," he has been willing to suffer
wrongfully in order to carry out his mission to those he believes he is obligated to
serve. R. Longenecker, *Paul*, pp. 247–48, similarly notes: "Now as a Roman citi-
zen, a Jew could escape the synagogue whippings for heresy or misconduct by an
appeal to the imperial authorities—though to do so would be not only to gain

operative issues of synagogue "authority" that I am asserting in the context of 13:1-7: to nurture and protect, to "praise good" and "discipline evil" so as "to bring offenders back into line."[113] And in Romans he states explicitly:

> For rulers are not a cause of fear for good behavior, but for evil. Do you want to have no fear of authority? Do what is good, and you will have praise from the same; for it is a minister of God to you for good. (Rom. 13:3-4)

Paul was not saying that the synagogue authorities were always "right" in the discipline they administered; he had done good and sought to give no offense; however, he had willingly submitted to unwarranted discipline, for he understood the "right" of the synagogue to protect its members from threat, which he had once been the most "zealous" in administering, wrongly, he now realized (2 Cor. 6:1-10).[114] They were, whether right or wrong, working within their "ordering" (Rom. 13:2) as the legitimate interpreters of Torah ("good" and "evil") to nurture and protect the community of the people of God, and in this sense they must be respected, even feared. The Christian gentiles, if

---

immunity from Judaism's jurisdiction but also to sever oneself from the ministry and fellowship of the synagogue. Undoubtedly Rabbi Saul, even though he possessed Roman citizenship, would never have thought of such an appeal had there ever come a time when he was to be judged for a breach of the Law. . . . In the case of these five whippings we have explicit evidence from the Apostle's own letters that at least at this point he did submit to Judaism's legislation even though he could theologically justify his escape from such punishment and could politically effect his release." Similarly noted by A. Harvey, "Forty Strokes Save One."

[113]Hultgren, "Paul's Pre-Christian Persecutions," p. 110.

[114]Sanders, *Paul, the Law*, p. 192: "The most important point to be derived from 2 Cor. 11:24 is that both Paul and the Jews who punished him regarded the Christian movement as falling within Judaism. Paul's converts were taken seriously enough by synagogue authorities to lead them to discipline the one who brought them into the people of God without requiring circumcision. . . . They punished Paul, and he submitted to the punishment, because they all agreed that the question of who constitutes Israel was a matter of crucial importance. Thus we see again that Paul was not consciously aiding in the foundation of a new religion. None of the parties who emerge in Paul's letters—Paul himself, his Gentile converts, the "false brethren," Peter and the other Jerusalem apostles, and the non-Christian Jews—looked on the Christian movement as outside the bounds of Judaism. *Punishment implies inclusion.* If Paul had considered that he had withdrawn from Judaism, he would not have attended synagogue. If the members of the synagogue had considered him an outsider, they would not have punished him."

they "behaved properly" and did "good," had nothing to fear; even martyrdom was not a threat to "good" deeds done in love with no intent to offend, even if they were misunderstood as a threat.[115]

Throughout this paraenesis Paul has urged them to pursue righteous behavior in the context of "loving" their "brethren" and "pleasing" their "neighbor," and thus, fulfilling the Law as it was applied in the synagogue for the "righteous gentile" in their midst, thus demonstrating that their claim of equal coparticipation was well founded indeed: they would "have praise from the same." We see that this was the clear intent of his own "subordination" to the "authorities" in Jerusalem (Acts 21:15-29, 30ff.), when he completed a vow of purification to demonstrate his fidelity to the Law and the Jewish people ("walk orderly, keeping the Law" in v. 24) in the face of accusations that he was teaching apostasy.[116] Note this principle guided his response upon learning that Ananias was a high priest: "You shall not speak evil of a ruler of your people" (Acts 23:2-5). And this was his appeal before Felix when he challenged his accusers and stated in his defense (Acts 24:16; cf. vv. 10-21):

[115]Justin's polemical description of the Jews who are "cursing in your synagogues those that believe in Christ" indicates the changing relationship with the Jewish authorities as the church became a separate institution in the middle of the second century. Perhaps Justin's following comments should be read in this light as an indication of just how important and fresh this issue of synagogue authority over the early Christian movement was some one hundred years later (*Dialogue with Trypho* 16.4): "For you have not the power to lay hands upon us, on account of those who now have the mastery. But as often as you could, you did so." Note that Justin had lived in Rome and perhaps settled there.

[116]The accusations were "that you are teaching all the Jews who are among the Gentiles to forsake Moses, telling them not to circumcise their children nor to walk according to the customs" in 21:21, and "This is the man who preaches to all men everywhere against our people, and the Law, and this place; and besides he has even brought Greeks into the temple and has defiled this holy place" in 21:28. For an excellent discussion of the authority of the Sanhedrin see Sherwin-White, *Roman Society*. Note pp. 41–42: "The Sanhedrin was allowed in the procuratorial period a limited criminal jurisdiction, both for police purposes in the Temple area and for the maintenance of the Jewish law." Elsewhere (p. 75) Sherwin-White notes: "It is probable that for the purpose of keeping the peace local magistrates of privileged communities such as 'coloniae' were allowed a minor degree of police-court jurisdiction in the early empire . . . the Sanhedrin of Jerusalem had at least the power of inflicting the 'thirty-nine stripes,' though this may be a special case," and he footnotes that 2 Cor. 11:25 "might refer to the jurisdiction of local sanhedrins of the Diaspora."

> I also do my best to maintain always a blameless conscience both before God and before men.

The very same appeal he now makes in Romans to the "strong" as the measure of their responsibility to the "stumbling" (14:18):

> For he who in this way serves Christ is acceptable to God and approved by men.

SUMMARY

If there was no separate institution of the church in Rome when Paul wrote Romans, we can see the gravity of the situation that compelled Paul's epideictic letter, and in particular, we can understand why he addressed, without restraint, the matter of "subordination" to the "authorities" "appointed by God" by "*every* person," that is, by *gentiles* as well as by Jews. The Christian gentiles were newly involved in synagogue attendance, and even the meetings in their homes took place under the authority of the synagogue. Thus the initial stirring of presumptuous and contentious attitudes toward the "stumbling" non-Christian Jews coupled with the temptation to resist the legitimacy of the synagogue leaders (or at least the suggestions of some party to such effect: 16:17-18) concerned Paul deeply and convinced him they were in need of being reminded "boldly" of their obligation to "increase the intensity of adherence" to righteous behavior (i.e., continue to obey the apostolic decree [Noahide Commandments] and pay community obligations [e.g., taxes]) on behalf of (rather than over against) their "brethren" (who may appear to be but "neighbors" or even "enemies"), for the failure to do so would hinder the very restoration of Israel that they were "indebted," as was Paul, to promote.

Paul thus hoped by writing this thorough letter to promote the seeking of peace, as far as they were "able" to do so (12:18), in order that the Jewish community would not be alienated prior to his arrival in Rome to preach the gospel. He would then institute his "customary" two-step pattern (Acts 17:1-2) for establishing the restoration of Jacob, preaching first in the synagogues of Rome, followed by turning to the gentiles with the "good news" of their inclusion by faith in Christ Jesus ("the fulness of the Gentiles begins") with the specific intention of provoking the children of Jacob to "jealousy" when they see

that the promised salvation had begun in Paul's eschatological ministry as the "light to the nations" while they were missing out on this
privilege if they failed to heed the "good news" (Rom. 11:11-15, 16ff.;
10:10-16, 17ff.; 9:30-33; Acts 13:40-48). The Romans addressed were
thus obligated to be "subordinate" to those in "authority" by the "ordering" of God among his people, both in terms of their institutional
responsibility (for "the sake of wrath"), and in terms of their ethical responsibility (for "conscience' sake") that they might serve Christ in a
manner "acceptable to God *and* approved by men" (Rom. 14:18) to
the end that both circumcised and uncircumcised might worship together in harmony in fulfillment of the promises:

> Now may the God who gives perseverance and encouragement grant
> you to be of the same mind with one another according to Christ
> Jesus; that with one accord you may with one voice glorify the God
> and Father of our Lord Jesus Christ. (15:5-6, 7ff.)

AN EXPANDED CONTEXTUAL TRANSLATION OF 13:1-7, 8

1 Every one ("righteous gentile" as well as Jew) should subordinate
themselves to the synagogue leaders (ἐξουσίαις ὑπερεχούσαις:
higher authorities). For they would not have their current authority
(over the congregation of God's people) unless God had arranged it
thus (in the past).

2 Therefore, if any of you oppose the legitimacy (of the synagogue
leaders) you are actually opposing the way God has chosen to work
(among his people since the election of Israel and the giving of Torah
[the ordinances of God] by angels), and you bring upon yourselves the
judgment you receive (for opposing the instructions of the synagogue
leaders).

3 For the (synagogue) rulers (ἄρχοντες: responsible for congregational
order) are not a threat to good behavior (obeying halakhah for the
"righteous gentile" worshiping the One God: v. 13) but to evil (deeds
of darkness associated with idolatry: v. 12). Do you want to have no
reason to be afraid of those in authority (in the congregation of God's
people)? You must but keep on practicing the halakhah of the "righteous gentile" (i.e., the apostolic decree [Noahide Commandments]

and community obligations [e.g., taxes]) and you will have their admiration.

₄ For the servant (διάκονός) of God (the synagogue leader overseeing table-fellowship halakhah for the "righteous gentile") is responsible to serve you in the practice of proper behavior as a "righteous gentile." However, if you practice improper behavior (claiming the right to pursue dietary and other practices that are associated with idolatry), you should rightly be afraid, for he is not empowered for interpreting God's word (Torah) for the congregation of his people without purpose, but as God's servant he defends the congregation from those practicing the behavior of idolatry (as the agent of God entrusted with interpreting God's wrath [discipline] in the congregation, including matters related to halakhah for the "righteous gentile").

₅ Moreover, it is incumbent upon you (Christian gentiles who are "enabled" by faith) to subordinate yourselves (to the synagogue leaders) not only for the sake of fulfilling your institutional responsibilities without being disciplined (for the sake of wrath), but also because you are responsible to demonstrate (bear witness to) the truth of your claim of now sharing in the promised blessings through faith in Jesus as the Christ of Israel and Savior of the world without becoming Jews through circumcision or the concomitant observance of Torah as entrance requirement (for the sake of conscience).

₆ That is also why you must pay the two-drachma Temple tax to those servants of God (λειτουργοί) in the congregation who are continually devoted to the thorough execution of this responsibility (the privilege granted by Caesar for "carrying" the Temple tax: collecting, treasuring, and ensuring safe distribution to Jerusalem for the support of the community sacrifices).

₇ You are indebted (to those who have been entrusted with the responsibility for the congregation of God's people) to demonstrate (your confession of faith in the One God) by paying that which is required of you (by those responsible for interpreting halakhah for the "righteous gentile" joining the congregation of Israel): the Temple tax to the servant responsible for its collection (λειτουργοί); proper behavior to the ministers responsible for judging the results of proper behavior for the "righteous gentile," particularly in matters of table-fellowship (διάκονός); respect for the synagogue rulers as demonstrated in your uncompromising subordination to their interpretation of your community obligations (ἄρχοντες); and honor, as demonstrated in your conscientious effort to go the second mile in the pursuit of peace by respecting the legitimacy of the synagogue leaders' authority (ἐξουσίαις ὑπερεχούσαις) over you.

8 Do not let yourself be indebted to any one for anything (that might allow their suspicion of your new status as "righteous gentiles" and equal coparticipants in the promised blessings through faith in Christ Jesus to be suspect [14:16]), except the responsibility (to do halakhah, v. 13) befitting your new standing by faith in Christ to love one another (particularly those "stumbling" so as to be devoted to their salvation, as was Paul). For when you walk (obey the halakhah for the "righteous gentile") in love you actually fulfill the Torah's ultimate intentions for the people of God (whether Jew or "righteous gentile") to love the other (even though you are not really under obligation to fulfill Torah, as you are not Jews, you must live in the new reality where your status as defined by the Law does not separate you from your full obligation to those on either side of the "dividing wall" of the Law, for in Christ it no longer really divides, for God is One).

PETER'S HYPOCRISY (GAL. 2:11-21) IN THE LIGHT OF PAUL'S ANXIETY (ROM. 7)

This portrait of Paul and his intentions and message as expressed in Romans has called into question not only the traditional interpretation of this letter, but also the presuppositions that frame contemporary Pauline theology. Where a Law-free gospel has been categorically presupposed, this reading has uncovered a Law-observant one for Jews and a Law-respectful one for gentiles. Where it has been assumed that Paul disregarded Torah and taught Christian Jews as well as gentiles to do the same, or at least that continued observance was a sign of a lack of complete trust in the liberating work of Christ (the "weakness of the weak"), this study found Paul respectful of and engaged in encouraging the continued observance of Torah for Jews in Rome, in fact, teaching that they ought to practice their convictions in faith "fully convinced" that God welcomed such behavior. In addition, we have seen that he actually taught the gentiles in Rome not to judge such convictions or behavior, but instead to welcome those so persuaded even as God welcomes them (14:1, 3; 15:7).

Moreover, we have seen that Paul taught the gentiles in Rome not merely to patronize or tolerate such behavior, but to accommodate it, even to adopt it. They were to observe the halakhic behavioral requirements of "righteous gentiles" in their relationship with Jews, whether Christian or not. In other words, we have found that Paul not only maintained "the teaching" of the apostolic decree, but insisted that disregard for such "obedience of faith" amounted to hurting "him for whom Christ died" in a manner that might "destroy him." Such arrogant disregard for the "stumbling" would result not only in the shove that might cause the destruction of the historical people of God, but it might result in the cutting off of the newly grafted-in gentiles as well. Instead, it was the responsibility of those Paul addressed to live in such a manner as to "hold up" those "stumbling" and ensure that they "stand" rather than "fall." Even Paul's apostleship to the gentiles was to be understood in this light: Paul turned to the gentiles with the gospel so that the "stumbling" of Israel might reconsider the arrival of the promised times and the message of good news for themselves and for the world.

We also found that when Paul argued for gentile inclusion in Christ without becoming Jews that he did not appeal to the nullifying of Torah because of the supersession of Christ. He appealed instead to the inherent truth of monotheism and developed his position within the context of the Shema: "Or is God the God of Jews *only*? Is He not the God of Gentiles *also*?" "Of course, for He is the One God of all" was Paul's uncompromising reply. The Paul of Romans believed that faith in Christ "established" Torah; it certainly did not make it obsolete. Even his most anguished moment was punctuated by praise for the gift of God's Torah; his complaint was with his own failure to overcome the impulse to "covet" (Rom. 7:7-25).

We did not find the Paul of Romans seeking to disassociate the new Christian movement from the synagogues, as many assume, but quite the opposite. We found him encouraging subordination to the leaders of the synagogues and to their interpretation of the proper behavior incumbent upon "righteous gentiles" as operative in guiding the behavior of the Christian gentiles of Rome. They were to obey applicable halakhah and pay Temple taxes, subordinating themselves to the interpretation of Torah by the authorities of the synagogues, not only from fear of punishment, but also to ensure the "approv[al] by men" of their claim to now share in the "good things" promised to Abraham's seed, that is, for "the sake of conscience." "Praise" rather than "blasphemy" would be the glorious unifying result, creating a situation ripe for Paul's arrival when he intends to implement the two-step pattern for the preaching of the gospel in Rome. That is, the early Roman Christian communities were functioning as subgroups within the larger synagogue communities at the time of Paul's letter, and Paul hoped that they would hear (*shema*) his epideictic message in a manner that would enhance their adherence to righteousness and the worship of the One God of Israel as the One God of the world even before his arrival. They would then be found fulfilling the eschatological expectation of Israel: gentiles declaring the Shema in the midst of the congregation of Israel to the glory of God, the One God of all.

I have tried to demonstrate that this reconstruction of the specific message of Romans is internally consistent and also that it is coherent with the portrait of Paul recorded in Acts. I believe it to be a plausible interpretation of the situation in Rome as well as the purpose of Paul's letter and intended visit. As a result, this portrayal of Paul has significant implications for Pauline theology and calls for a reevaluation of his other letters free of some of the traditional presuppositions. In other words, I propose that this interpretation will square with the message and portrait of Paul found in the balance of the Pauline corpus. Obviously it is not within the scope of this study to consider all the Pauline literature that would enhance this proposed reading of Paul, or that might appear to challenge it, for each letter would take a similarly involved study of the contingent features in order to be interpreted. I will carefully examine the one example that may perhaps cast the longest shadow of doubt upon this reading of Romans: the Antioch incident in Paul's letter to the Galatians (2:11-21).[1]

Galatians has often been "regarded as the closest thing we have to 'pure paulinism.'"[2] In this letter Paul presented a reconstruction of "the Antioch incident" to function, arguably, as the hermeneutical center of his message to the churches in Galatia with the result that Paul's description of this incident has figured significantly over the centuries in the interpretation of Paul's theology.[3] Further, this passage has become one of the most definitive paragraphs in modern New

[1]See H. Betz, *Galatians*, pp. 113–14, for discussion of whether the episode at Antioch ends with 2:14 or goes on to include 2:15-21 as the summary of the speech at Antioch, concluding that 2:15-21 "sums up the 'narratio's' [2:11-14] material content. But it is not part of the 'narratio,' and it sets up the arguments to be discussed later in the 'probatio' (chapters 3 and 4)." Tomson, *Paul*, p. 229: "Gal 2:11-14 must be read together with the ensuing 'sermon'; or in other words v14b is the beginning of the sermon." J. Dunn, *The Theology of Paul's Letter to the Galatians*, pp. 72–73, makes the interesting proposal that 2:15-21, indeed, the balance of Galatians, addresses "the challenge he failed to meet at Antioch—how can Christian Jews compel the Gentiles to judaize (2:14)? Galatians is what he should have said to Peter at Antioch had time and sufficient reflection allowed it." Dunn further notes on p. 75: "The issue here between Paul and the other Christian Jews at Antioch, and now at Galatia, comes to clearest focus in 2:16." But see L. Gaston, "Paul and the Law in Galatians 2–3," pp. 37-57.

[2]Dunn, *Theology*, p. 133.

[3]R. Hays, "Crucified with Christ," p. 242, notes: "Issues concerning the law and justification are present in Galatians, to be sure, but they appear to belong to the contingent level of argumentation rather than to the theological hermeneutic out of which Paul responds to the questions at hand. Gal 2:20-21, with its emphasis on union with Christ's grace-giving death, looks more and more like the hermeneutical center of the letter." Dunn, *Theology*, pp. 72–73: "If then we look for the distinctive theology of Paul as found in Galatians we cannot avoid focusing on the Antioch incident." For a review of the influence of Galatians in different periods and along different lines see Dunn, "The Influence of Galatians in

Testament studies for reconstructing Pauline thought vis-à-vis the development of early Jewish Christianity in Jerusalem and the Diaspora.[4] When we approach Paul's message here, carefully considering the results of this study of Romans and questioning the presuppositions of traditional Pauline theology, there is tension at points, but not to the degree one might expect. In fact, at critical points this approach reconciles important contradictions that have become commonplace in Pauline studies. Surprisingly, this example is quite instructive and can serve to sharpen the plausible edge of my proposal for reinterpreting the intentions and message of the Paul of Romans apart from the traditional Pauline presuppositions.

In Paul's letter to the Galatian churches he retells the story of the Antioch incident in order to explain his opposition to those seeking to persuade the Galatians to be circumcised and become Jews as a *helpful* obligation concomitant with their faith in Christ (2:12; 3:1; 4:17; 5:1-12; 6:12-13),[5] a proposal Paul fears that they are finding persua-

---

Christian Thought," in *Theology*, pp. 133–45. See also the review of Hill, *Hellenists and Hebrews*, pp. 126–42.

Charles Cosgrove, *The Cross and the Spirit*, p. 13, cautions against the traditional approach, which takes Gal. 2:15-21 "as a starting point for reconstructing the occasion of the letter": "Galatians 2:15-21 is notoriously difficult to interpret, and not simply because of the density of its argument. The more basic interpretive difficulty concerns its function in the letter as a whole. It is simply not evident from the passage itself how the argument, which takes its point of departure from the Antioch episode, touches specifically on the situation at Galatia." On pp. 24–31 Cosgrove concludes that 1:11—2:21 should be considered the "apostolic autobiography" which "affords no entree into the epistolary occasion, inasmuch as it is far from self evident how this personal history applies to the Galatians" (p. 31). These important observations need not prohibit the approach herein because I am interested in understanding Paul and his views better with respect to traditional and widely held views derived from or supported by this passage and not the larger interpretation of the setting of Galatians.

[4]Dunn, *Theology*, pp. 143–45.

[5]For various views of the outsiders "disturbing" the Galatians as opponents, agitators, teachers etc. see J. L. Martyn, "A Law-Observant Mission to Gentiles: The Background of Galatians," who notes among other things that "the Teachers" should not be regarded so much as Paul's opponents motivated by a desire to correct Paul, but "by a passion to share with the entire world the only gift they believed to have the power to liberate humankind from the grip of evil, the Law of God's Messiah" (p. 323); see Jewett, "Agitators"; Cosgrove, *The Cross and the Spirit*, p. 16, for an important exegetical caveat regarding the limited place of reconstructions of the opponents' position versus the more essential task of clarifying what Paul sees as the real issue in Galatia; and the full discussion of

sive.[6] My reading of Paul appears to be challenged at several important points by this episode in which Paul rebuked Peter for "hypocrisy" and Peter's failure to be "straightforward about the truth of the gospel"[7] because Peter "began to withdraw and hold himself aloof" from the gentiles with whom he "used to eat" after the "arrival of certain men from James" due to Peter's "fearing the ones of the circumcision" (Gal. 2:11-14, 15ff.). Paul then states explicitly: "If you, being a Jew, live like the Gentiles and not like the Jews, how is it that you compel the Gentiles to live like Jews?" (2:14).

The traditional interpretation finds Paul to be saying that Peter had not been observing Torah or halakhah as he was living "*like a gentile*" (ἐθνικῶς) when he was eating with gentiles prior to his withdrawal after "the coming of certain men from James": that is, "the ones of the circumcision."[8] And Paul does appear to believe that when Peter was "living like a gentile and not like a Jew [οὐχὶ Ἰουδαϊκῶς]" that he was living "like" or the same "as" one believing in Christ ought to live: Peter's withdrawal and aloofness he condemns as a denial of the gospel and outright "hypocrisy." Paul's *we* language further suggests that he too was living "like a gentile and not like a Jew": "*We* who are Jews by nature, and not sinners from among the Gentiles . . . *even we* have believed in Christ Jesus, that *we* may be justified by faith in Christ, and not by the works of the Law; since by the works of the Law shall no flesh be justified" (2:15-16). Paul went on to argue that faith in Christ had certainly not made Peter or Paul (as Jews) into "gentile sinners," but if they "rebuild" what they "have once destroyed" they

---

R. Longenecker, *Galatians*, pp. lxxxviii–c. See also Borgen, "Catalogues of Vices," for a discussion of the prevailing view that circumcision was "understood to portray the removal of passions, desires, and evil inclination" (p. 127); idem, "Paul Preaches Circumcision and Pleases Men," in *Paul and Paulinism*, pp. 37–46.

[6]Betz, *Galatians*, pp. 8–9. Cosgrove, *The Cross and the Spirit*, p. 125, makes the point that Paul utilizes the Antioch incident to "express his loyalty to the Gentile cause at Antioch": "Thus Paul's narrative is designed to reinforce the Galatians' trust in him, when they hear how none of the Jewish believers stood by the Gentiles at Antioch—'except Paul alone'. The 'speech' that he delivers on their behalf ('before them all', v. 14) provides a dramatic instance of both Paul's loyalty to the gospel and his fidelity to the Gentile cause. Moreover, it serves as a model to the Galatians. They should stand up to the agitators just like Paul did to the Judaizers at Antioch."

[7]The issue is not only theological but also halakhic, as Paul's choice of the verb ὀρθοποδοῦσιν ("walking straight") helps to indicate. See Dunn, "Echoes," pp. 461–62, 467; Tomson, *Paul*, p. 236.

[8]Betz, *Galatians*, pp. 111–12.

would "prove" themselves to be "transgressor[s]": "For through the Law I [we] died to the Law, that I [we] might live to God" (2:17-19). Paul (and Peter and the others in Christ) now "live in the flesh by faith in the Son of God" since they have been "crucified with Christ"; to "*live*" otherwise would be to "nullify the grace of God; for if righteousness comes through the Law, then Christ died needlessly" (2:20-21).

Paul's comments in Galatians 2:11-21 suggest at least the following problems with the Pauline thought portrayed in my reading of Romans:

1. The accommodation of Jewish practices urged in Romans 14 appears to have been followed to some degree by Peter in Antioch, yet Paul condemns Peter's actions on behalf of "the ones of the circumcision" as hypocrisy and a denial of the truth of the gospel.[9]

2. Paul, Peter, and the other Christian Jews appear not to have continued to eat according to Torah and Jewish halakhah, and Paul ostensibly condemns the return to Torah-observant behavior on the part of Peter and other Jews in Christ when they readopt it as appropriate.

3. Paul believed that both Jews and gentiles in Christ have "died" to the Law through the work of Christ so that Torah observance was (as early as the Antioch incident) obsolete not only for Christian gentiles, but also for Christian Jews.

4. Paul (and Peter and "the men from James" [and thus James?]) ostensibly opposed or at least disregarded the apostolic decree or any other such Noahide Commandments or Jewish purity behavior for Christians, whether Jews or gentiles.

5. Paul's preeminent concern was apparently not with winning the respect of "stumbling" Jews in such a manner that they would reconsider the gospel, nor with any two-step pattern such as Luke proposed and I have sought to clarify as operative in Romans: his concern appears to have been exclusively with the salvation of gentiles.

6. The Paul who confronted Peter seems unlikely to consider it proper for Christians to function as a subgroup within the context of the synagogues subordinating themselves to synagogue authorities, or obligated, for example, to pay Temple taxes.

The traditional assumption is of course that Paul opposed Peter in

[9]Richardson, "Pauline Inconsistency," pp. 347–62, discusses this same kind of tension with respect to Paul's discussion in 1 Corinthians, although he reads the issues differently and comes to different conclusions than I will propose.

Antioch because of Peter's change of behavior with respect to *food*:[10]
Peter (and Paul and the other Christian Jews in Antioch) presumably
ate like gentiles prior to the "coming of certain men from James," thereafter they "withdrew" and *ate like Jews* again as they had before they
had believed in Christ. This change in their way of "living" (ζῆς: "you
are living") implies much more than a change in Peter's habits regarding table-fellowship with Christian gentiles: "it suggests that the table
fellowship was only the external symbol of Cephas' total emancipation
from Judaism" and "in Paul's view, ἰουδαΐζειν ('judaize') includes
more than submitting to Jewish dietary laws; it describes forcing one
to become a convert obliged to keep the whole Torah (cf. 5:3)."[11] Paul
condemns this action as "hypocrisy" and a denial of "the truth of the
gospel" as it "nullifies the grace of God" and in effect means "Christ
died needlessly." Jews in Christ have "died to the Law" and now
ought to continue to "live like a gentile and not like a Jew" even as
they had before the arrival of "the ones of the circumcision."

If indeed Paul's language in this context is properly interpreted as
opposing Jews in Christ *eating like Jews*, or for that matter *living like Jews*
in that they observe Torah and halakhah, then one can hardly argue
with the traditional interpretation of Pauline thought derived from this
context: Paul must have taught, very early in his ministry, that the Law
was nullified for Jews as well as gentiles in Christ—Jews became, as it

---

[10]J. Dunn, "Theology of Galatians," p. 138: "*Galatians is Paul's first sustained attempt to deal with the issue of covenantal nomism within the new movement we call
Christianity.* The main ground for the claim is that covenantal nomism does not
seem to have been an issue before the Antioch incident (2:11-14). Here the relation between 2:1-10 and 2:11-14 is important. What had been settled at Jerusalem
(2:1-10) was the issue of circumcision. What emerged at Antioch (2:11-14) was a
different issue—*food laws*. Just how different these issues were lay at the heart of
the disagreement" (emphasis added). Betz, *Galatians*, p. 31: "Cephas and other
Jewish-Christian missionaries, but not Paul, 'withdrew' from the table fellowship.
Doubtless this withdrawal from fellowship with other Christians *served to uphold
the Jewish dietary and purity laws*, an act which Paul termed 'hypocrisy'" (emphasis
added). Sanders, *Paul, the Law*, p. 177: "Paul expected all Christians to share meals
(presumably the Lord's supper). The Antioch incident would seem to show that,
if Jews were present, Paul would expect them *not to observe the Jewish dietary laws*"
(emphasis added). See Dunn, "The Incident at Antioch (Gal. 2.11-18)," in *Jesus,
Paul*, pp. 129–82, for a complete discussion of this incident from the perspective
of the food requirements and Dunn's conclusion that this incident may have provoked Paul's realization that they have been obviated through justification by faith
(pp. 158–63).

[11]Betz, *Galatians*, p. 112.

were, gentiles through faith in Christ, and Christianity is properly regarded as a gentile religion where Paul is concerned.[12] Although other
passages may suggest that some "lean[ing] on the crutches of particular customs and not on God alone, as though they were an integral part
of that trust"[13] may be tolerated until Christian Jews have realized the
true freedom of the Law-free gospel in Christ, the language of the
Antioch incident has certainly been interpreted to mean that at the
center of Paul's thinking was the conviction that when a Jew believed
in Jesus as the Christ he or she no longer functioned as a Jew—Torah
and halakhah should no longer be operative in guiding their faith or
behavior. In fact, they should be eventually disregarded if one was to
avoid making a mockery of the death of Christ.

It can hardly be argued that Paul believed that a gentile must now
become a Jew through circumcision and Torah observance in order to
be in Christ or even to live in Christ (yet Gal. 1:6-10; 5:11 indicate that
those who had come to Galatia were arguing in this way, that is, they
were appealing to the Galatians that Paul himself taught circumcision);[14] we have seen this as a central point in Romans, and it is clear
in Galatians and elsewhere. But I have maintained that this was consistent with his monotheistic insistence that to do so would be to compromise God's oneness, for the One God of Israel was the One God of
non-Israel too. However, if the traditional reading of Paul's language
in the Antioch incident is correct, then certainly Paul compromised
God's oneness on the side of the gentiles, for it would be Paul's intention and practice that a Jew became a gentile through faith in Christ.
They were no longer the circumcision; they no longer practiced Torah
or halakhah. They were saved as gentiles, not as Jews. And they ought
now to disregard Jewish behavior and convictions. Indeed, Christ has
superseded Torah, and those who believed in Christ but sought to live
as Jews rather than to live as gentiles nullified the work of Christ. This
would of course contradict Paul's message in Romans 3:29-31, and
Galatians 3:28, and elsewhere,[15] for it would mean that Paul main-

---

[12]Räisänen, *Paul*, pp. 258–61.

[13]Dunn, *Romans*, p. 798. See the discussion in chapter 3 above on "Luther's
trap."

[14]Cf. R. Longenecker, *Galatians*, pp. 12–20.

[15]For example, in 1 Cor. 7:17-24 Paul teaches that each is to remain in the condition in which they were called, and he explicitly notes that this is to be the case
for circumcised and uncircumcised. But the effect of the traditional reading has
been to assume that while Paul meant that the uncircumcised must remain uncircumcised, he really meant that the circumcised were not to remain circumcised

tained that faith nullified the Torah and that while God was the One God of gentiles he was not the One God of Jews, for Jews became gentiles through faith in Christ.

In effect, this position maintains that when Paul argued that there was neither Jew nor gentile in Christ he actually meant that there was no Jew in Christ, for they became gentiles, as it were, in that they disregarded Torah and lived and even ate *as* gentiles. By this reasoning the One God of the nations hardly appears to be the One God of Israel. Was that Paul's position? Isn't his argument rather that Jews remain Jews in Christ, and gentiles remain gentiles in Christ, but they are equal: "for you are all one in Christ Jesus"? (3:28). Certainly this is the point in the case of men and women, slaves and free: they are to regard each other as equals in Christ even though their fleshly distinctions call for different lifestyles and responsibilities.[16]

Another problem with the traditional interpretation of Paul's convictions as revealed in his retelling of the Antioch incident is that it positions Paul in a contradiction of the traditional reading of Romans 14, not to mention the interpretation I have suggested, to tolerate or accommodate Jewish opinions and behavior. In Romans, Paul is understood to side with the Torah-observant Christian Jews, the "weak in faith" according to most. On the one hand, Paul clearly encourages these Jews to *continue* in their convictions and only challenges them to welcome Christians who do not practice Torah as welcome by God; on the other hand, Paul instructs the supposedly non-Torah-observant Christians ("the strong") to *accommodate* the sensitivities of the Torah-observant. Thus, while Paul classified himself with the "strong" in Rome, he was much harder on the "strong" than he was on the "weak"

---

and thereby obligated to observe the whole Law (yet the implication of Paul's logic in Gal. 5:3 is that Jews in Christ would be Torah observant). In other words, it is assumed that Jews in Christ were to change to uncircumcision in their faith and practice, even if the surgical issue was ignored (1 Cor. 7:18).

[16]Gal. 3:28 is often used to argue that Paul disregarded all distinctions for those in Christ, but the point of this text is to highlight that while these distinctions remain important they no longer are to represent inequality as they had in the past, at least in the congregation of those who believe Jesus is the Christ. So too Gaston, *Paul*, pp. 33-34, commenting on Gal. 3:28: "That means that in Christ there is both Jew and Greek, both male and female. Just as women do not need to become men nor men women to attain their full humanity, so Jews do not need to become Gentiles nor do Gentiles need to become Jews." See also Campbell, "Religious Identity and Ethnic Origin in the earliest Christian Communities," in *Intercultural Context*, pp. 98–121.

when it came to changing their behavior to accommodate the convictions of the other. The "strong" were not to "eat" in a manner that would cause the "weak" to stumble. Even though the "strong" may be entitled to eat all things in Christ, they are to follow Christ in abandoning their own interests as they seek to hold up the other, desisting from behavior that may seem legitimate but that is not in view of their responsibility toward "him for whom Christ died," that is, toward the "weak."

The implications of this instruction in Romans, that Jews are to continue to be Torah-observant and gentiles are to be Torah-respectful when in the company of Jews, are seldom elaborated on, particularly in the context of Paul's language in Galatians, but this direct contradiction is an important anomaly in Pauline theology. Isn't Peter in Antioch adopting precisely the behavior that Paul some ten or more years later outlined as proper in Romans, namely, to accommodate Jewish opinions of proper behavior when in the company of Jews who believed such behavior appropriate so as not to cause them to "stumble"? Yet Paul ostensibly opposed Peter in Antioch years earlier for just such behavior in no uncertain terms, calling Peter no less than a hypocrite for thereby denigrating the work of Christ, or so the traditional interpretation goes. In Romans Jews are urged to be Jews fully convinced that what they do they do in faith toward God; in Galatians they are condemned for such behavior. In Romans gentiles are told to accommodate Jewish opinions of proper behavior when in the company of Jews; in Galatians even Jews are rebuked for doing so. Paul looks to be the one guilty of hypocrisy, at least according to the traditional readings of these two passages.

Of course, one can take the easy way out by suggesting that Paul had radically changed his thought between the two letters, or that this is but another example of his inconsistency, even incoherence. And indeed it can hardly be argued that Paul would not have changed his opinion on some matters over the approximately five to ten years between Galatians (late 40s to early 50s [of course the Antioch incident is earlier])[17] and Romans (mid- to late 50s), however, this does not seem to be the logical direction we would expect his opinions to change, particularly if traditional Pauline theology is considered valid. That is, while Paul may have changed his opinion on the relevance of Torah observance for Christian Jews and Torah-respectful behavior for

[17]See R. Longenecker, *Galatians*, pp. lxxii–lxxxviii, for a full discussion of the dating of Galatians.

Christian gentiles, it hardly seems likely that he would have changed in the direction of more respect for Torah in later years, particularly as he moved farther out into the Diaspora and the composition of the churches became ever more gentile. If anything, one would expect him to move in the other direction between his letters to the Galatians and Romans. Do the prevailing Pauline theological assumptions based on the early years of Paul's ministry risk neglecting his more mature thinking? Or are the traditional assumptions perhaps wrong at both ends of Paul's career?

I have already shown how the presuppositions of Luther's trap have obscured consideration of the dynamic situation in Rome where Christian Jews and gentiles were functioning within the context of the synagogue communities and where Paul's language hardly suggests that Jews who believed in Christ were weakened by their continued regard for Torah and halakhah. I have considered Paul's respectful adaptation of the label ἀσθενείς to describe the current state of "stumbling" on the part of some Jews with respect to Jesus as the Christ and the claims of equal coparticipation for gentiles in Christ, rather than the traditional condescending assumption (Luther's trap) that Paul judged the faith of Torah-observant Christian Jews as weaker because they were still (mistakenly) observing Torah as meaningful while the "strong" (like Paul) were more mature in that they disregarded such practices as obsolete. This study has instead shown that his adaptation of the label "strong/able" carried the implicit criticism of those so addressed, for they had received grace and a "measure of faith" by which they ought to be "strengthened" to serve the interests of the one "stumbling" and "unable" to yet believe, but they were instead asserting their "ability" in the service of their own selfish interests, quite unlike the One they confessed faith in. I believe Paul's development of the Antioch incident in his message to the Galatians has been similarly misinterpreted by assumptions brought to the text, thereby obscuring the purpose of his criticism of Peter's actions and the structure of Paul's thought on the role of Torah for both Jews and gentiles in Christ.

As already mentioned, the traditional interpretation of Paul's rebuke of Peter turns on the issue of *food*. Although the balance of the letter is read with respect to the issue of justification by faith in Christ, and the explicit use of justification language in Galatians is concentrated around relating this incident,[18] yet the traditional interpretation

[18]Cosgrove, *The Cross and the Spirit*, p. 32.

obscures this focus on justification in verse 14. I suggest that the language of Paul's rebuke centers on the same justification language as the surrounding context, namely, the position of one *justified*, that is, *living* "in Christ" *by faith*, whether "Jews by nature" ("even we" of 2:16) or "gentile sinners," as *equals*. It is thus Peter's *withdrawal*, not food, that is at issue in Antioch; what was eaten or how it was eaten was not the reason for Peter's withdrawal.[19] The issue entirely concerned those with *whom* he had been eating and then withdrawn; his exclusion of gentiles was because they were gentiles, not because they ate offensive food or in offensive ways.[20] The issue was status: "In ordinary society any occasion on which people of different social levels ate together was likely to become an occasion for exhibiting the distance between them."[21] They were gentiles; Peter was a Jew. Peter's actions implied that the community of Christ was a Jewish community

[19]Tomson, *Paul*, p. 228, observes: "If Paul really would have violated the food laws and induced others to do so in the presence of Barnabas, Peter and the Antioch Jews, he would have made the agreement null and void and his own apostolate impossible. But not only does this classical interpretation [Chrysostom] not respect the integrity of Paul's letter to the Galatians. It also portrays Paul as the Apostle who indeed severed Christianity from Judaism and hence excommunicated Jewish followers of Jesus. Chrysostom was conscious of this. As he wrote elsewhere, abrogating the food laws amounts to an abrogation of Judaism itself. Modern commentators may be less familiar with Jewish Law than Chrysostom, but that is no excuse for not reading Paul according to his own intentions."

[20]G. Howard, *Paul: crisis in Galatia*, p. xix, similarly observes: "It should be noted, however, that nothing in the text of this passage explicitly says that Paul and Peter had ever given up Jewish food laws. The issue presented here is about Jewish Christians eating with Gentiles, not about 'what' they ate when they ate with Gentiles." On p. xx Howard further observes: "Peter's withdrawal, then, was a withdrawal from Gentiles without any implication that he withdrew from eating unclean food." Note also the comment of Gaston, "Paul and the Law in Galatians 2–3," p. 43 n. 10: "Nothing is said at all about the food eaten but only about the company." Differently, Sanders, "Jewish Association," p. 187, concludes his discussion by noting that he doubts "that biblical law was actually being transgressed." Sanders suggests that the issue in Antioch was James's concern that "too much fraternization with Gentiles would have bad results, and that Peter's mission would be discredited if he were known to engage in it himself": "Being 'strict' included reluctance to associate *too much* with Gentiles, since close association might lead to contact with idolatry or transgression of one of the biblical food laws. 'Too much association' is not a law, but a worry about the results of fraternization. How much was too much would be judged differently by different people and groups, and it would vary with the circumstances."

[21]Meeks, *Origins*, p. 96.

only, at least in terms of status; thus gentiles could only be equals in Christ if they became Jews.[22]

As I have discussed several times, certainly a Jew could eat with gentiles without disregarding or compromising the observance of Torah or halakhah in matters of food. Likewise, "righteous gentiles" could eat with Jews without concluding it was necessary to become Jews: they merely ate according to the halakhot that obtained for "righteous gentiles." Nothing in Paul's language suggests that Peter or the other Christian Jews or even Paul himself did not eat according to Jewish conventions for table-fellowship with gentiles.[23] Nor is there any suggestion that gentiles in Antioch (in particular)[24] were resistant

[22]Betz, *Galatians*, p. 112: "Ironically, therefore, by attempting to preserve the integrity of the Jewish Christians as Jews, Cephas destroys the integrity of the Gentile Christians as believers in Christ. Instead of welcoming them as converts to Christianity, he wants to make them into converts of Judaism. This contradicts the principles of the doctrine of justification by faith, which had been the basis of the faith thus far (see 2:15-16)."

[23]Segal, *Paul*, pp. 230–33, points out this problem in traditional presuppositions also: "Many New Testament scholars miss subtleties in this argument by assuming with Luke (Acts 10:27-48) that Jews could have no intercourse with gentiles at all and especially could not sit at table with gentiles. To the contrary, there is no law in rabbinic literature that prevents a Jew from eating with a gentile. . . . Since there was no explicit law forbidding Jews and gentile [*sic*] from eating together, we must assume that some, possibly many, ate with gentiles, despite qualms. There was obviously a range of practice that we cannot precisely reconstruct, since we have to rely on the mishnaic laws, codified a century and a half after Paul, which represent a prescriptive idealization by the successors to the Pharisees. We can find some hints in rabbinic literature. It is too inexact to consider that the issue separating Peter and Paul is *kashrut*, the special food laws for Jews, as many scholars have done." See Tomson, *Paul*, pp. 229–36, for another excellent discussion of the fact that Jews did eat with gentiles in the main, particularly in the Diaspora where purity issues were not as restrictive, and that this would have been expected in Antioch; although some Jews would have had a negative view of this activity for fear of idolatry, they would have represented the minority view. Tomson notes on p. 229: "According to Gal 2:11-13 the majority of Jews of Antioch, as Peter and Barnabas and also Paul, thought it possible for Jews and gentiles to eat together without transgressing the Jewish Law." See also Howard, *Paul*, pp. xix–xxii; Sanders, "Jewish Association"; and the discussions in chapters 2 and 4 above.

[24]The comment of Josephus regarding the successful experience of the Jews in Antioch during this period suggests that just such association of righteous gentiles with the Jewish community was notable: "Moreover, they were constantly attracting to their religious ceremonies multitudes of Greeks, and these they had in some measure incorporated with themselves" (*War* 7.3.3 [45]).

to accommodating Jewish sensitivities;[25] if anything they were tempted to take this practice a bit too far in considering that the next logical step was circumcision. That was precisely the temptation Paul was quick to challenge, for unlike "righteous gentiles" who were regarded as prospective proselytes by "the ones of the circumcision," gentiles "in Christ" were already equal coparticipants among the people of God according to "the truth of the gospel."[26] Peter's actions resulted in confusion on this otherwise clear point of equal justification ("living") through faith in Christ and not according to fleshly distinctions (Jew as circumcised "by nature"—gentile as uncircumcised "sinner").

In other words, the situation Paul confronted in Antioch (and Galatia) does not presuppose that Christian gentiles had been disregarding Jewish opinions in matters of food or other issues of proper behavior for "righteous gentiles," but implies exactly the opposite. It

[25]Dunn, "Theology of Galatians," p. 145, even observes this logic: "Certainly it is hard to believe that Jew and Gentile believers in Messiah Jesus had completely abandoned the law in Antioch for a decade or more before it came to the attention of the more conservative brothers in Judea or caused any kind of surprise or comment." In "Incident at Antioch," pp. 129–82, Dunn believes that the gentiles in Antioch were probably observing Noahide Commandments and even that the Jews were observing food regulations; however, he concludes that the issue was the matter of the degree of their observance as insufficient in the opinion of the men from James (pp. 154ff.). Dunn's final conclusion is, however, along traditional lines: this incident awakened in Paul the realization that "to live life 'in Christ' *and* 'in accordance with the law' was not possible; it involved a basic contradiction in terms and in the understanding of what made someone acceptable to God. . . . To begin with the Spirit and through faith rules out not just justification by works of law, but life lived by law (covenantal nomism) also—the very argument which he develops in the rest of Galatians" (p. 159). See also Hill, *Hellenists and Hebrews*, pp. 138–40.

[26]Tomson, *Paul*, p. 236, ties together Paul's defense of the gospel with his openness to table-fellowship with gentiles: "It appears that the traditions of R. Shimon ben Elazar offer us an illuminating parallel to the motivation of the men of James. Even with such precautions as the majority of Jews thought effective in preventing cooperation with idolatry, R. Shimon pronounces a diaspora Jew dining with gentiles guilty of idolatry. His motivation appears to have been excessive fear of idolatry. Similarly, James' emissaries probably could not perceive the gentile Christians as being free from the sphere of idolatry. Unlike Peter and Barnabas, who were uncertain when it came to a crisis, Paul stood up for 'the truth of the gospel' (Gal 2:14). This is usually taken as a purely *theological* statement, but we can now understand that it had a *halakhic* basis. It was in the Tannaic tradition supported by most Sages in post-Temple times, and apparently already shared by the majority of Jews of first century Antioch" (emphasis added).

appears that Peter's withdrawal in Antioch is characterized by the fact that even though Peter, the other Christian Jews, and the Christian gentiles were accommodating Jewish opinions of proper behavior, "the ones of the circumcision" were suggesting that their *indiscriminate* fellowship was obscuring the priority of the Jews and at the same time was not enough to ensure the equality of the gentiles: they may be in Christ by faith while remaining gentiles, but they were merely "righteous gentiles" at best and not equals, because if they were to fellowship as equals they had to be circumcised.[27] The believers in Christ must have still been operating within the framework of the Jewish community for this dynamic to be so compelling, hence the temptation to "judaize," earlier in Antioch, and now presumably in Galatia.

The traditional reading of this text understands Paul confronting Peter as a hypocrite for changing back to eating like a Jew because it was no longer appropriate for a Jew *in Christ* to so eat. But Paul's rebuke does not mean that Peter was eating like the gentiles and then he withdrew to eat like the Jews. In fact, Paul still speaks to Peter *after* his withdrawal of "living [ζῆς] like a gentile" *in the present tense*, as though he is *still* living like a gentile even *after* he has withdrawn and his Jewish exclusiveness has begun to "compel gentiles to live as Jews."[28] If Peter's ζῆς refers to his lifestyle in matters of food, then Paul could not accuse him of still living like a gentile at the point of this confrontation when Peter had already withdrawn and was living like a Jew! Paul's discussion of *living* should be understood in the context of his polemical development of a phrase that had probably been used by the "men from James" to persuade Peter's withdrawal: "you being a Jew, live like a gentile and not like a Jew?"[29] Paul developed the implicit justification language present in *their* turn of phrase ("live like a gentile") around the issue of how one who believes in Christ is

---

[27]S. Cohen, "Crossing the Boundary," pp. 26–33, notes on p. 27: "The Greek-speaking Jews of the second temple period and the Hebrew- (and Aramaic-) speaking Jews after 70 CE debated the meaning of circumcision and the ritual's exact place in the conversion process, but as far as is known no (non-Christian) Jewish community in antiquity accepted male proselytes who were not circumcised. Perhaps the god of the Jews would be pleased with gentiles who venerated him and practiced some of his laws, and perhaps in the day of the eschaton gentiles would not need to be circumcised to be part of god's holy people; but if those gentiles wanted to join the Jewish community in the here and now, they had to accept circumcision."

[28]See Dunn, "Echoes," p. 468, for discussion.

[29]Ibid., pp. 468–70.

justified, that is, how they "live": one who relies on the faith of Christ
to live before God and thus before others justified in Christ (cf. 2:20;
3:11; Rom. 1:16-17), versus one who relies on some other means to live
before God and thus before others, in this case justified by "the works
[status] of the Law"[30] (Gal. 2:16; cf. 3:11-14, 21). Paul's rebuke is of
Peter's withdrawal from eating with the gentiles to eating only with
the Jews, which implicitly as well as explicitly suggests that the gentiles are *not equals* "in Christ" with the Jews, regardless of how properly the gentiles might have been eating or living.[31] It is recreating the

[30]Similarly, though addressing a slightly different point, H. Boers, "'We Who
Are by Inheritance Jews; not from the Gentiles, Sinners,'" pp. 278–79, notes:
"Justification by faith is not a negation of justification through the doing of good
works—good works are neither required nor negated—but justification without
prior entrance into a favored community—justification as a Gentile; in contemporary language, justification as a heathen. . . . Faith does not stand in opposition to
justification for the doing of good works, but to justification through works of the
law as *the distinguishing mark of belonging to an exclusively favored community*" (emphasis added). For a thorough discussion of this phrase see Dunn, "Works of the
Law and the Curse of the Law" in *Jesus, Paul*, pp. 215–41; idem, *Theology*, p. 80,
though I am offering a slightly different view in this study.

[31]Betz, *Galatians*, p. 107, in a way recognizes that the distinction is operative
between gentiles and the gentiles in Christ: "In the beginning Cephas and the
others had agreed that Christian Gentiles are non-Jews, but that because of their
faith in Christ they are not to be regarded as 'sinners out of the Gentiles' (cf. 2:15).
For the conscientious Jew, therefore, they could not be regarded as impure. It
must have been for this reason that Cephas ate with them." However, based on
the presupposition that "the point of concern is the Jewish purity requirements
which must be observed whatever meals were involved," Betz concludes that "the
issue at stake was not Cephas' breaking of fellowship by first participation in and
subsequent withdrawal from the meal, but his shifting attitude with regard to the
Jewish dietary and purity laws." Betz's argument, free of this presupposition that
does not follow the logic of his observations, actually supports the contention that
what Paul opposed was the shifting attitude toward the gentiles in Christ, not to
what was being eaten. Gentiles who had been accepted as equals, as "righteous
gentiles" who may well have observed applicable halakhah in matters of food
when in the company of Jews (the context does not tell us otherwise), were no
longer regarded as equals unless they became Jews in Christ—at least that was the
implication of Peter's withdrawal from fellowship with them. So too Dunn,
"Echoes," p. 475, concludes that "by withdrawing from table fellowship they
effectively excluded the Christian Gentiles from the one covenant community
(2:11-14). In the Galatian churches, then, the tactic of the other missionaries had
clearly been to draw again these firm boundaries as laid down by the Torah and to
point out the (to them) inevitable corollary: that the Gentile converts were still
outside them."

Tomson, *Paul*, p. 230, joins me in objecting to the traditional interpretation

wall of separation that had excluded gentiles from the people of God ("gentile sinners" versus "Jews by nature").[32] It is, at the very least, cliquish behavior that implies gentiles ought to become Jews if they are to be insiders fully accepted as equals. Paul appears to believe it is not even so subtle as to be construed as an inference; for Paul it is a clear demonstration of covetousness, of turning back to the "works of the Law" as the status symbols by which the people of God are defined: Jews are in, gentiles are not.[33]

Peter's withdrawal suggests that gentiles are second-class citizens, not really equals through faith in Christ. Unless they become Jews they are deficient. This position, however, is far different from what either Paul *or* Peter teaches; thus it is labeled "hypocrisy," and Paul openly rebukes Peter's behavior as a denial of the work of Christ. For was not Peter justified "like a gentile," that is, in the same way as the gentiles, even though he was "a Jew by nature and not a gentile sinner"? For that matter, aren't the gentiles justified "like Jews" in the sense that they are justified in the same way, namely, by faith in Christ? In other words, what has been taken to mean that Jews are justified as gentiles and thus live or behave as gentiles, abandoning their Jewishness when they believe in Christ, is not what Paul was commu-

---

here and suggests a solution similar to the one I am proposing, yet different: "The whole sentence [v. 14] is charged with rhetoric and functions as a power centre of Paul's argument against forced circumcision in Galatia. At this point the representatives of James disagreed, and Paul seems to rhetorically adopt their speech, 'live like a gentile'. The sentence may then be paraphrased: 'Before, you agreed to live and eat as a Jew together with the gentiles, and although some call that 'living like a gentile', why do you now separate and wish to eat with them only if they become Jews?' This interpretation concurs with our analysis of Paul's report on the Jerusalem agreement: the agreement was based on mutual trust in view of Paul's law-free gospel to the gentiles and Peter's law-abiding one for the Jews. The conclusion is that here Paul does not urge Peter to join him again in a non-Jewish way of life. On the contrary: he urges for a Jewish life which does not force gentiles to judaize, in line with the agreement."

[32]Dunn, *Theology*, p. 74: "This was the seriousness of the Antioch incident: that Gentile converts were being seen as a threat to Jewish covenant status and hope of salvation; that association of Christian Jews and Christian Gentiles was being seen not as drawing Gentiles within the sphere of covenant righteousness, but as causing Jews to be accounted sinners along with the Gentiles."

[33]Tomson, *Paul*, pp. 229–30: "'Ἰουδαϊσμός signifies the way of life according to the 'Law of the Jews'; correspondingly ἰουδαΐζειν means 'to live as a Jew', to adopt a Jewish life style, as opposed to ἐθνικῶς ζῆς. This terminological complex reflects the central concern of the letter: the pressure exerted on Galatian gentiles to become Jewish proselytes."

nicating to Peter, or to the Galatians. Paul is merely saying that both Jews and gentiles live justified in the same manner, through faith in Christ, and thus "in Christ" they may live as Jews or gentiles; however, they live together justified as equals (cf. 1 Cor. 7:17-24). Peter, even after his withdrawal, still lived justified by faith in Christ (just like a gentile) though he lived as a Jew, and thus he must not live so as to imply that gentiles justified by faith in Christ must live as Jews in order to be equals in Christ. The *exclusive* lifestyle Peter had adopted is the issue, not the *Jewish* lifestyle per se. Their historical context is so full of Jews in Christ living Torah-observant lives that Paul is not concerned to address the misunderstanding of the later gentile interpreters of Paul that Jews were not to live Torah-observant lives. The problem involved the inclusion of gentiles, and clarification was called for on two points: the position of the gentiles in Christ as equals, and the hypocrisy of the Jews in Christ who would deny the gentiles in Christ equality without *also* becoming Jews.

Paul accuses Peter of hypocrisy, not apostasy. There is no argument about what the gospel teaches between Peter and Paul. For Peter also teaches (like Paul) that the truth of the gospel is equal justification for both Jews and gentiles through faith in Christ, yet he has adopted a lifestyle that denies this equality in Christ for gentiles who do not become Jews.[34] When he withdrew from table-fellowship with gentiles to meet exclusively with Jews he denied the truth of the very gospel he taught; Peter *taught* that gentiles were equal but he now *lived* as though they were not, that is, as though the boundary marking the people of God had not changed with the coming of Jesus as the Christ. Peter's diet need not have changed, nor his formal teaching on (not) circumcising gentiles in Christ;[35] his behavior with respect to indiscriminate (equal) fellowship certainly has. It no longer represents the inclusiveness he and Paul have been teaching, namely, that the wall

---

[34]See Betz, *Galatians*, pp. 115–19, for discussion of the fact that Paul approaches the theme of justification by faith as a pre-Pauline Jewish-Christian theology "based upon the self-definition of Jewish Christians as Jews" (p. 115) for whom "believing *(fides qua creditur)* that the Messiah is Jesus becomes the channel which mediates 'justification' before the throne of God, instead of 'doing' the works of the Torah" (p. 117). Dunn, "Theology of Galatians," p. 141, notes: "'What is expressed here [2:16] is the viewpoint of Peter and the other Jewish Christians at Antioch'. They are all at one so far as the gospel's call for faith in Jesus Christ is concerned."

[35]Contra Howard, *Paul*, pp. 24–25. Cosgrove *The Cross and the Spirit*, pp. 129–30, follows the subtle distinction well.

had been broken down in Christ so that there was no need for gentiles who believed in Christ to become Jews in order to be regarded as equal recipients of the promised blessings, indeed, equal members in the people of God.[36]

To paraphrase this extremely compact argument, Paul was saying to Peter that if he lived (justified) as (an equal, that is, justified in the same manner as) a gentile (through faith in Christ) and not like (those) Jews (who still relied on the works [status] of the Law for their justification), then why would he now withdraw in such a way as to compel the gentiles (also justified by faith in Christ) to believe that they are not equals unless they also live (justified) as Jews (by the works [status] of the Law).

Those who persuaded Peter to withdraw perhaps argued that he was saved in Christ as a Jew, not as a gentile, and that he must maintain the priority of the Jew in Christ. This line of argument and Peter's response to it are understandable in the "limited-good" culture of the first-century in which it was important to maintain inherited status: Peter's withdrawal was the action of an honorable Jew.[37] But the gentiles were shamed by this withdrawal. Paul unmasks the implicit hypocrisy of this position as covetousness by showing the failure of the internal logic: "Has accepting equality with gentiles in Christ meant that Christ has made Jews into gentile sinners? No, of course not."[38]

---

[36]Dunn, "Theology of Galatians," pp. 140–41, recognizes that "Paul expresses himself in traditionally Jewish terms ('we are Jews by nature'). 'He speaks as one who is consciously within Judaism' and conscious of his distinctiveness from the Gentile; he speaks as one within the law, who has traditionally seen the Gentile as outside the bounds marked out by the law—and so by definition a 'sinner'. Since it is this very distinction that he will be going on to question, it must be that Paul is trying to argue from an agreed position and perspective within Judaism to a new position and perspective. It is probable also that the movement in self-understanding which he is thereby trying to encourage was a reflection of his own changed self-understanding. But he remains a Jew; 'it is still an inner-Jewish dispute'. He is still able to identify himself with the older mind-set, which suggests that the full implications of his own changed perspective are still only becoming clear to him."

[37]B. Malina, *New Testament World*, pp. 25–48, 71–90, summarizes on p. 90: "The honorable man in the world of limited good was one who knew how to preserve his inherited status."

[38]That Paul does not challenge such opinions of gentiles as sinners, and even argues that "we are Jews by nature, and not sinners from among the Gentiles," should not be overlooked. Paul still functioned within a Jewish worldview, albeit altered by his conviction that Jesus was the Christ of Israel and savior of the

But to take the position that gentile sinners must become Jews in addition to faith in Christ in order to be equal participants in fellowship is to suggest just such a position. This could never be. Jews remain Jews; gentiles remain gentiles, though equals in Christ—that is "the truth of the gospel." Christ does not make Jews into gentiles or gentiles into Jews. He makes both into one family as equals: by faith in Christ they both live to God. The distinction remains; however, discrimination does not. Peter's actions have jeopardized this truth and so he stands condemned.

It is important to note that Paul does not suggest that these "men from James" sought Paul's withdrawal, only Peter's; some of the other Christian Jews then "joined him in hypocrisy, with the result that even Barnabas was carried away by their hypocrisy" (2:13).[39] But Paul was a Christian Jew as well. It would also be apostasy for Paul to flagrantly violate Torah and halakhah and presumably teach other Jews (in this case Peter and those joining him) to do the same (cf. Acts 21:17-31). Why wouldn't Paul be similarly approached?[40] The answer lies in their different apostolic ministries that Paul has clarified just prior to the retelling of the Antioch incident: Peter was an apostle to the circumcision, Paul was an apostle to the gentiles (Gal. 2:7-9).[41] This need not mean that they accepted gentile behavior on the part of Paul. In fact, the context of the recognition of Paul's apostleship by the leaders in Jerusalem suggests just the opposite: they would certainly oppose

---

nations, equally accessed by faith. A Jew might sin, but they were not sinners, they were within the boundary of the people of God. A gentile was categorically outside this boundary until the coming of Christ. See the discussion of Dunn, "Echoes," pp. 462–65.

[39]Betz, *Galatians*, p. 7.

[40]The suggestion of Jewett, "Agitators," that the agitators were Jewish Christians from Judea who were "stimulated by Zealotic pressure into a nomistic campaign among their fellow Christians in the late forties and early fifties," who "convinced themselves that circumcision of Gentile Christians would thwart Zealot reprisals," who first went to Antioch and then later to Galatia (pp. 205–6), is extremely interesting and tenable; however, it fails to qualify this discrimination with regard to Paul. Wouldn't Paul's behavior, in that he too was a Jew, have involved them (upon their return to Judea) in the same compromising position and thus still in a threatened position, particularly if Paul taught a Law-free gospel with the approval of the Jerusalem leaders? Yet the political dimension of Peter's choice is quite clear. See also Betz, *Galatians*, pp. 109–10.

[41]Martyn, "Law-Observant Mission," for an interesting view of the dynamics of the situation in Galatia which takes full account of 2:7-9. See also Howard, *Paul*, pp. 40–42.

Paul abandoning Torah if that was implied in his table fellowship with the gentiles in Antioch, for Paul too represented the position of the Jerusalem leaders—by agreement![42] But it does suggest that they were prepared to recognize Paul's indiscriminate fellowship with gentiles: the new reality that grew out of "the truth of the gospel" that they maintained as well, that is, that they were justified in Christ just as gentiles were: by faith in Christ, not by their status as Jews. Nevertheless, they were not yet prepared to recognize the implications of this for Peter and other Christian Jews, much less for themselves. Paul confronts Peter for hypocrisy, but not the other Christian Jews who "joined him in hypocrisy, with the result that even Barnabas was carried away by their hypocrisy."[43] He appears more restrained toward them, perhaps because this is new territory, but this is not new ground for Peter. Peter already understands the implications of "the truth of the gospel," and he has already adjusted to the new reality of gentile inclusion as equals in Christ.[44] Peter therefore stands

[42]Tomson, *Paul*, p. 227, observes: "Paul implies here [Gal. 2:7-10] that his 'Law-free gospel' for Galatian gentiles was founded on his respect for Law-observance by Jewish Christians. All would be well as long as two separate domains remained." Howard, *Paul*, pp. 52–53, recognizes the implications of this fact and notes: "If Jewish Christianity practised the law while accepting faith in Jesus Christ as the way to salvation, how can it be said that the early church, including Paul, considered the two as mutually exclusive principles of life?. . . The conclusion is inescapable that if Jewish Christianity continued to keep the law, and the evidence of the New Testament shows that it did, there is nothing incompatible in faith in Christ and works of the law when each is kept in its proper place. . . . His preclusion of circumcision to the Galatians under any circumstances, in spite of the fact that from his meeting with the Jerusalem 'pillars' he obviously knew that they would continue to observe the law, strongly suggests that his concern was not with the incompatibility of the principles of faith and works but rather and 'only' with the notion of Gentiles accepting circumcision and the Mosaic law." See also pp. 61-62; Boers, "We Who Are by Inheritance Jews."

[43]But see 5:10-12; 6:7-8, 12-13 for his opinion of "the men from James" disturbing the Galatians. That Paul did not confront James or his representatives by appealing to the apostolic decree of the Jerusalem Conference, or accuse them of hypocrisy in the manner of Peter, suggests that the incident in Antioch, and perhaps even the writing of Galatians, precede the events recorded in Acts 15.

[44]Tomson, *Paul*, p. 227: "The question was: can Jews and gentiles eat together without endangering either the Law-observance of the former or the freedom from the Law of the latter? James' representatives apparently thought they could not, but Paul and Barnabas, as well as the other Antioch Jews and Peter, thought they could. According to Gal 2:11-13 the majority of Jews of Antioch, as Peter and Barnabas and also Paul, thought it possible for Jews and gentiles to eat together without transgressing the Jewish Law."

condemned for returning to discrimination as the basis of fellowship in Christ.[45] The issue is not food; the issue is fellowship with gentiles as equals in Christ because they are justified as equals in Christ.

The balance of Paul's argument bears out this point further. In fact, Paul's argument follows the same lines as Romans 7,[46] namely, that this *covetous* insistence on Jewish priority among Jews in Christ is the one human sin that the Law cannot help one overcome.[47] Through the

[45]The current trend among scholars is to assume that Paul lost this argument with Peter (e.g., Dunn, "Incident at Antioch," in *Jesus, Paul*, p. 160 and n. 126; Brown and Meier, *Antioch and Rome*, p. 39). However, this solution is weakened when it is recognized that the issue is not about a Law-free gospel versus a Law-observant one as is usually assumed. Paul accused Peter of hypocrisy, not apostasy, which indicates that they both agree about the gospel and its relationship with the Law, leaving Peter no choice but to acquiesce or to argue against justification by faith for both Jew (Law observant) and gentile (Law respectful). Moreover, Paul need not explicitly declare his victory; it is implied. Testimonials are chosen for their persuasive weight. They are constructed to instill trust by demonstrating through concrete, verifiable evidence that what is being proposed has already succeeded in the past. After all, it is Paul who puts forward this example to make his point with the Galatians, thereby hoping to win their allegiance. If Paul had lost in Antioch, he would not appeal to this incident to illustrate his point, and he could hardly expect his audience in Galatia not to know that he was appealing to an incident that would only assert his position while failing to strengthen it, because they would know he had not won the day. This would fly in the face of the tactics of persuasion. Surely Paul had some more successful examples from which he could draw to illustrate such an important point. It seems unlikely that Paul's purpose for recalling this incident was self-serving, that is, to show his was an isolated view revealed directly by God. Paul's purpose is rather to illustrate that he has had to stand up for the importance of this particular, but often missed point before, with none less than Peter, Barnabas, and many others, including the men from James, to the end that they have come to realize through Paul's diligence the implications of the truth of the gospel they teach as well, so now in Galatia.

[46]G. Theissen, *Psychological Aspects of Pauline Theology*, pp. 197–201, demonstrates the formal structural similarities between Gal. 2:15-20 and Rom. 7:4-14, 15ff., though denying contextual comparison.

[47]Segal, *Paul*, pp. 243–44, broke through the traditional assumptions of New Testament scholars in approaching the issue in Rom. 7 as Paul's discussion of his religious impulse and not some lustful impulse in the sense of sexual desire or the like: "When Paul quotes the tenth commandment, 'Thou shalt not covet' (*ouk epithumeseis*), many scholars have assumed that he is speaking specifically about lust, following an exegesis of Eve in the Garden of Eden. But the term *epithumia* is a general term, more like desire than lust in Greek, thus covering all kinds of desires including religious ones. Josephus uses the same term to discuss the satisfaction of his religious desires during his stay with Bannus. And Paul uses *epithumia* in a positive sense in I Thess. 2:17. Paul could be thinking of Israel's rebellion

Law, which taught love of and service to the neighbor, one was in-
eluctably caught in the concomitant trap of judging the other as an
outsider, less equal, one might say. This was Paul's struggle in Romans
7 with his failure to keep the tenth commandment: "You shall not
covet" (7:7-13),[48] and in this context it is precisely the point of his rebuke of Peter in Galatians 2:18-19. And we find his exclamation of the
new life in Christ in Romans 7:25—8:17, 18ff. paralleling his concluding statements in Galatians 2:20-21, namely, in Christ this discrimination (of Jew from gentile in the flesh, i.e., by circumcision) is removed
in a manner that the Law is unable by its very nature (as the gift to the
circumcision) to do. Of course the Law does not cause this sin, nor
does Paul say that the Law killed:

> But if I do the very thing I do not wish to do, I agree with the Law,
> confessing that it is good. . . . For I joyfully concur with the law of
> God in the inner man, but I see a different law in the members of my

in Num. 11:4-34, where the people crave the meat of Egypt, as he does in I Cor.
10:6-10. Paul is speaking about desire in general (*pasan epithumian* [Rom. 7:8]), including the covetousness of depending on fleshly marks for religious justification—desiring the benefits of Torah—while ignoring the spiritual value of being
made over in the image of Christ. The desire to be justified by keeping the law is
one that he understands. It is a desire that he still has and that he now sees as a
misguided emotion. Paul is talking about the joy and security of doing Torah, a
feeling with which most New Testament scholars cannot empathize and therefore
miss. Paul is saying that he enjoys doing the ceremonial Torah, but it is a trap for
him. . . . He speaks of covetousness, envy of the position of religious surety presented by a life under the commandments, because he wishes to contrast the life
of ceremonial Torah, a life of the body, with the life of transformation in Christ, a
life of the spirit." See also P. Meyer, "The Worm at the Core of the Apple:
Exegetical Reflections on Romans 7," pp. 75–76.

[48]J. Ziesler, "The Role of the Tenth Commandment in Romans 7," observes
that Paul is concerned specifically with the tenth commandment and that this
must be kept in focus to interpret the passage correctly. Ziesler shows convincingly that no other single commandment could fit Paul's argument. The issue is
not to be confused with the traditional interpretation that Paul is referring to the
assumed Jewish seeking of self-justification by observing the Law completely
(pp. 42–43). However, contra Ziesler, the point does not seem to be "wanting what
is not one's own, and especially wanting it at the expense of one's neighbour"
(p. 47), but precisely wanting what *is* one's own *but ought to be no longer regarded as
only* one's own so as to *be denied* to the neighbor *also*: the coveted status that the
"works of the Law" had provided for defining oneself as in and the other as out,
in this case the denial of the privilege of sonship for gentile neighbors (cf. Rom.
8:9-17, 18ff., and the examples of the prodigal son [Luke 15:11-32], and the
"envious [evil] eye" of the laborers in the vineyard [Matt. 20:1-16]).

body, waging war against the law of my mind, and making me a prisoner of the law of sin which is in my members. Wretched man that I
am! Who will set me free from the body of this death? (Rom. 7:24-25)

The power of human sin is unable to be overcome as the Law
teases this judgmental nerve, and one kills oneself: "for the mind set
on the flesh is death" (Rom. 8:6). Paul argued that in this way sin still
lives under the Law and sin leads to final separation, death.

In Romans Paul wrote:

Therefore did that which is good become a cause of death for me?
May it never be! Rather it was sin, in order that it might be shown to
be sin by effecting my death through that which is good, that through
the commandment sin might become utterly sinful. (Rom. 7:13)

In Galatians he had earlier summarized the issue with Peter:

For through the Law I died to the Law, that I might live to God.
(Gal. 2:19)

Peter's covetous sin was to bring back discrimination on the basis of
circumcision and thus to find the uncircumcised wanting in spite of
confessing that Peter had been justified (lived) in the same way as the
uncircumcised: through faith in Christ. Paul's struggle with sin in
Romans 7 was with the similar temptation Paul knew to covet the status of circumcision and the gift of Torah,[49] thereby excluding the

---

[49]Segal, *Paul*, pp. 241-50, having recognized that the tension is in the arena of
religious covetousness, concludes that Paul found "that attempting to follow the
ceremonial Torah 'as a Christian' inevitably leads to sin, whether intentional or not.
. . . He might not have foreseen at first that the effects of his compromise put him
in real danger (7:15). . . . It is the self-description of a man relating his personal
experience: his attempt to find a compromise between the two sociological groupings in Christianity and discovery that he could not. . . . His perception that the law
of sin dwells in his members arises from his diplomatic struggle to find an accommodation to ceremonial laws in the new Christian community. It is a struggle that
Paul cannot win, because he cannot both observe the laws and ignore them at once,
and both communities appear to be watching him for guidance or criticism. It is a
struggle that no Christian can win as long as Torah observance is a serious option
within the Christian community. But Christianity can win the battle by ignoring
observance of the special laws of Torah entirely. A lawless gospel is the only
Christian solution that will yield a single community" (pp. 244-45).
　Whether Segal is correct that Paul, and hence Christianity, had to arrive at a
Law-free gospel presupposes that Paul abandoned Torah observance. However,

uncircumcised from equality, a struggle he was able to overcome only through faith in Christ and the recognition that this was the same for gentiles: gentiles were now equal in Christ, and the sting of this covetous discrimination was overcome. In this light we can see why Paul developed the illustration of Abraham in Romans 4. Paul sought to clarify the function of justification "by faith apart from the works of the Law" after remarking that the works of the Law *did not* exclude boasting against the one who does not also have the status conferred by them, that is, gentile sinners (3:27-28).[50]

Paul understood Peter's choice only too well. It was another form of his own earlier persecution of the believers in Christ of the Damascus synagogues;[51] that is why he challenged it so strongly. Peter's choice

---

his reading of Paul's tension as the positive and desirable practice of Torah observance is similar at the point of recognizing that the issue is the religious impulse to observe Torah. Where we depart completely is in his assumption that Paul concluded not to observe Torah to resolve the tension. I see that Paul is saying he resolved the tension by accepting the equality of those who do not observe Torah but fulfill it nevertheless through faith in Christ (Rom. 7:25; 8:1-4). Paul did not resolve the dilemma by abandoning Torah, by forsaking his circumcision; but by accepting Christ he was freed from the concomitant judgment of gentiles according to fleshly distinction, a freedom that "some" of the Roman Jews among those he is addressing in this letter did not share as they judged the gentiles by "the works [status] of the Law." Paul did not give up Torah; he gave up the "works [status] of the Law" as the distinguishing marks of the people of God. He could now live the life of Torah, free of judging those who did not. Paul is not describing his final compromise, but his final victory that allows him to now begin doing the good he wishes to do, namely, the Law of God with which his inner man joyfully concurs, though now free of the judgmental covetousness that had formerly led to separation or death. Paul thereby explains the tension that the Christian gentiles in Rome have been unable to understand in their relationship with non-Christian Jews who may be questioning the legitimacy of their claims of coparticipation through faith in Christ without Jewish conversion. The solution is not to become Jews, but to refrain from the temptation to undertake the same covetous judgmentalism in response, rather than extending the spirit of lovingkindness that has been extended to themselves (Rom. 2:1-4, 5ff.; 8:5-39; 11:7—12:3, 4ff.; 15:1-3).

[50]This remark of Paul's that boasting is not excluded by works of Law, where traditional Lutheran theology would suggest that boasting would indeed be excluded (because, it is presumed, no one could have done them), helps to clarify that the issue is not the doing of good deeds, but the boasting that comes from having status, an honored and desirable position, though one with the inherent problem Paul is addressing in Rom. 7. See the exegesis of J. Lambrecht, "Why Is Boasting Excluded? A Note on Rom 3,27 and 4,2," in *Pauline Studies*, pp. 27–31, although his conclusions are different.

[51]See discussion and references in chapter 6 above.

struck at the very heart of faith in Christ in a manner that would ultimately prevail if left unchecked, for it would have nullified the work
of Christ to bring the promise of God to all the world equally. It would
have compromised God's oneness and made faith in Christ an entrance requirement into Israel, along with circumcision and Torah, for
there would be no place for those outside Israel in Christ. It would
have killed the truth that the gospel was for all, everywhere, as equals
through faith in Christ.[52]

Paul related to the Galatians what he would seek to express some
five to ten years later in Romans 7, that the one who embraces the Law
is trapped by the human impulse to covet into discriminating by the
Law against the one who does not also embrace the Law. Thus one
kills oneself in seeking to observe the very gift of God, judging the
other instead of serving them—not because the Law kills, nor because
the Law fails, but because of human nature, the inability to live free
of judging the other. Thus one kills oneself by wielding the Law to
one's own purpose. Such people do violence with the very gift of God
that is "holy and righteous and good," that calls them to spirituality
but gives them also the weapon by which to judge according to fleshly
distinctions (circumcision and Torah observance). What Paul attacked
was not Peter's observance of Torah, which Paul also observed, but his
indulgence of covetousness (judging by "the works [status] of the
Law") evident in his withdrawal. The issue in Antioch illustrates the
sin Paul later expressed in the anguished prose of Romans 7, a sin regarding purity of motive, for which the rabbinic literature likewise indicates concern among those who love Torah.[53]

[52]Howard, *Paul*, pp. 61–62, appears to be arguing along very similar lines with
respect to interpreting Gal. 3:10, 13: "They [Jews] were redeemed from the sup-
pressing force of the law which separated Jew from Gentile and held back the universal unity which was destined to come. In our judgment the context points to
this sense, and none other, that all men, both Jews and Gentiles, were redeemed
from the law. In Christ's redemptive act the law lost its divisive power and uncircumcised Gentiles were ushered into God's kingdom on equal terms with the
Jews. This was salvation for Paul, for in that moment Yahweh became the God of
all men, and all men became his people."

[53]Moore, *Judaism*, 2.100, notes the rabbinic concern that "love of God should be
the sole motive. So Sifrè on Deut. 11, 13: '"To love the Lord your God." Should
you say, I will learn Torah that I may become rich, or that I may be called Rabbi,
or that I may acquire a reward, the Scripture says, "To love the Lord your God"—
whatever you do, do not do it except from love.' The same more at large in a
Baraita, quoting Deut. 30, 26: 'That a man say not, I will study the Scriptures that
men may call me a learned man (חכם), I will study tradition that I may become

We see then that Paul's phrase "through the Law I died to the Law" (Gal. 2:19) should not be interpreted as though this dying is a good thing, as though it pleased Paul to be finished with Torah observance, as though Paul had said "through *Christ* I *escaped* the Law," which would suggest that Christ has fulfilled and superseded the Law so that this presumably undesirable burden is no longer valid. Paul was not saying this at all. Paul said that "through the Law [which taught me to love God and my neighbor] I died to the Law," that is, I was unable to fulfill the service of God and my neighbor: "the good

---

an elder and sit in the session house; but learn out of love, and honor will come in the end' (Prov. 7, 3; 3, 17; 3, 18)."

The discussion of this religious dynamic by Heschel, *God in Search of Man*, is powerful (for additional rabbinic citations see pp. 391–92). For example, on pp. 387–88, he observes: "Anyone capable of self-examination knows that the regard for the self is present in every cell of our brain; that it is extremely hard to disentangle oneself from the intricate plexus of selfish interests. Thus, not only our evil deeds, but also our good deeds precipitate a problem. . . . In addition to our being uncertain of whether our motivation prior to the act is pure, and to our being embarrassed during the act by 'alien thoughts,' one is not even safe after the act. We are urged by Jewish tradition to conceal from others our acts of charity; but are we able to conceal them from ourselves? Are we able to overcome the danger of pride, self-righteousness, vanity, and the sense of superiority, derived from what are supposed to be acts of dedication to God? It is easier to discipline the body than to control the soul. The pious man knows that his inner life is full of pitfalls. The ego, 'the evil drive,' is constantly trying to enchant him. The temptations are fierce, yet his resistance is unyielding. And so he proves his spiritual strength and stands victorious, unconquerable. Does not his situation look glorious? But then the 'evil drive' employs a more subtle device, approaching him with congratulations: what a pious man you are!—He begins to feel proud of himself. And there he is caught in the trap."

And on pp. 392–93 Heschel continues: "Disguised polytheism is also the religion of him who combines with the worship of God the devotion to his own gain, as it is said, 'There shall be no strange god in thee' (Psalms 81:10), on which our teachers remarked that it meant the strange god in the very self of man. . . . 'For there is not a righteous man upon the earth, that does good and sins not' (Ecclesiastes 7:20). The commentators take this verse to mean that even a righteous man sins on occasion, suggesting that his life is a mosaic of perfect deeds with a few sins strewn about. The Baal Shem, however, reads the verse: For there is not a righteous man upon earth that does good and there is no sin in the good. 'It is impossible that the good should be free of sin and self-interest' [*Toldot Yaakov Yosef*]. Empirically, our spiritual situation looks hopeless. 'We are all as an unclean thing, and all our deeds of righteousness are as filthy rags.' (Isaiah 64:5) 'Even our good deeds are not pleasing but revolting, for we perform them out of the desire for self-aggrandizement and pride, and in order to impress our neighbors' [David Kimhi, *Commentary on Isaiah*]."

that I wish, I do not do" (Rom. 7:19). Even Paul's following comment, "I have been crucified with Christ," must be read in this context: "and it is no longer I who live, but Christ lives in me" (Gal. 2:20). In other words, Paul is saying: I (the Jew as defined by the works of the Law over against the gentile sinner) have been crucified with Christ and I (the Jew in Christ) am now justified/free to live the life that fulfills the Law without covetousness"; that is, he can now "subject [himself] to the righteousness of God" without "seeking to establish [his] *own* [Jewish vs. gentile] righteousness" (Rom. 10:3-4).

Paul's language is perhaps best understood in the light of Philippians 2:3-11, for the issue is that of learning to regard humbly the interests of the other, of taking on the "attitude in yourselves which was also in Christ Jesus, who although He existed in the form of God, did not regard equality with God a thing to be grasped [i.e., coveted]." Paul was saying that the Law could not finally empower him to overcome covetousness toward the one outside the Law because his judgmental nature was stirred up by the "works [status] of the Law," which led him to judge himself in and the other out. In this way, Paul argued, the status conferred upon those having the Law ("the works of the Law") stirs this covetousness impulse that rests in the human soul side by side with the desirable impulse to obey the Law, excluding or denigrating those not of the Law, as illustrated in Peter's recent hypocrisy. It is in this way that Paul spoke of dying to the Law through the covetousness stirred by the fleshly distinctions made through the Law. Thus Paul declared his need for and faith in Christ Jesus: "Wretched man that I am! Who will set me free from the body of this death?[54] Thanks be to God through Jesus Christ our Lord!" (Rom. 7:24-25). Paul's argument is that Peter's covetous action as illustrated in his withdrawal nullified the purpose of the death of Christ, which brings God's grace equally to all, to the Jew first and also to the gentile.

In summary, Paul "agree[d] with the Law," confessing that it was "holy and righteous and good"; moreover, the Law was "spiritual" and could do many things for those who embrace it (Rom. 7:12-16). Paul certainly "wished" to "do" Torah (7:11-23); he "joyfully concur[red] with the law of God in the inner man" (7:22). It ought to be obeyed, fulfilled, established, for the Law calls one to love, not covet; indeed, the Law calls one to Christ (10:4). But the Law cannot finally overcome covetousness of the privileged status of those who have it (i.e.,

---

[54]Note that Paul did *not* say "Who will set me free from the Law?"!

through the "works [status] of the Law" their "*own* righteousness" is established), because even when they do the good that the Law prescribes they find themselves immediately looking upon the other who does not have or does not do the Law as less "holy and righteous and good" than themselves—boasting is not excluded (3:27ff.). In other words, the covetous impulse of human nature ultimately stands in the way of the complete good to which the Law calls one because the status conferred by the Law does not exclude boasting, a state captured succinctly by Paul in his confrontation with Peter: "We are Jews by nature, and not sinners from among the Gentiles" (Gal. 2:15, 17). Paul concluded that this is where faith in Christ came into focus for those who believed in him (Gal. 2:16-21; Rom. 10:2-4). If one allows that Christ calls all equally, without discrimination as to their status as Jew or gentile, then this covetousness is obviated: "He condemned sin in the flesh in order that the requirement of the Law might be fulfilled in us, who do not walk according to the flesh, but according to the Spirit" (8:3-4).[55] Equal access means that the impulse to judge the other outside can be overcome and the Law can be fulfilled by those who walk "according to the Spirit." Paul can now do the very "good that [he] wishes" to do "in Christ" and not the "very thing [he] do[es] not wish."[56] Paul is not describing what is wrong with the Law or Judaism; he is simply explaining how he can now fulfill the Torah as a Jew in Christ free of the covetous exclusion of gentiles, something he apparently had not been able to do before believing in Christ, and something that he accused Peter of at Antioch.

Peter's action merely adumbrates what became all too obvious in Christian history: faith in Christ can still be made to function in the same covetous way as faith in the works of the Law for the one who

---

[55]Ziesler, "Role of the Tenth Commandment," p. 50, makes the important observation in Rom. 8:4 of the use of the singular δικαίωμα ("requirement") in Paul's conclusion: "having talked in 7.1-6 about dying to the Law, Paul now in a notably bald statement appears to bring us back to life again in relation to the Law, if not under it. We died to the Law in order to keep it better." He further suggests that this singular reference keeps the singular sin of covetousness in perspective (pp. 50–51).

[56]Snodgrass, "Spheres of Influence," p. 107, states: "If the law is not involved in salvation, then sin is a victor because it defeated God's law which was for life (7.12, 10). But now the law is placed within the sphere of the Spirit (cf. 8.4), where it belongs (7.14). The law in the right sphere frees us from the tyranny of the law in the sphere of sin. I do not think we can ignore a reference to the OT law. It is through the law that Paul died to the law."

looks to the other to judge him or her an outsider, "for the mind set on the flesh" discriminates, excluding instead of embracing. Covetousness is not the special domain of those obeying Torah; it is the universal plight of humankind.[57] Paul rebuked a manifestation on the Jewish side of this exclusivism in Antioch; in Romans we find him confronting this same covetous sin on the Christian gentile side. "Through the Law I died to the Law that I might live to God [and to the other as my equal]" is a universal program at the heart of Paul's theology that strikes at the heart of human sin manifest in judgmentalism, not Torah, through the profound themes elegantly captured in the Shema: the oneness of the Lord and the oneness of those who believe in the Lord, regardless of fleshly distinctions.

In Galatians, as in Romans, Paul does not ask Jews who believe in Christ to abandon their Jewish convictions. While Romans does not address Christian Jews directly (the context being concerned with Christian gentiles offending Christian and non-Christian Jews), in Galatians he retells an encounter with Christian Jews (Peter and "the rest") in which Paul told them not to let their Jewish status come in the way of equality with gentiles who believe in Christ. Galatians, unlike Romans, does not address the issue of the apostolic decree; however, the details of the Antioch incident suggest that some format was in place for guiding table-fellowship between Jews and gentiles because there are not charges of apostasy and no defense of such charges, and gentiles seriously considering "judaizing" were probably already functioning as "righteous gentiles" in their interaction with Jews.

Paul's position on the apostolic decree cannot be argued with certainty from Galatians, indeed, it is likely that the Antioch incident and the letter to the Galatians precede the Jerusalem conference of Acts 15.[58] It simply appears that the operative format of the apostolic decree and Noahide Commandments was not a matter of dispute and thus

---

[57]Heschel, *Between God and Man*, p. 414, again puts this most eloquently: "Religion becomes sinful when it begins to advocate the segregation of God, to forget that the true sanctuary has no walls. Religion has always suffered from the tendency to become an end in itself, to seclude the holy, to become parochial, self-indulgent, self-seeking; as if the task were not to ennoble human nature but to enhance the power and beauty of its institutions or to enlarge the body of doctrines. It has often done more to canonize prejudices than to wrestle for truth."

[58]R. Longenecker, *Galatians*, pp. lxxii–lxxxviii, makes a good argument for identifying the events of Gal. 2:1-10 with Acts 11:27-30, preceding the Jerusalem Conference of Acts 15. See also D. Wenham, "Acts and the Pauline Corpus II," pp. 215–58.

was not mentioned. Certainly Jews and gentiles were eating together, and as we have seen, for Jews to eat with gentiles would have involved such accommodating behavior and the acceptance of it by the Jewish community as sufficient. There is no indication that food was at issue in Antioch or Galatia, and gentiles considering circumcision would certainly(!)[59] be well down the road traveled by the "righteous gentile" in matters of food, no doubt well beyond pagan practices, particularly when in the company of Jews.

In other words, what has traditionally been assumed to tell us that Paul, and for that matter Peter, no longer invested Torah observance with any real significance, and that they even disregarded the practice of Torah and halakhah in Antioch and presumably elsewhere, does nothing of the sort. None of Paul's language suggests that they were not eating like Jews when they were eating with gentiles. And none of his language suggests that for Jews in Christ to continue to obey Torah as meaningful was wrong or even undesirable. On the contrary, his faith in Christ has permitted him to fulfill the Torah with which he "joyfully concurred" free of the covetous denial of the equal justification of the other in a way for which his former "life" according to "the works of the Law" had failed to provide the basis. What Paul opposes among those in Christ is returning to rebuilding, on the basis of circumcision and Torah, the boundary for excluding or judging gentiles in Christ as outsiders or inferior. Jews are Jews in Christ, gentiles are gentiles in Christ, because God is one and those in Christ are one, equals without the former discrimination. Jews do Jewish things unto the Lord, but not over against those who are not Jews—which involves them in the startling new reality of functioning as equals. Gentiles do gentile things unto the Lord, but not over against those who are Jews—therefore they must abandon gentile things that are actually pagan things and learn the ways of righteousness, which involves them in some Jewish or semi-Jewish "righteous gentile" behavior, both for doing righteousness unto the Lord and in service of Jewish sensitivities. They must accommodate and seek to "serve Christ in a manner acceptable to God *and* approved by men."

[59]One did not begin the process of becoming a Jew with the most difficult issue of circumcision, particularly notable in the context of first-century prejudices, fears, and medical considerations. This would be the final step, and it was being considered because the initial steps had not provided the equality of status desired, even if they had provided the level of purity necessary for preliminary inclusion (before Peter's withdrawal).

In conclusion, I find in the Antioch incident, recorded to instruct the Galatians, no challenge to this proposed reading of Romans. In fact, I find it corroborating my proposal even at the points where traditional interpretation seemed to suggest my portrayal of Pauline thought was not plausible.

1. Peter was not really accommodating Jewish practices in the manner Paul had called for among the gentiles in Romans 14; Peter was still observing Jewish practices as a practicing Jew in Antioch. Peter's hypocrisy in Antioch was in accommodating the opinion of those Jews who still maintained discrimination by the "works of the Law" when such discrimination had been made obsolete by the work of Christ for all those who were now living/justified "in Christ" by faith.

2. Peter and the other Christian Jews did not readopt Jewish behavior as appropriate upon the arrival of "the men from James." They had, along with Paul also, continued to observe Jewish lifestyles, including eating according to Torah and Jewish halakhah in the company of the Christian "righteous gentiles" in Antioch; however, they had not sought thereby to exclude the gentiles from equality in the community. One might say they did not *put on the Jew* when in mixed fellowship, instead they *put on Christ*.[60] Peter's withdrawal was condemned not for observance of Torah but for rebuilding the wall of fleshly distinction that he, along with Paul, had been tearing down since their recognition of equal access for all through faith in Christ Jesus.

3. Paul did not believe that Jews had died to the Law through the work of Christ, that is, that Torah is nullified, nor would he have desired to obviate the keeping of that which he so dearly loved. He believed, however, that Jews "in Christ" had died to the covetous judg-

---

[60]What I mean to suggest is that those in positions of power or social status are faced with a choice when in the company of those not similarly distinguished: they may "pull rank" so to speak or they may chose to relate on an "equal" basis. This would be illustrated, for example, in the choice of a professor when relating to a student outside the classroom. Will they play the professor and student and thus maintain some distinction and distance, or will they relate on some other level as equally human, or equally learners, etc. Will they be called "Dr." or by their first name in such a situation? Will they "put on" the professor or will they "put on" the friend, for example. This kind of choice is also quite clear in how a father relates to his adolescent son, on, say, a fishing trip. In this sense Paul speaks of how he relates to Jews as Jews and gentiles as gentiles (1 Cor. 9:19-23). He need not cease Jewish behavior when in the company of gentiles, but he does not make any more of it than necessary so as to minimize the distinction.

mentalism stirred by their observance of the Law against those who did not embrace the Law also, that is, "gentile sinners." They had been unable to overcome by the Law the seductive grip of the "works [status] of the Law," the boundary excluding gentiles from the privileges of the people of God, a boundary to which Peter had returned in his withdrawal in Antioch. Thus, Paul argued, through faith in Christ it was now possible truly to fulfill what the Law made him want so dearly, to do righteousness on behalf of and not over against the other. Justification in Christ made it possible to fulfill the Law as one people obeying the One God in harmony with gentiles who did not have the Law (and who must not compromise God's oneness by becoming Jews), but who, in Christ by faith, also fulfilled the intentions of the Law (who no longer behave as pagans).

4. Paul, Peter, James, and those who represented him all believed that gentiles in Christ were obligated to observe the halakhah appropriate for "righteous gentiles" in their fellowship with Jews. Although the dating of the Jerusalem conference with respect to the Antioch incident and the writing of Galatians is difficult to resolve,[61] the operative format that became known as the apostolic decree in Christianity and the Noahide Commandments in rabbinic Judaism was being observed. The issue in Antioch was not apostasy: Jews were not eating with pagans or in pagan ways. The issue was the failure to recognize the full implications of "the truth of the gospel": gentiles in Christ were not on the path of becoming Jews; rather, they had become one with Jews through their faith in Israel's king as the savior of the world.

5. Paul was careful not to condemn the other Jews involved in the Antioch incident, perhaps because he realized that they had not yet recognized the implications of justification in Christ as Peter had. It is difficult to comment on the two-step pattern for Paul or the others in Antioch or Galatia with respect to a mission to the Jews there first. The nature of the issues addressed in Galatians does not clarify the degree of involvement with non-Christian Jews who had not yet heard the gospel. However, Paul had been present in Antioch and in Galatia

---

[61]Paul's failure to use the results reached at the Jerusalem Conference in confronting Peter or the Galatians suggest that the Antioch incident and the writing of Galatians precede the conference of Acts 15 and thus the formal decision that gentiles need not become Jews in order to become Christians as equals and the apostolic decree. For a full discussion of the many proposals for resolving the issues of dating and reconciling the accounts in Acts with Paul's language in Galatians see R. Longenecker, *Galatians*, pp. lxxii–lxxxviii.

prior to writing this letter, unlike the case of Romans, and the two-step pattern may very well have been the operative methodology at that time. Certainly Acts 13:14-52 shows this to be the case in Paul's initial preaching in the synagogues there.[62]

6. The nature of the tensions in Antioch and Galatia suggests that gentiles were still aware of having joined the Jewish community's movement.[63] Their desire to "judaize" in order to be regarded as equals only makes sense in a Jewish environment dominated by Jewish behavior and leadership (cf. Gal. 2:2, 14-15; 6:12-13). This does not tell us whether the communities of believers in Christ in Antioch or Galatia were still operating under the synagogue authorities and obligated, for example, to pay Temple taxes. But the context certainly does not preclude this possibility, and the authority of the Jerusalem leadership was clearly operative, even in these Diaspora settings. It is likely that "Christianity" was still a subgroup identity in the context of the tensions Paul addressed, albeit one more distinguishable than perhaps was the case in Rome (Acts 11:26).

There is little tension between the Paul of Romans and the Paul revealed in the Antioch incident of Galatians. In each letter he is confronting the opposite sides of arrogant triumphalism with the same essential truths: the gospel is to the Jew *first* but to the gentile *also*—as equals. The Christian movement may be a very Jewish movement, but it is not an exclusively Jewish one. By the same reasoning the Christian movement may have become a very gentile movement, but it ought not to become an exclusively gentile one. Those who believe in the gospel are responsible to adopt the way of the Christ they have believed in who made the interests and rights of the other more

---

[62]Acts 11:19-21 has the two-step pattern operative in Antioch even before Paul followed the same custom there in Acts 13:14-52.

[63]Josephus *War* 7.3.3 (43–45), notes both that there were many Jewish inhabitants in Antioch during this period (estimates generally run similar to those for Rome of 20,000–50,000) and that there were many gentile proselytes who in some manner became a portion of the Jewish community (Josephus's language suggests that some kind of discrimination may have persisted toward these proselytes; perhaps this is similar to the lines drawn by Peter and the men from James). He also discusses the political climate in which the synagogues were afforded special privileges generally reserved for citizens; thus one must expect the same political realities I discussed with respect to Rome, which suggests that it would have also been unlikely for the earliest believers in Christ of Antioch to have functioned entirely separate from the Jewish communities and synagogues.

important than his own interests or rights. They are not called to judge the other, but to *hear* the intention of the One God and serve them, to join as one in reciting the Shema:

> that with one accord you may with one voice glorify the God and Father of our Lord Jesus Christ. (Rom. 15:6)

SOME PROBLEMS WITH READING ROMANS THROUGH THE LENS OF THE EDICT OF CLAUDIUS

Luke understood the leadership of the Jewish communities in Rome to be aware of, yet to have relatively little firsthand negative knowledge about, the Christian message and movement at the time of Paul's arrival (ca. 58–62 c.e.; cf. Acts 28:17-22). They do not appear to harbor any personal hostility; however, they are concerned about this "sect," having heard some disturbing news. When Paul concluded the introductory defense of his unwarranted imprisonment in the context of suffering "for the sake of the hope of Israel," he received the following response from the Jewish leadership in Rome:

> We have neither received letters from Judea concerning you, nor have any of the brethren come here and reported or spoken anything bad about you. But we desire to hear from you what your views are; for concerning this sect, it is known to us that it is spoken against everywhere.[1] (Acts 28:21-22)

This raises an interesting question concerning the historical backdrop of the conflict between Christian and Jews that is presumed by modern scholars to have led to the complete, or at least extensive, expulsion of the Jews (including Christian Jews and God-fearing [judaized] gentiles in most constructs) from Rome in 49 c.e. during the reign of Claudius, followed by their presumed return to Rome after the death of Claudius in 54 c.e.[2] The framework for the *Sitz im Leben*

---

[1]Note that Luke understands them to have some knowledge of this message and group that causes concern; however, what they know does not completely put them off and preclude their interest, which would be likely if what they did know led them to believe that it represented an entirely new religion.

[2]The dates for the reign of Claudius are fixed (41–54 c.e.); however, the later histories of Luke, Suetonius, and Dio Cassius do not include dates for the incidents recording the so-called edict of Claudius or its withdrawal, or even if it was withdrawn. It is assumed to have been no longer operative after the death of Claudius in 54 c.e.

of Romans projected through this historical construct[3] highlights a dramatic separation of Christianity and Judaism by the time of Paul's letter to and arrival in Rome in the late 50s or early 60s, although, interestingly, some interpreters allow that prior to the edict of Claudius the social setting in Rome was as I have argued in this study. That is, some interpreters recognize that operating in the background of Romans was the fact that the Christians in Rome had met prior to the edict "as a 'special synagogue' under the protection of the Jewish religious and legal privileges."[4]

The edict of Claudius construct suggests that house-churches, composed largely of Christian gentiles, developed rapidly in Rome and functioned independently of and at considerable distance from the synagogues and Jewish communities after the expulsion of 49 c.e.

[3]There are many modern proponents of the edict of Claudius construct I am discussing, many with their own unique twist. However, almost all share the same basic views I am generalizing herein. Some modern scholars use a good deal of caution, recognizing the possibility of this construct but also the paucity of the information and corroborating evidence, as well as the various ways the information could be construed to make quite different points. For example, Scramuzza, "Policy," pp. 295–96, drew careful conclusions similar to those I argue herein. Some scholars note that these tensions should or could be located between Jews and Christians as early as the beginning of the reign of Claudius in 41 c.e. See Smallwood, *Jews*, pp. 210–16, who argues decidedly that Suetonius's Chrestus reference is to Christianity (p. 11), but also cautions that it need not suggest that more than some, i.e., the actual rioters, were expelled (p. 216); see Dunn, *Romans*, pp. xlviii–liv, for an excellent discussion. For Dahl, *Studies in Paul*, p. 142, it constituted a three-sentence note to consider. Many modern scholars, however, appeal to the construct extensively, often without a substantial caveat, and it has become extremely influential for outlining the development of Christianity in Rome as well as for interpreting Romans. See Kümmel, *Introduction*, pp. 217–19, for an essential standard treatment. For historical development of the implications see Wiefel, "Jewish Community," pp. 92–96, an often noted article that develops the "possibility" this construct holds for specifying the *Sitz im Leben* of Romans (e.g., R. Jewett, *Tolerance*, pp. 27–29, builds on the reconstruction of Wiefel). Other recent examples of the importance of this construct for interpreting Romans include: Watson, *Paul*, pp. 88–98; Wedderburn, *Reasons*, pp. 54–59, 64–65; Campbell, *Intercultural Context*, pp. 180–82, and n. 96, 185–87, 200–204 and nn. 18, 20 (it is interesting to note the change in tone from Campbell's 1972 dissertation at Edinburgh, "Purpose of Paul," pp. 467–75, wherein he balanced the ideas of Wiefel's construct with the very different observations of Judge and Thomas and drew highly nuanced conclusions where the implications of this construct are concerned). J. Walters, *Ethnic Issues in Paul's Letter to the Romans*, has built an entire book around this construct and its historical significance for interpreting Romans.

[4]Stuhlmacher, *Paul's Letter to the Romans*, p. 7; Dunn, *Romans*, pp. xlviii–liv.

This construct is derived by harmonizing information provided in three references to the so-called edict of Claudius.

1. Luke's account in Acts 18:2:

And he [Paul] found a certain Jew named Aquila, a native of Pontus, having recently come from Italy with his wife Priscilla, because Claudius had commanded all the Jews to leave Rome.

2. The second-century note in Suetonius *Claudius* 25.4:

Since the Jews constantly made disturbances at the instigation of Chrestus, he [Claudius] expelled them from Rome.[5]

This note may also be interpreted:

He [Claudius] expelled from Rome the Jews constantly making disturbances at the instigation of Chrestus.

3. The third-century note in Dio Cassius 60.6.6-7:

As for the Jews, who had again increased so greatly that by reason of their multitude it would have been hard without raising a tumult to bar them from the city, he [Claudius] did not drive them out, but ordered them, while continuing their traditional mode of life, not to hold meetings.[6]

This expulsion is assumed by many modern scholars to lie behind the tensions addressed in Romans,[7] particularly between the "weak" and the "strong" (14:1—15:3).[8] The conflicts Paul addressed presum-

---

[5]Loeb Classic Library translation by J. C. Rolfe of Suetonius, *The Lives of the Caesars*: "'Iudaeos impulsore Chresto assidue tumultuantes Roma expulit.'"

[6]Loeb Classic Library translation by E. Cary of Dio Cassius, *Roman History*.

[7]D. Slingerland extensively, and I think convincingly, undercuts the tentative foundations upon which these "arbitrary" harmonizations of the citations and their historical importance rest. See his detailed arguments in "Suetonius *Claudius* 25.4, Acts 18, and Paulus Orosius' *Historiarum Adversum Paganos Libri VII*: Dating the Claudian Expulsion(s) of Roman Jews," pp. 127-44; "Suetonius *Claudius* 25.4 and the Account in Cassius Dio," pp. 305–22; and "Chrestus: Christus?" pp. 133–44.

[8]This construct, however, ignores the condescending and anti-Judaic implications of Luther's trap by suggesting that the "weak" are Christian Jews presumably weak because of their continued practice of Torah and Jewish customs as meaningful expressions of faith for those who believed in Christ. See chapter 3 above for the many problems with this view for both Paul and his audience.

ably grew out of the resocialization of Christian Jews (the "weak"), who were formerly in the majority and in prominent positions when Christianity was beginning in Rome, particularly when a synagogue environment is assumed for the earliest Christians who were Jews and God-fearing (judaized) gentiles. However, they were now returning to Rome only to find the Christian communities functioning independent of the synagogues, which were supposedly not operative again until this same time (54 c.e. and thereafter) since all (or almost all) of the Jews were banished from Rome. The newly formed house-churches, with Christian gentiles (the "strong") in the majority and in authority, had developed their own patterns of Christian practice that were presumably not very Jewish, perhaps even anti-Judaic. These Christian gentiles did not entirely welcome the returning Christian Jews, rejecting their continued practice of Jewish Law and customs, not to mention their desire to continue to be a part of the larger Jewish community(s), which they did not see being supplanted because of their new Christian persuasion, but rather restored. Nor did the Christian gentiles care to comply with their Jewish opinions about applicable halakhah for "righteous gentiles."

However, if the historical situation had been as profoundly affected by the edict of Claudius as is assumed in such a construct, then why does Luke not build on the irreconcilable animosity of the Jewish community(s) toward the Christian message (particularly as this would fit with the assumption of many scholars that it was Luke's intention to show Jews rejecting the gospel, thereby losing their place among God's people),[9] or at least, why doesn't Luke make the logical connection between their *firsthand, extensive, and extremely negative* knowledge of the gospel and its proclaimers and the situation in Rome upon Paul's arrival.[10] After all, Paul approached the very Jews who would have been severely affected and only recently returned to Rome when the edict expired. The Jewish leaders in Rome would certainly not have forgotten such a group if they had been victims of an expulsion

---

[9]Cf. J. T. Sanders, *Jews in Luke-Acts*. See the summaries of Gager, *Origins*, pp. 149–51; Kümmel, *Introduction*, p. 115. For a full discussion of the flaws in these assumptions see the reading of Luke's intentions by Jervell, *Luke*, pp. 41–74; Evans, "Is Luke's View"; see also chapter 5 herein.

[10]Some might argue that Luke is intentionally avoiding such a scenario for political reasons, but then why did Luke include the comment regarding the expulsion in the first place? Was it really necessary? Wouldn't this reference actually suggest that Luke does not connect the expulsion with any Jewish-Christian tensions?

because of them![11] Yet Luke portrays the Jewish leaders in Rome as essentially aware of this "sect" yet unfamiliar with the reasons that it is "spoken against everywhere," nor have they heard specifically of Paul's message (Acts 28:22). Would the same Luke who communicated the information upon which the lens of the Claudian edict constructs are ground (Acts 18:2) have been so totally blind to the extensive results that it would have precipitated in Rome (which are clear to modern scholars), namely, that the Jewish communities in Rome were highly aware of and antagonistic toward the Christian communities and their gospel by the time of Paul's arrival in the late 50s?[12] Following the modern scholars' development of the programmatic nature of Luke's intentions in constructing Acts, one must surely ask why Luke would not use this for all its worth, setting up the Jewish community in Rome as already rejecting, or at least predisposed to reject, on the basis of its own experience, the Pauline gospel. At least one must ask why Luke does not acknowledge such a highly agitated situation between Jews and Christians if he knew the expulsion under Claudius to have been the result of disturbances arising from the proclamation of the gospel in the synagogues of Rome. In other words, any historical inferences drawn with regard to the cause or extent of the expulsion under Claudius must address the internal contradiction they create within Luke's own account of the situation in Rome, regardless of Luke's historical reliability.

First of all, is it possible that Luke did not mean to communicate that all Jews had been expelled under Claudius? Perhaps "all the Jews" refers to a specific group of Jews in Rome: πάντας τοὺς Ἰουδαίους, with πάντας in the predicate position need not imply "every"; it may be translated indefinitely as "Jews," that is, "some Jews," or definitely as "the Jews," that is, "all the Jews."[13] This reading is supported by the alternate translation of Suetonius's report which does not suggest that all the Jews were expelled; only "the Jews constantly making disturbances" would have been affected. Along the same lines, where does Luke suggest that the expulsion had anything

[11]This point is similarly noted by S. Benko, "The Edict of Claudius of A.D. 49 and the Instigator Chrestus," pp. 417–18.

[12]The cunning, or at least purposed, intentions of Luke in his development of Luke-Acts presupposed by modern scholarship would seem to preclude such naiveté on Luke's part regarding the extensive knowledge of this expulsion among his readers.

[13]Slingerland, "Suetonius *Claudius* 25.4, Acts 18, and Paulus Orosius" p. 134.

to do with Christian matters, or that Aquila and Priscilla were "Christian" Jews? Luke identifies them as Jews and by trade tent-makers with whom Paul stayed "because he was of the same trade" (Acts 18:3), but not as Christians per se.[14] Note that after they met in Corinth Paul was engaged in preaching within the synagogue there (v. 4); he met them while he was working in the context of the syna-gogues, not churches. It certainly takes no stretch of the imagination to see them learning of and believing in Christ in response to Paul's influence.

To press this point further, Luke does not even indicate that all the Jews who were expelled included Christians among them; for that matter neither does Suetonius or Dio. Perhaps it was only the mem-bers of the offending synagogue (which likely would have constituted no more than a house meeting),[15] or even only the offending members of a particular synagogue, who were expelled. After all, Jews had been expelled several times from Rome well before Christ or Christianity were on the scene.[16] Even more likely, Luke may have seen clearly (known?) that the edict of Claudius had nothing to do with a negative Jewish response to Christ or to the Christian message or even to the Christian Jews among the synagogue communities, even if some "Christian" Jews (and Christian gentiles) may have been included among the members expelled (as Jews or judaized gentiles). Luke appears to believe that the Jewish leaders in Rome are largely (but not completely) unaware of the gospel message at the time of Paul's arrival, at least with respect to why this "sect" is spoken against else-

[14]Similarly noted by Benko, "Edict," p. 413.

[15]There is no evidence of independent synagogue structures in the Diaspora during this period. Private homes were adapted for meetings, and since the Jews of Rome of this period were not often wealthy, most if not all of their homes would have accommodated only small groups. See White, *Building God's House*, pp. 60–101; Meyers and Kraabel, "Archaeology, Iconography," pp. 177–89, cf. pp. 184–85, and Meyers and Strange, *Archaeology, the Rabbis*, pp. 140–54; S. Zeitlin, "Origins," pp. 14–26; L. I. Levine, "Synagogues of the Diaspora"; P. Lampe, *Die stadtrömischen Christen*.

[16]See Rutgers, "Roman Policy," pp. 56–74, for a discussion of the various ex-pulsions during the first century c.e. Also discussed by Benko, "Edict," pp. 412–17, who notes on p. 412: "The only reason why the expulsion of the Jews from Rome by Claudius may be connected with the Christian movement is be-cause of the occurrence of the name Chrestus in Suetonius. Otherwise the years leading up to the Jewish revolt of A.D. 66–70 are filled with Jewish-Gentile clashes in various parts of the empire and with various measures against Jewish excesses which had absolutely nothing to do with Christianity."

where, though apparently not among their own congregations in Rome. For that matter, Luke appears to know of an expulsion of Jews from Rome that does not seem to include any Christian involvement and that does not result in any direct knowledge of the dangers of this group among the Roman authorities with whom Paul deals: Gallio, Felix, Agrippa, or the prison authorities in Rome, where even as a prisoner he appears to be involved in the kind of behavior that is assumed to have stirred up exactly such riots—they regard Paul's activities as a purely intra-Jewish affair outside the confines of normal official Roman action. This is a startling circumstance, for if they did not know of such an extensive expulsion resulting from the tumultuous nature of this faction in Rome (is that really possible?), Paul's accusers would have certainly made them aware of such former incidents in seeking Paul's conviction (cf. 24:5), that is, if they applied.[17] Luke indicates that the leaders of the Jewish communities of Rome have first-hand knowledge of this faction, yet this knowledge provides no basis for understanding why they have heard that it is spoken against in other locations.

Further, perhaps "Chrestus" is not a reference to Christ or the Christian message or Christians at all, since Chrestus was a common Greco-Roman name, and in the case of Suetonius he does write later of the *christiani*, not *chrestiani*, when referring to this new religion:[18] "a consideration which might lead to the conclusion that Suetonius saw no association between the previously mentioned Chrestus and the religion of the christianorum."[19] We must also consider that Tacitus, who

---

[17]See Acts 18:12-17 for Gallio, proconsul of Achaia; chaps. 23–26 for Felix, governor, and King Agrippa II, son of Herod Agrippa I; chap. 28 for his freedom to move among the Jewish communities in Rome while still a prisoner for allegedly stirring up dissension (24:5). This point bears weight because Luke does report the expulsion in 18:2 (it does not appear necessary to have done so—was Luke so naive that he would include unnecessarily this historical point in 18:2, yet so cunning as to seek to obscure its significance for his reader at these other places in his narrative?), yet he does not link it with either official Roman or Jewish knowledge of the Christian movement as the source of riots in the Jewish communities that have been so threatening to the pax Romana that they have already resulted in expulsions such as the one by Claudius. Cf. Judge and Thomas, "Origin," p. 88; Campbell, "Purpose of Paul," p. 470. See also D. Gill and B. Winter, "Acts and Roman Religion," pp. 98–103.

[18]*Nero*, 16.2. See Benko, "Edict," pp. 410–12.

[19]Slingerland, "Chrestus: Christus?" pp. 136–37, and the complete article for a very strong argument against taking the reference to Chrestus as a reference to Christ or Christians, including a discussion of the fact that the text does not indi-

was "active before Suetonius, already knew the origin of the name and its correct spelling,"[20] and initially introduced the Christians only under the reign of Nero in 64 c.e. in a way that "rules out any prior treatment of them in his work,"[21] thus corroborating the possibility that "the Chrestus of Suetonius may therefore safely be left as some religious star whose appearance at Rome caused an upheaval among the Jews, but whose fame was sufficiently ephemeral for his precise identity to have been lost."[22]

Besides the obvious possibility that Chrestus was the name of a person in Rome, there is the possibility that it refers to a messianic person or movement, but not necessarily Jesus or his followers.[23] For example, Judge and Thomas argue that "Chrestus" should be understood as a messianic title that was

> taken by Suetonius or his source as a personal name. But if the Messiah concerned had been Jesus, we not only sharpen the problem of Suetonius' failure to see the point (even if his source did not), but come up with a quite different obstacle . . . we have to suppose that the Jewish lobby completely missed a unique opportunity of settling their account with the Christians by laying the blame firmly where it belonged. They failed to have the Christians as such named as political agitators, and at the same time allowed to pass into the record the title that implicitly conceded to Jesus the status they were at most pains to deny.[24]

Was Luke, who included such a specific detail as the expulsion of Jews from Rome under Claudius in Acts 18:2 (the very basis for this construct) completely unable to see the reasons for or implications of

---

cate that the issue is with those preaching about Chrestus: Suetonius appears to believe that this Chrestus is personally present in Rome (pp. 137–38). See also Benko, "Edict," pp. 406–18.

[20]Benko, "Edict," p. 412.

[21]Judge and Thomas, "Origin," p. 86.

[22]Ibid., p. 87.

[23]Borg, "New Context," pp. 211–12, points out "that Chrestus should be read as Christus (= Messiah) . . . [which] suggests that Suetonius' reference is to Jewish messianic agitation in Rome, provoked both by the expulsion of the Roman Jews and sympathy with the contemporaneous aspirations of and outrages suffered by Palestinian Jews." Benko, "Edict," pp. 412ff., suggests that Chrestus "was a rabble-rouser who incited the Jews to various riots" and links him with extreme nationalists who "expected the kingdom of God to come through violence" (pp. 413ff.), concluding that "Chrestus, in all probability, was an extremist ('zealot') leader in the Jewish community of Rome" (p. 418).

[24]Judge and Thomas, "Origin," p. 86.

the expulsion as they applied to Paul's arrival in Rome, or even how this detail could have been woven into his supposedly programmatic (even anti-Jewish?)[25] legitimization of Christianity as Israel's true heir?[26] Furthermore, we should not overlook the fact that this important historical detail apparently escaped the notice (or at least notations) of several important historians of the time such as Josephus, the Jewish historian concerned with just such Jewish matters,[27] and Tacitus, who officially documented this period of Roman history.[28] Neither mentions this Jewish expulsion in Rome under Claudius. This fact seems particularly strange since the Jewish residents of Rome numbered 20,000 to 50,000 at the time,[29] a sizable number of people to expel without significant historical notice, particularly if many Jews in Rome were citizens (freed slaves), as is noted by Philo.[30] Consider also that Dio appears to be denying just such a (mis)understanding of these events in stating that "he [Claudius] did not drive

[25]Cf. J. Sanders, *Jews in Luke-Acts*. But see Evans, "Luke's View."

[26]In Acts 28 the Jews of Rome are represented as honorable truth seekers, not contentious or riotous. Constructs that suggest a replacement theology for Luke should expect to find the Jews hardened against and rejecting violently the message of Paul, particularly in view of the edict of Claudius, shouldn't they? See the various essays (particularly on the twelve thrones of Israel) in Jervell, *Luke*; C. A. Evans and J. A. Sanders, *Luke and Scripture: The Function of Sacred Tradition in Luke-Acts.*

[27]Josephus does, however, mention the expulsion of 19 c.e. under Tiberius (*Ant.* 18.3.4–5 [65, 81–84]). For a discussion of the many problems with the reference attributed to Josephus by Orosius (fifth-century Christian writer), and thus why it should be disregarded in the constructs we are exploring, see Slingerland, "Suetonius *Claudius* 25.4, Acts 18, and Paulus Orosius," pp. 136–42.

[28]Tacitus, *Annals*, a second-century Roman historian's account of 47–54 c.e. As Slingerland points out, Tacitus would have been able to make excellent use of this information in his diatribe (*Hist.* 5.5.9); instead he is silent (Slingerland, "Suetonius *Claudius* 25.4, Acts 18, and Paulus Orosius," pp. 128–29, 135–36).

[29]Leon, *Jews*, pp. 135–37, and chapter 2 above.

[30]*Legatione Ad Gaium* 23.155, which was composed most likely after the death of Gaius (14.107) and the assumption of power by Claudius (30.206), according to Slingerland, "Suetonius *Claudius* 25.4 and the Account in Cassius Dio," pp. 314–15. On the status of Jews with respect to citizenship, etc., see Rutgers, "Roman Policy," pp. 59–60. See also Scramuzza, "Policy," pp. 296, who points out also the "practical difficulty of expelling all the Jews" in concluding that "only those individuals were expelled who took part in the disorders" and "the main body of the Jews was left unmolested." The obvious question is: How were those Jews who were citizens expelled on other than an individual-by-individual basis and with great difficulty in each case at that?

them out," although Dio may be discussing an entirely different event in the reign of Claudius.[31]

While there are tensions in Rome according to both Luke's account and Paul's letter, they do not seem to have degenerated to the perilous and irreversible degree suggested by such a construct.[32] There is not the monolithic hostility we would expect; there is instead the strain of different opinions developing within communities concerned with proper belief and behavior for the people of God. Nor do Christian gentiles (wild olive branches) appear to be in positions of authority in Rome to a greater degree than Christian Jews (the root that supports the branches) as this construct suggests, either by way of Paul's argument[33] or by way of the list of individuals in Romans 16. In fact, of the

[31]It seems a curious negative comment for Dio at this point. Why would he note what did not happen when writing the history of what did happen unless he was challenging another version of the event(s) at this point? But see Slingerland, "Suetonius *Claudius* 25.4 and the Account in Cassius Dio," pp. 305–22, who argues for separate incidents by demonstrating several problems including the circular reasoning involved in arbitrarily harmonizing the references (pp. 317–22): Dio describing an event in 41 c.e. and Suetonius an event that took place at another (uncertain) time under Claudius, Suetonius having written in a topical rather than annalistic style. See also Slingerland, "Suetonius *Claudius* 25.4, Acts 18, and Paulus Orosius," pp. 127–44, in which he argues further that it is not certain that Luke and Suetonius refer to the same incident (pp. 132–36), and if they do it provides only a range of dates between late 47 and 54 c.e. (p. 134 n. 31).

[32]Slingerland, "Suetonius *Claudius* 25.4 and the Account in Cassius Dio," p. 321, notes that the following harmonizations have been proposed: "Claudius restricted Roman Jewish worship and expelled rioters [Scramuzza]; he closed one synagogue and expelled some of its members [Penna, Luedemann]; he closed some synagogues and expelled rioters [Haenchen]; he closed all synagogues but expelled no one [Juster, Guterman]; he closed all synagogues and threatened expulsion [Harnack]; he closed all synagogues, threatened expulsion, and some Jews did leave or were expelled [Stern]; he closed all synagogues, and religious Jews left the city [Bruce, Schürer, Vogelstein, Suhl]; he closed all synagogues and expelled rioters [Leon, Berliner, Hoerber, May]; he closed synagogues and expelled all Jews [Benko; Smallwood in 'Jews and Romans' but not in *Jews*]; all Jews were simply expelled [Zielinski, Janne, Borg]" (brackets added for footnote references). To these many can be added from modern interpreters of Romans who largely see the complete, or at least extensive, expulsion of Jews in 49 c.e. as a result of Christian controversies in the synagogues of Rome (usually assuming a monolithic development of relations between Jews and Christians in Rome).

[33]See the discussion of Rom. 13:1-7 in chapter 6 above that proposes that the situation addressed suggests Christian gentiles are to subordinate themselves to the synagogue authorities. Note also that while the Christian gentiles are

APPENDIX 2

five Christian Jews mentioned, two (Aquila and Prisca) have meetings in their house (16:3-5) and two are apostles who were in Christ before Paul (16:7). Thus 80 percent of the Christian Jews mentioned are associated with authority roles in Rome within a few years after the edict of Claudius would have expired.

Moreover, if Christian gentiles were indistinguishably connected to the synagogues of Rome, or at least so from the standpoint of the Roman officials who apparently did not know much about the situation, (mis)citing *Chrestus* as though this individual was present (not to mention the obvious misspelling if they meant to refer to *Christus* or *Christiani*),[34] why wouldn't the (judaized) gentiles have been expelled along with the Jews?[35] Why would (Jewish or semi-Jewish [judaized]) gentiles have been permitted to remain in Rome, particularly when

---

challenged for their arrogant and high-minded attitudes toward Jews or the "weak" they are not confronted with the kind of instructions that would be directed to those guilty of abusing positions of power. They are dealt with rather as those who were resentful of the sustained privileges of Jews who have not "seen" what they have now seen so that they might recognize the awful error of nurturing such an uninformed and ungrateful attitude toward those whose very blindness has paradoxically served their own clarity of vision (11:1; 11:11—12:3). Note also that the "weak" are in the position to legitimately "approve" or "blaspheme" the behavior of the "strong" and not the other way around (14:16-18). It is also notable that Romans does not address any officials in Rome directly or even indirectly with respect to their position of authority or its proper execution (except full service of gifts in 12:6-8), not even among the many addressed in chap. 16, with the exception of Phoebe, a διάκονον of the church at Cenchrea, the port city of Corinth (v. 1), who was sent by Paul, and the two Christian *Jewish* apostles Andronicus and Junias (v. 7). See examples in Paul's other letters of those in authority and the continued expression of their responsibilities (e.g., throughout 1 Corinthians; apostles in 2 Cor. 8:23; 11:5, 13; 12:11; elders in Phil. 1:1; Titus 1:5-9; 1 Tim. 3:2; responsibilities of those in power, e.g., 2 Thess. 5:12-14; 1 Tim. 3; see Burtchaell, *From Synagogue to Church*, pp. 288–312, for full discussion of early church authorities).

[34]But see Wiefel, "Jewish Community," pp. 92–93, who argues that *Chrestiani* was commonly used for *Christiani* in the first two centuries, citing Tacitus, *Ann.* 15.44.2-4. See also Tertullian, *Apol.* 3.5; Justin, *Apol.* 1.4. Later Christian writers also played with the nuance provided by intentionally switching the ι for an η, for example, Clement of Alexandria in *Stromata* 2.5 writes: "Now those who believe in Christ both are and are called Chrestoi (good)," but this only proves that they were not confused about such a misspelling (Benko, "Edict," p. 410).

[35]Cohen, "Crossing the Boundary," pp. 13–33, especially pp. 20–21, discusses the indications that even in the second and third centuries gentiles who practiced Jewish rituals or lived in Jewish ways were still being referred to as Jews by gentile writers such as Juvenal, Plutarch, and Dio Cassius, even if they were not necessarily considered Jews by members of the Jewish community.

they were supposedly at the center of the controversy? Was the
Roman government able to make such a highly nuanced distinction at
such an early date between the gentile adherents to the synagogues
that they could expel gentile God-fearers and proselytes who were not
Christians, but not those who were? Could they distinguish Christians
from Jews at any level?[36] Would they even bother to try?[37] If so, this
would suggest a heightened discriminatory policy on the part of the
Romans toward Jews and Judaism, a viewpoint that modern scholarship has challenged.[38] Further, it necessitates a far more extensive
knowledge of the Christian movement than even the proponents of
this construct otherwise suggest.[39]

Along the same line, were the leaders of the synagogues even able
to make such a clear distinction among the gentile sympathizers in
Rome, for example, between gentiles believing in Christ and other
God-fearing gentiles who did not? Even if they could, would they
have done so to the benefit of Christian gentiles (with whom the hostility had supposedly become so fierce) so that they were excluded
from the expulsion? This is counter-intuitive and highly unlikely. In
other words, it follows logically that if the Jews were expelled, so too
were the Christian gentiles,[40] who would most likely have been classified at this time as Jews or semi-Jews (judaized gentiles) by both the
synagogue leaders and Roman officials.

[36]The continuing uncertainty among modern scholars about the identity of
Clemens and Domitilla as referred to by Dio Cassius for the charge by Domitian
in 95 c.e. of "'atheism', for which also many others were condemned who had
drifted into the practices of the Jews" (*Roman History* 67.14) bears witness to the
unlikelihood that there was a clear distinction between Christians and Jews among
the Roman rulers or historians of the period. The (arguable) conclusion that
Domitilla's "crime" was actually conversion to Christianity based on late documentary evidence (Eusebius) and especially archeological evidence is discussed at
length by Jeffers, *Conflict*, chaps. 1–4; cf. pp. 25–28.

[37]Rutgers, "Roman Policy," pp. 67–69, 70ff., 73–74, argues that Roman authorities primarily persecuted Roman Jews to suppress unrest and maintain law and
order and not because of their religious practices and beliefs: Roman authors reflect a "general antipathy to un-Roman religious practices" (p. 67). In order to research these details at the level necessary to make such discriminating choices
they would have had to operate with great care and effort in matters probably of
minor interest.

[38]Cf. Gager, *Origins*, and see discussion above in chapter 2.

[39]Most of these same scholars can be found recognizing that Roman authorities
do not identify or appear to formally recognize Christianity as a separate movement until 64 c.e. at the earliest.

[40]See Scramuzza, "Policy," p. 296, for a similar conclusion.

In addition, this construct still leaves open the problem of how the Christian gentiles would have procured official Roman permission to meet during this time. They had no rights if they operated outside the jurisdiction of the synagogues and their recognized privileges,[41] a problem that quickly came into focus in later years when Christians did meet outside such sanctions at great expense. Even if they had wanted to operate under the authority of the synagogues during this period, it would have been entirely impossible if all the Jews had been expelled, because naturally all synagogue privileges would have been suspended.

The tensions addressed in Romans are better explained when we recognize that these are precisely the kinds of tensions that would have been unfolding in synagogues as the Christian adherents grew in number and developed a subgroup identity (with additional meetings in their homes for worship and instruction). This would particularly be the case when more and more gentiles sought association as equals, without becoming Jews, with some even questioning the need to comply with the requirements of "righteous gentile" behavior in view of their perceived freedoms in Christ.

I suggest, for Luke, that the expulsion of Jews from Rome and the lack of extensive familiarity with the gospel among the Jewish leaders are compatible because (1) the expulsion had nothing to do with Christians and their message; or (2) if the expulsion was related to Christians and their message, it was a minor incident involving a specific and limited group of people (a house-synagogue?) so that it did not significantly affect the larger Jewish community(s). This makes sense of the situation addressed in Romans, the interpretation of which is perhaps best served apart from constructs dependent upon the harmonization of the limited historical details of the so-called edict of Claudius.[42]

---

[41]See the discussion in chapter 2 herein. Wiefel, "Jewish Community," pp. 92–96, sees this shaping the situation in Rome; however, he fails to note the political problems involved in forming a new assembly outside the synagogue's privileges, which he sees under the ban, not to mention his problematic view of the early Christians' intentions: "Christians could only assemble in Rome if they, as a group, had broken ties with the synagogue" (p. 94) and thus: "House churches provided a setting similar to that of congregations in the East who had also formed them in order to be independent of the synagogue" (p. 95).

[42]In fact, the evidence is so limited that it is not really clear that Jews were involved in any disturbances. The report by Suetonius, who was often given to sensationalism, the contrary report of Dio, and the absence of comment by Josephus

This suggestion also makes better sense of later evidence for positive Jewish and Christian interaction in Rome,[43] and the observation that Christianity in Rome developed with a distinctively Jewish *bent* (Ambrosiaster, ca. 375), which included loyalty to its Jewish heritage[44] and perhaps even continued synagogue involvement (cf. *Shepherd of Hermas* 11.9-14),[45] as well as the fact that Christian people do not appear to have an identity distinct from Jewish people in Roman sources until possibly 64 c.e., and even then they appear to have been regarded only as members of a faction within Judaism.[46]

It is likely that the Christians in Rome (gentiles as well as Jews) were much more Jewish and much more involved within the normal context of synagogue association than has been recognized in the past. Further, the tensions known to both Paul and the Jewish leadership, not to mention Luke, were perhaps much more intra-Jewish and manageable within the context of Judaism, precluding a parting of the ways as early as the Claudian edict dependent constructs seem logically, and necessarily, to promote.[47] This would make sense of Paul's

---

and Tacitus all lead one to wonder if this accusation was grounded in any real disturbance in the Jewish community. Perhaps it was an entirely false or fabricated accusation to serve some other purpose, or perhaps the report of Suetonius itself should be questioned.

[43]Rutgers, "Archaeological Evidence," pp. 101–18, discusses a wide range of third- and fourth-century evidence pointing to extensive positive interaction.

[44]See Brown and Meier, *Antioch and Rome*, and the discussion above in chapters 1, 2, and 4, including indications of continued application of some of the food concerns of the apostolic decree.

[45]There are several references to synagogue meetings in *Shepherd of Hermas* (ca. 100–140 c.e.). Perhaps even Hebrews was written to the Christians in Rome still meeting in synagogues; cf. Glaze, *No Easy Salvation*, pp. 22–28; Brown and Meier, *Antioch and Rome*, pp. 139-58; Judge and Thomas, "Origin," p. 92; Lane, *Hebrews 1–8*, pp. xviii–lx, cxxv–cxxviii.

[46]The persecution and fire of the 64 c.e. are the first indications of Roman government's awareness of a separation between Christians and Jews, and even this may be simply the awareness of a new sect of Judaism known as "Christiani" (Tacitus, *Annals*, 15.44.2-8; M. Grant, *Nero*, pp. 151–61; Benko as cited by Dunn, *Romans*, p. 1). Benko, *Pagan Rome*, p. 16, notes that "Tacitus saw Christianity as a 'superstition' of Jewish origin. . . . It seems that he drew no distinction between Jews and Christians"; and on p. 20 he summarizes: "In 64 Christians were still known as Jews."

[47]Paul was, after all, close to Aquila and Priscilla and thus would have been well aware of the profound implications of the Claudian edict constructs proposed cataclysmic separation between Jews and Christians. Judge and Thomas, "Origin," p. 88, note the issue similarly. A most instructive example of the depth of

appeal in Romans to the unifying essence of the Shema as the central
governing principle of their obligation no longer to entertain poten-
tially crippling behavior in the assertion of their special place in God's
design, but rather to welcome and serve each other in the same grace
that the One God has acted in toward themselves, without discrimination, as equals—as one:

> Now may the God who gives perseverance and encouragement grant
> you to be of the same mind with one another according to Christ
> Jesus; that with one accord you may with one voice glorify the God
> and Father of our Lord Jesus Christ. Wherefore, accept one another,
> just as Christ also accepted us to the glory of God. (Rom. 15:5-7)

By way of contrast, reading Romans through the lens of the edict of
Claudius projects an irreversible hostility and separation between
Jewish and Christian communities by the time of Paul's letter,[48] not to
mention an unforgivable level of self-serving intentions between those
Jews and gentiles believing in Christ.[49] Such scenarios fail to make
sense of Paul's optimism and light-handed treatment of the implied
tensions, (e.g., 1:8; 15:14; 16:19)[50] believing in spite of the emergence
of alarming trends that progress could be made, by way of this reminder
and his imminent trip, toward the restoration of all Israel in Rome.

When we look closely at the details of Luke's understanding of the
situation in Rome wherein the synagogue leaders were aware of but
not alienated from the Jewish faction believing Jesus to be the Christ,

---

synagogue involvement allowed before the edict of Claudius construct impacts
the assumptions of the social setting in Rome is found in Stuhlmacher, *Romans*,
p. 7: "They [Gentile Christians] now no longer had any possibility of meeting in
their congregational gatherings as a 'special synagogue' under the protection of
the Jewish religious and legal privileges, but had to form their own freely constituted assemblies without leaning on the Jewish synagogues."

[48]A point that, at the very least, ought to cause proponents of this construct to
reconsider Paul's projected role as the catalyst for the separation of Christianity
from its Jewish roots, since he has not been to or personally influenced these developments in Rome. In this case he is clearly the one seeking to mitigate differences and bridge a gap that others have already widened ostensibly beyond repair.

[49]Watson, *Paul*, pp. 94–98.

[50]Interpreters relying on this construct often note Paul's oblique handling of the
tensions, including indirect labels such as "weak" and "strong," yet they fail to see
the logical inconsistency of this approach for Paul if the hostilities were among
Christian Jews and gentiles and were as heightened as they suggest (e.g., Walters,
Ethnic Issues, pp. 86–92).

even in the light of the expulsion of some of the Jews of Rome by Claudius, we perhaps gain a new insight into the historical situation confronting Paul as he wrote to and later visited the Christians living within the context of the synagogues of Rome. Perhaps Paul's bold reminder of the need to continue to observe "the teaching" of the apostolic decree ("the obedience of faith") with the intention of winning the respect of the synagogue leaders was initially heeded by those he addressed in Romans. Perhaps Paul's letter actually succeeded in convincing the Christian gentiles in Rome to "serve Christ in a manner acceptable to God *and* approved by men" (Rom. 14:18), making them coworkers in the mystery designed to ensure simultaneously both of Paul's ultimate goals: "the fulness of the Gentiles" and the certain restoration of "all Israel."

BIBLIOGRAPHY

Allison, D. C. 1980. "The Background of Romans 11:11-15 in Apocalyptic and Rabbinic Literature." *Studia Biblica et Theologica* 10:229–34.

Alon, Gedaliah. 1989. *The Jews in Their Land in the Talmudic Age.* Trans. and ed. Gershon Levi. Cambridge, Mass., and London: Harvard University Press.

Aune, David E. 1983. *Prophecy in Early Christianity and the Ancient Mediterranean World.* Grand Rapids: Eerdmans.

——. 1991. "Romans as a *Logos Protreptikos.*" In *The Romans Debate.* Ed. Karl P. Donfried. Rev. ed. Peabody, Mass.: Hendrickson. Pp. 278–96.

Aus, Roger D. 1979. "Paul's Travel Plans to Spain and the 'Full Number of the Gentiles' of Rom. XI 25." *Novum Testamentum* 21/3:232–62.

Bacchiocchi, Samuele. 1977. *From Sabbath to Sunday: A Historical Investigation of the Rise of Sunday Observance in Early Christianity.* Rome: Pontifical Gregorian University Press; Greenwood, S.C.: Attic Press.

Badenas, Robert. 1985. *Christ the End of the Law: Romans 10.4 in Pauline Perspective.* Sheffield: JSOT Press.

Bammel, Ernst. 1985 (1984). "Romans 13." In *Jesus and the Politics of His Day.* Ed. Ernst Bammel and C. F. D. Moule. Cambridge: Cambridge University Press. Pp. 365–84.

Barnes, Arthur Stapylton. 1971 (1938). *Christianity at Rome in the Apostolic Age: An Attempt at Reconstruction of History.* Westport, Conn.: Greenwood Press.

Barre, Michael L. 1975. "Paul as 'Eschatological Person': A New Look at 2 Cor 11:29." *Catholic Biblical Quarterly* 37:500–526.

——. 1980. "Qumran and the 'Weakness' of Paul." *Catholic Biblical Quarterly* 42:216–27.

Barrett, C. K. 1991 (1957). *The Epistle to the Romans.* Hendrickson.

——. 1982. *Essays on Paul.* Philadelphia: Westminster.

Barth, Karl. 1968 (1933). *The Epistle to the Romans.* London, Oxford, and New York: Oxford University Press.

Barth, Markus. 1983. *The People of God.* Sheffield: University of Sheffield.

——. 1979. "St. Paul—A Good Jew." *Horizons in Biblical Theology* 1:7–45.

Bartsch, Hans-Werner. 1968. "The Concept of Faith in Paul's Letter to the Romans." *Biblical Research.* 13:41–53.

Bauer, Walter. 1979. *A Greek-English Lexicon of the New Testament and Other Early Christian Literature.* 2nd ed. Rev. by F. Wilbur Gingrich and Frederick W. Danker. Chicago and London: University of Chicago Press.

Baxter, A. G., and Ziesler, J. A. 1985. "Paul and Arboriculture: Romans 11.17-24." *Journal for the Study of the New Testament* 24.25–32.

Beker, J. Christiaan. 1991. "The Faithfulness of God and the Priority of Israel in Paul's Letter to the Romans." In *The Romans Debate*. Ed. Karl P. Donfried. Rev. ed. Peabody, Mass.: Hendrickson Publishers. Pp. 327-32.

———. 1993. "Luke's Paul as the Legacy of Paul." In *Society of Biblical Literature 1993 Seminar Papers*. Ed. E. H. Lovering, Jr. Atlanta: Scholars Press. 32:511–19.

———. 1990. "The New Testament View of Judaism." In *Jews and Christians: Exploring the Past, Present, and Future*. Ed. James H. Charlesworth. New York: Crossroads. Pp. 60–75.

———. 1980. *Paul the Apostle: The Triumph of God in Life and Thought*. Philadelphia: Fortress Press.

———. 1985. "Suffering and Triumph in Paul's Letter to the Romans." *Horizons in Biblical Theology* 1/7:105–19.

———. 1990. *The Triumph of God: The Essence of Paul's Thought*. Minneapolis: Fortress.

Bell, Richard H. 1994. *Provoked to Jealousy: The Origin and Purpose of the Jealousy Motif in Romans 9–11*. Tübingen: J. C. B. Mohr (Paul Siebeck).

Benko, Stephen. 1969. "The Edict of Claudius of A.D. 49 and the Instigator Chrestus." *Theologische Zeitschrift* 25/6:406–18.

———. 1985. *Pagan Rome and the Early Christians*. London: B. T. Batsford.

Betz, Hans Dieter. 1977. *Galatians: A Commentary on Paul's Letter to the Churches in Galatia*. Hermeneia. Philadelphia: Fortress Press.

Bjerkelund, C. J. 1967. *Parakalô: Form, Funktion und Sinn der parakalô-Sätze in den paulinischen Briefen*. Oslo: Universitetsforlaget.

Black, David Alan. 1984. *Paul, Apostle of Weakness: Astheneia and Its Cognates in the Pauline Literature*. New York: Peter Lang.

Bockmuehl, Markus. 1995. "The Noachide Commandments and New Testament Ethics with Special Reference to Acts 15 and Pauline Halakhah." *Revue Biblique* 102/1:72–101.

Boers, Hendrikus. 1982. "The Problem of Jews and Gentiles in the Macro-Structure of Romans." *Svensk Exegetisk Årsbok* 47:184–96.

———. 1992. "'We Who Are by Inheritance Jews; Not from the Gentiles, Sinners.'" *Journal of Biblical Literature*. III/2:273–81.

Borg, Marcus. 1972-73. "A New Context for Romans XIII." *New Testament Studies* 19:205–18.

Borgen, Peter. 1988. "Catalogues of Vices, The Apostolic Decree, and the Jerusalem Meeting." In *The Social World of Formative Christianity and Judaism: Essays in Tribute to Howard Clark Kee*. Ed. Jacob Neusner et al. Philadelphia: Fortress Press. Pp. 126–41.

——. 1982. "Paul Preaches Circumcision and Pleases Men." In *Paul and Paulinism: Essays in Honour of C. K. Barrett.* Ed. M. D. Hooker and S. G. Wilson. London: SPCK. Pp. 37-46.

Bornkamm, Günther. 1991. "The Letter to the Romans as Paul's Last Will and Testament." In *The Romans Debate.* Ed. Karl P. Donfried. Rev. ed. Peabody, Mass.: Hendrickson. Pp. 16–28.

Botha, Jan. 1994. *Subject to Whose Authority? Multiple Readings of Romans 13.* Atlanta: Scholars Press.

Bowers, W. P. 1975. "Jewish Communities in Spain in the Time of Paul the Apostle." *Journal of Theological Studies* 26/2:395–402.

Brichto, Herbert Chanan. 1973. "Kin, Cult, Land and Afterlife—A Biblical Complex." *Hebrew Union College Annual* 44:1–54.

Brown, Colin, ed. 1975. *The New International Dictionary of New Testament Theology.* 3 vols. Grand Rapids: Zondervan.

Brown, Raymond E. 1990. "Further Reflections on the Origins of the Church of Rome." In *The Conversation Continues: Studies in Paul and John in Honor of J. Louis Martyn.* Ed. Robert T. Fortna and Beverly R. Gaventa. Nashville: Abingdon. Pp. 98–115.

——, and Meier, John P. 1983. *Antioch and Rome: New Testament Cradles of Catholic Christianity.* New York: Paulist.

——; Fitzmyer, Joseph A.; and Murphy, Roland E., eds. 1990. *The New Jerome Biblical Commentary.* Englewood Cliffs: Prentice-Hall.

Bruce, F. F. 1984. "Paul and 'The Powers That Be.'" *Bulletin of the John Rylands University Library of Manchester* 66/2:78-96.

——. 1991 (1977). *Paul: Apostle of the Heart Set Free.* Grand Rapids: Eerdmans.

Brunt, John C. 1985. "Rejected, Ignored, or Misunderstood? The Fate of Paul's Approach to the Problem of Food Offered to Idols in Early Christianity." *New Testament Studies* 31:113–24.

Bruyn, Theodore De. 1993. *Pelagius's Commentary on St. Paul's Epistle to the Romans.* Trans. with Introduction and Notes. Oxford: Clarendon.

Burkitt, F. C. 1924. *Christian Beginnings.* London: University of London Press.

Burtchaell, James Tunstead. 1992. *From Synagogue to Church: Public Services and Offices in the Earliest Christian Communities.* Cambridge: Cambridge University Press.

Callan, Terrance. 1993. "The Background of the Apostolic Decree (Acts 15:20, 29; 21:25)." *Catholic Biblical Quarterly* 55:284–97.

Callaway, Mary C. 1993. "A Hammer That Breaks Rock in Pieces: Prophetic Critique in the Hebrew Bible." *Anti-Semitism and Early Christianity: Issues of Polemic and Faith.* Ed. Craig A. Evans and Donald A. Hagner. Minneapolis: Fortress Press. Pp. 21–38.

Cambell, Douglas A. 1992. *The Rhetoric of Righteousness in Romans 3.21-26.* Sheffield: Sheffield Academic Press.

Campbell, William S. 1992. *Paul's Gospel in an Intercultural Context: Jew and Gentile in the Letter to the Romans*. Frankfurt am Main: Peter Lang.

———. 1972. "The Purpose of Paul in the Letter to the Romans: A Survey of Romans I–XI with Special Reference to Chapters IX–XI." Dissertation, University of Edinburgh.

———. 1991. "Romans III as a Key to the Structure and Thought of Romans." In *The Romans Debate*. Ed. Karl P. Donfried. Rev. ed. Peabody, Mass.: Hendrickson. Pp. 251–64.

———. 1993. "The Rule of Faith in Romans 12:1—15:13." Paper presented at the 1993 SBL meeting, Washington D.C.

———. 1980. "Salvation for Jews and Gentiles: Krister Stendahl and Paul's Letter to the Romans." In *Studia Biblica 1978: III. Papers on Paul and Other New Testament Authors. Sixth International Congress on Biblical Studies*. Ed. E. A. Livingston. Sheffield: JSOT Press. Pp. 65–72.

Carrington, Philip. 1957. *The Early Christian Church*. Vol. 1: *The First Christian Century*. Cambridge: Cambridge University Press.

———. 1940. *The Primitive Christian Catechism*. Cambridge: Cambridge University Press.

Carter, Warren. 1989. "Rome (and Jerusalem): The Contingency of Romans 3:21-26." *Irish Biblical Studies* 11:54–68.

Catchpole, David R. 1977. "Paul, James and the Apostolic Decree." *New Testament Studies* 23:428–44.

Chance, J. Bradley. 1993. "The Seed of Abraham and the People of God: A Study of Two Pauls." In *Society of Biblical Literature 1993 Seminar Papers*. Ed. E. H. Lovering, Jr. Atlanta: Scholars Press. 32:384–411.

Charlesworth, James H. 1990. "Exploring Opportunities for Rethinking Relations among Jews and Christians." *Jews and Christians: Exploring the Past, Present, and Future*. Ed. James H. Charlesworth. New York: Crossroads. Pp. 35–59.

———. 1985. *The Old Testament Pseudepigrapha and the New Testament*. Cambridge: Cambridge University Press.

———, ed. 1992. *The Messiah: Developments in Earliest Judaism and Christianity*. Minneapolis: Fortress Press.

———, ed. 1983–85. *The Old Testament Pseudepigrapha*. 2 vols. Garden City, N.Y.: Doubleday.

Chilton, Bruce. 1992. *The Temple of Jesus: His Sacrificial Program Within a Cultural History of Sacrifice*. University Park, Pa.: Pennsylvania State University.

Clorfene, Chaim, and Rogalsky, Yakov. 1987. *The Path of the Righteous Gentile: An Introduction to the Seven Laws of the Children of Noah*. Jerusalem: Targum Press.

Cohen, Norman J. 1992. "Judaism and Christianity: The Parting of the Ways." *Thought* 67:409–19.

Cohen, Shaye J. D. 1989. "Crossing the Boundary and Becoming a Jew." *Harvard Theological Review* 82/1:13–33.

———. 1987. "Respect for Judaism by Gentiles according to Josephus." *Harvard Theological Review* 80/4:409–30.

Collins, J. J. 1983. *Between Athens and Jerusalem: Jewish Identity in the Hellenistic Diaspora.* New York: Crossroads.

Conzelmann, Hans. 1987 (1963). *Acts of the Apostles.* Ed. Eldon Jay Epp with Christopher R. Matthews. Trans. James Limburg, A. Thomas Kraabel, and Donald H. Juel. Hermeneia. Philadelphia: Fortress Press.

Cosgrove, Charles H. 1988. *The Cross and the Spirit: A Study in the Argument and Theology of Galatians.* Macon, Ga.: Mercer University Press.

Cranfield, C. E. B. 1975–79. *A Critical and Exegetical Commentary on Romans.* 2 vols. International Critical Commentary. Edinburgh: T. & T. Clark.

Dahl, Nils Alstrup. 1991. *Jesus the Christ: The Historical Origins of Christological Doctrine.* Ed. Donald H. Juel. Minneapolis: Fortress Press.

———. 1957–58. "A People for His Name." *New Testament Studies* 4/4:319–27.

———. 1977. *Studies in Paul: Theology for the Early Christian Mission.* Minneapolis: Augsburg Publishing House.

Davies, Glenn N. 1990. *Faith and Obedience in Romans: A Study in Romans 1–4.* Sheffield: Sheffield Academic Press.

Davies, W. D. 1974. *The Gospel and the Land: Early Christianity and Jewish Territorial Doctrine.* Berkeley: University of California Press.

———. 1984. *Jewish and Pauline Studies.* Philadelphia: Fortress Press.

———. 1948. *Paul and Rabbinic Judaism: Some Rabbinic Elements in Pauline Theology.* New York and Evanston: Harper and Row.

———. 1991 (1982). *The Territorial Dimension of Judaism.* Minneapolis: Fortress Press.

———. 1952. *Torah in the Messianic Age and/or the Age to Come.* Philadelphia: Society of Biblical Literature.

Donaldson, Terence L. 1988. "Preaching Circumcision: Gal 5:11 and the Origin of Paul's Gentile Mission." Paper presented at the Canadian SBL, 1988 meeting.

———. 1990. "Proselytes or 'Righteous Gentiles'? The Status of Gentiles in Eschatological Pilgrimage Patterns of Thought." *Journal for the Study of the Pseudepigrapha* 7:3–27.

Donfried, Karl P., ed. 1991. *The Romans Debate.* Rev. ed. Peabody, Mass.: Hendrickson.

Donin, Halevy. 1980. *To Pray as a Jew: A Guide to the Prayer Book and the Synagogue Service.* New York: Basic Books.

Drane, John W. 1975. *Paul Libertine or Legalist? A Study in the Theology of the Major Pauline Epistles.* London: SPCK.

Dunn, James D. G. 1993. "Echoes of Intra-Jewish Polemic in Paul's Letter to the Galatians." *Journal of Biblical Literature* 112/3:459–77.

———. 1991. "The Formal and Theological Coherence of Romans." In *The Romans Debate*. Ed. Karl Donfried. Rev. ed. Peabody, Mass.: Hendrickson. Pp. 245–50.

———. 1990. *Jesus, Paul and the Law: Studies in Mark and Galatians*. Louisville: Westminster/John Knox.

———. 1991. "The New Perspective on Paul: Paul and the Law." In *The Romans Debate*. Ed Karl Donfried. Rev. ed. Peabody, Mass.: Hendrickson. Pp. 299–308.

———. 1991. *The Partings of the Ways Between Christianity and Judaism and Their Significance for the Character of Christianity*. London: SCM; Philadelphia: Trinity Press International.

———. 1988a. *Romans 1–8*. Word Biblical Commentary, vol. 38a. Dallas: Word Books.

———. 1988b. *Romans 9–16*. Word Biblical Commentary, vol. 38b. Dallas: Word Books.

———. 1986. "Romans 13.1-7—A Charter for Political Quietism?" *Ex Auditu*. 2:55–68.

———. 1991. "The Theology of Galatians: The Issue of Covenantal Nomism." In *Pauline Theology*. Vol. 1. Ed. Jouette M. Bassler. Minneapolis: Fortress Press.

———. 1993. *The Theology of Paul's Letter to the Galatians*. Cambridge: Cambridge University Press.

———. 1990 (1977). *Unity and Diversity in the New Testament: An Inquiry into the Character of Earliest Christianity*. 2nd ed. London: SCM; Valley Forge, Pa.: Trinity Press International.

Ehrhardt, Arnold. 1964. *The Framework of the New Testament Stories*. Manchester: Manchester University Press.

Elliott, Neil. 1990. *The Rhetoric of Romans: Argumentative Constraint and Strategy and Paul's Dialogue with Judaism*. Sheffield: Sheffield Academic Press.

Ellis, E. Earle. 1989. *Pauline Theology: Ministry and Society*. Grand Rapids: Eerdmans.

Ellul, Jacques. 1991 (1988). *Anarchy and Christianity*. Trans. Geoffrey W. Bromiley. Grand Rapids,: Eerdmans.

———. 1976. *The Ethics of Freedom*. Trans. and ed. Geoffrey W. Bromiley. Grand Rapids: Eerdmans.

———. 1970. *The Meaning of the City*. Trans. Dennis Pardee. Grand Rapids: Eerdmans.

———. 1972. *The Politics of God and the Politics of Man*. Trans. and ed. Geoffrey W. Bromiley. Grand Rapids: Eerdmans.

Epp, Eldon Jay. 1986. "Jewish-Gentile Continuity in Paul: Torah and/or Faith? (Romans 9:1-5)." In *Christians Among Jews and Gentiles: Essays in Honor of Krister Stendahl on His Sixty-fifth Birthday*. Ed. George W. E. Nickelsburg with George W. MacRae. Philadelphia: Fortress Press. Pp. 80-90.

Eschner, Werner. 1981. *Der Römerbrief: An die Juden der Synagogen in Rom?* 2 vols. Hannover: Werner Eschner.

Esler, Philip Francis. 1987. *Community and Gospel in Luke-Acts: The Social and Political Motivations of Lucan Theology.* Cambridge: Cambridge University Press.

Evans, Craig A. 1993. "Faith and Polemic: The New Testament and First-century Judaism." In *Anti-Semitism and Early Christianity: Issues of Polemic and Faith.* Ed. Craig A. Evans and Donald A. Hagner. Minneapolis: Fortress Press. Pp. 1-20.

———. 1990. "Is Luke's View of the Jewish Rejection of Jesus Anti-Semitic?" In *Reimaging the Death of the Lukan Jesus.* Ed. Dennis D. Sylva. Bonner biblische Beiträge 73. Frankfurt am Main: Hain. Pp. 29-56.

———, and Sanders, James A. 1993. *Luke and Scripture: The Function of Sacred Tradition in Luke-Acts.* Minneapolis: Fortress Press.

Feldman, Louis H. 1993. *Jew and Gentile in the Ancient World: Attitudes and Interactions from Alexander to Justinian.* Princeton: Princeton University Press.

———. 1986. "The Omnipresence of the God-Fearers." *Biblical Archaeology Review* 12/5:58–63.

Fischer, U. 1978. *Eschatologie und Jenseitserwartung im hellenistischen Diasporajudentum,* Zeitschrift für die Neutestamentliche Wissenschaft Beiheft. 44. Berlin: de Gruyter.

Fitzmyer, Joseph A. 1990 (1968). "Romans." *The New Jerome Biblical Commentary.* Ed. Raymond E. Brown, Joseph A. Fitzmyer, and Roland E. Murphy. Englewood Cliffs: Prentice Hall.

———. 1993. *Romans: A New Translation with Introduction and Commentary.* Anchor Bible, vol. 33. New York: Doubleday.

Flusser, David. 1988. *Judaism and the Origins of Christianity.* Jerusalem: Magnes.

Foakes Jackson, F. J. 1933. *The Beginnings of Christianity.* Part I: *The Acts of the Apostles.* Vol. 5. Ed. F. J. Foakes Jackson and Kirsopp Lake. London: Macmillan.

Forster, Roger T., and Marston, V. Paul. 1973. *God's Strategy in Human History.* Wheaton, Ill.: Tyndale House.

Fortna, Robert T., and Gaventa, Beverly R., eds. 1990. *The Conversation Continues: Studies in Paul and John In Honor of J. Louis Martyn.* Nashville: Abingdon.

Fraikin, Daniel. 1986. "The Rhetorical Function of the Jews in Romans." In *Anti-Judaism in Early Christianity.* Vol. 1: *Paul and the Gospels.* Ed. Peter Richardson with David Granskou. Waterloo, Ont.: Wilfrid Laurier University Press. Pp. 91–106.

Fredriksen, Paula. 1988. *From Jesus to Christ: The Origins of the New Testament Images of Jesus.* New Haven and London: Yale University Press.

Friedrich, J., Pöhlmann, W., and Stuhlmacher, P. 1976. "Zür historischen Situation und Intention von Röm 13:1-7." *Zeitschrift für Theologie und Kirche* 73:131–66.

Gager, John G. 1986. "Jews, Gentiles, and Synagogues in the Book of Acts." In *Christians Among Jews and Gentiles: Essays in Honor of Krister Stendahl on His Sixty-fifth Birthday.* Ed. George W. E. Nickelsburg with George W. MacRae. Philadelphia: Fortress Press. Pp. 91–99.

——. 1986. "Judaism as Seen by Outsiders." In *Early Judaism and Its Modern Interpreters.* Ed. Robert A. Kraft and George W. E. Nickelsburg. Philadelphia: Fortress Press; Atlanta: Scholars Press. Pp. 99–116.

——. 1985 (1983). *The Origins of Anti-Semitism: Attitudes toward Judaism in Pagan and Christian Antiquity.* New York and Oxford: Oxford University Press.

Gamble, Harry, Jr. 1977. *The Textual History of the Letter to the Romans: A Study in Textual and Literary Criticism.* Studies and Documents 42. Grand Rapids: Eerdmans.

Garlington, Don B. 1991. *"The Obedience of Faith": A Pauline Phrase in Historical Context.* Tübingen: J. C. B. Mohr (Paul Siebeck).

——. 1990. "The Obedience of Faith in the Letter to the Romans: Part I: The Meaning of ὑπακοὴ πίστεως (Rom 1:5; 16:26)." *Westminster Theological Journal* 52:201–24.

——. 1991. "The Obedience of Faith in the Letter to the Romans: Part II: The Obedience of Faith and Judgment by Works." *Westminster Theological Journal* 53:47–72.

——. 1993. "The Obedience of Faith in the Letter to the Romans: Part III: The Obedience of Christ and the Obedience of the Christian." *Westminster Theological Journal* 55:87–112.

Gaston, Lloyd. 1991. "Israel's Misstep in the Eyes of Paul." In *The Romans Debate.* Ed. Karl P. Donfried. Rev. ed. Peabody, Mass.: Hendrickson. Pp. 309–26.

——. 1970. *No Stone on Another: Studies in the Significance of the Fall of Jerusalem in the Synoptic Gospels.* Leiden: Brill.

——. 1986. "Paul and the Law in Galatians 2–3." In *Anti-Judaism in Early Christianity.* Vol. 1: *Paul and the Gospels.* Ed. Peter Richardson with David Granskou. Waterloo, Ont.: Wilfrid Laurier University Press. Pp. 37–58.

——. 1987. *Paul and the Torah.* Vancouver: University of British Columbia Press.

Getty, Mary Ann. 1988. "Paul and the Salvation of Israel: A Perspective on Romans 9–11." *Catholic Biblical Quarterly* 50/3:456–69.

Gill, David W. J., and Winter, Bruce W. 1994. "Acts and Roman Religion." *The Book of Acts in Its Graeco-Roman Setting.* Vol. 2: *The Book of Acts in Its First-Century Setting.* Ed. David W. J. Gill and C. Gempf. Grand Rapids: Eerdmans; Carlisle: Paternoster. Pp. 79–104.

Glaze, R. E., Jr. 1966. *No Easy Salvation*. Nashville: Broadman.

Gooch, Peter D. 1993. *Dangerous Food: I Corinthians 8–10 in Its Context*. Waterloo, Ont.: Wilfrid Laurier University Press.

Goodman, Martin. 1994. *Mission and Conversion: Proselytizing in the Religious History of the Roman Empire*. Oxford: Clarendon.

Grant, Michael. 1970. *Nero*. London: Weidenfeld and Nicolson.

Grant, Robert M. 1963. *A Historical Introduction to the New Testament*. New York: Harper & Row.

Green, Michael. 1970. *Evangelism in the Early Church*. Grand Rapids: Eerdmans.

Grunfeld, Isidor. 1972. *The Jewish Dietary Laws*. Vol. 1. London, Jerusalem, and New York: Soncino.

Guerra, Anthony J. 1990. "The One God Topos in Spec. Leg. 1.52." In *Society of Biblical Literature 1990 Seminar Papers*. Ed. David Lull. Atlanta: Scholars Press. 29:148-57.

———. 1995. *Romans and the Apologetic Tradition: The Purpose, Genre and Audience of Paul's Letter*. Cambridge: Cambridge University Press.

Gutmann, Joseph. 1975. "The Origin of the Synagogue: The Current State of the Research." In *The Synagogue: Studies in Origins, Archaeology and Architecture*. New York: KTAV. Pp. 72–76.

Hagner, Donald A. 1993. "Paul and Judaism—The Jewish Matrix of Early Christianity: Issues in the Current Debate." *Bulletin for Biblical Research* 3:111–30.

———. 1993. "Paul's Quarrel with Judaism." In *Anti-Semitism and Early Christianity: Issues of Polemic and Faith*. Ed. Craig A. Evans and Donald A. Hagner. Minneapolis: Fortress Press. Pp. 128–50.

Hare, Douglas R. A. 1967. *The Theme of Jewish Persecution of Christians in the Gospel According to St Matthew*. Cambridge: Cambridge University Press.

Harvey, A. E. 1985. "Forty Strokes Save One: Social Aspects of Judaizing and Apostasy." In *Alternative Approaches to New Testament Study*. Ed. A. E. Harvey. London: SPCK. Pp. 79–96.

Hays, Richard B. 1991. "Crucified with Christ: A Synthesis of the Theology of 1 and 2 Thessalonians, Philemon, Philippians, and Galatians." *Pauline Theology*. Vol. 1. Ed. Jouette M. Bassler. Minneapolis: Fortress Press. Pp. 227–46.

———. 1989. *Echoes of Scripture in the Letters of Paul*. New Haven and London: Yale University Press.

Hengel, Martin. 1991 (1974). *Judaism and Hellenism: Studies in Their Encounter in Palestine during the Early Hellenistic Period*. 2 vols. Trans. John Bowden. Philadelphia: Fortress Press.

———. 1991. *The Pre-Christian Paul*. London: SCM; Philadelphia: Trinity Press International.

Heschel, Abraham J. 1959. *Between God and Man: An Interpretation of Judaism.* Ed. Fritz A. Rothschild. New York: Free Press.

———. 1955. *God in Search of Man: A Philosophy of Judaism.* New York: Farrar, Straus and Giroux.

Hill, Craig C. 1992. *Hellenists and Hebrews: Reappraising Division within the Earliest Church.* Minneapolis: Fortress Press.

Hofius, Otfried. 1990. "'All Israel Will be Saved': Divine Salvation and Israel's Deliverance in Romans 9–11." *Princeton Seminary Bulletin.* Supplementary Issue no. 1. 1:19–39.

Horbury, William. 1985 (1984). "The Temple Tax." In *Jesus and the Politics of His Day.* Ed. Ernst Bammel and C. F. D. Moule. Cambridge: Cambridge University Press. Pp. 265–86.

Horsley, G. H. R. 1981. *New Documents Illustrating Early Christianity: A Review of the Greek Inscriptions and Papyri Published in 1976.* Vol. 1. North Ryde, Australia: The Ancient History Documentary Research Centre at Macquarie University.

Houston, Walter. 1993. *Purity and Monotheism: Clean and Unclean Animals in Biblical Law.* Sheffield: Sheffield Academic Press.

Howard, George. 1990. *Paul: Crisis in Galatia: A Study in Early Christian Theology.* 2nd ed. Cambridge: Cambridge University Press.

Hultgren, Arland J. 1976. "Paul's Pre-Christian Persecutions of the Church: Their Purpose, Locale, and Nature." *Journal of Biblical Literature* 95/1:97–111.

Hurd, John Coolidge, Jr. 1965. *The Origin of 1 Corinthians.* New York: Seabury.

Hurtado, Larry W. 1988. *One God, One Lord: Early Christian Devotion and Ancient Jewish Monotheism.* Philadelphia: Fortress Press.

———. 1993. "What Do We Mean by 'First-Century Jewish Monotheism'?" In *Society of Biblical Literature 1993 Seminar Papers.* Ed. E. H. Lovering, Jr. Atlanta: Scholars Press. 32:348–68.

Hvalvik, Reidar. 1990. "A 'Sonderweg' for Israel: A Critical Examination of a Current Interpretation of Romans 11.25-27." *Journal for the Study of the New Testament* 38:87–107.

———. 1989. "'To the Jew First and also to the Greek': The meaning of Romans 1:16b." *Mishkan* 10/1:1–8.

Jeffers, James S. 1991. *Conflict at Rome: Social Order and Hierarchy in Early Christianity.* Minneapolis: Fortress Press.

Jervell, Jacob. 1991. "The Letter to Jerusalem." In *The Romans Debate.* Ed. Karl P. Donfried. Rev. ed. Peabody, Mass.: Hendrickson. Pp. 53–64.

———. 1972. *Luke and the People of God: A New Look at Luke-Acts.* Minneapolis: Augsburg Publishing House.

———. 1980. "The Mighty Minority." *Studia Theologica* 34:13–38.

———. 1991. "Retrospect and Prospect in Luke-Acts Interpretation." In *Society of Biblical Literature: 1991 Seminar Papers*. Ed. Eugene H. Lovering, Jr. Atlanta: Scholars Press. 30:383–404.

———. 1984. *The Unknown Paul: Essays on Luke-Acts and Early Christian History*. Minneapolis: Augsburg Publishing House.

Jervis, L. Ann. 1991. *The Purpose of Romans: A Comparative Letter Structure Investigation*. Sheffield: Sheffield Academic Press.

Jewett, Robert. 1970–71. "The Agitators and the Galatian Congregation." *New Testament Studies* 17:198–212.

———. 1982. *Christian Tolerance: Paul's Message to the Modern Church*. Philadelphia: Westminster.

———. 1985. "The Law and the Coexistence of Jews and Gentiles in Romans." *Interpretation* 34:341–56.

———. 1988. "Paul, Phoebe, and the Spanish Mission." In *The Social World of Formative Christianity and Judaism: Essays in Tribute to Howard Clark Kee*. Ed. Jacob Neusner et al. Philadelphia: Fortress Press. Pp. 142–61.

———. 1971. *Paul's Anthropological Terms: A Study of Their Use in Conflict Settings*. Leiden: Brill.

———. 1993. "Tenement Churches and Communal Meals in the Early Church: The Implications of a Form-critical Analysis of 2 Thessalonians 3:10." *Biblical Research* 38:23–43.

Johnson, Dan G. 1984. "The Structure and Meaning of Romans 11." *Catholic Biblical Quarterly* 46:91–103.

Johnson, E. Elizabeth. 1989. *The Function of Apocalyptic and Wisdom Traditions in Romans 9–11*. Atlanta: Scholars Press.

Joubert, S. J. 1993. "A Bone of Contention in Recent Scholarship: The 'Birkat Ha-Minim' and the Separation of Church and Synagogue in the First Century AD." *Neotestamentica* 27/2:351–63.

Judge, E. A., and Thomas, G. S. R. 1966. "The Origin of the Church at Rome: A New Solution?" *Reformed Theological Review* 25/3:81–94.

Juel, Donald. 1992 (1988). *Messianic Exegesis: Christological Interpretation of the Old Testament in Early Christianity*. Philadelphia: Fortress Press.

Kallas, James. 1964. "Romans XIII. 1-7: An Interpolation." *New Testament Studies* 11/4:365–74.

Karris, Robert J. 1991. "Romans 14:1—15:13 and the Occasion of Romans." In *The Romans Debate*. Ed. Karl P. Donfried. Rev. ed. Peabody, Mass.: Hendrickson. Pp. 65–84.

Käsemann, Ernst. 1980. *Commentary on Romans*. Trans. and ed. Geoffrey W. Bromiley. Grand Rapids: Eerdmans.

———. 1971. *Perspectives on Paul*. Trans. Margaret Kohl. Philadelphia: Fortress Press.

Katz, Jacob. 1962 (1961). *Exclusiveness and Tolerance: Jewish-Gentile Relations in Medieval and Modern Times*. New York: Schocken.

Katz, Steven T. 1984. "Issues in the Separation of Judaism and Christianity after 70 C.E.: A Reconsideration." *Journal of Biblical Literature* 103/1:43–76.

Kaylor, David R. 1988. *Paul's Covenant Community: Jew and Gentile in Romans.* Atlanta: John Knox.

Kee, Howard Clark. 1990. "The Transformation of the Synagogue after 70 C.E.: Its Import for Early Christianity." *New Testament Studies* 36:1–24.

Kimelman, R. 1981. "Birkat Ha-Minim and the Lack of Evidence for an Anti-Christian Jewish Prayer in Antiquity." In *Jewish and Christian Self-Definition.* Vol. 2: *Aspects of Judaism in the Graeco-Roman Period.* Ed. E. P. Sanders with A. I. Baumgarten and Alan Mendelson. Philadelphia: Fortress Press. Pp. 226–44.

Kittel, G., and Friedrich, G. eds. 1964–76. *Theological Dictionary of the New Testament.* Trans. and ed. G. W. Bromiley. Grand Rapids: Eerdmans.

Klein, Günter. 1991. "Paul's Purpose in Writing the Epistle to the Romans." In *The Romans Debate.* Ed. Karl P. Donfried. Rev. ed. Peabody, Mass.: Hendrickson. Pp. 29–43.

Knox, John. 1950. *Chapters in a Life of Paul.* New York and Nashville: Abingdon-Cokesbury.

Kraabel, A. Thomas. 1991. "The God-fearers Meet the Beloved Disciple." In *The Future of Early Christianity: Essays in Honor of Helmut Koester.* Ed. Birger A. Pearson. Minneapolis: Fortress Press. Pp. 276–84.

Kümmel, Werner Georg. 1966. *Introduction to the New Testament.* Trans. A. J. Mattill, Jr. Nashville: Abingdon.

La Piana, George. 1927. "Foreign Groups in Rome During the First Centuries of the Empire." *Harvard Theological Review* 20/4:183–403.

Ladd, George Eldon. 1968. *The Pattern of New Testament Truth.* Grand Rapids: Eerdmans.

Lake, Kirsopp. 1933. "The Apostolic Council of Jerusalem." *The Beginnings of Christianity.* Part 1: *The Acts of the Apostles.* Vol. 5. Additional Notes: XVI. Ed. F. J. Foakes Jackson and Kirsopp Lake. London: Macmillan. Pp. 195–212.

———. 1933. "Proselytes and God-Fearers." In *The Beginnings of Christianity.* Part 1: *The Acts of the Apostles.* Vol. 5. Additional Notes: VIII. Eds. F. J. Foakes Jackson and Kirsopp Lake. London: Macmillan. Pp. 74–96.

Lambrecht, J. 1994. *Pauline Studies: Collected Essays.* Leuven: Leuven University Press and Uitgeverij Peeters.

Lampe, Peter. 1991. "The Roman Christians of Romans 16." In *The Romans Debate.* Ed. Karl P. Donfried. Rev. ed. Peabody, Mass.: Hendrickson. Pp. 216-30.

———. 1989. *Die stadtrömischen Christen in den ersten beiden Jahrhunderten: Untersuchungen zur Sozialgeschichte.* Tübingen: J. C. B. Mohr (Paul Siebeck). English trans. forthcoming, Fortress Press.

Lane, William L. 1991. *Hebrews 1-8.* Word Biblical Commentary. vol. 47A. Dallas: Word Books.

Lapide, Pinchas, and Stuhlmacher, Peter. 1984. *Paul: Rabbi and Apostle*. Trans. Lawrence W. Denef. Minneapolis: Augsburg Publishing House.

Leon, Harry J. 1960. *The Jews of Ancient Rome*. Philadelphia: The Jewish Publication Society of America.

Levine, Lee I., ed. 1982. *Ancient Synagogues Revealed*. Jerusalem: Israel Exploration Society; Detroit: Wayne State University Press.

Lightstone, Jack. 1986. "Christian Anti-Judaism in Its Judaic Mirror: The Judaic Context of Early Christianity Revised." In *Anti-Judaism in Early Christianity*. Vol. 2. Ed. Steven G. Wilson. Waterloo, Ont.: Wilfrid Laurier University Press. Pp. 103–32.

Longenecker, Bruce W. 1991. *Eschatology and the Covenant: A Comparison of 4 Ezra and Romans 1–11*. Sheffield: Sheffield Academic Press.

Longenecker, Richard N. 1990. *Galatians*. Word Biblical Commentary, vol. 41. Dallas: Word Books.

——. 1964. *Paul, Apostle of Liberty: The Origin and Nature of Paul's Christianity*. New York, Evanston, and London: Harper & Row.

Luedemann, Gerd. 1989. *Opposition to Paul in Jewish Christianity*. Trans. M. Eugene Boring. Minneapolis: Fortress Press.

——. 1984. *Paul, Apostle to the Gentiles: Studies in Chronology*. Trans. F. Stanley Jones. Minneapolis: Fortress Press.

Luther, Martin. 1976. *Commentary of the Epistle to the Romans*. Trans. J. Theodore Mueller. Grand Rapids: Kregel.

MacLennan, Robert. 1989. "Four Christian Writers on Jews and Judaism in the Second Century." In *From Ancient Israel to Modern Judaism: Intellect in Quest of Understanding: Essays in Honor of Marvin Fox*. Vol. 1. Ed. Jacob Neusner, Ernest S. Frerichs, Nahum M. Sarna. Atlanta: Scholars Press. Pp. 187-202.

——, and Kraabel, A. Thomas. 1986. "The God-Fearers—A Literary and Theological Invention." *Biblical Archaeology Review* 12/5:46–53.

MacMullen, Ramsay. 1981. *Paganism in the Roman Empire*. New Haven and London: Yale University Press.

——. 1974. *Roman Social Relations: 50 B.C. to A.D. 284*. New Haven and London: Yale University Press.

Maier, Harry O. 1991. *The Social Setting of the Ministry as Reflected in the Writings of Hermas, Clement and Ignatius*. Waterloo, Ont.: Wilfrid Laurier University Press.

Malina, Bruce J. 1981. *The New Testament World: Insights from Cultural Anthropology*. Atlanta: John Knox.

Manns, F. 1993. "A Survey of Recent Studies on Early Christianity." In *Early Christianity in Context: Monuments and Documents*. Ed. F. Manns and E. Alliata. Jerusalem: Franciscan Printing Press. Pp. 17–25.

Manson, T. W. 1991. "St. Paul's Letter to the Romans—and Others." In *The Romans Debate*. Ed. Karl P. Donfried. Rev. ed. Peabody, Mass.: Hendrickson. Pp. 3–15.

Marcus, Joel. 1989. "The Circumcision and the Uncircumcision in Rome." *New Testament Studies* 35:67–81.

Martens, Elmer A. 1992. "Embracing the Law: A Biblical Theological Perspective." *Bulletin for Biblical Research* 2:1–28.

Martyn, J. Louis. 1985. "A Law-Observant Mission to Gentiles: The Background of Galatians." *Scottish Journal of Theology* 38:307–24.

McDonald, J. I. H. 1989. "Romans 13.1-7: A Test Case for New Testament Interpretation." *New Testament Studies* 35:540–49.

McKnight, Scot. 1991. *A Light Among the Gentiles: Jewish Missionary Activity in the Second Temple Period*. Minneapolis: Fortress Press.

Meagher, John C. 1979. "As the Twig Was Bent: Antisemitism in Greco-Roman and Earliest Christian Times." In *AntiSemitism and the Foundations of Christianity*. Ed. Alan T. Davies. New York: Paulist. Pp. 1–26.

Meeks, Wayne A. 1983. *The First Urban Christians*. New Haven and London: Yale University Press.

———. 1987. "Judgment and the Brother: Romans 14:1—15:13." In *Tradition and Interpretation in the New Testament: Essays in Honor of E. Earle Ellis for His 60th Birthday*. Ed. Gerald F. Hawthorne with Otto Betz. Grand Rapids: Eerdmans; Tübingen: J. C. B. Mohr (Paul Siebeck). Pp. 290–300.

———. 1986. *The Moral World of the First Christians*. Philadelphia: Westminster Press.

———. 1993. *The Origins of Christian Morality: The First Two Centuries*. New Haven and London: Yale University Press.

Meyer, Paul W. 1990. "The Worm at the Core of the Apple: Exegetical Reflections on Romans 7." In *The Conversation Continues: Studies in Paul and John in Honor of J. Louis Martyn*. Ed. Robert T. Fortna and Beverly R. Gaventa. Nashville: Abingdon. Pp. 62–84.

Meyers, Eric M. 1988. "Early Judaism and Christianity in the Light of Archaeology." *Biblical Archaeologist* 51/2:69–79.

———, and Kraabel, A. Thomas. 1986. "Archaeology, Iconography, and Nonliterary Written Remains." In *Early Judaism and Its Modern Interpreters*. Ed. Robert A. Kraft and George W. E. Nickelsburg. Philadelphia: Fortress Press; Atlanta: Scholars Press. Pp. 175–210.

———, and Strange, James F. 1981. *Archaeology, the Rabbis and Early Christianity*. Nashville: Abingdon.

Millgram, Abraham. 1971. *Jewish Worship*. Philadelphia: Jewish Publication Society of America.

Minear, Paul S. 1971. *The Obedience of Faith: The Purposes of Paul in the Epistle to the Romans*. London: SCM.

Moore, George Foot. 1971 (1958). *Judaism in the First Centuries of the Christian Era: The Age of the Tannaim*. 2 vols. New York: Schocken.

Müller, K. 1991. "Torah für die Völker: Die Noachidischen Gebote im Beziehungsfeld zwischen Judentum und Christentum." 1991 Dissertation. Heidelberg: Reprecht-Karls-Universität.

Munck, Johannes. 1967. *Christ and Israel: An Interpretation of Romans 9–11.* Trans. Ingeborg Nixon. Philadelphia: Fortress Press.

Munro, Winsome. 1983. *Authority in Paul and Peter: The Identification of a Pastoral Stratum in the Pauline Corpus and 1 Peter.* Cambridge: Cambridge University Press.

Murphy-O'Connor, Jerome. "Prisca and Aquila: Traveling Tentmakers and Church Builders." *Bible Review* 8/6:40–51.

Myers, Charles D., Jr. 1993. "Chiastic Inversion in the Argument of Romans 3-8." *Novum Testamentum et Orbis Antiquus* 35/1:30–47.

Neusner, Jacob. 1973. *From Politics to Piety: The Emergence of Pharisaic Judaism.* Englewood Cliffs, N.J.: Prentice-Hall.

———. 1975. "The Idea of Purity in Ancient Judaism." *Journal of the American Academy of Religion* 43:15–26.

———. 1984. *Judaism in the Beginning of Christianity.* Philadelphia: Fortress Press.

———. 1988. *The Mishnah: A New Translation.* New Haven and London: Yale University Press.

Newton, Michael. 1985. *The Concept of Purity at Qumran and in the Letters of Paul.* Cambridge: Cambridge University Press.

Neyrey, Jerome H. 1990. *Paul, in Other Words: A Cultural Reading of His Letters.* Louisville: Westminster/John Knox.

Nickle, Keith F. 1966. *The Collection: A Study in Paul's Strategy.* Naperville, Ill.: Allenson.

Nolland, John. 1981. "Uncircumcised Proselytes?" *Journal for the Study of the New Testament* 12/2:173–94.

Novak, David. 1983. *The Image of the Non-Jew in Judaism: An Historical and Constructive Study of the Noahide Laws.* New York and Toronto: Edwin Mellen.

———. 1989. *Jewish-Christian Dialogue: A Jewish Justification.* New York and London: Oxford University Press.

Ogle, Bud. 1978. "What is Left for Caesar? A Look at Mark 12:13-17 and Romans 13:1-7." *Theology Today* 35:254–64.

O'Neill, J. C. 1975. *Paul's Letter to the Romans.* Harmondsworth: Penguin.

Osborn, Robert T. 1990. "The Christian Blasphemy: A Non-Jewish Jesus." In *Jews and Christians: Exploring the Past, Present, and Future.* Ed. James H. Charlesworth. New York: Crossroads. Pp. 211–39.

Oster, Richard E., Jr. 1993. "Supposed Anachronism in Luke-Acts' Use of ΣΨΝΑΓΩΓΗ." *New Testament Studies* 39:178–208.

Parkes, James. 1979. *The Conflict of the Church and the Synagogue: A Study in the Origins of Antisemitism.* New York: Atheneum.

Parsons, Wilfrid. 1941. "The Influence of Romans XIII on Christian Political Thought II: Augustine to Hincmar." *Theological Studies* 2:325–46.

———. 1940. "The Influence of Romans XIII on Pre-Augustinian Christian Political Thought." *Theological Studies* 1/4:337–64.

Perelman, Chaim, and Olbrechts-Tyteca, L. 1969. *The New Rhetoric: A Treatise on Argumentation.* Trans. J. Wilkinson and P. Weaver. Notre Dame: Notre Dame University Press.

Porter, Calvin L. 1978. "A New Paradigm for Reading Romans." *Encounter* 39/3:257–72.

Pucci Ben Zeev, Miriam. 1995. "Caesar and Jewish Law." *Revue Biblique* 102/1:28–37.

Räisänen, Heikki. 1985. "Galatians 2.16 and Paul's Break with Judaism." *New Testament Studies* 31:543–53.

———. 1992. *Jesus, Paul and Torah: Collected Essays.* Trans. David E. Orton. Sheffield: Sheffield Academic Press.

———. 1986. *Paul and the Law.* Philadelphia: Fortress Press (reprint of 1983 by J. C. B. Mohr [Paul Siebeck]).

———. 1988. "Paul, God, and Israel: Romans 9–11 in Recent Research." In *The Social World of Formative Christianity and Judaism: Essays in Tribute to Howard Clark Kee.* Ed. Jacob Neusner et al. Philadelphia: Fortress Press. Pp. 178–206.

Rajak, Tessa. 1994. "Inscription and Context: Reading the Jewish Catacombs of Rome." In *Studies in Early Jewish Epigraphy.* Ed. J. W. Van Henten and P. W. Van der Horst. Leiden, New York, and Cologne: Brill. Pp. 226–41.

Richardson, Peter. 1969. *Israel in the Apostolic Church.* Cambridge: Cambridge University Press.

———. 1979. "Pauline Inconsistency: 1 Corinthians 9:19-23 and Galatians 2:11-14." *New Testament Studies* 26:347–62.

———, ed. 1986. *Anti-Judaism in Early Christianity.* Vol. 1. *Paul and the Gospels.* Waterloo, Ont.: Wilfrid Laurier University Press.

Ridderbos, Herman. 1975. *Paul: An Outline of His Theology.* Trans. John Richard De Witt. Grand Rapids: Eerdmans.

Rinaldi, G. 1989. *Biblia Gentium: Primo contributo per un indice delle citazioni dei riferimenti e delle allusioni alla Bibbia negli autori pagani, greci e latini, di età imperiale.* Rome: Libreria Sacre Scritture.

Rivkin, Ellis. 1978. *A Hidden Revolution.* Nashville: Abingdon.

Robinson, D. W. B. 1974. "The Priesthood of Paul in the Gospel of Hope." In *Reconciliation and Hope: New Testament Essays on Atonement and Eschatology Presented to L. L. Morris on His 60th Birthday.* Ed. Robert Banks. Grand Rapids: Eerdmans. Pp. 231–45.

———. 1967. "The Salvation of Israel in Romans 9–11." *Reformed Theological Review.* 26/3:81–96.

Robinson, John A.T. 1979. *Wrestling with Romans.* Philadelphia: Westminster.

Ruether, Rosemary Radford. 1974. *Faith and Fratricide: The Theological Roots of Anti-Semitism*. New York: Seabury.

Rutgers, Leonard Victor. 1992. "Archaeological Evidence for the Interaction of Jews and Non-Jews in Late Antiquity." *American Journal of Archaeology* 96:101–18.

———. 1995. "Attitudes to Judaism in the Greco-Roman Period: Reflections on Feldman's *Jew and Gentile in the Ancient World*." *Jewish Quarterly Review* (forthcoming).

———. 1993. "The Jews in Late Ancient Rome: An Archaeological and Historical Study on the Interaction of Jews and Non-Jews in the Roman Diaspora." Dissertation, Duke University.

———. 1994. "Roman Policy Towards the Jews: Expulsions from the City of Rome during the First Century C.E." *Classical Antiquity* 13/1:56–74.

Safrai, S., and Stern, M., eds. 1974–76. *The Jewish People in the First Century*. Compendia Rerum Iudaicarum ad Novum Testamentum et Orbis Antiquus, section 1. 2 vols. Assen: Van Gorcum; Philadelphia: Fortress Press.

Sanday, W., and Headlam, A. C. 1926. *A Critical and Exegetical Commentary on the Epistle to the Romans*. International Critical Commentary. New York: Charles Scribner's Sons.

Sanders, E. P. 1985. *Jesus and Judaism*. Philadelphia: Fortress Press.

———. 1990. "Jewish Association with Gentiles and Galatians 2:11-14." In *The Conversation Continues: Studies in Paul and John In Honor of J. Louis Martyn*. Ed. Robert T. Fortna and Beverly R. Gaventa. Nashville: Abingdon. Pp. 170–88.

———. 1990. *Jewish Law from Jesus to the Mishnah: Five Studies*. London: SCM; Philadelphia: Trinity Press International.

———. 1992. *Judaism: Practice and Belief 63 BCE–66 CE*. London: SCM; Philadelphia: Trinity Press International.

———. 1978. "On the Question of Fulfilling the Law in Paul and Rabbinic Judaism." In *Donum Gentilicium: New Testament Studies in Honour of David Daube*. Ed. E. Bammel, C. K. Barrett, and W. D. Davies. Oxford: Clarendon. Pp. 103–26.

———. 1977. *Paul and Palestinian Judaism: A Comparison of Patterns of Religion*. Philadelphia: Fortress Press.

———. 1985 (1983). *Paul, the Law, and the Jewish People*. Philadelphia: Fortress Press.

Sanders, Jack T. 1987. *The Jews in Luke-Acts*. Philadelphia: Fortress Press.

———. 1993. *Schismatics, Sectarians, Dissidents, Deviants: The First One Hundred Years of Jewish-Christian Relations*. London: SCM.

Schiffman, Lawrence H. 1981. "At the Crossroads: Tannaitic Perspectives on the Jewish-Christian Schism." In *Jewish and Christian Self-Definition*. Vol. 2: *Aspects of Judaism in the Graeco-Roman Period*. Ed. E. P. Sanders with A. I. Baumgarten and Alan Mendelson. Philadelphia: Fortress Press. Pp. 115–56.

Schmithals, Walther. 1965 (1963). *Paul and James*. Trans. Dorothea M. Barton. Naperville, Ill.: Allenson.

Schoeps, H. J. 1961. *Paul: The Theology of the Apostle in the Light of Jewish Religious History*. Trans. H. Knight. Philadelphia: Westminster.

Schottroff, Luise. 1992. "'Give to Caesar What Belongs to Caesar and to God What Belongs to God': A Theological Response of the Early Christian Church to Its Social and Political Environment." In *The Love of Enemy and Nonretaliation in the New Testament*. Ed. Willard M. Swartley. Louisville: Westminster/John Knox Press. Pp. 223–57.

Schultz, Joseph P. 1981. *Judaism and the Gentile Faiths: Comparative Studies in Religion*. New Jersey: Associated University Press.

———. 1975. "Two Views of the Patriarchs: Noahides and Pre-Sinai Israelites." In *Texts and Responses: Studies Presented to Nahum N. Glatzer on the Occasion of His Seventieth Birthday by His Students*. Ed. Michael A. Fishbane and Paul R. Flohr. Leiden: Brill. Pp. 43–59.

Scramuzza, Vincent M. 1933. "The Policy of the Early Roman Emperors towards Judaism." *The Beginnings of Christianity*. Part 1: *The Acts of the Apostles*. Vol. 5. Additional Notes: XXV. Ed. F. J. Foakes Jackson and Kirsopp Lake. London: Macmillan. Pp. 277–97.

Seager, Andrew. 1992. "The Architecture of the Dura and Sardis Synagogues." In *The Dura-Europos Synagogue: A Re-evaluation (1932–1992)*. Ed. Joseph Gutmann. Atlanta: Scholars Press. Pp. 79–116.

Segal, Alan F. 1992. "Conversion and Messianism: Outline for a New Approach." *The Messiah: Developments in Earliest Judaism and Christianity*. Ed. James H. Charlesworth. Minneapolis: Fortress Press. Pp. 296–340.

———. 1990. *Paul the Convert: The Apostolate and Apostasy of Saul the Pharisee*. New Haven and London: Yale University Press.

———. 1986. *Rebecca's Children: Judaism and Christianity in the Roman World*. Cambridge, Mass., and London: Harvard University Press.

———. 1995. "Universalism in Judaism and Christianity." In *Paul in His Hellenistic Context*. Ed. Troels Engberg-Pedersen. Minneapolis: Fortress Press. Pp. 1–29.

Seifrid, Mark A. 1992. *Justification by Faith: The Origin and Development of a Central Pauline Theme*. Leiden, New York, and Cologne: Brill.

Setzer, Claudia J. 1994. *Jewish Responses to Early Christians: History and Polemics, 30–150 C.E.* Minneapolis: Fortress Press.

Sherwin-White, A. N. 1967. *Racial Prejudice in Imperial Rome*. Cambridge: Cambridge University Press.

——. 1963. *Roman Society and Roman Law in the New Testament*. Oxford: Clarendon.

Simon, Marcel. 1970. "The Apostolic Decree and Its Setting in the Ancient Church." *Bulletin of the John Rylands Library* 52/2:437–60.

——. 1986 (1964 French). *Verus Israel: A Study of the Relations Between Christians and Jews in the Roman Empire (135–425)*. Trans. H. McKeating. New York: Oxford University Press.

Sky, Hyman I. 1992. *Development of the Office of Hazzan through the Talmudic Period*. San Francisco: Mellen Research University Press.

Slingerland, Dixon. 1989. "Chrestus: Christus?" In *New Perspectives on Ancient Judaism*. Vol. 4: *The Literature of Early Rabbinic Judaism: Issues in Talmudic Redaction and Interpretation*. Ed. Alan J. Avery-Peck. Lanham: University Press of America. Pp. 133–44.

——. 1992. "Suetonius *Claudius* 25.4, Acts 18, and Paulus Orosius' *Historiarum Adversum Paganos Libri VII*: Dating the Claudian Expulsion(s) of Roman Jews." *Jewish Quarterly Review* 83/1-2:127–44.

——. 1989. "Suetonius *Claudius* 25.4 and the Account in Cassius Dio." *Jewish Quarterly Review* 79/4:305–22.

Smallwood, E. Mary. 1981. *The Jews Under Roman Rule: From Pompey to Diocletian*. Leiden: Brill.

Smith, Morton. 1967. "The Reason for the Persecution of Paul and the Obscurity of Acts." In *Studies in Mysticism and Religion Presented to Gershom G. Scholem on His Seventieth Birthday by Pupils, Colleagues and Friends*. Ed. E. E. Urbach, R. J. Zwi Werblowsky, and Ch. Wirszubski. Jerusalem: Magnes, The Hebrew University Press. Pp. 261–68.

Snider, Theodore M. 1984. *The Continuity of Salvation*. Jefferson, N.C.: McFarland.

Snodgrass, Klyne R. 1986. "Justification by Grace—To the Doers: An Analysis of the Place of Romans 2 in the Theology of Paul." *New Testament Studies* 32:72–93.

——. 1988. "Spheres of Influence: A Possible Solution to the Problem of Paul and the Law." *Journal for the Study of the New Testament* 32:93–113.

Squarciapino, Maria Floriani. 1963. "The Synagogue at Ostia." *Archaeology* 16/3:194–203.

Stambaugh, John E., and Balch, David L. 1986. *The New Testament in Its Social Environment*. Library of Early Christianity. Philadelphia: Westminster.

Stanley, Christopher D. 1992. *Paul and the Language of Scripture: Citation Technique in the Pauline Epistles and Contemporary Literature*. Cambridge: Cambridge University Press.

——. 1993. "'The Redeemer Will Come ἐκ Ζιων': Romans 11.26-27 Revisited." In *Paul and the Scriptures of Israel*. Ed. Craig A. Evans and James A. Sanders. Studies in Scripture in Early Judaism and Christianity 1. Sheffield: JSOT Press. Pp. 118–42.

Stein, Robert H. 1989. "The Argument of Romans 13:1-7." *Novum Testamentum et Orbis Antiquus* 31/4:325–43.

Steinmetz, David C. 1986. "Calvin and Melanchthon on Romans 13:1-7." *Ex Auditu* 2:74–81.

Stendahl, Krister. 1976. *Paul Among Jews and Gentiles and Other Essays.* Philadelphia: Fortress Press.

Stern, Menahem. 1974–84. *Greek and Latin Authors on Jews and Judaism.* 3 vols. Jerusalem: Israel Academy of Sciences and Humanities.

Stowers, Stanley Kent. 1981. *The Diatribe and Paul's Letter to the Romans.* Chico, Calif.: Scholars Press.

———. 1994. *A Rereading of Romans: Justice, Jews, and Gentiles.* New Haven and London: Yale University Press.

Stuhlmacher, Peter. 1994 (1989). *Paul's Letter to the Romans: A Commentary.* Trans. Scott J. Hafemann. Louisville: Westminster/John Knox Press.

———. 1991. "The Purpose of Romans." In *The Romans Debate.* Ed. Karl P. Donfried. Rev. ed. Peabody, Mass.: Hendrickson. Pp. 231–42.

Tannenbaum, Robert F. 1986. "Jews and God-Fearers in the Holy City of Aphrodite." *Biblical Archaeology Review* 12/5:54–57.

Tcherikover, Victor. 1961. *Hellenistic Civilization and the Jews.* Trans. by S. Applebaum. Philadelphia: Jewish Publication Society of America; Jerusalem: Magnes, The Hebrew University.

Theissen, Gerd. 1987 (1983). *Psychological Aspects of Pauline Theology.* Trans. John P. Galvin. Philadelphia: Fortress Press.

———. 1992. *Social Reality and the Early Christians: Theology, Ethics, and the World of the New Testament.* Trans. Margaret Kohl. Minneapolis: Fortress Press.

Tomson, Peter J. 1990. *Paul and the Jewish Law: Halakha in the Letters of the Apostle to the Gentiles.* Compendia Rerum Iudaicarum ad Novum Testamentum, section 3: Jewish Traditions in Early Christian Literature. Vol. 1. Assen: Van Gorcum; Minneapolis: Fortress Press.

Towner, W. Sibley. 1984. "Tribulation and Peace: The Fate of Shalom in Jewish Apocalyptic." *Horizons in Biblical Theology* 6/2:1–26.

Urbach, Ephraim E. 1979 (1975). *The Sages: Their Concepts and Beliefs.* Trans. Israel Abrahams. Cambridge, Mass., and London: Harvard University Press.

Vermes, Geza. 1983. *Jesus and the World of Judaism.* Philadelphia: Fortress Press.

———. 1981 (1973). *Jesus the Jew: A Historian's Reading of the Gospels.* Philadelphia: Fortress Press.

Verneput, D. J. 1993. "Paul's Gentile Mission and the Jewish Christian Community: A Study of the Narrative in Galatians 1 and 2." *New Testament Studies* 39:36–58.

Veyne, Paul. 1987 (1985). "The Roman Empire." In *A History of Private Life.* Vol. 1: From Pagan Rome to Byzantium. Ed. Paul Veyne. Trans. Arthur Goldhammer. General editors Philippe Aries and Georges Duby. Cambridge, Mass., and London: Belknap Press of Harvard University Press. Pp. 5–234.

Walters, James C. 1993. *Ethnic Issues in Paul's Letter to the Romans: Changing Self-Definition in Earliest Roman Christianity.* Valley Forge, Pa.: Trinity Press International.

Watson, Francis. 1989 (1986). *Paul, Judaism and the Gentiles: A Sociological Approach.* Cambridge: Cambridge University Press.

——. 1991. "The Two Roman Congregations: Romans 14:1—15:13." In *The Romans Debate.* Ed. Karl P. Donfried. Rev. ed. Peabody, Mass.: Hendrickson. Pp. 203–15.

Webster, Alexander F. C. 1981. "St. Paul's Political Advice to the Haughty Gentile Christians in Rome: An Exegesis of Romans 13:1-7." *St. Vladimir's Theological Quarterly* 24/4:259–82.

Wedderburn, A. J. M. 1991. "Like an Ever-Rolling Stream: Some Recent Commentaries on Romans." *Scottish Journal of Theology* 44:367–90.

——. 1991. "Purpose and Occasion of Romans Again." In *The Romans Debate.* Ed. Karl P. Donfried. Rev. ed. Peabody, Mass.: Hendrickson. Pp. 195–202.

——. 1991 (1988). *The Reasons for Romans.* Minneapolis: Fortress Press.

Wenham, David. 1993. "Acts and the Pauline Corpus II: The Evidence of Parallels." In *The Book of Acts in Its Ancient Literary Setting.* Vol. 1. Ed. Bruce W. Winter and Andrew D. Clarke. Grand Rapids: Eerdmans; Carlisle: Paternoster. Pp. 215–58.

Westerholm, Stephen. 1988. *Israel's Law and the Church's Faith: Paul and His Recent Interpreters.* Grand Rapids: Eerdmans.

White, L. Michael. 1990. *Building God's House in the Roman World.* Baltimore and London: Johns Hopkins University Press.

Whittaker, Molly. 1984. *Jews and Christians: Graeco-Roman Views.* Cambridge: Cambridge University Press.

Wiefel, Wolfgang. 1991. "The Jewish Community in Ancient Rome and the Origins of Roman Christianity." In *The Romans Debate.* Ed. Karl P. Donfried. Rev. ed. Peabody, Mass.: Hendrickson. Pp. 85–101.

Williamson, Clark M. 1978. "The *Adversus Judaeos* Tradition in Christian Theology." *Encounter* 39/3:273–96.

Wilson, S. G. 1983. *Luke and the Law.* Cambridge: Cambridge University Press.

——, ed. 1986. *Anti-Judaism in Early Christianity.* Vol. 2: Separation and Polemic. Waterloo, Ont.: Wilfrid Laurier University Press.

Wilson, Walter T. 1991. *Love without Pretense: Romans 12.9-21 and Hellenistic-Jewish Wisdom Literature.* Tübingen: J. C. B. Mohr (Paul Siebeck).

Wright, N. T. 1992 (1991). *The Climax of the Covenant*. Minneapolis: Fortress Press.

———. 1992. *The New Testament and the People of God*. Vol. 1: *Christian Origins and the Question of God*. Minneapolis: Fortress Press.

———. 1991. "One God, One Lord, One People." *Ex Auditu* 7:45–58.

———. 1992. "Romans and the Theology of Paul." In *Society of Biblical Literature: 1992 Seminar Papers*. Ed. Eugene H. Lovering, Jr. Atlanta: Scholars Press. 31:184–213.

Wuellner, Wilhelm. 1991. "Paul's Rhetoric of Argumentation in Romans: An Alternative to the Donfried-Karris Debate Over Romans." In *The Romans Debate*. Ed. Karl P. Donfried. Rev. ed. Peabody, Mass.: Hendrickson. Pp. 128–46.

Yoder, John Howard. 1972. *The Politics of Jesus*. Grand Rapids: Eerdmans.

Zeitlin, Solomon. 1975. "The Origin of the Synagogue." In *The Synagogue: Studies in Origins, Archaeology and Architecture*. Ed. Joseph Gutmann. New York: KTAV. Pp. 14–26.

Zerbe, Gordon. 1992. "Paul's Ethic of Nonretaliation and Peace." In *The Love of Enemy and Nonretaliation in the New Testament*. Ed. Willard M. Swartley. Louisville: Westminster/John Knox Press. Pp. 177–222.

Ziesler, John. 1989. *Paul's Letter to the Romans*. London: SCM; Philadelphia: Trinity Press International.

———. 1988. "The Role of the Tenth Commandment in Romans 7." *Journal for the Study of the New Testament* 33:41–56.

INDEXES

Index of Passages

INDEX OF SELECTED SUBJECTS

Abraham: seed(s) of, 112, 140-44, 164, 286, 338; faith of, *see* "Weak"; "Strong"
Adam: temptation of, 98, 101, 106, 197, 199-201, 217, 219, 230, 234-35
Agitators: in Antioch and Galatia, 340-41, 356; in Rome, 14, 35-36, 83-84, 101, 128, 201, 208, 216-17, 234-35, 293; *See also* "Judaizers"
Agrippa II, 378
Akedah, 253
Ambrosiaster, 12, 33, 385
Ananias, 303
Andronicus, 382
Anti-Jewish, 4, 6, 64-68, 100-1, 374-75
Antioch incident, Appendix 1 *passim*
Apocalyptic. *See* Paul; Israel
Apostolic decree, Noahide Commandments, Mosaic model for "strangers within the gates": definitions of, 50-56, 166-79, 192-93, ch. 4 *passim*; fluid nature of, 19, 52, 206; initial response to, 209-12; parallels in Romans, 209-22, 228-38, ch. 4 *passim*; purity intentions of, 192-201, ch. 4 *passim*
Apostrophic "Jew," 10-12, 80, 82, 101, 127, 148, 295
Apuleius, 65
Aquila. *See* Prisca
Aurelius, Marcus, 65
Audience for Romans: definition of (implied and explicit), 75-84; attitudes toward non-Christian Jews, *see* Gentiles; as "righteous gentiles,"

see Gentiles; as subgroups within the synagogues of Rome, 13-14, 23-26, 25, 30-40, 68-75, 82-84, 110, 136, 163-65, ch. 4 *passim*, 285, ch. 6 *passim*, 327-38, 347, 384, 386-87; as subordinate to synagogue authorities, 75, 163-65, 177, 198-99, ch. 6 *passim*, 337-38
Augustine, 12, 301
Authorities. *See* Synagogue

Baal Shem, 363
Babylon, 290, 297
bar-Kochba, 64
Barnabas, 202, 209, 348-50, 356-58
Birkat-ha-Minim, 69 n. 98
Blasphemy: of gentile's claims, 26, 98, 104, 127, 152-53, 219, 226, 284-85, 323, 325, 338; of Paul, 129-130
Buber, Martin, 185

Caesar: Julius, 44-45, 73-75; worship of, 66-67, 75
Calvin, John, 298, 301
Cassius, Dio, 65, 372, 374, 380-83
Chiasmus, 180, 315, 320
Chrestus, Christus, 373-79, 382
Chrestiani, Christiani, 68, 378, 382, 385
Christian: definition of usage, 21 n. 1
Christian gentiles in Rome. *See* Gentiles
Chrysostom, 348
Cicero, 65
Claudius: 44; edict of, Appendix 2 *passim*
Clemens, Flavius, 69, 383

INDEX OF GREEK AND HEBREW WORDS

INDEX OF AUTHORS